Andalucía

John Noble, Susan Forsyth, Paula Hardy

Contents

Destination Andalucía

It's no secret that in this most southerly extreme of the European mainland you're guaranteed, for at least half of the year, to get a great suntan reclining on beaches fronted by sparkling seas. Fewer people know that easily the best and least populated of Andalucía's beaches lie at its extremities – the Costa de la Luz in the west and the Cabo de Gata in the east. As celebrated as Andalucía's sunshine are its hot-blooded people. Andalucians love socialising and partying, whether nibbling tasty tapas in their convivial bars or raging all night at one of the innumerable fiestas. Gregarious, emotional and in love with colour and action, they live life to the full. Their intense vivacity reaches its peak in the passion of Andalucía's own art form, flamenco, an electric combination of dance, song and music.

Andalucía's cities and towns combine modern glitz with an incomparable legacy of centuries-old Islamic and Christian monuments – the Alhambra of Granada, the Alcázar of Seville, the Mezquita of Córdoba, the great cathedrals, monasteries and castles – all delighting the senses with their interplay of shapes and colours. Get away from the cities and coastal resorts to the villages and hills and you enter a different land, one that still moves to the rhythms of the seasons, nurturing the olive, the grape, the orange and the almond through broiling summers and chilly winters. Andalucía possesses majestic landscapes – 3000m snowcapped mountains, bottomless gorges where vultures nest, rolling hills covered in endless forests of cork oaks. This magnificent outdoors country presents exciting possibilities not only for walkers but also for climbers, wildlife watchers, horse riders, windsurfers, sailors and skiers.

The marvellous heritage from over 2000 years of history is one of Andalucía's most exciting attractions. The Romans left impressive remains at **Itálica** (p123) near Seville and **Baelo Claudia** (p203) in Bolonia. Treasures from the Islamic era (AD 711–1492) include palaces such as Córdoba's **Medina Azahara** (p283), castles such as Almería's **Alcazaba** (p375), and fascinating vernacular architecture like Granada's **Albayzín** (p311). The legacy of Gothic, Renaissance and baroque architecture from the centuries after the Reconquista (Christian reconquest) is also superb: don't miss Seville's **cathedral** (p91). The old quarters of **Úbeda** (p357) and **Baeza** (p353) in Jaén, and **Carmona** (p125) and **Écija** (p128) in Sevilla are so full of fine old churches, mansions and monasteries that they're almost living museums. History buffs will also love the **Lugares Colombinos** (p143), a group of sites connected with the great voyages of Christopher Columbus.

Delight in the magnificent Islamic architecture and the striking detail of Córdoba's Mezquita (p279)

DAMIEN SIMONIS

PAUL BERNHARDT

Gaze up at Seville's exquisitely proportioned Giralda (p91)

Connect with the Catholic Monarchs, Isabel and Fernando, at Granada's Capilla Real (p310)

CHRISTOPHER WOOD

JENNY JONES

Marvel at the intricate detail of Granada's world-famous Islamic monument, the Alhambra (p305)

Immerse yourself in the beauty of Seville's Islamic-era Alcázar (p94)

DAN HERRICK

The Andalucian calendar is filled with colour and pageantry. Most famous are the celebrations of **Semana Santa** (Holy Week; p406). Many of Andalucía's festivals disguise deeply rooted pagan beliefs, others are linked to local traditions. The whole religious cycle comes to an end in February or March with joyous **Carnaval** (p406) – the biggest is in **Cádiz** (p171) – in time for sober Lent.

Religion aside, Andalucía hosts innumerable music, dancing and sporting events such as the **Bienal de Flamenco** (p108), the **Motorcycle Grand Prix** (p188) and the **Festival Internacional de Música y Danza** (p317).

GUY MOBERLY

Dance up a storm during Seville's Feria de Abril (p108)

Soak up the atmosphere at Andalucía's most exuberant fair, the Feria de Málaga (p238)

ROBIN CHAPMAN

JENNY JONES

Absorb the solemn fervour of Seville's Semana Santa processions (p107), the most intense in Spain

STEVE DAVEY

Honour Ronda's bullfighting past at its bullring, one of the oldest in Spain, during the Feria de Pedro Romero (p261)

Join in festivities at Granada's Feria de Corpus Christi (p317)

BETHUNE CARMICHAEL

NEIL SETCHFIELD

Watch lavish holy images pass by at Málaga's Semana Santa processions (p238)

Andalucía's two *parques nacionales* (national parks) and 24 *parques naturales* (natural parks) occupy over 15,000 sq km of spectacular territory. Supreme in ecological importance is the **Parque Nacional de Doñana** (p148), vital to millions of birds and many mammals. The upper reaches of the **Sierra Nevada** (p327), with unique alpine vegetation, are a national park, while the lower slopes, with picturesque villages, are a fascinating natural park. Don't miss the rugged mountains of the **Parque Natural Sierra de Grazalema** (p192) or the wooded, rolling hills of the **Parque Natural Sierra de Aracena y Picos de Aroche** (p159).

Gaze out over the Alpujarran villages of Bubión and Capileira (p332) in the Parque Natural Sierra Nevada

DAVID TOMLINSON

JOHN NOBLE

Explore the spectacular mountains of the Parque Natural de Cazorla (p365)

Traverse the dramatic landscape of the Parque Natural Cabo de Gata-Níjar (p385)

JESSE MECH

Getting Started

Andalucía is as big as Portugal so you need to give some thought to where and how you want to spend your time. Take account of the travel time between destinations: you could drive right across Andalucía along the main highways in seven or eight hours, but cross-country roads and coastal routes are slower. The Itineraries chapter (p13) gives suggestions for routes geared to different interests and periods of time. Don't try to do *too* much: hurrying is a waste of your time here. A good strategy is to build your trip around a few chosen destinations but also allow time for following up unexpected discoveries.

Andalucía has accommodation and eating options for all budgets, ranging from youth hostels to super-luxury hotels. Travellers on mid-range budgets will find some charming options available to them. Public transport services are mostly good, but car hire is generally inexpensive and uncomplicated, and the roads good, so this is one of the best ways to get around.

WHEN TO GO

Andalucía can be enjoyable any time of year, though the weather between November and Easter is hit or miss. Climatically, the ideal months to visit are May, June, September and October, when the countryside is at its most colourful and you can rely on good to excellent weather. Some of the hotter inland places such as Seville, Córdoba and Ronda are at their busiest, tourism-wise, during these spring and autumn months because peak summer there is just too hot for many people. The shoulder months are also generally the most comfortable for land-based outdoor activities such as walking, horse riding and golf (see p61 for more information).

See Climate Charts (p402) for more information.

July and August temperatures can be extreme, up to 45°C inland, but these are the high-season months in many places, especially on and near the coast, where the crush of tourists can sometimes make rooms scarce and push room prices up.

From late October to Easter (with a brief exception over Christmas and New Year) crowds are few and many hotels reduce their prices. But the weather is unpredictable and can be downright cold inland.

The majority of special events – festivals, fairs, religious processions and pilgrimages, sports events, big concerts – happen in the warmer months from Easter to September. Every city, town and village has a *feria* (fair)

DON'T LEAVE HOME WITHOUT...

- Checking the visa situation (see p413)
- Adequate travel insurance (see p407)
- Warning triangles and a reflective jacket if you're going by car (see p425)
- An inconspicuous container for money and valuables, such as a small, slim wallet or an under-the-clothes pouch or money belt (see p403)
- A small Spanish dictionary and/or phrase book
- A small daypack
- Your favourite sunglasses!
- Clothes to cope with cold snaps or rain between October and May

at some time during this period. Along the coast, many events happen in July or August; inland, the cooler months either side of the summer peak are favoured. See p406 and the sections on individual cities and towns for more on the timing of Andalucian festivals.

COSTS & MONEY

Andalucía is refreshingly economical by European standards. Accommodation, meals, drinks, transport, car hire and entertainment all, as a rule, cost noticeably less than in the UK or France.

If you are extremely frugal, it's just possible to scrape by on €30 to €40 a day by staying in the cheapest accommodation, avoiding restaurants except for an inexpensive set lunch, and keeping a close eye on what you spend on museums, entertainment and bars. A comfortable mid-range budget would be €60 to €100 a day. This would allow you €20 to €40 for accommodation; €3 or €4 for a light breakfast; €15 to €25 for one full meal and one lighter one; €6 to €15 for public transport and admission fees; and the rest for a drink or two, intercity travel and some shopping.

If you have €150 to €200 a day, you can stay in excellent accommodation and eat some of the best food Andalucía has to offer.

Two people can travel more cheaply (per person) than one by sharing rooms. Rooms, apartments and villas for up to six people, available in many places, work out even cheaper per person – good value for families, especially when they have a kitchen where you can prepare some meals. You'll also save by avoiding the peak tourist seasons, when most room prices go up.

Children benefit from reduced admission fees at many museums, monuments and attractions, as do, in fewer cases, students and seniors. A few museums have free-admission days – worth bearing in mind if you're taking the whole family.

TRAVEL LITERATURE

In the 1920s Englishman Gerald Brenan settled in remote Yegen, Granada province, aiming to educate himself unimpeded by British traditions. *South from Granada* (1957) is his acutely perceptive, humorous account of village life punctuated by visits from the Bloomsbury set.

Laurie Lee set off from his Gloucestershire home on foot in 1934. He walked from northern Spain to Andalucía, playing his violin for a living. *As I Walked Out One Midsummer Morning* (1969) delightfully evokes the sights, smells and moods of turbulent pre–civil war Spain.

Driving Over Lemons (1999) is the entertaining, anecdotal, bestselling tale of a small farm south of Granada by a more recent British emigrant, amiable drummer-turned-farmer-turned-writer Chris Stewart.

Andalucía's own greatest writer was Federico García Lorca (1898–1936). The three great tragedies for which he is best known, *Blood Wedding, Yerma* (which translates as 'Barren') and *The House of Bernarda Alba,* are collected in English in several editions called *Three Plays* or *Three Tragedies.*

Jason Webster uncovers what's left of the medieval Islamic legacy as he travels across contemporary Andalucía with an illegal immigrant from Morocco in *Andalus* (2004) – a book both comical and serious that combines adventure, travel and history.

American Washington Irving took up residence in Granada's Alhambra palace when it was in an abandoned state in the 1820s. *Tales of the Alhambra* (1832) weaves a series of enchanting stories around the folk with whom he shared his life there.

HOW MUCH?

Two-hour bus or train ride €12

Admission to major monument or museum €5-7

Mid-range double room in high season €60-110

Decorative fan €10

Souvenir bullfight poster with your name on it €5

LONELY PLANET INDEX

Litre of petrol €0.90

1.5L bottled water €0.45

Bottle of San Miguel beer €1.50

Souvenir T-shirt €10

Tapas €1.80

TOP TENS

FESTIVALS & EVENTS

Andalucians love to celebrate, and there's always something exciting going on somewhere. For more festivals and events around Andalucía through the year, see p406 and individual destination sections.

- **Carnaval** (Carnival; p171)
  February or March; wildest in
  Cádiz

- **Semana Santa** (Holy Week; p107)
  March or April; grandest in
  Seville

- **Feria de Abril** (April Fair; p108)
  April or early May; Seville

- **Motorcycle Grand Prix** (p188)
  April or May; Jerez de la Frontera,
  Cádiz province

- **Feria del Caballo** (Horse Fair; p185)
  early May; Jerez de la Frontera,
  Cádiz province

- **Concurso de Patios Cordobeses**
  (Patio Competition; p287)
  first half of May; Córdoba

- **Romería del Rocío**
  (Pilgrimage to El Rocío; p150)
  May or June; El Rocío, Huelva province

- **Festival Internacional de Guitarra**
  (International Guitar Festival; p286)
  late June or early July; Córdoba

- **Feria de Málaga** (Málaga Fair; p238)
  mid-August; Málaga

- **Bienal de Flamenco** (p108)
  September of even-numbered years;
  Seville

ROOMS WITH A VIEW

The vistas from these establishments are priceless:

- **Cortijo Catifalarga** (p334)
  Capileira, Granada province

- **Las Chimeneas** (p336)
  Mairena, Granada province

- **Parador de Ronda** (p261)
  Ronda, Málaga province

- **La Casa Grande** (p191)
  Arcos de la Frontera,
  Cádiz province

- **Hostal Mamabel's** (p391)
  Mojácar, Almería province

- **Hotel Toruño** (p151)
  El Rocío, Huelva province

- **Hotel Dos Mares** (p208)
  Tarifa, Cádiz province

- **Hotel Gran Sol** (p202)
  Zahara de los Atunes,
  Cádiz province

- **Refugio Poqueira** (p330)
  Mulhacén, Granada province

- **Hotel Arco de la Villa** (p196)
  Zahara de la Sierra, Cádiz province

PUEBLOS

For beauty, setting and atmosphere you can't beat these small-scale country and coastal retreats:

- **Capileira** (p332) Granada province

- **Bolonia** (p203) Cádiz province

- **Los Caños de Meca** (p199)
  Cádiz province

- **Ferreirola** (p334) Granada province

- **Cazalla de la Sierra** (p132)
  Sevilla province

- **Grazalema** (p194) Cádiz province

- **Zahara de la Sierra** (p195)
  Cádiz province

- **Zuheros** (p295) Córdoba province

- **Segura de la Sierra** (p369)
  Jaén province

- **Alájar** (p160) Huelva province

Andalucía (1998) by Michael Jacobs runs comprehensively, eruditely and irreverently through the region's culture and history – great for those who wonder whether their hotel is named after a 16th-century playwright or a 19th-century general, but knowledgeable about modern Andalucía too. Jacobs' The Factory of Light (2003) is an extended love letter to his adopted home of Frailes, in Jaén province.

INTERNET RESOURCES

Andalucía There's Only One (www.andalucia.org) Encyclopedic official tourism site of Turismo Andaluz, with detailed information on every city, town and village, directories of everything from accommodation to recommended hikes, and around 100 maps.

Andalucia.com (www.andalucia.com) Broad compendium of practical and background information.

Embassy of Spain in London (www.tourspain.co.uk) Good practical information.

Lonely Planet (www.lonelyplanet.com) Succinct summaries on travel in Andalucía; the popular Thorn Tree bulletin board; travel news; and the Subwwway section with links to other Internet travel resources.

OKSpain (www.okspain.org) Site of the Spanish tourist offices in the USA, with good links.

Turespaña (www.spain.info) Site of the Spanish overseas tourism promotion body: lots of useful stuff.

Itineraries

CLASSIC ROUTES

THE BIG THREE
10 Days to Two Weeks

Capture the essence of Andalucía's culture and history by visiting its three great World Heritage cities: **Seville** (p86), **Córdoba** (p278) and **Granada** (p302). It's possible to fly in or out of Seville or Granada, though it may turn out more economical to get a return flight to Málaga and journey overland to Seville at the start of your trip.

Each of the three cities is home to one of Andalucía's three outstanding Islamic monuments – Seville's **Alcázar** (p94), Córdoba's **Mezquita** (p279), Granada's **Alhambra** (p305) – as well as an array of other treasures, from Seville's baroque churches and **Museo de Bellas Artes** (p100) to Córdoba's **Alcázar de los Reyes Cristianos** (p284) to Granada's historic **Capilla Real** (p310) and old Islamic quarter, the **Albayzín** (p311). Modern Andalucian culture and entertainment is at its strongest in these university cities.

For a change of pace and scenery, venture outside the cities to the great Roman site of **Itálica** (p123) near Seville, or the caliphs' palace **Medina Azahara** (p283) near Córdoba, or to mainland Spain's highest mountains, the **Sierra Nevada** (p327), outside Granada.

Seville to Granada via Córdoba is only 300km. Allowing for one night in Málaga at the start or end of the trip, and half a day for travel on each leg of the route, you can see a lot with four nights in Seville, two in Córdoba and three in Granada. If you have extra days, so much the better.

WARRIORS & CASTLES   Three Weeks

Much of Andalucía's vibrant history comes from two principal eras: the eight centuries of Islamic rule (AD 711–1492) and the subsequent Reconquista (Christian reconquest). This eastern itinerary allows you to explore the history of these two key periods.

Start in **Málaga** (p231), principal port to the region, dominated by the monumental **Castillo de Gibralfaro** (p235) and the massive post-reconquest **cathedral** (p234). Then head north to the architectural gem of **Antequera** (p267), home to some 30 churches and a history that stretches back nearly 5000 years to its prehistoric **dolmens** (p268). Heading north again brings you to **Córdoba** (p278), whose famous **Mezquita** (p279) epitomises the clash of Islamic and Christian cultures. Take time to explore the dramatic hilltop castles that stood near the Muslim-Christian frontier in later Islamic times, such as those at **Almodóvar del Río** (p292) and **Zuheros** (p295), and Jaén's fantastically sited **Castillo de Santa Catalina** (p349). The rolling countryside you pass through nurtured wealthy rural towns such as **Priego de Córdoba** (p296) and the unique Renaissance showcases of **Úbeda** (p357) and **Baeza** (p353).

Turning south, head on to **Granada** (p302), home to the peerless **Alhambra** (p305), the last Islamic fortress to fall in the Reconquista. Then make for **Almería** (p374), overlooked by one of Andalucía's finest fortresses, the **Alcazaba** (p375). Before returning to Málaga take a few relaxing days to enjoy the unspoilt beaches along the unique **Cabo de Gata** (p385) coastline.

Three weeks should give you ample time to get round this circuit. Public transport links most of the towns but timetables can be restrictive, making travel by your own car preferable.

From mist-shrouded mountains and swathes of olive green to Europe's only desert, this eastern route is full of contrasts; no less in the wildly different architecture of the heavy fortified castles versus Baroque extravagance. The 850km can be done in three weeks, which should enable you to really get off the beaten track.

SIERRAS, SHERRY, SAND & SEA
Three to Four Weeks

Start this western loop with a couple of nights in **Málaga** (p231), an always vivacious city whose new **Museo Picasso** (p235) is finally drawing attention to its cultural depths. Make your way to the awesome **El Chorro Gorge** (p265) and the Mozarabic site of **Bobastro** (p267), then head across to spectacular, historic **Ronda** (p256). Move west into Cádiz province to the little village of **Grazalema** (p193), base for some marvellous walks.

Continuing westward, stop off at the dramatic and ancient cliff-top town of **Arcos de la Frontera** (p189), before you reach **Jerez de la Frontera** (p182), home of sherry and fine horses, and a hotbed of flamenco. See at least one of the two other highly individual towns of the 'sherry triangle', **Sanlúcar de Barrameda** (p179) and **El Puerto de Santa María** (p175), before plunging into the historic, atmospheric port city of **Cádiz** (p166). Then head down the Costa de la Luz, where Andalucía's most glorious stretches of sand front the Atlantic Ocean. The small coastal getaways of **Los Caños de Meca** (p199), **Zahara de los Atunes** (p202) and **Bolonia** (p203) are all ideal for chilling out before you reach **Tarifa** (p204), an ancient town at Spain's southern tip with a hip international scene based loosely around windsurfing and kitesurfing.

En route back to Málaga, stop into the spectacular historical anomaly of **Gibraltar** (p216) and, if the Costa del Sol tweaks your curiosity, **Marbella** (p250).

This circuit can all be done by train and bus, although from Bobastro you would have to return to El Chorro for a train to Ronda (see individual destination sections for transport information).

This western circuit around some of Andalucía's best natural and cultural attractions is 600km. Three weeks is sufficient to enjoy it but four weeks allows you to savour more of the spectacular scenery, explore the historic towns in greater depth, linger longer in the sherry houses and truly relax on the beaches.

TAILORED TRIPS

WILDLIFE WATCH

Andalucía is great for observing wildlife. From Málaga, head first for **Gibraltar** (p216) for an encounter with the Gibraltar apes and a dolphin-spotting boat trip in the bay. The coast along the **Strait of Gibraltar** (p212) is great for spotting migrating birds for several months of the year. **Tarifa** (p204) is a starting point for dolphin- and whale-watching trips in the strait. Head up to Seville then southwest to **La Cañada de los Pájaros** (p124) and **Dehesa de Abajo** (p124) for some first-class bird-watching en route to the mecca of wildlife lovers in Andalucía, the **Parque Nacional de Doñana** (p148), with its deer, wild boar, millions of birds and a few Iberian lynx (you're unlikely to spot these last). If you're keen on birds, continue a little further west to the **Paraje Natural Marismas del Odiel** (p143) before heading back east to see the spectacular griffon vulture colony and maybe some ibex in the **Parque Natural Sierra de Grazalema** (p192).

Continue east across central Andalucía to **Laguna de Fuente de Piedra** (p270), Spain's biggest breeding ground for the glorious greater flamingo. Then, if it's summer, make for the upper reaches of the **Parque Nacional Sierra Nevada** (p327), home to some 5000 ibex, of which you stand a good chance of seeing a reasonable number. Last stop is the wonderful **Parque Natural de Cazorla** (p365), with Andalucía's greatest numbers of visible large mammals – red and fallow deer, wild boar, mouflon, ibex – plus plenty of birds.

ANDALUCÍA FOR KIDS

Kids of all ages will be excited by the attractions that lie along the Costa del Sol west from Málaga: **Aquapark** (p248) in Torremolinos; **Tivoli World** (p248) amusement park and **SeaLife** (p248) aquarium at Benalmádena; **Parque Acuático Mijas** (p248) in Fuengirola; the **Aquarium de Puerto Banús** (p255) in Puerto Banús; and **Selwo Aventura** (p256) wildlife park at Estepona.

In **Gibraltar** (p216) kids love the cable car, the apes and the caves and tunnels in the upper rock. Next stop: Jerez de la Frontera for its **zoo** (p185) and the prancing horses of the **Real Escuela Andaluza del Arte Ecuestre** (p185). In Seville, **Isla Mágica** (p105) is a sure-fire highlight for all white-knuckle thrill-seekers.

Head west to the enormous opencast mine and vintage train at **Minas de Riotinto** (p155) and the **Gruta de las Maravillas** (p157) at Aracena. Call in at the **Reserva Natural Castillo de las Guardas** (p107) on your way east to Granada's science museum, **Parque de las Ciencias** (p316), and **Mini Hollywood** (p382), a Wild West movie town in the desert north of Almería. En route back to Málaga, stop in at the **Parque Ornitológico Loro-Sexi** (p338), Almuñécar's tropical bird aviary, and the spectacular **Cueva de Nerja** (p274).

FLAVOURS OF THE SOUTH

Dine at some of Andalucía's best restaurants in **Málaga** (p239) and mountainous **Ronda** (p262) before travelling west to **Cádiz** (p172) to sample a prodigious array of seafood. Then head to **El Puerto de Santa María** (p178) for a cornucopia of shellfish and on to **Sanlúcar de Barrameda** (p181) for succulent prawns. At **Jerez de la Frontera** (p186), try *riñones al jerez* (kidneys braised in sherry), and stock up on the finest sherries and brandies. For more titillating sea fare head further west to **Huelva** (p141) before heading north for a change of pace in the gamey heart of the **Parque Natural Sierra de Aracena y Picos de Aroche** (p157). Gorge yourself on succulent *jamón ibérico de bellota* (ham from the Iberian breed of pig fed solely on acorns) at **Jabugo** (p160) or sign up for a hands-on course in sierra cuisine at the **Finca Buen Vino** (p162). Then turning east head to **Córdoba** (p288) to sample Mozarabic dishes such as *cordero mozárabe* (lamb braised with honey). Buy olive oil direct from the producers in **Baena** (p294) or soft cheeses from the factory at **Zuheros** (p295) and wash it down with some light **Montilla** (p294) wine. As a grand finale head for **Seville** (p115) whose cosmopolitan tapas bars encapsulate the very best of Andalucian cooking.

The Authors

JOHN NOBLE Coordinating Author, Cádiz, Granada, Sevilla

In the mid-1990s John, originally from England's Ribble Valley, and his wife Susan Forsyth decided to try life in an Andalucian mountain village and they're still there, along with their now bilingual children Isabella and Jack. A writer specialising in Spain and Latin America, John has travelled throughout Andalucía and loves its music, dance, architecture, history, tapas, wine, labyrinthine villages and wild, dramatic countryside. John co-wrote the first two editions of *Andalucía* with Susan and he is also author of the Andalucía chapter of Lonely Planet's *Walking in Spain*. For this guide John wrote most of the introductory chapters and covered most of Sevilla province, as well as parts of Cádiz and Granada provinces.

My Andalucía

Give me 10 days footloose in Andalucía and I'll head for the valleys of Las Alpujarras (p331). The beautiful white villages here, clinging to the sides of deep ravines, have a unique atmosphere and a special place in history as the last redoubt of the Andalucian Muslims. I'll start with a few days walking the ancient pathways from one fantastically named village to another – Pampaneira, Capileira, Ferreirola, Cástaras, Cádiar, Jorairátar, Ugíjar, Mairena, Yegen, Mecina Bombarón, Bérchules, Trevélez. Then I'll head for the hills:

Sierra Nevada ○○ Las Alpujarras

the mighty Sierra Nevada (p327), rising above the north side of the Alpujarras. In three days' walking I can top Mulhacén (3479m), Veleta (3395m) and Alcazaba (3366m), the highest, third-highest and fifth-highest peaks in mainland Spain, and be back down in a comfy bed in Capileira (p332) on night three.

SUSAN FORSYTH Cádiz, Granada

Susan, an Australian, has spent the last decade based in Andalucía, and travelling, researching and writing in Spain, Mexico and Central America. The Hispanicisation of her life continues apace with her two children totally immersed in local life. Andalucian culture, lifestyle and the Spanish language continue to fascinate her: she marvels at Andalucía's architectural and artistic heritage, loves its varied landscapes and finds many similarities with Australia including the ocean beaches, open spaces and big blue skies. Susan co-wrote the first two editions of *Andalucía* with John Noble and has written substantial sections of all editions of Lonely Planet's *Spain*. For this guide Susan covered Granada city and most of Cádiz province.

PAULA HARDY Almería, Córdoba, Gibraltar, Huelva, Jaén, Málaga

Fascinated by the self-contained culture of the Mediterranean, Paula has spent the last four years living in and writing her way round its fringes, from a cultural history of Libya to Lonely Planet postings in Sicily, Morocco and Andalucía. Researching the chapters for Málaga, Almería, Huelva, Jaén and Córdoba provinces gave her the perfect excuse to delve deeper into the complex composite of Eastern and Western culture which makes Andalucía endlessly fascinating, as well as turning up a couple of good retreats for post-write-up relaxation. As a freelance journalist, Paula has also contributed travel articles to the *Telegraph*, *Independent* and *Express*. For this guide Paula also wrote the Food & Drink chapter.

CONTRIBUTING AUTHORS

Heather Dickson wrote the Eating, Drinking, Entertainment and Shopping sections for the Seville and Granada city sections. Heather is Lonely Planet's Commissioning Editor for Spain and Portugal titles, and has spoken about planning trips in Spain at a number of events and exhibitions.

Dr Caroline Evans wrote the Health chapter. Caroline studied medicine at the University of London, and completed General Practice training in Cambridge. She is the medical adviser to Nomad Travel clinic, a private travel-health clinic in London, and also a GP specialising in travel medicine. Caroline has been an expedition doctor for Raleigh International and Coral Cay expeditions.

Snapshot

Andalucians are basking in the warm glow of their biggest economic boom since Christopher Columbus found America and turned Seville into the richest city on earth. Ongoing growth in tourism and industry, massive subsidies for Andalucian agriculture since Spain joined the EU in 1986, and a construction boom that began in the mid-1990s and still showed no sign of tailing off by 2005, have seen unemployment fall to its lowest levels in memory.

The Spanish national elections in 2004, which brought the left-of-centre Partido Socialista Obrero Español (PSOE; Spanish Socialist Workers' Party) back to power in Madrid after an eight-year absence, boded well for Andalucía since the regional government in Seville is also in the hands of the PSOE. Andalucía could look forward to improved cooperation over a range of issues, from strategies to save the Iberian lynx (a beautiful feline on the verge of extinction – see p52) to payment of Madrid's €2.5 billion debt to Andalucía. Vegetable growers in eastern Andalucía were less happy, however, about the PSOE's decision to stop planned diversions of water from the Río Ebro in northern Spain to their arid region.

The 2004 election took place just three days after the 11 March Madrid train bombings which killed nearly 200 people and injured almost 2000, and were thought to have been perpetrated by a group of Islamic extremists mainly from Morocco. Like others throughout Spain, Andalucians poured onto their streets in massive demonstrations of grief and solidarity the day after the attacks. Being so close to Morocco – just 15km away across the Strait of Gibraltar – Andalucía has always been the Muslim world's gateway to Spain and today it is home to perhaps 100,000 of the 600,000 Muslims in Spain. The majority of these people, in Andalucía as elsewhere in Spain, are Moroccan migrant workers. Ethnic harmony is something all of Spain is striving doubly hard to maintain in the wake of the Madrid attacks and high levels of immigration from Africa, Latin America and eastern Europe in recent years. Muslim leaders throughout Spain were quick to condemn the bombings and Andalucía, which has a long tradition of racial integration, will be looking to avoid any resurgence of the racist attacks on Moroccans which occurred in the El Ejido area in 2000.

In the half-century since tourism was launched on the Costa del Sol, Andalucía has been transformed from an impoverished, hungry, highly traditional rural backwater with a barren coastline to an increasingly prosperous region with glitzy shopping centres, fast cars, high levels of consumption, a coast lined with international holiday resorts, universal schooling, large universities and much more relaxed social codes. Wages and educational levels still remain below the Spanish average, but the air of confidence and economic progress is palpable. Yet Andalucians remain a close-knit bunch, deeply rooted in their families and communities, and age-old traditions such as religious festivals, fairs and flamenco music. The new good times have not yet lasted long enough to obliterate the memory of the bad ones or weaken the strong traditions of mutual support among families and communities that they generated.

FAST FACTS

Area: 87,000 sq km
(Portugal: 92,000 sq km)

Human population:
7.4 million
(Spain: 41 million)

Lynx population:
between 150 and 400

Ibex population:
12,000 (estimated)

Wolf population:
50 (estimated)

Olive trees: 80 million

Registered unemployment (2004): 18%
(Spain: 11%)

Average monthly wage (2003): €1452
(Spain: €1599)

Hotel beds: 210,000
(Spain: 1.4 million)

History

Andalucía stands where the Mediterranean Sea meets the Atlantic Ocean and Europe gives way to Africa. From prehistoric times to the 17th century, this location put it at the forefront of Spanish history and at times made it a mover in world history. Then several centuries of economic mismanagement turned Andalucía into a backwater, a condition from which it has only emerged since the 1960s.

IN THE BEGINNING

A bone fragment found in 1982 near Orce (Granada province) could be the oldest known human remnant in Europe. It is probably one to two million years old and is believed to be from the skull of an ancestor of the modern *Homo sapiens*.

The Palaeolithic or Old Stone Age, which lasted beyond the end of the last Ice Age to about 8000 BC, was not as cold in Andalucía as in more northerly regions, permitting hunter-gatherers to live here in reasonable numbers. They left impressive rock paintings at the Cueva de Ardales (p265), the Cueva de la Pileta (p264) near Ronda, and elsewhere.

The Neolithic or New Stone Age reached eastern Spain from Egypt and Mesopotamia around 6000 BC, bringing innovations such as the plough, crops, domesticated livestock, pottery, textiles and villages. Between 3000 and 2000 BC, metalworking culture arose at Los Millares, near Almería. This Chalcolithic or Copper Age gave rise to a megalithic culture, during which tombs known as dolmens were built of large rocks. Spain's best dolmens are near Antequera (p268), Málaga province.

The next big technological advance came around 1900 BC, when the people of El Argar in Almería province learned to make bronze, an alloy of copper and tin that is stronger than copper. El Argar was probably the first Bronze-Age settlement on the Iberian Peninsula.

TARTESSOS

By about 1000 BC, a flourishing culture rich in agriculture, animals and metals had arisen in western Andalucía. Phoenician traders, largely from Tyre and Sidon in present-day Lebanon, arrived to exchange perfumes, ivory, jewellery, oil, wine and textiles for Andalucian silver and bronze. The Phoenicians set up coastal trading settlements at Adra (west of Almería), Almuñécar (which they called Ex or Sex), Málaga (Malaca), Cádiz (Gadir) and Huelva (Onuba). In the 7th century BC the Greeks came too, trading much the same goods.

The Phoenician- and Greek-influenced culture of western Andalucía in the 8th and 7th centuries BC, with Phoenician-type gods and advanced methods of working gold, is known as the Tartessos culture. Iron replaced bronze as the most important metal. Tartessos was described centuries later by Greek, Roman and biblical writers as the source of fabulous riches. Whether Tartessos was a city, a state or just a region no-one knows. Some argue that it was a trading settlement near modern Huelva; others believe it may lie beneath the marshes near the mouth of the Río Guadalquivir.

DID YOU KNOW?

The olive tree, the vine, the donkey, writing and the potter's wheel were all brought to Andalucía by the Phoenicians and Greeks.

TIMELINE

8th & 7th centuries BC	206 BC
Phoenician- and Greek-influenced Tartessos culture flourishes in western Andalucía	Itálica, first Roman town in Spain, founded near modern Seville

From the 6th century BC the Phoenicians and Greeks were pushed out of the western Mediterranean by a former Phoenician colony in modern Tunisia – Carthage. The people known as Iberians, from further north in Spain, set up a number of small, often one-village statelets in Andalucía.

ROMAN ANDALUCÍA

'Andalucía settled quickly into Roman ways and became one of the most civilised and wealthiest areas of the empire out-side Italy'

The Carthaginians inevitably came into conflict with the next new Mediterranean power, Rome. After losing out to Rome in the First Punic War (264–241 BC), fought for control of Sicily, Carthage conquered southern Spain. The Second Punic War (218–201 BC) not only saw Carthaginian general Hannibal march his elephants over the Alps towards Rome, but also brought Roman legions to fight Carthage in Spain. Rome's victory at Ilipa, near modern Seville, in 206 BC, was conclusive. The first Roman town in Spain, Itálica (p123), was founded near the battlefield soon afterwards.

Andalucía settled quickly into Roman ways and became one of the most civilised and wealthiest areas of the empire outside Italy. Rome imported Andalucian products such as wheat, vegetables, grapes, olives, copper, silver, lead, fish and garum (a spicy seasoning derived from fish, made in factories whose remains can still be seen at Bolonia, p203, and Almuñécar, p338). Andalucía also gave Rome two emperors, Trajan and Hadrian, both from Itálica. Rome brought to Andalucía and the rest of Spain aqueducts, temples, theatres, amphitheatres, baths, their language (Spanish is basically colloquial Latin 2000 years on), the basis of their legal system, a sizable Jewish population (Jews spread throughout the Mediterranean part of the Roman Empire), and Christianity, which probably arrived in the 3rd century AD with soldiers from North Africa and also with merchants.

The Roman province of Baetica, with its capital at Corduba (Córdoba), covered most of Andalucía plus neighbouring southern Extremadura and southwestern Castilla-La Mancha.

THE VISIGOTHS

When the Huns arrived in Europe from Asia in the late 4th century AD, displaced Germanic peoples moved westwards across the weakening Roman Empire, some overrunning the Iberian Peninsula. One Germanic group, the Visigoths, took Rome in AD 410. Having spared the emperor, they made a pact with him to rid the Iberian Peninsula of other invaders in return for lands in southern Gaul (France), where they then settled. Early in the 6th century, the Visigoths were pushed out of Gaul by another Germanic people, the Franks. The Visigoths then settled in the Iberian Peninsula, making Toledo, in central Spain, their capital.

The long-haired Visigoths, numbering about 200,000, had little culture of their own and their precarious rule over the relatively sophisticated Hispano-Romans was undermined by strife among their own nobility. But ties between the Visigoth monarchy and the Hispano-Romans were strengthened in 587 when King Reccared converted to Catholicism from the Visigoths' Aryan version of Christianity (which denied that Christ was God).

6th century AD	AD 711
Visigoths, a Christian Germanic people, take control of Iberian Peninsula	Muslim invaders land at Gibraltar and overrun Iberian Peninsula within a few years

AL-ANDALUS

Following the death of the prophet Mohammed in 632, Arabs spread through the Middle East and North Africa, bringing their new religion, Islam, with them. If you believe the myth, they were ushered onto the Iberian Peninsula by the sexual exploits of the last Visigoth king, Roderic (Rodrigo). Chronicles relate how Roderic seduced young Florinda, the daughter of Julian, the Visigothic governor of Ceuta in North Africa; and how Julian sought revenge by approaching the Muslims with a plan to invade Spain. In reality, Roderic's rivals probably just sought outside help in the ongoing struggle for the Visigothic throne.

In 711 Tariq ibn Ziyad, the Muslim governor of Tangier, landed at Gibraltar with around 10,000 men, mostly Berbers (indigenous North Africans) and he had some of Roderic's Visigoth rivals as allies. Roderic's army was decimated, probably near the Río Guadalete or Río Barbate in Cádiz province, and he is thought to have drowned as he fled. Within a few years, the Muslims had taken over all of the Iberian Peninsula except for small areas in the Asturian mountains in the far north. The Muslims (sometimes referred to as the Moors) were to be the dominant force on the Iberian Peninsula for nearly four centuries and a potent force for a further four. Between wars and rebellions, the Islamic areas of the peninsula developed the most cultured society in medieval Europe. The name given to these Muslim territories as a whole was Al-Andalus, which lives on today in the modern name of what was always the Muslim heartland – Andalucía.

Al-Andalus' frontiers were constantly shifting as the Christians strove to regain territory in the stuttering 800-year Reconquista (Christian reconquest). Up to the mid-11th century, the frontier between Christians and Muslims stretched across the Iberian Peninsula from just south of Barcelona to what's now northern Portugal. The small Christian states developing north of this frontier were too weak and quarrelsome to pose much of a threat to Al-Andalus. Although the Muslims also had their internal conflicts, and at times Muslims and Christians even struck up alliances with each other against others of their own kind.

Islamic political power and culture centred first on Córdoba (756–1031), then Seville (c 1040–1248) and lastly Granada (1248–1492). In the main cities, the Muslims built beautiful palaces, mosques and gardens, established bustling *zocos* (markets) and public bathhouses (which most people attended about once a week), and opened universities. In the countryside, they improved irrigation and introduced new fruits and crops such as oranges, lemons, sugar cane and rice.

Although military campaigns against the northern Christians could be bloodthirsty affairs, the rulers of Al-Andalus allowed freedom of worship to Jews and Christians under their rule. Jews, on the whole, flourished, but Christians in Muslim territory (Mozarabs; *mozárabes* in Spanish) had to pay a special tax, so most either converted to Islam (to become known as *muladíes*, or Muwallads) or left for the Christian north.

The Muslim ruling class was composed of various Arab groups prone to factional friction. Below them was a larger group of Berbers, holding mainly second-rank positions and living on second-grade land and they rebelled on numerous occasions.

Moorish Spain by Richard Fletcher is an excellent short history of Al-Andalus, concentrating to a large extent on Andalucía.

756–929	929–1031
Muslim Emirate of Córdoba rules most of Iberian Peninsula	Caliphate of Córdoba, the political and cultural apogee of Al-Andalus (Muslim-ruled parts of Spain and Portugal)

Before long, Muslim and local blood merged. There was frequent politically motivated intermarriage between leading families from the Islamic south and the Christian north.

The Cordoban Emirate (756–929)

Initially, Muslim Spain was a province of the emirate of North Africa. In 750 the Omayyad caliphal dynasty in Damascus, supreme rulers of the Muslim world, was overthrown by a revolutionary group called the Abbasids, who shifted the caliphate to Baghdad. One Omayyad, Abd ar-Rahman, escaped the slaughter and somehow made his way to Córdoba, where in 756 he set himself up as an independent emir. Abd ar-Rahman I's Omayyad dynasty more or less unified Al-Andalus for long periods, although prolonged resistance was waged by Omar ibn Hafsun, a Muwallad rebel based at the hilltop hideout of Bobastro (Málaga province), who at one stage controlled territory from Cartagena to the Strait of Gibraltar.

The Cordoban Caliphate (929–1031)

In 929 Abd ar-Rahman III (r 912–61) bestowed upon himself the title of caliph (meaning deputy to Mohammed and therefore supreme leader of the Muslim world) to assert his authority in the face of the Fatimids, a growing Muslim power in North Africa. Thus Abd ar-Rahman III launched the caliphate of Córdoba, which at its peak encompassed most of the Iberian Peninsula south of the Río Duero, plus the Balearic Islands and some of North Africa. Córdoba became the biggest, most dazzling and most cultured city in Western Europe. Abd ar-Rahman III's court was frequented by Jewish, Arabian and Christian scholars. Astronomy, medicine, mathematics, philosophy, history and botany flourished.

Later in the 10th century, the fearsome Cordoban general Al-Mansur (or Almanzor) terrorised the Christian north with 50-odd *razzias* (forays) in 20 years. In 997 he destroyed the cathedral at Santiago de Compostela in northwestern Spain – home of the cult of Santiago Matamoros (St James the Moor-Slayer), a crucial inspiration to Christian warriors. After Al-Mansur's death, the caliphate disintegrated into dozens of *taifas* (small kingdoms), ruled by local potentates, who were often Berber generals.

The Almoravids & Almohads

In the 1040s Seville, in the wealthy lower Guadalquivir valley, began to emerge as the strongest *taifa* in Andalucía. By 1078 the writ of its Abbasid dynasty ran all the way from southern Portugal to Murcia, restoring a measure of peace and prosperity to Andalucía.

Meanwhile, the northern Christian states were getting themselves into more threatening shape. When one of them, Castile (Castilla in Spanish), took Toledo from its Muslim rulers in 1085, a scared Seville begged for help from the Almoravids, a strict Muslim sect of Saharan Berbers who had conquered Morocco. The Almoravids came, defeated the Castilian king Alfonso VI, and ended up taking over Al-Andalus too, ruling it from Marrakesh as a colony and persecuting Jews and Christians. But the charms of Al-Andalus seemed to relax the Almoravids' austere grip: revolts spread across the territory from 1143 and within a few years it had again split into *taifas*.

1212	1248
Battle of Las Navas de Tolosa: northern Spanish Christian army defeats Almohad rulers of Al-Andalus	Seville falls to Fernando III of Castile

In Morocco, the Almoravids were displaced by a new, strict Muslim Berber sect, the Almohads, who in turn invaded Al-Andalus in 1160, bringing it under full control by 1173. But Al-Andalus was by now considerably reduced from its 10th-century heyday: the frontier now ran from south of Lisbon to north of Valencia. The Almohads made Seville capital of their whole realm and revived arts and learning in Al-Andalus. In 1195, their king Yusuf Yacub al-Mansur thrashed Castile's army at Alarcos, south of Toledo, but this only spurred the northern Christian states to join forces against him. In 1212 the combined armies of Castile, Aragón and Navarra routed a large Almohad force at Las Navas de Tolosa in northeastern Andalucía. Then, with the Almohad state riven by a succession dispute after 1224, the Christians pressed home their advantage.

As the Christian kingdoms of Portugal, León and Aragón moved down the southwest, central west and east of the Iberian Peninsula respectively, Castile's Fernando III (El Santo; the Saint) moved into Andalucía, taking strategic Baeza in 1227, Córdoba in 1236 and Seville, after a two-year siege, in 1248.

The Nasrid Emirate of Granada

The Granada emirate was a wedge of territory carved out of the disintegrating Almohad realm by Mohammed ibn Yusuf ibn Nasr, after whom it's known as the Nasrid emirate. Comprising the modern provinces of Granada, Málaga and Almería, plus neighbouring bits of Cádiz, Sevilla, Córdoba and Jaén, with a population of about 300,000, it held out for nearly 250 years as the last Muslim state on the Iberian Peninsula.

The Nasrids ruled from the lavish Alhambra palace in Granada city, which witnessed the final flowering of Islamic culture in Spain. The emirate reached its greatest glory in the 14th century under Yusuf I and Mohammed V, creators of the chief splendours of the Alhambra. In between bouts of fighting, Granada continued trading with Christian Spain, selling silk, dried fruits, sugar and spices, and buying salt, oil and other staples.

Granada's downfall was precipitated by two incidents. One was Emir Abu al-Hasan's refusal in 1476 to pay any more tribute to Castile (Ibn Nasr had agreed back in 1246 to pay half his income to Castile). The other was the unification in 1479 of Castile and Aragón, the peninsula's biggest Christian states, through the marriage of their monarchs Isabel and Fernando (Isabella and Ferdinand). The Reyes Católicos (Catholic Monarchs), as the pair are known, launched the final crusade of the Reconquista – against Granada – in 1482 (see p302).

Harem jealousies and other feuds between Granada's rulers degenerated into a civil war which allowed the Christians to push across the emirate, besieging towns and devastating the countryside. They captured Málaga in 1487, and Granada itself, after an eight-month siege, on 2 January 1492.

The surrender terms were fairly generous to the last emir, Boabdil (p302), who received Las Alpujarras valleys south of Granada as a personal fiefdom. He stayed there only a year, however, before leaving for Africa. The Muslims were promised respect for their religion, culture and property, but this didn't last long.

'Harem jealousies and other feuds between Granada's rulers degenerated into a civil war'

1248–1492	1469
Emirate of Granada remains as last Muslim state on the Iberian Peninsula	Isabel, heir to Castile, marries Fernando, heir to Aragón, uniting the peninsula's two most powerful Christian states

THE MUSLIM LEGACY

The medieval Muslims left a deep imprint on Andalucía, and not just because of their great architectural monuments. For a start, most Spaniards today are, through medieval intermarriage, partly descended from the Muslims. The narrow, labyrinthine street plans of many Andalucian villages and towns date from the Islamic period, as does the predilection for fountains, running water and decorative plants.

Many Andalucian churches were originally built centuries ago as mosques, and flamenco song, too, has clear Islamic roots. The Spanish language contains numerous words of Arabic origin, including *arroz* (rice), *alcalde* (mayor), *naranja* (orange) and *azúcar* (sugar). Many of the foods eaten in Andalucía today were introduced by the Muslims, and are still grown on irrigated terracing systems that date back to Muslim times.

It was through Al-Andalus that much of the learning of ancient Greece was transmitted to Christian Europe. The Arabs, during their conquests in the eastern Mediterranean, absorbed Greek science and philosophy, translating classical works into Arabic and developing such sciences as astronomy and medicine. There were two places in medieval southern Europe where the Islamic and Christian worlds met and where this knowledge could find its way northwards – one was southern Italy and the other was Al-Andalus.

Isabel and Fernando succeeded in uniting Spain under one rule for the first time since the Visigothic days. Both are buried in Granada's Capilla Real (p310) – an indication of the importance attached to their conquest of the city.

RECONQUEST ANDALUCÍA

In areas that fell to the Christians in the 13th century, many of the Muslim population fled to Granada or North Africa. Those who remained became known as Mudejars. The new Christian rulers handed large tracts of land to their nobility and to the knightly crusading orders – such as the Orden (Order) de Santiago and Orden de Calatrava – who had played a vital part in the Reconquista. Muslim raids from Granada caused lesser Christian settlers to flee or sell their smallholdings to the nobility and orders, whose holdings thereby increased. Thus originated the *latifundia* (huge estates) that have been a problematic feature of rural Andalucía ever since. The landowners turned much of their estates over to sheep, ruining former food-growing land and by 1300, rural Christian Andalucía was almost empty.

Fernando III's son Alfonso X (El Sabio, The Learned; r 1252–84) made Seville one of Castile's capitals and launched something of a cultural revival, gathering scholars around him, particularly Jews, who knew Arabic and Latin and could translate ancient texts into Castilian Spanish. With the Castilian nobility content to sit back and count the profits from wool production on their huge estates, Jews and foreigners, especially Genoese, came to dominate Castilian commerce and finance.

Persecution of the Jews

After the Black Death and a series of bad harvests in the 14th century, discontent found its scapegoat in the Jews, who were subjected to pogroms around the peninsula in the 1390s. As a result, some Jews converted to

Spanish History Index (vlib.iue.it/hist-spain /index.html) provides countless Internet leads for those who want to dig deeper.

1481	1492
First tribunal of the Spanish Inquisition, held in Seville	Catholic Monarchs, Isabel and Fernando, conquer Granada, expel Jews from their territories and fund Columbus' voyage to the Americas

Christianity (they became known as *conversos*); others found refuge in Muslim Granada. In the 1480s the *conversos* became the main target of the Spanish Inquisition, founded by the Catholic Monarchs, pious Isabel and Machiavellian Fernando, to root out those who didn't practise Christianity as the Catholic Church wished them to. Many *conversos* were accused of continuing to practise Judaism in secret. Of the estimated 12,000 deaths for which the Inquisition was responsible in its three centuries of existence, 2000 took place in the 1480s.

In 1492 Isabel and Fernando ordered the expulsion from their territories of every Jew who refused Christian baptism. Around 50,000 to 100,000 converted, but some 200,000, the first Sephardic Jews (Jews of Spanish origin), left for other Mediterranean destinations. The monarchy seized all unsold Jewish property and a talented urban middle class was decimated.

Morisco Revolts & Expulsion

The task of converting the Muslims of the conquered Granada emirate to Christianity was handed to Cardinal Cisneros, Isabel's confessor and overseer of the Inquisition. He carried out forced mass baptisms, burnt Islamic books and banned the Arabic language. As Muslims found their land being expropriated too, a revolt that began in 1500 in Las Alpujarras valleys spread right across the former emirate, from Ronda to Almería. Afterwards, Muslims were ordered to convert to Christianity or leave. Most, an estimated 300,000, underwent baptism and stayed, becoming known as Moriscos (converted Muslims), but they never assimilated to Christian culture. When the fanatically Catholic king Felipe II (Philip II; r 1556–98) forbade them in 1567 to use the Arabic language, Arabic names or Morisco dress, a new revolt in the Alpujarras spread across southern Andalucía and took two years to put down. The Moriscos were then deported from eastern to western Andalucía and more northerly parts of Spain. Among other things, this ruined the Granada silk industry. The Moriscos were finally expelled altogether from Spain by Felipe III between 1609 and 1614.

For a colourful and not over-long survey of the whole saga of Spanish history, read *The Story of Spain* by Mark Williams.

SEVILLE & THE AMERICAS: BOOM & BUST

In April 1492 the Catholic Monarchs granted the Genoese sailor Christopher Columbus (Cristóbal Colón to Spaniards) funds for a voyage across the Atlantic in search of a new trade route to the Orient. Columbus' finding of the Americas (see p144) opened up a whole new hemisphere of opportunity for Spain, especially the river port of Seville.

During the reign of Carlos I (Charles I; r 1516–56), the first of Spain's new Habsburg dynasty, the ruthless but brilliant conquerors Hernán Cortés and Francisco Pizarro subdued the Aztec and Inca empires respectively with small bands of adventurers, and other Spanish conquerors and colonists occupied further vast tracts of the American mainland. The new colonies sent huge quantities of silver, gold and other treasure back to Spain, where the crown was entitled to one-fifth of the bullion (the *quinto real,* or royal fifth).

Seville became the hub of world trade, a cosmopolitan melting pot of money-seekers, and remained the major city in Spain until late in the

16th century	17th century
Most remaining Muslims convert to Christianity to avoid expulsion; Seville grows into one of Europe's biggest and richest cities	Moriscos expelled from Spain (1609–14); economic depression, epidemics and famines

17th century, even though a small country town called Madrid was named the national capital in 1561. Seville's cosmopolitan status opened up urban Andalucía to new European ideas and artistic movements and made the city a focus of Spain's artistic golden age (see p102). The prosperity was shared to some extent by Cádiz and the lower Guadalquivir area, and less so by cities such as Jaén, Córdoba and Granada. But in rural Andalucía a small number of big landowners did little with large tracts of territory except run sheep on them. Those peasants who still lived off the land lacked any way of improving their lot and most Andalucians owned no land or property.

'The country spent too much on European wars, wasting any chance of becoming an early industrial power'

Spain never developed any strategy for absorbing the American wealth, or to cope with the inflation it brought. The country spent too much on European wars, wasting any chance of becoming an early industrial power. The gentry's disdain for commerce and industry allowed Genoese and German merchants to dominate trade, and Spain ran a trade deficit because grain had to be imported while sheep and cattle roamed its countryside.

In the 17th century, silver shipments from the Americas shrank disastrously and epidemics and bad harvests killed some 300,000 people, including half of Seville in 1649. Coming after the expulsions of the Jews and Moriscos, this left Andalucía distinctly underpopulated. The lower Guadalquivir, Seville's lifeline to the Atlantic, became increasingly silted-up and in 1717 the Casa de la Contratación, the government office controlling commerce with the Americas, was transferred to the seaport of Cádiz.

THE BOURBONS

Under the new Bourbon dynasty (still in place today) Spain made a limited recovery in the 18th century. The monarchy financed incipient industries, such as Seville's tobacco factory. A new road, the Carretera General de Andalucía, was built from Madrid to Seville and Cádiz. New land was opened up for wheat and barley, and trade through Cádiz (which was in its heyday) grew. Free-trade decrees in 1765 and 1778 permitted additional Spanish ports to conduct commerce with the Americas, which stimulated the growth of Málaga. New settlers from other parts of Spain boosted Andalucía's population to about 1.8 million by 1787.

NAPOLEONIC INVASION

When Louis XVI of France (a cousin of Spain's Carlos IV) was guillotined in 1793, Spain declared war on France. Two years later, with French forces occupying northern Spain, the country switched sides, pledging military support for France against Britain in return for French withdrawal from Spain. In 1805 a combined Spanish-French navy was beaten by a British fleet under Admiral Nelson off Cape Trafalgar (at Los Caños de Meca, Cádiz province), putting an end to Spanish sea power.

Two years later, France's Napoleon Bonaparte and Spain agreed to divide Portugal, Britain's ally, between the two of them. French forces poured into Spain, supposedly on the way to Portugal, but by 1808 this had become a French occupation of Spain. In the ensuing Spanish War of Independence, or Peninsular War, the Spanish populace took up arms

1717	1810–12
Control of commerce with the Americas transferred from Seville to Cádiz	Cortes de Cádiz: Spanish parliament meets in Cádiz, holding out under French siege

in guerrilla fashion and, with help from British and Portuguese forces led by the Duke of Wellington, drove the French out by 1813. The city of Cádiz withstood a two-year siege from 1810 to 1812, during which a national parliament that convened in the city adopted a new constitution for Spain, proclaiming sovereignty of the people and reducing the rights of the monarchy, nobility and church.

SOCIAL POLARISATION

The Cádiz constitution set the scene for a century of struggle in Spain between liberals, who wanted vaguely democratic reforms, and conservatives who wanted to maintain the status quo. King Fernando VII (r 1814–33) revoked the new constitution, persecuted opponents and even temporarily re-established the Inquisition. During his reign Mexico and most of Spain's South and Central American colonies took advantage of Spain's weakness to win their independence – desperate news for Cádiz, which had been totally reliant on trade with the colonies.

The Disentailments of 1836 and 1855, when liberal governments auctioned off church and municipal lands to reduce the national debt, pleased the bourgeoisie, who could build up new estates. But they were a disaster for the peasants, who lost municipal grazing lands. Despite being home to a quarter of Spain's 12 million people in 1877, Andalucía declined into one of Europe's most backward, socially polarised areas. At one social extreme were the few bourgeoisie and rich aristocratic landowners; at the other was a very large number of impoverished *jornaleros* – landless agricultural day labourers who were without work for a good half of the year. Illiteracy, disease and hunger were rife.

In 1873 a liberal government proclaimed Spain a republic – a federal grouping of 17 states – but this 'First Republic' was totally unable to control its provinces and lasted only 11 months, with the army ultimately restoring the monarchy.

In the face of lost grazing lands, erratic, miserably paid work and hunger, Andalucian peasants began to stage uprisings, always brutally quashed. The anarchist ideas of the Russian Mikhail Bakunin gained a big following, especially in the lower Guadalquivir area, where the estate owners' monopoly on cultivable land was most complete. Bakunin advocated strikes, sabotage and revolts as the path to a spontaneous revolution of the oppressed that would usher in a free society governed by voluntary cooperation.

The powerful anarchist union, the Confederación Nacional del Trabajo (CNT; National Labour Confederation), was founded in Seville in 1910. By 1919, it had 93,000 members in Andalucía. Anarchist trade unionists, known as syndicalists, saw the general strike as the main weapon to achieve an anarchist society.

In 1923 an eccentric general from Jerez de la Frontera, Miguel Primo de Rivera, launched a mild military dictatorship, which won the cooperation of the big socialist union the Unión General de Trabajadores (UGT; General Union of Workers), while the anarchists went underground. Primo achieved more industrialisation, better roads, punctual trains, new dams and power plants, but he was unseated in 1930 as a result of an economic downturn and discontent in the army.

DID YOU KNOW?

During the First Republic some Spanish cities declared themselves independent states and some, such as Seville and nearby Utrera, even declared war on each other.

1891–1918	1936–39
Impoverished Andalucian rural workers launch waves of anarchist strikes	Spanish Civil War: right-wing Nationalists led by General Franco rebel against left-wing Republican government and win control

THE SECOND REPUBLIC

When the republican movement scored sweeping victories in Spain's municipal elections in April 1931, King Alfonso XIII departed in exile to Italy. The ensuing Second Republic (1931–36) was an idealistic, tumultuous period that ended in civil war. Leftists and the poor welcomed the republican system, but conservatives were alarmed. Elections in 1931 brought in a mixed government, including socialists, centrists and Republicans. A new constitution in December 1931 outraged Catholics by stopping government payment of priests' salaries, legalising divorce and banning clerical orders from teaching.

Anarchist disruption, an economic slump, the alienation of big business and disunity on the left all helped the right win new elections in 1933. The left, including the emerging Communists, called increasingly for revolution and by 1934 violence was spiralling out of control. When the workers' committees that had taken over the northern Spanish mining region of Asturias were viciously quashed by the army, all Spain was polarised into left and right.

In the February 1936 elections a left-wing coalition narrowly defeated the right-wing National Front. Violence continued on both sides of the political divide. The anarchist CNT now had over one million members and the peasants were on the verge of revolution.

On 17 July 1936 the Spanish garrison at Melilla in North Africa revolted against the leftist government, followed the next day by some garrisons on the mainland. The leaders of the plot were five generals. On 19 July one of them, Francisco Franco, flew from the Canary Islands to Morocco to take command of his legionnaires. The Spanish Civil War had begun.

THE CIVIL WAR

The civil war split communities, families and friends. Both sides committed atrocious massacres and reprisals, in the early weeks especially. The rebels, who called themselves Nationalists, shot or hanged tens of thousands of supporters of the Republic. Republicans did likewise to those they considered Franco sympathisers, including some 7000 priests, monks and nuns. Political affiliation often provided a convenient cover for settling old scores. Altogether, around 350,000 Spaniards died in the war.

In Republican-controlled areas, anarchists, Communists or socialists ended up running many towns and cities. Social revolution followed. In Andalucía this tended to be anarchist, with private property abolished and churches and convents often burned and wrecked. Large estates were occupied by the peasants and around 100 agrarian communes were established. The Nationalist campaign, meanwhile, quickly took on overtones of a holy crusade against the enemies of God.

The basic battle lines were drawn within a week of the rebellion at Melilla. Cities whose garrisons backed the rebels (most did) and were strong enough to overcome any resistance fell immediately into Nationalist hands – as happened at Cádiz, Córdoba, Algeciras and Jerez. Seville was in Nationalist hands within three days and Granada within a few more. The Nationalists executed an estimated 4000 people in and around Granada after they took the city. There was slaughter in Republican areas, too. An estimated 2500 were murdered in a few months in

The politics and social movements of pre–civil war Spain are fascinatingly unravelled in Gerald Brenan's The Spanish Labyrinth.

1939–75	1975–78
Spain under right-wing Franco dictatorship; civil war followed by the 'years of hunger'; mass tourism launched on Costa del Sol	Transition to democracy following Franco's death

anarchist Málaga. A gang from Málaga killed over 500 people in Ronda in the first month of the war.

From Seville, Nationalist troops mopped up most of western Andalucía by the end of July. Málaga fell to Nationalist troops and their allies from Fascist Italy in February 1937. When the Nationalists captured Republican towns they took bloody revenge for any supposed atrocities carried out there: thousands were executed after they took Málaga.

After the fall of Málaga there was little shift in the military position in Andalucía for the rest of the war. Almería and Jaén provinces, the eastern half of Granada province and the north of Córdoba province all remained Republican until the end of the war.

Franco emerged as the undisputed Nationalist leader in late 1936, styling himself Generalísimo (Supreme General). Before long, he also adopted the title Caudillo, roughly equivalent to the German Führer.

The scales of the war were tipped in the Nationalists' favour by support from Nazi Germany and Fascist Italy in the form of weapons, planes and 92,000 men (most of them from Italy). The Republicans had some Soviet planes, tanks, artillery and advisers, and 25,000 or so French soldiers fought with them, along with a similar number of other foreigners in the International Brigades.

Hugh Thomas' *The Spanish Civil War* is the classic account of the war; it's long and dense, yet readable and humane.

The Republican government moved from besieged Madrid to Valencia in late 1936, then to Barcelona in autumn 1937. The diversity of left-wing groupings on the Republican side erupted into fierce street fighting in Barcelona in May 1937, with the Soviet-backed Communists crushing the anarchists and Trotskyites. In 1938 Franco swept eastwards, isolating Barcelona from Valencia, and the USSR withdrew from the war. The Nationalists took Barcelona in January 1939 and Madrid in March. Franco declared the war won on 1 April 1939.

FRANCO'S SPAIN

After the civil war, instead of reconciliation, more blood-letting ensued and the jails filled up with political prisoners. An estimated 100,000 Spaniards were killed, or died in prison, after the war. A few Communists and Republicans continued their hopeless struggle in small guerrilla units in the Andalucian mountains and elsewhere until the 1950s.

Franco kept Spain out of WWII, but afterwards Spain was excluded from the United Nations (UN) until 1955 and suffered a UN-sponsored trade boycott which helped turn the late 1940s into the *años de hambre* (years of hunger) – which were particularly hungry in poor areas such as Andalucía where, at times, peasants subsisted on soup made from grass and wild herbs.

Franco ruled absolutely. He was commander of the army and leader of the sole political party, the Movimiento Nacional (National Movement). Army garrisons were maintained outside every large city, strikes and divorce were banned, secondary schools were entrusted to the Jesuits and church weddings became compulsory.

In Andalucía, some new industries were founded and mass foreign tourism was launched on the Costa del Sol in the late 1950s, but by the 1970s many villages still lacked electricity, reliable water supplies and paved roads.

1982–96	1982
Sevillan Felipe González, of the left-of-centre PSOE party, is Spain's prime minister	Under Spain's new regional autonomy system, Andalucía gets own regional parliament, dominated ever since by PSOE

NEW DEMOCRACY

Franco's chosen successor, Alfonso XIII's grandson Prince Juan Carlos, took the throne, aged 37, two days after Franco's death in 1975. Much of the credit for the ensuing transition to democracy goes to the king. The man he appointed prime minister, Adolfo Suárez, pushed through Spain's Francoist-filled Cortes (Parliament) a proposal for a new, two-chamber parliamentary system. In 1977 political parties, trade unions and strikes were legalised, the Movimiento Nacional was abolished and Suárez's centrist party won nearly half the seats in elections to the new Cortes. The left-of-centre Partido Socialista Obrero Español (PSOE; Spanish Socialist Workers' Party), led by a young lawyer from Seville, Felipe González, came second.

Spain enjoyed a sudden social liberation after Franco. Contraceptives, homosexuality, adultery and divorce were legalised, and it was during this era that the *movida* – the late-night bar and club scene that enables people anywhere in Spain to party all night – emerged.

In 1982 Spain made a final break with the past by voting the PSOE into power. Felipe González was to be prime minister for 14 years, taking several other Andalucians into high office with him. The party's young, educated leadership came from the generation that had opened the cracks in the Franco regime in the late 1960s and early 1970s. The PSOE made big improvements in education, launched a national health system and basked in an economic boom after Spain joined the European Community (now the European Union; EU) in 1986.

The PSOE, sometimes in coalition with the communist Izquierda Unida (United Left), has also dominated Andalucía's regional government in Seville ever since it was inaugurated in 1982, as part of a post-Franco devolution of limited autonomy to the 17 Spanish regions. Manuel Chaves of the PSOE has headed the Andalucian executive, known as the Junta de Andalucía, since 1990. PSOE government at national and regional level eradicated the worst of Andalucian poverty in the 1980s and early 1990s with grants, community works schemes and a generous dole system.

By the mid-1990s, however, the PSOE nationally was facing a series of damaging scandals and an economic slump. It lost the 1996 national elections to the centre-right Partido Popular (PP; People's Party), led by former tax inspector José María Aznar. Aznar presided over eight years of steady economic progress for Spain. Registered unemployment in Andalucía remains the highest in Spain (18% in 2003), but the rate almost halved in the PP years, and there is no doubt that many Andalucians work while registered as unemployed. The Andalucian economy has benefited from steady growth in tourism and industry, massive EU subsidies for agriculture (which still provides one job in eight) and a decade-long construction boom intensified by the introduction of the euro in 2002, which saw large amounts of 'black' cash invested in property.

José María Aznar's high-handed style of governing did not go down well with a lot of Spaniards, however. His strong support for the US-led invasion of Iraq in 2003 was highly unpopular, as was his decision to send 1300 Spanish troops to join the US-led coalition forces in Iraq after the war.

1986	1992
Spain joins EC (now EU), launching five-year economic boom	Expo '92 world fair in Seville; high-speed AVE Madrid–Seville rail link opens

The PP was unseated by the PSOE in the 2004 national election, which took place three days after the Madrid train bombings of 11 March in which nearly 200 people were killed and at least 1800 injured. The PP's defeat was widely attributed to its policy on Iraq and to what many Spaniards perceived as its attempt to mislead voters by initially blaming the bombings on the Basque terrorist group ETA, when available evidence pointed at least equally strongly to Islamic extremists. One of PSOE leader José Luis Rodríguez Zapatero's campaign promises had been to pull Spanish troops out of Iraq – a promise he carried out within two weeks of taking office the following month.

Within three weeks of the bombings the government had named an organisation called the Moroccan Islamic Combatant Group, thought to have connections with Al-Qaeda, as the main focus of investigations. Of 16 people charged in connection with the bombings by the end of April 2004, 14 were Moroccan.

Spain governed by right-of-centre PP party; Andalucía enjoys economic progress fuelled by construction boom

Andalucians stage massive peace marches following Madrid train bombings; PSOE wins national and Andalucian regional elections

The Culture

REGIONAL IDENTITY

Andalucians have a great capacity for enjoying themselves, but that doesn't mean they don't like to work. As someone put it, they work, but they don't have a work ethic. Work simply takes its allotted place alongside other equally important aspects of life, such as socialising, entertainment and relaxation. Timetables and schedules are a little less important than in many other Western cultures, but things that Andalucians consider important do get done, and if anything really needs a fixed time (eg trains, cinemas, weddings, sporting events), it gets one.

Andalucians are gregarious people, to whom the family is of paramount importance (children are always a good talking point). Andalucians who live away from home – students, people with jobs in other cities – make frequent visits back home at weekends and on the numerous fiestas and public holidays. Local fairs, religious festivals and family fiestas such as baptisms, first communions and weddings are all important opportunities for families and communities to get together and mark the rhythms of the seasons and of their lives. Andalucians get high on fun, noise and each other's company, and any excuse for a party is eagerly seized.

With some exceptions – think of the elaborate formal dress donned by Sevillan society for their fiestas and bullfights – Andalucians are fairly informal in both dress and etiquette, more so as you move away from the cities. The Spanish *'gracias'* is heard far less often than 'thank you' in English-speaking countries, but this does not signify unfriendliness. Most Andalucians are, however, unlikely to display much personal interest in the average tourist stuttering out a few syllables of Spanish, much as they welcome the fact that millions of foreigners come to spend their holidays and their money in Andalucía each year. Invitations to Andalucian homes are something special.

'Andalucians get high on fun, noise and each other's company, and any excuse for a party is eagerly seized'

LIFESTYLE

Home for most Andalucians is an apartment in a city or town, furnished in the most modern, nontraditional way its occupants can afford. Middle-class families may live in modern terraced or detached houses in the suburbs or in dormitory towns. Lifestyle progress for many Andalucians is still a matter of getting away from the rural backwardness of their forebears, even though they may maintain personal ties to villages or country towns, or even a small *finca* (country property) to which they return for weekends. It's only in the last decade or so that rural tourism has taken off, as city-dwellers rediscover the pleasures of fresh air, greenery and open space. Andalucians – not, as a rule, great travellers – typically opt for a week or so at a seaside resort for their annual holiday.

Though they still attach great importance to their extended families, Andalucians increasingly live in small nuclear groups. In 1975 the average Andalucian woman would give birth to 3.1 children; today she has just 1.3 – above the Spanish national average but still not enough to balance the death rate. Divorces, illegal under Franco, are becoming more common and now exceed 4000 a year in Andalucía (below the national average rate).

Social life is vitally important to any Andalucian, and perhaps especially to teens and those in their twenties, for most of whom it's *de rigueur* to stay out partying deep into the *madrugada* (early hours) on weekends. Teenagers like to gather in large groups in squares and plazas, bringing their own booze to avoid age restrictions and the high cost of drinks in bars. The mobile phone is another *sine qua non* of adolescent social life.

Gender roles tend to be more traditionally defined here than in northern Europe and North America. Though many women have paid jobs, their wages are only around 70% of men's and they tend to do most of the domestic work, too. In the villages it's still unusual to see men shopping for food or women standing at bars.

Openly gay and lesbian life is easier in the bigger cities where gay scenes are bigger and attitudes more cosmopolitan.

DID YOU KNOW?

Andalucians, according to one recent survey, are the least sexually faithful of all Spaniards, with an average of 10.9 sexual partners per lifetime (national average: 5.5).

POPULATION

Andalucía's population of 7.4 million comprises 18% of the Spanish total and Andalucía is the most populous of Spain's 17 regions. The population is very much weighted to the provincial capitals. Seville (population 710,000), Málaga (547,000), Córdoba (319,000), Granada (238,000) and Huelva (145,000) are all five times as big as any other town in their provinces. About one-fifth of Andalucians live in villages or small towns. Country farmsteads and cottages are rarely actually lived in these days – their owners will travel out to them daily from their villages, or just use them on weekends.

Andalucians' ancestors include prehistoric hunters from Africa; Phoenicians, Jews and Arabs from the Middle East; Carthaginians and Berbers from North Africa; Visigoths from the Balkans; Celts from central Europe; Romans; and northern Spaniards, themselves descended from a similar mix of ancient peoples. All these influences were deeply intermingled by late medieval times. Since then there have been just three major additions to the Andalucian ethnic soup: the *gitanos* (Roma people, formerly called Gypsies), the northern European expats, and the developing world migrants.

Spain has around 600,000 *gitanos* – more than any other country in Western Europe – and about half of them live in Andalucía. The *gitanos* are thought to have come from India, from where they headed west in about the 9th century AD, reaching Spain in the 15th century.

By 2002 Andalucía had 212,000 legal foreign residents (about 17% of the legal foreign population in Spain), of whom some 91,000 were from Western Europe (principally Britain, Germany, Scandinavia and France); 53,000 from Africa (chiefly Morocco); 38,000 from Latin America; and 13,000 from Eastern Europe. The numbers, especially in the last three groups, are growing fast and estimates of the total for 2004 were around 280,000. The numbers of legal foreign residents are probably approached by the numbers of others who live full-time in Andalucía without legal documentation.

SPORT
Football

Fútbol (soccer) rivals bullfighting as Spain's national sport. Every weekend from September to May, millions follow the national Primera División (First Division) on TV, which devotes acres of airtime to every game.

Andalucía's three best teams are Sevilla and Real Betis (both of Seville; see p120), and Málaga (see p242), all usually found around the middle of the Primera División table. Many Andalucians also support Real Madrid. The Segunda División (Second Division) usually has a further half-dozen Andalucian teams. League games are mostly played on Sunday, with a few on Saturday. For upcoming fixtures see the local press or the sports papers *AS* or *Marca,* or the website **Planet Fútbol** (planetfutbol.diariosur.es).

DID YOU KNOW?

It was at Huelva, Andalucía, that soccer was introduced to Spain in the 1870s by British sailors; Recreativo de Huelva (founded 1899) is the oldest club in the country.

Bullfighting

The *corrida de toros* (bullfight) is a pageant with a long history and many rules, not just a ghoulish alternative to the slaughterhouse. Many people feel ill at the sight of the kill, and the preceding few minutes' torture is undoubtedly cruel, but aficionados will say that fighting bulls have been bred for conflict and that before the fateful day they are treated like kings. The *corrida* is also about many other things – bravery, skill, performance and a direct confrontation with death. The bullfighters face very real danger. So deeply ingrained in Spanish culture is this sport-cum-art-cum-fiesta that the question of whether it's cruel just doesn't frame itself to many Andalucians. Plenty of people are uninterested in the activity, but few actively oppose it. The anti-bullfighting lobby is much bigger and more influential in parts of northern Spain, where the Barcelona city council voted to ban bullfighting in 2004. Spanish animal-rights and anti-bullfighting organisations include the **Asociación para la Defensa de los Derechos del Animal** (ADDA, Association for the Defence of Animal Rights; ☎ 934 59 16 01; www.addaong.org; Calle Bailén 164, Local 2 interior, 08037 Barcelona). Another anti-bullfighting organisation is the **World Society for the Protection of Animals** (☎ 020-7587 5000; www.wspa.org.uk; 89 Albert Embankment, London SE1 7TP, UK).

For the latest information on the next bullfight near you, biographies of toreros and more, check out www.portaltaurino .com/nuevo/toros_en _espana.htm.

It was probably the Romans who staged Spain's first bullfights. *La lidia*, as the modern art of bullfighting on foot is known, took off in an organised fashion in Spain in the mid-18th century. Three generations of the Romero family from Ronda, in Málaga province, established most of the basics of bullfighting on foot, and Andalucía has been one of its hotbeds ever since. Before then, bullfighting on horseback was a kind of cavalry-training-cum-sport for the gentry. (Horseback bullfights, known as *corridas de rejones*, still take place, with some marvellous equestrian skills involved.)

EL MATADOR & LA CUADRILLA

Only champion matadors make good money, and some make a loss. The matador must pay a *cuadrilla* (supporting team), pay for the right to fight a bull, and rent or buy an outfit and equipment.

The *cuadrilla* has quite a few members. Firstly, there are several *peones*, junior toreros (bullfighters), who come out to distract the bull with great capes, manoeuvre him into the desired position, and so on. Then come the banderilleros, who attempt to plunge a pair of banderillas (short prods with harpoon-style ends) into the bull's withers, to goad him into action. In the next stage of the fight, the horseback picadors shove a lance into the withers, greatly weakening the bull.

Then there is the matador. The matador's dress could be that of a flamenco dancer. At its most extravagant, the *traje de luces* (suit of lights) is an extraordinary display of bright, spangly colour. All the toreros (matadors, banderilleros and so on) wear the black *montera*, the hat that looks a little like a set of Mickey Mouse ears. Their standard weapons are the *estoque* or *espada* (sword) and the heavy silk and percale *capa* (cape). The matador alone also employs a different cape – the muleta, a smaller piece of cloth held with a bar of wood used for a number of different passes.

LA CORRIDA

Bullfights usually begin at about 6pm and, as a rule, six bulls are on the day's card, with three different matadors fighting two bulls each. Each fight takes about 15 minutes.

The spectacle begins with the bull entering the arena, then being moved about by the junior bullfighters. The matador then appears and displays *faenas* (moves) with the bull, such as pivoting before its horns.

The more closely and calmly the matador works with the bull, the greater the crowd's approbation. After a little of this, the matador strides off and leaves the stage first to the banderilleros, then to the picadors, before returning for the final session. When the bull seems tired out and unlikely to give a lot more, the matador chooses the moment for the kill. Facing the animal head-on, the matador aims to sink the sword cleanly into its neck for an instant kill – the *estocada*.

A good performance followed by a clean kill will have the crowd on its feet waving handkerchiefs in appeal to the president of the fight to award the matador an ear of the animal. The president usually waits to gauge the crowd's enthusiasm before finally flopping a white handkerchief onto his balcony. If the fight has been exceptional, the matador might *cortar dos orejas* – cut two ears off.

'A good performance will have the crowd on its feet waving handkerchiefs'

MATADORS

If you're spoiling for a fight, it's worth looking out for the big names among the matadors. They are no guarantee you'll see an exciting *corrida*, as that also depends on the animals themselves. Names to look for include: Enrique Ponce, a serious class act from Jaén province; Julián 'El Juli' López, born in Madrid in 1982 (he graduated to senior matador status at the extraordinarily early age of 15); José Tomás, another young superstar; Morante de la Puebla, highly popular in Seville, his home town; Finito de Córdoba, the great favourite of his city; and macho sex symbol Jesulín de Ubrique.

ETHICS OF THE FIGHT

People certainly do die in the ring. Today, however, the risk is reduced by the fraudulent practice known as the *afeitado* – filing down the bull's horns. Filing not only makes the bull slightly less anxious to attack its tormentors but also impairs its judgment of distance and angle. When moves were made to stop this practice in 1997, the matadors went on strike.

WHEN & WHERE

The main bullfighting season in Andalucía runs from Easter Sunday to October, though it's possible to see a *corrida* at other times of the year on the Costa del Sol and occasionally elsewhere. Most *corridas* are held as part of a city or town fiesta. Few rings (Seville is one) have regular fights right through the season.

The big bang that launches Andalucía's bullfighting year is Seville's Feria de Abril (April Fair; p108), with fights almost daily during the week of the fair and the week before it. It's Seville, too, where the year ends with a *corrida* on 12 October, Spain's National Day. Here are some of the other major fight seasons on the Andalucian bullfight calendar:

Fiesta de Jerez de la Frontera (late April/early May)

Feria de Nuestra Señora de la Salud (late May/early June) Held in Córdoba, a big bullfighting stronghold.

Feria de Corpus Christi (late May 2005, mid-June 2006; p317) In Granada.

Season in El Puerto de Santa María (June to August) Held on most Sundays.

Fights on the Costa del Sol (June to August) Most Sundays, in rings such as those at Fuengirola, Marbella, Torremolinos or Mijas.

Fiestas Colombinas (3-9 August; p141) In Huelva.

Feria de Málaga (mid-August; p238) Nine-day fair in Málaga.

Feria de la Virgen del Mar (last week of August) In Almería.

Corrida Goyesca (early September) Held in Ronda, with select matadors fighting in costumes such as those shown in Goya's bullfight engravings.

See city and towns later in this book for further details on local bullfights. Bullfighting magazines such as the weekly *6 Toros 6* carry details of who's fighting where and when, and posters advertise upcoming fights locally. In addition to the top *corridas,* which attract big-name matadors and big crowds, there are plenty of lesser ones in cities, towns and villages. Some of these are *novilladas,* in which *novillos* (immature bulls) are fought by *novilleros* (junior matadors).

Other Sports

The annual motorcycle Grand Prix at Jerez de la Frontera, in May, is one of Spain's biggest sporting events, attracting around 150,000 spectators (see p188).

Baloncesto (basketball) is also popular. Andalucía's most successful teams in the national professional league, the Liga ACB, are Unicaja of Málaga and Caja San Fernando of Seville.

Andalucía stages several major professional golf tournaments each year. The Volvo Masters, played in recent Novembers at Valderrama, near Sotogrande (northeast of Gibraltar), is traditionally the final tournament of the season on the European Circuit. In 1999, Andalucian Ryder Cup star Miguel Ángel Jiménez, from Churriana near Málaga, became the first Spaniard to win the Volvo.

MULTICULTURALISM

To find out more about Spanish *gitanos,* start with the trilingual (English, Spanish and Romany) website, Unión Romaní (www.union romani.org).

Spain's *gitanos,* victims of discrimination and official persecution until at least the 18th century, have always been on the fringes of society – a position that inspired them to invent flamenco music and dance (see p39). Today, most Andalucian *gitanos* lead a settled life in cities, towns and villages, but often in the poorest parts of town. *Gitanos* rub along all right with other Spaniards, but still tend to keep – and be kept – to themselves.

The numbers of immigrants in Andalucía and Spain as a whole, from other European countries and from the developing world, are growing fast (see p35). Many Spaniards accept that Spain needs immigrants to bolster its labour force and the younger age groups of the population, due to the low birth rate that would otherwise be insufficient to maintain the population at its current levels.

The major new challenge in ethnic relations is presented by developing world migrants, who come predominantly from Morocco and South America. Many of these migrants take great risk in the hope of finding work in Spain: every year dozens, and some years hundreds, of people drown attempting to cross the Strait of Gibraltar from Morocco in small boats to gain clandestine entry into Andalucía. Thousands more each year (19,000 in 2003) are intercepted by coastguards or police and sent back. Almost certainly, there are even higher numbers that escape capture. The beaches of Cádiz province, near towns such as Tarifa and Algeciras, are the favoured drop-off points, but Almería and Granada provinces are also the destinations of many boats. Once in Spain, illegal migrants are particularly vulnerable to exploitation – low wages, poor living conditions, enforced prostitution, threats of violence – because of their fear of repatriation.

An estimated 30,000 legal and illegal migrants, mainly illiterate North African males in their twenties, work on intensive vegetable cultivation in plastic-sheeted greenhouses in Almería province, often in extremely poor conditions and for much lower wages than Spaniards would receive for the same work. Relations between Spaniards and Moroccans in Almería's El Ejido area are tense: things boiled over in 2000 in a wave of violent attacks on Moroccans after three Spaniards were murdered by Moroccans.

RELIGION

Medieval Andalucía under Islamic rule is famed for its 'three cultures' tolerance in which Muslims, Christians and Jews lived together in harmony. In reality, Christians and Jews did at times suffer persecution or discriminatory taxes and Christian rebellions were not unknown. But there's no doubt that different religions were able to coexist and that fruitful cooperation took place under the aegis of such rulers as Abd ar-Rahman III of Córdoba. The 13th-century Christian king Alfonso X kept this going briefly, but later Christian rulers subjected Muslims and Jews to forced conversions, persecutions and finally mass expulsions. By the 17th century Spain had been turned into a one-religion state. The Protestant version of Christianity, too, was firmly stamped on before it could get a toehold in the 16th century.

According to surveys, 90% of Andalucians today say they are Catholics but only 20% consider themselves churchgoers. Andalucía also has a deep-rooted anticlerical tradition. The church was considered one of the main enemies by the anarchists and other 19th-century revolutionaries. This hostility reached a bloody crescendo in the civil war, when some 7000 priests, nuns and monks were killed in Spain. But the great majority of Andalucians today have church baptisms, weddings and funerals, and families spend an average of €2000 on special clothes and festivities for a child's first communion. There's still plenty of truth in the 20th-century philosopher Miguel Unamuno's quip: 'Here in Spain we are all Catholics, even the atheists.'

The number of Muslims in Spain has grown fast. By 2004 they numbered an estimated 600,000, of whom perhaps 100,000 are in Andalucía – predominantly Moroccan migrant workers but also a few thousand Spaniards, some of whom are naturalised immigrants while others are native Spaniards who have converted to Islam. Apart from the El Ejido area of Almería province, where many Moroccans work in agriculture, Andalucía's largest Muslim community, about 20,000 strong, is in Granada. Muslim leaders throughout Spain condemned the Madrid train bombings of March 2004.

The Jewish community numbers a few thousand people, many of them from Morocco.

ARTS
Flamenco

This constellation of singing, dancing and instrumental arts that is one of Andalucía's greatest gifts to the world first took recognisable form in the late 18th and early 19th centuries among *gitanos* in the lower Guadalquivir valley (still its heartland). Flamenco's origins may go back to songs brought to Spain earlier by the *gitanos,* to music and verses of medieval Muslim Andalucía, and even to the Byzantine chant used in Visigothic churches. The first flamenco was *cante jondo* (deep song), an anguished, passionate form of expression for a people on the margins of society. *Jondura* (depth) is still the essence of flamenco. A flamenco performer who successfully communicates their passion will have you unwittingly on the edge of your seat, oblivious to all else. The gift of evoking this kind of response is known as *duende* (spirit). Performers who, on the night, just don't have the spark, will fail to really engage their audience.

A flamenco singer is known as a *cantaor* (male) or *cantaora* (female); a dancer is a *bailaor/a*. Most of the songs and dances are performed to a blood-rush of guitar from the *tocaor/a*. Percussion is provided by tapping feet, clapping hands and sometimes castanets. Flamenco *coplas* (songs) come in many different *palos* (styles), from the anguished *soleá* or the intensely despairing *siguiriya*, to the livelier *alegría* or the upbeat *bulería*. Their scales and rhythms can be hard for the beginner to tune into: technically speaking, flamenco is in the Phrygian mode, in which the interval between the first and second notes of an eight-note scale is a semitone. In conventional Western music the interval is a whole tone.

The traditional flamenco costume – for women, the shawl, fan and long, frilly *bata de cola* dress; for men, flat Cordoban hats and tight black trousers – dates from Andalucian fashions in the late 19th century, when flamenco first took to the public stage.

The *sevillana*, a popular dance with high, twirling arm movements, often seen at fiestas, is not, despite superficial appearances, flamenco at all. Consisting of four parts each coming to an abrupt halt, the *sevillana* is probably an Andalucian version of a Castilian dance, the *seguidilla*.

FLAMENCO LEGENDS

The first person to make a living from flamenco was El Fillo, from the Cádiz area, born in about 1820. His name lives on in the term *voz afillá*, which refers to the classic raw, powerful, booze-and-baccy-soaked *jondo* voice. The great singers of the late 19th century were Silverio Franconetti, from Seville, and Antonio Chacón, from Jerez. The early 20th century threw up Seville's La Niña de los Peines, the first great *cantaora*, and Manuel Torre, from Jerez, whose singing, legend has it, could drive people to rip their shirts open and upturn tables.

La Macarrona, from Jerez, and Pastora Imperio, from Seville, the first great *bailaoras*, took flamenco to Paris and South America. Their successors, La Argentina and La Argentinita, formed dance troupes and turned flamenco dance into a theatrical show. The fast, dynamic, unfeminine dancing and wild lifestyle of Carmen Amaya (1913–63), from Barcelona, made her the *gitana* dance legend of all time. Her long-time partner Sabicas was the father of the modern solo flamenco guitar.

Singers Antonio Mairena and Manolo Caracol carried the flamenco torch through the mid-20th century, a period when it seemed that the lightweight, debased flamenco of the *tablaos* – touristy shows emphasising the sexy and the jolly – was in danger of taking over. *Flamenco puro* got a new lease of life in the 1970s through singers such as Terremoto and La Paquera from Jerez, Enrique Morente from Granada and above all, El Camarón de la Isla from San Fernando near Cádiz. Camarón's incredible vocal range and his wayward lifestyle made him a legend well before his tragically early death in 1992.

Paco de Lucía (1947–), from Algeciras, has transformed the guitar, formerly the junior partner of the flamenco trinity, into an instrument of solo expression far beyond traditional limits, with new techniques, scales, melodies and harmonies. De Lucía can sound like two or three people playing together. He has said that his 2004 world tour would be his last tour. Hopefully he'll reconsider. The double album *Paco de Lucía Antología* is an excellent introduction to his life's work.

Carlos Saura's *Flamenco* (1995) is a great film introduction to the subject, featuring many of the best artists, including Paco de Lucía, Manolo Sanlúcar and Joaquín Cortés.

FLAMENCO TODAY

Flamenco may be going through its true golden age right now. Never has it been so popular or so innovative. Long-established singers such as

Enrique Morente, Carmen Linares and Chano Lobato remain at the top of the profession, while new generations continue to broaden flamenco's audience. Perhaps most universally acclaimed is José Mercé, from Jerez, whose exciting albums *Del Amanecer* (Of the Dawn; 1999), *Aire* (Air; 2000) and *Lío* (Entanglement; 2002) have all been huge sellers. El Barrio from Cádiz, a kind of 21st-century urban poet, Estrella Morente from Granada (Enrique's daughter), Arcángel from Huelva and Miguel Poveda, a non-*gitano* from Barcelona, are carving out niches in the first rank of *cantaores*, with large followings among the young. Other top singers whose concerts will always be worth attending include José Menese, Remedios Amaya, Aurora Vargas and Juan 'El Lebrijano' Peña.

Dance, always the readiest of flamenco arts to cross boundaries, has reached its most adventurous horizons in the person of Joaquín Cortés, born in Córdoba in 1969. Cortés' fuses flamenco with contemporary dance, ballet and jazz, to music at rock-concert amplification; he may dance half-naked, or in women's clothes. He tours frequently both in Spain and all over the world with spectacular solo or ensemble shows.

The most exciting young dance talent is Farruquito from Seville (b 1983), grandson of legendary flamenco dancer, Farruco, who died in 1997. Other top-rank stars, who you may find dancing solo or with their own companies, are Sara Baras, Antonio Canales, Manuela Carrasco, Cristina Hoyos

Flamenco World (www.flamenco-world.com), Centro Andaluz de Flamenco (caf.cica.es) and Deflamenco.com (www.deflamenco.com) are all great resources on flamenco, with calendars of upcoming concerts and performances.

ANDALUCIAN FLAMENCO & MUSIC FESTIVALS

These are some of the best regular events:

■ **Festival de Jerez** (late February/early March; p185) Two-week flamenco bash in Jerez de la Frontera.

■ **Potaje Gitano** (June) In Utrera, this is the first of three big Saturday-night flamenco fests in Sevilla province.

■ **Festival Torre del Cante** (June) One-night flamenco festival at Alhaurín de la Torre, near Málaga.

■ **Festival Internacional de Guitarra** (late June and early July; p286) Two-week celebration of the guitar in Córdoba.

■ **Festival Internacional de Música y Danza** (late June to early July; p317) A 2½-week international festival of mainly classical music and dance in Granada.

■ **Caracolá Lebrijana** (June/July) In Lebrija, this is the second of three big Saturday-night flamenco festivals in Sevilla.

■ **Etnosur** (mid-July; www.etnosur.com) World music and multicultural event in Alcalá la Real, in Jaén province.

■ **Blues Cazorla** (late July; www.bluescazorla.com) Weekend blues festival in Cazorla, in Jaén province.

■ **Gazpacho Andaluz** (July/August) In Morón de la Frontera, this is the third of three big Saturday-night flamenco events in Sevilla.

■ **AV Festival** (July/August; www.avfestival.com) Weekend of electronic sound, cyber-jazz and post-rock at Castillo de Sohail, Fuengirola.

■ **Bienal de Flamenco** (September, even-numbered years; p108) Month-long megafest in Seville featuring just about every big star of the flamenco world.

■ **Festival Internacional de Jazz** (November) Jazz festival in several Andalucian cities.

■ **Fiesta Mayor de Verdiales** (28 December; p238) Celebration of an exhilarating brand of folk music unique to the Málaga area, at Puerto de la Torre.

and Eva La Yerbabuena. An innovative young dancer to watch for is Israel Galván from Seville, who has turned Kafka's *Metamorphosis* and the music of The Doors into flamenco – not to everyone's liking!

Guitarists to keep an eye out for include Manolo Sanlúcar, from Cádiz, José Mercé's accompanist Vicente Amigo, and Tomatito, from Almería, who used to accompany El Camarón de la Isla.

FLAMENCO FUSION

Given a cue, perhaps, by Paco de Lucía, 1970s musicians began mixing flamenco with jazz, rock, blues, rap and other genres. This *nuevo flamenco* (new flamenco) greatly broadened flamenco's appeal. The seminal recording was a 1977 flamenco-folk-rock album, *Veneno* (Poison), by the group of the same name centred on Kiko Veneno (see below) and Raimundo Amador, both from Seville. Amador and his brother Rafael formed Pata Negra, which produced four fine flamenco-jazz-blues albums culminating in *Blues de la Frontera* (1986). Raimundo is now a solo artist and his 2003 album *Isla Menor* adds rap, reggae and *pasos dobles* to the fusion.

In the hard-to-put-down *Duende* (2003), young author Jason Webster immerses his body and soul for two years in Spain's passionate and dangerous flamenco world in search of the true flamenco spirit.

The group Ketama, whose key members are all from the Montoya flamenco family of Granada, mixes flamenco with African, Cuban, Brazilian and other rhythms. Two of its best albums are *Songhai* (1987) and *Songhai 2* (1995). Radio Tarifa emerged in 1993 with a mesmerising mix of flamenco, North African and medieval Andalucian sounds on *Rumba Argelina* (Algerian Rumba; 1993) and has produced just three albums since then, the latest being *Fiebre* (Fever; 2003).

The latest generation is led by artists such as Cádiz's Niña Pastori, who arrived in the late 1990s singing jazz- and Latin-influenced flamenco. Her albums *Entre dos Puertos* (Between Two Ports; 1997), *Eres Luz* (You are Light; 1999), *Cañailla* (2000) and *María* (2002) are all great listening. Málaga group Chambao successfully combines flamenco with electronic beats on *Flamenco Chill* (2002) and *Endorfinas en la Mente* (Endorphins in the Mind; 2004). The most recent big crossover triumph has been the collaboration between flamenco singer Diego El Cigala and the octogenarian Cuban pianist Bebo Valdés on *Lágrimas Negras* (Black Tears; 2003).

SEEING FLAMENCO

Flamenco is easiest to catch in the summer when many Andalucian *ferias* and fiestas include flamenco performances, and some places stage special night-long flamenco festivals (see Andalucian Flamenco & Music Festivals, p41). The rest of the year there are intermittent big-name performances in theatres, occasional seasons of concerts, and regular flamenco nights at bars and clubs in some cities – often just for the price of your drinks. Flamenco fans also band together in clubs called *peñas*, which stage live performance nights – most will admit interested visitors and the atmosphere here can be very intimate. Seville, Jerez de la Frontera, Cádiz and Granada are flamenco hotbeds, but you'll often be able to find something in Málaga, Córdoba or Almería – and, erratically, in other places too.

Tablaos are regular shows put on for largely undiscriminating tourist audiences, usually with high prices. These are what tourist offices are likely to steer you towards unless asked otherwise.

Other Music

In this intensely musical land all the major cities have full calendars of musical events from classical to jazz to rock to pop to electronic, and there is usually quite a choice of musical entertainment at weekends. Live music of many types is also an essential ingredient of many Andalucian fiestas.

THE GUITAR IS BORN

Clapton, Santana and King owe everything to Andalucía. The 9th-century Córdoba court musician Ziryab added a fifth string to the four-string Arab lute, and this instrument was widespread in Spain for centuries. Around the 1790s a sixth string was added, probably by a Cádiz guitar maker called Pagés. In the 1870s Antonio de Torres of Almería brought the guitar to its modern shape by enlarging its two bulges and placing the bridge centrally over the lower one to give the instrument its carrying power.

Few Andalucian performers of any genre are completely untouched by the flamenco tradition. One of the most interesting and talented characters is singer-songwriter Kiko Veneno, who has spent most of his life around Seville and Cádiz. Though also a practitioner of flamenco fusion (see p42), he's more in a rock-R&B camp now, mixing rock, blues, African and flamenco rhythms with lyrics that range from humorous, *simpático* snatches of everyday life to Lorca poems. His compilation albums *Puro Veneno* (Pure Poison; 1997) and *Un Ratito de Gloria* (A Moment of Glory; 2001) are excellent introductions to his music.

Another evergreen is the iconoclastic Joaquín Sabina from Úbeda (Jaén province), a prolific producer of lyrical rock-folk with a protest theme for more than two decades. 'I'll always be against those in power' and 'I feel like vomiting every time I sit in front of a telly', he has proclaimed. His 2000 double album *Nos Sobran Los Motivos* (More Reasons Than We Need) is a good one to start with.

Other Andalucian performers worth watching out for include Seville's female rapper, La Mala Rodríguez; Granada indie band Los Planetas; Tabletom, a hippy band that has been mixing blues, jazz, Frank Zappa and Málaga hedonism since the 1970s; Granada technopunks Lagartija Nick, purveyors of what has been described as a 'tyrannical storm of sound'; Las Niñas, a Seville threesome who update Afroamerican R&B with elements of rap; and everlasting Córdoba heavy rockers Medina Azahara.

On the classical front, arguably the finest Spanish composer of all, Manuel de Falla, was born in Cádiz in 1876. He grew up in Andalucía before heading off to Madrid and Paris, then returned in about 1919 to live in Granada until the end of the civil war, when he left for Argentina. De Falla's three major works, all intended as ballet scores, have deep Andalucian roots: *Noches en los Jardines de España* (Nights in the Gardens of Spain) evokes the Muslim past and the sounds and sensations of a hot Andalucian night, while *El Amor Brujo* (Love, the Magician) and *El Sombrero de Tres Picos* (The Three-Cornered Hat) are rooted in flamenco. Andrés Segovia from Jaén province was one of the major classical guitarists of the 20th century, and Málaga's Carlos Álvarez ranks among the top baritones of the opera world today.

For all the gigs and festivals, log on to Indy Rock (www.indyrock.es). Clubbing Spain (www.clubbingspain) and Satisfaxion (www.satisfaxion.com) have what you need to know about house and techno events.

Literature

ISLAMIC PERIOD

The 11th century saw a flowering of both Arabic and Hebrew poetry in Andalucía. The Arabic was chiefly love poetry, by the likes of Ibn Hazm and Ibn Zaydun from Córdoba, and Ibn Ammar and Al-Mutamid, a king, from Seville. Outstanding among the Jewish poets was Judah Ha-Levi, considered one of the greatest of all post-biblical Hebrew writers. He divided his life between Granada, Seville, Toledo and Córdoba, before deciding that a return to Palestine was the only solution for Spanish Jews.

The philosopher Averroës, or Ibn Rushd (1126–98), from Córdoba, wrote commentaries on Aristotle that tried to reconcile science with religious faith, and had great influence on Christian thought in the 13th and 14th centuries. This remarkable polymath was also a judge, astronomer, mathematician and personal physician and adviser to two Almohad rulers.

SIGLO DE ORO

In Andalucía, Spain's literary Siglo de Oro (Golden Century), roughly the mid-16th to the mid-17th centuries, began with the circle that gathered in Seville around Christopher Columbus' great-grandson Álvaro Colón. The group included the playwrights Juan de la Cueva and Lope de Rueda.

Córdoba's Luis de Góngora (1561–1627) is considered the greatest Spanish sonneteer and, by many, the greatest Spanish poet. Góngora's metaphorical, descriptive verses are above all intended as a source of sensuous pleasure. Some of them celebrate the more idyllic aspects of the Guadalquivir valley.

'In his Andalucian years Cervantes procured for himself a number of lawsuits, spells in jail and even excommunications'

Miguel de Cervantes (1547–1616) was no Andalucian but he did spend 10 troubled years in Andalucía collecting unpaid taxes and procuring oil and wheat for the Spanish navy. In his Andalucian years Cervantes also procured for himself a number of lawsuits, spells in jail and even excommunications – no doubt grist to the mill of one of the inventors of the novel. His *El Ingenioso Hidalgo Don Quijote de La Mancha* (The Inventive Hidalgo Don Quijote of La Mancha) appeared in 1605. The comically insane knight Quijote and his comically dim companion, Sancho Panza, conducted most of their deranged ramblings on the plains of La Mancha, but did stray into the Sierra Morena for a few crazed episodes. Some of Cervantes' short *Novelas Ejemplares* (Exemplary Novels) chronicle turbulent 16th-century Seville.

THE GENERATIONS OF '98 & '27

Andalucian literary creativity didn't seriously flower again until the late 19th century. The Generation of '98 was a loose grouping of Spanish intellectuals who shared a deep disturbance about Spain's national decline, symbolised by the loss of its last colonies in 1898. Antonio Machado (1875–1939), the group's leading poet, was born in Seville but spent most of his adult life outside Andalucía, except for a few years as a teacher in Baeza, where he completed *Campos de Castilla* (Fields of Castile), a set of melancholy poems evoking the landscape of Castile. Machado's friend Juan Ramón Jiménez (1881–1958), from Moguer near Huelva, touchingly and amusingly brought to life his home town in *Platero y Yo* (Platero and I), a prose poem that tells of his childhood wanderings with his donkey and confidant, Platero. Jiménez, the 1956 Nobel literature laureate, stands as a kind of bridge between the Generation of '98 and the later Generation of '27, who took their name from the readings and talks they organised in Seville in 1927 for the tercentenary of the death of Luis de Góngora.

The loose-knit Generation of '27 included the poets Rafael Alberti, from El Puerto de Santa María, and Vicente Aleixandre (the 1977 Nobel literature laureate) and Luis Cernuda, both from Seville. Artist Salvador Dalí, film-maker Luis Buñuel and composer Manuel de Falla were also associated with them, but the outstanding literary figure – and for many, the major Spanish writer since Cervantes – was Federico García Lorca, from Granada.

LORCA

Federico García Lorca (1898–1936) was a musician, artist, theatre director, poet, playwright and much more. Though charming and popular, he felt alienated – by his homosexuality, his leftish outlook and, probably, his talent itself – from his home city Granada ('a wasteland populated by the worst bourgeoisie in Spain') and from Spanish society as a whole. Lorca identified with Andalucía's marginalised *gitanos* and longed for spontaneity and vivacity. He eulogised both Granada's Islamic past and what he considered the 'authentic' Andalucía (to be found in Málaga, Córdoba, Cádiz – anywhere except Granada).

Lorca first won major popularity with *El Romancero Gitano* (The Gypsy Ballads), a colourful 1928 collection of verses on *gitano* themes, full of startling metaphors and with the simplicity of flamenco song. This was followed between 1933 and 1936 by the three tragedies for which he is best known: *Bodas de Sangre* (Blood Wedding), *Yerma* (Barren) and *La Casa de Bernarda Alba* (The House of Bernarda Alba) – brooding, dark but dramatic works dealing with themes of entrapment and liberation, passion and repression. Lorca was executed by the Nationalists during the civil war.

Or was Lorca murdered after all? Miguel Hermoso's 2003 Andalucía-produced film *La Luz Prodigiosa* (Marvellous Light) revolves around a rumour that the great writer somehow survived the Nationalist executioners.

RECENT WRITING

Most of Spain's post–civil war literary lights have hailed from outside Andalucía, but Antonio Muñoz Molina (born in Úbeda, Jaén province, in 1956) is one of the country's leading contemporary novelists, a writer

---

THE ROMANCE OF ANDALUCÍA

Chris 'Driving Over Lemons' Stewart is not the first foreigner whom Andalucía has inspired to successful literary endeavours. Far from it. Just as Stewart and thousands of other recent ex-patriates have been attracted to Andalucía by the prospect of a slower-paced, less expensive life with more hours of sunshine in a vaguely exotic setting, so 19th-century travellers and writers were lured by Andalucía's combination of backwardness, poverty, mystery, sensuousness and its perceived spiritual wealth. The picturesque decay of Andalucía's cities, its flamenco music and dance, its legend-filled past, its people's love of fiesta, fun and bullfighting, its rugged, brigand-haunted mountains, its heat, its dark-haired, dark-eyed people – all these helped to give birth to the romantic image of Andalucía.

One of the first Romantic writings to be set in Andalucía (Seville, in this case) was *Don Juan*, the masterpiece of Lord Byron, who visited Andalucía in 1809 and wrote the mock-epic poem near the end of his life in the early 1820s. In 1826 France's Viscount Chateaubriand published a melancholic novella, *Les Aventures du Dernier Abencerage* (The Adventures of the Last Abencerraj), in which a Muslim prince returns to Granada after the Christian conquest. The Alhambra was established as the quintessential symbol of exotic Andalucía by *Les Orientales* (1829) by Victor Hugo (who didn't visit Granada), and *Tales of the Alhambra* (1832) by the American Washington Irving (who lived in the palace for a few months). *Carmen*, a violent novella of *gitano* love and revenge in Seville, written in the 1840s by Frenchman Prosper Mérimée, added subtropical sensuality to the Andalucian mystique.

Composers, too, felt the pull of the images Andalucía conjured up. The Don Juan story (originally written as a play by 17th-century Spanish playwright Tirso de Molina) inspired an operatic version, *Don Giovanni*, by Mozart in the 18th century. If the Don Juan story gave Andalucian men a reputation as chauvinist seducers, it was Georges Bizet's 1875 opera *Carmen*, based on Mérimée's novella, which fixed the stereotype of Andalucian women as full of fire, guile and flashing beauty.

Alexandre Dumas came close to summing it all up when he characterised Andalucía as a 'gay, lovely land with castanets in her hand and a garland on her brow'. The spell this image casts has hardly faded with the passing of more than a century.

Ian Gibson's *Federico García Lorca* (1990) is an excellent biography of Andalucía's most celebrated writer. Gibson also penned *The Assassination of Federico García Lorca* (1979), revealing the murky story of Lorca's murder near Granada in the civil war.

of depth, imagination and great story-telling ability. Probably his best novel to date is *El Jinete Polaco* (The Polish Jockey; 1991), set in 'Mágina', a fictionalised Úbeda, in the mid-20th century.

Poet, novelist and essayist José Manuel Caballero Bonald was born in Jerez de la Frontera in 1926. His 1962 novel *Dos Días de Septiembre* (Two Days in September) treats the social inequalities of rural Andalucía using experimental narrative techniques such as stream of consciousness. *Ágata Ojo de Gato* (Agate, Cat's Eye; 1974) is an almost magical-realist work that's set in Andalucía although not in any recognisable time or place.

Playwright, poet and novelist Antonio Gala (1930–), from Córdoba, sets much of his work in the past, which he uses to illuminate the present. *La Pasión Turca* (Turkish Passion; 1993) is his best-known novel.

Architecture

Andalucía's most celebrated buildings – the Alhambra (p305) in Granada and the Mezquita (p279) in Córdoba – represent the supreme lasting achievements of the Islamic period (AD 711–1492). For a detailed look at Islamic architecture in Andalucía, see p68.

Andalucía's most significant pre-Islamic structures are Roman – notably at Itálica (p123), near Seville, which possesses the biggest of all Roman amphitheatres; Baelo Claudia (Bolonia; p203), with its theatre; and Carmona (p125), with its necropolis. The Romans bequeathed Andalucía the happy invention of the interior patio, an idea later taken up by the Muslims.

GOTHIC

Christian architecture reached northern and western Andalucía with the Reconquista (Christian reconquest) in the 13th century. The prevailing style at the time was Gothic, with its pointed arches, ribbed ceilings, flying buttresses and fancy window tracery. Seville's cathedral (p91), the biggest in Spain, is almost entirely Gothic. Dozens of Gothic or part-Gothic churches, castles and mansions are dotted around Andalucía. Many buildings that began life in Gothic times were finished or added to later, so they ended up as a stylistic hotchpotch. Such are the cathedrals at Jerez de la Frontera (Gothic, Mudejar, baroque and neoclassical; p184) and Málaga (Gothic, Renaissance and baroque; p234).

The final flourish of Spanish Gothic was Isabelline Gothic, from the time of the Catholic Monarchs, whose own burial chapel – the Capilla Real (p93) in Granada – is the supreme work in this style. Isabelline Gothic features sinuously curved arches and tracery, and façades with lacelike ornament and low-relief sculptures (including lots of heraldic shields). A fine example is the Palacio de Jabalquinto (p355) in Baeza.

RENAISSANCE

The Renaissance in architecture was an Italian-originated return to classical ideals of harmony and proportion, dominated by columns and shapes such as the square, circle and triangle.

Spanish Renaissance architecture had three phases. First came plateresque, taking its name from the Spanish for silversmith, *platero*, because it was primarily a decorative genre, with effects resembling those of silverware. Round-arched portals were framed by classical columns and stone sculpture.

Next came a more purist style whose ultimate expression is the Palacio de Carlos V (p309) in Granada's Alhambra, designed by the Rome-trained Pedro Machuca.

The last and plainest phase was Herreresque, after Juan de Herrera (1530–97), creator of the austere palace-monastery complex of El Escorial, near Madrid, and Seville's Archivo de Indias (p96).

All three phases were spanned in Jaén province by Andrés de Vandelvira (1509–75), who gave the town of Úbeda one of the finest ensembles of Renaissance buildings in Spain (see p360). Vandelvira was much influenced by Burgos-born Diego de Siloé (1495–1563), who was chiefly responsible for the cathedrals of Granada, Málaga and Guadix.

This was an era in which the gentry could build themselves gorgeous urban mansions with delightful central patios surrounded by harmonious arched galleries – such as the Palacio de la Condesa de Lebrija (p101) and Casa de Pilatos (p103) in Seville or the Palacio de Vázquez de Molina (p359) in Úbeda.

BAROQUE

The reaction to Renaissance sobriety came in the colours and movement of baroque, which reached its peak of elaboration in the 18th century. Andalucía was one of the places where baroque blossomed most brilliantly.

Baroque was at root classical, but it crammed a great deal of ornament onto façades and stuffed interiors full of ornate stucco sculpture and gilt paint. Retables – the large, sculptural altarpieces that adorn many Spanish churches to illustrate Christian stories and teachings – reached extremes of gilded extravagance.

Before full-blown baroque there was a kind of transitional stage, exemplified by more sober works such as Alonso Cano's 17th-century façade for the Granada cathedral (p311). The most extravagant work is termed Churrigueresque after a Barcelona family of sculptors and architects named Churriguera.

Seville has probably as many baroque churches per square kilometre as any city in the world. However, the church at Monasterio de La Cartuja (p316) in Granada, by Francisco Hurtado Izquierdo (1669–1728), is one of the most lavish baroque creations in all of Spain. Hurtado's followers adorned the small town of Priego de Córdoba (p296) with seven or eight baroque churches.

'Andalucía was one of the places where baroque blossomed most brilliantly'

NEOCLASSICISM

Throughout Europe in the mid-18th century, the cleaner, restrained lines of neoclassicism came into fashion – another return to Greek and Roman ideals, expressing the Enlightenment philosophy of the era. Cádiz has the biggest neoclassical heritage in Andalucía. But the single most notable neoclassical building is Seville's enormous, almost monastic Antigua Fábrica de Tabacos (Old Tobacco Factory; p103), built to house an early state-supported industry.

19TH & 20TH CENTURIES

The 19th century saw revivals of all sorts of earlier architectural styles: Andalucía experienced some neo-Gothic, and even a bit of neobaroque, but most prevalent were neo-Mudejar and neo-Islamic. Mansions such as the Palacio de Orleans y Borbón (p180), in Sanlúcar de Barrameda, and public buildings ranging from train stations in Seville to markets in Málaga and Tarifa were constructed in pleasing imitation of past Islamic architectural styles. For the 1929 Exposición Iberoamericana, fancy buildings in almost every past Andalucian style were concocted in Seville.

During the Franco period, drab, Soviet-style blocks of workers' housing sprang up in many cities. New public buildings such as Huelva's town hall exhibited a bland classicism similar to that favoured by Stalin and Mussolini. Long stretches of Andalucía's coasts began to be lined with scrappy concrete hotels and resorts, controlled only by piecemeal, hotchpotch urban planning.

Since Franco, the major positive impetus has been Expo '92 in Seville, which brought the city a sea of avant-garde exhibition pavilions and several spectacular new bridges over the Guadalquivir.

Painting, Sculpture & Metalwork

Andalucian art goes back to the Stone Age and reached its creative peak during the 17th century.

'Andalucían art reached its creative peak during the 17th century'

PRE-CHRISTIAN ART

Stone Age hunter-gatherers left impressive rock paintings of animals, people and mythical figures in caves such as the Cueva de la Pileta (p264) near Ronda, in Málaga province, and the Cueva de Los Letreros (p396) near Vélez Blanco, in Almería province. The later Iberians carved stone sculptures of animals, deities and other figures, often with Carthaginian or Greek influence. The archaeological museums in Seville (p103) and Córdoba (p285), and Jaén's Museo Provincial (p349) have good Iberian collections.

The artistic legacy of the Romans is at its best in mosaics and sculpture, with some wonderful examples at Itálica, Écija and Carmona (all in Sevilla province), and in Seville's Palacio de la Condesa de Lebrija and the Córdoba and Seville archaeological museums.

In Andalucía's Islamic era (AD 711–1492) the decorative arts reached great heights in the service of architecture – see p68 for further information on Islamic architecture.

GOTHIC & RENAISSANCE ART

Seville has been Andalucía's artistic epicentre ever since the Reconquista. One of the earliest masterpieces of Andalucian Christian art is Seville cathedral's huge Gothic main retable (1482), designed by a Flemish sculptor, Pieter Dancart, and carved with more than 1000 biblical figures. Around this time, Frenchman Lorenzo Mercadante de Bretaña and his local disciple, Pedro Millán, brought a new naturalism and detail into Sevillan religious sculpture. Then Seville's 16th-century boom threw it open to the humanist and classical trends of the Renaissance. Alejo Fernández (1470–1545), an artist of probable German origin, ushered in the Renaissance in painting; the Italian Pietro Torrigiano (1472–1528) did the same for sculpture.

A 16th-century master artisan known as Maestro Bartolomé created some of Spain's loveliest *rejas* (wrought-iron grilles) in churches in Granada and Jaén province.

SIGLO DE ORO

Early in the 17th century Sevillan artists such as Francisco Pacheco and Juan de Roelas began to paint in a more naturalistic style, heralding baroque. With its large, colourful, accessible images, the baroque movement took deep root in Andalucía. Great Seville artists of this, Spain's artistic Siglo de Oro (Golden Century), included the mystical Francisco de Zurbarán; Diego Velázquez, who left Seville in his 20s to become an official court painter in Madrid and ultimately the major artist of Spain's cultural golden age; and the masters of full-blown baroque Bartolomé Esteban Murillo, Juan de Valdés Leal and sculptors Juan Martínez Montañés and Pedro Roldán. See p102 for more on all these major figures.

Velázquez's friend Alonso Cano (1601–77), a gifted architect, painter and sculptor, studied under Pacheco in Seville, but did some of his best work on Granada and Málaga cathedrals. Málaga-based Pedro de Mena (1628–88), the most sought-after Andalucian sculptor of his time, produced a welter of saints, child Christs and other religious work.

18TH & 19TH CENTURIES

An impoverished Spain in this period produced just one outstanding artist – Francisco de Goya (1746–1828), from Aragón in northern Spain. Goya recorded Andalucian bullfights at Ronda, and tradition has it that he painted his famous *La Maja Vestida* and *La Maja Desnuda* – near-identical portraits of one woman, clothed and unclothed – at a royal hunting lodge in what is now the Parque Nacional de Doñana. A few Goya works are on view in Andalucía in places such as Seville cathedral and the Oratorio de la Santa Cueva in Cádiz.

20TH CENTURY

Pablo Picasso (1881–1973) was born in Málaga, but moved to northern Spain when he was nine. Picasso's career involved many abrupt changes. His sombre Blue Period (1901–04) was followed by the cheerier Pink Period; later, with Georges Braque, Picasso pioneered cubism. A major Picasso museum finally opened in Málaga in 2003 (see p235), with a large collection of his works donated by his daughter-in-law, Christine Ruiz-Picasso, at last giving his native city a slice of the Picasso pie.

Other talented 20th-century artists followed Picasso's footsteps out of Andalucía, among them the Granada-born abstract expressionist José Guerrero (1914–91), who found fame in New York in the 1950s. A museum dedicated to him opened in Granada in 2000. Among the more notable artists who actually worked in Andalucía were Córdoba's Julio Romero de Torres (1880–1930), a painter of dark, sensual female nudes; portraitist Daniel Vázquez Díaz (1882–1969) from Huelva; and Carmen Laffón, a realistic, intimate painter of everyday things, born in Seville in 1934. Leading contemporary artists working in Andalucía include Chema Cobo, born in Tarifa in 1952, and Pedro García Romero, born in Aracena in 1964.

DID YOU KNOW?

Picasso revisited Málaga for annual holidays from 1891 to 1900, but never returned thereafter, settling in France for good in 1904.

Cinema

Andalucía is not in the forefront of the film scene in a country whose creative but short-of-funds cinema industry is heavily concentrated in Madrid. Even an Andalucian accent is a disadvantage for actors trying to make their way in the national capital. Nevertheless some good films are coming out of Andalucía even if they are not reaching vast international audiences. The Andalucian TV company Canal Sur has been involved in the production of several recent movies, including *Nadie Conoce a Nadie* (Nobody Knows Anybody; 1999), Mateo Gil's psychological thriller set in Semana Santa (Holy Week) in Seville, and *Carlos Contra el Mundo* (Carlos Against the World; 2002), Chiqui Carabante's comic film about a Málaga teenager thrust into unwelcome responsibility when his father dies. Another successful Andalucian production to look out for is Pablo Carbonell's comic *Atún y Chocolate* (Tuna and Chocolate; 2004), filmed in the Cádiz town of Barbate (p201), with a plot revolving around weddings, tuna fishing and hashish smuggling.

Non-Andalucian productions with Andalucian themes have included the charming *Al Sur de Granada* (South from Granada; 2003), a version of English writer Gerald Brenan's book about his life in an Andalucian village in the 1920s (directed by Fernando Colomo), and *800 Balas* (800 Bullets; 2002), a tribute by Alex de la Iglesia (director of *Dance with the Devil*) to the 'spaghetti Westerns' that are probably Andalucía's greatest claim to cinematic fame. It was in the early 1960s that makers of Westerns realised that the desert landscape around Tabernas, Almería, provided them with a perfect location and that they could shoot films there at much lower cost than in Hollywood. The Clint Eastwood 'Man with No Name' trilogy – *A Fistful of Dollars, For a Few Dollars More* and *The Good, the Bad and the Ugly* – directed by Italian Sergio Leone (hence the 'spaghetti' label) were the most celebrated of over 150 films made in 10 years in Almería. Three Wild West town sets remain today as tourist attractions (see the boxed text The Wild West, p382).

> 'Spaghetti Westerns are probably Andalucía's greatest claim to cinematic fame'

The 1960s saw several other celebrated films shot, or partly shot, in Andalucía – notably *Lawrence of Arabia*, in which Seville buildings such as the Casa de Pilatos (p103) and Plaza de España (p103) were used for scenes in Cairo, Jerusalem and Damascus. For Lawrence's attack on Aqaba, a whole fake town was built on the Almería coast near Carboneras. British director Ridley Scott (*Alien, Gladiator, Blade Runner* and *Black Hawk Down*) came to the Casa de Pilatos and Seville's Alcázar (p94) in 2004 for medieval-Jerusalem sequences in his crusades film *The Kingdom of Heaven*, with Orlando Bloom. The Tabernas desert and Almería's Cabo de Gata promontory also provide the backdrop for parts of such classics as *Cleopatra, Dr Zhivago* and *Indiana Jones and the Last Crusade*.

The one Andalucian movie name that everyone today knows is Antonio Banderas. Born in Málaga in 1960, the dashing and talented Banderas made his name with some very challenging parts in films directed by the doyen of modern Spanish cinema, Pedro Almodóvar, including *Women on the Verge of a Nervous Breakdown* and *Tie Me Up! Tie Me Down!*, before moving to Hollywood and a string of hits such as *Philadelphia, The Mask of Zorro* and *Spy Kids*.

The rising Andalucian star most likely to make it as big as Banderas is Paz Vega, from Seville, who won Cannes' best new actress award for her lead in the steamy but serious *Lucía y el Sexo* (Lucía and Sex; 2001) and followed up with another success in the lighter *El Otro Lado de la Cama* (The Other Side of the Bed; 2002).

Another increasingly important Andalucian contribution to Spanish cinema is Málaga's annual Festival de Cine Español. Held over a week in late April and early May, this event began in 1998 and grows in size and importance each year.

Environment

THE LAND

Andalucía has four main geographic regions, all running roughly east–west across it: the Sierra Morena, the Guadalquivir valley, the mountains and the coastal plain.

The Sierra Morena, a range of hills that rarely tops 1000m, rolls across the north of Andalucía. The area is sparsely populated and divided between evergreen oak woodlands and scrub, and rough pasture used for grazing.

The fertile valley of the 660km-long Río Guadalquivir, Andalucía's longest river, stretches across Andalucía south of the Sierra Morena. The Guadalquivir rises in Jaén province, flows westward through Córdoba and Seville and enters the Atlantic at Sanlúcar de Barrameda. The lower Guadalquivir is straddled by a broad plain: before entering the ocean, the river splits into a marshy delta known as Las Marismas del Guadalquivir, which includes the Parque Nacional de Doñana. The Guadalquivir is navigable as far upstream as Seville.

Between the Guadalquivir valley and the Mediterranean coast rises the Cordillera Bética, a band of rugged mountains which widens out from its beginnings in southwest Andalucía to a breadth of 125km or so in the east. The Cordillera Bética continues east from Andalucía across the Murcia and Valencia regions, then re-emerges from the Mediterranean as the Balearic islands of Ibiza and Mallorca. It was pushed up by pressure of the African tectonic plate on the Iberian subplate 15 to 20 million years ago. Much of it is composed of limestone, yielding some wonderful karstic rock formations.

In Andalucía, the cordillera (mountain range) divides into two main chains: the more northerly Sistema Subbético and the southerly Sistema Penibético. The two chains are separated by a series of valleys, plains and basins. The Sistema Penibético includes the 75km-long Sierra Nevada, southeast of Granada, with a series of 3000m-plus peaks, including Mulhacén (3479m), the highest mountain on mainland Spain.

Andalucía's coastal plain varies in width from 50km in the far west to virtually nothing in parts of Granada and Almería provinces, where the Sierra de la Contraviesa and Sierra de Cabo de Gata drop away in sheer cliffs to the Mediterranean.

WILDLIFE

Andalucía's wildlife is among the most diverse in Europe, thanks to its varied, often untamed terrain, which has allowed the survival of several species that have died out in other countries.

Animals

Many animals are nocturnal but if you want to see wildlife, and know where to look, you're unlikely to go home disappointed. See p16 for an itinerary incorporating the best wildlife-watching sites.

MAMMALS

Andalucía has perhaps 10,000 to 12,000 ibex (cabra montés), a stocky mountain goat whose males have distinctive long horns. The ibex spends summer hopping agilely around high-altitude precipices and descends to lower elevations in winter. Around 5000 ibex live in the Sierra Nevada,

> **DID YOU KNOW?**
>
> The name Guadalquivir derives from the Arabic Wadi al-Kabir (Great River). The Romans called it the Betis and the ancient Greeks the Tartessos.

> *Wildlife Travelling Companion Spain* by John Measures covers 150 of Spain's best sites for viewing flora and fauna – many of them in Andalucía – with details of how to reach them. It also contains a basic field guide to some common animals and plants.

2000 or more in the Cazorla natural park, 1500 in the Sierras de Tejeda y Almijara and 1000 in the Sierra de las Nieves.

Only about 50 wolves *(lobos)* now survive in the Sierra Morena, mostly in Jaén province's Parque Natural Sierra de Andújar. In 1986 the wolf was declared in danger of extinction in Andalucía and, in an effort to protect

MISSING LYNX?

The Iberian (or pardel) lynx *(lince ibérico* to Spaniards, *Lynx pardina* to scientists) is a beautiful feline un-ique to the Iberian Peninsula. It's twice the size of a domestic cat, with a black-spotted brown coat, a short, black-tipped tail, and ears with distinctively pointed black tufts. It lives for up to 15 years and eats little but rabbit, which it catches with great agility and a burst of lightning speed. The lynx likes to inhabit thick Mediterranean woodland interspersed with patches of scrub and open ground; however, it's on the verge of becoming the first extinct feline since the sabre-tooth tiger.

The lynx was still common enough to be legally hunted until 1966, but by 1988 its numbers were down to between 1000 and 1200. Today, optimists argue that there might be 400 left. Pessimists think there are less than 200. The only known breeding populations are in two areas of Andalucía: one is the eastern Sierra Morena, with at least 100 and possibly more than 200 lynxes, chiefly in the Parque Natural Sierra de Andújar and neighbouring Parque Natural Sierra de Cardeña y Montoro; the other is the Parque Nacional de Doñana and adjoining Parque Natural de Doñana, with around 50 lynxes.

The reasons for this sad decline are several:

- disastrous epidemics that have decimated the rabbit population
- loss of habitat due to new farmland, roads, dams and pine or eucalyptus plantations
- illegal traps and snares set for other animals
- road accidents

It took Spain's politicians a very long time to face up to the emergency. Research, conferences and strategy proposals abounded, but action was scarce and uncoordinated. From 1996 to 2004 the two major actors in the saga, the national environment ministry in Madrid and the Andalucian environment department in Seville, were in the hands of opposing political parties – the Partido Popular (PP; People's Party) and the Partido Socialista Obrero Español (PSOE; Spanish Socialist Workers' Party) respectively – which seemed incapable of cooperating on anything.

Special facilities for an in-captivity breeding programme were built at El Acebuche in Doñana national park as long ago as 1992, but not until 2001 did the National Nature Protection Com-mission finally approve a captive-breeding project. And by late 2002 the Andalucian environment department was still refusing permission for wild lynxes to be captured for this purpose. It was around then that Nicolás Guzmán, coordinator of the National Lynx Conservation Strategy, an-nounced that recent studies indicated there were only 160 lynxes left. In mid-2003 Seville and Madrid at last signed a coordination agreement and decided to accelerate the captive-breeding programme. On 31 December 2003 a breeding-age male from the Sierra Morena, nicknamed Garfio (Hook), was finally brought to El Acebuche to join four females (Esperanza, Sali, Aura and Morena) already gathered there. Garfio was joined in March 2004 by Cromo, a young male who had been found on the verge of starvation in the Sierra de Andújar the year before, but had made a recovery in the company of an American lynx (bobcat) cub at the zoo at Jerez de la Frontera. Another male was due to be captured in Doñana to join the breeding programme.

Meanwhile efforts continue to try to help the wild lynx population to recover. Since most lynxes live on privately-owned land, the national and regional governments and some conser-vation organisations have signed over 100 agreements with landowners to improve lynx habitat and allow rabbit populations to grow.

Between 2000 and 2006, the Andalucian and Spanish governments and the EU are spending over €30 million on assorted programmes to help save the Iberian lynx. That's somewhere bet-ween €75,000 and €150,000 per lynx, depending how many lynxes you think are left.

it from hunters and farmers, farmers are now awarded compensation if their animals are attacked by wolves. But the wolf population has still sunk to levels that are probably fatally low. Around 1500 to 2000 wolves survive in northern Spain. See Missing Lynx? (p52) for the story of Andalucía's other famously endangered species.

More common beasts include the mainly nocturnal wild boar (jabalí), which are found in thick woods, marshes and farmers' root crops; the red deer (ciervo), roe deer (corzo) and fallow deer (gamo), in forests and woodlands; the genet (gineta), rather like a nocturnal, short-legged cat with a black-spotted white coat and a long, striped tail, in woodland and scrub; the mainly nocturnal Egyptian mongoose (meloncillo), in woods, scrub and marshes, especially in southwestern Andalucía; the red squirrel (ardilla), in mountain forests; the nocturnal badger (tejón), in woods with thick undergrowth; the fox (zorro), common in scattered areas; the otter (nutria), along some rivers; and the beech marten (garduña), in deciduous forests and on rocky outcrops and cliffs. The mouflon (muflón), a wild sheep, has been introduced to the Cazorla natural park and a couple of other areas in the region to help satisfy rural Spaniards' passion for hunting.

Gibraltar is famous for its colony of Barbary apes (see p223), the only wild primates in Europe. The Bahía de Algeciras and Strait of Gibraltar harbour plenty of dolphins (delfines; common, striped and bottlenose) and some whales (ballenas; pilot, killer and even sperm) – see p224.

BIRDS
Andalucía is a magnet for bird-watchers. The rugged mountains ranges and many coastal wetlands provide ideal habitats for many species.

Raptors
Andalucía has 13 resident raptor (bird-of-prey) species and several other summer visitors from Africa. You'll see some of them circling or hovering over the hills in many areas.

The Sierra Morena is a stronghold of Europe's biggest bird, the rare black vulture (buitre negro). The few hundred pairs in Spain are probably the world's biggest population.

Another emblematic and extremely rare bird is the Spanish imperial eagle (águila imperial), found in no other country. Its white shoulders distinguish it from other imperial eagles. Of the 130 pairs remaining, about 30 are in Andalucía, of which seven (at the last count) are in the Parque Nacional de Doñana. Like the lynx, the imperial has suffered from the decline in the rabbit population, but poisoned bait put out by farmers or hunters is its greatest enemy.

Other large birds of prey in Andalucía include the golden eagle (águila real) and several other eagles, and the griffon vulture (buitre leonado) and Egyptian vulture (alimoche), all found in mountain regions. Among smaller birds of prey, many of them found around woodlands and forests, are the kestrel (cernícalo), buzzard (ratonero), sparrowhawk (gavilán), various harriers (aguiluchos) and the red kite (milano real). You may see the acrobatic black kite (milano negro) over open ground near marshes, rivers and rubbish dumps.

Storks
The large, ungainly white stork (cigüeña blanca), actually black-and-white, nests from spring to summer on electricity pylons, trees and towers – sometimes right in the middle of towns – in western Andalucía. Your attention will be drawn to it by the loud clacking of beaks from these

DID YOU KNOW?
Wolves have killed about 1500 head of livestock in Andalucía since 1990; farmers complain that compensation from the regional government is insufficient and takes years to be paid.

Bird-watchers will also need a field guide such as the Collins Field Guide: Birds of Britain and Europe by Roger Tory Peterson, Guy Mountfort and PAD Hollom, or the slimmer Collins Pocket Guide: Birds of Britain & Europe.

lofty perches. A few pairs of the much rarer black stork *(cigüeña negra)*, all black, also nest in western Andalucía, typically on cliff ledges. In spring both types of stork migrate north from Africa across the Strait of Gibraltar (see p212).

Water Birds

Andalucía is a haven for water birds, mainly thanks to extensive wetlands along the Atlantic coast, such as those at the mouths of the Guadalquivir and Odiel rivers. Hundreds of thousands of migratory birds, including an estimated 80% of Western Europe's wild ducks *(patos)*, winter in the Doñana wetlands at the mouth of the Guadalquivir, and many more call in during spring and autumn migrations.

Laguna de Fuente de Piedra, near Antequera, is Europe's main breeding site for the greater flamingo *(flamenco)*, with as many as 20,000 pairs rearing chicks in spring and summer. This beautiful pink bird can also be seen in several other places, including Cabo de Gata, Doñana and the Marismas del Odiel.

Other Birds

Andalucía's many other colourful birds are the golden oriole *(oropéndola)*, seen in orchards and deciduous woodlands in summer (the male has an unmistakable bright- yellow body); the orange-and-black *hoopoe (abubilla)*, with its distinctive crest, common in open woodlands, on farmland and golf courses; and the gold, brown and turquoise bee-eater *(abejaruco)*, which nests in sandy banks in summer.

OTHER FAUNA

From spring to autumn, Andalucía is a paradise for butterfly and moth enthusiasts. Most of Europe's butterflies *(mariposas)* are found in Spain. Also here are several bat *(murciélago)* species, salamanders *(salamandras)*, chameleons *(camaleones*; most numerous in the Axarquía region), numerous lizards *(lagartos)*, and snakes *(serpientes)*.

Plants

The variety of Andalucian flora is astonishing, as anyone who witnesses the spectacular wild-flower displays in spring and early summer will testify. Andalucía has around 5000 plant species, some 150 of them unique – an abundance largely due to the fact that, during the last ice age, many plants that died out further north were able to survive at this southerly latitude.

HIGH-ALTITUDE PLANTS

The Sierra Nevada, southeast of Granada, with several 3000m-plus peaks, is home to 2100 plant species. About 60 of these are unique to the Sierra Nevada. The Cazorla natural park in northeast Andalucía, another mountainous region, has 2300 plant species, 24 of them found nowhere else. When the snows melt, the alpine and subalpine zones above the tree line bloom with small, rock-clinging plants and high pastures full of gentians, orchids, crocuses and narcissuses.

FOREST & WOODLANDS

Many mountain slopes are clothed in pine *(pino)* forests, often commercially grown. The tall black pine *(pino laricio)*, with horizontally spreading branches clustering near the top, likes terrain above 1300m. The maritime pine *(pino resinero or pino marítimo)*, with its rounded top, can grow all the way up to elevations of 1500m. The Aleppo pine *(pino carrasco)*, with a bushy top and separated, often bare branches, flourishes below 1000m. The lovely umbrella pine *(pino piñonero)*, with its broad, umbrella-like top and edible kernels, prefers low-lying and coastal areas – it's characteristic of the Doñana area.

The natural vegetation of many lower slopes and gentler hill country is Mediterranean woodland, with trees adapted to a warm, fairly dry climate, such as the wild olive *(acebuche)*, carob *(algarrobo)*, the holm or ilex oak *(encina)*, the cork oak *(alcornoque)* and the gall oak *(quejigo)*. These oaks are more gnarled and smaller and pricklier in the leaf than the tall oaks of more temperate regions. The best surviving stands of Mediterranean woodland are in the Sierra de Grazalema and Los Alcornocales natural parks in Cádiz province. Large expanses of woodland in these areas, and in the Sierra Morena, have been converted over the centuries into woodland-pastures known as *dehesas*, which provide a fine example of sustainable symbiosis between humans, plants and animals. The cork oak's thick outer bark is stripped every ninth summer for cork; you'll see the visible scars – a bright terracotta colour if they're new – on some trees. The holm oak can be pruned about every four years and the offcuts used for charcoal. Meanwhile, livestock can graze the pastures, and in autumn pigs are turned out to hungrily gobble up the fallen acorns, a diet considered to produce the tastiest ham of all.

The rare Spanish fir *(pinsapo)*, a handsome, dark-green relic of the extensive fir forests around the Mediterranean in the Tertiary period (which ended approximately 2.5 million years ago), survives in significant numbers only in the Sierra de Grazalema, Sierra de las Nieves and Sierra Bermeja, all in southwest Andalucía, and in northern Morocco. It likes north-facing slopes up to 1800m. It can grow to 30m high and lives for up to 500 years.

At ground level Andalucía's forests sprout some 2000 species of fungi *(setas)* in autumn. Many are edible and appear in markets and restaurants; others are poisonous – and the decisions on which are which are best left to the local experts!

Definitely not wild but in some areas the dominant feature of the landscape – especially in Jaén and Córdoba provinces – are the lines upon lines of olive trees *(olivos)*, rolling over the horizon and far beyond. Andalucía produces about 20% of the world's olive oil (see p345). Other food-bearing trees grown in many parts of Andalucía are the almond *(almendro)*, with beautiful pink winter blossom, and the chestnut *(castaño)*, with incredible star-bursts of catkins in midsummer. Widely cultivated for timber, though now unfashionable because of its insatiable thirst, is the eucalyptus *(eucalipto)*.

In summer many watercourses are lined with the unmistakable bright pink flowers of oleander *(adelfa)* bushes.

SCRUB & STEPPE
Where there are no trees and no agriculture, the land is likely to be either scrub *(matorral)* or steppe *(estepa)*. Typical scrub plants include gorse *(tojo)*, juniper *(enebro)*, shrubs of the cistus *(jara)* family and herbs such as lavender *(lavanda)*, rosemary *(romero)*, fennel *(hinojo)* and thyme *(tomillo)*. Orchids, gladioli and irises may flower beneath these shrubs.

Steppe is either produced by overgrazing or occurs naturally in hot, very dry areas such as the southeast of Almería province. Plant life in Andalucía is sparse, often mostly cacti, but some areas can bloom with colour after rain.

Flower lovers should carry Betty Molesworth Allen's *A Selection of Wildflowers of Southern Spain* and, if possible, the classic *Flowers of South-West Europe* by Oleg Polunin and BE Smythies.

PARKS & OTHER PROTECTED AREAS

Much of Andalucía remains either wilderness barely touched by human hand, or countryside managed in traditional and sustainable ways. Its landscapes never cease to surprise with their beauty, and nearly all of the most spectacular and ecologically important country is under official protection.

Andalucía has the biggest environmental protection programme in Spain, possessing more than 90 protected areas covering some 17,000 sq km. This amounts to 20% of Andalucian territory and more than 60% of the total protected area in Spain.

Along with official protection (largely an achievement of the regional government, the Junta de Andalucía, since the 1980s) have come infinitely improved levels of public information and access to these often remote and challenging areas – visitors centres and information points, better maps, marked footpaths, more (and better) rural accommodation, active-tourism firms that will take you walking, riding, wildlife watching, climbing, caving, canyoning etc.

Responsibility for nature conservation in Spain is divided between the national government in Madrid and regional governments such as the Junta de Andalucía. There are at least 17 different categories of protected area. All of them can be visited, but degrees of access vary. So do degrees of actual protection: many parks still lack a proper legal framework for their management, and environmentalists and dedicated officials wage an endless struggle against illicit building, quarrying, hunting and so on in protected areas.

Parques nacionales (national parks), administered jointly by the national and regional governments, are areas of exceptional importance for their fauna, flora, geomorphology or landscape and are the most strictly controlled protected areas. They tend to have sparse human population and may include reserve areas closed to the public, or restricted areas that can only be visited with permission. Some unscrupulous or (to give them the benefit of the doubt) ignorant tourism operators will make out that every little nature reserve or periurban park on their doorstep is a 'national park'. Take no notice of them: Spain has just 13 *parques nacionales*, two of which are in Andalucía.

Parques naturales (natural parks) are declared and administered by regional governments. Andalucía's 24 natural parks account for most of its protected territory and include nearly all of its most spectacular country. They are intended to protect cultural heritage as well as nature, and to promote economic development that's compatible with conservation. Many of them include roads, villages or even small towns, with accommodation often available within the park. Camping is often restricted to organised camping grounds. In some parks there are networks of marked walking trails. Like national parks, they may include areas which can only be visited with permission.

Other types of protected areas in Andalucía include *parajes naturales* (natural areas; there are 32 of these) and *reservas naturales* (nature reserves; numbering 28). These are generally smaller, little-inhabited areas, with much the same goals as natural parks. Some Spanish wilderness areas – about 900 sq km in Andalucía – are *reservas nacionales de caza* (national hunting reserves). Hunting, though subject to restrictions, is a deeply ingrained aspect of Spanish life. Hunting reserves are often located inside protected areas such as *parques naturales,* and you might walk or drive across one without even knowing it. If you hear gunshots, exercise caution!

For official information on protected areas, visit the websites of the Ministerio de Medio Ambiente, Spain's environment ministry (www.mma .es), or the Consejería de Medio Ambiente, the Junta de Andalucía's environmental department (www.juntadeandalucia .es/medioambiente).

ANDALUCÍA'S TOP PARKS & PROTECTED AREAS

Park	Features	Activities	Best Time To Visit	Page
Parque Nacional de Doñana	wetlands, dunes, beaches & woodlands; vital to birds	4WD tours	any	p148
Parque Natural de Doñana	buffer zone for Parque Nacional Doñana with similar habitats & wildlife	wildlife watching, 4WD trips, horse riding & walking	any	p148
Parque Nacional Sierra Nevada	spectacular high-mountain wilderness with many ibex & endemic plants	walking	Jul–early Sep	p327
Parque Natural Sierra Nevada	Nevada lower slopes of Sierra Nevada with timeless villages & tumbling streams	walking, horse riding, mountain biking, skiing & climbing	depends on activity	p327
Parque Natural Cabo de Gata-Níjar	coastal park with sandy beaches, volcanic cliffs, flamingo colony & semidesert vegetation	swimming, bird-watching, walking, horse riding, diving and snorkelling	any	p385
Parque Natural Los Alcornocales	rolling hills covered in great cork oak forests	walking	Apr-Oct	p211
Parque Natural Sierra de Aracena y Picos de Aroche	rolling Sierra Morena country with old stone villages	walking & horse riding	Apr-Oct	p159
Parque Natural Sierra de Grazalema	beautiful, damp, hilly region with vultures, Mediterranean woodlands & Spanish firs	walking, wildlife watching, climbing, caving, canyon-ing & paragliding	Oct-Jun	p192
Parque Natural Sierra de las Nieves	mountain region with deep valleys, ibex, Spanish firs & spectacular vistas	walking	Apr-Jun, Sep-Nov	p264
Parque Natural Sierra Norte	rolling Sierra Morena country, ancient villages, long panoramas & gorgeous spring wild flowers	walking & horse riding	Mar-Oct	p131
Parque Natural Sierras de Cazorla, Segura y Las Villas	craggy mountains, deep valleys, thick forests & abundant visible wildlife	walking, horse riding, 4WD tours	Mar-Nov	p365
Paraje Natural Desfiladero de los Gaitanes	dramatic gorge of El Chorro	climbing	Sep-Jun	p265
Paraje Natural Torcal de Antequera	mountain covered in spectacular limestone formations	walking & climbing	Mar-Nov	p269
Reserva Natural Laguna de Fuente de Piedra	shallow lake with Spain's biggest flamingo population	bird-watching	Feb-Aug	p270

PARKS & OTHER PROTECTED AREAS

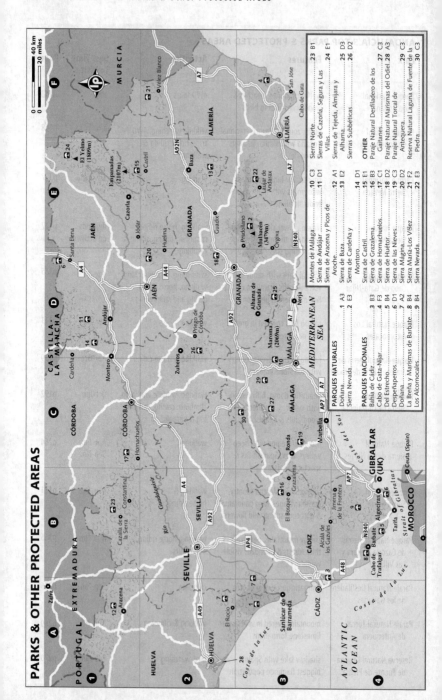

Montes de Málaga	10 C3
Sierra de Andújar	11 D1
Sierra de Aracena y Picos de	
Aroche	12 A1
Sierra de Baza	13 E2
Sierra de Cardeña y	
Montoro	14 D1
Sierra de Castril	15 E1
Sierra de Grazalema	16 B3
Sierra de Hornachuelos	17 C1
Sierra de Huétor	18 D2
Sierra de las Nieves	19 C3
Sierra Mágina	20 D2
Sierra María-Los Vélez	21 F2
Sierra Nevada	22 E3

Sierra Norte	23 B1
Sierras de Cazorla, Segura y Las	
Villas	24 E1
Sierras de Tejeda, Almijara y	
Alhama	25 D3
Sierras Subbéticas	26 D2

OTHER
Paraje Natural Desfiladero de los	
Gaitanes	27 C3
Paraje Natural Marismas del Odiel	28 A3
Paraje Natural Torcal de	
Antequera	29 C3
Reserva Natural Laguna de Fuente de la	
Piedra	30 C3

PARQUES NATURALES
| Doñana | 1 A3 |
| Sierra Nevada | 2 E3 |

PARQUES NACIONALES
Bahía de Cádiz	3 B3
Cabo de Gata-Níjar	4 F3
Del Estrecho	5 B4
Despeñaperros	6 D1
Doñana	7 A2
La Brena y Marismas de Barbate	8 B4
Los Alcornocales	9 B4

ENVIRONMENTAL ISSUES

Andalucía's relative lack of industry and, until recently, its fairly trad-itional agriculture have left it with a pretty clean environment. There are, however, problem areas. Potentially, Andalucía's worst environmental problem is drought, which struck in the 1950s and '60s and the early 1990s. This is despite huge investment in reservoirs (which cover a higher proportion of Spain than of any other country in the world).

Environmental awareness in Andalucía and Spain in general took a leap forward in the 1980s under the Partido Socialista Obrero Español (PSOE; Spanish Socialist Workers' Party) national government, which gave regional administrations responsibility for most environmental mat-ters. In 1981 Spain had 35 environmentally protected areas, covering 2200 sq km. Today there are over 400, covering more than 25,000 sq km, and Andalucía is the leader in this field (see p56). But slack controls on construction, often tourism-based and especially near the coasts, still leads to the destruction of woodlands, wetlands and other coastal eco-systems, pressure on water supplies, unsightly, haphazard development and some pollution of the seas. The environmental state of Andalucía's beaches – so crucial to the tourism industry – is mixed. In 2004, 60 of them proudly flew the blue flag of the Foundation for Environmen-tal Education, an international body that annually awards the flags to beaches that satisfy certain criteria of water quality, safety and services, including that 'no industrial or sewage-related discharges may affect the beach area'. On the other hand 34 Andalucian beaches, mainly in Málaga and Cádiz provinces, were given environmental *banderas negras* (black flags) by the local environmental group Ecologistas en Acción, mainly for pollution by raw sewage entering the sea or for counter-ecological coastal building developments. In Cádiz province, for example, said Ecologistas en Acción, there were no purification facilities for sewage entering the sea anywhere in the municipalities of Algeciras, Tarifa, Barbate, Vejer de la Frontera or Chipiona.

Air pollution by industry is a concern in the Huelva area. Intensive vegetable growing under enormous expanses (270 sq km) of ugly plastic greenhouses in the arid Almería region is drying up the underground aquifers on which it depends, produces enormous quantities of non-biodegradable rubbish and has resulted in hundreds of hospital cases of workers with pesticide poisoning (see p384). The PP national govern-ment in power from 1996 to 2004 planned to divert water from the Río Ebro in northern Spain to help agriculture in Almería and the Murcia and Valencia regions of eastern Spain. But this was strongly opposed by the Ebro area inhabitants and by ecologists concerned about the delicate balance of the large Ebro delta. The PSOE government that replaced the PP in 2004 cancelled the water transfer, intending to construct a series of desalination plants instead.

Andalucía's worst single environmental disaster of recent times was in 1998 when the Río Guadiamar, one of the most important waterways feed-ing the vital Doñana wetlands, was flooded with toxic mining wastes after a dam broke at Los Frailes mine, Aznalcóllar. Hastily erected dikes kept the poisonous tide out of all but a small corner of the national park, but up to 100 sq km of neighbouring wetlands were contaminated and 70km of the river's course was devastated. Since then, an expensive clean-up pro-gramme seems to have set these areas on the road to ecological recovery.

It was the Romans who began to cut Andalucía's extensive woodlands and forests for timber, fuel, weapons and space for agriculture. They and the Muslims opened up large areas to agriculture through irrigation

Visit the Foundation for Environmental Education (www.fee-international .org) for the list of blue-flag beaches, and Ecologistas en Acción (www.ecologistasen accion.org in Spanish) for the list of unsavoury black-flag beaches.

DID YOU KNOW?

Andalucía aims to gener-ate 15% of its electricity from renewable sources by 2006. Wind will be by far the biggest source of this, with thousands of new windmills being constructed around the region.

and terracing of the hillsides. Later, overgrazing by huge sheep flocks eroded much topsoil, imperial Spain's demand for shipbuilding timber decimated many native forests, and many wetlands were drained for agriculture (the last in the past couple of centuries). Such loss of habitat has contributed, along with hunting, to drastic depletion of many animal and bird species.

Andalucía's largest and most active environmental organisation is **Ecologistas en Acción** (www.ecologistasenaccion.org in Spanish). **SEO/BirdLife** (www.seo.org in Spanish), the Spanish Ornithological Society, is also active in conservation. International organisations involved in Andalucía include **WWF** (www.panda.org).

Andalucía Outdoors

Andalucía's varied terrain and long coastline beckon action-lovers with the promise of endless adventures. Here we introduce some of the most popular and exciting activities you can pursue in the region. You'll find further detail in destination sections.

WATER SPORTS
Windsurfing
Tarifa (see Surfers' Paradise, p204), on the Strait of Gibraltar, is one of, if not *the,* top spot in Europe for windsurfing, thanks to the strong breezes blowing one way or other through the strait almost year-round. The long, sandy beaches are an added attraction and there's a hip international scene to go with the boards and waves. Rental of board, sail and wetsuit costs around €35 per hour or €65 per day, with tuition at around €50 per two hours. Other spots with good winds are Los Caños de Meca (p199), Sancti Petri (p197) and El Puerto de Santa María (p175), further up the Atlantic coast of Cádiz province. Along the Mediterranean coast conditions are often less exciting, though perhaps better for beginners, and there are facilities at several Costa del Sol resorts and places further east such as La Herradura (p339) and Roquetas de Mar (p385).

Kitesurfing
Kitesurfers (also known as flysurfers or kiteboarders) use boards like windsurfers but they catch the wind by means of a kitelike sail high in the air, to which they're attached by a harness and long strings. This fast-growing sport can be practiced in lighter winds than are needed for windsurfing. Experts can reach high speeds and perform tricky manoeuvres while 'hanging' in the air. Tarifa (see Surfers' Paradise, p204) is the hub, with equipment rental and sales, and classes available: classes and equipment rental generally cost a bit more than for windsurfing. Beginners definitely need tuition, as out-of-control kitesurfers can be a danger to themselves and everyone else. A six-hour beginner's course should cost about €175 to €200. If you have the gear you can kitesurf on the Mediterranean coast too.

Surfing
Andalucía's waves don't rival those of northern Spain, but the surf can be good in winter on the Atlantic coast of Cádiz province, especially at El Palmar (p199), where waves can reach 3m, and Los Caños de Meca (p199). Some of the Mediterranean beaches are good for beginners – those around Estepona (p256) are popular. Bodyboarding (boogie-boarding) is popular all along the Andalucian coasts and boards are for sale everywhere.

Diving & Snorkelling
Andalucía's coasts don't provide all the spectacular sights of tropical waters but there is still some interesting diving here, and plenty of diving schools and shops to help you enjoy it. Most establishments offer courses under the aegis of international diving organisations such as **PADI** (www.padi.com) or **NAUI** (www.nauiww.org), as well as dives for qualified divers. A single dive with full equipment costs around €40. Introductory 'baptism' and 'discover scuba diving' courses for up to three hours run from about €35 to €75. The five-day PADI open-water certification course will cost you around €350.

Andalucía There's Only One (www.andalucia.org) lists 20 dive outfits.

For an idea of what diving is available, have a look at websites such as www.simplydiving.com, www.indalosub.com (in Spanish) or www .divehire.co.uk.

The following are Andalucía's best diving areas, from west to east:
Tarifa (p207) Wrecks and varied marine fauna, but low temperatures and some strong currents – better for experienced divers.
Gibraltar (p224) Great for wrecks.
Coast of Granada province Especially La Herradura/Marina del Este (p339) and around the towns of Calahonda and Castell de Ferro (p336); steep cliffs, deep water, some caves.
Cabo de Gata (p385)

Snorkelling is best along the rockier parts of the Mediterranean coast – between Nerja and Adra, and from Cabo de Gata to Mojácar.

Sailing

More than 40 marinas and mooring places are strung along Andalucía's coast from Ayamonte on the Portuguese border to Garrucha in Almería province. Voyages along the Mediterranean coast, through the Strait of Gibraltar to the Costa de la Luz or Portugal, or across to Morocco, are all popular. Andalucía's biggest marinas are the flashy Puerto Banús (p255) and Benalmádena (p245) on the Costa del Sol, and Almerimar near Almería, each with over 900 moorings, but there are plenty of smaller, more relaxed ports such as San José (p387) on Cabo de Gata, or Marina del Este (p339) near La Herradura. Information on marinas, moorings and sailing clubs is available from **Andalucía There's Only One** (www.andalucia.org), **Andalucia.com** (www.andalucia.com) and the **Federación Andaluza de Vela** (Andalucian Sailing Federation; www.federacionandaluzavela.com in Spanish). Boat hire of some kind is possible at many marinas. For yacht charter, check **Costa del Sol Charter** (www.costadelsolcharter.com) or **Viento y Mar** (www.vientoymar.com in Spanish).

This is largely an activity for those with experience, or at least friends in the field. Opportunities for beginners are not easy to come by, but the **Gibraltar Sailing Centre** (www.gibraltar-sailing.com) offers courses approved by the UK's Royal Yachting Association – around UK£500 for a six-day course.

HORSE RIDING

Andalucía is steeped in equestrian tradition. The horse has been part of rural life since time immemorial and Andalucía is the chief breeding ground of the elegant and internationally esteemed Spanish thorough-bred horse, also known as the Cartujano or Andalusian. Countless good riding tracks crisscross its marvellous landscapes, and an ever-growing number of *picaderos* (stables) are ready to take you on a guided ride for any duration between an hour and a week or give you classes. Many of the mounts are Andalusians or Andalusian-Arab crosses – medium-sized, intelligent, good in traffic and, as a rule, easy to handle and sure-footed. At many stables you'll be using Andalucian saddles and stirrups: the sad-dles are bigger than the British variety, with high front and rear pieces, but sheepskin-covered for more comfort, while the stirrups are heavy and triangular, with room for the whole foot.

Typical prices for a ride or lesson are €20 to €25 for one hour, €50 to €60 for a half day and €80 to €100 for a full day. Most stables cater for all levels of experience, from lessons for beginners or children, upwards. As with walking, the ideal months to ride in Andalucía are May, June, September and October, when the weather is likely to be good but not too hot.

The provinces of Sevilla and Cádiz have perhaps the highest horse populations and concentrations of stables, but there are riding opportun-ities throughout the region. The Junta de Andalucía's tourism website, **Andalucía There's Only One** (www.andalucia.org), has a directory of over 90 stables and other equestrian establishments.

Two of the many highlight riding experiences in Andalucía are trail rides in the Alpujarras (p333) and Sierra Nevada (p329), and beach and dune riding just out of Tarifa on Cádiz's Costa de la Luz (p207). See this book's sections on Alájar (p160), Baeza (p356), Cazalla de la Sierra (p133), Cómpeta (p271), El Rocío (p151), Grazalema (p194), Los Caños de Meca (p199), Parque Natural de Cazorla (p369), Parque Natural Sierra de Hornachuelos (p293), Ronda (p260) and San José (p387) for recommended stables.

All horse-lovers should put Jerez de la Frontera (p182) high on their itinerary. The town holds a number of exciting annual equine events – especially its Feria del Caballo (Horse Fair) in May – and its famous Real Escuela Andaluza del Arte Ecuestre (Royal Andalucian School of Equestrian Art) and the nearby Yeguada del Hierro del Bocado (p189) breeding centre are fascinating to visit at any time.

CLIMBING

Mountainous Andalucía is full of crags, walls and slabs that invite *escalada* (climbing), a fast-growing sport here. Thanks to the southern Mediterranean climate, this is a good region for winter climbing. In fact there's good climbing year-round, though July and August temperatures are too high for some spots. Most of the climbing is on limestone and there's more sport climbing than classical.

The sheer walls of El Chorro Gorge (p265), one of several great sites in the north of Málaga province, are the biggest magnet, with over 600 routes of almost every grade of difficulty. El Chorro presents a great variety of both classical and sport climbing, from slab climbs to towering walls to bolted multipitch routes. If this isn't enough, several nearby spots provide fine climbing too. There's accommodation for all budgets in the El Chorro area, and a climbers' scene at Bar Isabel at El Chorro train station. Rockfax's successful *Costa Blanca, Mallorca & El Chorro* climbing guide recently went out of print (you might still find a few copies in bookshops) but the British publisher is producing a dedicated El Chorro guide in 2005. In the meantime, you can obtain an El Chorro mini-guide through www.rockfax.com.

The following are among the most notable sites:

Benaocaz (p196; Cádiz province) One hundred routes, mainly sport-climbing, grades V–7, good in winter.

Los Cahorros (p330; near Monachil, Granada province) Three hundred sport and classical routes, grades 6–8, climbable year-round.

El Torcal (p269; Málaga province) Three hundred sport and classical routes of grade 6–7 in weird limestone landscape, best in spring and autumn.

Parque Natural Sierra de Grazalema (p192; Cádiz province) Fine classical climbs on Peñón Grande crag, spring to autumn.

La Cueva de Archidona (Archidona, northern Málaga province) Superb grade 7–9 sport climbing, spring to autumn.

Loja (Granada province) Has 175 grade 6–7 mainly sport routes, best from autumn to spring.

Mijas (p249; Málaga province) Around 100 grade V–7 climbs, good for winter.

San Bartolo (p203; near Bolonia, Cádiz province) Rare sandstone crag with 300 routes up to grade 6, good in winter.

Villanueva del Rosario (Málaga province) Best boulder climbing in Andalucía; also sport and classical routes.

Short courses for beginners are available at **Finca La Campana** (www.el-chorro .com) and **Girasol Andalusian Tours** (p207; www.girasol-adventure.com) in Tarifa. You can buy climbing equipment at sports shops in cities; try **Deportes La Trucha** (Map p234; ☎ 952 21 22 03; Calle Carretería 100) in Málaga.

Desnivel (www.escuelas deescalada.com) has comprehensive listings of Andalucian climbing sites with lots of detail in English and Spanish.

Andalusian Rock Climbs by Chris Craggs is still a useful guide, though published in 1992.

WALKING IN ANDALUCÍA

The thousands of kilometres of paths and tracks wending their way along Andalucía's verdant valleys and across its rugged hills provide marvellous walking of any length or difficulty you like. In some areas you can string together day walks into a trek of several days, sleeping along the way in a variety of hotels, *hostales* (simple guesthouses or small places offering hotel-like accommodation), camping grounds or occasionally mountain refuges, or wild camping. For about half the year the climate is ideal, and in most areas the best months for walking are May, June, September and October. Walking in Andalucía is increasingly popular among both Spaniards and foreigners (and a growing number of specialist firms in northern Europe offer walking holidays here), but you'll rarely encounter anything like a crowd on any walk.

Trail marking is erratic: some routes are well signed with route numbers, on others just the odd dab of red paint might tell you you're heading in the right direction, and on yet others you're left entirely to your own devices. You'll certainly have opportunities to use navigational skills!

The two main categories of marked walking routes in Spain (not always well marked) are *senderos de gran recorrido* (GRs, long-distance footpaths) and *senderos de pequeño recorrido* (PRs, shorter routes of a few hours or one or two days). There are also plenty of paths that are neither GRs nor PRs. The GR-7 long-distance path runs the length of Spain from Andorra in the north to Tarifa in the south, and is part of the European E-4 route from Greece to Andalucía. It enters Andalucía near Almaciles in northeast Granada province, then divides at Puebla de Don Fadrique, with one branch heading through Jaén and Córdoba provinces and the other through Las Alpujarras southeast of Granada before the two rejoin near Antequera in Málaga province. Signposting of this path throughout Andalucía is still in progress.

Further information on walking is given in this book's regional chapters. Some walking guides to specific areas are available locally. Tourist offices and visitors centres can often help with information on routes and conditions. For information on maps, see p408.

La Axarquía

Hill villages such as Cómpeta, Canillas de Albaida, Canillas de Aceituno and Alfarnate, in the eastern district of Málaga province known as La Axarquía (p270), give access to many good tracks and paths. You can choose from climbs to summits with majestic views or gentle valley strolls close to the villages.

Access cities, towns and villages: Málaga (p231), Vélez Málaga (p270), Cómpeta (p271), Nerja (p272)

Las Alpujarras

One of the most picturesque corners of Andalucía, Las Alpujarras (p331) is a 70km-long jumble of valleys along the south flank of the Sierra Nevada, stretching from Granada province into neighbouring Almería. Arid hillsides split by deep ravines alternate with oasislike white villages surrounded by vegetable gardens, orchards, rapid streams and woodlands. Ancient paths wind up and down through constantly changing scenery between labyrinthine, Berber-style villages. Many villages have hotels, *hostales* or camping grounds, enabling you to string together routes of several days or do a number of day walks from a single base.

Access cities and towns: Granada (p302), Órgiva (p332), Laujar de Andarax (p383)

Parque Natural Cabo de Gata-Níjar

The combination of a dry, desert climate with volcanic cliffs plunging into azure Mediterranean waters produces a landscape of stark grandeur around the Cabo de Gata (p385) promontory southeast of Almería. Between the cliffs and headlands are strung some of Spain's best and least crowded beaches, and by combining paths, dirt roads and occasional sections of paved road, you can walk right round the 60km coast in three or four days. There's plenty of accommodation, including four camping grounds, along the way. September and October are good months to walk here: the searing temperatures of July and August have abated, but the sea is still warm (it's warmer in October than June).

Access city: Almería (p374)

Parque Natural de Cazorla

Parque Natural de Cazorla (p365) is the largest protected area in Spain (2143 sq km), a crinkled, pinnacled region of several complicated mountain ranges – not extraordinarily high, but memorably beautiful – divided by high plains and deep river valleys. Much of the park is thickly forested and wild animals are abundant and visible. The ideal way to explore it is with a vehicle to reach day walks in some of its more remote areas. Wild camping is not permitted and with accommodation and camping grounds concentrated in certain areas, multiday walks are not really feasible.

Main access town: Cazorla (p363)

Parque Natural Sierra de Aracena y Picos de Aroche

This sometimes lush, sometimes severe region of Parque Natural Sierra de Aracena y Picos de Aroche (p159) in far northwest Andalucía (Huelva province), dotted with timeless stone villages, has an extensive network of marked walking trails. It's another lovely area to spend a few days. Many villages have accommodation, enabling you to string together routes of several days.

Main access town: Aracena (p157)

Parque Natural Sierra de Grazalema

The hills of Parque Natural Sierra de Grazalema (p192) in Cádiz province encompass a variety of beautiful landscapes, from pastoral river valleys and dense Mediterranean woodlands to rocky summits and precipitous gorges. Some of the best walks are within a reserve area for which permits or guides are required: you may need to arrange these a few days ahead. There's plenty of accommodation in nearby villages.

Access villages: Grazalema (p194), El Bosque (p194), Zahara de la Sierra (p195), Benamahoma (p194), Benaocaz (p196)

Parque Natural Sierra de las Nieves

Southeast of the interesting old town of Ronda, the Sierra de las Nieves (p264) includes the highest peak in the western half of Andalucía, Torrecilla (1919m), climbable in a day trip from Ronda. Lower altitudes have extensive evergreen woodlands.

Access towns: Ronda (p256), Yunquera (p264), El Burgo (p264)

Parque Natural Sierra Norte

The rolling Sierra Morena country in the north of Sevilla province presents ever-changing vistas of green valleys and hills, woodlands, rivers and atmospheric old towns and villages (see p131). The spring wild flowers are spectacular here. There are a variety of day and half-day walks marked around the region and, with a range of attractive accommodation, it's a delightful area to spend a few days.

Access towns: Cazalla de la Sierra (p132), Constantina (p134), El Pedroso (p132)

Sierra Nevada

This snowcapped mountain range southeast of Granada includes mainland Spain's highest peak, Mulhacén (3479m), and many other summits over 3000m. The Sierra Nevada (p327) is Andalucía's ultimate walking experience in terms of altitude and climatic conditions and also for its forbidding, wild aspect: large tracts are a rugged wilderness of black rock and stones, with plenty of sheer faces and jagged crags. During July, August and early September – the best months for walking up here, though high-altitude weather is never very predictable – a national park bus service gives walkers access to the upper reaches of the range from both the north and south sides. It's quite feasible to cap Mulhacén or the second-highest peak, Veleta (3395m), in a day trip. There are many other possible routes as well as a limited number of refuges if you want to stay the night in the mountains. Camping in the Sierra Nevada is allowed above 1600m, subject to certain conditions (see p329).

Main access towns: Granada (p302), Estación de Esquí Sierra Nevada (p327), Capileira (p332), Trevélez (p335)

SKIING & SNOWBOARDING

Andalucía's only ski station, the highly popular Estación de Esquí Sierra Nevada (Sierra Nevada Ski Station; see p327), 33km southeast of Granada, is the most southerly ski resort in Europe, and its runs and facilities are of championship quality. The season normally runs from December to April, and it gets pretty crowded (with a thriving nightlife) at weekends for most of that period and around the Christmas–New Year and Día de Andalucía (28 February) holidays.

Walking in Andalucía by Guy Hunter-Watts has detailed descriptions and maps of 34 good day walks.

The resort has 67 marked downhill runs of varied difficulty, totalling 76km, plus cross-country routes and a dedicated snowboarding area. Some runs start almost at the top of Veleta (3395m), the second highest peak in the Sierra Nevada.

A day pass plus rental of skis, boots and poles, or snowboard and boots, costs between €40 and €55, depending when you go. Six hours of group classes at ski school are €57.

There's plenty of accommodation at the station, but reservations are always advisable: double rooms start at about €80. The best deals are ski packages, bookable through the station's website or phone number, which start at around €150 for two days and two nights with half board (bed, breakfast and either lunch or dinner).

CYCLING & MOUNTAIN BIKING

Andalucía's combination of plains, rolling hills and mountain ranges makes all kinds of cycling trips possible, from cruises along the *carriles de cicloturismo* (roads adapted for cycle touring) in the flat lands surrounding the Doñana national park (see p124 for more information about the Carril de Cicloturismo Pinares de Aznalcázar–La Puebla) to tough off-road mountain routes. Road cycling has always been popular in Spain, and mountain biking is ever more popular. Thousands of kilometres of good and bad off-road routes await the adventurous, while the relatively little-trafficked country roads offer endless opportunities for cycle touring. Spring and autumn are the best seasons, with their moderate temperatures.

Many tourist offices have route information and **Andalucía There's Only One** (www.andalucia.org) details 15 mountain bike routes in each of Andalucía's eight provinces, with sketch maps. The same routes are covered in the *Mountain Bike* booklet sold by Junta de Andalucía tourist offices. The **Vías Verdes** (www.viasverdes.com), abandoned railway lines turned into cycle and walking tracks, provide several hundred kilometres of attractive cross-country routes.

You can buy a reasonably good touring or mountain bike for around €200 in hypermarkets or bike shops (of which there's at least one in every sizeable town), though a quality machine might cost double that. A growing number of places rent out mountain bikes in Andalucía, usually for around €10 to €12 a day, and you can join guided group rides in a growing number of places.

ESCAPE

Pamper yourself and get a feel for life in medieval Islamic Andalucía at one of the new Baños Árabes (Arab Baths) that have opened in cities such as Granada (p316), Córdoba (p286) and Málaga (p237), recreating a key institution of Al-Andalus (medieval Córdoba had more than 60 bathhouses). The scent of herbal oils wafts through the air as you move between pools of varied temperatures. Indulge in aromatherapy or another massage then round things off with a pot of mint tea!

Some recommended bike hire and tour firms can be found in Monachil (p330), the Sierra Nevada (p329), Pampaneira, Bubión and Capileira (p333) and La Herradura (p340) in Granada province; Vejer de la Frontera (p198) and Tarifa (p207) in Cádiz province; Ronda (p260), Ardales and El Chorro (p265) and Estepona (p256) in Málaga province; and in San José (p387) in Almería.

GOLF

Over 700,000 people a year come to Andalucía primarily to play golf, and more and more Andalucians are taking to the fairways. Andalucía has 69 golf courses, more than half of them dotted along or near the Costa del Sol between Málaga and Gibraltar. The fine climate and the many beautifully landscaped, well-kept courses designed by the top golf-course designers are among the special pleasures of golf here. There's even one completely floodlit night-time course, La Dama de Noche at Marbella. Flat terrain is fairly rare in Andalucía, so most courses have a certain amount of slope to contend with. Green fees are comparable to Britain: between €45 and €70 at most clubs. Top courses on the Costa del Sol, such as Valderrama (proud host to the Ryder Cup in 1997), Sotogrande, and Las Brisas and Aloha at Marbella, are more costly (€250 to €275 at Valderrama, the most expensive). Professional tuition (typically around €25 an hour) and hire of clubs (around €15 per round), trolleys (around €5) and buggies (around €30) are available at almost every course.

Useful information sources include **Andalucía There's Only One** (www.andalucia.org) and the **Federación Andaluza de Golf** (www.golf-andalucia.com), both with directories of the region's courses, and the free paper *Andalucía Costa del Golf*, available from some tourist offices. Many golfers from other countries come on organised golf holidays, with tee times, accommodation and everything else booked in advance, but it's perfectly feasible to organise your own golf: English-speakers are available almost everywhere. **Golf Service** (www.golf-service.com) offers discounted green fees and tee-off time reservations.

OTHER ACTIVITIES

Tennis, caving, canyoning, canoeing, kayaking, rowing, fishing, paragliding, hang-gliding and microlighting are some of the other sports and activities you can do in Andalucía. For introductory information see websites such as **Andalucia.com** (www.andalucia.com) and **Andalucía There's Only One** (www.andalucia.org). The region is also exciting for those who like watching birds and other wildlife – for information about wildlife and wildlife watching in Andalucía see p51 and p16.

Over two weeks' worth of the best walking is described in detail in the Andalucía chapter of Lonely Planet's *Walking in Spain*, written by John Noble.

Islamic Architecture in Andalucía

Andalucía was always the heartland of Al-Andalus (as the Muslim-ruled areas of the Iberian Peninsula were known) and the Islamic centuries (AD 711–1492) left a heritage of exotic and beautiful buildings – palaces, mosques, minarets, fortresses – that make this region visually unique in Europe.

After the Reconquista (Christian reconquest) of Andalucía, which happened in fits and starts between 1227 and 1492, many Islamic buildings were put directly to Christian use. As a result, many Andalucian churches today are converted mosques (as most famously at Córdoba), many church towers were originally built as minarets, and the tangled streets of many an old town (Granada's Albayzín district is just one famous case) have their origins in labyrinthine Islamic-era street plans.

The wonderfully illustrated *Moorish Architecture in Andalusia* by Marianne Barrucand and Achim Bednorz, with a learned but readable text, will whet your appetite for the region's Islamic heritage.

THE OMAYYADS

Islam – the word means 'Surrender' or 'Acceptance' (of the will of Allah, the Muslim name for God) – was founded by the prophet Mohammed in the Arabian city of Mecca in the 7th century AD. It spread rapidly to the north, east and west, reaching Spain in 711. After Mohammed died in 632, the leader of Islam was known as the caliph (deputy). The first caliphs were chosen from among Mohammed's companions, but in about 660 Muawiya, a late convert to Islam from one of Mecca's richest families, seized power and instituted a hereditary caliphate. This was the Omayyad dynasty, which governed from Damascus, Syria, from 661. In 750 the Omayyads were massacred by a group of non-Arab Muslim revolutionaries known as the Abbasids. Just one of the Omayyad family, Abu'l-Mutarrif Abd ar-Rahman bin Muawiya, escaped. Aged only 20, he made for Morocco and thence to Spain, where in 756 he managed to set himself up as an independent emir, Abd ar-Rahman I, in Córdoba. Thus began the Omayyad dynasty of Al-Andalus, which lasted till 1009.

The Abbasids set up their caliphal capital far to the east, at Baghdad. Al-Andalus, at the western extremity of the Islamic world, became the last outpost of Omayyad culture.

The Mezquita of Córdoba

The oldest significant surviving Spanish Islamic building is also arguably the most magnificent and the most influential. The Mezquita (Mosque; p279) of Córdoba was founded by Abd ar-Rahman I in AD 785 and underwent major extensions under his successors Abd ar-Rahman II in the first half of the 9th century, Al-Hakim II in the 960s and Al-Mansur in the 970s.

THE HORSESHOE ARCH

Omayyad architecture in Spain was enriched by styles and techniques taken up from the Christian Visigoths, whom the Omayyads had replaced as rulers of the Iberian Peninsula. Chief among these was what became almost the hallmark of Spanish Islamic architecture, the horseshoe arch – so called because it narrows at the bottom like a horseshoe, rather than being a simple semicircle.

THE ALMORAVIDS & ALMOHADS

The rule of the Berber Almoravids from Morocco from the late 11th to mid-12th centuries yielded few notable new buildings in Spain, but the second wave of Moroccan Berbers to conquer Al-Andalus, the Almohads, constructed huge Friday mosques in the main cities of their empire, among them Seville. The design was simple and purist, with large prayer halls conforming to the T-plan of Al-Hakim II's extension to the Córdoba Mezquita. The bays where the naves meet the qibla transept were surmounted by cupolas or stucco *muqarnas* (stalactite or honeycomb vaulting), composed of hundreds or thousands of tiny cells or niches. On walls, large brick panels with designs of interwoven lozenges were created. From the late 12th century, tall, square, richly decorated minarets appear. The Giralda (p93), the minaret of the Seville mosque, is the masterpiece of surviving Almohad building in Spain, with its beautiful brick panels. The prayer hall of the Seville mosque was demolished in the 15th century to make way for the city's cathedral, but the mosque's courtyard (now called the Patio de los Naranjos; p94) and its northern gate, the Puerta del Perdón (p91), survive.

Another Almohad mosque, more palace chapel than a large congregational affair, stands inside the Alcázar (p184) of Jerez de la Frontera. This tall, austere brick building is based on an unusual octagonal plan inscribed within a square. Many rooms and patios in Seville's Alcázar (p94) palace-fortress date from Almohad times, but only the Patio del Yeso has substantial surviving Almohad remains. One side of this courtyard, with its flower beds and a water channel, is adorned with a superbly delicate trelliswork of multiple interlocking arches.

DID YOU KNOW?

Muqarnas (honeycomb or stalactite vaulting) originated in Syria or Iran: the Almoravid mosque at Tlemcen, Morocco, was the first western Islamic building to feature it.

THE ALHAMBRA

Granada's magnificent palace-fortress is the only surviving large medieval Islamic palace. The Alhambra (p305) was the redoubt of the Nasrid emirs of Granada, whose state – the last Muslim state on the Iberian Peninsula – endured from 1249 to 1492. It's a palace-city in the tradition

---

BATHHOUSES

Cleanliness and the public *hammam* (bathhouse) were such features of life in Al-Andalus that the Muslims' Christian enemies came to view washing with huge suspicion and believed bathhouses to be dens of wild orgies. To make their point, some Spanish monks took pride in wearing the same woollen habit uninterrupted for a whole year, and the phrase 'Olor de Santidad' (Odour of Sanctity) became a euphemism for particularly offensive BO. After the Reconquista (Christian reconquest) of Andalucía, the Moriscos (Muslims who converted to Christianity) were expressly forbidden to take baths.

Nevertheless medieval Islamic bathhouses have been preserved in some Andalucian towns today. They generally contain a changing room, cold room, temperate room and hot room, in succession, with the heat in the hot rooms being provided by underfloor systems called hypocausts. Good examples of bathhouses, with their rooms lined by arched galleries and lit by star-shaped skylights, include the following:

- **Baño de Comares** (p309) Alhambra, Granada
- **Baños Árabes El Bañuelo** (p313) Albayzín, Granada
- **Baños Árabes** (p184) Alcázar, Jerez de la Frontera
- **Baños Árabes** (p348) Palacio de Villardompardo, Jaén
- **Baños Árabes** (p259) Ronda
- **Baño Moro** (p369) Segura de la Sierra

of Medina Azahara but also a fortress, with 2km of walls, 23 towers, four gates and a fort-within-a-fort, the Alcazaba. Also within its walls were seven separate palaces, mosques, garrisons, houses, offices, baths, a summer residence (the Generalife) and exquisite gardens.

The Alhambra's designers were supremely talented landscape architects, combining nature and architecture by the use of pools, running water, meticulously clipped trees and bushes, flower beds, windows framing vistas, carefully placed lookout points, and contrasts between heat and cool and light and dark. The conjunction of fountains, pools and gardens with domed reception halls was developed to a degree of perfection suggestive of the paradise described in the Quran. In keeping with the Alhambra's partial role as a pleasure palace, many of its defensive towers also functioned as miniature summer palaces.

Michael Jacobs' *Alhambra* is a close look at the greatest of all works of Islamic architecture in Andalucía.

A great variety of densely ornamented arches adorns the Alhambra. The Nasrid architects refined existing decorative techniques to new peaks of delicacy, elegance and harmony. Their media included sculptured stucco, marble panels, carved and inlaid wood, epigraphy (with endlessly repeated inscriptions of 'There is no conqueror but Allah') and colourful tiles. Plaited star patterns in tile mosaic have since covered walls the length and breadth of the Islamic world, and Nasrid Granada is the dominant artistic influence in the Maghreb (Northwest Africa) even today.

FORTIFICATIONS

With its borders constantly under threat and its subjects often rebellious, it's hardly surprising that Al-Andalus boasts more Islamic castles and forts than any comparably sized territory in the world.

Caliphate Era

Designs were fairly simple, with no outer walls and rectangular towers that were rarely higher than the walls. Two of the finest Caliphate-era forts are the oval one at Baños de la Encina (p353) in Jaén province and the hilltop Alcazaba (p375) dominating Almería.

Taifa Period

In this 11th-century era of internal strife, many towns bolstered their defences. A fine example is Niebla (p146) in Huelva province, which was strengthened by walls with massive round and rectangular towers. So was the Albayzín (p308) area of Granada. Niebla's gates show a new sophistication, with barbicans (double towers defending the gates) and bends in their passageways to impede attackers.

Almohad Fortifications

The Almohads, in the 12th and early 13th centuries, rebuilt many city defences, such as those at Córdoba, Seville and Jerez de la Frontera. Córdoba's Torre de la Calahorra (p284) and Seville's Torre del Oro (p97) are well constructed bridgehead towers. The Torre del Oro, at a corner of the city wall, did not actually guard a bridge but probably had a sister tower on the far bank of the Río Guadalquivir, enabling a chain to be stretched across for defensive purposes.

Nasrid Fortifications

Many defensive fortifications – as at Antequera (p267) and Ronda (p256), and Málaga's Castillo de Gibralfaro (p235) – were restored as the Nasrid emirate of Granada strove to survive in the 13th, 14th and 15th centuries. Big rectangular corner towers such as those at Málaga and Antequera suggest the influence of the Christian enemy. The most spectacular fort of the era – though better known as a palace – is Granada's Alhambra (p305).

Cathedral (p91),
Seville

PAUL BERNHARDT

PAUL BERNHARDT

Typical building interior, Barrio de Santa Cruz (p97),
Seville

Torre del Oro (p97), Seville
INGRID RODDIS

MARTIN MOOS

Semana Santa procession
(p107), Seville

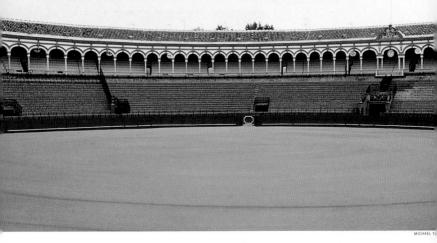

Plaza de Toros de la Real Maestranza (p100), Seville

Plaza de España (p103), Seville

Flamenco haunt (p119), Seville

The peak of Granada's splendour came under emirs Yusuf I (r 1333–54) and Mohammed V (r 1354–59 and 1362–91). Yusuf I was responsible for the Alhambra's Palacio de Comares (Comares Palace) and Mohammed V for its Palacio de los Leones (Palace of the Lions). The brilliant marquetry ceiling of the Salón de Comares (Comares Hall), representing the seven levels of the Islamic heavens, capped by a cupola representing the throne of Allah, served as the model for Islamic-style ceilings in state rooms for centuries afterwards.

DID YOU KNOW?

The marquetry ceiling of the Alhambra's Salón de Comares employs more than 8000 small wooden panels.

The Palacio de los Leones focuses on the celebrated Patio de los Leones (Patio of the Lions), with its colonnaded gallery and pavilions, and a central fountain channelling water through the mouths of 12 stone lions. The Sala de Dos Hermanas (Hall of Two Sisters) reception room features a fantastic *muqarnas* dome of 5000 tiny cells, recalling the constellations.

MUDEJAR & MOZARABIC ARCHITECTURE

The label Mudejar – from Arabic *mudayan*, 'domesticated' – was given to Muslims who stayed on in areas reconquered by the Christians, who often employed the talents of gifted Muslim artisans. Mudejar buildings are effectively part of Spain's Islamic heritage. You'll find Mudejar or part-Mudejar churches and monasteries all over Andalucía but the classic Mudejar building is the exotic Palacio de Don Pedro (p95), built in the 14th century inside the Alcázar of Seville for Christian Pedro I of Castile. Pedro's friend Mohammed V of Granada sent many of his best artisans to work on Pedro's palace, and as a result the Palacio de Don Pedro is effectively a Nasrid building, and one of the best of its kind.

One hallmark of Mudejar style is geometrical decorative designs in brick or stucco, often further embellished with tiles. Elaborately carved timber ceilings are also a mark of the Mudejar hand. *Artesonado* is the word used to describe ceilings with interlaced beams leaving regular spaces for decorative insertions. True Mudejar *artesonados* generally bear floral or simple geometric patterns. Mudejar is often found side by side with the Christian Gothic style in the same building.

The term Mozarabic, from *musta'rib* (Arabised), refers to Christians who lived or had lived in Muslim-controlled territories in the Iberian Peninsula. Mozarabic architecture was, unsurprisingly, much influenced by Islamic styles. It includes, for instance, the horseshoe arch. It was in more northerly reconquered territories such as León that most Mozarabic architecture was constructed. The only significant remaining Mozarabic structure in Andalucía – but well worth seeking out for its picturesque setting and poignant history – is the rock-cut church at Bobastro (p267).

Food & Drink

When someone mentions Spanish – and by extension Andalucian – cooking, what comes to mind is not usually artichokes with mandarin sauce, sardines with angel-hair pasta or citrus blinis but a reassuring combination of paella, tortilla, gazpacho and tapas. However, in the last decade a new wave of contemporary restaurants, spearheaded by the likes of Martín Berasategui, Juan Mari Arzak and Ferran Adriá, has set in motion a revolution in Spanish cooking.

World Food Spain by Richard Sterling is a trip into Spain's culinary soul, from tapas to *postres* (desserts), with a comprehensive culinary dictionary.

Admittedly, Andalucía has come late to this culinary boom. Encompassing the high sierras and the tropical southern coastline, this vast region has tremendous advantages in terms of culinary traditions and raw materials. The cooking itself bears Roman, Jewish, *gitano* (Romany), New World and above all Arabian influences, and lends itself superbly to experimentation. Among other things the palette includes exotic ingredients such as oranges, lemons, apricots, aubergines (eggplants), mint, spinach and spices such as cinnamon and cumin, as well as the solid staples of gamey meats and seafood.

But this new wave of Spanish cooking is not about modernity per se but about the refinement and celebration of traditions and ingredients. In restaurants such as Restaurante Tragabuches (p262) and Café de Paris (p239), both in Málaga province, regional dishes have been given a radical twist, breathing exciting new life into provincial cooking.

STAPLES & SPECIALITIES

Andalucian cooking is typically Mediterranean in its liberal use of olive oil, garlic, onions, tomatoes and peppers – it is simple peasant food based on fresh ingredients, with a hint of herbs and spices. In the hill country, cured hams and game dishes abound. Stews based on various types of beans are a traditional staple of home cooking, while on the coasts, seafood predominates.

Bread

No meal is eaten in Spain without *pan* (bread). Every district has a *panadería* (bakery) where bread of all shapes and sizes is produced daily. For breakfast *bollos* or *molletes* (small, soft rolls) are consumed as well as *tostadas* (toasted bread often served with a variety of toppings such as tomatoes and olive oil). Simple country bread, *pan de campo*, is the perfect companion for any meal. What isn't eaten is then used to thicken soups and sauces.

Cheese

Spain's most famous cheese, the *manchego* originates from the central region of La Mancha. Traditionally made from goat's milk, it is salty and full of flavour and is frequently served as a *tapa* (snack). When still fresh, *manchego* cheese has a creamy and mild consistency; semicured ones are firmer and have a stronger flavour, while those aged more than three months have a distinctive tang. Typical Andalucian cheeses include *Grazalema*, from the mountains of Cádiz, made from ewe's milk and similar to *manchego*, *Málaga* a goat's milk cheese preserved in olive oil and *Cádiz* a strong fresh goat's milk cheese made in the countryside around Cádiz. Another cheese found throughout Spain is *Burgos*, a very mild ewe's milk cheese often served as a dessert with honey, nuts and fruit.

Fish & Seafood

The variety of fish and seafood in the coastal towns of Andalucía can be intimidating. *Boquerones* (anchovies) marinated in garlic, olive oil and vinegar, and grilled sardines are the staple of any coastal tapas, as are *gambas* (prawns), which can be grilled, fried in garlic or served cold with a bowl of fresh mayonnaise (the smallest ones are used in paellas or soups, while the king prawns for grilling are called *langostinos*). Other Andalucian obsessions include *chipirones* or *chopitos* (baby squid) and in Málaga they would also add *chanquetes* (similar to whitebait and served deep-fried) to the list. *Ostras* (oysters) are plentiful in and around Cádiz.

The Flavor of Andalusia by Pepita Aris (1996) gives recipes for some 50 typical Andalucian dishes, plus interesting background on the region's food, but is hard to find. Otherwise, try *Spanish Cooking* by the same author.

Fruit & Vegetables

Andalucía has arguably the finest fruits and vegetables in Spain due to its generous climate. Along the subtropical coastal plains you can find *plátanos* (bananas), *aguacates* (avocadoes), *mangos* (mangoes) and even *caña de azúcar* (sugar cane). Almería province, east of Málaga, is Europe's winter garden with miles of plastic-covered hothouses of intensively grown vegetables. Fruit and almond trees cover the lower slopes of the sierras alongside the famous bitter *naranjas* (oranges) – used solely to produce marmalade – introduced by the Arabs.

Córdoba province is famous for its vegetable dishes such as *alcachofas con almejas* (artichokes with clams), *esparragos revueltos* (wild asparagus with scrambled eggs), and lots of deep purple *berenjenas* (aubergines).

THE TAPAS TALE

The saucer-sized snacks known as tapas are part of the Spanish way of life and come in infinite variety. The word *tapa* means 'lid'. Today's snacks supposedly originated in the sherry area of Andalucía (Cádiz province) in the 19th century, when bar owners placed a piece of bread on top of a drink to deter flies; this developed into the custom of putting a salty titbit such as olives or a piece of sausage, on the bread to encourage drinking.

Simple tapas include olives, cheese, omelette and *charcutería* or *chacinas* (pork products). Other varieties include *garbanzos con espinacas* (chickpeas with spinach), a small serving of pork *solomillo* (sirloin) or *lomo* (loin) with garnish, *brochetas* or *pinchos* (mini-kebabs on sticks), *flamenquines* (deep-fried, breaded veal or ham) or *boquerones* (anchovies), which might be marinated in vinegar or fried in batter. There's infinite scope for adventurous chefs to combine flavours and textures. Seville is out in front, where you can sample courgettes (zucchinis) with Roquefort cheese, or mushroom-filled artichoke hearts.

Seafood tapas are a highlight. Sample the best shellfish in the sherry triangle of Cádiz province (see p175) – from Atlantic *conchas finas* (Venus shell, the biggest of the clams) to *cangrejos* (tiny crabs, cooked whole) or *búsanos* (sea snails or whelks). *Langostinos a la plancha*, king prawns grilled with coarse-grained salt, are wonderful.

Offal such as *sesos* (brains), *callos* (tripe), *criadillas* (bull or sheep testicles), *riñones* (kidneys) and *hígado* (liver) may appear in a small earthenware dish, simmering in a tomato sauce or gravy. More to some people's taste are salad tapas such as *pipirrana* (based on diced tomatoes and red peppers), *salpicón* (the same with bits of seafood), *ensaladilla* (Russian salad; a salad of cold diced vegetables mixed with Russian dressing) and *aliño* (any salad in a vinegar-and-oil dressing).

Bars usually display a range of tapas on the counter. They may also have a menu or a blackboard listing what's available. Otherwise, things can be a mite confusing. A place that appears not to have tapas may actually specialise in them! You just have to ask what tapas are available.

A *ración* is a meal-sized serving of these snacks. A *media-ración* is half a *ración*. Two different *media-raciones* amount to something like a full meal. A *tabla* is a selection of tapas – typically a combination of hams, sausages, cheeses and *ahmudos* (smoked fish); like a *ración*, it's good for a group of people to share.

Ham & Sausages

To most Spaniards there is no more mouthwatering prospect than a few thin, succulent slices of cured *jamón* (ham). Most of these hams are *jamón serrano* (mountain-cured ham). The best is *jamón ibérico*, also called *pata negra* (black leg), from the black Iberian breed of pig, and the best is *jamón ibérico de bellota*, from pigs fed on *bellotas* (acorns). Considered to be the best *jamón* of all is the *jamón ibérico* of Jabugo, in Andalucía's Huelva province (see p160), which comes from pigs free-ranging in the Sierra Morena oak forests. The best Jabugo hams are graded from one to five *jotas* (Js), and *cinco jotas* (JJJJJ) hams are said to come from pigs that have never eaten anything but acorns.

Ordinary, uncured ham, is called *jamón York*, and tends to be as un-inspiring as British supermarket ham.

Olive Oil

Originally planted by the Romans, the vast olive groves of Córdoba, Jaén and Sevilla provinces contribute to making Spain the world's largest olive-oil producer. The production of *az-zait* (juice of the olive) – from which we derive *aceite*, the modern generic word for olive oil – was further developed by the Muslims and both olives and olive oil continue to be a staple of the Andalucian kitchen. For quality-control purposes there are now six accredited Denominación de Origen (DO; domains that consistently produce high-quality olive oils) labels in Spain and four of these are in Andalucía: Baena and Priego de Córdoba in Córdoba, and Sierra de Segura and Sierra Mágina in Jaén. The absolute finest of these, such as Núñez de Prado (see p294), have nearly zero acidity.

DID YOU KNOW?

Spain is the world's largest producer of olive oil.

Rice

With the advent of the Arabs, Andalucía gained a new staple, *arroz* (rice). Although Spain's most famous dish, paella, is not an Andalucian speciality (its true home is Valencia), it is still in much demand in local restaurants.

Andalucian versions of paella often include seafood and/or chicken. On the Costa del Sol, peas, clams, mussels and prawns, and a garnish of red peppers and lemon slices is a popular combination. In Sevilla and Cádiz provinces, big prawns and sometimes lobster are added. Paella is cooked in a wide, two-handled metal pan – best on a wood fire outdoors. Its flavour comes from the simmering rice absorbing the juices of the other ingredients, and the yellow colour traditionally comes from saffron, although this is often substituted by the cheaper *pimentón* (paprika).

Other variations include *arroz a la Sevillana*, a seafood rice from Sevilla with crab, sausage and ham; *arroz con almejas* (rice with clams); and *calamares en su tinta* (squid cooked in its own ink with rice).

Stews

In the past the *cocido*, a one-pot feast of meat, sausage, beans and vegetables, was a mainstay of the Andalucian diet. It's time-consuming to prepare, but in Andalucian villages the smell still wafts through the streets. A *cocido* can actually provide a three-course meal, with the broth eaten first, followed by the vegetables and then the meat.

More usual nowadays is a simpler kind of stew, the *guiso*, which comes in three traditional types – *las berzas*, with cabbage and either beef or pork; *el puchero*, chicken and bacon broth with turnips and mint; and *los potajes*, with dried beans and chorizo (spicy pork sausage). Dishes which Granada is famous for include *habas con jamón* (broad beans with ham) and the ubiquitous *rabo de toro* (oxtail stew).

Soups

True gazpacho, a typical Andalucian dish, is a chilled soup of blended tomatoes, peppers, cucumber, garlic, breadcrumbs, lemon and oil. It is sometimes served in a jug with ice cubes, with side dishes of chopped raw vegetables such as cucumber and onion. Its close relatives – all chilled soups containing oil, garlic and breadcrumbs – include *salmorejo cordobés*, Cordoban gazpacho cream, made without peppers or cucumber, served with chopped hard-boiled eggs, and *ajo blanco*, pounded almond and garlic soup from Málaga province, often garnished with grapes.

Gazpacho developed in Andalucía among the *jornaleros*, agricultural day labourers, who were given rations of bread and oil. They soaked the bread in water to form the basis of a soup and then added oil, garlic and whatever fresh vegetables were at hand. All of the ingredients were pounded using a pestle and mortar resulting in a refreshing and nourishing dish.

DRINKS
Wine

Vino (wine) production in Andalucía was introduced by the Phoenicians, possibly as early as 1100 BC. Nowadays, almost every village throughout Andalucía has its own simple wine, known simply as *mosto*. Eight areas in the region produce distinctive, good, non-DO wines that can be sampled locally: Aljarafe and Los Palacios (Sevilla province); Bailén, Lopera and Torreperogil (Jaén province); Costa Albondón (Granada province); Laujar de Andarax (Almería province); and Villaviciosa (Córdoba province).

A Traveler's Wine Guide to Spain by Desmond Begg (1998) is an authoritative and well-illustrated guide through the wine country of Spain.

The Montilla-Morales DO in southern Córdoba province produces a wine that is similar to sherry but, unlike sherry, is not fortified by the addition of brandy – the fino variety is the most acclaimed. Andalucía's other DO is Málaga province: sweet, velvety Málaga Dulce pleased palates from Virgil to the ladies of Victorian England, until the vines were blighted around the beginning of the 20th century. Today the Málaga DO area is Andalucía's smallest. You can sample Málaga wine straight from the barrel in some of the city's numerous bars.

Wine not only accompanies your meals but is also a popular bar drink – and it's cheap: a bottle costing €5 from a supermarket or €12 in a restaurant will be a decent wine. Cheap *vino de mesa* (table wine) may sell for less than €1.50 a litre in shops. You can order wine by the *copa* (glass) in bars and restaurants: the *vino de la casa* (house wine) may come from a barrel or jug at around €1.

WHAT'S IN A LABEL?

You can judge the quality of Spanish wine to a certain extent from the label. Apart from sherry, most of Spain's best wines come from the north of the country. DOC stands for Denominación de Origen Calificada and refers to wine from areas that have maintained high quality over a long period. Rioja, in northern Spain, is the only DOC so far. DO, Denominación de Origen, is one step down from DOC. There are 50-odd DO areas. A DOC or DO label tells you that the wine has been produced by serious wine growers, although each DOC and DO covers a range of wines of varying quality.

Young wine for immediate drinking is called *vino joven*, while *vino de crianza* has been stored for certain minimum periods: if red, for two full years with a minimum of six months in oak; if white or rosé, for one year. A Reserva requires three years' storage for reds and two for whites and rosés. Gran Reserva wines are particularly good vintages, mostly reds which must have spent at least two years in storage and three in the bottle.

Sherry

The website www.sherry .org provides a good introduction on the subject of sherry and the firms that make it.

Sherry, Andalucía's celebrated fortified wine, is produced in the towns of Jerez de la Frontera, El Puerto de Santa María and Sanlúcar de Barrameda, which make up the 'sherry triangle' of Cádiz province (see p175). A combination of climate, chalky soils that soak up the sun but retain moisture, and a special maturing process called the *solera* process (see p184) produces these unique wines.

The main distinction in sherry is between fino (dry and straw-coloured) and oloroso (sweet and dark, with a strong bouquet). An amontillado is an amber, moderately dry fino with a nutty flavour and a higher alcohol content. An oloroso combined with a sweet wine results in a cream sherry. A manzanilla – officially not sherry – is a camomile-coloured, unfortified fino produced in Sanlúcar de Barrameda; its delicate flavour is reckoned to come from sea breezes wafting into the bodegas (wineries).

Beer

The most common ways to order a *cerveza* (beer) is to ask for a *caña* (a small draught beer; 250mL) or a *tubo* (a larger draught beer; about 300mL), which come in a straight glass. If you just ask for a *cerveza* you may get bottled beer, which tends to be more expensive. A small bottle (250mL) is called a *botellín* or a *quinto*; a bigger one (330mL) is a *tercio*. San Miguel, Cruzcampo and Victoria are all decent Andalucian beers.

Coffee

In Andalucía the coffee is good, and strong unless you specify otherwise. A *café con leche* is about 50% coffee, 50% hot milk; ask for a *grande* or *doble* if you want a large cup, *en vaso* if you want it in a glass and *sombra* if you want lots of milk. A *café solo* is short and black; *café cortado* is short with a dash of milk.

DID YOU KNOW?

The round-bottomed sherry glass with its narrow mouth is an Arab invention, attributed to Ziryah, court musician to Abd ar-Rahman II.

Tea

In cafés and bars, *té* (tea) is invariably weak. Ask for *leche aparte* (milk to be separate), otherwise you'll end up with a cup of lukewarm milky water with a tea bag thrown in. Many places also have *té de manzanilla* (camomile tea). *Teterías* (Arabian-style tearooms) are fashionable in some cities, serving all manner of teas and herbal *infusiones*.

Hot Chocolate

The Spaniards brought chocolate back from Mexico in the mid-16th century and adopted it enthusiastically. As a drink, *caliente* (hot chocolate) is served thick; sometimes it even appears among *postres* (desserts) on menus. Generally, it's a breakfast drink consumed with *churros* (long thin doughnuts with sugar).

Water

Clear, cold water from a public fountain or tap is an Andalucian favourite – but check that it's drinkable. For tap water in restaurants, ask for *agua de grifo*. *Agua mineral* (bottled water) comes in innumerable brands, either *con gas* (fizzy) or *sin gas* (still).

CELEBRATIONS

The act of celebrating is integral to Spanish cuisine and there is always something to celebrate. Most celebrations are family affairs with religious overtones, usually a fiesta honouring a patron saint. Bigger celebrations such as Semana Santa (Holy Week) or Christmas call forth specialities from the larder. At Easter you will see *monas de Pascua* (figures made out of chocolate), *torrijas* (French toast) or *torta pascualina* (spinach-and-egg pie). You know its All Saints' Day when the *huessos santos* (saints' bones; sweet breads) appear, and at Christmas all children devour a *roscón de Reyes* (spongy doughnut decorated with dried fruit and sugar). But of all seasons, Christmas is the gastronomic timepiece calling for the famous *turrón* (nougat made of almonds, honey and egg whites) and a host of other *pasteles* (pastries or cakes). While most families still tuck into turkey, there are those who prefer the traditional *bacalao* (cod) or *besugo* (red bream).

WHERE TO EAT & DRINK

If you want to live like locals, you'll spend plenty of time in bars and cafés. Bars come in many guises, such as *bodegas* (traditional wine bars), *cervecerías* (beer bars), *tascas* (bars specialising in tapas), *tabernas* (taverns) and even *pubs* (pubs). In many of them you'll find tapas to eat; others may serve more substantial fare too. You'll often save 10% to 20% by eating at the bar rather than at a table.

The *restaurantes* (restaurants) of Andalucía serve good, straightforward food at affordable prices. A *mesón* is a simple restaurant attached to a bar with home-style cooking, and a *comedor* is usually the dining room of a bar or *hostal* (a simple guesthouse or small place offering hotel-like accommodation) – the food is likely to be functional and cheap. A *venta* is (or once was) a roadside inn – the food can be delectable and inexpensive. A *marisquería* is a seafood restaurant, while a *chiringuito* is a small open-air bar or kiosk, or sometimes a beachside restaurant.

Log on to www.vegetarian guides.co.uk to order *The New Spain: Vegan and Vegetarian Restaurants*, a guide to over 100 vegetarian restaurants throughout Spain.

VEGETARIANS & VEGANS

Throughout Andalucía the fruit and vegetables are delicious, and fresh nearly all year-round, but unfortunately the region boasts only a handful of avowedly vegetarian restaurants. A word of warning: 'vegetable' dishes may contain more than just vegetables (eg beans with bits of ham). Vegetarians will find that salads in most restaurants are a good bet, as are gazpacho and *ajo blanco*. Another reliable dish is *pisto*, a fry-up of courgettes, green peppers, onions and potatoes; *esparragos trigueros* (a thin wild asparagus) grilled or with *revueltos* (scrambled eggs) also make a satisfying meal. By and large, though, tapas such as *pimientos asados* (roasted red peppers), *alcachofas* (artichokes) and, for vegetarians, cheese are the best bet.

WHINING & DINING

Spanish restaurants tend to be extremely child friendly as it is customary for children to accompany adults for dinner from a very young age. As a result local children are expected to be well behaved and allow the adults to enjoy their meal in peace. Few restaurants provide a special children's menu but are happy to downsize their portions to a *medio plato* (half plate) on request. Highchairs are available in many restaurants but it is advisable to ask in advance or even bring one along if you can.

HABITS & CUSTOMS

The Spanish eating timetable is at its most extreme in Andalucía, so it's a good idea to reset your stomach clock unless you want to eat only with other tourists. Andalucians, like most Spaniards, usually start the day with a light *desayuno* (breakfast), usually consisting of coffee with a *tostada*. Another popular choice is *churros con chocolate* – long, thin doughnuts to dip in thick hot chocolate. If you're hungry, a *tortilla* (omelette) is a good option. *Huevos* (eggs) also come *fritos* (fried), *revueltos* (scrambled)

DOS & DON'TS

- *Buenos días* (good morning) or *buenas tardes* (good afternoon) is the basic greeting in any bar or restaurant.

- Andalucians tend not to stand on ceremony so when you're enjoying your pre-prandial sherry it is not uncommon for people passing your table to say *¡Buen provecho!* ('Enjoy your meal!').

- Tapas are usually eaten with a fork or *palillo* (toothpick) but not with one's hands, although dipping your bread in any saucy plate is a must.

- One word of warning, you won't find many nonsmoking sections in Andalucian restaurants or bars. Smoking is still very much a national pastime.

---

or *cocidos* (boiled). Head to a bar or café for a *merienda* (snack) at around 11am or noon and again at 6pm or 7pm for an apéritif. Tapas apart, one great Spanish snack is the *bocadillo,* a long white roll filled with anything from cheese or ham to *tortilla.*

Comida or *almuerzo* (lunch) is usually the main meal of the day, eaten between 2pm and 4pm. It can consist of several courses, starting with a soup or salad, continuing with a main course of meat or fish with vegetables, or a rice dish or bean stew, and ending with dessert. As well as ordering from *la carta* (the main menu), you nearly always have the option of the budget traveller's best friend, the *menú del día* (daily set meal). Some restaurants also offer *platos combinados* combining several items on one plate. Note that prices for fish and seafood are sometimes given by weight, which can be misleading. Desserts have a low profile – *helado* (ice cream), *arroz con leche* (rice pudding) and *flan* (creme caramel) are often the only choices.

La cena (the evening meal) tends to be lighter than lunch and may be eaten as late as 10pm or 11pm. Andalucians sometimes go out for a bigger dinner in a restaurant, but before about 9pm you're unlikely to see anyone but foreigners.

'Quality cooking courses are beginning to make their mark'

COOKING COURSES

Given the renaissance taking place in top Spanish restaurants and the growing desire of travellers to engage more fully with local culture, it is hardly surprising that quality cookery courses are beginning to make their mark. Two excellent courses are:

Finca Buen Vino (☎ 959 12 40 34; www.fincabuenvino.com) A wonderfully warm kitchen and an excellent course in the stunning rural setting of the Parque Natural Sierra de Aracena y Picos de Aroche (see p162).

Turismo Rural Hidalgo (☎ 954 88 35 81; www.turismoruralhidalgo.com) Want to get to grips with the new Spanish creative cuisine? Try this week-long course in the old-fashioned town of Cazalla de la Sierra (see p133).

EAT YOUR WORDS

Andalucía has such a variety of foods and food names that you could travel for years and still find unfamiliar items on almost every menu. The following guide should help you sort out what's what. For pronunciation guidelines, see p431.

Useful Phrases

Table for ..., please.   *Una mesa para ..., por favor.*
oo-na me-sa pa-ra ..., por fa-vor

Can I see the menu please?   *¿Puedo ver el menú, por favor?*
pwe-do ver el me-noo, por fa-vor

Do you have a menu in English?
tye-nen oon me-*noo* en een-*gles*
I'm a vegetarian.
soy ve-khe-ta-*rya*-no/a
What would you recommend?
ke re-ko-*myen*-da
What's the speciality here?
kwal es la es-pe-sya-lee-*dad* de es-te res-to-*ran*-te
I'd like the set lunch, please.
kee-*sye*-ra el me-*noo* del *dee*-a, por fa-*vor*
The bill, please.
la *kwen*-ta por fa-*vor*
Do you accept credit cards?
a-*thep*-tan tar-*khe*-tas de *kre*-dee-to

¿Tienen un menú en inglés?

Soy vegetariano/a.

¿Qué recomienda?

¿Cuál es la especialidad de este restaurante?

Quisiera el menú del día, por favor.

La cuenta, por favor.

¿Aceptan tarjetas de crédito?

To learn about the food and drink of Andalucía visit www.andalucia .com/gastronomy.

Food Glossary
BASICS & STAPLES
arroz – rice
bocadillo – filled roll
bollo – small soft roll; also *mollete*
gazpacho – chilled soup of blended tomatoes, peppers, cucumber, garlic, breadcrumbs, lemon and oil
huevo – egg
media-ración – half a ración
menú del día – fixed-price meal
mollete – small soft roll; also *bollo*
montadito – open sandwich
paella – rice dish with shellfish, chicken and vegetables

pan – bread
plato combinado – 'combined plate'; seafood/omelette/meat with trimmings
queso – cheese
ración – meal-sized serving of tapas
revueltos – scrambled eggs
rosquilla – toasted roll
tapas – light snacks, usually eaten with drinks
tortilla – omelette
tostada – toasted bread often served with a variety of toppings such as tomatoes and olive oil

CARNE (MEAT)
cabra – goat
cabrito – kid; also *choto*
carne de monte – 'meat of the mountain'; local game
carne de vaca – beef
caza – game
charcutería – cured meat
choto – kid; also *cabrito*
chorizo – spicy pork sausage
codorniz – quail
conejo – rabbit
cordero – lamb
hígado – liver

jamón – ham
jamón ibérico – ham from the black Iberian breed of pig
jamón ibérico de bellota – ham from Iberian pigs fed on acorns
jamón serrano – mountain-cured ham
jamón York – uncured ham
liebre – hare
ato – duck
pavo – turkey
pollo – chicken
riñón, riñones (pl) – kidney
ternera – veal

www.spaingourmetour .com is the most authoritative and comprehensive periodical on Spanish gastronomy.

FRUTA & VERDURAS (FRUIT & VEGETABLES)
aceituna – olive
aguacate – avocado
ajo – garlic
alcachofa – artichoke
apio – celery
berenjena – aubergine (eggplant)
calabacín – courgette (zucchini)
calabaza – pumpkin

cebolla – onion
cereza – cherry
frambuesa – raspberry
fresa – strawberry
lima – lime
limón – lemon
manzana – apple
manzanilla – camomile

melocotón – peach
naranja – orange
piña – pineapple

plátano – banana
sandía – watermelon
uva – grape

PESCADO & MARISCOS (FISH & SEAFOOD)

almeja – clam
anochoa – anchovy; also boquerón
atún – tuna
bacalao – cod
bogavante – lobster; also langosta
boquerón – anchovy; also anochoa
caballa – mackerel
cangrejo – crab
chipirón, chipirones (pl) – baby squid;
also chopito

chopito – baby squid;
also chipirón
gamba – prawn
langosta – lobster; also bogavante
langostino – king prawn
mellijón, mejillones (pl) – mussel
merluza – hake
ostra – oyster
sardina – sardine
trucha – trout

TARTAS & POSTRES (CAKES & DESSERTS)

arroz con leche – rice pudding
churro – long thin doughnut
with sugar
flan – creme caramel

helado – ice cream
pastel – pastry or cake
torta – pie or tart
turrón – nougat

DID YOU KNOW?

Muslim rulers liked their
ices to be made with
snow from the mountains
which was carried down
perilous tracks in the
panniers of donkeys.

TÉNICAS (COOKING TECHNIQUES)

a la brasa – grilled or barbecued
a la parrilla – grilled or barbecued
a la plancha – grilled on a hotplate
ahumado/a – smoked
al carbón – char-grilled
asado – roast
cocido – cooked or boiled; also hotpot/stew

crudo – raw
frito/a – fried
guiso – stew
rebozado/a – battered and fried
relleno/a – stuffed
salado/a – salted, salty
seco/a – dry, dried

Drinks Glossary

NONALCOHOLIC DRINKS

agua de grifo – tap water
agua mineral – bottled water
agua potable – drinking water
café con leche – 50% coffee, 50% hot milk
café cortado – short black with a dash of milk
café solo – short black

caliente – hot chocolate
con gas – fizzy (bottled water)
refresco – soft drink
sin gas – still (bottled water)
té – tea
zumo – fruit juice

CERVEZA (BEER)

botellín – bottled beer (250mL);
also quinto
caña – draught beer (250mL) served in
a straight glass

quinto – bottled beer (250mL); also botellín
tercio – bottled beer (330mL)
tubo – draught beer (300mL) served in a
straight glass

VINO (WINE)

blanco – white
de la casa – house
rosado – rosé

tinto – red
vino de la casa – house wine
vino de mesa – table wine

OTHER ALCOHOLIC DRINKS

aguardiente – grape-based spirit
(similar to grappa)
anís – aniseed liqueur

coñac – brandy
sangría – wine and fruit punch

Sevilla Province

Andalucía's biggest and most vibrant city, proud and historic Seville (Sevilla in Spanish), is the highlight of the province, with its great architecture and art, famous Easter and spring festivals, fascinating barrios (districts), creative entertainment scene, mouthwatering tapas bars and all-night nightlife. All the excitement of a buzzing modern city is played out against a matchless backdrop of heritage and tradition – from the exquisitely proportioned Almohad minaret (the Giralda) and the delicate Mudejar work of the Alcázar palace to the great flowering of baroque art, sculpture and architecture in the city's churches and museums.

But there's more to Sevilla province than Seville. Straddling the fertile valley of the lower Río Guadalquivir, this region has been Andalucía's cultural and economic vanguard ever since the Tartessos culture flourished here centuries before Christ. Outside the capital city you'll find Andalucía's most impressive Roman ruins at Itálica, and, on the rolling agricultural plains in the east of the province (known as La Campiña), fascinating old towns such as Carmona, Écija and Osuna, whose architecture and monuments speak of many epochs of history. Countryside-lovers will be charmed by the ever-changing Sierra Morena hill country of the sparsely populated Sierra Norte region, where you'll find fine walking and bird-watching, beautiful spring wild flowers, and quaint old towns and villages to explore.

HIGHLIGHTS

■ Immersing yourself in the beauty of the **Alcázar** (p94), the **cathedral** (p91) and the **Giralda** (p91), the city of Seville's greatest buildings

■ Enjoying the golden age of Spanish art at Seville's **Museo de Bellas Artes** (p100)

■ Taking a tapas crawl: joining locals and touring Seville's tempting **tapas bars** (p115)

■ Soaking up the solemn fervour of Seville's **Semana Santa** (p108) processions and the fun of the **Feria de Abril** (p108)

■ Walking, watching birds and marvelling at the wild flowers and rolling hill scenery of the **Parque Natural Sierra Norte** (p131)

★ Parque Natural Sierra Norte

★ Itálica ★ Carmona ★ Écija
★ Seville
★ Osuna

■ Travelling through millennia of history at Roman **Itálica** (p123) and the towns of La Campiña: **Carmona** (p125), **Écija** (p128) and **Osuna** (p130)

■ Feeling the passion at Seville's **flamenco haunts** (p119) and its **Bienal de Flamenco** (p108) festival

■ POPULATION:	■ SEVILLE AVERAGE DAILY HIGH:	■ ALTITUDE RANGE:
1.78 MILLION	JAN/AUG 15°C/36°C	0m–959m

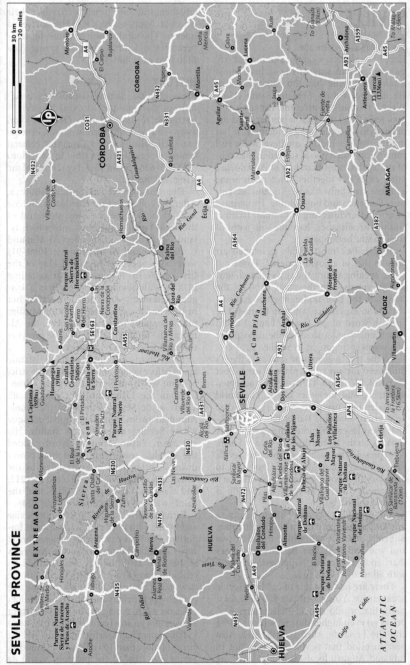

SEVILLA PROVINCE

SEVILLE

pop 710,000 / elevation 30m

Here in Andalucía's capital and biggest city the Andalucian way of life is lived most intensely. Seville has the most passionate and portentous Semana Santa (Holy Week), the most festive and romantic annual *feria* (fair), the best tapas bars and the most stylish people in all Andalucía. It has more narrow, winding, medieval lanes and romantic, hidden plazas soaked in the scent of orange blossom than half of Andalucía's other cities put together. It's a main home of those two bulwarks of Andalucian culture: flamenco and bullfighting. Its heritage of art and architecture – Roman, Islamic, Gothic, Renaissance, baroque – is without rival in southern Spain.

But Seville's most highly developed art form is that of enjoying oneself. To be out for an evening among the city's relaxed, fun-loving crowds – in the tapas bars, on the streets, in the after-midnight clubs and discos – is an experience you won't forget. The Spanish word *alegre* (joyful, happy) could have been coined to describe the atmosphere of a warm spring night in Seville.

To the true *sevillano* or *sevillana,* there's little need for any other place to exist. Poet Fernando Villalón (1881–1930) accepted that there was one other place: 'The world is divided into two parts: Seville and Cádiz,' he averred. Matador Rafael Guerra (1862–1941) was less ambiguous: after a fight in A Coruña, on the far northwestern tip of Spain, he expressed the wish to get back to Seville that same evening. '*Maestro*', they said to him, 'Seville is very far away.' 'Seville, far?' countered Guerra. 'Here is far. Seville is where it should be.'

A non-*sevillano* cannot hope to become a *sevillano* except perhaps in another lifetime. But walk out in Seville with a friend or two and you will find that the city has more than enough *alegría* (happiness) to share with all who set foot in it.

There are just a couple of catches. Seville is expensive. You might pay €80 here for a room that would cost €50 elsewhere. And prices go even higher during Semana Santa and the Feria de Abril (April Fair). Also bear in mind that Seville gets *very* hot in July and August: locals, sensibly, leave the city then, and some hotels even reduce their prices to tempt visitors into the breezeless inferno. The ideal season to come, for temperatures and atmosphere, is spring (late March to early June).

HISTORY

Roman Seville, named Hispalis, was a significant port on the Río Guadalquivir – navigable to the Atlantic Ocean 100km away – but was overshadowed by Córdoba. Later, Hispalis became a Visigothic cultural centre, especially in the time of St Isidoro (AD 565–636), Spain's leading scholar of the Visigothic period.

The Muslims called Seville Ishbiliya. After the collapse of the Córdoba caliphate in 1031, it became the most powerful of the *taifas* (small kingdoms) into which Islamic Spain broke up. Its rulers Al-Mutadid (r 1042–69) and Al-Mutamid (r 1069–91) were both poets. Al-Mutamid, one of the first people in history recorded as falling in love with Seville, presided over a languid, hedonistic court in the Alcázar, but in 1085 had to call in help from the Muslim fundamentalist rulers of Morocco, the Almoravids, for support against the growing threat of Christian reconquest.

The Almoravids took over all Islamic Spain before being replaced by another strict Muslim sect from North Africa, the Almohads, in the 12th century. Caliph Yacub Yusuf made Seville capital of the whole Almohad realm, building a great mosque where Seville cathedral now stands. His successor, Yusuf Yacub al-Mansur, added the Giralda tower. But Almohad power dwindled after the disastrous defeat by the Christians at Las Navas de Tolosa in 1212, and Castile's Fernando III (El Santo; the Saint) went on to capture Seville in 1248.

Fernando brought 24,000 settlers to Seville and by the 14th century it was the most important Castilian city. Seville's biggest break was Columbus' discovery of the Americas in 1492. In 1503 the city was awarded an official monopoly on Spanish trade with the new-found continent. It rapidly became one of the biggest, richest and most cosmopolitan cities on earth, a magnet for everyone from beggars and *pícaros* (card and dice tricksters) to Italian merchants, artists of genius and the clergy of more than 100 religious institutions. Seville was labelled the *puerto y puerta de*

Indias (port and gateway of the Indies), the Babylon of Spain and even the new Rome. Lavish Renaissance and baroque buildings sprouted and the city's population jumped about 40,000 in 1500 to 150,000 in 1600.

But a plague in 1649 killed half the city and, as the 17th century wore on, the Río Guadalquivir became more silted up and less navigable for the bigger ships of the day; many ships foundered on a sandbar at the river mouth near Sanlúcar de Barrameda. In 1717 the Casa de la Contratación (the government office controlling commerce with the Americas) was transferred to Cádiz. Another Seville plague in 1800 killed 13,000 people. Napoleonic troops occupied the city from 1810 to 1812, stealing, it's said, 999 works of art when they left.

The beginnings of industry in the mid-19th century brought a measure of prosperity for some. The first bridge across the Guadalquivir, the Puente de Triana (or Puente de Isabel II), was built in 1852, and the old Almohad walls were knocked down in 1869 to let the city expand. However, the majority of people in the city and countryside remained impoverished. In 1936 Seville fell very quickly to the Nationalists at the start of the Spanish Civil War, despite resistance in working-class areas (which brought savage reprisals).

Things finally looked up in the 1980s when Seville was named capital of the new autonomous Andalucía within democratic Spain, and the left-of-centre Partido Socialista Obrero Español (PSOE) party, led by Sevillan Felipe González, came to power in Madrid. The Expo '92 international exhibition, marking the 500th anniversary of Columbus' great voyage, brought Seville millions of visitors, eight new bridges across the Guadalquivir, the super-fast AVE (Alta Velocidad Española) rail link to Madrid, an opera house and thousands of new hotel rooms. The Expo party had its hangover during the succeeding years of economic recession, but Seville's economy is now steadily improving with a mix of tourism, commerce, technology and industry.

ORIENTATION

Seville straddles the Río Guadalquivir, with most places of interest on the eastern bank. The central area is mostly a tangle of narrow, twisting old streets and small squares, with the exceptions of Plaza Nueva and broad, straight Avenida de la Constitución. The *avenida* runs south from Plaza Nueva to the Puerta de Jerez, which is a busy intersection marking the southern edge of the central area. Just east of Avenida de la Constitución are the city's major monuments: the cathedral, the Giralda tower and the Alcázar fortress-palace. The quaint Barrio de Santa Cruz, east of the cathedral and Alcázar, is a popular place to sleep and eat. The true centre of Seville, El Centro, is a little further north, around Plaza de San Francisco and Plaza Salvador. The area between Avenida de la Constitución and the river is El Arenal.

The bus and train stations are on the periphery of the central area, all served by city buses that circle the centre (see p123): Prado de San Sebastián bus station is on Plaza San Sebastián, 650m southeast of the cathedral and within walking distance of the Barrio de Santa Cruz; Plaza de Armas bus station is 900m northwest of the cathedral, within walking distance of El Arenal; Santa Justa train station is 1.5km northeast of the cathedral, on Avenida Kansas City.

INFORMATION
Bookshops

Casa del Libro (Map pp98-100; ☎ 954 50 29 50; Calle Velázquez 8; ☼ 9.30am-9.30pm Mon-Sat) Guidebooks in several languages, novels in English, maps, dictionaries, Spanish course books.

Librería Beta Constitución 9 (Map pp98-100; ☎ 954 56 28 17; Avenida de la Constitución 9) Constitución 27 (Map pp98-100; ☎ 954 56 07 03; Avenida de la Constitución 27) Guidebooks in several languages, novels in English, maps.

LTC (Map pp98-100; ☎ 954 42 59 64; Avenida Menéndez Pelayo 42-44; ☼ closed Sat) Best map shop in Andalucía; also sells Spanish-language guidebooks.

Vértice International Bookshop (Map pp88-90; ☎ 954 21 16 54; Calle San Fernando 33) Novels in many languages, some guidebooks.

Emergency

Ambulance (☎ 061)
Fire (☎ 085)
Policía Local (Local Police; ☎ 092)
Policía Nacional (National Police; ☎ 091)

Internet Access

Ciber Alcázar (Map pp88-90; ☎ 954 21 04 01; Calle San Fernando 35; per hr €1.80; ☼ 10.15am-10.30pm Mon-Fri, noon-10.30pm Sat & Sun)

SEVILLE

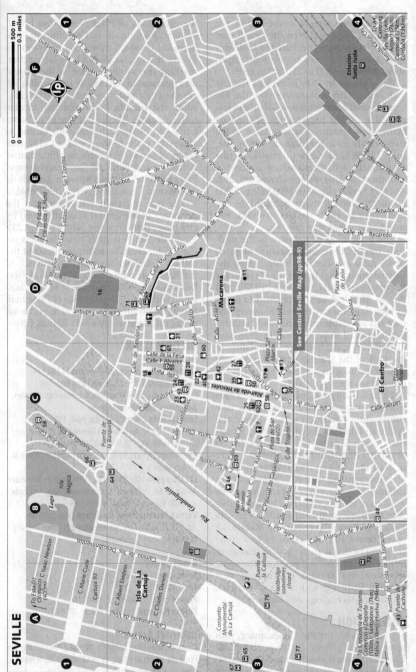

0	500 m
0	0.3 miles

To Estadio
Olímpico (1.3km)

C Isaac Newton

C Marie Curie

Cartuja 93

C Albert Einstein

Calle Leonardo da Vinci

C Charles Darwin

Calle América Vespucio

Isla de La Cartuja

Camino de los Descubrimientos

Lago

Isla Mágica

Calle José Gálvez

Río Guadalquivir

Puente de la Barqueta

Avenida de la Ribera

To Estadio
Olímpico (1.3km)

Dr Marañón

Dr Leal Castaño

San Juan de Ribera

Calle Don Fadrique

Calle Resolana

Ronda de Po XIV

Sor Dorotea

Avenida de Pino Montano

Calle San Juan de La Salle

Manuel Villalobos

C de la Albaida

Avenida de la Cruz Roja

Carretera de Carmona

San Juan Bosco

Avenida de Capuchinos

Avenida de Miraflores

Ronda de Capuchinos

Calle de Recaredo

Macarena

Calle Arrayán

Calle Castellar

Plaza San Martín

Calle Féria

Calle Relator

Calle San Luis

Calle Aduana

Calle Muñoz León

Calle de la Féria

Calle F Álvarez

Calle Peral

Alameda de Hércules

Calle Lumbreras

Calle Calatrava

Calle Santa Clara

Calle Santa Ana

Calle de San Vicente

Plaza San Antonio de Padua

C Juan Rabadán

Plaza de San Lorenzo

Calle Trajano

Calle Amor de Dios

Calle del Torneo

Calle Marqués de Parades

El Centro

Plaza Salvador

Calle Sierpes

Plaza Ponce de León

CA Apodaca

Plaza Alfonso XII

Puente de la Cartuja

Footbridge
sometimes
closed

Conjunto Monumental de La Cartuja

To Consejería de Turismo,
Comercio y Deporte
(100m); Santiponce (7km);
Italica (8km); Huelva (94km)

Avenida del Costa de la Exposición

Puente del Cachorro

Estación
Santa Justa

Calle Saturno

Calle Amador de

C Medul Castrejo

Calle José Laguillo

Antonio Cesalpino

Calle José

To A4;
Cámping
Sevilla (6km);
Airport (7km);
Carmona (15km);
Córdoba (136km)

See Central Seville Map (pp98–9)

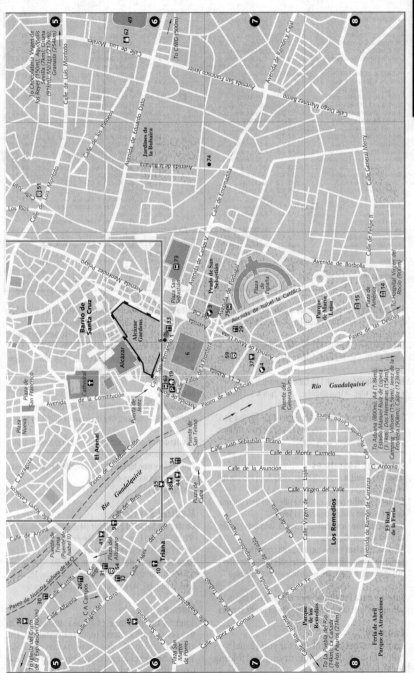

First Center (Map pp98-100; Avenida de la Constitución 34; per hr €2; 9am-10pm Mon-Fri, 10am-9.30pm Sat, noon-9pm Sun)

Internetia (Map pp98-100; Avenida Menéndez Pelayo 46; per hr €2.20; 10.30am-1.30am Mon-Fri, noon-1.30am Sat & Sun)

Interpublic (Map pp98-100; Calle O'Donnell 3; per hr €1.80; 10am-11pm Mon-Fri, 10am-3pm & 5-11pm Sat, 5-11pm Sun)

Seville Internet Center (Map pp98-100; 954 50 02 75; Calle Almirantazgo 2; per min €0.05; 9am-10pm Mon-Fri, 10am-10pm Sat & Sun)

Internet Resources

Discover Sevilla (www.discoversevilla.com) Hip site full of ways for tourists and students to enjoy Seville.

Explore Seville (www.exploreseville.com) Very informative for anyone visiting or living in Seville.

Sevilla Online (www.sol.com) Sights, language schools, accommodation, festivals.

Seville Tourism (www.turismo.sevilla.org) The city's useful official tourism site; its 'Accessible Guide' contains lists of hotels, restaurants, museums, etc with disabled access.

Turismo de la Provincia (www.turismosevilla.org) Informative official tourist information site for Sevilla province.

Laundry

Laundries here do the job for you (usually in half a day), with washing, drying and folding included in their prices.

Auto-Servicio de Lavandería Sevilla (Map pp98-100; 954 21 05 35; Calle Castelar 2C; per load €6; 9.30am-1.30pm & 5-8.30pm Mon-Fri, 9am-2pm Sat)

La Segunda Vera (Map pp98-100; 954 54 11 48; Calle Alejo Fernández 3; per load €7.80; 9.30am-1.30pm & 5-8pm Mon-Fri, 10am-1.30pm Sat)

Media

El Giraldillo Andalucía-wide what's-on mag with a strong Seville emphasis, free from tourist offices and some hotels.

Sevilladc The *ayuntamiento's* (town hall's) free cultural-events magazine.

Tourist Free mag for tourists, with worthwhile information about what to see and do.

Welcome & Olé Ditto.

Medical Services

Centro de Salud El Porvenir (Map pp98-100; 955 03 78 17; cnr Avenidas Menéndez Pelayo & de Cádiz) Public clinic with emergency service.

Hospital Virgen del Rocío (Map pp88-90; 955 01 20 00; Avenida de Manuel Siurot s/n) The main general hospital, 1km south of Parque de María Luisa.

Money

There's no shortage of banks and ATMs in the central area. Santa Justa train station, the airport and both bus stations have ATMs. You'll find exchange offices on Avenida de la Constitución and at Estación Santa Justa.

American Express (Map pp98-100; ☎ 954 21 16 17; Plaza Nueva 8; ☉ 9.30am-1.30pm & 4.30-7.30pm Mon-Fri, 10am-1pm Sat)

Post

Main post office (Map pp98-100; Avenida de la Constitución 32; ☉ 8.30am-8.30pm Mon-Fri, 9.30am-2pm Sat)

Telephone

There are plenty of pay phones around the centre. The following call centres offer cheap international calls (per minute €0.20 or less to Western Europe, USA, Canada or Australia):

Ciber Alcázar (Map pp88-90; ☎ 954 21 04 01; Calle San Fernando 35; ☉ 10.15am-10.30pm Mon-Fri, noon-10.30pm Sat & Sun)

First Center (Map pp98-100; Avenida de la Constitución 34; ☉ 9am-10pm Mon-Fri, 10am-9.30pm Sat, noon-9pm Sun)

Tourist Information

Inhfor (Map pp88-90; ☎ 954 54 19 52; Estación Santa Justa; ☉ 8am-10pm Mon-Fri, 8am-2pm & 4-10pm Sat, 8am-2pm & 6-10pm Sun & holidays) Independent tourist office at the train station.

Municipal tourist office (Map pp98-100; ☎ 954 22 17 14; barranco.turismo@sevilla.org; Calle de Arjona 28; ☉ 9am-9pm Mon-Fri, 9am-2pm Sat & Sun, reduced hours during Semana Santa & Feria de Abril)

Regional tourist office Constitución (Map pp98-100; ☎ 954 22 14 04; otsevilla@andalucia.org; Avenida de la Constitución 21; ☉ 9am-7pm Mon-Fri, 10am-2pm & 3-7pm Sat, 10am-2pm Sun, closed holidays); Estación Santa Justa (Map pp88-90; ☎ 954 53 76 26; Santa Justa; ☉ 9am-8pm Mon-Fri, 10am-2pm Sat & Sun, closed holidays; airport (☎ 954 44 91 28; ☉ 9am-8.30pm Mon-Fri, 10am-6pm Sat, 10am-2pm Sun, closed holidays). The staff at the Constitución office are well informed but often very busy.

Turismo Sevilla (Map pp98-100; ☎ 954 21 00 05; Plaza del Triunfo 1; ☉ 10.30am-7pm Mon-Fri) Information on all Sevilla province.

DANGERS & ANNOYANCES

Seville has a bit of a reputation for petty crime against tourists – pickpockets, bag snatchers and the like. In reality the risks seem no greater here than in any other large Andalucian city. Stay awake to those around you. For general tips on safety in Andalucía see p403.

SIGHTS

The city's major monuments – the cathedral, the Giralda and the Alcázar – are all just east of Avenida de la Constitución and south of the city's true centre (El Centro). But there's plenty to see in El Centro and in the neighbouring El Arenal area too, as well as in the areas to the south, north and west.

Cathedral & Giralda

Seville's immense **cathedral** (Map pp98-100; ☎ 954 21 49 71; www.catedralsevilla.org in Spanish; adult/child under 12/disabled/student/senior €7/free/free/1.50/1.50, Sun free; ☉ 11am-6pm Mon-Sat, 2.30-7pm Sun Sep-Jun, 9.30am-4.30pm Mon-Sat, 2.30-7pm Sun Jul & Aug, closed 1 & 6 Jan, Palm Sunday, Corpus Christi, 15 Aug & 8 & 25 Dec), one of the biggest in the world, stands on the site of the great 12th-century Almohad mosque, with the mosque's minaret (the Giralda) still towering beside it. After Seville fell to the Christians in 1248 the mosque was used as a church until 1401. Then, in view of its decaying state, the church authorities decided to knock it down and start again. 'Let us create such a building that future generations will take us for lunatics,' they decided (or so legend has it). They certainly got themselves a big church – 126m long and 83m wide. It was completed by 1507, all in Gothic style, though later work done after its central dome collapsed in 1511 was mostly in Renaissance style.

The enormity of the broad, five-naved cathedral is disguised by a welter of interior structures and decoration that is typical of Spanish cathedrals and adds up to a storehouse of art and artisanry as rich as that of any church in Spain.

The entry system and timetable for visiting Seville's cathedral change frequently. Current regulations are usually posted up fairly clearly. At the time of writing the main entrance was next to the Puerta de los Príncipes on the southern side of the cathedral.

EXTERIOR

From close up, the bulky exterior of the cathedral gives few hints of the treasures within. But have a look at the **Puerta del Perdón** on Calle Alemanes (a legacy of the Islamic mosque) and the two 15th-century Gothic **doorways**, with terracotta reliefs and statues by Lorenzo Mercadante de Bretaña and Pedro Millán, on Avenida de la Constitución.

The **Giralda**, the 90m decorative brick tower on the northeastern side of the cathedral, was the minaret of the mosque, constructed between 1184 and 1198 at the height of Almohad power. Its proportions, its delicate brick-pattern decoration, and its colour, which changes with the light, make it perhaps Spain's most perfect Islamic building. The top-most parts of the Giralda – from the bell level up – were added in the 16th century, when Spanish Christians were busy 'improving on' surviving Islamic buildings. At the very top is **El Giraldillo**, a 16th-century bronze weathervane representing Faith that has become a symbol of Seville. (The entrance to the Giralda is inside the cathedral – see p91).

SALA DEL PABELLÓN

Selected treasures from the cathedral's art collection are exhibited in this room, the first after the ticket office. Much of what's displayed here, as elsewhere in the cathedral, is the work of masters from Seville's 17th-century artistic golden age (see p102).

SOUTHERN & NORTHERN CHAPELS

The chapels along the southern and northern sides of the cathedral hold riches of sculpture and painting. Near the western end of the northern side is the **Capilla de San Antonio**, housing Murillo's large 1666 canvas depicting the vision of St Anthony of Padua; thieves cut out the kneeling saint in 1874 but he was later found in New York and put back.

VAULTING & STAINED GLASS

Don't forget to look up from time to time to admire the cathedral's marvellous Gothic vaulting and rich-hued stained glass. The oldest stained glass, with markedly different colour tones, was done between 1478 and 1483 by a German known as Enrique Alemán. This master artisan takes credit for the glass above the five westernmost chapels on both sides of the nave and the glass in the four westernmost bays on either side of the uppermost storey of the nave.

COLUMBUS' TOMB

Inside the **Puerta de los Príncipes** stands the monumental tomb of Christopher Columbus (Cristóbal Colón) – though the remains

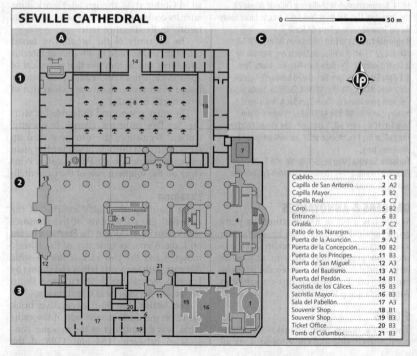

SEVILLE CATHEDRAL

0 ————— 50 m

Cabildo..1	C3
Capilla de San Antonio..................2	A2
Capilla Mayor..................................3	B2
Capilla Real......................................4	C2
Coro..5	B2
Entrance...6	B3
Giralda..7	C2
Patio de los Naranjos....................8	B1
Puerta de la Asunción...................9	A2
Puerta de la Concepción............10	B2
Puerta de los Príncipes...............11	B3
Puerta de San Miguel..................12	A3
Puerta del Bautismo....................13	A2
Puerta del Perdón........................14	B1
Sacristía de los Cálices...............15	B3
Sacristía Mayor..............................16	B3
Sala del Pabellón..........................17	A3
Souvenir Shop...............................18	B1
Souvenir Shop...............................19	B3
Ticket Office..................................20	B3
Tomb of Columbus......................21	B3

inside are probably not those of the great explorer at all. The monument, dating from 1902, shows four sepulchre bearers representing the four kingdoms of Spain at the time of Columbus' famous 1492 voyage: Castile (carrying Granada on the point of its spear), León, Aragón and Navarra. After their initial interment in Valladolid, Spain, in 1506, Columbus' remains were moved to several different locations, but it is known that human remains inside the Seville cathedral tomb arrived from Cuba in 1899. The Dominican Republic made strong claims that it housed Columbus' remains, so in 2003 investigators began tests to identify the remains in Seville cathedral. In August 2004 international newspapers reported that the remains were those of a man who had died about 15 years earlier than did Columbus and were probably those of one of his sons, Diego. It's likely that the great explorer himself rests in the Dominican Republic.

CORO

In the middle of the cathedral you'll find the large *coro* (choir), which has 117 carved Gothic-Mudejar choir stalls. The lower ones have marquetry representations of the Giralda. Vices and sins are depicted on their misericords.

CAPILLA MAYOR

East of the choir is the Capilla Mayor (Main Chapel). Its Gothic retable is the jewel of the cathedral and reckoned to be the biggest altarpiece in the world. Begun by Flemish sculptor Pieter Dancart in 1482 and finished by others in 1564, this sea of gilded and polychromed wood holds over 1000 carved biblical figures. At the centre of the lowest level is the tiny 13th-century silver-plated cedar image of the Virgen de la Sede (Virgin of the See), patron of the cathedral.

EASTERN CHAPELS

East of the Capilla Mayor, situated against the eastern wall of the cathedral, are some more chapels. These chapels are normally closed to visitors, which is a shame, because the central one is the **Capilla Real** (Royal Chapel), which contains the tombs of two great Castilian kings – Fernando III and Alfonso X.

SACRISTÍA DE LOS CÁLICES

South of the Capilla Mayor are rooms containing some of the cathedral's main art treasures. The westernmost of these is the Sacristy of the Chalices, where Francisco de Goya's painting of the Seville martyrs, *Santas Justa y Rufina* (1817), hangs above the altar. These two potters, one depicted with a lion licking her feet, died at the hands of the Romans in AD 287.

SACRISTÍA MAYOR

This large room with a finely carved stone dome, east of the Sacristía de los Cálices, is a plateresque (a decorative genre, with effects resembling those of silverware) creation of 1528–47: the arch over its portal has carvings of 16th-century foods. Pedro de Campaña's 1547 *Descendimiento* (Descent from the Cross), above the central altar at the southern end, and Francisco de Zurbarán's *Santa Teresa*, to its right, are two of the cathedral's most precious paintings. The room's centrepiece is the **Custodia de Juan de Arfe**, a huge 475kg silver monstrance made in the 1580s by Renaissance metalsmith Juan de Arfe. Also here are Pedro Roldán's 1671 statue *San Fernando* (Fernando III) and Alonso Martínez's *La Inmaculada* (Mary, the Immaculate) of 1657, both of which are carried with the Custodia in Seville's Corpus Christi processions. In one of the glass cases are the city keys that were handed over to the conquering Fernando III in 1248.

CABILDO

The beautifully domed chapter house, also called the Sala Capitular, in the southeastern corner, was built between 1558 and 1592 for meetings of the cathedral hierarchy. It was designed by Hernán Ruiz, architect of the Giralda belfry. High above the archbishop's throne at the southern end is a Murillo masterpiece, *La Inmaculada*. Eight Murillo saints adorn the dome at the same level.

GIRALDA

In the northeastern corner of the cathedral you'll find the passage for the climb up to the belfry of the Giralda. The ascent is quite easy, as a series of ramps – built so that the guards could ride up on horseback – goes all the way up. The climb affords great views of the buttresses and pinnacles surrounding the cathedral, as well as of the city beyond.

PATIO DE LOS NARANJOS

Outside the cathedral's northern side, this patio was originally the courtyard of the mosque. It's planted with 66 *naranjos* (orange trees), and a Visigothic fountain remains in the centre. Hanging from the ceiling in the patio's southeastern corner is a replica stuffed crocodile – the original was a gift to Alfonso X from the Sultan of Egypt. On the northern side of the patio is the beautiful Islamic Puerta del Perdón.

Alcázar

The beautiful, not-to-be-missed **Alcázar** (Map pp98-100; ☎ 954 50 23 23; www.patronato-alcazarsevilla .es; adult/child under 16/student/senior/disabled €5/free/ free/free/free; ⌚ 9.30am-8pm Tue-Sat, 9.30am-6pm Sun & holidays Apr-Sep, 9.30am-6pm Tue-Sat, 9.30am-2.30pm Sun & holidays Oct-Mar) stands south of the cathedral across Plaza del Triunfo.

Originally founded as a fort for the Cordoban governors of Seville in 913, the Alcázar is intimately associated with the lives and loves of several later rulers. These include the extraordinary Christian king Pedro I of Castile (r 1350–69), who was known either as Pedro el Cruel or as Pedro el Justiciero (the Justice-Dispenser), depending which side of him you were on.

The Alcázar has been expanded or reconstructed many times in its 11 centuries of existence, making it a complicated building to understand, but in the end this only increases its fascination. In the 11th century, Seville's prosperous Muslim *taifa* rulers developed the original fort by building a palace called Al-Muwarak (The Blessed) in what's now the western part of the Alcázar. The 12th-century Almohad rulers added another palace east of this, around what's now the Patio del Crucero. Christian Fernando III moved into the Alcázar when he captured Seville in 1248, and several later Christian monarchs used it as their main residence. Fernando's son Alfonso X replaced much of the Almohad palace with a Gothic one. Between 1364 and 1366 Pedro I created the Alcázar's crown jewel, the sumptuous Mudejar Palacio de Don Pedro, partly on the site of the old Al-Muwarak palace. The Catholic Monarchs, Fernando and Isabel, set up court here in the 1480s as they prepared

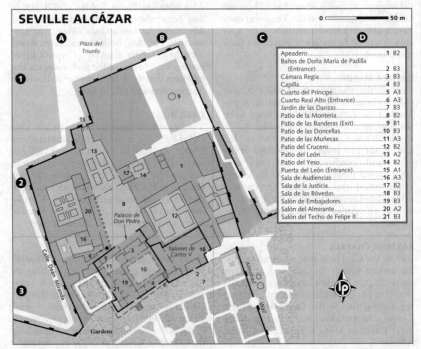

SEVILLE ALCÁZAR

0 ⸻ 50 m

Apeadero......................................**1** B2	
Baños de Doña María de Padilla	
(Entrance).............................**2** B3	
Cámara Regia..............................**3** B3	
Capilla...**4** B3	
Cuarto del Príncipe......................**5** A3	
Cuarto Real Alto (Entrance)..........**6** A3	
Jardín de las Danzas.....................**7** B3	
Patio de la Montería.....................**8** B2	
Patio de las Banderas (Exit)..........**9** B1	
Patio de las Doncellas..................**10** B3	
Patio de las Muñecas....................**11** A3	
Patio del Crucero.........................**12** B2	
Patio del León..............................**13** A2	
Patio del Yeso..............................**14** B2	
Puerta del León (Entrance)...........**15** A1	
Sala de Audiencias.......................**16** A3	
Sala de la Justicia.........................**17** B2	
Sala de las Bóvedas......................**18** B3	
Salón de Embajadores..................**19** B3	
Salón del Almirante......................**20** A2	
Salón del Techo de Felipe II..........**21** B3	

for the conquest of Granada. Later rulers created the Alcázar's lovely gardens.

PATIO DEL LEÓN

From the ticket office inside the **Puerta del León** (Lion Gate) you emerge into the Patio del León (Lion Patio), which was the garrison yard of the original Al-Muwarak palace. Off here is the **Sala de la Justicia** (Hall of Justice), with beautiful Mudejar plasterwork and an *artesonado* (a ceiling of interlaced beams with decorative insertions); this room was built in the 1340s by Christian king Alfonso XI, who disported here with one of his mistresses, Leonor de Guzmán, reputedly the most beautiful woman in Spain. Alfonso's many dalliances left his heir, Pedro I, with five illegitimate half-brothers and a severe case of sibling rivalry. Pedro had a dozen relatives and friends murdered in his efforts to stay on the throne. One of them, Pedro's half-brother Don Fadrique, met his maker right here in the Sala de la Justicia.

The room gives on to the pretty **Patio del Yeso**, part of the 12th-century Almohad palace reconstructed in the 19th century.

PATIO DE LA MONTERÍA

The rooms on the western side of this patio were part of the Casa de la Contratación (Contracting House) founded by the Catholic Monarchs in 1503 to control trade with Spain's American colonies. The **Salón del Almirante** (Admiral's Hall) houses 19th- and 20th-century paintings showing historical events and personages associated with Seville; the room off its northern end has an international collection of strikingly pretty fans. The **Sala de Audiencias** (Audience Hall) is hung with tapestry representations of the shields of Spanish admirals and Alejo Fernández's 1530s painting *Virgen de los Mareantes* (Virgin of Sailors), the earliest known painting about the discovery of the Americas. The Virgin shelters Columbus, Fernando El Católico, Carlos I, Amerigo Vespucci and native Americans beneath her cloak. This room also contains a model of one of Columbus' ships, the *Santa María*.

CUARTO REAL ALTO

The Alcázar is still a royal palace. In 1995 it staged the wedding feast of the Infanta Elena, daughter of King Juan Carlos I, after her marriage in Seville's cathedral. The Cuarto Real Alto (Upper Royal Quarters), the rooms used by the Spanish royal family on their visits to Seville, are open for around 12 half-hour tours (€3), some in Spanish, some in English. The tours are for a maximum of 15 people: if you're keen, it's best to book ahead on ☎ 954 56 00 40. Any unreserved tickets are sold at the main ticket office. The tours start in the southwestern corner of the Patio de la Montería: highlights include the 14th-century Salón de Audiencias, still the monarch's reception room, and Pedro I's bedroom, with marvellous Mudejar tiles and plasterwork.

PALACIO DE DON PEDRO

Whatever else Pedro I may have done, posterity owes him a big thank you for creating this palace (also called the Palacio Mudéjar), which rivals Granada's Alhambra (p305) in its splendid decoration. Though at odds with many of his fellow Christians, Pedro had a long-standing alliance with the Muslim emir of Granada, Mohammed V, the man responsible for much of the Alhambra's finest decoration. So in 1364, when Pedro decided to build a new palace within the Alcázar, Mohammed sent along many of his best artisans. These were joined by others from Seville and Toledo. Their work, drawing on the Islamic traditions of the Almohads and caliphal Córdoba, is a unique synthesis of Iberian Islamic art.

Inscriptions on the palace's **façade**, facing the Patio de la Montería, encapsulate the collaborative nature of the enterprise. While one announces in Spanish that the building's creator was 'the very high, noble and conquering Don Pedro, by the grace of God king of Castile and León', another proclaims repeatedly in Arabic that 'There is no conqueror but Allah'.

At the heart of the palace is the wonderful **Patio de las Doncellas** (Patio of the Maidens), surrounded by beautiful arches, plasterwork and tiling. The doors at its two ends are among the finest made by Toledo's carpenters. The sunken garden in the centre was uncovered by archaeologists in 2004 from beneath a 16th-century marble covering.

The **Cámara Regia** (King's Quarters), on the northern side of the patio, has stunningly beautiful ceilings and wonderful plaster- and tile-work. Its rear room was probably the monarch's summer bedroom.

From here you can move west into the little **Patio de las Muñecas** (Patio of the Dolls), the heart of the palace's private quarters, with delicate Granada-style decoration; indeed, plasterwork was actually brought here from the Alhambra in the 19th century when the mezzanine and top gallery were added for Queen Isabel II. The **Cuarto del Príncipe** (Prince's Room), to its north, has superb ceilings and was probably the queen's bedroom.

The spectacular **Salón de Embajadores** (Hall of Ambassadors), at the western end of the Patio de las Doncellas, was the throne room of Pedro I's palace – as it had been, in earlier form, of Al-Muwarak palace (from which Pedro retained the horseshoe-arched doorways). The room's fabulous wooden dome of multiple star patterns, symbolising the universe, was added in 1427. The dome's shape gives the room its alternative name, *Sala de la Media Naranja* (Hall of the Half Orange). The coloured plasterwork is magnificent. It was in this room that Pedro laid a trap for the so-called Red King, who had temporarily deposed Pedro's buddy Mohammed V in Granada. During a banquet, armed men suddenly leapt from hiding and seized the Red King and his retinue of 37, all of whom were executed outside Seville a few days later.

On the western side of the Salón de Embajadores the beautiful **Arco de Pavones**, named after its peacock motifs, leads into the **Salón del Techo de Felipe II**, with a Renaissance ceiling (1589–91). The **Capilla** (chapel), along the southern side of the Patio de las Doncellas, has another fine ceiling (1540s).

SALONES DE CARLOS V

Reached by a staircase from the southeastern corner of the Patio de las Doncellas, these are the much-remodelled rooms of Alfonso X's 13th-century Gothic palace. It was here that Alfonso's intellectual court gathered and, a century later, Pedro I installed the mistress he loved, María de Padilla. The rooms are now named after the 16th-century Spanish king Carlos I, using his title as Holy Roman Emperor, Charles V. His wedding feast was held here on 11 March 1526 and the **Sala de las Bóvedas** (Hall of the Vault) is adorned with beautiful tiles by Cristóbal de Augusta, commissioned in memory of that event by his son, Felipe II, in the 1570s.

PATIO DEL CRUCERO

This patio outside the Salones de Carlos V was originally the upper storey of the patio of the 12th-century Almohad palace. Originally it had consisted only of raised walkways along the four sides and two cross-walkways that met in the middle. Below grew orange trees, whose fruit could be plucked at hand height by the lucky folk strolling along the walkways. The patio's lower level was built over in the 18th century after earthquake damage.

GARDENS & EXIT

From the Salones de Carlos V you can go out into the Alcázar's large and peaceful gardens. The gardens in front of the Salones de Carlos V and Palacio de Don Pedro date in their present form from the 16th and 17th centuries. Immediately in front of the buildings is a series of small linked gardens, some with pools and fountains. From one, the **Jardín de las Danzas** (Garden of the Dances), a passage runs beneath the Salones de Carlos V to the **Baños de Doña María de Padilla** (María de Padilla Baths). These are the vaults beneath the Patio del Crucero – originally that patio's lower level – with a grotto that replaced the patio's original pool.

The gardens to the east, beyond a long wall, are 20th-century creations. The way out is via the **Apeadero**, a 17th-century entrance hall, and the **Patio de las Banderas** (Patio of the Flags).

Archivo de Indias

Found on the western side of Plaza del Triunfo, the **Archivo de Indias** (Archive of the Indies; Map pp98–100; ☎ 954 21 12 34; Calle Santo Tomás) has been the main archive on Spain's American empire since 1785. The 16th-century building, designed by Juan de Herrera, was originally Seville's Lonja (Exchange) for commerce with the Americas. Its 8km of shelves hold 80 million pages of documents dating from 1492 through to the end of the empire in the 19th century. It was closed for restoration at the time of writing; for an update on schedules, check at a tourist office.

Normally, the archive exhibits rotating displays of fascinating maps and documents, including manuscripts written by the likes of Columbus, Cervantes, Cortés or Pizarro.

Barrio de Santa Cruz
Map pp98–100

East of the cathedral and Alcázar extends a tangle of quaint, winding streets and lovely squares with flowers and orange trees, the Barrio de Santa Cruz. It's a favourite tourist locale, with numerous popular places to stay, eat and drink and plenty of souvenir shops. A wander through it is well worthwhile. After the Christian conquest of Seville in 1248, this became the city's *judería* (Jewish quarter), flourishing especially under Pedro I, whose court included many Jewish financiers and tax collectors. Racial jealousies led eventually to a pogrom that emptied the *judería* in 1391.

One of the prettiest squares, down narrow lanes from Plaza del Triunfo, is **Plaza Doña Elvira**, surrounded by restaurants and with tiled benches beneath the orange trees. A few steps east is Plaza de los Venerables, where you can visit the 17th-century **Hospital de los Venerables Sacerdotes** (☎ 954 56 26 96; adult/child under 12/student/senior €4.75/free/2.40/2.40, Sun afternoon free; ☉ 10am-2pm & 4-8pm). Used until the 1960s as a residence for aged priests, this has a lovely central courtyard and several exhibition rooms, one with a collection of prints of Seville. Don't miss the church with murals by Juan de Valdés Leal and fine sculptures by Pedro Roldán.

Through a couple more narrow lanes eastward is the pretty **Plaza de Santa Cruz**, whose central cross, made in 1692, gives the barrio its name and ranks as one of the finest examples of Seville wrought-iron work. A short distance north from here is the **Casa de la Memoria de Al-Andalus** (☎ 954 56 06 70; Calle Ximénez de Enciso 28; admission €1; ☉ 9am-2pm & 6-7.30pm), an 18th-century mansion on the site of a medieval Jewish house, with an exhibition on Sephardim (Jews of Spanish origin).

El Arenal
Map pp98–100

A short walk west from Avenida de la Constitución brings you to the Río Guadalquivir, with a pleasant riverside footpath. This district, El Arenal, is home to some of Seville's most interesting sights.

TORRE DEL ORO

The 'Tower of Gold' is a 13th-century Almohad watchtower on the riverbank. It once crowned a corner of the city walls that stretched here from the Alcázar, and its dome was, by legend, covered in golden tiles. Inside is a small **maritime museum** (☎ 954 22 24 19; admission €1; ☉ 10am-2pm Tue-Fri, 11am-2pm Sat & Sun, closed Aug). The collection of models of famous boats merits a visit.

HOSPITAL DE LA CARIDAD

A marvellous sample of Sevillan golden-age art adorns the church in this **Hospital de la Caridad** (Hospice for the Elderly; ☎ 954 22 32 32; Calle Temprado 3; admission €4, free Sun & holidays; ☉ 9am-1.30pm & 3.30-7.30pm Mon-Sat, 9am-1pm Sun & holidays), a block east of the river. The Hospital de la Caridad was founded by Miguel de Mañara, by legend a notorious libertine who changed his ways after seeing a vision of his own funeral procession. In the 1670s Mañara commissioned a series of works on the theme of death and redemption from Seville's three finest artists of the day, Bartolomé Esteban Murillo, Juan de Valdés Leal and Pedro Roldán, for the church here. The juxtaposition of Murillo's optimistic paintings with the suffering depicted by Roldán and the unforgiving vision of Valdés Leal makes for fascinating contrasts.

Valdés Leal's two masterpieces, chillingly illustrating the futility of worldly glory, are at the western end of the church. In *Finis Gloriae Mundi* (The End of Earthly Glory), above the door by which you enter, a bishop, a king and a knight are devoured in their coffins by worms and cockroaches, while Christ's hand weighs their virtues and sins in the balance. *In Ictu Oculi* (In the Blink of an Eye), on the opposite wall, shows a skeletal Death figure extinguishing the candle of life while trampling symbols of power, glory, wealth and knowledge. On this same, northern, side of the church are Murillo's *San Juan de Dios* (St John of God), *Anunciación* (Annunciation) and *Moises Haciendo Brotar el Agua de la Roca* (Moses Drawing Water from the Rock). Beneath this last is a cute little infant Christ by Murillo (facing an equally cute infant St John the Baptist on the opposite wall).

The sculpture on the elaborate baroque high altar illustrates the final act of compassion – the burial of the dead (in this case Christ). The tableau, with its strong sense of movement, is Pedro Roldán's masterpiece. To the left of the high altar, steps descend to the crypt where Miguel de Mañara is buried.

CENTRAL SEVILLE

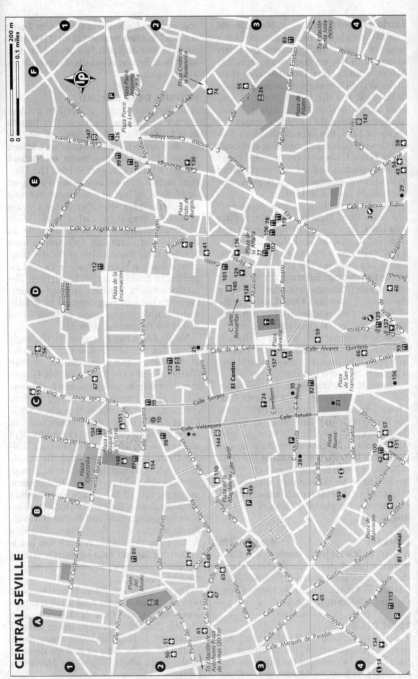

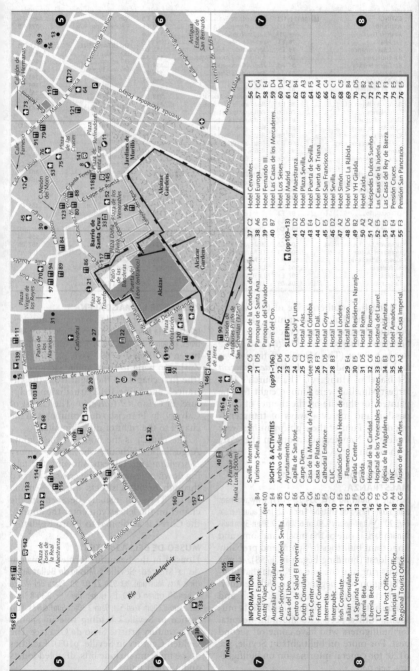

EATING	🎬 (pp113–17)
Alfalfa 10	**77** D3
Altamira Bar-Café	(see 91)
Bar Alfalfa	**78** E3
Bar Casa Fernando	**79** E5
Bar Entrecalles	**80** E5
Bar Gloria Bendita	**81** A5
Bar Laredo	**82** C4
Bar Pepe-Hillo	(see 81)
Bodega Extremeña	**83** F3
Bodega Santa Cruz	**84** D5
Bodegón Alfonso XII	**85** B2
Cafe Alianza	**86** D5
Cafe Bar Duque	**87** B2
Café Bar Las Teresas	**88** E5
Café-Bar Campanario	**89** D5
Café-Bar Puerta de Jerez	**90** D7
Carmela	**91** E5
Casa de la Moneda	**92** C6
Casa Robles	**93** C4
Cervecería Giralda	**94** D5
Confitería La Campana	**95** C2
Corral del Agua	**96** E6
El Giraldillo	**97** D5
El Patio San Eloy	**98** C2
El Rinconcillo	**99** E2
Enrique Becerra	**100** C4
Habanita	**101** D3
Horno de San Buenaventura	**102** D3
Horno de San Buenaventura	**103** C5
Horno del Duque	**104** C1
Kiosco de las Flores	**105** A7
La Bodega	**106** E3
La Giganta	**107** E2
La Gitana	**108** B5
La Tienda de Eva	**109** C5
La Trastienda	**110** E3
Las Escobas	**111** D5
Los Alcazáres	(see 112)
Mercado de la Encarnación (Market)	**112** D1
Mercado del Arenal (Market)	**113** A4
Mesón Cinco Jotas	**114** B5
Mesón de la Infanta	**115** B5
Mesón Serranito	**116** B5
Restaurant La Cueva	**117** D5
Restaurante La Albahaca	**118** E5
Restaurante La Judería	**119** F5
Restaurante Las Lapas	**120** D6
Restaurante Modesto	**121** F5
Restaurante San Marco	**122** C2
Restaurante San Marco	**123** E5
Ristorante Cosa Nostra	**124** A7
Robles Placentines	**125** D4
Taberna Los Terceros	**126** E2

DRINKING	🍸 (pp117–19)
Antigüedades	**127** D4
Bar Europa	**128** D3
Bare Nostrum	**129** D3
Cabo Loco	(see 129)
Café Lisboa	**130** E2
Cervecería International	**131** C4
Clan Scottish Pub	**132** B5
Elefunk	**133** B5
Isbiliyya Café	**134** A4
La Antigua Bodeguita	**135** C3
La Rebótica	**136** D3
La Soportales	**137** C3
La Subasta	(see 127)
Maya Soul	**138** A6

Nao	(see 129)
P Flaherty Irish Pub	**139** C5

ENTERTAINMENT	🎭 (pp117–21)
El Mundo	**140** D3
El Tamboril	**141** E5
Empresa Pagés	**142** B5
La Carbonería	**143** F4
La Teatral	**144** C3
Los Gallos	**145** E5
Sala La Fundición	**146** C6
Sol Café Cantante	**147** E1

SHOPPING	🛍 (p121)
El Corte Inglés	**148** B2
El Corte Inglés	**149** B3
El Corte Inglés	**150** B3
El Corte Inglés	**151** C2
El Postigo	**152** C5
Record Sevilla	**153** C1
Sevilla Rock	**154** B2

TRANSPORT	
ATA Rent A Car	**155** C7
Cruceros Turísticos Torre del Oro	(see 157)
Good Rent A Car	(see 161)
Halcón Viajes	**156** C4
Jetty	**157** B6
Parking Paseo de Colón	**158** A5
Renfe Office	**159** B4
Sevilla Tour & Tour Por Sevilla Bus Stop	**160** B6
Triana Rent A Car	**161** C7

Along the southern side of the church, another fine Roldán sculpture, of Christ praying before being crucified, stands between Murillo's *La Multiplicación de Panes y Peces* (The Miracle of the Loaves and Fishes) and *Santa Isabel de Húngria* (St Isabel of Hungary). The church's four largest Murillos were among eight that he painted for this site on the themes of compassion and mercy – ways of transcending death. Four of the eight paintings were looted by Napoleonic troops in the early 19th century.

PLAZA DE TOROS DE LA REAL MAESTRANZA

Seville's **bullring** (☎ 954 22 45 77; www.realmaestranza.com; Paseo de Cristóbal Colón 12; tour adult/senior €4/3.20; ☽ half-hourly 9.30am-6.30pm, 9.30am-3pm bullfighting days) is one of the most handsome and important bullrings in Spain, and probably the oldest (building began in 1758). It was in this ring and the one at Ronda that bullfighting on foot began in the 18th century. Interesting guided visits, in English and Spanish, take you into the ring and its museum, with a peep into the mini-hospital for bullfighters who have come off second best. For more on bullfights in Seville, see p120; for general information on bullfighting, see p36.

IGLESIA DE LA MAGDALENA

A jewel among Seville's baroque churches, **Iglesia de la Magdalena** (Calle San Pablo 12; ☽ Mass times, usually 8-11.30am & 6.30-9pm) was built between 1691 and 1709. Two paintings by Zurbarán hang in the Capilla Sacramental (the first chapel on the right from the entrance), and a fine 1612 Crucifixion sculpture, *El Cristo del Calvario* (The Christ of Calvary) by Francisco de Ocampo, is in the chapel to the right of the main altar.

The church is the home of the Quinta Angustia brotherhood, whose 17th-century *Descendimiento* tableau, showing the taking down of Jesus from the cross, is carried through Seville's streets during Semana Santa. This can usually be seen in the chapel on the left as you enter the church: the Christ is attributed to Pedro Roldán.

MUSEO DE BELLAS ARTES

Housed in the beautiful former Convento de la Merced, Seville's **Museo de Bellas Artes** (Fine Arts Museum; ☎ 954 22 07 90; Plaza del Museo 9; non-EU citizen €1.50, EU citizen free; ☽ 2.30-8.30pm Tue, 9am-8.30pm Wed-Sat, 9am-2.30pm Sun) does full justice to Seville's leading role in Spain's 17th-century artistic Siglo de Oro (see The Golden Century in Seville, p102). Facilities at the museum include lifts, disabled toilets and a wheelchair.

Room I exemplifies the 15th-century beginnings of the Sevillan school: the best exhibits are Pedro Millán's terracotta sculptures, displaying a realism that was then rare in Spanish art.

Room II, the dining hall of the convent, displays Renaissance work from Seville and elsewhere, including sculptures by Pietro Torrigiano, an Italian who came to Seville in 1522 and was the major artistic figure of the early Renaissance here.

Room III exhibits Sevillan Renaissance retables and early 17th-century Sevillan paintings. The penetrating portrait of Don Cristóbal Suárez de Ribera by the young Velázquez grabs the attention, as does Alonso Cano's striking *Las Ánimas del Purgatorio* (Souls in Purgatory), in the corner between rooms III and IV.

In room IV, devoted mainly to Mannerism (the transition from Renaissance to baroque), Alonso Vázquez's large *Sagrada Cena* (Last Supper) is the outstanding canvas. The cute anonymous statuettes of the child Jesus and child St John the Baptist contrast markedly with the grisly head of St John the Baptist (1591) by Gaspar Núñez Delgado in the centre of the room. From here you move through the beautiful cloister to room V, the convent church, which is hung with paintings by masters of Sevillan baroque, above all Murillo. His *Inmaculada Concepción Grande* at the head of the church, depicting the Virgin borne aloft by cherubs, displays all the curving, twisting movement that is so central to baroque art.

Upstairs, highlights of room VI include José de Ribera's very Spanish-looking *Santiago Apóstol* (St James the Apostle) and Zurbarán's deeply sombre *Cristo Crucificado* (Christ Crucified), perhaps the most disturbing picture in the whole museum. Room VII is devoted to Murillo and disciples, room VIII to Valdés Leal, and room IX to European baroque art.

Room X has a few carvings by Juan Martínez Montañés and Juan de Mesa but is otherwise all Zurbarán, with a masterly depiction of the contrast between the worldly Pope Urban II and the ascetic St Bruno in *Visita de San Bruno a Urbano II*.

Room XI, the closed-in gallery around the upper storey of the cloister, displays Spanish painting of the 18th century, a time of little creative verve, though Domingo Martínez's Seville carnival scenes are interesting in their detail. Rooms XII to XIV show 19th- and 20th-century painting, mainly Sevillan but also with Goya's 1824 portrait of Don José Duaso. Among the Sevillan work, don't miss the Romantic portraits of Antonio María Esquivel (1806–57), the early flamenco scenes by Manuel Cabral Bejarano (1827–91), or the eclectic work of impressionist-influenced Gonzalo Bilbao (1860–1938).

El Centro   Map pp98–100

The real centre of Seville is the densely packed zone of narrow streets north of the cathedral, broken up here and there by squares around which the city's life has revolved for aeons.

PLAZA DE SAN FRANCISCO & CALLE SIERPES

Scene of a market in Muslim times and later of Inquisition burnings, Plaza de San Francisco has been Seville's main public square since the 16th century. The **ayuntamiento** (town hall), on its western side, is a building of contrasting characters: its southern end is encrusted with lovely Renaissance carving from the 1520s and '30s, while its northern end, a 19th-century extension, is bare.

The pedestrianised Calle Sierpes, which runs north from the square, and the parallel Calle Tetuán/Velázquez are the hub of Seville's fanciest shopping zone. Between the two streets, on Calle Jovellanos, look into the **Capilla de San José** (8am-12.30pm & 6.30-8.30pm). This small 18th-century chapel, created by the city's carpenters' guild, is a world unto itself of breathtakingly intense baroque ornamentation.

The **Palacio de la Condesa de Lebrija** (954 22 78 02; www.palaciodelebrija.com; Calle de la Cuna 8; admission ground fl only €4, whole bldg €7; 10.30am-1.30pm & 4.30-7pm Mon-Fri, 10am-1pm Sat Oct-Apr, 10.30am-1.30pm & 5-7.30pm Mon-Fri, 10am-1pm Sat May-Sep), a block east of Calle Sierpes, is a 16th-century mansion with a rich collection of art and artisanry, and a beautiful Renaissance-Mudejar courtyard. If you want to see the top floor, you must wait for the guided tour, but it's worth it. The late Countess of Lebrija, an archaeologist, remodelled the house in 1914 and filled many of the rooms with treasures from her travels. Ancient Rome was the Countess' speciality, so the library is full of books on antiquity and there are plenty of remains from Roman Itálica (p123), including some marvellous mosaics – especially the large one in the main patio. Upstairs are Arabic, baroque and Spanish rooms. The three-flight main staircase is lined with 16th- and 17th-century Sevillan tiles, and has a coffered ceiling imported from a now-demolished palace at Marchena. A delightful touch is added by the sound of birds twittering, right here in the city centre.

PLAZA SALVADOR

A couple of blocks northeast of Plaza de San Francisco, this plaza was once the main forum of Roman Hispalis. It's dominated by the **Parroquia del Salvador**, a big baroque church built between 1674 and 1712 following the demolition of Muslim Ishbiliya's main mosque at this site. Before the mosque, early Christian churches had stood here, and before them, a Roman temple. At the time of writing the church was closed for restoration work and investigations by archaeologists, who hoped to establish the exact age of the mosque here. Walkways may be installed for the public to view the excavations. Hundreds of 18th-century burials, just beneath the church floor, were among the archaeologists' first discoveries in 2003. On the northern side of the church, the mosque's small **patio** remains, with orange trees, font, and a few half-buried Roman columns.

THE GOLDEN CENTURY IN SEVILLE

Seville played a lead role in Spain's artistic Siglo de Oro (Golden Century), from the late 16th to the late 17th century. At this time Seville was Spain's richest and most important city and open to important artistic influences from Italy. The 17th century dawned with painters such as Juan de Roelas (1560–1625) and Francisco Pacheco (1564–1644) adopting an increasingly naturalistic approach that heralded the move from the idealised schemes of Mannerism to the flowing curves of baroque. Pacheco's studio was the centre of a humanist circle that influenced most significant Andalucian artists of the century. He advised his pupils to 'go to nature for everything'.

The mystically inclined Francisco de Zurbarán (1598–1664), born in Extremadura, lived most of his life in and around Seville, though he eventually died in poverty in Madrid. Zurbarán's clear, spiritual paintings of saints, churchmen and monastic life often utilise strong light/shadow contrasts comparable with the work of two contemporaries, the Italian Caravaggio and José de Ribera, a Spaniard who spent most of his life in Italy.

Pacheco's son-in-law, Seville-born Diego Rodríguez de Silva y Velázquez (1599–1660), also showed a strong naturalistic leaning and masterly use of light and shadow in the early works he painted in Seville – religious scenes (using models drawn from the city's streets), kitchen scenes and portraits. But Velázquez left Seville in 1623 to become a painter at the royal court in Madrid and, ultimately, Spain's major artist of the epoch.

Bartolomé Esteban Murillo (1617–82) and his friend Juan de Valdés Leal (1622–94), both Seville-born, led the way to full-blown baroque art. Murillo was the youngest of 14 children and orphaned at the age of nine. His fine technique and soft-focus children and religious scenes, emphasising the positive, hopeful aspects of biblical stories, made him highly popular in a time of economic decline. Valdés Leal could be both humorous and bitterly pessimistic. His greatest works hang alongside several Murillos in Seville's Hospital de la Caridad (p97).

Sevillan sculptor Juan Martínez Montañés (1568–1649) carved such dramatic and lifelike wooden images that contemporaries called him 'El Dios de la Madera' (The God of Wood). You'll find his carvings in many Andalucian churches, and many of the statues still carried in Seville's Semana Santa (Holy Week) processions are his work. Martínez provided models for generations of sculptors to follow. Among his many disciples, Juan de Mesa (1583–1627) stands out for the pathos of his images, particularly his Crucifixions.

The leading Sevillan sculptor of the later 17th century was Pedro Roldán (1624–99), whose best work is in the Hospital de la Caridad. It was his daughter María Luisa Roldán, 'La Roldana' (1654–1704), who, according to tradition, created La Macarena, the powerful Virgin image that takes the place of honour in Seville's Semana Santa.

CASA DE PILATOS

Another of Seville's finest noble mansions, the **Casa de Pilatos** (☎ 954 22 52 98; admission ground fl only €5, whole house €8, EU citizen 1-5pm Tue free; ☺ 9am-7pm Mar-Sep, 9am-6pm Oct-Feb) is still occupied by the ducal Medinaceli family. It's a mixture of Mudejar, Gothic and Renaissance styles, with some beautiful tilework and *artesonado*. The overall effect is similar to that of the Alcázar.

One explanation for the building's name ('Pilate's House') is that its 16th-century creator, Don Fadrique Enríquez de Ribera, was trying to imitate Pontius Pilate's palace in Jerusalem, to which city he had made a pilgrimage. A rival theory is that the house served as the first station of a Via Crucis (Way of the Cross) route, in which penitents symbolically retraced Christ's steps to the Crucifixion. The first station would represent Christ's appearance before Pilate.

The **Patio Principal** has lots of wonderful 16th-century tiles and intricate Mudejar plasterwork. The armless statue of Athene is ancient Greek; the statues in the other corners are Roman. Around the walls are busts of Roman historical and mythical figures, plus King Carlos I of Spain.

The names of the rooms off the Patio Principal recall the supposed Pontius Pilate connection. The **Descanso de los Jueces** (Judges' Retiring Room), **Salón Pretorio** (Palace Hall) and **Gabinete de Pilatos** (Pilate's Study) have *artesonado*. Beyond the Salón Pretorio is the **Zaquizami**, a corridor with Roman sculptures and inscriptions. The Gabinete de Pilatos leads into the **Jardín Grande** (Big Garden), with Italian-style loggias.

The **staircase** to the upper floor has the most magnificent tiles in the building, and a great golden *artesonado* dome above. Visits to the **upper floor** itself, still partly inhabited by the Medinacelis, are guided. Of interest are the several centuries' worth of Medinaceli portraits and a small Goya bullfighting painting.

South of the Centre   Map pp88–90

ANTIGUA FÁBRICA DE TABACOS

Seville's massive 250m by 180m former tobacco factory, **Antigua Fabrica de Tabacos** (Old Tobacco Factory; Calle San Fernando; ☺ 8am-9.30pm Mon-Fri, 8am-2pm Sat) – the workplace of Bizet's operatic heroine Carmen – was built in the 18th century and served its original purpose until the mid-20th century. Long a cornerstone of the city's economy, the factory had its own jail, stables for 400 mules, 21 fountains, 24 patios and even a nursery for the children of its mostly female workers.

It's an impressive if rather gloomy building, in neoclassical style. The main portal sports carvings on the theme of the discovery of the Americas, where tobacco came from: among them are Columbus, Cortés (conqueror of the Aztecs) and two Native Americans, one of them smoking a pipe. At the top of the portal is Fame, blowing a trumpet.

The tobacco factory is now part of the Universidad de Sevilla (Seville University). You're free to wander through and take a look.

PARQUE DE MARÍA LUISA & PLAZA DE ESPAÑA

A large area south of the tobacco factory was transformed for Seville's first international fair, the 1929 Exposición Iberoamericana, when architects spattered it with all sorts of fine, fancy and funny buildings, many of them in styles harking back to Seville's eras of past glory. In their midst, the **Parque de María Luisa** (☺ 8am-10pm Sep-Jun, 8am-midnight Jul & Aug), with its maze of paths, flowers, fountains, lawns and 3500 magnificent trees, is a beautiful respite from the hustle of the city.

Plaza de España, one of the city's favourite relaxation spots with its fountains and minicanals, faces the northeastern side of the park across Avenida de Isabel la Católica. Curving round the plaza is the most grandiose of the 1929 buildings, a brick-and-tile confection featuring Seville tilework at its gaudiest, with a map and historical scene for each Spanish province – all designed by the leading Exposición Iberoamericana architect, Sevillan Aníbal González.

On **Plaza de América** at the southern end of the park is a large flock of white doves (they'll clamber all over you if you buy a €1.50 bag of seed from vendors) and two interesting museums. Highlights of the big **Museo Arqueológico** (☎ 954 23 24 01; non-EU citizen €1.50, EU citizen free; ☺ 3-8pm Tue, 9am-8pm Wed-Sat, 9am-2pm Sun & holidays) include a room of gold jewellery from the mysterious Tartessos culture, and fine collections of Iberian animal sculptures and beautiful Roman mosaics. Large quantities of Roman sculpture include statues of the two emperors from Itálica near Seville – Hadrian (Adriano) and Trajan (Trajano, with the top half of his head missing).

Facing the Museo Arqueológico is the **Museo de Artes y Costumbres Populares** (☎ 954 23 25 76; non-EU citizen €1.50, EU citizen free; ☼ 3-8pm Tue, 9am-8pm Wed-Sat, 9am-2pm Sun & holidays), in the 1929 exhibition's Mudejar pavilion (which appeared as an Arab palace in *Lawrence of Arabia*). Its collection includes mock workshops of local crafts, and some really beautiful old festival costumes.

Triana

The barrio of Triana, across the Río Guadalquivir from central Seville, used to be the quarter of the city's *gitanos* (Roma people, formerly called Gypsies) and was one of the birthplaces of flamenco and the home of Sevillan ceramics. The *gitanos* were moved out to new suburban areas in the 1960s and '70s, but Triana retains a distinct character and is an intriguing place to wander around. There are plenty of atmospheric places to eat or drink, and in the evening there's often flamenco in at least one of the bars.

The heart of the **pottery and tile-making area**, with a dozen shops and workshops still offering charming and artistic ceramics, is around the meeting of Calles Alfarería and Antillano Campos (Map pp88–90). Four diversely interesting churches and chapels provide a further focus for your explorations. At the northern end of Triana the **Iglesia del Cristo de la Expiración** (Map pp88-90; ☎ 954 33 33 41; Calle Castilla 182; ☼ 10.30am-1.30pm & 6-9.30pm Tue-Sat, 10.30am-1.30pm Sun) houses a much loved figure of the dead Christ, dating from 1682, that takes an honoured place in Seville's Semana Santa processions. The image is known as El Cachorro (The Puppy): sculptor Antonio Ruiz Gijón was reputedly inspired by the agonised body of a *gitano* singer of that name who had died in a fight in this street. In the southern part of Triana, the **Capilla del Rocío** (Map pp88-90; Calle Evangelista 23) is home to the Hermandad del Rocío de Triana. The departure of this brotherhood's procession of horses and covered wagons to El Rocío (see The Romería del Rocío, p150) on the Thursday before Pentecost is one of the most colourful and emotive events in the Seville calendar. At the **Capilla de los Marineros** (Map pp88-90; ☎ 954 33 26 45; Calle de la Pureza 53; ☼ 9am-1pm & 5.30-9pm Mon-Sat) you'll find the gorgeously bedecked, much adored image of the Virgen de la Esperanza (Virgin of Hope), patroness of Triana sailors, another who has an honoured role in the Semana Santa processions. The **Parroquia de Santa Ana** (Map pp98-100; Calle de la Pureza 80), dating from 1280, has a wealth of antique religious imagery. A strange tradition has it that every woman who kicks 'El Negro', a 16th-century tomb that has tiles depicting a recumbent knight, will find a husband. Despite benches and other obstacles placed to prevent damage to this precious artwork, women still come here to do just that.

Isla de la Cartuja   Map pp88–90

North of Triana, this northern part of an island between two branches of the Guadalquivir was the site of Expo '92. Today it's home to Isla Mágica theme park, Cartuja 93 technology business park and the historic La Cartuja monastery. Bus Nos C1 and C2 (p123) serve the Isla de la Cartuja.

CONJUNTO MONUMENTAL DE LA CARTUJA
Founded in 1399, the **Conjunto Monumental de la Cartuja** (Cartuja Monastery; ☎ 955 03 70 70; admission incl/excl temporary exhibitions €3/1.80, EU citizen free Tue; ☼ 10am-9pm Mon-Fri, 11am-9pm Sat, 10am-3pm Sun, to 8pm Mon-Fri Oct-Mar, last admission 1hr before closing time) became the favourite Sevillan lodging place for Columbus, King Felipe II and other luminaries. Columbus' remains lay here from 1509 to 1536. Over the centuries benefactors endowed the monastery with a rich collection of Sevillan art, but in 1836 the monks were expelled during the Disentailment (when church property was auctioned off by the state). In 1839 the complex was bought by a Liverpudlian, Charles Pickman, who turned it into a porcelain factory, building the tall bottle-shaped kilns that stand incongruously beside the monastery buildings. The porcelain factory functioned until 1982.

The whole complex was restored for Expo '92. The entrance is on the monastery's western side on Calle Américo Vespucio. The monastery features a now rather bare 15th-century **church**; a pretty 15th-century Mudejar **cloister**; and the **Capilla de Santa Ana**, which was built as the Columbus family tomb. It also features the **Capítulo de Monjes** (Chapter House), full of disarmingly realistic 16th-century funerary sculptures of members of the Ribera family, who were among the

Mezquita (p279), Córdoba

Building detail, Córdoba (p278)

Torre de la Calahorra (p284), Córdoba

DAVID PEEVERS

Gitano (Romany) musician, Granada (p302)

Generalife (p310), Alhambra, Granada

MARK AVELLINO

Bullfighting (p36)

MICHAEL TAYLOR

monastery's chief benefactors. Also here is the **Centro Andaluz de Arte Contemporáneo** (Andalucian Contemporary Art Centre), with a large collection of modern Andalucian art and frequent temporary exhibitions by contemporary artists.

CARTUJA 93

Many of the exotic Expo pavilions are now encompassed within this technology park, which is home to nearly 200 companies and organisations employing nearly 9000 people. Many of the pavilions still look futuristic, though the built-in obsolescence of a few is starting to show through. You can wander around the area during daylight hours but you may find that the gates are only open on the western side on Calle Américo Vespucio.

ISLA MÁGICA

The theme park **Isla Mágica** (☎ 902 16 17 16; www.islamagica.es in Spanish; adult/child under 13/senior €21/14.50/14.50 all day, €14.50/11/11 evening or night mid-Jun–mid-Sep, €19/13/13 all day, €13/10/10 evening or night rest of season; ☼ 11am-7pm Tue-Fri, 11am-10pm Sat & Sun Apr–mid-Jun; 11am-10pm Tue-Thu & Sun, 11am-midnight Fri & Sat mid-Jun–mid-Jul; 11am-10pm Sun-Thu, 11am-midnight Fri & Sat 2nd half Jul; 11am-midnight daily Aug; 11am-10pm daily 1st half of Sep; 11am-9pm Fri-Sun 2nd half of Sep; 11am-9pm Sat & Sun Oct, closed Nov-Mar) attracts a million visitors a year and is a great day's fun for kids and anyone who likes white-knuckle rides. Opening schedules vary a little from year to year, so it's always best to confirm times before going. Evening tickets are valid from 5pm to 9pm on days when the park closes at midnight and from 3pm or 4pm until closing on other days; night tickets, available when the park closes at midnight, run from 9pm to midnight.

The theme is the 16th-century Spanish colonial adventure. Highlight rides include **El Jaguar**, a roller coaster with high-speed 360-degree turns, and the **Anaconda** water roller coaster with vertiginous drops. At busy times you may have to wait 45 minutes for the big attractions. There are also pirate shows, virtual rides, bird-of-prey displays and lots of entertaining street-theatre-type stuff, plus plenty of places to eat and drink.

North of the Centre   Map pp88–90

The more working-class area north of Calle Alfonso XII and Plaza Ponce de León provides a fascinating contrast to the city centre. It has many intriguing nooks and crannies, one of the city's best street markets (on Calle de la Feria, Thursday morning – see p121) and some colourful spots to eat and drink.

BASÍLICA DE JESÚS DEL GRAN PODER

Found behind a large baroque portal in the corner of Plaza de San Lorenzo, the **Basílica de Jesús del Gran Poder** (☎ 954 91 56 72; Plaza de San Lorenzo 13; ☼ 8am-1.30pm & 6-9pm Sat-Thu, 7.30am-10pm Fri) church dates only from the 1960s but houses a famous and far older sculpture of the cross-bearing Christ (after which it's named). The almost wizened Christ image, sculpted in 1620 by Juan de Mesa, inspires much Sevillan devotion and takes a place of honour in the Semana Santa processions on Good Friday morning. On either side of the altar are a sculpture of St John the Evangelist, also by de Mesa, and an anonymous *Virgen del Mayor Dolor* (Virgin of the Deepest Grief) of the 18th century or earlier.

ALAMEDA DE HÉRCULES

This dusty 350m-long parklike strip was created in the 1570s by draining a marsh. Two columns from a ruined Roman temple were erected at its southern end and topped with statues of Hercules and Julius Caesar by Diego de Pesquera. Planted with avenues of *álamo* (poplar) trees – hence the name – the Alameda became a fashionable meeting place in the 17th century, sank to little more than a red-light zone by the 1980s, and has since come back up in the world as one of the city's liveliest nightlife areas, with a bohemian, alternative scene.

BASÍLICA DE LA MACARENA

You can get an inkling of the fervour inspired by Semana Santa in Seville at the **Basílica de la Macarena** (☎ 954 90 18 00; Calle Bécquer 1; ☼ 9am-2pm & 5-9pm), off Calle San Luis. This 1940s church contains the most adored religious image in Seville, the *Virgen de la Esperanza Macarena* (Macarena Virgin of Hope), believed to have been sculpted in the mid-17th century by María Luisa Roldán ('La Roldana'). Commonly known just as La Macarena, this Virgin is patron of bullfighters and is Seville's supreme representation of the grieving, yet hoping, mother of Christ. She stands in splendour behind the main altarpiece, adorned with a golden crown, lavish vestments, and five diamond-and-emerald brooches donated by a famous 20th-century matador, Joselito El Gallo.

A beautiful 1654 statue of *El Cristo de la Sentencia* (Christ of the Sentence) by Felipe Morales is normally positioned in a chapel on the left of the church. Both statues are carried from the church at midnight at the start of every Good Friday. Their journey through the city is the climax of Semana Santa in Seville, and their return to the church around 1.30pm is attended by enormous crowds.

The church's **museum** (adult/student/senior €3/1.50/1.50; ⊙ 9.30am-2pm & 5-8pm) displays some of La Macarena's extraordinarily lavish vestments, plus bullfighters' suits donated by famous matadors and the Semana Santa *pasos* (platforms) on which both images are carried. The *paso* of *El Cristo de la Sentencia* is a tableau showing Pontius Pilate washing his hands while the order for Christ's Crucifixion is read out.

Bus Nos C1, C2, C3 and C4 (p123) stop on Calle Andueza, near the Basílica de la Macarena. Across this street is the **Parlamento de Andalucía**, Andalucía's regional parliament (generally not open to visitors). East of the church extends the longest surviving stretch of Seville's 12th-century **Almohad walls**.

IGLESIA DE SAN LUIS
One of Seville's most magnificent churches, **Iglesia de San Luis** (☎ 954 55 02 07; Calle San Luis s/n; admission free; ⊙ 9am-2pm Tue-Thu, 9am-2pm & 5-8pm Fri & Sat, closed Aug) stands 500m south of the Basílica de la Macarena. Designed for the Jesuits by Leonardo de Figueroa in 1731, the baroque San Luis has an unusual equal-armed cross plan, 16 twisting stone pillars and a superb soaring dome. Statues of saints and virtues by Pedro de Mena perch very precariously on pedestals around the lower levels of the dome. Religio (Religion) looks as if she's about to topple over and crash to the church floor. Only in use as a church for a few decades, San Luis became a hospice before being abandoned in 1877, but has recently been restored and opened for visits.

COURSES
Flamenco & Dance
The city has many dance and flamenco schools. Check these out:

Espacio Meteora (Map pp88-90; ☎ 954 90 14 83; www.espaciometeora.com; Calle Duque Cornejo 16A) Innovative arts centre where flamenco and other dance courses are usually ongoing.
Fundación Cristina Heeren de Arte Flamenco (Map pp98-100; ☎ 954 21 70 58; www.flamencoheeren.com; Calle Fabiola 1) Long-term courses in all flamenco arts; also one-month intensive summer courses.
Sevilla Dance Centre (Map pp88-90; ☎ 954 38 39 02; Calle Conde de Torrejón 19) Salsa, flamenco, classical, hip-hop, contemporary.
Taller Flamenco (Map pp88-90; ☎ 954 56 42 34; www.tallerflamenco.com; Calle Peral 49) Flamenco dance and guitar and Spanish language courses.

Tourist offices and *El Giraldillo* magazine (p90) have further information.

Language
Along with Granada, Seville is one of the two most popular cities in Andalucía for foreigners to study Spanish. The following are among the best schools: all offer short- and long-term courses at a variety of levels, nearly always with a range of excursions and other spare-time and social activities.
Carpe Diem (Map pp98-100; ☎ 954 21 85 15; www .carpediemsevilla.com; Calle de la Cuna 13) Small, friendly school with courses also available in arts, culture, translation and Spanish for business.
CLIC (Map pp98-100; ☎ 954 50 21 31; www.clic.es; Calle Albareda 19) Well-established language centre with good social scene; courses in business Spanish and Hispanic studies available.
Giralda Center (Map pp98-100; ☎ 954 21 31 65; www .giraldacenter.com; Calle Mateos Gago 17) Friendly atmosphere, plenty of excursions, reputation for good teaching.
Lenguaviva (Map pp88-90; ☎ 954 90 51 31; www .lenguaviva.es; Calle Viriato 24) Good on spare-time activities; courses in business Spanish available.
LINC (Map pp98-100; ☎ 954 50 04 59; www.linc.tv; Calle General Polavieja 13) Small, popular school, good on cultural activities and excursions.

SEVILLE FOR CHILDREN
The riverbank of the **Guadalquivir** and **Parque de María Luisa** (p103) are good places for younger children to run off some steam, and they'll enjoy feeding the doves in Parque de María Luisa. **Isla Mágica** (p104) gives kids of all ages a great day of fun, though those aged over about 10 will get the most out of the rides. Another likely hit is a **city tour** in an open-topped double-decker bus or horse-drawn carriage (p107). On Sunday

morning visit the **pet market** in Plaza de la Alfalfa (Map pp98–100).

The **Teatro Alameda** (p120) and other venues stage regular theatre for children.

Also recommended:

Aquópolis Sevilla (Map pp88-90; ☎ 954 40 66 22; www.aquopolis.es in Spanish; Avenida del Deporte s/n; adult/child under 11 €12.90/8.90; 🕙 11am-7 or 8pm approx late May–early Sep) Waterslides and wave pools, in Barrio Las Delicias in the east of the city (off the A92 towards Málaga).

Reserva Natural Castillo de las Guardas (☎ 955 95 25 68; Finca Herrerías Bajas s/n, Carretera A476 Km 6.82; adult/child under 13 €14/10; 🕙 10.30am-6pm Tue-Sun, last admission 4.30pm) About 1000 animals from around the planet roam in semi-liberty and can be viewed from your own vehicle or the park's road-train. There are also bird-of-prey demonstrations. It's 58km northwest of Seville in the village of El Castillo de las Guardas, off the N433 towards Aracena.

TOURS

Cruceros Turísticos Torre del Oro (Map pp98-100; ☎ 954 56 16 92; child over 14/child under 14 €12/free) One-hour sightseeing river cruises every half-hour from 11am from the riverbank by the Torre del Oro, with loudspeaker commentary in Spanish, English and German; last departure can range from 6pm in winter to 10pm in summer. From around May to September, there are also Saturday & Sunday round-trip day cruises to Sanlúcar de Barrameda, 100km downriver (adult/child under 14 /senior €27/15/21); it's 4½ hours each way, usually with 4½ hours in Sanlúcar in between.

Discover Sevilla (☎ 954 22 66 42; www.discoversevilla .com) Out-of-town adventure trips, including horse riding on Doñana beaches and whale- and dolphin-watching in the Strait of Gibraltar, with prices from €35 to €75.

Horse-drawn Carriages These wait around near the cathedral, Plaza de España and Puerta de Jerez, charging €30 for up to four people for a one-hour trot around the Barrio de Santa Cruz and Parque de María Luisa areas. Prices are posted on boards near their stops.

Sevilla Tour (☎ 902 10 10 81; www.citysightseeing -spain.com) Open-topped double-decker buses and converted trams make one-hour city tours, with earphone commentary in a choice of languages. The €11 ticket is valid for 48 hours and you can hop on or off along Paseo de Cristóbal Colón (Map pp98-100; near the Torre del Oro), Avenida de Portugal behind Plaza de España (Map pp88-90), or the Isla de La Cartuja (Map pp88-90). Buses typically leave every 30 minutes from 7am to 8pm.

Sevilla Walking Tours (☎ 902 15 82 26; www.sevilla walkingtours.com) English-language tours of the main monumental area, lasting about 1½ hours, at 9.30am and 11.30am daily. The same people also offer tours of the cathedral and Alcázar.

Tour por Sevilla/Guide Friday (☎ 954 56 06 93; sevirama.cjb.net) Same deal as Sevilla Tour but doesn't start until 10am.

Walking in Seville with Carmen This is a 90-minute combination of walking tour, street theatre and history lesson given in English by a lively and amusing young woman several days a week from March to October (except July). Look for her flyers around the Barrio de Santa Cruz telling where and when to meet. Your donation is up to you.

FESTIVALS & EVENTS
Semana Santa

Nowhere in Spain is Semana Santa marked with quite such intense spectacle, anguish and solemnity, and quite such overriding adoration of the Virgin, as in Seville. Holy Week here gives a special insight into both Spanish Catholicism and the enormous strength of tradition in Seville.

Every day from Palm Sunday to Easter Sunday, large, richly bedecked images and life-sized tableaux of scenes from the Easter story are carried from Seville's churches through the streets to the cathedral. They're accompanied by long processions, which may take more than an hour to pass, and watched by vast crowds. These rites go back to the 14th century but they took their present form in the 17th, when many of the images – some of them supreme works of art – were created.

Programmes showing each procession's schedule and route are widely available before and during Semana Santa. *ABC* newspaper prints maps showing the churches, recommended viewing spots and other details. **Semana-Santa.org** (www.semana-santa.org) is devoted to Semana Santa in Seville. It's not too hard to work out which procession will be where and when, so you can pick up one in its own barrio or as it leaves or re-enters its church – always an emotional moment. Crowds along most of the *carrera oficial* (official route) in the city centre make it hard to get much of a view there, unless you can manage to get yourself a seat. These are sold at nearby ticket windows for anything from about €10 on Plaza Virgen de los Reyes behind the cathedral to €25 or more on Good Friday morning on Calle Sierpes. But if you arrive early in the evening, you can usually get close enough to the cathedral to see plenty for free.

See Inside Semana Santa (p108) for more on this unique week.

INSIDE SEMANA SANTA

Seville's Holy Week processions are organised by more than 50 different *hermandades* or *cofradías* (brotherhoods, some of which include women). Each brotherhood normally carries two lavishly decorated *pasos* (platforms). The first bears a statue of Christ, crucified, bearing the cross, or in a tableau from the Passion; the second carries an image of the Virgin. They are carried by teams of about 40 bearers called *costaleros*, who work in relays. The *pasos* are heavy – each *costalero* normally carries about 50kg – and they move with a hypnotic swaying motion to the rhythm of their brass-and-drum bands and the commands of their *capataz* (leader), who strikes a bell to start and stop the *paso*.

Each pair of *pasos* has up to 2500 costumed followers, known as *nazarenos*. Many *nazarenos* wear tall Ku Klux Klan-like capes. The most contrite go barefoot and carry crosses. Membership of a *hermandad* is an honour keenly sought, even by some who rarely attend Mass.

Each day from Palm Sunday to Good Friday seven or eight *hermandades* leave their churches around the city in the afternoon or early evening. They arrive between 5pm and 11pm at Calle Campana at the northern end of Calle Sierpes in the city centre. This is the start of the *carrera oficial* (official route) along Calle Sierpes, through Plaza San Francisco and along Avenida de la Constitución to the cathedral. The processions enter the cathedral at its western end and leave by its eastern doors, emerging on Plaza Virgen de los Reyes. They get back to their churches some time between 10pm and 3am.

The climax of the week is the *madrugada* (early hours) of Good Friday, when some of the most respected and popular *hermandades* file through the city. The first to reach the *carrera oficial*, about 1.30am, is the oldest *hermandad*, El Silencio, which goes in complete silence. At about 2am comes Jesús del Gran Poder, whose 17th-century Christ is one of the masterpieces of Sevillan sculpture. This is followed at about 3am by La Macarena, whose passionately adored Virgin evokes the greatest emotion among the watching crowds. Then come El Calvario from the Iglesia de la Magdalena, Esperanza de Triana, and lastly, at about 6am, Los Gitanos, the *gitano* brotherhood.

On the Saturday evening just four *hermandades* make their way to the cathedral, and finally, on Easter Sunday morning, the Hermandad de la Resurrección.

City-centre brotherhoods, such as El Silencio, are traditionally linked with the bourgeoisie. They are austere, with little or no music, and wear black tunics, usually without capes. *Hermandades* from the working-class districts outside the centre (such as La Macarena) have bands and more brightly bedecked *pasos*. Their *nazarenos* wear coloured, caped tunics, often of satin, velvet or wool. They also have to come from further away, and some are on the streets for more than 12 hours.

Feria de Abril

The April Fair, which is held in the second half of the month (sometimes edging into May), is a kind of release after the solemnity of Semana Santa. The biggest and most colourful of all Andalucía's *ferias*, it takes place on a special site, El Real de la Feria, in the Los Remedios area west of the Guadalquivir. The ceremonial lighting-up of the fairgrounds on the opening Monday night is the starting gun for six nights of festivities: eating, drinking, talking, fabulous flouncy dresses, and music and dancing till dawn. Much of the site is taken up by private areas for clubs, associations, families and groups of friends. But there are public areas, too, where much the same fun goes on.

In the afternoons, from about 1pm, those who have horses and carriages parade about the site – and the city at large – in their finery (many of the horses are dressed up too). Seville's major bullfighting season also takes place during the *feria*.

Other Festivals & Events

Other major Seville events include:

Bienal de Flamenco (September of even-numbered years; www.bienal-flamenco.org) Most of the big names of the flamenco world participate in this major flamenco festival, with events every night for a month in the Alcázar or the city's theatres.

Corpus Christi (late May or June – 26 May 2005, 15 June 2006) An important early-morning procession of the Custodia de Juan de Arfe and accompanying images from the cathedral.

SLEEPING

The attractive Barrio de Santa Cruz, which is close to the cathedral, Alcázar and Prado de San Sebastián bus station, has many places to stay in all price brackets. So do El Arenal (west of Santa Cruz towards the river, near Plaza de Armas bus station) and El Centro (the true city centre north of Santa Cruz).

Room rates in this section are for each establishment's high season – typically from about March to June and again in September and October, though every place seems to have its own idiosyncratic seasons. Budget hotels and *hostales* (simple guesthouses or small places offering hotel-like accommodation) may keep the same prices almost year-round. On the other hand, just about every room in Seville costs extra during Semana Santa and the Feria de Abril. The typical increase is between 30% and 60% over normal high-season rates, but a few places even double their prices. A few hotels extend this *temporada extra* (extra-high season) for a whole month from the start of Semana Santa to the end of the *feria*. It's vital to book ahead for rooms in Seville at this time, if you can afford them. Even at normal times, it's always worth ringing ahead.

Barrio de Santa Cruz   Map pp98–100
BUDGET
Huéspedes Dulces Sueños (☎ 954 41 93 93; Calle Santa María La Blanca 21; s/d €40/50, with shared bathroom €20/40; 🐱) 'Sweet Dreams' is a friendly little *hostal* with seven spotless rooms. Those overlooking the street are good and bright. Doubles have air-con, singles don't.

Hostal Arias (☎ 954 22 68 40; www.hostalarias .com; Calle Mariana de Pineda 9; s/d €41/56; 🐱) Floral-print bedspreads and a tiled foyer lend a cute note to the friendly Arias, which has a lift to all floors. All 14 rooms have a phone and a safe.

Pensión San Pancracio (☎/fax 954 41 31 04; Plaza de las Cruces 9; d €42, s/d with shared bathroom €18/30) This nine-room, family-run budget option is on a small, quiet square that gets a bit of a breeze in summer. The furnishings are almost as old as the rambling house, but it's all kept good and clean.

Pensión Cruces (☎ 954 22 60 41; Plaza de las Cruces 10) Across the square from the San Pancracio, this lovely old house has two patios sporting attractive tiles and lots of greenery.

It was closed for renovations at the time of writing but is expected to re-open in 2005.

MID-RANGE
Hostal Córdoba (☎ 954 22 74 98; Calle Farnesio 12; s/d €50/70, with shared bathroom €40/60; 🐱) Twelve bright, spotless rooms surround a plant-draped three-storey atrium. The Córdoba is run by a friendly older couple and situated on a quiet pedestrian street.

Hostal Goya (☎ 954 21 11 70; hgoya@hostalgoya .e.telefonica.net; Calle Mateos Gago 31; s/d with shower €43/60, d with bathroom €70) The 20 medium-sized rooms are cheered up with pretty tiling and a few paintings and prints. It's a popular, clean, well-run place – highly advisable to book head.

Hotel YH Giralda (☎ 954 22 83 24; www.yh-hoteles .com; Calle Abadés 30; r €69.55; P 🐱 🖵) This is not a youth hostel but a pleasant small hotel in an 18th-century abbot's house. The 14 rooms, with good-sized beds, phones and marble or tile floors, are simple but tasteful and in perfect condition.

Hotel Alcántara (☎ 954 50 05 95; www.hotel alcantara.net; Calle Ximénez de Enciso 28; s/d €64/80; 🐱) This small, friendly, new hotel on a pedestrianised street has 21 bright rooms with bathtub, phone, windows looking on to the hotel's patio, and pretty flower-print curtains. Breakfast is available and there's a lift and a room equipped for the disabled.

Hotel Amadeus (☎ 954 50 14 43; www.hotelamadeus sevilla.com; Calle Farnesio 6; s/d €65.50/81.30; P 🐱 🖵) A charming musician family converted their 18th-century mansion into this unique hotel geared to musicians and music lovers. There's a soundproofed practice room with piano, and a piano in the foyer where classical concerts are held monthly. Each of the 14 very comfortable and impeccably tasteful rooms and suites is named after a different composer (one has its own piano), and a variety of fascinating art decorates the whole house. A glassed-in lift rises from the foyer, and the roof terrace has great views to the Giralda.

Hotel Puerta de Sevilla (☎ 954 98 72 70; www.hotel puertadesevilla.com; Calle Santa María la Blanca 36; s/d €64.20/83.45; P 🐱) A small new hotel in a handy location, the Puerta de Sevilla is in pleasing, traditional style with flower-pattern textiles, pretty tiled bathrooms and an antique-dotted foyer. Rooms are clean and comfortable. A lift connects the three floors.

Hostería del Laurel (☎ 954 22 02 95; www.hosteria dellaurel.com in Spanish; Plaza de los Venerables 5; s/d incl breakfast €71.70/103.80; 🔀) Above a characterful old bar on a small Santa Cruz plaza, the Laurel has 21 simple, spacious and bright rooms with cool marble floors and good-sized bathrooms. Legend has it that during a stay here in 1844 playwright José Zorrilla was inspired to write *Don Juan Tenorio*, one of the most popular versions of the Don Juan story, and each room is named after a character in the play. Prices fall by about a quarter in July and August and from November to February.

Hostal Dalí (☎ 954 22 95 05; Puerta de Jerez 3; r €85.10; 🔀) Most of the 18 cheerful rooms in blue-and-apricot tones overlook busy streets but double-glazing keeps traffic noise at bay. Staff are friendly and prices come down by a quarter or more from June to August and November to February. All rooms are upstairs and there's no lift.

Hostal Picasso (☎ 954 21 08 64; Calle San Gregorio 1; r €85.10; 🔀) The bright green foyer at the foot of a three-storey atrium is more exciting than the 17 rooms, which are pretty, with comfy wrought-iron beds, but small. The Picasso is in the same small *hostal* group as Hostal Dalí and with the same seasonal price structure.

TOP END

Las Casas de la Judería (☎ 954 41 51 50; www.casas ypalacios.com; Callejón de Dos Hermanas 7; s/d from €108.05/166.90; 🅿 🔀) This charming hotel is comprised of a series of restored houses and mansions around several lovely patios and fountains. Most of the 116 comfortable, traditional-style rooms and suites sport four-poster beds, bath *and* shower, writing table, cable TV, phone and safe, and an amazing range of art decks the walls. In the evening, relax in the cosy piano bar. Breakfast is available.

Hotel Fernando III (☎ 954 21 73 07; www.fernando3 .com; Calle San José 21; s/d €132.70/156.20; 🅿 🔀 🖳 🔊) The Fernando III is a dependable hotel whose 155 comfortable if unimaginative rooms all have balcony, phone, TV and safe. It also has a restaurant, bar, spacious lounge, garage and rooftop pool open in spring and summer.

Hotel Los Seises (☎ 954 22 94 95; www.hotellos seises.com; Calle Segovias 6; s/d €147.65/202.25; 🔀 🔊) This 42-room luxury hotel was once part of the 16th-century Archbishop's Palace. The large rooms, all looking on to interior patios, have attractive terracotta-tile floors, spacious bathrooms and all the expected luxury touches. There's also a good restaurant and a rooftop pool with great Giralda views.

Hotel Alfonso XIII (Map pp88-90; ☎ 954 91 70 00; www.westin.com/hotelalfonso; Calle San Fernando 2; s/d €371.30/486.85; 🅿 🔀 🔀 🖳 🔊) Break the bank in style at this palatial confection of old Sevillan styles in mahogany, marble and tiles, just south of the Alcázar. Built to house heads of state visiting the Exposición Iberoamericana of 1929, it has 147 ultra-elegant rooms and suites with every amenity you could imagine, an outdoor pool, a fine restaurant and a sophisticated bar.

El Arenal
Map pp98–100

BUDGET

Hostal Residencia Naranjo (☎ 954 22 58 40; fax 954 21 69 43; Calle San Roque 11; s/d €30/44; 🔀) Colourful bedspreads and pine furniture add a touch of warmth to this *hostal* that's almost opposite Hotel Zaida. The 27 rooms are all equipped with TV and phone.

Hotel Zaida (☎ 954 21 11 38; www.hotelzaida.com; Calle San Roque 26; s/d €36.50/55; 🔀) The 27 rooms here are plain but decent, with phone, and reading lamps. A lovely Mudejar-style arched patio remains from the original 18th-century town house here. There's a lift to the upper floor, and the street is quiet, but ground-floor rooms open straight onto the foyer.

Hotel Madrid (☎ 954 21 43 07; fax 954 21 43 06; Calle San Pedro Mártir 22; s/d €40/55; 🅿 🔀) This friendly, family-run, small hotel offers pretty good value, with 21 pale yellow rooms all equipped with firm beds, nice blue-tiled bathrooms, and little balconies overlooking quiet streets. Rates may dip in slow periods, and there are no single rooms so solo travellers enjoy doubles at a single price.

Hostal Roma (☎ 954 50 13 00; www.sol.com /hostales-sp; Calle Gravina 34; s/d €48.15/55.65; 🅿 🔀) An attractive *hostal* with 17 rooms and a lift linking its three floors. Rooms all boast phone, writing table, prints on the walls and double glazing. The owners have three other *hostales* close by.

Also recommended:

Hostal Londres (☎ 954 50 27 45; www.londreshotel.com; Calle San Pedro Mártir 1; s/d €43.85/57.80; 🔀) Plain but decent 23-room *hostal* with pretty tiled foyer; rooms have phone and TV and, in some cases, little balconies.

Hostal Romero (☎ 954 21 13 53; Calle Gravina 21; d €40, s/d with shared bathroom €18/30) Friendly low-budget choice; firm beds in a dozen very plain, clean rooms.

MID-RANGE

Hotel Simón (☎ 954 22 66 60; www.hotelsimonsevilla .com; Calle García de Vinuesa 19; s/d €49.65/74.45; ❄) The charming Hotel Simón, a small hotel in a fine 18th-century house, is extremely popular so it's recommended that you book well ahead. It's built around a lovely patio with fountain, and antiques and beautiful Sevillan tilework adorn the passages, sitting areas and broad staircase. Tiling is also a feature of some of the 29 good-sized, spotless and comfortable rooms. All have phone and desk.

Hotel Puerta de Triana (☎ 954 21 54 04; www .hotelpuertadetriana.com; Calle Reyes Católicos 5; s/d €64.20/85.60; ❄) The Puerta de Triana is a good 65-room hotel with traditional fittings but modern comfort. The rooms here are cosy and medium-sized, with marble floors, desk and telephone, all with windows that look out onto the street or interior patios. There are spacious lounge areas downstairs. Breakfast is available.

Hotel Maestranza (☎ 954 56 10 70; www.hotel -maestranza.com; Calle Gamazo 12; s/d €49/87; ❄ 💻) A small and friendly hotel on a quietish street, the Maestranza has just 18 spotless but plain rooms, all equipped with phone and safe. The singles are small. Doubles go down to €65 or less from June to August and November to February.

Also recommended:

Hotel Europa (☎ 954 21 43 05; www.hoteleuropasevilla .com; Calle Jimios 5; s/d €77.05/95.25; Ⓟ ❄) Comfortable, sizable, marble-floored rooms with phone, in a fine 18th-century house.

Hotel Plaza Sevilla (☎ 954 21 71 49; info@hotelplaza sevilla.com; Calle Canalejas 2; s/d incl breakfast €47/67; Ⓟ ❄) Efficiently run hotel with cosy rooms.

TOP END

Hotel Vincci La Rábida (☎ 954 50 12 80; www.vincci hoteles.com; Calle Castelar 24; s/d €154.10/181.90; Ⓟ ❄ 💻) A beautiful four-storey columned atrium-lounge greets you in this converted 18th-century palace, now a classy four-star hotel. Most of the 81 extremely comfortable rooms, with terracotta and marble floors and attractive prints, surround this central focus. The hotel boasts a seasonal rooftop

bar-café with Jacuzzi and magnificent views of the cathedral. Service is professional and polished.

El Centro
Map pp98–100

BUDGET

Casa Sol y Luna (☎ 954 21 06 82; casasolyluna@auna .com; Calle Pérez Galdós 1A; d €42, s/d/tr with shared bathroom €22/35/54) This is a first-rate *hostal* in a characterful, attractively modernised, old town house. Your welcoming young hosts speak fluent English, Italian and Spanish and will make you feel right at home. Most of the nine rooms surround a sociable central lounge. Special touches such as pretty paintings, good-sized mirrors, desks and reading lamps bespeak the care of the owners, and the shared bathrooms (none shared by more than two rooms) are the biggest and most beautiful you'll find in any *hostal* in Andalucía!

Hostal Lis (☎ 954 21 30 88; www.hostallis.com; Calle Escarpín 10; s/d/tr €21/42/63; 💻) The friendly Lis was once owned by a tile manufacturer and is adorned with richly colourful old Sevillan tiling throughout. Most rooms are around a two-storey, sky-lit patio and they're well kept, with fans. There's a roof terrace and free Internet access for guests.

MID-RANGE

Hotel San Francisco (☎ /fax 954 50 15 41; Calle Álvarez Quintero 38; s/d €55/68; ❄) On a pedestrian street linking El Centro with the Barrio de Santa Cruz, the friendly, good-value Hotel San Francisco is a recently converted 18th-century family home. Nearly all the 16 good-sized rooms look on to the street or an interior patio; all have marble floors, TV and heating.

TOP END

Hotel Las Casas de los Mercaderes (☎ 954 22 58 58; www.casasypalacios.com; Calle Álvarez Quintero 9-13; s/d €94.15/136.95; Ⓟ ❄) Centred on a lovely two-storey, 18th-century patio with stained-glass roof, this hotel has 47 tasteful rooms, plus café and breakfast service.

Las Casas del Rey de Baeza (☎ 954 56 14 96; www .hospes.es; Plaza Jesús de la Redención 2; s/d €162.65/189.40; Ⓟ ❄ 💻 🐾) This tranquil, expertly run and marvellously designed hotel occupies former communal housing patios dating from the 18th century. The 41 large rooms, in tasteful blue, white, orange and red hues, boast attractive modern art, CD player, DVD and modem line. Public areas include a super-comfortable lounge and reading room, an attractive restaurant featuring Sevillan food, and a gorgeous pool. The décor uses such traditional Andalucian features as exterior blinds made of *esparto* (grass).

Hotel Casa Imperial (☎ 954 50 03 00; www.casaimperial.com; Calle Imperial 29; s/d €235.40/256.80; P ✹) One of Seville's most luxurious and atmospheric hotels, the Casa Imperial is a 16th-century palace with three lovely plant-filled patios – one with a fountain and sometimes a guitarist. Decoration is sumptuous; the 24 luxurious suites and junior suites in various bold colours all have kitchenette and sitting area, though not all are as big as you might hope. The hotel has a good restaurant and a roof terrace with gorgeous views.

North of the Centre
BUDGET
Hotel Sevilla (Map pp98-100; ☎ 954 38 41 61; www.hotel-sevilla.com; Calle Daoíz 5; s/d €35/55; ✹) The recently modernised Hotel Sevilla, on a quiet little plaza, is not bad value. The 30 medium-sized rooms in pink-and-green colour schemes have good bathrooms, large mirrors, desk, reading lamps and phone. There's a pretty little greenery-filled patio off the broad foyer.

MID-RANGE
Hotel Corregidor (Map pp88-90; ☎ 954 38 51 11; fax 954 38 42 38; Calle Morgado 17; s/d €77.05/96.30; P ✹) On a quiet little street up towards the Alameda de Hércules, the 77-room Corregidor is comfortable and dependable. It has pleasant, reasonable-sized rooms with phone, TV and a spot of art on the walls. Singles are a decent size. Downstairs are spacious sitting areas and a little open-air patio. Breakfast is available.

Patio de la Cartuja (Map pp88-90; ☎ 954 90 02 00; www.patiosdesevilla.com; Calle Lumbreras 8-10; s/d €69/97.90; P ✹) Just off the northern end of Alameda de Hércules, this apartment hotel occupies a former *corral* – a three-storey patio community that was once the typical form of Sevillan lower-middle-class housing. Renovated into 30 cosy apartments, it's a pleasant place to stay if you don't mind being this far north. Each apartment has a double bedroom, kitchen and sitting room with double sofa bed. There's a café, too.

Patio de la Alameda (Map pp88-90; ☎ 954 90 49 99; www.patiosdesevilla.com; Alameda de Hércules 56; s/d €69/97.90; P ✹) A branch of the Patio de la Cartuja, with the same facilities and prices.

TOP END
Hotel Cervantes (Map pp88-100; ☎ 954 90 02 80; www.hotel-cervantes.com; Calle Cervantes 10; s/d €85.95/122; P ✹) The Cervantes is a charming, modern, 54-room hotel on a quiet street in a rather quaint old part of the city, up towards Alameda de Hércules. The rooms have pretty furnishings, parquet floors and bright modern art on the walls, and come with phone, desk and bathtub. Buffet breakfast is available.

Hotel San Gil (Map pp88-90; ☎ 954 90 68 11; www.fp-hoteles.com; Calle Parras 28; s/d €125.20/157.30; P ✹ ☎) Just around the corner from the Basílica de la Macarena, San Gil is one of the city's hidden gems. The renovated early-20th-century building focuses on a pretty garden-courtyard and combines acclaimed modern design with beautiful antique tiling and other traditional touches. The 61 cosy, tasteful rooms and suites feature marble-tiled bathrooms; public areas include restaurant, bar and pool.

TOURIST APARTMENTS IN SEVILLE

Four people can rent a clean, comfortable, tasteful, well-located and well-equipped apartment in Seville for well under €100 a night. Two people normally pay between €30 and €70. The accommodation will usually compare well with what you get for the same money in a hotel or *hostal* (a simple guesthouse or small place offering hotel-like accommodation).

There are several websites that provide details of a range of apartments in Seville: they don't usually offer immediate online booking, but provide the chance to request availability and await email confirmation. Try the following:

Apartamentos Embrujo de Sevilla (☎ 625 060 937; www.embrujodesevilla.com)
Sevilla5.com (☎ 637 011 091; www.sevilla5.com)
Sol (www.sol.com)

There's further information available at **Explore Seville** (www.exploreseville.com).

Other Areas

Camping Villsom (Map pp88–90; ☎ /fax 954 72 08 28; Carretera Sevilla-Cádiz Km 554.8; camping 2 people, tent & car €15.45) is a well-equipped camping ground with plenty of trees, in Dos Hermanas, 15km south of Seville towards Cádiz. **Camping Sevilla** (Map pp88–90; ☎ 954 51 43 79; camping 2 people, tent & car €14) is only 6km from the city but on a less attractive site on the A4 just before Seville airport.

EATING

To catch the atmosphere of the city, plunge straight in and follow the winding tapas trail that links scores of spirited bars and bodegas. Classier modern eateries also abound but most give in to their Spanish roots, offering similar tasty titbits with an *alta cocina* (haute cuisine) edge.

Restaurants

BARRIO DE SANTA CRUZ & AROUND   **Map pp98–100**

The interlacing narrow streets and squares just east of the Alcázar make a convenient spot to stop and fill up, though you'll have to cope with the rabble that gets here first. The restaurants are touristy, but thankfully some still have character.

Restaurant La Cueva (☎ 954 21 31 43; Calle Rodrigo Caro 18; mains €10.75-23.50) As you stroll through Plaza Doña Elvira, inhale the whiff of orange blossom and sizzling fish, which wafts from this popular seafood eatery. It cooks up a storming fish casserole (€23.50 for two people), and a hearty *caldereta* (lamb stew; €10.75), if something meatier takes your fancy.

Hostería del Laurel (☎ 954 22 02 95; Plaza de los Venerables 5; mains €10-20) Arm-in-arm with the tapas bar and hotel (p110), the restaurant here offers charming service, a bustling atmosphere and average fare. The grandly named *pollo a la Sevillana* (€11.50) is more like chicken and chips in gravy but it's tasty nonetheless.

Corral del Agua (☎ 954 22 07 14; Callejón del Agua 6; mains €12-18, menú €23; ☯ noon-4pm & 8pm-midnight Mon-Sat) If you're hankering after inventive food on a hot day, then opt to book a table at Corral del Agua. Its leafy courtyard makes a pleasant spot to sample traditional stews and Arabic-inspired desserts (such as orange, carrot and cinnamon!).

Restaurante La Albahaca (☎ 954 22 07 14; Plaza de Santa Cruz 12; mains €18-22, menú €27) Gas-

tronomic inventions are the mainstay of this swish restaurant. Try pork trotter with mushroom, young garlic and mousse of peas (€18) if your sense of adventure is running high.

El Giraldillo (☎ 954 21 45 25; Plaza Virgen de los Reyes 2; menú €27) A stone's throw from the cathedral, El Giraldillo is one of the sightseers' favourites but the Andalucian-style paella (€19 per person) is delicious, which goes to show that it doesn't just cook up tourist fare.

Cervecería Giralda (☎ 954 22 74 35; Calle Mateos Gago 1; breakfast €3-5) Conquer the effects of the night before with one of the recommended breakfasts here. Munch on your *tostadas* (toasted rolls; €1.10 to €4.20) and imagine the place in its former guise – an Islamic bathhouse. (See also p116.)

Restaurante Las Lapas (☎ 954 21 11 04; Calle San Gregorio 6; menú €9; ☯ closed Sun) Lying in the path of incessant horse-drawn traffic and, it seems, the whole of Seville's student population, you might find this eatery rather noisy outside and in. But sit back and enjoy the hubbub with a chorizo and potato mixed dish (€7.50).

Restaurante San Marco (☎ 954 21 43 90; Calle Mesón del Moro 6; mains €5.90-8.90; ☯ closed Mon) Although San Marco occupies a flash refurbished Islamic bathhouse (worth seeing), it's really just one of the many homogenised pizza and pasta places that dot the city. You'll be forgiven for thinking that the food doesn't quite match the exotic surrounds.

Ordinary Calle Santa María La Blanca has a throng of eateries, whose muddle of outdoor seating is invariably crammed with diners.

Carmela (Calle Santa María La Blanca 6; menú €7) The rustic-looking waiting staff, dressed in headscarves and aprons, give this establishment a rather earthy feel. It cooks up a wholesome quiche Lorraine (€6).

Altamira Bar-Café (☎ 954 42 50 30; Calle Santa María La Blanca 4; raciones €7.20-8.10) One of the snazzier options along this little stretch, Altamira serves up tempting seafood *raciones* (meal-sized servings of tapas) to chirpy diners.

Bar Casa Fernando (Calle Santa María La Blanca; menú €7) This place bustles with punters, most of whom are trying out the good-value menu of the day. There is a variety of options but a small dish of paella, followed by fried fish and a dreamy caramel flan will set you up nicely.

Restaurante Modesto (☎ 954 41 68 11; www.grupo modesto.com; Calle Cano y Cueto 5; mains €7.35-42.60) Modesto is a classy place (so don't let the name fool you) that twitters with pleased diners and teams up with Restaurante La Judería to present a full range of fish dishes, such as Sevillan-style cod (€12.60).

Restaurante La Judería (☎ 954 41 20 52; Calle Cano y Cueto 13A; menú around €28) This is Modesto's sister restaurant and gives fans a change of scenery, though the dishes are basically the same.

The dizzily bright lights of the restaurants north of the cathedral function to attract and trap buzzing sightseers, so be prepared. Eateries here include:

Las Escobas (☎ 954 21 94 08; Calle Álvarez Quintero 62; mains around €15) Sweep your plate clean at Las Escobas. The à la carte dinner, with various dishes (such as gazpacho and a dessert flan), beer and coffee costs €26.

Casa Robles (☎ 954 21 31 50; Calle Álvarez Quintero 58; mains around €20) An upmarket choice, Casa Robles prides itself on its natural food and elegantly styled restaurant. Its dishes, which range from braised bulls' tails to seasonal salads, are beautifully presented.

EL ARENAL
Map pp98–100

Mesón Serranito (☎ 954 21 12 43; Calle Antonia Díaz 9; platos combinados around €8) Boasting an eye-popping collection of gargantuan bulls' heads that stare down at diners, this restaurant is especially well stocked in the ham department. A *media-ración* (half a *ración*) of *jamón serrano* (mountain-cured ham) costs €8.

Enrique Becerra (☎ 954 21 30 49; Calle Gamazo 2; mains €14.50-20.20; ☽ closed Sun) Adding a smart touch to El Arenal, Enrique Becerra cooks up hearty Andalucian dishes to rave about. The lamb drenched in honey sauce and stuffed with spinach and pine nuts (€17.50) is just one of the delectable offerings.

Bar Gloria Bendita (Calle de Adriano 24; platos combinados around €8) This place smells of strong coffee and strong cheese, and will happily ply you with both. Share the intimate bar with a few locals or escape with your *bocadillo* (filled roll; €3.60) to the tables outside.

EL CENTRO
Map pp98–100

Confitería La Campana (cnr Calles Sierpes & Martín Villa) Smother your face with crumbs and chocolate at the city's most famous bakery, which has been turning out scrumptious

cakes and pastries since 1885. Sit outside with a sweet treat and coffee (€1.60; or €1.10 standing inside), and watch the shoppers flounce by.

Bar Laredo (cnr Calle Sierpes & Plaza de San Francisco) Watch them slap together a variety of *bocadillos* (€3) for rapid consumption at this popular breakfast stop.

Restaurante San Marco (☎ 954 21 24 40; Calle de la Cuna 6; pizzas around €8, pasta dishes €8.95-11.95) Located in an 18th-century palace, this is the grandest of the San Marco batch of eateries. A run-of-the-mill *quattro staggioni* (four seasons) pizza costs €8.

Alfalfa 10 (☎ 954 21 38 41; Plaza de la Alfalfa 10) The health conscious might be tempted by the multivitamin breakfast (€4.75) or the natural yogurt and runny honey (€1.50) here. Both slip down a treat.

Horno de San Buenaventura (Plaza de la Alfalfa 10; branch cnr Calles Pagés del Corro & Covadonga) If one Buenaventura wasn't enough there are two branches to tempt cake lovers into submission. Their offerings are treated like precious jewels and showcased in particularly shiny glass cabinets. You can also pick up breakfast; a coffee and serrano ham *tostada* costs €2.80.

Habanita (☎ 606-716456; Calle Golfo 3; raciones €6-9; ☽ 12.30-4.30pm & 8pm-12.30am Mon-Sat, 12.30-4.30pm Sun) This top restaurant serves a winning variety of Cuban, Andalucian, vegetarian and vegan food. Wash down specialities, such as mozzarella, tomato and basil salad (*media-ración* €4), with a piña colada and chat to the people you met last time.

Bodegón Alfonso XII (☎ 954 21 12 51; Calle Alfonso XII 33; platos del día €6) For those visiting the Museo de Bellas Artes, this place is convenient for a sightseeing intermission. Coffee with a bacon *tostada* costs €3.

Horno del Duque (☎ 954 21 77 33; Plaza del Duque de la Victoria; mains around €7-11) The invariably busy Horno del Duque offers standard helpings of paella Valenciana with chicken (€10.50) to bag-laden shoppers.

Café Bar Duque (Plaza del Duque de la Victoria; platos combinados around €5) A stalwart in the ambrosial *churros con chocolate* (long, thin doughnuts to dip in thick hot chocolate) department, this café-bar churns them out with gusto (€1.80).

Los Alcazáres (Plaza de la Encarnación; tapas €1.80-3) A perfect, old-world haunt for those who need to fill a gap after visiting the nearby market.

NORTH OF THE CENTRE **Map pp88–90**
La Piola (cnr Alameda de Hércules & Calle Relator; mains around €4-7) A pair of trendy media spectacles would blend in splendidly at this comfortably hip Alameda joint. Drown the mixed salad (€3.80) with a freshly squeezed orange juice (€1.80) and leave glowing.

Badaluque (cnr Calles Calatrava & Pacheco y Núñez de Prado; breakfast €2.20-4, pizzas €6.80-9.50) Mull over the paper with a good-value breakfast at this earthy Alameda outpost. Tea with a ham-and-cheese *tostada* costs €2.20.

SOUTH OF THE CENTRE
Café-Bar Puerta de Jerez (Map pp98-100; Puerta de Jerez; tapas around €1.80) Cars and horses whizz around the fountain at Puerta de Jerez at great speed and it's fun to watch the spectacle at this café-bar; an accompanying coffee costs €1.60.

Restaurant San Fernando (Map pp98-100; ☎ 954 91 70 00; Calle San Fernando 2; ☻ 7-11am, 1-4pm & 8.30-11.30pm; mains €14-27) Guinea fowl, dahling? This posh restaurant, inside the posh Hotel Alfonso XIII, does a variety of fancy dishes for even fancier diners but it's good value too. The aforementioned bird, with grated potatoes and sautéed chanterelle mushrooms, costs €20.

Restaurante Egaña Oriza (Map pp88-90; ☎ 954 22 72 11; Calle San Fernando 41; mains €15-40; ☻ closed Sat lunch & Sun) Still one of the best restaurants in Seville, Egaña Oriza cooks up superb Andalucian-Basque cuisine, and big meaty dishes such as steak tartar (€23.45). While it's an undeniably good restaurant, it's a shame about the fume-choked location.

La Raza (Map pp88-90; ☎ 954 23 20 24, 954 23 38 30; Avenida de Isabel la Católica 2; mains €10-17) With tables spread out under the trees in leafy Parque de María Luisa, La Raza is a peaceful spot for morning coffee. Peckish patrons may fancy paella too (€11.50 per person; minimum two people).

TRIANA
Kiosco de las Flores (Map pp98-100; ☎ 954 27 45 76; Calle del Betis; media-raciones around €5, raciones around €9, mains €15-40; ☻ closed Sun evening & Mon) Still revelling in the transformation from 70-year-old shack to a glam conservatory (just take a look a the photos on display), this eatery doles out great *pescaíto frito* (fried fish).

Río Grande (Map pp88-90; ☎ 954 27 39 56, 954 27 83 71; Calle del Betis; seafood mains €15-28.50) This

CHOCS AWAY!

Slurping on thick hot chocolate is something Sevillans love to do, so blend in and get your very own chocolate moustache where you see the *chocolatería* sign. For that special cup of cocoa, head out to **Chocolatería Virgen de los Reyes** (Map pp88-90; ☎ 954 57 66 10; Virgen de los Reyes Hotel, Avenida Luís Montoto 131), which whisks up some of the best hot chocolate in the city. A cup costs €1.35.

restaurant wins the prize for most desirable location; many diners spend their mealtime gazing at the Torre del Oro. If the menu does manage to catch your eye, try the cuttlefish (€10).

Ristorante Cosa Nostra (Map pp98-100; ☎ 954 27 07 52; Calle del Betis 52; pizzas €5.40-7.50; ☻ closed Mon) Although there are a few pizzerias and pasta parlours on Calle del Betis, Cosa Nostra has an intimate feel that the others lack. The tortellini with gorgonzola (€6.50) is tasty too.

Casa Cuesta (Map pp88-90; ☎ 954 33 33 37; Calle de Castilla 3-5; mains around €9-10) Something about the carefully buffed wooden bar and gleaming beer pumps gives a sense that the owners are proud of Casa Cuesta. Indeed they should be; it's a real find for food lovers and winebibbers alike.

La Triana (Map pp88-90; ☎ 954 33 38 19; Calle de Castilla 36; menú €10, mains €9.60-15.80) The hosts at La Triana are suave and courteous, and while the décor may be minimalist the dishes are not. Menu of the day options include *pisto* (an oily vegetable fry-up) and a meaty main dish. The restaurant also backs out onto a quieter stretch of the river.

Tapas
It's sociable, still in vogue and something that should be done with a few friends in tow. Yes, tapas-hopping in Seville is a way of life that goes on from lunchtime till bedtime (whenever that may be). In some bars your account is chalked on the counter in front of you and added up when you leave. For some tapas hints to get you started, see p75.

BARRIO DE SANTA CRUZ **Map pp98–100**
Bodega Santa Cruz (☎ 954 21 32 46; Calle Mateos Gago; tapas €1.40-1.70) A focal point for tapas

pilgrims, this bodega has a wonderful choice of flavoursome bites. Its popularity speaks volumes.

Cervecería Giralda (☎ 954 22 74 35; Calle Mateos Gago 1; tapas €1.60-2.10) Exotic variations are merged with traditional dishes, such as *pechuga bechamel* (chicken breast in bechamel sauce), at this central tapas bar. (See also p113.)

Café-Bar Campanario (☎ 954 56 41 89; Calle Mateos Gago 8; tapas €1.80-2.40) A hotchpotch of tapas favourites can be found here, including Spanish omelette, aubergines with cheese and divine croquettes with ham and bechamel. Unlike most of the old bars it has an airy feel.

Cafe Alianza (Plaza de la Alianza; tapas €1.80-2.50) Old-fashioned street lights, a trickling fountain and colourful wall plants make this small plaza a charming place to relax with a coffee, and Cafe Alianza is positioned perfectly for just that. Its tapas nibbles are also good.

Café Bar Las Teresas (☎ 954 21 30 69; Calle Santa Teresa 2; tapas €1.80-4, media-raciones €6-8) Hams dangle proudly from the ceiling at Las Teresas and punters are kept happy with plates of authentic tapas, which are just right for sopping up the beer.

Bar Entrecalles (Calle Ximénez de Enciso; tapas €2.20) If you're not on a date, try the very flavoursome potatoes in *alioli* (aïoli; garlic mayonnaise) at this well-established bar.

EL ARENAL   **Map pp98–100**
Mesón Cinco Jotas (☎ 954 21 05 21; Calle Castelar 1; tapas €3, media-raciones €6.95) Dine on succulent Jabugo ham, which comes from pigs that have snuffled out the finest acorns, at this restaurant owned by Sánchez Romero Carvajal – the biggest producer of Jabugo ham.

La Gitana (Calle Antonia Díaz; tapas €2, mains €9.60-13.20) Bow-tied waiters serve up a great selection of tapas at this bar, which heaves with chattering locals.

Bar Pepe-Hillo (☎ 954 21 53 90; Calle Adriano 24; tapas €1.65-2.10) For no-nonsense, quality tapas head for easy-going Bar Pepe-Hillo.

Mesón de la Infanta (Calle Dos de Mayo 26; tapas €1.80-3.10) Classier tapas-hunters can indulge in trendy dishes at this Sevillan favourite. Sherry drinkers are also very welcome.

La Tienda de Eva (Calle Arfe; tapas around €2) Decked out like a village shop, this place offers an escape from the norm. Settle down with a beer and a few slices of chorizo (€2.50)

and gape at the well-presented tinned goods and gourmet hams.

EL CENTRO   **Map pp98–100**
Plaza de la Alfalfa is the hub of the tapas scene, with a flush of first-rate bars. Hop from sea-themed **La Trastienda** (Calle Alfalfa; tapas €1.80-3), off the eastern end of the plaza, to **La Bodega** (Calle Alfalfa; tapas €1.60-2.10), where you can mix head-spinning quantities of ham and sherry. **Bar Alfalfa** (cnr Calles Alfalfa & Candilejo; tapas €1.80-3.10), perched snugly between the latter two places, serves authentic tapas in intimate surroundings.

Bodega Extremeña (☎ 954 41 70 60; Calle San Esteban 17; tapas €1.60-2.10) Decorated with rustic bits and bobs, Bodega Extremeña flexes its muscles in the meat department and offers mouthwatering *solomillo ibérico* (Iberian pork sirloin).

El Rinconcillo (☎ 954 22 31 83; Calle Gerona 40; tapas €1.60-4) Founded in 1670, this is Seville's oldest bar and is still going strong. The tapas dishes are fairly straightforward but El Rinconcillo has had plenty of time to perfect the Spanish omelette with *jamón serrano* (€4).

La Giganta (☎ 954 21 09 75; Calle Alhóndiga 6; tapas €1.80) This place equals El Rinconcillo's talent for tapas, despite being a lot newer. While you're here, marvel at the weeds sprouting from the roof of the old church of Santa Catalina nearby.

Taberna los Terceros (Calle del Sol; tapas €2.20-2.40) Completing the hat-trick of tapas bars in this area, Los Terceros pulls a more energetic crowd and serves up fine tapas.

El Patio San Eloy (Calle San Eloy 9; tapas €1.30-1.60) Hams hang like stalactites in a cave at El Patio San Eloy, where you can feast on the usual mix of tapas and *burguillos* (small filled rolls).

Robles Placentines (☎ 954 21 31 62; Calle Placentines 2; tapas around €2) Modelled on a Jerez wine cellar, this popular haunt serves up tempting dishes such as white asparagus from the Sierra de Córdoba.

NORTH OF THE CENTRE   **Map pp88–90**
La Ilustre Víctima (Calle Doctor Letamendi 35; tapas €2.20, raciones €6.60) This hip, offbeat place has just the right atmosphere for some *pinchos de pollo* (small grilled-chicken kebabs; €3.40). The celebrated vegetarian tapas, including *calabacines al roque* (courgettes with

Roquefort cheese; €2.20), are as tasty as ever. Quit the brooding with a mint tea (€1.25).

Bar-Restaurante Las Columnas (Alameda de Hércules; tapas €1.35-2.10) Beefy men and tasty tapas are brought together at this low-key restaurant, which serves down-to-earth fare such as *albondigas* (meatballs; €2.20).

TRIANA
Map pp88–90

Las Columnas (Calle San Jacinto 29; tapas €2.20-3) Brought to us by the inventors of El Patio San Eloy (p116), Las Columnas purveys more of the same good-quality food.

Mariscos Emilio (☎ 954 33 25 42; Calle San Jacinto 39; www.mariscos-emilio.com in Spanish; tapas around €1.80) This seafood supremo steams, grills and fries an assortment of aquatic creatures. A few other branches dot the city.

Self-Catering

EL CENTRO
Map pp98–100

Mercado del Arenal (Calle Pastor y Landero) and the **Mercado de la Encarnación** (Plaza de la Encarnación) are central Seville's two food markets. The Encarnación, which mainly sells fruit, veg and fish, has been in its current 'temporary' quarters, awaiting construction of a new permanent building, since 1973!

El Corte Inglés (Plaza del Duque de la Victoria) has a well-stocked supermarket in the basement.

DRINKING & ENTERTAINMENT

Seville proudly presents a feast of nighttime delights, from beer-fuelled bopping and thumping live beats to experimental theatre and steamy flamenco. Bars usually open from 6pm to 2am weekdays and 8pm to 4am on the weekend. Drinking and partying get going at midnight on Friday and Saturday (daily when it's hot) and ups tempo as the night goes on. Pockets of bodegas such as those in Plaza del Salvador give rise to crowds of young boozers, often gathered around bottle-covered cars and scooters. You can find a range of live music most days, and some bars have space for grooving. DJs mix a range of beats every night, with soulful and jazzy house still big on the decks.

Get to grips with the latest action by picking up *Welcome & Olé* or *¿Qué Hacer?* (both monthly and free from tourist offices) or logging onto www.discoversevilla.com, a great resource, or www.exploreseville.com. For flamenco listings and events try www .tallerflamenco.com.

Bars

Thirst-quenching *cerveza* (beer) is just as important to Spaniards as tapas. So grab a bar stool in one of the bodegas and make the most of both.

In summer, dozens of *terrazas de verano* (summer terraces; temporary, open-air, late-night bars), many of them with live music and plenty of room to dance, spring up along both banks of the river. They change names and ambience from year to year.

BARRIO DE SANTA CRUZ
& AROUND
Map pp98–100

P Flaherty Irish Pub (☎ 954 21 04 15; Calle Alemanes 7) Paddy Flaherty certainly knows a thing or two about location, which makes this one of the busiest bars around. Drench your innards with a Guinness and watch the football (or whatever major sporting event is on).

Antigüedades (Calle Argote de Molina 40) Blending mellow beats with weird mannequin parts and skewered bread rolls that hang from the ceiling, this is a strange but cool place. Wander past and it'll suck you in.

La Subasta (Calle Argote de Molina 36; ☾ 8pm-3am) A smattering of antique paraphernalia gives this place a rather conservative feel but it's popular nonetheless.

Casa de la Moneda (Calle Adolfo Jurado) Part of a group of rambling old buildings, Casa de la Moneda is a fine watering hole that offers old-world charm, tapas (€1.80 to €2.10), and football on TV.

Bodega Santa Cruz (p115), **Bar Entrecalles** (p116) and **Café Bar Las Teresas** (p116), in the heart of the Barrio de Santa Cruz, is a much-loved bunch of beer (and tapas) haunts.

EL ARENAL
Map pp98–100

Isbiliyya Café (☎ 954 21 04 60; Paseo de Cristóbal Colón 2) Cupid welcomes you to this busy gay music bar, which puts on extravagant drag-queen shows on Thursday and Sunday nights.

Calle de Adriano has a couple of bars for drinkers who aren't so fussy. **Clan Scottish Pub** (Calle de Adriano 3) is busy in sporadic bursts and caters to a grungy mob. **Elefunk** (Calle de Adriano 10), on the other hand, is packed with dizzy young things fluttering around to the latest dance tunes.

EL CENTRO
Map pp98–100

Plaza del Salvador throbs with drinkers from mid-evening to 1am and is a great place to experience Cruzcampo (the local beer) al fresco. Grab a drink from **La Antigua Bodeguita** (☎ 954 56 18 33) or **La Saportales**, next door, and sit on the steps of the Parroquia del Salvador.

Bar Europa (☎ 954 22 13 54; Calle Siete Revueltas 35) With its soothingly colourful tiling, Bar Europa is a pleasant place for a drink and a chat. It also does tea (€0.90) and croissants (€1.05) if you want a break from alcohol and tapas.

Cervecería International (☎ 954 21 17 17; Calle Gamazo 3) Stare goggle-eyed at the glittering display of bottled beer as you drink yours (€1.50 from the pumps) and socialise with the crowd.

Calle Pérez Galdós, off Plaza de la Alfalfa, has a handful of pulsating bars: **Bare Nostrum** (Calle Pérez Galdós 26); **Cabo Loco** (Calle Pérez Galdós 26); **Nao** (Calle Pérez Galdós 28); and **La Rebótica** (Calle Pérez Galdós 11). If you're in a party mood, you should find at least one with a scene that takes your fancy.

ALAMEDA DE HÉRCULES — Map pp98–100

At first glance, Alameda de Hércules is nothing more than a dusty wasteland with a few seedy characters lurking about. However, it is home to a bohemian and alternative mix of bars and live-music venues.

Bulebar Café (☎ 954 90 19 54; Alameda de Hércules 83; ☉ 4pm-late) This place fills up with young sweaty bodies at night, though it has a pleasantly chilled atmosphere in the early evening. Lounge around on the old furniture or sit in the courtyard out front.

El Corto Maltés (Alameda de Hércules 66) The first in a bunch of three good bars clustered at the northeastern end of Alameda, El Corto is a laid-back saloon by day and a boisterous drinking den by night.

Café Central (☎ 954 38 73 12; Alameda de Hércules 64) Sit under the yellow bar lights with a bevy of bright young things at Café Central, one of Seville's hippest bars.

La Ilustre Víctima (Calle Doctor Letamendi 35) Buzzing with an international crowd, this place plays good jazzy house music. (See also p116.)

TRIANA

For a real treat, prop yourself up with a drink by the banks of the Guadalquivir in Triana; the wall along Calle del Betis forms a fantastic makeshift bar. Carry your drink out

from one of the following watering holes: **Alambique**, **Big Ben**, **Sirocca** and **Mú d'Aquí**. They are all clustered on Calle del Betis 54 (Map pp88–90) and open from 9pm.

Maya Soul (Map pp98-100; Calle del Betis 41-42) Beat-up leather sofas and soulful house music make this a soporific afternoon stop-off. Things get livelier in the evening.

Café de la Prensa (Map pp88-90; Calle del Betis 8) Weary souls can mellow out with a beer or two and even have a game of cards at this popular Betis bar.

North of Calle del Betis, Calle de Castilla has more good bars, brimming with a mixed local crowd on weekend nights, including **Casa Cuesta** (Map pp88-90; Calle de Castilla 3-5) and **Aníbal Café** (Map pp88-90; Calle de Castilla 98).

La Otra Orilla (Map pp88-90; Paseo de Nuestra Señora de la O) A couple of passages lead through to the river bank, where you'll find this buzzing music bar blessed with a great outdoor terrace.

Madigan's (Map pp88-90; ☎ 954 27 49 66; Plaza de Cuba 2; ☉ from noon) This raucous Irish pub is the best on Plaza de Cuba, and is now one of the hip places for mass youth gatherings.

Shiva (Map pp88-90; Calle San Jacinto 68) Handsome barmen aside, you'll be swooning from the candlelight and incense (and maybe the alcohol) before you know it. Calm things down with a green tea (€1.50) if need be.

Nightclubs

Clubs in Seville come and go with amazing rapidity but a few have stood the test of time. The partying starts between 2am and 4am at the weekend, so make the most of your siesta.

If a club flyer is thrust into your hand, keep hold of it – you're more likely to get in for free. Dress smarter (so no sportswear) at the weekend as clubs become much pickier about their punters and prices are hiked up dramatically if you don't fit the scene.

All of the following venues are on the Seville map (pp88–90).

Boss (Calle del Betis 67; admission free with flyer; ☉ 8pm-7am Tue-Sun) Make it past the two gruff bouncers wedged in the doorway and you'll find Boss to be a top dance spot. The music is a total mix but mainly appeals to the masses.

Weekend (☎ 954 37 88 73; Calle del Torneo 43; admission around €7; ☉ 11pm-8am Thu-Sat) Just across the road from the Guadalquivir, Weekend is one of Seville's top live-music and DJ spots.

Lisboa Music Club (Calle Faustino Álvarez 27; admission €6; ☾ midnight-6am Wed-Sat) LMC, near the Alameda de Hércules, is a fashionable club for house and techno lovers. Stylish, '60s-inspired décor spars with modernity; it's very hip.

Apandau (Avenida de María Luisa s/n; ☾ 8pm-late Sat & Sun summer) Looking more like a palatial greenhouse than a disco, Apandau has three separate halls in which to salsa the night away.

Aduana (☎ 954 23 85 82; www.aduana.net; Avenida de la Raza s/n; ☾ midnight-late Thu, Fri & Sat) Located 1km south of Parque de María Luisa, this huge dance venue plays nonstop grooves for manic party people.

Live Music

Tickets for some major events are sold at the music shop **Sevilla Rock** (Map pp98-100; Calle Alfonso XII 1). For information on flamenco in Seville, see below.

Fun Club (Map pp88-90; ☎ 95 825 02 49; Alameda de Hércules 86; admission live-band nights €3-6, other nights free; ☾ around 11.30pm-late Thu-Sun, from 9.30pm live-band nights) When it comes to music, this little dance warehouse is deadly serious. With a host of funk, Latino, hip-hop and jazz bands gracing the small stage it's not surprising that it's a music-lovers' favourite. Live bands play Friday and/or Saturday.

Naima Café Jazz (Map pp88-90; ☎ 954 38 24 85; Calle Trajano 47; admission free; live performances from 10pm) This intimate place sways to the sound of (occasionally live) mellow jazz. Time it right and you might be able to see an entrancing live act.

La Buena Estrella (Map pp88-90; Calle Trajano 51) Tap along to weekly jazz sessions in the evening or sip tea by day at this chilled café.

FLAMENCO HAUNTS OF SEVILLE

Seville is one of Spain's flamenco capitals. Its Triana barrio (district) on the western bank of the Guadalquivir, once the quarter of the city's *gitanos* (Roma people, formerly called Gypsies), was one of flamenco's birthplaces. Impromptu flamenco in small, smoky bars in Triana or around the Alameda de Hércules is pretty much a thing of the past, but there are plenty of spots where you can catch live flamenco song, dance or guitar. Hotels and tourist offices tend to steer you towards *tablaos* (expensive, tourist-oriented flamenco venues), which put on nightly shows, sometimes including dinner. These can be inauthentic and lacking in atmosphere, but **Los Gallos** (☎ 954 21 69 81; www.tablaolosgallos.com; Plaza de Santa Cruz 11) in the Barrio de Santa Cruz is a cut above average. Some top-notch flamenco artists have trodden Los Gallos' boards in the early stages of their careers. There are two-hour shows at 9pm and 11.30pm nightly for €27, including one drink.

In general, you'll catch a more spontaneous atmosphere in one of the bars that stage regular nights of flamenco, usually with no admission charge. Quality is unpredictable. At the time of writing, these bars offered some good shows:

Casa de la Memoria de Al-Andalus (Map pp98-100; ☎ 954 56 06 70; Calle Ximénez de Encisco 28; adult/child/concession €11/5/9; ☾ 9pm daily) Highly recommended show in a great patio setting.

El Mundo (Map pp98-100; Calle Siete Revueltas 5; admission free; ☾ 11pm Tue) Convenient El Centro flamenco joint.

El Tamboril (Map pp98-100; Plaza de Santa Cruz; admission free; ☾ from 10pm) Pack in to watch Sevillans flamenco-ing the night away.

La Carbonería (Map pp98-100; ☎ 954 21 44 60; Calle Levíes 18; admission free; ☾ about 8pm-4am) A converted coal yard in the Barrio de Santa Cruz with two large rooms, each with a bar, that gets thronged nearly every night with locals and visitors who come to enjoy the social scene and hear live music – nearly always flamenco.

La Sonanta (Map pp88-90; ☎ 954 34 48 54; Calle San Jacinto 31; admission free; ☾ 10pm Thu) A Triana bar with flamenco on Thursday.

Sol Café Cantante (Map pp98-100; ☎ 954 22 51 65; Calle Sol 5; adult/concession €18/11) Up-and-coming flamenco performers and guitarists head to this popular café for shows on Wednesday, Thursday, Friday and Saturday nights at 9pm.

Well-known flamenco artists make fairly frequent appearances at some theatres, especially the Teatro Central (p120), which runs flamenco seasons under the name Flamenco Viene del Sur. Seville also stages one of Spain's major flamenco festivals, the Bienal de Flamenco (p108), and, if you're present for the Feria de Abril, you'll find plenty going on then, too.

Jazz Corner (Map pp88–90; Calle Juan Antonio Cavestany; ☻ 7pm-late Tue-Sat, 5pm-late Sun) A big venue for jazz aficionados.

La Imperdible (Map pp88–90; ☎ 954 38 82 19; sala@imperdible.org; Plaza San Antonio de Padua 9; admission €4.80-6) A few blocks west of Alameda de Hércules is an epicentre of experimental arts in Seville. Its small theatre stages lots of contemporary dance and a bit of drama and music, usually at 9pm. Its bar, the **Almacén** (☎ 954 90 04 34; admission free), hosts varied music events from around 11pm Thursday to Saturday – from soul or blues bands to psychedelic punks to DJs mixing everything from soulful house to industrial breakbeat.

Theatre

Seville is big on cultural entertainment, be it classic drama, contemporary dance, flamenco or world music. Catch performances at the following venues:

Auditorio de la Cartuja (Map pp88–90; ☎ 954 50 56 56; Isla de La Cartuja) Huge venue for big-name acts.

Teatro Central (Map pp88–90; ☎ 95 503 72 00; Calle José Gálvez s/n) From top-end flamenco productions to plays and contemporary dance.

Teatro de la Maestranza (Map pp98–100; ☎ 954 22 65 73; Paseo de Cristóbal Colón 22) Opera and classical-music buffs should head here for stirring concerts.

Teatro Lope de Vega (Map pp88–90; ☎ 954 59 08 53/54; Avenida de María Luisa s/n) This theatre will seduce you with its ornate-looking exterior and its wide range of shows.

A couple of municipally run but innovative experimental theatres include:

Sala La Fundición (Map pp98–100; ☎ 954 22 58 44; Calle Matienzo s/n) Has offbeat offerings.

Teatro Alameda (Map pp88–90; ☎ 954 90 01 64; Calle Crédito 13) Located just off the northern end of Alameda de Hércules.

Cinemas

Avenida 5 Cines (Map pp88–90; ☎ 954 29 30 25; Calle Marqués de Paradas 15 s/n; admission €4.80) This is the best cinema for v.o. (*versión original*) films in Seville, with around 14 film options from which to choose. It has around three showings per day.

Cine Nervión Plaza (☎ 954 42 61 93; Avenida de Luis Morales s/n; tickets €3.90 Mon-Fri, €4.80 Sat & Sun) This massive 20-screen cinema is within the Nervión Plaza shopping complex. It has between three and six showings per day.

Sport

Seville's modern 60,000-seat Estadio Olímpico (Map pp88–90) is at the northern end of the Isla de La Cartuja. It wasn't enough to secure Seville's bid for the 2012 Olympics but there's always 2016.

La Teatral (Map pp98–100; ☎ 954 22 82 29; Calle Velázquez 12) Based in El Centro, this ticket agency sells tickets for bullfights, football matches and some concerts at a mark-up of a few euros. You need to book well in advance for the most popular events.

BULLFIGHTING

Fights at Seville's **Plaza de Toros de la Real Maestranza** (Map pp98–100; Paseo de Cristóbal Colón 12; www.realmaestranza.com) are among the best in Spain. The ring, which holds 14,000 spectators, is one of the country's oldest and most elegant, and its crowds some of the most knowledgeable. The season runs from Easter Sunday to early October, with fights every Sunday, usually at 6.30pm, and every day during the Feria de Abril and the week before it.

From the start of the season until late June/early July, nearly all the fights are by fully fledged matadors (every big star in the bullfighting firmament appears at least once a year in the Maestranza). These are the *abono* (subscription) fights, for which locals buy up the best seats on season tickets. Often only *sol* seats (in the sun at the start of proceedings) are available to nonsubscribers attending these fights. The cheapest seats in the ring cost between €20 and €28. The most expensive tickets, if available, cost a whopping €100. Most of the rest of the season, the fights are *novilleras* (novice bullfights), with young bulls and junior bullfighters; tickets for these cost from €9 to €42. Tickets are sold in advance at **Empresa Pagés** (Map pp98–100; ☎ 954 50 13 82; Calle de Adriano 37), and from 4.30pm on fight days at the *taquillas* (ticket windows) at the bullring itself.

For more on the Plaza de Toros de la Real Maestranza, see p97.

FOOTBALL

Seville has two professional – and very passionate – clubs, **Real Betis** (www.realbetisbalompie.es) and **Sevilla** (www.sevillafc.es). Despite Betis having the upper hand over the past decade, both teams are well established in the Primera Liga and are accustomed to Top 10 finishes. Players on Betis' books include

Joaquín, whose missed penalty against South Korea eliminated Spain from the 2002 World Cup, and Juanito, the international central defender.

Betis plays at the Estadio Manuel Ruiz de Lopera (Map pp98–100), beside Avenida de Jerez (the Cádiz road), 1.5km south of Parque María Luisa (bus No 34 southbound from opposite the main tourist office). Sevilla's home is the **Estadio Sánchez Pizjuán** (Calle de Luis Morales), east of the centre.

Except for the biggest games – against Real Madrid or Barcelona, or when the Seville clubs meet each other – tickets cost between €25 and €60, payable at the gates.

SHOPPING

Seville has one of the prettiest clusters of pedestrianised shopping streets in Europe. Calles Sierpes, Velázquez/Tetuán and de la Cuna (all on Map pp98–100) have retained their charm with a host of small shops selling everything from polka-dot *trajes de flamenca* (flamenco dresses) and trendy Camper shoes to diamond rings and antique fans. Most shops open between 9am and 9pm but expect ghostly quiet between 2pm and 5pm when they close for siesta.

You can have an interesting browse on Calle Amor de Dias and Calle Doctor Letamendi, near the hub of the city's alternative scene, Alameda de Hércules (Map pp88–90). Shops along these two streets specialise in fabrics, jewellery and artefacts from Africa and Asia, rare music recordings, secondhand clothes, and so on.

Tourist-oriented craft shops are dotted all around the Barrio de Santa Cruz (Map pp98–100), east of the Alcázar. Many sell attractive local tiles and ceramics with colourful Islamic designs, scenes of old rural life etc, as well as a lot of gaudy T-shirts.

El Postigo (cnr Calles Arfe & Dos de Mayo) This indoor arts-and-crafts market houses a few shops selling a range of goods from pottery and textiles to silverware.

Sevilla Rock (Map pp98–100; Calle Alfonso XII No 1) If you're looking for a great music store then look no further than Sevilla Rock. The CDs are good value but be sure to check out the super-cheap bargain room at the back.

Record Sevilla (Map pp98–100; Calle Amor de Dias 27) Fancy mixing flamenco with house? Then grab your vinyl here. Staff are knowledgeable about the music scene, too.

Nervión Plaza (Map pp88–90; ☎ 954 98 91 41; Avenida Luis de Morales s/n) A large shopping complex, 1.5km east of the Barrio de Santa Cruz, off Avenida de Eduardo Dato.

El Corte Inglés department store – the best single shop to look for almost anything – occupies four separate buildings in central Seville: two on Plaza de la Magdalena and two on Plaza del Duque de la Victoria. There is also a large branch located on Calle Montoto.

Markets

The most colourful street market is **El Jueves Market** (Map pp88–90; Calle de la Feria; ☽ Thu), east of Alameda de Hércules, where you can find everything from hat stands to antiquated household appliances. It's as interesting for those who like people-watching as it is for those with an eye for a bargain. Alternatively, lose yourself among the leather bags and hippie-type necklaces on Plaza del Duque de la Victoria and Plaza de la Magdalena, which both stage **markets** (☽ Thu-Sat).

GETTING THERE & AWAY
Air
Seville's **Aeropuerto San Pablo** (Map pp88–90; ☎ 954 44 90 00) has a fair range of international and domestic flights, though at the time of writing there were no low-cost airlines flying here. **Iberia** (Map pp088–90; city ☎ 902 40 05 00; Avenida de la Buhaira 8; airport ☎ 954 26 09 15) flies daily nonstop between Seville and London, Paris, Madrid, Barcelona, Valencia and Bilbao, and Santiago de Compostela six days a week. **Spanair** (☎ 954 44 91 38, 902 131415; Airport) and **Air Europa** (☎ 902 40 15 01, 954 44 91 79; tickets from Halcón Viajes, Avenida de la Constitución 5) both fly nonstop daily to/from Barcelona. There are also daily nonstop flights to/from the following cities: London on **British Airways** (☎ 902 11 13 33, 954 44 90 69; Airport), Paris on **Air France** (☎ 901 11 22 66, 954 44 92 52; Airport), and Brussels on **Brussels Airlines** (☎ 902 90 14 92, 954 44 91 86; Airport). **Air Berlin** (☎ 901 11 64 02; Airport), **LTU** (☎ 954 44 91 99, 901 33 03 20; Airport) and **Hapag-Lloyd Express** (☎ 902 02 00 69; www.hlx.com; Airport) fly to German and Austrian cities, sometimes with a connection en route.

Bus
Seville has two bus stations. Buses to/from the north of Sevilla province, Huelva province,

Portugal, Madrid, Extremadura and north-west Spain use the **Estación de Autobuses Plaza de Armas** (Map pp88-90; ☎ 954 90 80 40, 954 90 77 37) by the Puente del Cachorro. Other buses use the **Estación de Autobuses Prado de San Sebastián** (Map pp88-90; ☎ 954 41 71 11; Plaza San Sebastián), just southeast of the Barrio de Santa Cruz.

Destinations from Plaza de Armas include Aracena (€5.35, 1¼ hours, two daily), Ayamonte (€9.40, two hours, four to six daily), Cáceres (€14.15, four hours, six or more daily), El Rocío (€4.50, 1½ hours, three to five daily), Huelva (€6.10, 1¼ hours, at least 18 daily), Isla Cristina (€8.95, two hours, one to three daily), Madrid (€15.95, six hours, 14 daily), Matalascañas (€5.45, two hours, three to five daily), Mérida (€10.50, three hours, 12 daily) and Minas de Riotinto (€4, one hour, three daily).

For information on buses to/from Portugal, see p417. Plaza de Armas is also the station for buses to Santiponce (€0.80, 30 minutes), and Sevilla province's Sierra Norte (p135).

Buses from Prado de San Sebastián include 10 or more daily to Cádiz (€9.50, 1¾ hours), Córdoba (€8.60, 1¾ hours), Granada (€16.45, three hours), Jerez de la Frontera (€5.40, 1¼ hours) and Málaga (€13.05, 2½ hours). Other destinations include Carmona (€1.80, 45 minutes), Écija (€5.05, 1¼ hours), Osuna (€5.65, 1¼ hours), Sanlúcar de Barrameda (€7.40, 1½ hours, five or more daily), El Puerto de Santa María (€7.50, 1½ hours, five daily), Vejer de la Frontera (€10.80, three hours, five daily), Tarifa (€14, three hours, four daily), Algeciras (€13.35 to €14.75, 3½ hours, four daily), Arcos de la Frontera (€6.35, two hours, two daily), Ronda (€8.40, 2½ hours, five or more daily), Antequera (€9.90, two hours, six daily), Jaén (€15.25, three hours, three to five daily), destinations along the Mediterranean coast from the Costa del Sol to Barcelona, and one bus at 5.30pm Monday to Friday to Conil (€10.10, two hours), Los Caños de Meca (€11.55, 2½ hours), Barbate (€12.45, three hours) and Zahara de los Atunes (€13.25, 3½ hours).

Car & Motorcycle

Some local car-rental firms are cheaper than the big international companies, though booking before you come (see p423) is usu-ally the cheapest option of all. Several local firms have their offices on Calle Almirante Lobo off the Puerta de Jerez: most of them are open on Sunday morning in addition to the typical office hours from Monday to Saturday:

ATA Rent A Car (Map pp98-100; ☎ 954 22 17 77; Calle Almirante Lobo 2)

Good Rent A Car (Map pp98-100; ☎ 954 21 03 44; Calle Almirante Lobo 11)

Triana Rent A Car (Map pp98-100; ☎ 954 56 44 39; Calle Almirante Lobo 7)

You'll find larger companies at the transport terminals:

Atesa (☎ 954 41 26 40; Airport)

Avis airport (☎ 954 44 91 21); Estación Santa Justa (☎ 954 53 78 61)

Europcar airport (☎ 954 25 42 98); Estación Santa Justa (☎ 954 53 39 14)

Hertz (☎ 954 51 47 20; Airport)

Train

Seville's **Estación Santa Justa** (Map pp88-90; ☎ 954 41 41 11; Avenida Kansas City) is 1.5km northeast of the centre. There's also a city-centre **Renfe information & ticket office** (Map pp98-100; Calle Zaragoza 29).

Fourteen or more super-fast AVEs, reaching speeds of 280km/h, whizz daily to/from Madrid (€59 to €65, 2½ hours). The two daily 'Altaria' services are a little cheaper and about one hour slower. (For fares and other information see p420.)

Other destinations include Antequera (€10.60, 1¾ hours, three daily), Barcelona (€50 to €77.50, 10½ to 13 hours, three daily), Cáceres (€14.65, 5¾ hours, one daily), Cádiz (€8.40 to €22.50, 1¾ hours, nine or more daily), Córdoba (€7 to €24, 40 minutes to 1½ hours, 21 or more daily), El Puerto de Santa María (€7 to €20, one to 1½ hours, 10 or more daily), Granada (€17.65, three hours, four daily), Huelva (€6.40 to €15.50, 1½ hours, four daily), Jaén (€14.70, three hours, one daily), Jerez de la Frontera (€5.85 to €19, one to 1¼ hours, nine or more daily), Málaga (€13.15, 2½ hours, five daily), Mérida (€11, 3¾ hours, one daily), Osuna (€5.85 to €6.55, one hour, six daily) and Zafra (€8.25, 3¾ hours, one daily). For Ronda or Algeciras, take a Málaga train and change at Bobadilla. For Lisbon (€49.65 2nd-class, 16 hours), you must change in the middle of the night at Cáceres.

GETTING AROUND
To/From the Airport
Seville airport is about 7km east of the centre on the A4 Córdoba road. From Monday to Friday, buses of **Amarillos Tour** (☎ 902 21 03 17) make the trip from Puerta de Jerez to the airport (€2.30, 30 to 40 minutes) every 30 minutes from 6.15am to 2.45pm and 4.30pm to 11pm, and from the airport (arrivals terminal) to Puerta de Jerez 30 minutes later. On Saturday, Sunday and holidays, the service is reduced to 15 buses in each direction daily. The buses stop at Santa Justa train station en route.

A taxi costs €15 (€18 from 10pm to 6am and on Saturday, Sunday and holidays).

Bus
Bus Nos C1, C2, C3 and C4 do useful circular routes linking the main transport terminals and the city centre. The No C1, going east from in front of Santa Justa train station, follows a clockwise route via Avenida de Carlos V (close to Prado de San Sebastián bus station and the Barrio de Santa Cruz), Avenida de María Luisa, Triana, the Isla de la Cartuja (including Isla Mágica) and Calle de Resolana. The No C2 follows the same route in reverse. Bus No 32, from the same stop as No C2 outside Santa Justa station, runs to/from Plaza de la Encarnación in the northern part of the centre.

The clockwise No C3 goes from Avenida Menéndez Pelayo (near Prado de San Sebastián bus station) to the Puerta de Jerez, Triana, Plaza de Armas bus station, Calle del Torneo, Calle de Resolana and Calle de Recaredo. The No C4 does the same circuit anticlockwise except that from Plaza de Armas bus station it heads south along Calle de Arjona and Paseo de Cristóbal Colón, instead of crossing the river to Triana.

A single bus ride is €1. You can pick up a route map, the *Guía del Transporte Urbano de Sevilla*, from tourist offices or from information booths at major stops, including Plaza Nueva, Plaza de la Encarnación and Avenida de Carlos V.

Car & Motorcycle
Seville's system of one-way and pedestrian streets is no fun for drivers. Hotels usually charge €10 to €15 a day for parking - no cheaper than some public car parks, but at least your vehicle will be close at hand. Most underground car parks charge around €16 for 24 hours – see the Seville map (pp88–90) and Central Seville map (pp98–100) for locations. **Parking Paseo de Colón** (Map pp98-100; cnr Paseo de Colón & Calle Adriano; up to 10 hr €1.15 per hr, 10-24 hr €11.40) is a little cheaper.

Taxi
From 6am to 10pm Monday to Friday, taxis cost €0.95 plus €0.65 per kilometre. At other times and on public holidays, it's €1.15 plus €0.80 per kilometre.

AROUND SEVILLE

SANTIPONCE
pop 7000 / elevation 20m
The small town of Santiponce, about 8km northwest of Seville, is the location of Itálica, the most impressive Roman site in Andalucía, and of the historic and artistically fascinating Monasterio de San Isidoro del Campo. There's a **tourist office** (☎ 955 99 80 28; Calle La Feria s/n; ☼ 9am-4pm Tue-Fri & Sun) next to the Roman theatre.

Itálica (☎ 955 99 65 83; Avenida de Extremadura 2; non-EU citizen €1.50, EU citizen free; ☼ 8.30am-8.30pm Tue-Sat, 9am-3pm Sun & holidays Apr-Sep; 9am-5.30pm Tue-Sat, 10am-4pm Sun & holidays Oct-Mar, closed 1 & 6 Jan, 28 Feb, Good Friday, 1 May, 15 Aug, 1 Nov, 25 Dec) was the first Roman town in Spain, founded in 206 BC for soldiers wounded in the Battle of Ilipa, nearby, in which a Roman army under General Scipio Africanus extinguished Carthaginian ambitions on the Iberian Peninsula. Itálica was the birthplace of the 2nd-century-AD Roman emperor Trajan, and probably of his adopted son and successor Hadrian (he of the wall across northern England).

Most of the Romans' original *vetus urbs* (old town) now lies beneath Santiponce. The main area to visit is the *nova urbs* (new town), added by Hadrian, at the northern end of town. The site includes broad paved streets, one of the biggest of all Roman amphitheatres (able to hold 20,000 spectators), and ruins of several houses built around patios adorned with beautiful mosaics. The most notable of these houses are the **Casa del Planetario** (House of the Planetarium), with a mosaic depicting the gods of the seven days of the week, and the **Casa de los Pájaros** (House of the Birds).

To the south, in the old town, you can also visit a restored **Roman theatre**. In April or May each year this is the setting for a European youth festival of Greco-Latin theatre, with plays by classical playwrights. Itálica has been heavily recycled over the centuries and parts of its buildings have been reused in Santiponce, Seville and elsewhere. You can see statuary and further mosaics from here in Seville's Palacio de la Condesa de Lebrija (p101) and Museo Arqueológico (p103).

The **Monasterio de San Isidoro del Campo** (☎ 955 99 69 20; admission €2; ✆ 10am-2pm Wed & Thu, 10am-2pm & 5.30-8.30pm Fri & Sat, 10am-3pm Sun & holidays, also 4-7pm Fri & Sat Oct-Mar) is at the southern end of Santiponce, 1.5km from the Itálica entrance. The monastery was founded in 1301 by Guzmán El Bueno, hero of the defence of Tarifa in 1294 (see p205). In the 15th century its order of hermitic Hieronymite monks decorated the Patio de Evangelistas

and central cloister with a rare set of mural paintings of saints and Mudejar geometric and floral designs. By the 16th century the monastery had one of Spain's best libraries, and one monk, Casiodoro de Reina, did the first translation of the Bible into Spanish (published 1559). But Reina and others were too much influenced by Lutheran ideas for the liking of the Inquisition, which dissolved the nascent Protestant community, imprisoning and executing some monks while others managed to escape into exile.

In 1568 the monastery was occupied by a different (nonhermitic) order of Hieronymites, for whom the great 17th-century Sevillan sculptor Juan Martínez Montañés carved one of his masterpieces – the retable in the larger of the monastery's twin churches – as well as the effigies of Guzmán El Bueno and his wife María Alonso Coronel that lie in wall niches either side of the retable, above their tombs. In the outer 'twin church' are

---

DETOUR: BIRDS & PINE FORESTS

A detour through the northeast fringes of the Doñana area en route to El Rocío (p151), or a day trip into the same territory from Seville, will reward any nature lover. You'll see plenty of large birds – flamingos, storks, eagles, hawks, herons – even before you get out of your car.

Leave Seville southwestward by Avenida de la República Argentina and the A3122 to Coria del Río and La Puebla del Río. For information about the Doñana area, stop for a chat with the friendly, knowledgeable, English-speaking folk at the **Punto de Información Puebla del Río** (☎ 955 77 20 03; www.rutasdedonana.com; Avenida Pozo Concejo s/n; ✆ 9am-2pm & 5-7.30pm), beside the A3122 in La Puebla del Río, 15km from central Seville. Seven kilometres further along the road is **La Cañada de los Pájaros** (☎ 955 77 21 84; www.canadadelospajaros.com; Carretera Puebla del Río-Isla Mayor Km 8; adult/child under 5/child under 13 student/senior €6/free/€4/5/5; ✆ 10am-dusk), a nature reserve with thousands of easy-to-see birds of 150-plus species, including flamingos and many others that inhabit the Parque Natural de Doñana.

Time for lunch? **Venta El Cruce** (☎ 955 77 01 19; Carretera Puebla del Río-Isla Mayor Km 9.5; raciones €10), 1.75km beyond Cañada de los Pájaros at the turn-off for Villafranco del Guadalquivir, serves a typical duck of meat and fish dishes but the speciality, in this area of rice fields and wildfowl, is *pato con arroz* (duck with rice), served on Saturday and Sunday. If you'd prefer to picnic outdoors, continue past the Villafranco junction and fork right after 600m along the signposted 'Carril de Cicloturismo Pinares de Aznalcázar–La Puebla'. This road running through lovely tall pine woods towards the village of Aznalcázar has been turned into a *vía paisajística* (landscape route), with speed bumps to restrict motor vehicles to 40 km/h and special roadside reflectors to warn wildlife of traffic at night. About 6km along is the **Área Recreativa Pozo del Conejo**, with picnic tables beneath the trees.

Return 6km to the main road and turn right (southwest). On the right after 4km is **Dehesa de Abajo**, a 1.5 sq km nature reserve with walkways to observation points over Europe's largest woodland nesting colony of white storks (400 pairs) and hides overlooking a lake. A variety of raptors also nest here. To continue to El Rocío, carry on southwest from Dehesa de Abajo to the Vado de Don Simón causeway across the shallow Río Guadiamar. At the far end of the causeway turn right (northward) to Villamanrique de la Condesa, from where it's 20km southwest to El Rocío by unpaved road, or 43km on paved roads via Pilas, Hinojos and Almonte.

the tombs of Guzmán's son Juan Alonso Pérez de Guzmán, 'El Gran Batallador,' and his wife Urraca Ossorio de Lara, who was burned alive by Pedro El Cruel in Seville for refusing to hand over her treasures.

In the 19th century the monks were again expelled from this monastery. It subsequently served as a women's prison, brewery and tobacco factory. Finally, after a 12-year Junta de Andalucía restoration project, it was recently opened for visits.

Santiponce has several spots for a meal. **Casa Venancio/Gran Venta Itálica** (☎ 955 99 67 06; Avenida Extremadura 9; mains €6-13), opposite the Itálica entrance, has a reasonably varied menu. Try its rabbit or partridge with rice (€16.50 for two). For seafood or more rice dishes, head to the slightly fancier **La Caseta de Antonio** (☎ 955 99 63 06; Calle Rocío Vega 10; mains €10-18; ☺ closed Sun night, Mon & all Aug), a few steps south of Casa Venancio then a minute's walk along a side street.

Buses run to Santiponce (€0.80, 30 minutes) from Seville's Plaza de Armas bus station at least twice an hour from 6.30am to 11pm Monday to Friday, a little less often on weekends. In Santiponce they make a stop near the monastery, and terminate at the petrol station outside the Itálica entrance.

LA CAMPIÑA

La Campiña – the rolling plains east of Seville and south of the Río Guadalquivir, crossed by the A4 to Córdoba and the A92 towards Granada and Málaga – is still a land of huge agricultural estates belonging to a few landowners, dotted with scattered towns and villages. History goes back a long way here: you'll find traces of Tartessians, Iberians, Carthaginians, Romans, early Christians, Visigoths, Muslims and many others. Three towns – Carmona and Écija on the A4 and Osuna on the A92 – are especially worth visiting for their architecture, art and fascinating histories.

CARMONA

pop 27,000 / elevation 250m

Carmona stands on a low hill just off the A4, 38km east of Seville. Its charming old town has impressive monuments from many different epochs, fine views and some classy places to stay and eat. This strategic site was important as long ago as Carthaginian times. The Romans laid out a street plan that survives to this day: their Via Augusta, running from Rome to Cádiz, entered Carmona by the eastern Puerta de Córdoba and left by the western Puerta de Sevilla. The Muslims built a strong defensive wall around Carmona but it fell in 1247 to Fernando III. The town was later adorned with fine churches, convents and mansions by Mudejar and Christian artisans.

Orientation & Information

Old Carmona stands on the hill at the eastern end of the modern town: the Puerta de Sevilla marks the beginning of the old town. The helpful **tourist office** (☎ 954 19 09 55; www .turismo.carmona.org; ☺ 10am-6pm Mon-Sat, 10am-3pm Sun & holidays) is inside the Puerta de Sevilla. There are banks with ATMs on Paseo del Estatuto and Calle San Pedro, west of the Puerta de Sevilla, and on Plaza de San Fernando, the main square of the old town.

Sights

NECRÓPOLIS ROMANA

If you head just over 1km southwest of the Puerta de Sevilla you'll find the impressive **Necrópolis Romana** (Roman cemetery; ☎ 954 14 08 11; Avenida de Jorge Bonsor s/n; admission free; ☺ 9am-2pm Tue-Sat 15 Jun–14 Sep; 9am-5pm Tue-Fri, 10am-2pm Sat & Sun rest of year, closed holidays). You can climb down into a dozen or more family tombs, hewn from the rock in the 1st and 2nd centuries AD, some of them elaborate and many-chambered (a torch is useful). Most of the dead were cremated and in the tombs are wall niches for the boxlike stone urns containing the ashes.

Don't miss the **Tumba de Servilia**, as big as a temple (it was the tomb of a family of Hispano-Roman bigwigs), or the **Tumba del Elefante**, with a small elephant statue.

Across the street, you can overlook a 1st-century-BC Roman **amphitheatre**.

PUERTA DE SEVILLA & AROUND

This impressive main gate of the old town has been fortified for well over 2000 years. Today it also houses the tourist office, which sells tickets for the interesting upper levels of the structure, the **Alcázar de la Puerta de Sevilla** (adult/child/student/senior €2/1/1/1; ☺ 10am-6pm Mon-Sat, 10am-3pm Sun & holidays). This affords fine views and includes an upstairs Almohad

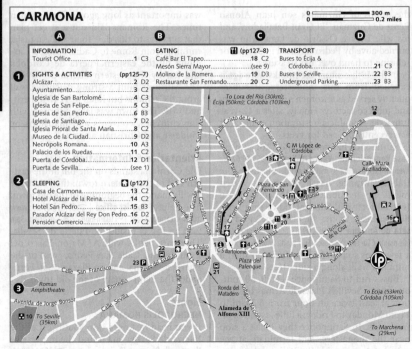

CARMONA

INFORMATION		EATING	(pp127–8)	TRANSPORT	
Tourist Office	1 C3	Café Bar El Tapeo	18 C2	Buses to Écija &	
		Mesón Sierra Mayor	(see 9)	Córdoba	21 C3
SIGHTS & ACTIVITIES	(pp125–7)	Molino de la Romera	19 D3	Buses to Sevilla	22 B3
Alcázar	2 D2	Restaurante San Fernando	20 C2	Underground Parking	23 B3
Ayuntamiento	3 C2				
Iglesia de San Bartolomé	4 C3				
Iglesia de San Felipe	5 C3				
Iglesia de San Pedro	6 B3				
Iglesia de Santiago	7 D2				
Iglesia Prioral de Santa María	8 C2				
Museo de la Ciudad	9 D2				
Necrópolis Romana	10 A3				
Palacio de los Ruedas	11 C2				
Puerta de Córdoba	12 D1				
Puerta de Sevilla	(see 1)				
SLEEPING	(p127)				
Casa de Carmona	13 C2				
Hotel Alcázar de la Reina	14 C2				
Hotel San Pedro	15 B3				
Parador Alcázar del Rey Don Pedro	16 D2				
Pensión Comercio	17 C2				

patio with traces of a Roman temple. An informative leaflet helps you identify the various Carthaginian, Roman, Islamic and Christian stages of the construction of the Alcázar.

Lengthy sections of Carmona's **walls** extend from the Puerta de Sevilla. The **Iglesia de San Pedro** (☎ 954 14 12 77; Calle San Pedro; admission €1.20; ☽ 11am-2pm Thu-Mon), west of the Puerta de Sevilla, is worth a look for its richly decorated baroque interior – and if its tower looks familiar, that's because it's an imitation of Seville's Giralda (p91).

OLD TOWN WALKING TOUR

From the Puerta de Sevilla, Calle Prim leads up to Plaza de San Fernando (or Plaza Mayor), whose 16th-century buildings are painted a quaint variety of colours. Just off this square, the patio of the 17th-century **ayuntamiento** (☎ 954 14 00 11; Calle El Salvador; admission free; ☽ 8am-3pm Mon-Fri, 4-6pm Tue & Thu) contains a large, very fine Roman mosaic showing the Gorgon Medusa.

Calle Martín López de Córdoba leads northeast off Plaza de San Fernando past

the noble **Palacio de los Ruedas** to the splendid **Iglesia Prioral de Santa María** (☎ 954 19 14 82; admission €3; ☽ 9am-2pm & 5.30-7.30pm Mon-Fri, 9am-2pm Sat 1 Apr–20 Aug, 9am-2pm & 5-7pm Mon-Fri, 9am-2pm Sat 22 Sep–31 Mar, closed 21 Aug–21 Sep). Santa María was built, mainly in the 15th and 16th centuries, on the site of the former main mosque in a typical Carmona combination of brick and stone. The Patio de los Naranjos by which you enter (formerly the mosque's ablutions courtyard) has a 6th-century Visigothic calendar carved into one of its pillars. Inside the church, don't miss the fine Gothic pillars and ceiling tracery, and the plateresque main retable.

Behind Santa María is the **Museo de la Ciudad** (City History Museum; ☎ 954 14 01 28; www .museociudad.carmona.org; Calle San Ildefonso 1; adult/child/student/senior €2/1/1/1, free Tue; ☽ 10am-2pm & 4.30-9.30pm Wed-Mon, 10am-2pm Tue 16 Jun–31 Aug, 11am-7pm Wed-Mon, 11am-2pm Tue rest of year). The archaeological and historical displays here, housed in a 16th- to 18th-century mansion, provide extensive background for an exploration of the town. Most impressive are the Roman and Tartessos sections, the latter including a unique collection of large earthenware vessels with Middle Eastern decorative motifs.

From the Iglesia de Santa María, Calle Santa María de Gracia and Calle de Dolores Quintanilla continue to the **Puerta de Córdoba**, an originally Roman gate, with good eastward panoramas.

Moving back uphill and turning southwest down Calle Calatrava, you reach the **Iglesia de Santiago**, with a pretty Mudejar tower. South of here are the ruins of the **Alcázar** fortress, with the luxury parador (state-run hotel) built within its precinct in the 1970s. It was Pedro I who turned the original Almohad fort into a Mudejar-style country palace, similar to his parts of the Seville Alcázar, in the 14th century. The Catholic Monarchs further embellished the Alcázar before it was severely damaged by earthquakes in 1504 and 1755. With great views and a lovely patio, this is a good place to stop for a drink or meal.

Start back along Puerta de Marchena on the southern rim of the town, then head into the tangle of streets to see the 14th-century **Iglesia de San Felipe**, with a pretty brick Mudejar tower and Renaissance façade, and the 15th- to 18th-century **Iglesia de San Bartolomé**.

Sleeping

At all the following except the parador, expect to pay one-third or 50% more during Semana Santa and Seville's Feria de Abril.

Hotel San Pedro (☎ /fax 954 14 16 06; Calle San Pedro 3; r €42; ✖) Shorter on atmosphere than the similarly priced Pensión Comercio, the San Pedro nevertheless provides comfortable, refurbished rooms with TV.

Pensión Comercio (☎ /fax 954 14 00 18; Calle Torre del Oro 56; s/d €32/45; ✖) A lovely tiled old building with a Mudejar-style arch and patio, the Comercio is easily the best bet in its price range, with 14 cosy, clean rooms. The in-house restaurant (closed Sunday) has very reasonable prices (*menú* €6.60).

Hotel Alcázar de la Reina (☎ 954 19 62 00; www.alcazar-reina.es; Plaza de Lasso 2; s/d incl breakfast €100.05/126.80; P ✖ 🖳 🖳) This luxurious, modern, 68-room hotel is built in what was a monastery garden in the old town. One of its two patios holds a pool and there's a good restaurant.

Parador Alcázar del Rey Don Pedro (☎ 954 14 10 10; www.parador.es; Alcázar s/n; s/d €100.05/128.10;

P ✖ 🖳 🖳) Built amid the remains of the Alcázar of Pedro I, in a medieval fortress-palace style that mixes Islamic and Christian influences, Carmona's parador exudes historic atmosphere. The 63 spacious rooms and the public spaces are luxuriously equipped with antique and antique-style furnishings, the restaurant is excellent, and few Andalucian swimming pools are more spectacularly sited.

Casa de Carmona (☎ 954 14 41 51; www.casade carmona.com; Plaza de Lasso 1; r incl breakfast from €160; P ✖ 🖳) A luxury hotel in a beautiful 16th-century palace, the Casa de Carmona has the genuine feel of the aristocratic home that it used to be – four pretty patios, spacious lounges, library, restaurant, antiques, creaking floorboards. The staff are welcoming and each of the 33 rooms is unique and equipped with reading matter, CDs and videos.

Eating

Parador Alcázar del Rey Don Pedro (☎ 954 14 10 10; www.parador.es; Alcázar s/n; menú €26.80) The refectory-style dining room here is one of the best in town. Try the speciality *espinacas de Carmona* (spicy spinach) or *cartuja de perdiz* (partridge and vegetables).

Casa de Carmona (☎ 954 14 41 51; www.casade carmona.com; Plaza de Lasso 1; mains €16-22, menú €24-48) The elegant restaurant at this luxurious hotel serves true haute cuisine with an Andalucian touch, and has a fine wine list.

Restaurante San Fernando (☎ 954 14 35 56; Calle Sacramento 3; mains €12-15, menú €25; ⏰ 1.30-4pm Tue-Sun, 9pm-midnight Tue-Sat) The *menú* (set menu) at this classy restaurant overlooking Plaza de San Fernando offers a taste of five or so different dishes, perhaps beginning with cream of green apple soup followed by stuffed salmon pastries, then pears in red wine to finish. One or two other morsels are fitted in along the way.

Mesón Sierra Mayor (☎ 954 14 44 04; Calle San Ildefonso 1; tapas €1.25-2.25) This place serves excellent tapas and *raciones* in a little patio inside the Museo de la Ciudad building. Ham products and cheese from the hills of Huelva province are the specialities.

Molino de la Romera (☎ 954 14 20 00; Calle Sor Ángela de la Cruz 8; 4-course menú incl 2 drinks €17.50; ⏰ closed Sun evening) Serves hearty, well-prepared Andalucian meals in an interesting 15th-century oil mill building. It has a bar and café if you fancy something light.

Several bars and cafés on and around Plaza de San Fernando do *raciones* and tapas; **Café Bar El Tapeo** (☎ 954 14 43 21; Calle Prim 9; tapas/raciones €1.50/5, menú €9) is friendly, down-to-earth and popular.

Getting There & Away

Casal (☎ 954 41 06 58) runs buses to Carmona from Seville's Prado de San Sebastián bus station (€1.80, 45 minutes, 20 a day Monday to Friday, 10 Saturday, seven Sunday). The stop in Carmona is on Paseo del Estatuto, 300m west of the Puerta de Sevilla. **Alsina Graells** (☎ 954 41 86 11) runs buses to Écija (€3.30, 45 minutes) and Córdoba (€6.75, two hours) at 8am and 2.30pm, from an empty lot outside Puerta de Sevilla.

There's around-the-clock underground parking on Paseo del Estatuto (three/six/10/ 24 hours for €2/4.25/7.25/11.75).

ÉCIJA

pop 38,000 / elevation 110m

Écija (*ess*-i-ha), 53km east along the A4 from Carmona, is known both as *la ciudad de las torres* (the city of towers), for its many fine baroque church towers studded with colourful tiles, and as *la sartén de Andalucía* (the frying pan of Andalucía), for its summer temperatures, which have topped 50°C. With some remarkable archaeological excavations going on, a growing number of monuments and museums to visit, and a spruce-up campaign making the town centre progressively more attractive, Écija is well worth a visit. It owes most of its architectural splendours to the 18th century, when the local gentry, rich from wheat and oil production, splashed out on large mansions, and the church towers were rebuilt after an earthquake in 1757. Écija's long and fascinating earlier history is still coming to light through archaeology.

Information

The helpful **tourist office** (☎ 955 90 29 33; www .ecija.org; Plaza de España 1; 🕑 9.30am-3pm Mon-Fri, to 2pm Jul & Aug, 10.30am-1.30pm Sat, Sun & holidays) is in the front of the ayuntamiento on the central plaza. Its good tourist map will guide you around the sights.

Sights

Recent excavations in the central **Plaza de España** (also called El Salón) have yielded spectacular finds. When the plaza was dug up for an intended underground car park, its western half (nearest the ayuntamiento) turned out to be the site of a 9th- to 12th-century Muslim cemetery with 4000 burials. At the eastern end were Roman baths with a swimming pool stuffed with pieces of sculpture hidden there since the 3rd century AD. At the time of writing the Roman baths were temporarily covered over pending further excavations, while the Muslim cemetery was being explored prior to eventual replacement by the car park.

The **ayuntamiento** (Plaza de España 1; 🕑 9.30am-3pm Mon-Fri, to 2pm Jul & Aug, 10.30am-1.30pm Sat, Sun & holidays) boasts a fine Roman mosaic depicting the punishment of Queen Dirce, tied to the horns of a bull. To see it, ask at the tourist office: a staff member will accompany you and, when possible, show you the art treasures in the building's 19th-century Sala Capitular (Chapter House). Additionally, tourist office staff operate a **cámara oscura** (camera obscura; admission €2.50; 🕑 10.30am-1.30pm), which projects live, moving images of the town onto a screen – a uniquely complete panorama of Écija's wonderful spires, belfries and palaces and the main square below.

The **Iglesia de Santa María** (Plaza Santa María), just off Plaza de España, has one of Écija's finest church towers. A block south from Plaza de España along Calle Cintería is the fascinating **Museo Histórico Municipal** (☎ 955 90 29 19; Plaza de la Constitución; admission free; 🕑 9am-2pm Tue-Sun Jun-Sep; 9.30am-1.30pm & 4.30-6.30pm Tue-Fri, 9am-2pm Sat, Sun & holidays Oct-May), in the handsome 18th-century Palacio de Benamejí. Pride of place goes to the best finds of Roman sculpture from Plaza de España, including a full-sized sculpture of an Amazon (see p129), an athlete's torso and a white marble male head (possibly the god Mars). The rest of the museum has absorbing displays covering the full spectrum of Écija's history, including Iberian sculptures and Roman mosaics.

A couple of blocks east, the huge 18th-century **Palacio de Peñaflor** (Calle Emilio Castelar 26; admission free; 🕑 9am-1.30pm Mon-Fri Jun-Sep, 10am-1pm & 4.30-7.30pm Mon-Fri, 11am-1pm Sat & Sun Oct-May) lines one side of the street with frescoes along its curved façade. Enter to see the grand staircase and the pretty two-storey patio, which houses the town library and two exhibition rooms. Across the street corner, the **Palacio de Valhermoso** has a lovely

Renaissance façade. Turn down Calle Cadenas opposite the Palacio de Valhermoso and head for the elegant tower of the **Iglesia de San Gil** (Calle San Antonio). Just past this church, on the right, is the **Plaza de Armas**, where Écija's 12th-century Islamic Alcazaba (fortress), and, below that, Roman and Tartessos levels, are being excavated. Fine Phoenician ceramics and the only known mosaic depicting the Roman god of the year, Annus, have been found here, and the site is projected to become an *in-situ* museum.

Head back past the Palacio de Valhermoso to check out the towers of the **Iglesia de San Juan** (Plaza San Juan) and the **Convento de San Pablo y Santo Domingo** (Plazuela de Santo Domingo) – the latter hung with a gigantic set of rosary beads – en route to the **Parroquia Mayor de Santa Cruz** (Plazuela de Nuestra Señora del Valle; admission free; 9am-1pm & 6-9pm Mon-Sat, 10am-1pm & 6-9.30pm Sun Jun-Sep; 9am-1pm & 5-9pm Mon-Sat, 10am-1pm & 6-8pm Sun Oct-May). Santa Cruz is Écija's parish church but was once the town's principal mosque and still has traces of Islamic features and some Arabic inscriptions. Arches, fountains and patios from now-roofless parts of the building surround three sides with romantic effect. The main altar is a lovely 5th-century early Christian stone sarcophagus, carved with Greek script and the images of Abraham, Isaac, Christ the Good Shepherd and Daniel. Across the street is the 16th- to 18th-century **Palacio de los Palma** (955 90 20 82; Calle Espíritu Santo 10; admission €3; 10am-2pm), with a porticoed patio and richly decorated halls with Mudejar *artesonados*. From here it's four blocks south back to Plaza de España.

Sleeping & Eating

Pensión Santa Cruz (954 83 02 22; Calle Practicante Romero Gordillo 8; s/d with shared bathroom €13/26) A low-budget but friendly option with ancient furnishings in very ancient rooms around a pretty patio.

Hotel Platería (955 90 27 54; hotelplateria@ret-email.es; Calle Platería 4; s/d €35.30/59.90;) Just a block east of Plaza de España, this hotel is excellent value. Most of the 18 tasteful, good-sized rooms look on to a pleasant central courtyard, and the restaurant, open for all meals, does terrific food at good prices (mains €7 to €11).

Hotel Palacio de los Granados (955 90 10 50; www.palaciogranados.com; Calle Emilio Castelar 42; r/ste incl breakfast €120/160;) This 18th-century mansion set around two patios provides 11 palatial-style rooms and suites, all unique and designed with great care in a traditional-modern mix. Contemporary art decks many walls. Dinner is available on request, and the hotel can organise visits to Écija's archaeological digs, churches and horse breeding centres.

Las Ninfas (955 90 45 92; Calle Elvira; 3-course menú €9; closed Mon;) Around the corner from the Museo Histórico Municipal and decorated with local art treasures, this welcoming restaurant offers excellent Andalucian and local specialities.

Bisturí (954 83 10 66; Plaza de España 23; menú €10 & €15;) Right on the central square, Bisturí has something for everyone, at reasonable prices. Eat out on the *terraza* (terrace) or in the air-conditioned interior restaurant.

Bodegón del Gallego (954 83 26 18; Calle Arcipreste Juan Aparicio 3; mains €10-13) This busy,

---

THE AMAZON OF ÉCIJA

Écija's superb marble figure of an Amazon (legendary female warrior) stands 2.11m high, still bearing traces of her original decorative red paint. Looking surprisingly unwarlike and carved with great delicacy, she is thought to have once stood in Rome with a handful of other Roman copies of the same 5th-century-BC Greek original. The original, by sculptor Policletus, adorned the Temple of Artemis at Ephesus (Turkey), one of the seven wonders of the ancient world. One of the Roman copies was, for some reason, brought to Colonia Augusta Firma Astigi (as Écija was then known) in the 1st century AD and then hidden, along with other prized sculptures, in the swimming pool of the town's forum baths in the 3rd century AD when early Christians were on a pagan-idol-smashing rampage. The pool turned out to be such a secure hiding place that the Écija Amazon did not see the light of day again until excited archaeologists scraped away the earth from the pool on 7 February 2002.

Other copies of Policletus' original, unearthed in Rome in the 17th and 19th centuries, are in museums in Berlin, Copenhagen and New York.

wood-beamed restaurant is the place for fine seafood.

Getting There & Away

Linesur runs up to 11 buses daily to/from Seville (Prado de San Sebastián; €5.05, 1¼ hours). Alsina Graells has three or more buses to Córdoba (€3.40, 1¼ hours), and two or three to Carmona (€3.30, 45 minutes). The **bus stop** (☎ 954 83 02 39) is by the football ground on Avenida de Andalucía, six blocks south of Plaza de España.

OSUNA

pop 18,000 / elevation 330m

Osuna, 91km southeast of Seville, doesn't look much from the A92 but you'll find it a handsome old place with many lovely stone buildings from the 16th to 18th centuries. Several of the most impressive were created by the ducal family of Osuna, one of Spain's richest since the 16th century.

Information

On the central Plaza Mayor, the **Oficina Municipal de Turismo** (☎ 954 81 57 32; www.ayto-osuna .es; ☼ 9am-2pm Mon-Sat) and the **Asociación Turístico Cultural Ossuna** (☎ 954 81 28 52; ☼ 10am-2pm & 5-8pm Mon-Fri, 10am-2pm Sat & Sun) provide tourist information and hand out useful guides detailing the town's monuments in various languages. The Asociación Turístico can also provide English-, French- or Spanish-speaking guides (per half/full day €50/100).

Sights

PLAZA MAYOR

The leafy square has the partly modernised 16th-century **ayuntamiento** on one side, a large **market building** on the other, and the 16th-century church of the **Convento de la Concepción** at the end.

BAROQUE MANSIONS

You can't go inside most of Osuna's mansions, but the façades of a few are worth hunting out. One is the **Palacio de los Cepeda** (Calle de la Huerta), behind the town hall, with rows of Churrigueresque columns topped by stone halberdiers holding the Cepeda family coat of arms. It's now a courthouse. The 1737 portal of the **Palacio de Puente Hermoso** (Palacio de Govantes y Herdara; Calle Sevilla 44), a couple of blocks west of Plaza Mayor, has twisted pillars encrusted with grapes and vine leaves.

Moving north from Plaza Mayor up Calle Caballos and its continuation Calle Carrera, you pass the **Iglesia de Santo Domingo** (1531) before you reach the corner of Calle San Pedro. The **Cilla del Cabildo Colegial** (Calle San Pedro 16) bears a sculpted representation of Seville's Giralda, flanked by the Seville martyrs Santa Justa and Santa Rufina. Further down, the **Palacio del Marqués de La Gomera** (Calle San Pedro 20) has elaborate clustered pillars, with the family shield at the top of the façade. This is now a hotel (p131) – step inside for a drink.

MUSEO ARQUEOLÓGICO

The Torre del Agua, a 12th-century Almohad tower, just east uphill from the Plaza Mayor, houses Osuna's **Museo Arqueológico** (Archaeological Museum; ☎ 954 81 12 07; Plaza de la Duquesa; admission €1.60; ☼ 11.30am-1.30pm & 4.30-6.30pm Tue-Sun Oct-Apr; 11.30am-1.30pm & 5-7pm Tue-Sun May-Sep, closed Sun afternoon Jul & Aug). The collection of mainly Iberian and Roman artefacts found in the vicinity is well worth seeing: it includes copies of the celebrated Iberian Toro de Osuna (Osuna bull) and the Roman Osuna bronzes, whose originals are in the Louvre in Paris and Spain's national archaeological museum in Madrid.

COLEGIATA & AROUND

Osuna's most impressive monuments overlook the centre from the hill above the Museo Arqueológico. The **Colegiata de Santa María de la Asunción** (☎ 954 81 04 44; Plaza de la Encarnación; admission by guided tour only €2; ☼ 10am-1.30pm & 3.30-6.30pm Tue-Sun Oct-Apr, 10am-1.30pm & 4-7pm Tue-Sun May-Sep, closed Sun afternoon Jul & Aug), a large 16th-century former collegiate church, contains a wealth of fine art collected by the Duques de Osuna, descendants of its founder, Juan Téllez Girón, the Conde de Ureña.

In the main body of the church are José de Ribera's *Cristo de la Expiración,* a marvellous example of this 17th-century painter's use of light/dark contrast; an elaborate baroque main retable; a contrasting 14th-century retable in the Capilla de la Virgen de los Reyes; and, in the Capilla de la Inmaculada, a Crucifixion sculpture of 1623 by Juan de Mesa. The church's sacristy contains four more Riberas. The tour also includes the lugubrious underground Sepulcro Ducal, created in 1548 with its own chapel as the family vault of the Os-unas, who are entombed in wall niches.

Opposite the Colegiata is the **Monasterio de la Encarnación** (☎ 954 81 11 21; Plaza de la Encarnación; admission €2; ⊙ same as Colegiata), now Osuna's museum of religious art and well worth a visit. The 18th-century tiles in the cloister, representing the five senses, the seasons, the Alameda de Hércules in Seville and diverse biblical, hunting, bullfighting and monastic scenes, are among the most beautiful of all Sevillan tilework, and the monastery church is richly decked with baroque sculpture and art. One upstairs room has a cute collection of 18th-century child Christs.

On the hill-top just above the Colegiata is the **Universidad de Osuna**, a square building with pointed towers and a stately Renaissance patio, founded in 1548 by the Conde de Ureña to help combat Protestantism. It's now an outpost of Seville University, providing courses in nursing and business studies. Down behind the Monasterio de la Encarnación, the 17th-century **Iglesia de la Merced** (Cuesta Marruecos) has a lovely baroque tower and portal.

Sleeping & Eating

Hostal 5 Puertas (☎ 954 81 12 43; Calle Carrera 79; s/d €22/41; 🅿) The 14 smallish but decent rooms here have TV, phone and heating. Some are let to university students.

Hostal Esmeralda (☎ 955 82 10 73; www.hostal-esmeralda.com; Calle Tesorero 7; s/d with shower cubicle & washbasin €21/33, with bathroom €24/36; 🅿 🖳) Clean, friendly and family-run, the Esmeralda is about 200m south of Plaza Mayor. Rooms are simple and reasonably sized, with TV, and open on to tiled passageways off a small sky-lit patio.

Hostal Caballo Blanco (☎ 954 81 01 84; Calle Granada 1; s/d €28.35/44.40; 🅿 🅿) An old coaching inn on the corner of Calle Carrera, 350m north of Plaza Mayor, the friendly 'White Horse Inn' has courtyard parking and 13 comfy rooms in deep red or blue, with reading lamps and tasteful prints. There's a restaurant here too (open Monday to Saturday).

Hotel Palacio Marqués de la Gomera (☎ 954 81 22 23; www.hotelpalaciodelmarques.com; Calle San Pedro 20; s/d €77.05/96.30; 🅿 🅿 🖳) This luxury hotel occupies one of Osuna's finest baroque mansions, with 20 large, lovely and varied rooms and suites around a beautiful, arcaded, two-storey central patio. Its

elegant restaurant, **La Casa del Marqués** (mains €9-18), provides a tempting Andalucian and Spanish menu, while its **Asador de Osuna** grill specialises in charcoal-grilled meats.

Restaurante Doña Guadalupe (☎ 954 81 05 58; Plaza Guadalupe 6; 4-course menú €12.30, mains €11-16; ⊙ closed Tue & 1-15 Aug; 🅿) On a small square between Calle Quijada and Calle Gordillo (both off Calle Carrera), Doña Guadalupe serves up quality Andalucian fare from partridge with rice to wild asparagus casserole. There's a good list of Spanish wines too. Sit in green wicker chairs in the bar area, in the large restaurant behind, or out in the courtyard.

El Mesón del Duque (☎ 954 81 28 45; Plaza de la Duquesa 2; raciones €8-11) Enjoy well prepared Andalucian dishes on the terrace opposite the Museo Arqueológico, with views up to the Colegiata.

Getting There & Away

The **bus station** (☎ 954 81 01 46; Avenida de la Constitución) is 500m southeast of Plaza Mayor. Up to 11 daily buses run to/from Seville (Prado de San Sebastián; €5.65, 1¼ hours). Four daily go to Fuente de Piedra (€3.90, 45 minutes) and Antequera (€4.40, 1¼ hours), and two each to Málaga (€7.45, 2½ hours) and Granada (€10.40, 3¼ hours).

Six trains a day run to/from Seville (€5.80 to €6.55, one hour) and three each to/from Antequera (€5.55, one hour), Granada (€11.80, 2½ hours) and Málaga (€7.85, 1½ hours): the **train station** (Avenida de la Estación) is 1km southwest of the centre.

PARQUE NATURAL SIERRA NORTE

This 1648-sq-km natural park, stretching right across the north of Sevilla province, is beautiful, rolling, often wild Sierra Morena country. It's an ever-changing landscape of green valleys and hills, woodlands, rivers and atmospheric old towns and villages with Islamic-era forts or castles, part-Mudejar churches and narrow, zig-zagging white streets. It's a nature lover's delight that, so far, has been discovered by few foreigners. The spring wild flowers are among the most beautiful you'll see in Andalucía.

At least 14 walks of a few hours each are signposted in various areas. The routes are shown on the IGN/Junta de Andalucía 1:100,000 map *Parque Natural Sierra Norte*, and described in Spanish in the booklet *Cuaderno de Senderos*, available at the Centro de Interpretación El Robledo visitors centre (p134).

The two main towns, Cazalla de la Sierra and Constantina, lie 20km apart at the centre of the park.

EL PEDROSO
pop 2500 / elevation 415m

A pleasant village of broad cobbled streets, El Pedroso lies 16km south of Cazalla de la Sierra on the A432 from Seville. The 15th-century **Iglesia de Nuestra Señora de la Consolación** in the centre contains a 1608 *Inmaculada* by the great sculptor Juan Martínez Montañés (in the chapel to the right in front of the main altar). The **Sendero del Arroyo de las Cañas**, a 10km marked walking route around the flattish country west of El Pedroso, beginning opposite Bar Triana on the western side of town, is one of the prettiest walks in the park. It goes through a landscape strewn with boulders and, in spring, gorgeous wild flowers.

The eight-room **Hotel Casa Montehuéznar** (☎ 954 88 90 00; www.montehueznar.com; Avenida de la Estación 15; s/d incl breakfast €35/55; ✸) provides comfortable rooms with attractive wooden furnishings, around the upper floor of a pretty patio. The hotel is in the street leading up towards the village centre (500m away) opposite the train station. Its good restaurant is normally only open Friday to Sunday: at other times **Bar-Restaurante Serranía** (☎ 954 88 96 03; Avenida de la Estación 30; platos combinados €5-8), at the bottom of the street, is a reasonable fallback.

Restaurante Los Álamos (☎ 954 88 96 11; Carretera Cantillana Km 29.5; meat raciones €6), on the A432 just south of El Pedroso, makes a good lunch stop. You can dine al fresco on a large veranda looking out on a garden with lots of birds. Meats are a speciality and the local cheese is superb.

CAZALLA DE LA SIERRA
pop 5200 / elevation 600m

This attractive little white town, spread around a hill-top 85km northeast of Seville, has a great little selection of places to stay.

The site of an Islamic castle, it was conquered by Fernando III in 1247. In the 16th and 17th centuries Cazalla was celebrated for its wines and brandies, which were exported to the Americas.

Information

A new tourist office is being prepared on Plaza Mayor, next to the Iglesia de la Consolación. In the meantime tourist information is available at the **ayuntamiento** (☎ 954 88 42 36; Plaza Doctor Nosea s/n; ✷ 8am-3pm Mon-Fri). There are plenty of banks with ATMs on the central pedestrian street, Calle La Plazuela, and nearby on Calle Llana, the main road passing through town.

Sights

The outstanding building in Cazalla's tangle of old-fashioned streets is the fortresslike **Iglesia de Nuestra Señora de la Consolación** (Plaza Mayor; ✷ Mass 7.30pm Tue-Sat, noon Sun), a mainly 14th-and-15th-century construction in the region's typical red brick and yellow stone. Badly damaged in the civil war, it's actually more impressive outside than inside.

La Cartuja de Cazalla (☎ 954 88 45 16; adult/child €3/1; ✷ 9am-2pm & 4-8pm) is a large 15th-century monastery in a beautiful, secluded nook of the Sierra Morena, 4km from Cazalla (take the signposted turn-off the A455 Constantina road, 2.5km from Cazalla). Built on the site of an Islamic mill and mosque, the monastery fell into ruin in the 19th century. In 1977 it was bought by art lover Carmen Ladrón de Guevara, who is devotedly restoring it, in part as an arts centre – it has a ceramics' workshop and art gallery and the restored church functions as a concert hall. A good guesthouse is part of the project (see p133).

Activities
WALKING

Two tracks lead from Cazalla down to the Huéznar Valley and by combining them you can enjoy a round trip of 9km. They pass through typical Sierra Norte evergreen oak woodlands, olive groves and small cultivated plots, plus the odd chestnut wood and vineyard.

One track is the **Sendero de las Laderas**, which starts at El Chorrillo fountain on the eastern edge of Cazalla at the foot of Calle Parras. A 'Sendero Las Laderas 900m' sign on Paseo El Moro, just down from the

Posada del Moro, directs you to this starting point. The path leads down to the Puente de los Tres Ojos bridge on the Río Huéznar, from where you go up the western bank of the river a short way, then head west under the Puente del Castillejo railway bridge (first take a break at the picnic area on the far bank, if you like) and return to Cazalla by the **Camino Viejo de la Estación** (Old Station Track). You can also join this walk from Cazalla-Constantina station by following the 'Molino del Corcho' track down the Huéznar for 1km to the Puente del Castillejo.

HORSE RIDING

Experienced local horseman Ángel Conde runs the recommended stables **Cuadras Al Paso** (☎ 689-944451; www.al-paso.com; Plaza JM López-Cepero 3; per hr/day/week €18/100/600) with home-bred mounts that are a mix of Andalucian, Arab and English thoroughbreds.

Courses

Turismo Rural Hidalgo (☎ /fax 954 88 35 81; www.turismoruralhidalgo.com; Calle Virgen del Monte 19; courses incl hostal accommodation per week €260-310), run by a Dutch couple resident in Cazalla, organises an almost year-round programme of one-to-three-week workshop courses in flamenco dance and guitar, *sevillana* dance, painting, ceramics, Andalucian cooking and Spanish language, including some courses for kids.

Sleeping & Eating

Posada del Moro (☎ /fax 954 88 48 58; Paseo El Moro s/n; s/d incl breakfast €50/60; 🍴 🐾) Near the southern entrance to the town, this is a very welcoming hotel run by two sisters and their amiable staff. Most of the good-sized, comfortable rooms (with red marble floors and pretty cork-topped furnishings) overlook an appealing garden. The restaurant (mains €10 to €15) cooks up local specialities such as wild asparagus and assorted game. You can also eat economically in the convivial bar.

Las Navezuelas (☎ 954 88 47 64; www.lasnavezuelas.com; s/d incl breakfast €45.60/63.15, 4-person apt €117.70; ⚘ closed early Jan–late Feb; 🅿 🐾) This beautiful 16th-century farm in the countryside near Cazalla was once a winery and later an olive-oil mill. Human habitation on the site goes back to time immemorial. It's an exceptionally charming place to stay, from the friendly owners and the tranquil rural setting to the assorted tastefully simple rooms and apart-

ments and the excellent meals based on home-grown produce. Good walks start right here and your Italian host, Luca, can set up great bird-watching, horse riding and other activities. Altogether this is one of the best places to stay in Andalucía. From Cazalla, go 2km south towards Seville, then 1km east down a dirt road (signposted).

Hospedería de la Cartuja (☎ 954 88 45 16; www.skill.es/cartuja; s/d incl breakfast €58.85/96.30, dinner €21.40; 🅿 🍴 🐾) The guesthouse at the beautiful Cartuja de Cazalla (p132) has eight modern rooms hung with work by former resident artists, plus suites and a small house for families. There are two inviting pools, and riding stables on site (ride/class per hour €20/15). Much of the fare at the excellent dinner table, in the monastery's old pilgrims' hostel, is home-grown. Room rates go down if you stay longer than one night.

Palacio de San Benito (☎ 954 88 33 36; www.palaciodesanbenito.com; Paseo El Moro; r €128.40-224.70; 🅿 🍴) This luxurious, antique-filled boutique hotel occupies what was a 15th-century hermitage and pilgrims' hostel and still includes a Mudejar church. All 10 ultra-comfortable rooms are completely different. The restaurant (mains €14 to €20), open to all, serves all meals, with an emphasis on country specialities such as venison, partridge and salmon.

Also recommended:

Bodeguita Que Me Deje (Plaza JM López-Cepero y Muru; raciones €5-6) One of the best bets for tapas and *raciones* near the central pedestrian street, Calle La Plazuela.

Casa Palacio (☎ 955 60 02 07, 677-329526; casapala@terra.es; Calle Llana 2; 2-person apt €60; 🍴) Good apartments in a 16th-century mansion where Felipe V lodged during his 1730 summer holiday in Cazalla.

Hostal Castro Martínez (☎ 954 88 40 39; Calle Virgen del Monte 36; r €29-35; 🍴) Budget accommodation in the town centre; it can be noisy.

Shopping

Buy Cazalla's celebrated *anisados* (aniseed-based liqueurs), at the handicrafts shop **La Artesa** (Calle La Plazuela 1) or **La Destilería** (Calle Llana 1). The *guinda* (wild cherry) variety is a rich, heart-warming concoction.

HUÉZNAR VALLEY

The Río Huéznar (or Hucsna) runs north–south through the countryside about halfway between Cazalla de la Sierra and Constantina. The A455 Cazalla–Constantina road crosses the river just east of the Cazalla y Constantina train station. A 1km drivable track leads downstream from here to the Puente del Castillejo railway bridge and the Área Recreativa Molino del Corcho (p132). Upstream, the river is paralleled by the SE168 road, which runs 13km to the village of San Nicolás del Puerto. The **Isla Margarita picnic area** is about 1km up the river from the station. From Isla Margarita a walking path leads up the eastern side of the river all the way to San Nicolás del Puerto: after about 4km it meets the course of a disued railway running to San Nicolás and the old mines of Cerro del Hierro – you can walk along this instead of the path, if you like. Two kilometres before San Nicolás are the **Cascadas del Huesna**, a series of powerful waterfalls on the river.

There are three camping grounds along this stretch of the river:

Área de Acampada El Martinete (☎ 955 88 65 83; Carretera SE168 Km 12; camping per person/tent/car €3.20/3.50/free; **P**) Shady site 2km from San Nicolás; short paths lead to the Cascadas del Huesna and the good Restaurante El Martinete (*raciones* €7).

Camping La Fundición (☎ 955 95 41 17; Carretera SE168 Km 2; camping per person/tent/car €3.45/2.55/1.65; **P** **☒**) Large, shady site on the river's western bank, 1km up from Isla Margarita, with a restaurant, pool and bar.

Camping Batán de las Monjas (☎ 955 88 65 48; Carretera SE168 Km 7; camping per person/tent/car €2.80/2.80/2.70; **P**) Twenty-tent farm site east of the river; access by 1km vehicle track from the SE168, fording the river.

CONSTANTINA
pop 6900 / elevation 555m

The likable valley town of Constantina is the 'capital' of the Sierra Norte. The Parque Natural Sierra Norte's visitors centre, the **Centro de Interpretación El Robledo** (☎ 955 88 15 97; Carretera Constantina-El Pedroso Km 1; ☒ 10am-2pm Tue-Thu & Sun, 6-8pm Fri, 10am-2pm & 6-8pm Sat Oct-Jun; 11am-1pm Tue & Thu, 6-8pm Fri, 10am-2pm & 6-8pm Sat & Sun Jul-Sep; closed 1 & 6 Jan, extra hours some holidays) is 1km west along the A452 El Pedroso road from the southern end of Constantina. It has interesting displays on the park's flora, fauna and history, and a clearly labelled botanical garden of Andalucian plants that is a picture in spring and well worth a 20- to 30-minute wander. Also in the garden are a few enclosures with birds of prey that are unfit to be returned to the wild.

Buses stop at **Bar Gregorio** (☎ 955 88 10 43; Calle El Peso 9) in the town centre. There are several banks with ATMs on the pedestrianised main street, Calle Mesones.

Sights & Activities

The western side of Constantina is topped by a ruined Almoravid-era **Islamic fort** – worth the climb for the views alone. Below are the medieval streets and 18th-century mansions of the **Barrio de la Morería** district. The **Iglesia de Santa María de la Encarnación** (Plaza Llano del Sol), in the centre, is a Mudejar church

---

DETOUR: LA CAPITANA

If you're heading north into Extremadura, or just fancy a day out from Cazalla or Constantina, don't miss the magnificent vistas from the highest point in Sevilla province, La Capitana (959m).

Head north on the A432 from Cazalla or the SE163 from Constantina, pass Alanís and continue 11km along the A432 to Guadalcanal. At a junction as you enter this village, follow the 'Sendero de la Capitana' sign pointing to the right up a bypass road. After 1.5km, above the village, turn left down a minor road, then almost immediately right up an unpaved road with another 'Sendero de la Capitana' sign. Though signposted as a *sendero* (footpath) this is perfectly drivable, with a little care, in a car of normal clearance. Follow the track as it climbs in a general northwest direction along the Sierra del Viento (Windy Range), taking the major track at all forks. Expansive views open out as you pass an observatory on the left after 1.6km and TV towers up on the right after 2.1km and 4.3km. Keep your eyes open for vultures and birds of prey roaming the updraughts along this very breezy ridge. Some 500m after passing below the second TV tower you pass through a gate: just beyond it, park and follow the 'Mirador de la Sierra del Viento 300m' sign to the hill-top ahead of you. This is the summit of La Capitana, where the views in every direction are limited only by atmospheric conditions. To the south extend the many ranges of the Sierra Norte, to the north the endless plains of Extremadura. If you're lucky you'll have the entire hill to yourself and the only sounds you'll hear will be wind, birds and the bleating of sheep.

Return the way you came.

with a 16th-century plateresque portal and a belfry (popular with nesting storks) that was added in 1567 by Hernán Ruiz, who also did the one atop the Giralda in Seville.

The **Sendero Los Castañares**, a 7km marked walk, starts from the north end of Paseo de la Alameda in the north of town. It takes you up through thick chestnut woods to a hill-top viewpoint, then back into Constantina below the fort (about two hours, total).

Sleeping & Eating

Hotel San Blas (☎ 955 88 00 77; www.fp-hoteles.com; Calle Miraflores 4; s/d €44.95/62.05 Aug, Semana Santa & Sat all year, €33.15/46 other times; ✷ ☒) The large, tasteful rooms at this friendly, modern hotel have big bathrooms and either look out towards the castle or to the pool area. It's 200m off the main road from Cazalla and is clearly signposted.

Hotel Casa Rural Las Erillas (☎ 955 88 17 90; www .constantina.org/erillas; s/d incl breakfast €60/80; ℗ ☒) Found about 500m along the Sendero Los Castañares, these comfortable farmhouse lodgings stand in lovely gardens, with a pool. Good meals are available, using plenty of local produce.

Mesón de la Abuela Carmen (☎ 955 88 00 95; Paseo de la Alameda 39; raciones €7-11; ✷ 9.30am-late Tue-Sun) Locals flock into this large, barnlike eating hall near the northern end of town for its succulent grilled meats; salads and some sea-food provide options for noncarnivores.

Bodeguita Tomás (Calle El Peso 1; tapas/media-raciones €1.75/3.50) Come here, next to the bus stop, for tempting tapas of venison or fried potatoes and Roquefort.

GETTING THERE & AROUND
Bus

Linesur (☎ 954 98 82 20) runs buses from Seville (Plaza de Armas) three times daily (twice on Saturday and Sunday) to Cazalla de la Sierra (€5.45, 1¾ to 2¼ hours) and Guadalcanal (€6.90, 2¾ hours), and three to six times daily to El Pedroso (€4.65, 1¼ hours) and Constantina (€5.45, 1¾ hours).

Train

Cazalla y Constantina station is on the A455 Cazalla–Constantina road, 7km from Cazalla, 12km from Constantina. Two trains daily rattle to/from Seville (€4.35, 1¾ hours). All stop at El Pedroso en route and continue to/from Guadalcanal, and one goes to/from Zafra, Mérida and Cáceres in Extremadura. The 4.30pm train from Seville arrives at Cazalla y Constantina station at 6.22pm – in time to catch the Constantina–Cazalla bus that passes the station at about 7.30pm Monday to Friday – but you should con-firm current schedules.

Huelva
Province

Disconnected and distant, Huelva (*wel*-vah) province is the poor relation of its famous and glamorous neighbour, Seville. With a motorway beating a path to Portugal's door in the west it can also feel like the south of the province is a casualty of 'out-of-sight, out-of-mind' development. However, Huelva nurtures ancient roots – it is reputedly the site of the mysterious 7th century BC Tartessos civilisation, whose founding city is thought to lie somewhere amid the southern flood plains. The Tartessians grew rich on the mining of copper and bronze inland at the Río Tinto mines. Succeeding civilisations prospered from the metal-rich mines, and in recent times a global mining company even took its name from the rust red river, which cuts its bleeding path down to the southern ports of the Atlantic.

But the province is not all industry and iron ore: on the contrary, the rich red soil, soggy flood plains and benevolent climatic conditions make it the site of one of Andalucía's, and Europe's, foremost nature reserves – a 500-sq-km marshland which sees up to 80% of Europe's migratory birds. To the north a short drive transports you to the beautiful Parque Natural Sierra de Aracena y Picos de Aroche, a huge area of verdant hill country scattered with unprettified *pueblos blancos* (white villages), many still supporting an age-old way of rural life.

Lacking the drama of Seville, the romance of Granada and the energy of Málaga, Huelva presents the traveller with the authentic face of busy, down-to-earth Andalucía, a province of workers and farmers whose lives are little altered by the tourism bandwagon to the east.

HIGHLIGHTS

- Witnessing Andalucía's largest devotional pilgrimage, when over a million faithful Christians converge on **El Rocío** (p150) for huge religious celebrations
- Soaking up the peaceful, marshy hinterland of the **Parque Nacional de Doñana** (p148)
- Walking in Columbus' footsteps in the **Lugares Colombinos** (p143)
- Stepping back in time in the farming towns of the **Parque Natural Sierra de Aracena y Picos de Aroche** (p159) and indulging in some regional gastronomy at the **Finca Buen Vino** (p162)
- Losing your hat on the wild, windy beaches of the **Costa de la Luz** (p146)
- Exploring the mini-*mezquita* (mosque) of **Almonaster la Real** (p161), without the crowds

| POPULATION: 465,000 | HUELVA AVERAGE DAILY HIGH: JAN/AUG 12°C/24°C | ALTITUDE RANGE: 0m–913m |

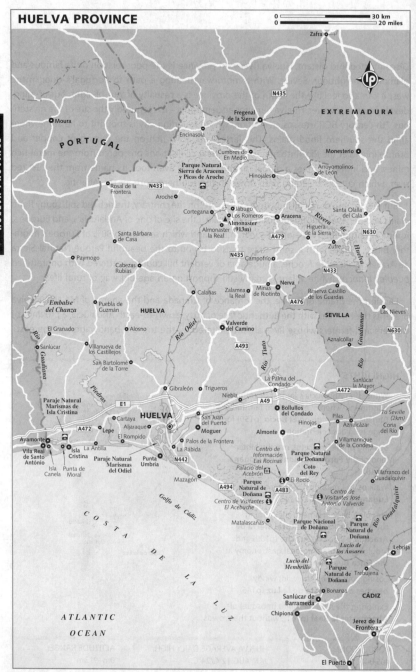

HUELVA PROVINCE

0 ——— 30 km
0 ——— 20 miles

Zafra

N435

Fregenal
de la Sierra

EXTREMADURA

Moura

PORTUGAL

Encinasola

Cumbres de
En Medio

Monesterio

Parque Natural
Sierra de Aracena
y Picos de Aroche

Hinojales

Arroyomolinos
de León

Rosal de la
Frontera

N433

Aroche

Jabugo
Los Romeros
Almonaster
(913m)

Aracena

Santa Olalla
del Cala

Cortegana

Almonaster
la Real

Higuera
de la Sierra

N630

Rivera

de

Santa Bárbara
de Casa

A479

Zufre

Huelva

Paymogo

N435

Campofrío

Cabezas
Rubias

N433

Embalse
del Chanza

El Granado

Puebla de
Guzmán

HUELVA

Calañas

Zalamea
la Real

Minas
de Riotinto

Nerva

Reserva Castillo
de los Guardas

A476

SEVILLA

Las Nieves

Río Odiel

Valverde
del Camino

Aznalcóllar

N630

Sanlúcar

Alosno

A493

Río

Guadiamar

Río Guadiana

Villanueva de
los Castillejos

San Bartolomé
de la Torre

Río Tinto

La Palma del
Condado

Sanlúcar
la Mayor

Piedras

Gibraleón

Trigueros

Niebla

A472

Paraje Natural
Marismas de
Isla Cristina

E1

A49

Bollullos
del Condado

Pilas

To Seville
(2km)

Ayamonte

Cartaya

A472

Lepe

HUELVA

San Juan
del Puerto

Moguer

Hinojos

Aznalcázar

Coria
del Río

Vila Real
de Santo
António

Isla
Cristina

La Antilla

El Rompido

Aljaraque

Palos de la Frontera

Almonte

Villamanrique
de la Condesa

Isla
Canela

Punta de
Moral

Paraje Natural
Marismas
del Odiel

Punta
Umbría

N442

La Rábida

Centro de
Información
Las Rocinas

Parque Natural
de Doñana

Villafranco del
Guadalquivir

Mazagón

A494

Palacio del
Acebrón

Coto
del Rey

El Rocío

Centro de
Visitantes José
Antonio Valverde

Río Guadalquivir

Parque
Natural de
Doñana

A483

Centro de Visitantes
El Acebuche

COSTA

Matalascañas

Parque Nacional
de Doñana

Parque
Natural de
Doñana

Lucio de
los Ánsares

Lebrija

DE

Golfo de Cádiz

Lucio del
Membrillo

Parque
Natural de
Doñana

Trebujena

LA

Bonanza

CÁDIZ

LUZ

Sanlúcar de
Barrameda

ATLANTIC

OCEAN

Chipiona

Jerez de la
Frontera

El Puerto

HUELVA

pop 145,000
The provincial capital of Huelva is a work-worn port lying between the Odiel and Tinto estuaries. Industry dominates the approaches to the city, but central Huelva is a likable place. Its history dates back an impressive 3000 years to the Phoenician town of Onuba, when its location at the mouth of the estuary made it a natural base for the export of inland minerals to the Mediterranean. Later expanded and developed by the Romans, the city grew rich on the mineral trade and initially dominated the gold and silver routes from the newly discovered American colonies. However, by 1503 it had lost this monopoly to the political heavyweight, Seville. Although devastated in the 1755 Lisbon earthquake, Huelva's subsequent renaissance and relentless industrialisation have produced a thoroughly modern and unsentimental city.

ORIENTATION

Huelva's central area is about 1km square, with the main bus station on Calle Doctor Rubio at its western edge, and the train station on Avenida de Italia at its southern edge. Plaza de las Monjas is the central square. From here the main street, Avenida Martín Alonso Pinzón (also called Gran Vía), leads east and becomes Alameda Sundheim. Parallel to Avenida Pinzón, one block south, is a long, narrow, pedestrianised shopping street that runs through several names, from Calle Concepción to Calle Berdigón.

INFORMATION

Bookshops
English Bookshop (☎ 959 28 10 94; Calle San Cristóbal 11) Sells bestselling fiction, guides and children's books.

Emergency
Policía Local (Local Police; ☎ 959 24 84 22; Avenida Tomás Domínguez 2) Opposite the main post office.
Policía Nacional (National Police; Avenida de Italia (☎ 959 24 84 22); Paseo Santa Fe (☎ 959 24 05 92)

Internet Access
Cyber Huelva (Calle Amado de Lázaro; per hr €1.50; ☯ 11am-2.30pm & 5-10.30pm Mon-Thu, to midnight Fri & Sat, 4.30-10.30pm Sun)

Left Luggage
There is a **baggage deposit** (per day €3; ☯ 8am-8pm Mon-Fri) at the main bus station, in the form of lockers. There are also lockers at the main train station, which are open similar hours.

Medical Services
Hospital General Juan Ramón Jiménez (☎ 959 20 10 88, emergency ☎ 959 20 10 00; Ronda Exterior Norte) The main general hospital, 4km north of the city centre.
Red Cross (Cruz Roja; ☎ 959 26 12 11; Paseo Buenos Aires s/n) Opposite the cathedral, offering emergency treatment.

Money
There are banks and ATMs all over the town centre. The main bus station has an ATM and an exchange booth, where you can change cash or travellers cheques Monday to Saturday.

Post
Post office (Avenida Tomás Domínguez 1; ☯ 8.30am-8.30pm Mon-Fri, 9.30am-2pm Sat)

Tourist Information
Tourist office (☎ 959 25 74 03; www.ayuntamiento huelva.es in Spanish; Avenida de Alemania 12; ☯ 9am-7pm Mon-Fri, 9am-2.30pm Sat) A few steps from the main bus station. The English-speaking staff have a great deal of information.

DANGERS & ANNOYANCES

Like most port cities Huelva can seem rough and ready at times, but most people are open and very friendly. There are a few dodgy characters around, however, and there's a seriously unhappy drugs scene, the results of which are sometimes bleakly visible in off-centre areas. Take care of belongings wherever you go and leave nothing in parked cars.

SIGHTS

Despite a past that is much-vaunted, Huelva's sights are few and far between. The city's main museum, **Museo de Huelva** (☎ 959 25 93 00; Alameda Sundheim 13; admission free; ☯ 3-8pm Tue, 9am-8pm Wed-Sat, 9am-2pm Sun) concentrates on its prehistoric pedigree, and houses an exhibition on the Tartessos civilisation (see p21) whose origins, along with its mythical city of Atlantida, are thought to be buried somewhere in the flood plains surrounding Huelva. The best exhibit – the Roman water wheel, powered by slaves and used to drain the Río Tinto mines – is now in storage and it is unclear when it might be on view again.

The mines (see p155) and their history represent a curious legacy of British expatriate life. Owned by Rio Tinto, British employees effectively colonised Huelva in the late 19th century, housed in Victorian-style suburbs built by the company. One such suburb is the **Barrio Reina Victoria** (Queen Victoria District) just off the eastern end of Alameda Sundheim.

A more surreal stroll is along the **Muelle Río Tinto**, an impressive iron pier curving out into the Odiel estuary about 500m south

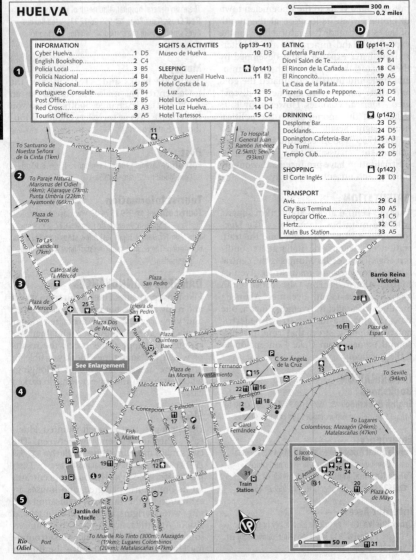

HUELVA

0 ————— 300 m
0 ————— 0.2 miles

INFORMATION	
Cyber Huelva	1 D5
English Bookshop	2 C4
Policia Local	3 B5
Policia Nacional	4 B4
Policia Nacional	5 B5
Portuguese Consulate	6 B4
Post Office	7 B5
Red Cross	8 A3
Tourist Office	9 A5

SIGHTS & ACTIVITIES	(pp139–41)
Museo de Huelva	10 D3

SLEEPING	(p141)
Albergue Juvenil Huelva	11 B2
Hotel Costa de la Luz	12 B5
Hotel Los Condes	13 D4
Hotel Luz Huelva	14 D4
Hotel Tartessos	15 C4

EATING	(pp141–2)
Cafetería Parral	16 C4
Dioni Salón de Te	17 B4
El Rincon de la Cañada	18 C4
El Rinconcito	19 A5
La Casa de la Patata	20 D5
Pizzeria Camillo e Peppone	21 D5
Taberna El Condado	22 C4

DRINKING	(p142)
Desplome Bar	23 D5
Docklands	24 D5
Donington Cafeteria-Bar	25 A3
Pub Tumi	26 D5
Templo Club	27 D5

SHOPPING	(p142)
El Corte Inglés	28 D3

TRANSPORT	
Avis	29 C4
City Bus Terminal	30 A5
Europcar Office	31 C5
Hertz	32 C5
Main Bus Station	33 A5

To Santuario de Nuestra Señora de la Cinta (1km)

Avenida de Manuel Siurot

Avenida Marchena Colombo

Calle JS Elcano

Avenida de Andalucía

To Hospital General Juan Ramón Jiménez (2.5km); Seville (93km)

To Paraje Natural Marismas del Odiel (4km); Aljaraque (7km); Punta Umbría (22km); Ayamonte (66km)

Plaza de Toros

To Las Candelas (7km)

Paseo de la Independencia

Catedral de la Merced

Plaza de la Merced

Av de Buenos Aires

C Fray Junípero Serra

C San Sebastián

Plaza San Pedro

Iglesia de San Pedro

Plaza Pablo Rada

Av. Federico Mayo

Barrio Reina Victoria

28

Plaza Dos de Mayo

C Ginés Martín

See Enlargement

Calle Doctor Rubio

Avenida de Alemania

Calle Puerto

Méndez Núñez

Avenida Pablo Rada

Paseo Santa Fe

Plaza Quintero Baez

Vía Paisajista

Plaza de las Monjas

C Fernando Católico

Ayuntamiento

15

Av Martín Alonso Pinzón

22 16

2

18

29

Via Cineasta Francisco Elías

10

Plaza de España

Alameda Sundheim

14

Miss Whitney

To Seville (94km)

Avenida Escultora

C Sor Ángela de la Cruz

A Sánchez

Avenida de Cádiz

Calle Orta

Calle Puerto

Plus Ultra

C Concepción

C Palacios

Calle Berdigón

C Miguel Redondo

To Lugares Colombinos; Mazagón (24km); Matalascañas (47km)

C Doctor Rubio

C Gravina

Fish Market

C Vázquez López

C Garci Fernández

32

C Jacobo del Barco

23

C Amado

Paseo de Lazaro

26

27

1

24

C Aragón

30

Avenida

Portugal

19

Duque de la Victoria

Amo

12

Calle Vendavala

C Gines Martin

C Palma

20

Plaza Dos de Mayo

31

Train Station

33

9

Avenida Noroeste

Av Sanlúcar de Barrameda

Av Tomás Domínguez

Avenida Sur

5

3

7

Jardín del Muelle

Río Odiel

Port

To Muelle Río Tinto (300m); Mazagón (19km); Lugares Colombinos (20km); Matalascañas (47km)

0 ————— 50 m

Calle La

Calle de la Independencia

C Isaac Peral

21

of the port. It was built for the Rio Tinto Company in the 1870s by George Barclay Bruce, a British disciple of tower specialist Gustave Eiffel.

Two kilometres north of the city centre, off Avenida de Manuel Siurot, is the **Santuario de Nuestra Señora de la Cinta** (☎ 959 25 93 00; admission free; ✆ 8am-6pm), a chapel where Columbus is reported to have prayed before setting off. The event is portrayed in tiles by artist Daniel Zuloaga and the chapel's hilltop position affords good views over the Odiel estuary and the wetlands to the west. City bus No 6 (€1) from the terminal outside the main bus station will take you here.

FESTIVALS & EVENTS

From 3 to 9 August each year, Huelva celebrates Columbus' departure for the Americas (3 August 1492) with its **Fiestas Colombinas**, a week of music, dancing, sport, cultural events and bullfighting.

SLEEPING

Huelva has a very limited range of accommodation and most of it caters for the business crowd.

Hotel Luz Huelva (☎ 959 25 00 11; Alameda Sundheim 26; s/d €84/99; **P** ✖) This is the best hotel Huelva has to offer – fairly bland but corporately comfortable in an astonishingly ugly, yellow building with concrete, scallop-shaped balconies. Ring ahead to make sure you get a parking spot.

Hotel Costa de la Luz (☎ 959 25 64 22; fax 959 25 32 14; Calle José María Amo 8; s/d €27/47.58) Despite its proximity to the fish market, the Costa de la Luz is reasonable and comfortable with a helpful reception. Obviously decorated in the '70s, the hotel remains locked in a furnishings time warp.

Hotel Los Condes (☎ 959 28 24 00; www.hotellos condes.com in Spanish; Alameda Sundheim 14; s/d €38.95/56.85; **P** ✖) Almost next door to Hotel Luz, Los Condes has 54 air-con rooms at about half the price. The décor is a bit spartan and drab but the rooms are adequate and the hotel has good facilities.

Hotel Tartessos (☎ 959 28 27 11; fax 959 25 06 17; Avenida Martín Alonso Pinzón 13; s/d €53.50/64; **P** ✖) A huge, modern hotel with over 100 well-appointed rooms. It's located on the main drag as you enter Huelva from the *autovía* (toll-free dual carriageway), which is a very

convenient location for those who don't want to get snarled up in the one-way system.

Albergue Juvenil Huelva (☎ 959 25 37 93; Avenida Marchena Colombo 14; dm under/over 26 €12.90/17.25) A modern youth hostel with a good standard of accommodation (all rooms have a bathroom). It is inconveniently located 2km north of the bus station but city bus No 6 (€1) from outside the main bus station stops just around the corner from the hostel, on Calle JS Elcano.

EATING

In the evening, many restaurants and tapas places don't open until after about 8.30pm.

El Rincon de la Cañada (☎ 959 54 03 21; Calle Garcí Fernández 5; mains €15) Unpretentious rustic furnishings and terracotta floors disguise a classy and popular place that is heaving with lunchgoers even at 5pm. The restaurant has another dining room across the street to accommodate all its hungry clients. Go for the fresh fish, which you can choose yourself from the cold counter.

Las Candelas (☎ 959 31 83 01; Carretera Punta Umbría; mains €8-14; ✆ closed Sun) Huelva's most renowned restaurant 7km west of the city in Aljaraque. Like La Cañada, it specialises in delicious fresh fish in a traditional inn setting.

Taberna El Condado (Calle Sor Ángela de la Cruz 3; tapas €1.50) An atmospheric tapas bar, little more than a single room dominated by its ham-heavy bar. Directors' chairs and tables out on the pedestrianised street are great for an evening beer.

La Casa de la Patata (☎ 959 28 25 75; Calle Ginés Martín; baked potatoes €1.20-3.30; ✆ Tue-Sun) Uptown in a classy street off Paseo de la Independencia is this neat modern diner, which serves up steaming baked potatoes to a hungry student crowd. Away from the centre of town, this is a tranquil setting for a filling and reasonably priced lunch.

El Rinconcito (Calle Marina 4; raciones €7-9) This is a rough and ready, male-oriented bar found down in the grimy, workaday streets around the fish market. Authentically cooked fresh fish and a heavy fisherman's atmosphere are the order of the day if you can nudge your way past all the old guys propping up the bar.

Cafetería Parral (Calle Sor Ángela de la Cruz 2; tapas €2.50, raciones €3-4) Opposite El Condado this is a straightforward workman's café which is popular for its *platos combinados* ('combined plates' of seafood, omelette or meat with trimmings; €5), three-course set lunch for €7, and meat and fish *raciones* (meal-sized servings of tapas) and tapas.

Pizzeria Camillo e Peppone (Calle Isaac Peral; pasta & pizza €4.50-7; ☺ closed Wed) Serves up pretty authentic pizzas and pasta, becoming very busy on weekends.

Dioni Salón de Te (Calle Palacios 3) This shiny, English-style tearoom is great to drop into for tea or coffee and a mouth-watering array of cakes and pastries from its glittering counters.

North of Plaza Quintero Baez, Avenida Pablo Rada is lined with many popular lunchtime eateries, many of them with terraces. You can eat snacks or a sit-down meal along here, but the Avenida is too wide and traffic-bound to lend much character to the strip.

DRINKING

After 9pm some of the tapas bars off Avenida Martín Alonso Pinzón, such as Taberna El Condado and Cafetería Parral (see p141), get quite lively. Later, crowds flock to the bars and terraces lining Avenida Pablo Rada and, to a lesser extent, the bars around Plaza de la Merced. Up around the university (Plaza de la Merced) there are a clutch of bars such as the Irish pub **Docklands** (Calle Aragón), classy **Donington Cafeteria-Bar** (Calle Aragón), **Desplome Bar** (Calle Jacobo del Barco), **Pub Tumi** (Calle Jacobo del Barco), and the weirdly decorated **Templo Club** (Calle Jacobo del Barco). All these bars are open in the evenings from about 8.30pm and cater largely to students.

SHOPPING

El Corte Inglés (Plaza de España) The ubiquitous superstore of every Spanish town, Corte Inglés runs the gamut of products from clothes to foodstuffs. A one-stop store.

Many smaller shops are strung along the pedestrianised street running from Calle Concepción to Calle Berdigón.

GETTING THERE & AROUND
Bus

There are buses operated by **Damas** (☎ 959 25 69 00; www.damas-sa.es) that run frequently to and from Seville (€6.15, 1¼ hours, 18 or more daily). The website gives timetables

for all services within the province and is useful for reduced weekend services (usually only one).

There are frequent services to all the surrounding towns including the seaside resorts of Mazagón (€1.55, 35 minutes, 15 daily Monday to Friday, 10 daily Saturday and Sunday), Matalascañas (€3.50, 50 minutes, five daily Monday to Friday, three daily Saturday and Sunday) and Isla Cristina (€3.45, one hour, 11 daily). There are also regular buses to La Rábida (€0.85, 25 minutes, seven or more daily), Minas de Riotinto (€4.85, 1¼ hours, five daily Monday to Saturday), Punta Umbría (€1.70, 30 minutes, 14 daily), Almonaster la Real (€5.75, 2½ hours, one daily Monday to Friday) and Ayamonte (€3.85, one hour, 11 daily Monday to Friday, six daily Saturday and Sunday), found just before the Portuguese border.

Buses also run to Madrid (€18.70, seven hours, three daily). For other major destinations outside Huelva province, you normally have to change in Seville. Buses depart from Huelva for Faro (2¼ hours, two daily Monday to Saturday) in Portugal. For more information on travelling to Portugal see p417.

Car & Motorcycle

Driving in Huelva is challenging, to say the least. There is street-side parking around the train and bus stations and at a 500-place secure car park just up from the bus station on Avenida de Italia. The car park charges are €0.30/1.10 for 35/122 minutes, or €12 for 24 hours. If your car is towed, go to the **Policía Local** (☎ 959 24 84 22; Avenida Tomás Domínguez 2) or call ☎ 959 24 93 50. Taxis wait by the main bus station, at Plaza de la Merced and Plaza de las Monjas, or call ☎ 959 28 13 13 or ☎ 959 25 00 22.

For car hire you can try **Avis** (☎ 959 28 38 36; Avenida de Italia 107), **Hertz** (☎ 959 26 04 60; Avenida de Italia), or **Europcar** (☎ 959 28 53 35) in the train station concourse.

Train

From the **train station** (☎ 959 24 56 14; www.renfe .com; Avenida de Italia) services run daily to Seville (€6.40, 1½ hours, three daily), and an afternoon Talgo 200 goes to Córdoba (€15.50, two hours, daily) and Madrid (€55, 4¼ hours, daily).

AROUND HUELVA

PARAJE NATURAL MARISMAS DEL ODIEL

Across the Odiel estuary from Huelva lies the Paraje Natural Marismas del Odiel, a 72-sq-km wetland reserve. It has a large, varied bird population, including up to 1000 greater flamingos in winter. There are about 4000 pairs of spoonbills, and other birds you may see include ospreys, grey herons and purple herons. Some of these birds are easily viewed from a 20km-long road that runs the length of the marshes.

The marshes can be reached by car along the A497 Punta Umbría road west from Huelva. Cross the bridge over the Río Odiel, then fork right at the sign to 'Ayamonte, Corrales, Dique Juan Carlos I', heading immediately left for Espigón. This curves you back towards Huelva, but instead of re-crossing the bridge take the right turn marked 'Dique Juan Carlos I' to reach **Centro de Visitantes Calatilla** (☎ 959 50 02 36; ☽ 10am-2pm & 5-9pm, closed holidays). Several paths strike off the more-southerly road, but check with the visitors centre to find out which paths are open.

Erebea SL (☎ 660 41 49 20; www.erebea.com in Spanish; Carretera Las Islas Km 2.5) runs guided trips in the reserve by boat (per person €25, four hours), 4WD (€4), on foot (€15) and on horseback (€6, 1½ hours). If you don't have transport, call to inquire about being collected from Huelva. (For additional tours see Punta Umbría, p152.)

LUGARES COLOMBINOS

Huelva's one claim to fame, its ultimate tourist lever, is its connection with the exploits of Christopher Columbus. The Lugares Colombinos (the 'place of Columbus') encapsulates the three townships of La Rábida, Palos de la Frontera and Moguer, all of which played a key role in the Columbus story.

The small towns lie along the eastern bank of the Tinto estuary and can all be visited in an enjoyable 40km return trip from Huelva. (See p145 for information on getting to the three sites.)

The first and most important of the sites is La Rábida, where Columbus retreated to take refuge in the Franciscan monastery, after his grand plans had been rejected by Portuguese King João II. It was here that he met Abbot Juan Pérez (former confessor to Queen Isabel) who took up his cause and helped him to find favour with the royal court.

La Rábida
pop 400

Critical to Columbus' success was the role of the Franciscan monks in the **Monasterio de la Rábida** (☎ 959 35 04 11; admission €2.50, with audio guide €3; ☽ 10am-1pm & 4-7pm Tue-Sat Apr-Sep, 10am-1pm & 4-6.15pm Tue-Sat Oct-Mar, 10am-1pm & 4.45-8pm Tue-Sat Aug, 10.45am-1pm Sun year-round). Here Columbus found support for his far-fetched ideas, and much of the planning of his voyage was dissected and agreed upon inside these walls.

Set amid pine trees, this 14th-century Mudejar monastery is a haven of tranquillity and is now devoted to the Columbus myth. Highlights of the 50-minute (Spanish only) tour include a series of 1930s murals by Huelvan artist Daniel Vázquez Díaz; the church, where Captain Martín Alonso Pinzón is buried; and a chapel with a 13th-century alabaster Virgin before which Columbus prayed. Upstairs, the **Sala Capitular** (Chapter House), with its ponderous atmosphere, is where the final plans for the voyage were drawn up by Columbus, Fray Pérez (the abbot of La Rábida) and Columbus' two fellow captains, the Pinzón brothers.

Even the enchanting gardens of the **Parque Botánico** (☎ 959 53 05 35; admission €1.50; ☽ 10am-9pm Tue-Sun Apr-Sep; 10am-7pm Tue-Sun Oct-Mar) are dedicated to an impressive collection of South American plants and flowers. Within the gardens of the monastery is an information point, the **Centro de Recepción** (☎ 959 53 05 35), which is open when the monastery is open. It has advice on all the sites in what is otherwise a poorly signposted area.

For more information on La Rábida in general try the **tourist office** (☎ 949 53 05 35; Paraje de la Rábida s/n; ☽ 10am-2pm & 5-9pm Tue-Sun Apr-Sep, 10am-3pm Tue-Sun Oct-Mar).

No Columbus tour would be complete without a walk down to the waterfront to the **Muelle de las Carabelas** (Wharf of the Caravels; ☎ 959 53 05 97; admission €3; ☽ 10am-2pm & 5-9pm Tue-Fri, 11am-8pm Sat, Sun & holidays Apr-Sep, 10am-7pm Tue-Sun Oct-Mar), with life-size replicas of Columbus' faithful fleet, set against a pseudo

15th-century quayside. The surprisingly small caravels, the *Niña, Pinta* and *Santa María,* can all be boarded. Their size (none of them is more than 30m long) and the evidently ghastly living conditions give you some idea of the huge achievement of the voyage. However, the comical mannequins, including some sorry naked natives, are impossible to take seriously.

Next to the monastery is the **Hostería de La Rábida** (☎ 959 35 03 12; d €51.30), a traditional hostelry with just five well-appointed rooms. It's an attractive place to stay amid the green gardens, but is usually booked up well in advance.

The only other hotel to be found near La Rábida is **Hotel Santa María** (☎ 959 53 00 01; fax 959 35 04 99; Carretera La Rábida-Palos, Km 16; s/d €20/40), which has 18 comfy rooms and is located 1km north on the Palos de la Frontera road.

Palos de la Frontera
pop 7900

The small town of Palos de la Frontera, 4km northeast of La Rábida, was the port from which Columbus set sail, and that provided two of his ships and more than half his crew. Palos' access to the Tinto estuary is now silted up and there is no momentous atmosphere in what has become a pleasant but everyday country town. However, Palos remains justifiably proud of its role in the European discovery of the Americas – especially the part played by the Pinzón brothers as expressed by the statue of Martín Alonso Pinzón in the central square. Moving northeast up Calle Cristóbal Colón, you soon reach **Casa Museo Martín Alonso Pinzón** (Calle Cristóbal Colón 24; admission free; ⊗ 10am-2pm & 5-7.30pm Mon-Fri), closed at the time of writing. It stands, inexplicably, between Nos 32 and 36, but you can't miss the fine old doorway. It was the home of the

---

THE FOUR VOYAGES OF CHRISTOPHER COLUMBUS

In April 1492 Christopher Columbus (Cristóbal Colón to Spaniards) finally won Spanish royal support for his proposed enterprise to the spice-rich Orient; a proposal that was to result in no fewer than four voyages, spanning the last decade of Columbus' life, and which was to result in a fabulous golden age for Spain.

On the 3 August 1492, Columbus embarked from Palos on his first expedition with only 100 men and three ships, the flagship, *Santa Maria,* the *Niña* and the *Pinta.* After a month in the Canary Islands, Columbus and his crew sailed west and 31 days later sighted the Bahamian island of Guanahaní. They landed there on 12 October, naming it San Salvador. The expedition went on to discover Cuba and Hispaniola, where the *Santa María* sank and its timbers were used to build a fort (Fuerte Navidad).

In January 1493 the remaining two ships sailed for home, leaving 33 Spaniards at Fuerte Navidad. The *Niña* and the *Pinta* reached Palos de la Frontera on 15 March. Columbus, with animals, plants, gold ornaments and six naked Caribbean Indians (so ludicrously modelled on the Muelle de las Carabelas, p143), received a hero's welcome, as all were convinced that he had reached the fabled East Indies (in fact, his calculations were some 12,800km out!).

Columbus made two further voyages in 1493 and 1498, discovering Jamaica, Trinidad and numerous other Caribbean islands. However, he proved disastrous as a colonial administrator, enslaving the native Indians and subjecting them to brutal forced labour in the gold mines in order to keep up with the insatiable demands of the Spanish treasury. Inevitably, his mishandling of the situation led to civil revolt on Hispaniola and before he could suppress the uprising he was arrested by a royal emissary from Spain and sent home in chains. In a final attempt to redeem himself and find a strait to India, he set out on his fourth and final voyage in April 1502. This time he reached Honduras and Panama, but then became stranded for a year in Jamaica, having lost his ships to sea worms.

With no more exciting discoveries to win him back the fame and fortune of his earlier trips, Columbus came to a sorry end. He died in 1506 in Valladolid, northern Spain – poor and apparently still believing he had reached Asia. His remains laid at La Cartuja monastery in Seville before being moved to Hispaniola in 1536. They were later transported to Cuba, then back again to Seville in 1899. Inside the city's cathedral stands the monumental tomb of Columbus – though the remains inside are probably not those of the great explorer at all (see p92).

captain of the *Pinta* and the place where, an inscription proudly claims, the discovery of America was organised.

Further along and downhill is the 14th-century **Iglesia de San Jorge** (Calle Cristóbal Colón; 10am-noon & 7-8pm Tue-Sun). Before leaving to set sail on 3 August 1492, Columbus and his men took communion by the Mudejar portal facing the small square. Ten weeks earlier, the royal document ordering Palos to help Columbus had been read out in the square. A monument in the square lists 35 Palos men who sailed with Columbus.

A little further down the street, now within a small park, is **La Fontanilla** (Calle Cristóbal Colón), a brick well where Columbus' crews drew water for their voyage. A viewing platform above has a plaque marking the site of the jetty from which the three ships sailed.

Just off Palos' central square is **Pensión Rábida** (959 35 01 63; Calle Rábida 9; s/d €9/20), a standard *pensión* (guesthouse) with ultra-cheap, clean, basic rooms. It has a cafeteria where *platos combinados* cost €5 to €7.

The bigger and pricier **Hotel La Pinta** (959 35 05 11; fax 959 53 01 64; Calle Rábida 79; s/d €24/48) is a few steps along the same street. It is certainly a step up from Pensión Rábida but is over-priced for its simple rooms. It also has a res-taurant serving a *menú* (set menu) for €10.

Moguer
pop 16,000

Like Palos, Moguer is an attractive white-washed village. It also shares a great deal of common history with Palos. However, the town is also charming in its own right, with an unmistakable flavour of Andalu-cian baroque – its sunny beauty fulsomely summed up by local poet laureate, Juan Ramón Jiménez (1881–1958), who won the Nobel prize for literature in 1956. The streets are dotted with plaques that bear quotes from Jiménez's *Platero y Yo* (Platero and I; see The Generations of '98 and '27, p44) and his old home is now a museum.

ORIENTATION

Finding your way into town can be tricky. If driving in from the south, look for parking signs that will lead you to the good car park that's alongside the tourist office and is handy for the centre. Coming from the northwest it may be best to park when you have a chance, then set off on foot. Once you have located

the central Plaza del Cabildo, with its statue of Juan Ramón Jiménez in a pretty little garden, things are straightforward.

INFORMATION

There's a helpful **tourist office** (959 37 18 98; www.aytomoguer.es in Spanish; Calle Castillo s/n; 10.30am-1.30pm & 6-8pm Mon-Fri Apr-Sep, 10.30am-1.30pm & 5-7pm Mon-Fri Oct-Mar) in Moguer's old castle, which is being restored. The office has lots of information including leaflets for those who wish to follow the Juan Ramón Jiménez trail. The castle and tourist office are a couple of blocks south of Plaza del Cabildo and are just off Calle Rábida.

SIGHTS

Simply taking a stroll round Moguer's busy morning streets is a pleasure. There are fine buildings everywhere, one of the best ex-amples being the 18th-century Italianate **ayuntamiento** (town hall; Plaza del Cabildo; 10.30am-2.30pm Mon-Fri), with its arcaded, two-storeyed, neoclassical façade. Pop your head inside to take a look at the beautiful patio.

Close by is the 14th-century **Monasterio de Santa Clara** (959 37 01 07; Plaza de las Monjas; guided tour €1.80; 11am-1pm & 5-7pm Tue-Fri), where Columbus kept a prayerful vigil the night after returning from his first voyage. He had vowed to do so when caught in a terrible storm off the Azores. You'll see a lovely Mudejar cloister, some of the nuns' old quar-ters and dormitories, and an impressive col-lection of Renaissance religious art including sculpture, tapestries and silverwork.

Five minutes' walk from Plaza del Ca-bildo (start along Calle Burgos y Mazo and keep going) is the **Casa Museo Zenobia y Juan Ramón** (959 37 21 48; Calle Juan Ramón Jiménez 10; admission €1.80; 10.15am-1.15pm & 5.15-7.15pm Tue-Sat, 10.15am-1.15pm Sun), the old home of Juan Ramón Jiménez. It now houses memora-bilia of the poet's life and that of his wife, Zenobia Camprubí. It is open for one-hour guided visits.

The 18th-century, baroque **Iglesia de Nues-tra Señora de la Granada**, one block southeast of Plaza del Marqués, has a tower that Jiménez immortalised as resembling Seville's Giralda tower from the hazy distance.

SLEEPING & EATING
Hostal Pedro Alonso Niño (959 37 23 92; Calle Pedro Alonso Niño 13; s/d €13.85/22) Close to the

HUELVA PROVINCE

DETOUR: NIEBLA

Forty-seven kilometres east of Huelva on the A472 to Seville lies the walled town of Niebla, hidden behind 2km-long red-ochre walls. Complete with 50 towers and five gates it is one of the most perfectly preserved medieval towns in Andalucía. To reach the city you cross the 2nd-century Roman bridge that was destroyed in the Civil War but that has been carefully restored.

Inside the walls the warren of streets is a pleasure to explore. In the heart of the old town the quaint **Mezquita-Iglesia Santa María de la Granada** (Plaza Santa María) combines the features of a 10th-century Gothic-Mudejar church and a mosque in one building. The key is available from the Casa de Cultura next to the church. The enormous **Castillo de los Guzmanes** (admission €4), a castle that dominates the town, was the original fortress although it was much added to in the 15th-century additions by Enrique de Guzmán. For a truly romantic evening take in one of the theatrical productions that are staged here in the summer months.

The municipal **tourist office** (☎ 959 36 22 70; Plaza Santa María; ☉ 10am-6pm), in the centre of the walled area, has information on all the town's historic buildings as well as performances as the *castillo* (castle).

Convento de Santa Clara at the end of Calle Monjas is the friendly Hostal Pedro, with an attractive tiled patio and comfortable rooms (with showers only). The best rooms overlook the patio.

Hostal Platero (☎ 959 37 21 59; Calle Aceña 4; s/d €15.20/26) Just around the corner from Hostel Pedro is another small *hostal* (a simple guesthouse or small place offering hotel-like accommodation) with clean, simply furnished rooms. However, the welcome at the Platero is not quite as friendly as at the Pedro.

Mesón El Lobito (Calle Rábida 31; raciones €4.50-9) This fun restaurant occupies an old bodega (cellar) and is an experience even without the food. The smoke-blackened walls are covered in customers' graffiti; huge cobwebs and curious artefacts dangle from the roof and locals occasionally sell fruit and vegetables. The fish and meat *a la brasa* (char-grilled) is good and the house wine is cheap (€0.15 per glass).

Mesón La Parralla (Plaza de las Monjas 22; mains €5-12) The town's best restaurant, located in Moguer's finest plaza (opposite the Santa Clara convent). A family-run tavern, it serves up excellent grills and fresh fish, as well as offering traditional tapas and a good-value, fixed-price *menú*.

Bodeguita de Los Raposo (Calle Fuente 60; platos small/medium/large €1/1.50/2.20) Another cracking place, where you order by plate size from a choice of more than 40 fish, meat and salad dishes. There's lots of local wine, too. Try the 'Licor de Viagra'; it works wonders, according to the ever-smiling host.

Getting There & Around

Buses leave Huelva daily, every half-hour for Palos (€0.90, 25 minutes, 12 daily), but less frequently on the weekend. There are three turnings into central Palos from the La Rábida–Moguer road; the northernmost is right by La Fontanilla (see p145).

At least 10 Damas buses run daily from Huelva bus station to La Rábida and Palos de la Frontera; some then continue to Mazagón, but most terminate at Moguer (€0.95, 30 minutes, 10 daily). In Moguer, buses leave from Calle Coronación to the north of Plaza Cabildo.

SOUTHEAST OF HUELVA

A wide, sandy beach runs 60km southeast from the outskirts of Huelva to the mouth of the Río Guadalquivir. The beach enjoys good weather for most of the year (although it can be windy) and shares many of the characteristics of the more famous beaches of the Cádiz province stretch of the Costa de la Luz: fine white sand, windswept dunes and a thick, protective barrier of pines. Frequented mainly by Spanish holidaymakers, the two resort towns of Mazagón and Matalascañas (at either end of the coastal road) are unpretentious if unremarkable places to stay.

MAZAGÓN
pop 3000

Mazagón is an unexciting resort by appearance, but its low-rise development is inoffensive and in summer the town develops a holiday buzz of its own. There's a **tourist office** (☎ 959 37 63 00; Carretera de la Playa; 10am-2pm Mon-Fri) on the main street. Carretera de la Playa runs 1km down from the N442 to the beach and to a large marina. Residential Mazagón stretches to the east, for three featureless kilometres, along the beachfront Avenida de los Conquistadores. The real off-beach action is around the mid-point of Carretera de la Playa, in the pedestrianised Avenida Fuentepiña, where there are good bars and restaurants.

East of Mazagón, you can reach the **beach** easily from beside Parador de Mazagón, 3km from the town. At **Cuesta de Maneli**, 9km beyond, a 1.2km boardwalk leads from a car park to the beach through glorious pines and junipers across 100m-high dunes. The Cuesta de Maneli beach has a naturist section.

Sleeping & Eating

Parador de Mazagón (☎ 959 53 63 00; www.parador .es in Spanish; Playa de Mazagón; d low/high season €106.80/123; P ⊠ ⊠) Three kilometres east of Mazagón, the creeper-clad Parador is a low-lying '70s classic. It is a cross between a Californian beach bungalow and a horsey ranch-house, with broad verandas, wooden ceilings, pale-lemon bedding and neatly manicured hedges and lawns. The bedrooms are luxurious and there is easy access to the beach below the cliff-top gardens.

Hotel Albaida (☎ 959 37 60 29; www.hotelalbaida .com; Carretera Huelva-Matalascañas Km 18.3; s/d €50/80; P ⊠) The most elegant of Mazagón's mid-range options, Hotel Albaida is housed in a classic-looking villa and offers comfortable, airy rooms tastefully kitted out in primary colours. It is situated 600m east of the town centre amid pine trees.

Hostal Álvarez Quintero (☎ 959 37 61 69; Calle Hernández de Soto 174; d €34; ⊠) A quiet and unassuming place just off the seaward end of Carretera de la Playa. Simple rooms verge on the monastic but there is air-con and the prices are very reasonable.

Hostal Hilaria (☎ 959 37 62 06; Calle Buenos Aires 20; d €51) Another cheap and cheerful *hostal* just off Carretera de la Playa, further up the hill from Álvarez. The rooms are located above the bar (and can be a little noisy in summer), opening onto a terrace. You can also hire bicycles here.

Camping Playa de Mazagón (☎ 959 37 62 08; Cuesta de la Barca s/n; camping per adult/tent/car €4/4/4; year-round) A huge camping ground just a couple of minutes' walk from the beach. The site is densely wooded, which provides welcome shade and a useful wind barrier in the hotter months.

There are dozens of places to eat in Mazagón, mainly on Carretera de la Playa and Avenida Fuentepiña. On summer evenings the seafront bristles with life.

Las Dunas (Avenida de los Conquistadores 178; mains €7-12) Right up at the western end of the seafront near the yacht harbour, Las Dunas cooks up lovely fresh fish, and the view of the marina puts you right in the mood.

El Remo (Avenida de los Conquistadores 123; mains €8-12) This seafood restaurant has a wide terrace for outdoor dining. The best options are always the simply fried or grilled fish – the succulent *dorada* (bream) and *merluza* (hake) are particularly good.

El Choco (Avenida Fuentepiña 47; tapas €1.50) A good place for tapas, El Choco does a roaring local trade and has great atmosphere.

Getting There & Away

Buses run daily from Huelva to Mazagón (€1.55, 35 minutes, 15 daily Monday to Friday, 10 daily Saturday and Sunday) via La Rábida and Palos de la Frontera, and vice versa. At weekends and on holidays there are reduced services in each direction. There's a bus stop on Carretera de la Playa near the junction with Avenida Fuentepiña.

MATALASCAÑAS

pop 500

This custom-built resort of candy-coloured high-rise hotels and low-rise apartments is a shocking contrast to the wilderness of the adjoining Doñana natural and national parks. Despite its unattractive aesthetic, Matalascañas is a favourite of escapees from Seville, for its terrific beach (the best section being at the eastern end towards the park) and plenty of summertime facilities. The Parque Dunar, an area of dune fields dotted with picnic areas and riddled with cycling and walking routes, is a new and relatively successful low-key development. Out of season, there's a hollow eeriness about the deserted shopping malls and streets.

Orientation & Information

Matalascañas extends 4km southeast from the junction of the A494 from Mazagón with the A483 from El Rocío. From this junction Avenida de las Adelfas heads south straight to the beach, passing the **tourist office** (☎ 959 43 00 86; www.aytoalmonte .es in Spanish; Avenida de las Adelfas s/n; ⏰ 9.30am-2pm Mon-Fri, 10am-2pm Sat). Buses stop by the big roundabout at the beach end of Avenida de las Adelfas, a spot known as Torre Higuera. The east side of the *avenida* is a wall of shops and restaurants a couple of blocks deep.

Sleeping & Eating

El Cortijo de los Mimbrales (☎ 959 42 22 37; www .cortijomimbrales.com in Spanish; Carretera del Rocío A483 Km 20; d/4-person cottage €125/350; P X 🛋) Some 10km north of Matalascañas, on the edge of Parque Nacional de Doñana, you will find this delightful hacienda-style *cortijo* (country property). Bold, vibrant colour washes and curious antiques combined in a uniquely contemporary fashion make this one of Huelva's best hotels. Accommodation is in double rooms or cottages, and the excellent restaurant (mains €8 to €15) is worth the trip even if you aren't a guest.

Hotel Flamero (☎ 959 44 80 20; Ronda Maestro Alonso; d €78.50; P X 🛋) One of the better-value large hotels, the Flamero has modern rooms as well as a range of facilities such as tennis courts and a pool.

Hostal Victoria (☎ 959 44 09 57; Sector O No 8; d €48; X) Located in Matalascañas, the Victoria is a fairly functional *hostal* although the rooms are well-appointed and have air-con to boot.

Camping Rocío Playa (☎ 959 43 02 40; 2 people, tent & car €22; ⏰ year-round) A huge place with room for 4000 pitches, Camping Rocío is in a fine position just above the beach although there is very limited shade. It is reached down a broad sandy track just before the entry roundabout to Matalascañas as you approach from Mazagón on the A494.

Other reasonably priced, decent accommodation is to be had at **Hostal Los Tamarindos** (☎ 959 43 01 19; Avenida de las Adelfas 31; d €60) and **Hostal El Duque** (☎ 959 43 00 58; Avenida de las Adelfas 34; d €48.25).

Several restaurants are clustered behind the beach near the end of Avenida de las Adelfas and offer a typical three-course *menú* for about €8.50 and *platos combinados* for €5.50.

Getting There & Away

There's a daily bus service from Huelva (€3.50, 50 minutes, five daily Monday to Friday, three daily Saturday and Sunday) via Mazagón, leaving Huelva at 2.45pm. There are only two return buses from Matalascañas, which leave at 7am and 4pm (Monday to Friday only). Extra services may run in summer. Buses also link Matalascañas with El Rocío and Seville (see p152).

PARQUE NACIONAL DE DOÑANA

Spain's largest wildlife reserve and one of Europe's last remaining great wetlands, the Parque Nacional de Doñana is a place of immense natural beauty and romantic myth. It was owned by the dukes of Medina Sidonia in the 16th century, and is named after Dona Aña, the wife of the seventh duke. She is believed to wander, lost forever, in the marshy forests of the lower Guadalquivir. There are also enduring claims that the areas was once the site of the fabled Tartessos, and these days the park even has its own patron saint, the deeply revered Nuestra Señora del Rocío (see p151) who, it is hoped, will safeguard the park from future environmental threat.

Much of the national park's boundary is bordered by the separate Parque Natural de Doñana, which consists of four distinct zones totalling 540 sq km and forming a buffer for the national park. The protected area (combined with the separate Parque Natural de Doñana) covers over 1080 sq km and provides a vital refuge for endangered species such as the Iberian lynx (with only 25 breeding pairs remaining) and Spanish imperial eagle (reduced to just 14 breeding pairs), and is a crucial habitat for millions of migrating birds. It was only in 1969 that the government transformed the area into a national park. The World Wide Fund for Nature – then called the World Wildlife Fund – raised much of the cash for the initial purchases of the land. James Michener, in *Iberia*, writes how members of one Danish shooting club were persuaded to dig deep: 'Gentlemen,' they were told, 'if the lakes of *Doñana* are allowed to disappear, within five years there will be no ducks in Denmark.'

However, the pressure of tourism and the threat of more industrial development are a continuing concern. Added to this, many locals believe the interests of the national park take unfair priority over their own concerns about much-needed jobs. In 1998 the fraught balance between industry and conservation collapsed when a dam broke at the Los Frailes heavy-metals mine at Aznalcóllar (50km to the north). Hastily erected dikes prevented the poisonous tide from entering all but a small corner of the national park, but up to 100 sq km of wetlands to the park's northeast were contaminated, and agricultural land bordering about 70km of the Río Guadiamar was devastated. Since then the area has largely recovered, although the repaired dams remain in place and plans for two new tourist resorts to the north of Sanlúcar de Barrameda in Cádiz province have been given the go-ahead.

Orientation & Information

Access to the national park itself is limited. Anyone may walk along the 28km stretch of Atlantic beach between Matalascañas and the mouth of the Guadalquivir (which can be crossed by boats from Sanlúcar de Barrameda in Cádiz province), as long they do not stray inland. To visit the park's interior, you will have to book a guided tour. These leave from the **Centro de Visitantes El Acebuche** (☎ 959 44 87 11; www.parquenacionaldonana.com in Spanish; Carretera A483 Almonte-Matalascañas Km 26; ☼ 8am-9pm May-Sep; 8am-7pm Oct-Apr), which is the park's main visitor centre, and from Sanlúcar de Barrameda (p179).

To reach El Acebuche, head 4km north from Matalascañas, or 12km south from El Rocío, on the A483, then go 1.6km west along an approach road. The centre has a café, shop and park exhibition, and can provide maps. Short paths lead to hides overlooking a lagoon.

Some of the best bird-watching in the Doñana area is to be had at the **Centro de Información Las Rocinas** (☎ 959 44 23 40; ☼ 9am-3pm & 4-8pm) where a 2km route, the 'Charco de la Boca', meanders through marshland to concealed hides along the riverbank.

The third visitors centre is the **Palacio del Acebrón** (☼ 9am-3pm & 4-8pm), a converted hunting lodge now housing an ethnographic exhibition of the park. Footpaths

disappear into the surrounding riverine forest and encircle Lake Acebrón. The Centro de Visitantes El Acebuche has maps of the park.

Just outside the park is the **Centro de Visitantes José Antonio Valverde** (Centro Cerrado Garrido; ☼ 10.30am-7.30pm). It is an excellent spot for bird-watching as it overlooks a year-round *lucio* (pond).

The best map of the park is IGN's 1:50,000 *Parque Nacional de Doñana* (1992), which is sold at the Acebuche centre.

Tours

Trips from El Acebuche into the national park are run, in all-terrain vehicles holding about 20 people each, by the **Cooperativa Marismas del Rocío** (☎ 959 43 04 32; per person €20; ☼ 8.30am Tue-Sun year-round, 3pm Oct-Apr, 5pm May-Sep). This is the only way for ordinary folk to get inside the park proper except for guided trips from Sanlúcar de Barrameda (see p180). You need to book ahead by telephone – the tours can be full more than a month before spring, summer and all holiday times. Bring binoculars, if you can, and carry plenty of drinking water in summer. Use mosquito repellent, except in winter. The tour lasts four hours and most guides speak Spanish only. The route of about 80km normally begins with a drive along the beach to the mouth of the Río Guadalquivir, then loops back through the south of the park, taking in moving dunes, marshlands and woods, where you can be pretty certain of seeing a good number of deer and boars. Serious ornithologists may be disappointed by the limited bird-watching opportunities.

Another reliable operator, offering guided tours of Doñana with English-speaking guides, is **Discovering Doñana** (☎ 959 44 24 66; www.discoveringdonana.com; Calle Acebuchal 14, El Rocío). Its regular excursions combine the natural park with the northern national park, focusing on bird-watching (for details of excursions, see p151).

For horseback trips in the national park contact **Club Hípico** (☎ 959 44 82 41; Sector G, Parcela 90, Matalascañas), which can arrange trips to suit all ages and abilities, with English-speaking guides. This is an absolutely great excursion to do with kids because it concentrates mainly on the beaches and dune fields.

HUELVA PROVINCE

Wildlife

The national park has been declared both a Unesco Biosphere Reserve and a World Heritage Site, and about six million birds spend at least part of each year in the park.

The many interwoven ecosystems that make up the park give rise to fantastic diversity. Nearly half the park consists of the marshes of the Guadalquivir delta, which enters the Atlantic Ocean at the southeastern corner of the park. The wetlands are almost dry from July to October. In autumn they start to fill with water, eventually leaving only a few islets of dry land. Over 500,000 water birds arrive from the north to winter here, including an estimated 80% of Western Europe's wild ducks. As the waters sink in spring, other birds – the greater flamingo, spoonbills, storks, herons, avocets, hoopoes, bee-eaters and stilts – arrive for the summer. Fledglings flock around *lucios* and as these dry up in July, herons, storks and kites move in to feast on trapped perch.

Between the marshlands and the park's 28km-long beach is a band of shifting sand dunes. Winds move the dunes inland at a rate of up to 6m per year. The shallow valleys between the dunes host pines and other trees favoured as nesting sites by raptors. When dune sand eventually reaches the marshlands, rivers carry it back down to the sea, which washes it up on the beach – the cycle then begins all over again. The beach and moving dunes make up 102 sq km of the park.

In other parts of the park, stable sand supports 144 sq km of *coto* (an area where hunting rights are reserved for a specific group of people), the favoured habitat of an abundant mammal population – 33 species including red and fallow deer, wild boar, mongoose and genets. *Coto* vegetation ranges from heather and scrub through to dense wooded thickets to stands of umbrella pine and cork oaks, known locally as aviaries due to the weight of nesting birds.

Getting There & Away

From Monday to Saturday, the first **Damas** (www.damas-sa.es) bus from El Rocío towards Matalascañas (about €0.90, 15 minutes), departing at 7am weekdays and 7.15am on Saturday, will get you to El Acebuche in time for the morning tour. However, check current bus schedules before you go.

THE ROMERÍA DEL ROCÍO

The Romería del Rocío is Spain's biggest religious pilgrimage, when hundreds of thousands of pilgrims and brotherhoods converge on the sanctuary of Nuestra Señora del Rocío (Our Lady of Dew), a sacred effigy of the Virgin, to commemorate the miracle-story of her discovery.

Like most of Spain's holiest images, the Nuestra Señora del Rocío – aqua La Blanca Paloma (White Dove) – has legendary origins. Back in the 13th century, a hunter from the village of Almonte found the effigy of the Virgin in a marshland tree and started to carry her home. But when he stopped for a rest, the Virgin magically returned to the tree.

Before long, a chapel was built on the site of the tree (El Rocío) and it became a place of pilgrimage. By the 17th century, *hermandades* (brotherhoods) were forming in nearby towns to make pilgrimages to El Rocío at Pentecost, the seventh weekend after Easter. Today, the **Romería del Rocío** (Pilgrimage to El Rocío) is a vast festive cult that draws people from all over Spain. There are over 90 *hermandades*, some with several thousand members, both men and women, who still travel to El Rocío on foot, on horseback and in gaily decorated covered wagons.

Solemn is the last word you'd apply to this quintessentially Andalucian event. In an atmosphere similar to Seville's Feria de Abril (p108), participants dress in Andalucian costume and sing, dance, drink, laugh and romance their way to El Rocío. The total number of people in the village on this special weekend can reach about a million.

The weekend comes to an ecstatic climax in the very early hours of Monday. Members of the *hermandad* of Almonte, which claims the Virgin as its own, barge into the church and bear her out on a float. Violent struggles ensue as others battle with the Almonte lads for the honour of carrying La Blanca Paloma. The crush and chaos are immense, but somehow good humour survives and the Virgin is carried round to each of the *hermandad* buildings before finally being returned to the church in the afternoon.

EL ROCÍO

pop 1500

North of Matalascañas, overlooking a picturesque *marisma* (wetland), you will come across the extraordinary village of El Rocío. As you drive into town the road peters out and gives way to wide sandy avenues, which cut between eerily quiet ranch-style houses. Hoof-prints, hitching posts and hat-clad honchos do nothing to dissipate the bizarre guns-at-noon atmosphere that pervades. But despite appearances the town is not contrived, but a bona fide piece of the Wild West where many of the Spanish pioneers to America originated. The quiet houses, with their sweeping verandas, are no show homes but are the well-tended properties of over 90 *hermandades* (brotherhoods) whose pilgrims converge on the town every Pentecost (Whitsuntide) for the Romería del Rocío (see p150).

Information

The **tourist office** (☎ 959 44 26 84; Avenida de la Canaliega s/n; ☒ 10am-2pm) can be found just south of the Hotel Puente del Rey at the western end of the village. The office supplies a town map and also has information on excursions in the national park.

An El Monte ATM on the northern side of the Ermita del Rocío takes major cards.

Sights & Activities

In the heart of the village, dominating the wide sandy square, is the attractive church – the **Ermita del Rocío** (admission free; ☒ 8.30am-2.30pm & 4.30-8pm). It houses the celebrated **Nuestra Señora del Rocío** (Our Lady of Rocío) –a small wooden image of the Virgin dressed in long, bejewelled robes, which normally stands above the main altar. People arrive to see the Virgin every day of the year. In the south wall of the church is a special chamber for votive candles. The heat is so ferocious and the fumes so dense that ventilator fans work nonstop to clear the air of what seems more like fire and brimstone than faith.

The **marshlands** at El Rocío contain water all year, thanks to the Río Madre de las Marismas, which flows through here. They are nearly always a good place to spot birds and animals. Deer and horses graze in the shallows and you may be lucky enough to see a flock of flamingos wheeling through the sky in a big pink cloud. The Spanish

Ornithological Society's observatory, the **Observatorio Madre del Rocío** (☎ 959 50 60 93; admission free; ☒ 10am-2pm & 4-7pm Tue-Sun), has telescopes and is found by the water, about 150m east of the Hotel Toruño.

The bridge over the river 1km south of the village on the A483 is another good viewing spot. Just past the bridge is the **Centro de Información Las Rocinas** (☎ 959 44 23 40; ☒ 9am-3pm & 4-8pm). From this national park information centre, short paths lead to bird-watching hides by a year-round creek. Though outside the park itself, this section of the creek is in a special *zona de protección* (protected zone) and has abundant bird life.

For a longer walk from El Rocío, cross the Puente del Ajolí, at the northeastern edge of the village, and head along the track into the woodland ahead. This is the **Coto del Rey**, a large woodland zone where you can wander freely for hours. It's crossed by numerous tracks that vehicles might manage in dry seasons. In early morning or late evening you may spot deer or boars.

Discovering Doñana (☎ 959 44 24 66; www.discover ingdonana.com; Calle Acebuchal 14, El Rocío; tour 3/6 people €110/140) runs daily bird-watching trips for small groups in the Parque Natural de Doñana. Trips are in all terrain vehicles and prices include a guide and binoculars. It also offers a variety of longer holiday packages that include accommodation and daily trips.

You can hire horses for hourly or daily trips. Ask at **Hotel Toruño** (☎ 959 44 23 23; hotel -toruno@terra.es; Plaza Acebuchal 22) or contact **Doñana Ecuestre** (☎ 959 44 24 74) or **Turismo a Caballo** (☎ 959 44 20 84; Calle Boca del Lobo 3). Charges are around €15 for one hour or €60 for a day. Doñana Ecuestre also arranges 4WD tours of the national park.

Sleeping & Eating

During Romería you will never be able to find an empty room. If you want to attend the festivities then you need to book well ahead, although hotel rooms are booked often at least a year in advance and prices go sky-high.

Hotel Toruño (☎ 959 44 23 23; hotel-toruno@terra .es; Plaza Acebuchal 22; d incl breakfast €75; **P** ☒) An attractive-looking villa overlooking the *marismas*, not far from the observatory and only 100m from the church. There are 30 well-appointed rooms, many of which have views over the marshland (odd-numbered rooms from 207 to 217), while 1st-floor rooms have balconies.

Pensión Cristina (☎ 959 44 24 13; Calle El Real 58; s/d €30/36) Located behind the church, this is one of El Rocío's two budget *hostales*. Rooms are reasonably comfortable and there is a decent restaurant with a *menú* for €9. Reception has lots of helpful information on Discovering Doñana's (p151) bird-watching trips.

Pensión Isidro (☎ 959 44 22 42; Avenida de los Ánsares 59; s/d €20/40) The town's other budget *hostal*, 400m north of the church.

The bars and restaurants of El Rocío do a roaring trade at most times, although in Wild West fashion the food is more about feeding the hungry punters than about culinary niceties. If you eat out in the evening, slap on some mosquito repellent.

Bar-Restaurante Toruño (Plaza Acebuchal; mains €9-17) This is one of the better options in town, and it overlooks the marshlands with handsome tile-and-wooden-beam décor. The quality fish and organic beef come from the national park.

Aires de Doñana (☎ 959 44 27 19; Avenida de la Canaliega 1; mains €11-16; ⏰ closed Mon & July) Light-filled floor-to-ceiling windows, an imaginative menu and a lovely, small veranda make this restaurant a pleasant change from the rustic salon-style restaurants in town. In spring the *marisma* is full of birds and you hardly need get up from your table to spot them.

Tapas is served at most of the friendly bars and restaurants along the main street. They offer hearty but very average food. For a wide choice of tapas, you could try **Bar Cafetería El Real** (raciones €8-11, tapas €1.50) facing the northern side of the church.

Getting There & Away

Damas buses runs from Seville to El Rocío (€4.50, 1½ hours, three to five daily) and then on to Matalascañas (€5.45, 1¾ hours). Buses also run each way along the A483 between Almonte and Matalascañas (€2.45, 40 minutes, three to six daily), stopping at El Rocío. All these buses will stop outside the Las Rocinas and El Acebuche national park visitor centres (you may have to request this).

To get to El Rocío from Huelva, take a Damas bus to Almonte (€3.65, 45 minutes, six daily Monday to Friday, with fewer services on weekends), then another from Almonte to El Rocío (€1.15, 18 minutes, five daily).

WEST OF HUELVA

The coast between Huelva and the Portuguese border, 53km to the west, alternates between estuaries, wetlands, good sandy beaches, and small- and medium-sized resorts and fishing ports. The coastal towns along this strip have few interesting sights and the area remains an enduringly Spanish holiday destination.

PUNTA UMBRÍA

pop 13,000

Established as a holiday resort in 1880 by the Rio Tinto Company (whose holidaying engineers used to travel to the coast in a paddle steamer), Punta Umbría continues to be a favourite summer destination for *onubenses* (people from Huelva), and the town can become extremely busy in July and August.

Despite the uninspiring, low-key development, the resort has an attractive location between the Atlantic coast and the Paraje Natural Marismas del Odiel (see p143), an area of flats declared a 'Landscape of National Interest' and which includes two breeding reserves for herons and spoonbills. As with the rest of the province there are wonderful, sandy beaches along the northern and southern sides of the *punta* (point), all of which have the ecofriendly blue-flag classification due to their pristine waters.

The town has a helpful **tourist office** (☎ 959 31 46 19; Avenida Ciudad de Huelva; 8am-3pm & 4-8pm Mon-Fri, 10am-2pm Sat & Sun) and you can arrange boat trips around the Odiel *marisma* and the estuary with **Turismar** (☎ 959 31 55 26).

Punta Umbría has a huge range of accommodation, although even these get booked up in July and August. Off the road from Huelva, a few kilometres out of town, there are also two camping grounds that are handy for good beaches.

Hotel Barceló Punta Umbría (☎ 959 49 54 00; puntaumbria@barcelo.com; Avenida Océano s/n; d €110.70; P ⏰ ⏰) is a large, Andalucian-style complex right on the Atlantic seaboard overlooking the beach. This modern hotel, part of the Barcelo chain, offers all the expected facilities and there is a large kidney-shaped pool.

Near the estuary on the eastern side of town, the newly refurbished **Hotel Emilio** (☎ 959 31 18 00; Calle Ancha 21; d €54.25; P ⊠), previously a *hostal*, has decent but ordinary rooms with TV. Its location on bar-filled Calle Ancha means rooms can be a little noisy.

Hostal Casa Manuela (☎ 959 31 07 60; Calle Carmen 8; d €30) is another recently refurbished *hostal* with simple, light rooms that are quieter than those in the Emilio.

For a popular drinks bar housed in a kitsch old ferry boat with plenty of atmosphere try **Bar Chimbito** (Paseo de Pascasio s/n; raciones €4-8). Unsurprisingly (as it is actually on the water) it serves up tasty seafood tapas and *raciones*.

From Huelva, buses run to Punta Umbría every hour from 7.15am to 9pm (€1.70, 30 minutes, 14 daily). In summer, hourly ferries (€1.80) sail from the Muelle de Levante at Huelva's port.

EL ROMPIDO

Sixteen kilometres northwest of Punta Umbría is the minor resort of El Rompido, currently a low-key, low-lying affair that continues to develop apace. However, it's still a quieter bet than the main resort. It's essentially a small fishing village grown big on the Río Piedras estuary. It has more sandy beaches with the characteristic backdrop of pines.

Several buses travel from Huelva to El Rompido (€1.80, 30 minutes, seven daily Monday to Friday).

ISLA CRISTINA

pop 19,000

As well as being a beach resort (packed in August), Isla Cristina has a fair-sized fishing fleet. The boats create a lively scene in the morning and evening as they land their catches at the **Puerto Pesquero** (fishing port), before the fish are whisked away to the markets of Seville, Córdoba and Madrid.

North of town, the road heading towards the A472 crosses the **Paraje Natural Marismas de Isla Cristina**, an area of watery estuaries and lagoons full of thriving bird life, including the greater flamingo and spoonbills. Signs 2km north of Isla Cristina indicate the **Sendero de Molino Mareal de Pozo del Camino**, a 1km walking track across the marshlands.

East of Isla Cristina is the resort of La Antilla, a collection of holiday chalets and apartments that stretches 9km along the fine, wide beach that runs all the way from Isla Cristina to the Río Piedras. It's a likeable resort that practically empties in the winter.

Orientation & Information

From the plaza, Gran Vía Román Pérez heads south for about 1km to the western end of Isla Cristina's blue-flagged beach. The **tourist office** (☎ 959 33 26 94; Avenida Madrid; ⊙ 10am-2pm & 5-9pm) is 150m east of Gran Vía Román Pérez.

Sleeping & Eating

Most hotels are in the mid- to top-end range and are around Avenida de la Playa near Playa Central.

Hotel Los Geranios (☎ 959 33 18 00; geraniosh@yahoo.com; Avenida de la Playa; s/d €66.98/96.98; P ⊠ ⊠) The modern, '70s-style block of the Los Geranios has been imaginatively refurbished – each room is individually decorated with cheerful colour washes. The hotel is only 150m from the beach and the English-speaking management is extremely friendly and helpful.

Hotel Paraíso Playa (☎ 959 33 02 35; www.hotelparaisoplaya.com; Avenida de la Playa; s/d €48/85; ⊠ ⊠) A seafront location, a jolly yellow and white exterior, pleasant rooms and friendly staff make the Paraíso a good mid-range option.

Camping Giralda (☎ 959 34 33 18; camping per adult/tent/car €4.80/4.50/4) Set among pine trees at the eastern edge of town, the Giralda has room for 2200 people. Playa Central is a stone's throw away and you can arrange a host of canoeing and sailing activities at the site.

La Palmera (Paseo de los Gavilanes; menú €7.25) is a cheerful, down-to-earth bar located just beside the big roundabout at the end of the approach road to Isla Canela from the A472. Likewise, **Acosta Bar-Restaurante** (Plaza de las Flores; seafood dishes €5-12) serves up good fish dishes. Otherwise, head over to the seafood bars and restaurants on the square outside the Puerto Pesquero, such as **Bar-Restaurante Hermanos Moreno**, which is definitely worth a try. There is a top-quality restaurant upstairs and a popular tapas bar below. There are also eateries at Playa Central.

Getting There & Away

Buses run to/from Huelva (€3.45, one hour, six daily), Ayamonte (€1.20, 25 minutes, three daily) and Seville (€8.95, two hours, one to three daily).

To get to La Antilla from El Rompido you must drive west and go inland to the A472 before turning south again at Lepe. There are 13 buses from Huelva (€1.70) which run on an hourly basis from 8.15am to 9pm.

AYAMONTE
pop 17,500

Ayamonte has a cheerful borderland buzz about it, although you can now pass it by and wheel your way into Portugal, customs-free and toll-free, across the splendid Puente del Guadiana that spans the Río Guadiana. Romantics can still enjoy the pace of times past, however, by taking the ferry across the Guadiana between Ayamonte and Vila Real de Santo António.

Orientation & Information

Ayamonte's heart is the Plaza de la Coronación and its seamless neighbour Plaza de Ribera, fronted by the main road (Avenida Vila Real de Santo António), which runs along the harbour.

The bus station is on Avenida de Andalucía, 700m east of the central plazas. The *muelle transbordador* (ferry dock) is on Avenida Muelle de Portugal, 300m northwest of the plazas.

Ayamonte's **tourist office** (☎ 959 32 18 71; La Casa Grande, Avenida Ramón y Cajal s/n; ☯ 10am–1pm & 6-9pm) is located in a restored mansion on Plaza del Rosario. The office has a plan of the town and can give you information on rental accommodation.

In the pedestrianised streets behind Plaza de Ribera are several banks with ATMs. The banks are open for exchange during banking hours from Monday to Friday.

Sights & Activities

Plaza de Ribera, with its handy tiled seats and cheeky cupid statues, and Plaza de la Coronación are the main centres of activity. Both plazas are lined with bars and restaurants, behind which narrow streets lead up to the old town that's crammed with shops and cafés. Worth a look within the old town are pleasant buildings and some fine churches such as **Iglesia de San Francisco** (Calle San Francisco) and the **Parroquia de El Salvador** (Calle San Francisco), with its leaning columns

(a legacy of the Lisbon earthquake of 1755). You can climb the tower of El Salvador to get a view over the harbour.

Old ferries ply the Guadiana half-hourly, connecting Ayamonte to neighbouring Vila Real de Santo António in Portugal. Other excursions travel up the river to Sanlúcar. This trip can be arranged through **Guadi Tour** (☎ 959 47 16 30; www.guaditour.com in Spanish; Avenida Andalucía 31).

ISLA CANELA

Six kilometres south of town is Ayamonte's beach resort, **Isla Canela**, which stretches as far as the old fishing village of **Punta del Moral**. The blue-flagged beach is wide, sandy and several kilometres long, with a reasonably undeveloped hinterland apart from low-rise apartments and one big, very expensive hotel, the Riu Canela (see p154).

Sleeping & Eating

Hotel Riu Canela (☎ 959 47 71 24; www.riu.com; Paseo de los Gavilanes s/n; s/d €135; P ⌘ ⌘) Opulent, over-the-top, ostentatious – just a few words that spring to mind when you first see the Riu Canela. This huge Andalucian complex has every imaginable comfort and convenience together with a seafront location.

Parador de Ayamonte (☎ 959 32 07 00; www.para dor.es in Spanish; El Castillito; d low/high season €74.40/97.10; P ⌘ ⌘) On a hill 1.5km north of the town centre, the Parador looks out over the broad estuary. The modern hotel, decked out in chichi peaches and mint greens, is well-appointed although fairly soulless.

Hotel Diego (☎ 959 47 02 50; Avenida Ramón y Cajal 2; s/d €51/65.50; P ⌘) Ayamonte's only real mid-range option is the nasty-pink confection of the Hotel Diego. Located east of the harbour, rooms come with TV (and air-con for extra €15).

Hostal Los Robles (☎ 959 47 09 59; Avenida de Andalucía 121; d with private/shared bathroom €30.65/24) An easygoing place in a bland modern block just west of the bus station. The rooms are decent and neat if not exactly welcoming. Its bar-restaurant serves *platos combinados* and *bocadillos* (filled rolls) for €2.50.

Casa Luciano (Calle Palma 2; menú €12) Great fish and a great atmosphere make Luciano the place to come for a slap-up meal. The restaurant itself is unassuming but everything on your plate is freshly cooked and only minutes out of the water.

Two other options are **Casa Barberi** (Plaza de la Coronación 12; mains €4-12) and **Mesón La Casona** (Calle Lusitania 2; menú €8). Both are popular and busy.

If in Ayamonte for a couple of days it is worth making your way to Punta del Moral, where the unpaved main street has a number of excellent tapas bars.

Getting There & Around

There are no customs or immigration checks heading in either direction by road or ferry.

BOAT

Transportes Fluvial del Guadiana SL (☎ 959 47 06 17) runs daily ferries to/from Vila Real de Santo António every half-hour from 9.30am to 9pm from July to September and every 40 minutes from 9am to 7pm, October to June. One-way fares are €3.50 for a car and driver and €1 for adult passengers. Fairly frequent buses and trains run through the Algarve from Vila Real de Santo António.

BUS

Several daily buses run from Huelva (€3.85, one hour, 11 daily Monday to Friday, five daily Saturday and Sunday), Seville (€9.40, two hours, four to six daily) and Madrid (€22.30, 8½ hours, four daily). There are also a few buses along the Algarve and to Lisbon. The **bus station** (☎ 959 32 11 71) has details. From June to September buses run to Isla Canela every half-hour from Ayamonte. The first bus from Ayamonte (€1.35) is at 9am; the last bus back from Isla Canela is 8.30pm. For the rest of the year the return bus leaves at 2.45pm.

CAR & MOTORCYCLE

The town isn't difficult to get around (except in summer when there is a lot more traffic). There is parking along the waterfront, opposite Plaza de la Coronación, but competition is fierce in the morning and early evening. There's a pay-for car park along the eastern end of the harbour.

THE NORTH

The rolling hills of Huelva's portion of the Sierra Morena are covered with a thick pelt of cork oaks and pine and chestnut trees, punctuated here and there by dramatic cliffs, enchanting villages and bustling market towns such as the area's 'capital', Aracena. These hills – relatively rainy and a little cooler than most of Andalucía in summer – form the 1840-sq-km **Parque Natural Sierra de Aracena y Picos de Aroche**, Andalucía's second-largest protected area. A world apart from the industrial sprawl around the southern coast, the darkly forested slopes draw you in with their detachment and timelessness.

MINAS DE RIOTINTO

pop 4500 / elevation 420m

Tucked away in the north of the province (68km northeast of Huelva), as if shielded from the gaze of the outside world, are the poisonous pits of the Minas de Riotinto, one of the world's oldest mining districts. Río Tinto takes its name, which means 'coloured river', from the stain of copper and iron oxides that wash into it from the mining zone and are carried all the way to the Atlantic.

Orientation

Minas de Riotinto is 5km east along the A461 off the N435 Huelva–Jabugo road. Entering the town, veer right at the first roundabout to reach the Museo Minero, about 400m uphill. Buses stop on Plaza de El Minero, a little beyond the same roundabout.

Sights

The museum and all the attractions are administered from the reception of the well-signposted Museo Minero. From here you can purchase tickets for the museum, the Corta Atalaya opencast mine and rides on the Ferrocarril Turístico-Minero. All three attractions come under the aegis of **Aventura Minaparque** (☎ 959 59 00 25). There are small discounts if you opt for combined tickets. It's worth ringing ahead to confirm timetables. It's especially if you plan to ride the train.

The **Museo Minero** (Plaza Ernest Lluch s/n; adult/child under 14 €3/2; ⏰ 10.30am-3pm & 4-7pm) is a figurative gold mine for devotees of industrial archaeology. But the best feature is the re-creation of a Roman mine that you are guided through (in Spanish) and which includes a reconstruction of one of the Roman water wheels. The tunnels are somewhat claustrophobic but the various displays along the way tell their own vivid story of a nightmarish world. Allow half an hour for the tour.

Another feature is the big display of the railways that the Rio Tinto Company built to serve the mines. At one time, 143 steam engines, mostly British-built, were puffing up and down these tracks. Pride of place goes to the **Vagón del Maharajah**, a luxurious carriage built in 1892 for a tour of India by Britain's Queen Victoria. That trip never happened, but the carriage was later used by Spain's Alfonso XIII for a visit to the mines.

The main tour from the museum takes you to the opencast mine of **Corta Atalaya** (adult/child €5/4, museum & mine adult/child €7/5), an awesome hole in the ground 1.2km long and 335m deep. It is one of the world's biggest opencast mines and its stepped sides are reminiscent of a huge amphitheatre, save for the lurid colours of its copper-bearing depths. It lies 1km west of the town and the rather long-winded commentary of the tour is in Spanish only.

Today's mining activities take place about 1km north of Minas de Riotinto at another opencast mine, the **Corta Cerro Colorado**, on the road towards Aracena. There's a viewing platform, the Mirador Cerro Colorado, from where you can view the current mining activities and ponder on the fact that only a century ago Cerro Colorado was a hill.

The easiest and most pleasurable way to view the mines (especially with children)

is on the **Ferrocarril Turístico-Minero** (adult/child €9/8, combined ticket for museum, mine & train adult/child €15/12), a restored steam train that takes visitors 22km through a surreal and scarred landscape. Trips start at Talleres Mina, the old railway repair workshops 2.5km east of Minas de Riotinto, just off the road to Nerva. From June to September they depart daily at 1.30pm, with an extra 5pm service in August only. Ring **Aventura Minaparque** (☎ 959 59 00 25) to confirm the winter schedule. You have to make your own way to the station and should leave yourself plenty of time to get there; ask at the museum about taxis.

The 19th-century Victorian-style houses where employees of the Rio Tinto Company were housed can still be seen on the left of the A461, coming from the west (opposite the turn-off into the town centre). Known as the **Barrio de Bella Vista**, the suburb has an unhappy history, effectively an English-only area where a fence (no longer in existence) kept the locals out.

Sleeping & Eating
Hotel Santa Bárbara (☎ 959 59 11 88; Cerro de los Embusteros s/n; d €52; P ✗ ✉) On a hill-top at the eastern end of town, the Santa Bárbara is a reliable, comfortable option with the town's best facilities. The rates include

---

RIVER OF FIRE

For centuries Huelva's mines have attracted a greedy and industrious line of entrepreneurs eager to exploit them for their hidden wealth. Popular legend would have us believe that they are the mines of King Solomon and there is evidence of copper mining in the area, which dates back to 3000 BC. What is certainly true is that around 1000 BC the Phoenicians sailed the length of the Mediterranean to begin the serious extraction of silver and iron ore. They named the river, where, according to myth, nuggets of ore floated to the very doors of their city, Ur-yero – River of Fire.

By the 4th century AD the Romans were going at it hammer and tongs, mining vast quantities of silver, described as a veritable mountain by Avienus who saw the 'slopes glint and shine in the light'. In order to keep up with demand, the Romans filled the mines with slaves, many of whom died within weeks from the wretched and poisonous conditions. Huge *norias* (water wheels) were built to drain the water, requiring an endless supply of forced labour to tread ceaselessly, lifting the buckets some 100m or more out of the depths. Inside, slaves worked in galleries only 1m wide, with light supplied by tiny oil lamps, a miserable environment now recreated in the museum. The 50 million tonnes of slag left behind by the Romans is a staggering testimony to the scale of the pre-industrial operation.

After the Romans, the lodes were largely neglected until they were bought by the British Río Tinto Company in 1872. The company turned the area into one of the world's great copper-mining centres, diverting rivers, digging away an entire metal-rich hill – Cerro Colorado – and founding the town of Minas de Riotinto to replace a village it had demolished. The mines returned to Spanish control in 1954, and today mining continues mainly at Cerro Colorado.

breakfast and the hotel has its own restaurant serving up a *menú* for €9.

Hostal Galán (☎ 959 59 08 40; Avenida La Esquila 10; s/d with bathroom €22.25/35.40) A cheaper option than Santa Bárbara and conveniently located just around the corner from the Museo Minero. The *hostal* has simple rooms (some of them with bathroom) and a handy restaurant with a *menú* for €7.80.

There are also some good accommodation options in the nearby town of Nerva:

La Estación (☎ 959 58 00 34; Carretera Nerva-Riotinto s/n; dm under/over 26 €11.10/14) Offers friendly and sparkling clean hostel-type accommodation in the converted railway station at Nerva. It also does full and half-board, can organise various trips and activities (such as biking tours in the mining zone) and has lots of local information.

Hotel Vázquez Díaz (☎ /fax 959 58 09 27; Calle Cañadilla 51; s/d €30/40) A friendly, modern hotel in Nerva with reasonable rooms and its own restaurant (*menú* for €7.80).

Getting There & Away

Damas buses run daily from Huelva to Minas de Riotinto (€4.85, 1¼ hours, five daily Monday to Saturday) and nearby Nerva. Casal runs services from Aracena to Minas de Riotinto (€2.20, 40 minutes, two daily Monday to Saturday) – the services depart early morning and early evening (check at the tourist office in Aracena for exact times).

From Seville (Plaza de Armas) there are **Casal** (Seville ☎ 954 99 92 90) buses to Minas de Riotinto (€4, one hour, three daily).

ARACENA

pop 7000 / elevation 730m

Travelling north from the yawning flat landscapes of southern Huelva into the picturesque mountains of the Parque Natural Sierra de Aracena y Picos de Aroche provides a welcome change. Humid, brine-filled breezes give way to crystal-clear mountain air, and straight highways become winding byways as the route takes you ever higher into dense, dark-green forests. In the heart of the Sierra is the thriving market town of Aracena, an appealing place, in a handsome location below a hill crowned by a medieval church and ruined castle. Surrounded by a series of similar rural towns, Aracena is an ideal base from which to explore.

Orientation

The town lies between the castle hill, Cerro del Castillo, in the south, and the N433 Seville–Portugal road that skirts it to the north and east. The main square is Plaza del Marqués de Aracena, from which the cobbled main street, Avenida de los Infantes Don Carlos y Doña Luisa (more simply known as Gran Vía), runs west. The bus office and stop for Casal and Damas buses is a few minutes' walk southeast of Plaza del Marqués de Aracena, on Avenida de Andalucía.

Information

Centro de Salud (☎ 959 12 62 56; Paseo Buenos Aires s/n) This health centre is located opposite the main bus station.

Centro de Turismo Rural y Reservas (☎ 959 12 82 06; Calle Pozo de la Nieve; ◷ 9am-2pm & 4-7pm) This tourist office faces the entrance to the Gruta de las Maravillas.

Centro de Visitantes Cabildo Viejo (☎ 959 12 88 25; Plaza Alta 5; ◷ 10am-2pm & 6-8pm Apr-Sep; 10am-2pm & 4-6pm Oct-Mar) The main information centre of the Parque Natural Sierra de Aracena y Picos de Aroche, but also has information on Aracena town.

Cybercafe Aranet (Calle José Nogales s/n; per hr €1.50; ◷ 10am-2.30pm & 6-10pm Mon-Fri) Internet access.

Policía Local (☎ 959 12 62 32; Plaza de Doña Elvira s/n)

Post office (☎ 959 12 81 52; Calle Juan del Cid 6; ◷ 8.30am-8.30pm Mon-Fri, 9.30am-2pm Sat)

Sights

Dramatically dominating the town are the tumbling ruins of the **castillo**, an atmospheric fort atop a steep hill that is now the site of the 13th-century **Iglesia Prioral de Nuestra Señora del Mayor Dolor** (admission free; ◷ 11am-7pm). The church is a Gothic-Mudejar hybrid that combines an interior of ribbed vaults with an attractive brick tracery exterior. The castle is reached up a steep road from Plaza Alta, a handsome, cobbled square that used to be the centre of the town. The plaza is now the location of the tourist office which is housed in the 15th-century **Cabildo Viejo** (Old Town Hall). Opposite the Cabildo Viejo is a huge, unfinished Renaissance church, the **Parroquia de la Asunción** (◷ hours of service).

Beneath the castle hill lies a maze of caves and passageways, full of stalagmites and stalactites. Attracting some 150,000 visitors a year, these form Aracena's premier tourist site, the **Gruta de las Maravillas** (Cave of

ARACENA

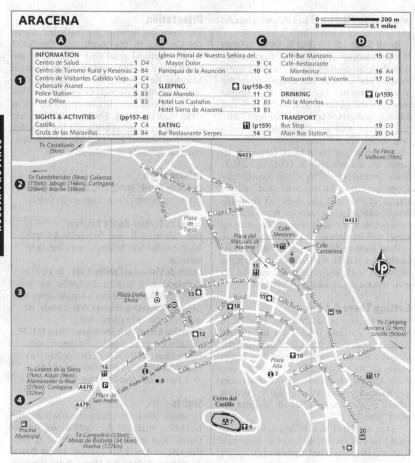

INFORMATION		
Centro de Salud	1	D4
Centro de Turismo Rural y Reservas	2	B4
Centro de Visitantes Cabildo Viejo	3	C4
Cybercafe Aranet	4	C3
Police Station	5	B3
Post Office	6	B3

SIGHTS & ACTIVITIES	(pp157–8)	
Castillo	7	C4
Gruta de las Maravillas	8	B4

Iglesia Prioral de Nuestra Señora del
Mayor Dolor.................9 C4
Parroquia de la Asunción.............10 C4

SLEEPING	🏠 (pp158–9)	
Casa Manolo	11	C3
Hotel Los Castaños	12	B3
Hotel Sierra de Aracena	13	B3

EATING	🍴 (p159)	
Bar Restaurante Sierpes	14	C3

Café-Bar Manzano	15	C3
Café-Restaurante Montecruz	16	A4
Restaurante José Vicente	17	D4

DRINKING	🍷 (p159)	
Pub la Moncloa	18	C3

TRANSPORT		
Bus Stop	19	D3
Main Bus Station	20	D4

Marvels; ☎ 959 12 83 55; Calle Pozo de la Nieve; hourly tour adult/child under 16 €7.70/5.50; ⏰ 10am-1.30pm & 3-6pm). The 1.2km route open to visitors features 12 chambers and six lakes, and has all sorts of weird and wonderful rock formations that provided the backdrop for the filming of *Journey to the Centre of the Earth*. Coloured lighting and piped music make you feel that this is still a lurid film set but the cave nevertheless manages to impress. The tour (in Spanish only) culminates at the aptly named **Sala de los Culos** (Chamber of the Backsides), usually met with roars of laughter from elderly Spanish ladies and bashful silence from their husbands.

Tour groups are limited to 35 people only and can get booked out in the after-noons and on weekends when busloads of visitors arrive in the town.

Sleeping

Finca Valbono (☎ 959 12 77 11; Carretera de Carboneras Km 1; d low/high season €63.10/83.15, 4-person apt low/high season €126/139; P 🐶 🚗) A converted farmhouse 1km northeast of Aracena, this is easily the most charming place in the area, with tasteful rustic rooms and tiled bathrooms. Facilities include a bar, a pool, riding stables and a good, medium-priced restaurant in a huge vaulted dining area.

Hotel Los Castaños (☎ 959 12 63 00; Avenida de Huelva 5; d low/high season €36/84; P 🐶) This 33-room hotel is the main hotel in town. It's not very exciting to look at but the rooms are a cut above the Hotel Sierra de Aracena and it has a restaurant serving a *menú* for €12.

Hotel Sierra de Aracena (☎ 959 12 61 75; Gran Vía 21; d weekend/week €52/47; **P** **⊠**) A reliable hotel due for an overhaul. Rooms are, however, perfectly comfortable, with TV. There are no evening meals (only breakfast) but the hotel is located close to a number of restaurants.

Casa Manolo (☎ 959 12 80 14; Calle Barbero 6; s/d €12.85/23.50) Just south of Plaza del Marqués de Aracena, this tiny little *pensión* has Aracena's only budget beds. It is a friendly place and there are seven basic rooms. However, there is no heating and it can get very cold in winter.

Eating

Restaurante José Vicente (☎ 959 12 84 55; Avenida de Andalucía 53; 3-course menú €15) Aracena's best restaurant and a good place to enjoy the area's famous specialities – the *jamón ibérico de bellota* (ham that comes from small, fat, black pigs who gorge themselves on acorns), mushrooms, pork loin and even snails. The proprietor is an expert on Sierra cuisine and even the fixed price *menú* (which includes a drink) is excellent.

Café-Restaurante Montecruz (☎ 959 12 60 13; Plaza de San Pedro; platos combinados €6-12) Perpetually busy and always open, the Montecruz might not be much to look at with its dark blue décor and swinging bunches of veg. However, it does a mean grilled steak and chips (€12) and when everything else in town is shut down this place is still humming.

Bar-Restaurant Sierpes (Calle Mesones 13; raciones €4.85) Located in a converted old house just up from the central Plaza del Marqués de Aracena, this pleasant bar has a sumptuous adjoining restaurant. It serves tapas for under €1 and has a restaurant *menú* for around €10.

Café-Bar Manzano (☎ 959 12 63 37; Plaza del Marqués de Aracena; tapas €1.20-1.80, platos combinados €6-9; ☼ Wed-Mon) This terrace café on the south side of Plaza del Marqués is a fine spot to watch the world go by and serves up varied tapas and *raciones*.

Several tourist-oriented restaurants line Plaza de San Pedro and Calle Pozo de la Nieve near the Gruta de las Maravillas.

Drinking

Pub La Moncloa (Calle Rosal; ☼ 10pm-4am Apr-Sep) Nightlife in Aracena is limited to the main bars, but for cool company and late-night drinking try the excellent La Mondoa. It's tucked away in a quiet side street and has a deep 16th-century *pozo* (well), preserved in one corner. Off-season it closes at about 1am and sometimes doesn't open at all.

Getting There & Away

Casal (Seville ☎ 954 99 92 90) runs buses to/from Seville's Plaza de Armas (€5.35, 1¼ hours, two daily). There are also buses from Aracena to Minas de Riotinto (€2.20, 40 minutes, two daily Monday to Saturday), to villages around northern Huelva province (see p163) and one daily bus at 10.30am to the Portuguese border (just beyond Rosal de la Frontera), where you can change to onward Portuguese buses. From the same Avenida de Andalucía stop, **Damas** (www.damas -sa.es) runs daily buses to/from Huelva (€6.80, two hours, two daily). Damas also has a service direct to Lisbon (3½ hours) that departs from the same bus stop at 10.30am Monday, Wednesday and Friday.

WEST OF ARACENA

Stretching west of Aracena is one of Andalucía's most unexpectedly beautiful landscapes, a sometimes lush, sometimes severe hill-country region dotted with old stone villages where time seems to have stood still. Many of the valleys are full of woodlands, while elsewhere are expanses of *dehesa* – evergreen oak groves where the region's famed black pigs forage for acorns.

There's an extensive network of marked walking trails throughout the **Parque Natural Sierra de Aracena y Picos de Aroche**, and particularly between Aracena and Aroche. Most of the villages are served by buses and many of them have accommodation, so you can make day hikes or string together a route of several days. It's advisable to phone ahead for rooms.

The N433 from Aracena to Aroche passes through Galaroza, and close to Fuenteheridos, Jabugo and Cortegana. A more scenic route as far as Cortegana (taking about an hour or just over, depending on speed as the road is quite narrow and windy) is along the A470 through Santa Ana la Real and Almonaster la Real (passing close to Linares de la Sierra and Alájar). Several roads and paths cut across the hills to link these two roads.

WEST OF ARACENA

Walking
The best information on walking routes in the Aracena area is in a leaflet called *Senderos de la Sierra de Aracena y Picos de Aroche* (Spanish only), which gives descriptions and directions to a number of linear and circular walks in the area. Ask at the Centro de Turismo Rural y Reservas in Aracena, or at Huelva city's tourist office before heading north. The map *Parque Natural Sierra de Aracena y Picos de Aroche* (1:75,000), published by the Junta de Andalucía, and the SGE 1:50,000 maps *Aracena*, *Aroche* and *Santa Olalla del Cala* give good overviews of the topography of the area but are not entirely helpful for route-finding. The former should be available locally, but SGE maps are usually only available at city outlets.

Linares de la Sierra
pop 300 / elevation 505m
Sunk in a river valley 7km west of Aracena on the A470, Linares appears to exist in another era. Cobbled streets, a minute unpaved bullring plaza, silent black-clad villagers, blind corners and oppressive silence pervade the tiny streets that are surrounded on all sides by a verdant river valley. There is no accommodation in the town but there is the famously good **Restaurant Al Arrieros** (☎ 959 46 37 17; Calle Arrieros 2; mains €9-11; ⏰ Thu-Tue Aug-Jun), with its summer terrace overlooking the valley and an enticing fire in winter. It is a great place to break the walk

from Aracena to Alájar (see p161), but be sure to reserve a table.

Alájar
pop 750 / elevation 574m
Five kilometres west of Linares de la Sierra is the region's most picturesque village, Alájar. Bigger than Linares, it still retains its tiny cobbled streets and cubist stone houses as well as a fine baroque church. Above the village a rocky spur, the **Peña de Arias Montano**, supports a 16th-century chapel, the **Ermita de Nuestra Señora Reina de los Ángeles** (⏰ hours of service) with magical views over the town. The *ermita* is 1km up the road towards Fuenteheridos. This road leaves the A470 almost opposite the Alájar turning. The church has a 13th-century carving of the Virgin and is the focus of a hectic pilgrimage on 7 September, when Alájar villagers race horses up the steep slope to the shrine.

La Posada (☎ 959 12 57 12; Calle Médico Emilio González 2; s/d €45/55) is a cosy place near Alájar's church, with eight rooms and a tiny restaurant. La Posada also hires out horses (per hour €7) and bicycles (per hour/day €3.50/10).

Jabugo
pop 2500
Famed throughout Spain for its mouthwateringly tender *jamón ibérico*, Jabugo even has its own system of classification. It grades hams from one to five *jotas* (Js), with five Js representing hams from pigs

---

DETOUR: LINARES DE LA SIERRA & ALÁJAR WALK

Many walking routes start from Aracena. A good round trip of about 12km can be made by leaving Aracena between the Piscina Municipal (municipal swimming pool) and the A470 road at the western end of town. This path rollercoasters down a verdant valley to Linares de la Sierra.

To return by the more southerly PRA39 path, find a small stone bridge over the river below Linares, beyond which the path goes round Cerro de la Molinilla, passing old iron mines, and then crosses a stream for a stony ascent to Aracena, bringing you out on the A479 in the southwest of town.

You could extend the walk by continuing 4km west along the PRA38 path from Linares to Alájar, via the hamlet of Los Madroñeros. There are fine views on this stretch. From Alájar you can walk back the way you came (30km round-trip) or catch the afternoon bus, daily except Sunday, to Aracena (for bus information, see p163).

HUELVA PROVINCE

who have only ever gorged themselves on the Sierra's acorns. The town itself in not much to look at and has ugly, sprawling ham-producing factories hemming it in on all sides, but then you come here for the taste-bud trail, not for sightseeing.

A line of bars and restaurants along on the eastern side of the village wait for you to sample the best *jamón* in the country. At **Mesón Cinco Jotas** (☎ 959 12 15 15; Carretera San Juan del Puerto), run by the biggest producer, Sánchez Romero Carvajal, a serving of the best ham, *cinco jotas* (5 Js), will set you back €7, or you could really 'pig out' on *cinco jotas* and fried eggs for about €10. At shops such as **de Jabugo la Cañada** (☎ 959 12 12 07; Carretera San Juan del Puerto 2) you can purchase almost every part of the pig in some form or other. *Jamón* to take away costs about €20 per kilogram and for a whole 7kg ham of the best quality, you will pay €250.

Finca la Silladilla (☎ 959 50 13 50; silladi@teleline .es; Los Romeros-Jabugo; d €89, cottages €108-178; P ⊠ ⊠), just west of Jabugo on the road to Los Romeros (turn left after 3km at the sign for La Silladilla) is a gorgeous little *finca* (farm) tucked away in a sea of cistus and oak trees. The house was originally a textile mill and you can stay here or in four self-catering farmhouses. The small shop has provisions and also serves tapas.

Almonaster la Real

pop 2000 / elevation 613m

Nestling in the shadow of the Sierra's highest peak, Almonaster (913m), Almonaster la Real is a solid workaday town but harbours a surprising gem of Islamic architecture. The mini **mezquita** (mosque; admission

free; ⊗ 9.30am-8pm) stands on a hill-top five minutes' walk up from the main square. If you find it shut, ask for the key at the town hall on the square.

Almost perfectly preserved, the mosque was built in the 10th century and is a miniature version of the great mosque at Córdoba. Despite being Christianised in the 13th century, the building retains nearly all of its original features: the huge horseshoe arches, the semicircular mihrab, an ablutions fountain and various Arabic inscriptions. The Christians added a Romanesque apse on the northern side, where parts of a broken Visigothic altar, carved with a dove and angels' wings, have been reassembled.

The original minaret, a square, three-level tower, adjoins the main building. You can climb to the upper chamber and look down on the Almonaster's 19th-century **bullring** (where a *corrida de toros* – bullfight – is held each August), but take care near the open, unprotected windows. In the village, the Mudejar **Iglesia de San Martín** (Placeta de San Cristóbal) has a 16th-century portal in the Portuguese Manueline style, unique in the region.

On the first weekend in May the town hosts the **Cruz de Mayo** flamenco festival, an excuse to show off the local fandango dancing and some fabulous traditional costumes. Throughout May similar festivals take place throughout the Sierra villages.

Hotel Casa García (☎ 959 14 31 09; fax 959 14 31 43; Avenida San Martín 2; s/d €35.40/51.45; P ⊠) is a stylish, small hotel at the entrance of the village from the A470. It provides some of the best accommodation in the Sierras. Rooms have a *Country Living* feel and some have

---

A QUESTION OF TASTE

The best ham in Spain comes from the Sierra Morena and the best of this from Jabugo. Throughout the Sierra the pampered pigs graze in a porcine paradise, snuffling out the acorns within the area's vast oak forests. In October, beaters knock the acorns off the trees and just as quickly knock off the greedy piggies to be transformed into gourmet hams. The traditional spring-time slaughter, known locally as the *matanza*, is a village affair where people travel from farm to farm helping with the strenuous task of preparing the meat into hams and *morcillas* (sausages). Anthony Bourdain gives a fantastic, if gory, account of a *matanza* in his book *Kitchen Confidential*. The innumerable tools required for the business are exhibited in Jaén's wonderful Museo de Artes y Costumbres Populares (see p348). The huge ham haunches are usually smothered in sea salt and hung to sweat. The longer they are hung – some up to two years – the higher the quality and the greater the value.

To immerse yourself in the history, traditions and etiquette of Sierra cuisine, book into the **Finca Buen Vino** (959 12 40 34; www.fincabuenvino.com; Los Marines, Carretera N433 Km 95; d €60, cottage per week low/high season €300/1015; P ⛽), a working farm. Would-be gourmets will be particularly interested in the week-long course run by cordon-bleu trained Jeannie, who will take you through a repertoire of Andalucian, Mediterranean and Moroccan dishes. Cooking days are interspersed with trips to local cheese and ham factories, food shops, sherry bodegas and restaurants. Wine-fuelled lunches are had in its fabulous wood-panelled dining room, where the requisite *jamón* sits in state on its *jamonera*. Courses run from autumn to spring and cost €1,200 for six nights, all inclusive. Some facilities are adapted for wheelchair users.

---

balconies. The restaurant is also highly regarded and specialises in local meat dishes (mains €9 to €12).

Located on a pleasant small plaza, **Hostal La Cruz** (☎ 959 14 31 35; Plaza El Llano 8; s/d €24/30) has a few simple rooms. It also has a bar-restaurant with *raciones* for around €5.

Cortegana
pop 5000 / elevation 673m

Six kilometres northwest of Almonaster is the village of Cortegana, which supplies much of the local *anís* (aniseed liqueur) for Almonaster's fiesta. It is a sizeable village overlooked by a 13th-century **castillo** (admission €1.25; ✹ 11am-2pm & 5-7pm) that now contains a rather boring exhibition on medieval fortifications in northern Huelva. Next to the castle is the 16th-century **Capilla de Nuestra Señora de la Piedad** and also worth a look is the Gothic-Mudejar **Iglesia del Divino Salvador** (Plaza del Divino Salvador). The best time to visit Cortegana is during the **Jornadas Medievales**, a huge fiesta in August where everyone dresses up in medieval costume and indulges in plenty of drinking and merry-making, including tournaments, falconry displays and archery competitions.

Hostal Cervantes (☎ 959 13 15 92; Calle Cervantes 27B; d without/with bathroom €18/24) is a good-value *hostal* with nice rooms, some of which overlook a garden. It is situated just off Plaza de la Constitución.

Aroche
pop 3500 / elevation 406m

A stone's throw away from the Portuguese border, Aroche has always been in disputed territory. Nowadays, however, it gets few visitors and is one of the least touristy villages reached from Cortegana along the N433 or the PRA2 footpath that runs along the broad, open valley. It is a cheerful, friendly place and is full of narrow, pebbled streets. There's a car park in Calle Dolores Losado beside the bus stop as you enter the town.

Aroche's 12th-century **castillo** (admission free; ✹ 10am-2pm & 5-7pm Sat, Sun & holidays), at the top of the village, has been remodelled as the town's unusual bullring. Outside the official opening hours ask at the **Casa Consistorial** (town hall; Plaza de Juan Carlos I) or **Cafetería Lalo** (☎ 959 14 02 61; ✹ 9.30am-2pm & 5-7pm), up the steps beside the Casa Consistorial, where local guide Manuel Amigo will take you up there.

Just below the castle is the large **Iglesia de Nuestra Señora de la Asunción**, which surprisingly, houses some 1st-class sculpture by La Roldana, the daughter of the famous Pedro Roldán, and Alonso Cano. The town's other main attraction – if you can call it that – is the bizarre **Museo del Santo Rosario** (☎ 959 13

16 31; Paseo Ordóñez Valdéz; ⓨ inquire at Cafetería Lalo). It has a collection of more than 1000 rosaries from around the world, from illustrious names such as Mother Theresa, former US president Richard Nixon and General Francisco Franco.

Hostal Picos de Aroche (☎ 959 14 04 75; Carretera de Aracena 12; s/d €18/30) is a serviceable *hostal* on the road up into town from the N433. It is spotless, if basic, and it's wise to book ahead.

Centro Cultural Las Peñas (Calle Real; tapas €1.20-1.50, raciones €8-11), full of men swigging the local *anís*, has a great local atmosphere and serves up tasty tapas and *raciones*.

Other Villages

Between Jabugo and Aracena are several attractive little villages that can be reached from the N433. Worth a visit, if you have time, are **Galaroza**, **Fuenteheridos** and especially **Castaño del Robledo**. The latter is a small, impoverished village, on a minor road between Fuenteheridos and the N435. It has a positively medieval feel, with two large churches in states of advanced disrepair overlooking a mass of sagging tiled roofs. You'll find a couple of bars on Plaza del Álamo, behind the Iglesia de Santiago el Mayor (the church with the pointier tower).

Getting There & Away

BUS

Many of the villages are served by **Casal** (in Seville ☎ 954 99 92 90) buses from Seville (Plaza de Armas) and Aracena. Buses run from Aracena to Cortegana (€2.20, 50 minutes, two daily Monday to Saturday), and back, via Linares de la Sierra (€0.70, 15 minutes, two daily Monday to Saturday), Alájar (€0.80, 20 minutes, two daily Monday to Saturday) and Almonaster la Real (€1.55, 40 minutes, two daily Monday to Saturday), with one of them continuing to/from Aroche (€2.95, 1¼ hours) and the other to/from Seville. Four buses run daily each way between Aracena and Cortegana via Fuenteheridos, Galaroza and Jabugo, with three continuing to/from Aroche and Rosal de la Frontera.

Damas buses run each way between Huelva and Almonaster la Real (€5.75, 2½ hours, daily Monday to Friday) and Aroche (€6.80, 2½ hours, two daily Monday to Friday).

TRAIN

There are services between Huelva and Almonaster-Cortegana (€4.95, 1¾ hours, two daily) and Jabugo-Galaroza (€5.50, two hours, two daily) stations. At the time of writing they leave Huelva at 9.35am and 1pm. Both of the outbound trains from Huelva terminate in Extremadura: one at Fregenal de la Sierra, the other at Zafra. Almonaster-Cortegana station is 1km off the Almonaster–Cortegana road, about halfway between the two villages. Jabugo-Galaroza station is in El Repilado, on the N433, 4km west of Jabugo.

Cádiz Province

Cádiz (*cad*-i, or if you've got a really good local accent, just *ca*-i) possesses perhaps the greatest variety of attractions of any of Andalucía's eight provinces. Its coast, stretching from the mouth of the region's biggest river, the Guadalquivir, to the Strait of Gibraltar, is blessed with the best string of beaches in Andalucía – one long strand after another of clean Atlantic sand. As you'd expect, mounds of tasty seafood wait to be sampled in the towns and villages along this shore. Even better news is that the property-development blight that afflicts some other sections of Andalucian coast is largely unknown here. Inland, Cádiz stretches to the beautiful Grazalema mountains and the majestic cork forests of Parque Natural Los Alcornocales. Its natural variety provides opportunities for windsurfing, kitesurfing, diving, scaling peaks, descending canyons, watching the large and varied bird population, or following assorted trails on horseback, mountain bike or foot.

The cities and towns of Cádiz province are among the most historically and culturally fascinating in Andalucía – from the age-old port of Cádiz itself, with its famously warm and cultivated people, or Jerez de la Frontera, with its sherry bodegas (wineries), horse displays and flamenco, to lesser but still historic ports such as Tarifa or El Puerto de Santa María; from small, laid-back beach towns such as Los Caños de Meca and Bolonia, to spectacularly sited mountain towns and villages such as Arcos de la Frontera, Grazalema and Zahara de la Sierra. The proliferation of 'de la Frontera' place names in Cádiz province dates from the Reconquista (Christian reconquest) when from the mid-13th to the late 15th century this was a *frontera* (frontier) of Christian territory.

HIGHLIGHTS

- Savouring the surf and beach scene at **Tarifa** (p204) – one of Europe's top wind-surfing and kitesurfing spots

- Enjoying the port city of **Cádiz** (p166), scene of Spain's wildest **Carnaval** (p171)

- Visiting **Jerez de la Frontera** (p182), famous for its sherry, horses, flamenco and festivals

- Touring the tapas bars of **El Puerto de Santa María** (p178) or enjoying a seafood dinner at **Sanlúcar de Barrameda** (p181)

- Exploring the white villages and craggy mountains of the **Parque Natural Sierra de Grazalema** (p192)

- Unwinding on the **Costa de la Luz** (p197) – long sandy beaches, laid-back coastal villages and the Roman ruins at **Baelo Claudia** (p203) in Bolonia

★ Sanlúcar de Barrameda
★ Parque Natural Sierra de Grazalema
★ Jerez de la Frontera
★ El Puerto de Santa María
★ Cádiz
★ Bolonia
★ Costa de la Luz
★ Tarifa

POPULATION:	CÁDIZ AVERAGE DAILY HIGH:	ALTITUDE RANGE:
1.6 MILLION	JAN/AUG 15°C/30°C	0m–1654m

CÁDIZ PROVINCE

CÁDIZ

pop 135,000

Once past the coastal marshes and industrial sprawl around Cádiz, you emerge into an elegant, civilised port city of largely 18th- and 19th-century construction, whose grandeur is now rapidly being restored by an energetic inner city restoration programme. Cádiz is crammed onto the head of a long promontory like some huge, crowded, ocean-going ship, and the tang of salty air and open ocean vistas are never far away. It has a long and fascinating history, plenty of absorbing monuments and museums, and a healthy quota of enjoyable places at which to eat and drink – yet it's the *gaditanos* (people of Cádiz) who make the place truly special. Warm, open, hospitable, cultured and independent-minded, most *gaditanos* are concerned above all to make the most of life – whether simply enjoying each other's company over a coffee or beer in one of the city's bars, staying out late to soak up the after-dark cool in the sweltering summer months, or indulging in Spain's most riotous carnival in late winter.

HISTORY

Cádiz may be the oldest city in Europe. It was founded under the name Gadir by the Phoenicians, who came here to exchange Baltic amber and British tin for Spanish silver.

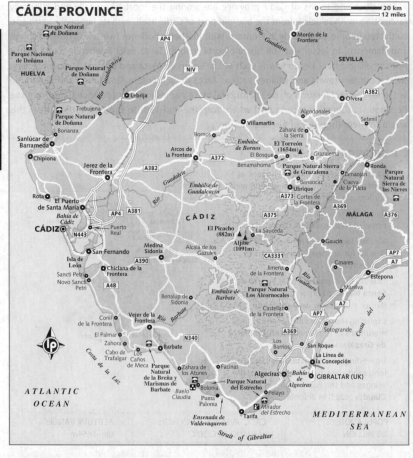

Classical sources speak of the founding of Gadir around 1100 BC. The archaeological evidence is that Gadir was in existence by at least the 8th century BC. Later, it became a naval base for the Romans, who called it Gades and heaped praise on its culinary, sexual and musical delights.

In more recent times, Cádiz began to boom with the discovery of America. Christopher Columbus sailed from here on his second and fourth voyages. Cádiz attracted Spain's enemies too: in 1587 England's Sir Francis Drake 'singed the king of Spain's beard' with a raid on the harbour, delaying the imminent Spanish Armada. In 1596 Anglo-Dutch attackers burnt almost the entire city.

Cádiz's golden age was the 18th century, when it enjoyed 75% of Spanish trade with the Americas. It grew into the richest and most cosmopolitan city in Spain and gave birth to the country's first progressive, liberal middle class. Most of its fine buildings date from this era.

The Napoleonic Wars brought British warships back to blockade and bombard the city and shatter the Spanish fleet at the Battle of Trafalgar, nearby, in 1805. After Spain turned against Napoleon, Cádiz underwent a two-year French siege from 1810. During this time a national parliament, known as the Cortes de Cádiz, convened here. This lopsidedly liberal gathering adopted Spain's 1812 constitution, proclaiming sovereignty of the people and setting the scene for a century of struggle between liberals and conservatives.

Spain's loss of its American colonies in the 19th century plunged Cádiz into a slump from which it is only now emerging. Cádiz province still has the highest unemployment figures in Spain (24% in 2004), partly due to a decline in shipbuilding and fishing. Tourism is an important part of the city's recovery plan, with more monuments being opened to the public, and an admirable renovation programme restoring the old city's splendour.

ORIENTATION

Breathing space between the huddled streets of the old city is provided by numerous squares, the four most important for short-term orientation being Plaza San Juan de Dios, Plaza de la Catedral and Plaza de Topete in an arc in the southeast, and Plaza de Mina in the north. Pedestrianised Calle San Francisco runs most of the way between Plaza San Juan de Dios and Plaza de Mina.

The train station is just east of the old city, off Plaza de Sevilla, with the main bus station (of the Comes line) 900m to its north on Plaza de la Hispanidad. The main harbour lies between the two.

The 18th-century Puertas de Tierra (Land Gates) mark the eastern boundary of the old city. Modern Cádiz extends back along the peninsula towards the town of San Fernando.

INFORMATION
Bookshops
QiQ (☎ 956 20 57 66; Calle San Francisco 31; ☼ 10am-2pm & 5.30-9pm Mon-Sat) Guidebooks in several languages, local-interest books.

Emergency
Ambulance (☎ 061)
Policía Nacional (National Police; ☎ 091; Avenida de Andalucía 28) Five hundred metres southeast of the Puertas de Tierra.

Internet Access
Enred@2 (cnr Calles Isabel La Católica & Antonio López; per hr €1.50; ☼ 11am-11pm Mon-Sat)

Medical Services
Hospital Puerta del Mar (☎ 956 00 21 00; Avenida Ana de Viya 21) The main general hospital, 2.25km southeast of the Puertas de Tierra.

Money
You'll find plenty of banks and ATMs along Calle San Francisco and the parallel Avenida Ramón de Carranza.

Post
Main post office (Plaza de Topete)

Tourist Information
Municipal tourist office main office (☎ 956 24 10 01; Plaza San Juan de Dios 11; ☼ 9am-2pm & 4-7pm Mon-Fri, afternoon hours 5-8pm mid-Jun–mid-Sep); information kiosk (Plaza San Juan de Dios; ☼ 10am-1.30pm & 4-6pm Sat, Sun & holidays, afternoon hours 5-7.30pm mid-Jun–mid-Sep)
Regional tourist office (☎ 956 25 86 46; Avenida Ramón de Carranza s/n; ☼ 9am-7pm Mon-Fri, 10am-1.30pm Sat, Sun & holidays)

CÁDIZ PROVINCE

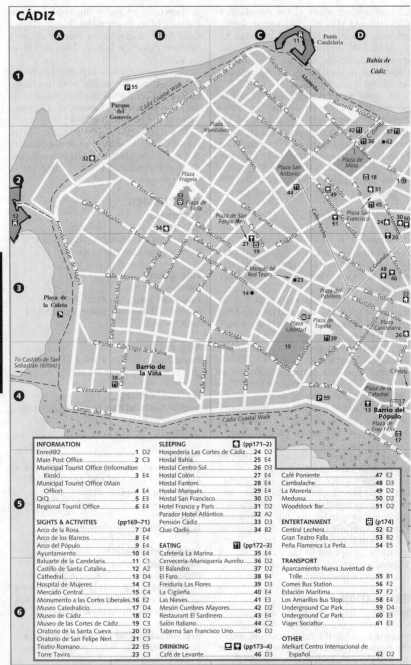

CÁDIZ

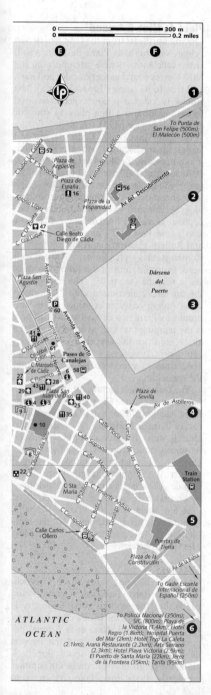

SIGHTS
Plaza San Juan de Dios & Barrio del Pópulo

Broad Plaza San Juan de Dios is surrounded by cafés and dominated by the imposing neoclassical **ayuntamiento** (city hall), which was built around 1800. Behind the *ayuntamiento*, the Barrio del Pópulo neighbourhood was the kernel of medieval Cádiz, a fortified enclosure wrecked by the Anglo-Dutch raiders in 1596. Its boundaries are still marked by three 13th-century gate arches, the **Arco de los Blancos**, **Arco de la Rosa** and **Arco del Pópulo**. Until recently shabby and run-down, the Barrio del Pópulo has been a focus of the city centre's restoration programme and its now clean and attractive streets, which are mostly pedestrianised, sport several craft shops and galleries.

On the seaward edge of the Barrio del Pópulo, pop into the excavated **Teatro Romano** (Roman Theatre; ☎ 956 21 22 81; Campo del Sur s/n; admission free; ⏰ 10am-2pm), where you can walk along the gallery beneath the tiers of seating. The remains of the stage are still buried beneath the adjacent buildings.

Cathedral & Around

The story of Cádiz's yellow-domed **cathedral** (☎ 956 25 98 12; Plaza de la Catedral; adult/child €4/2.50; ⏰ 10am-1.30pm & 4.30-7pm Tue-Fri, 10am-12.30pm Sat), fronting a handsome, broad and pedestrianised plaza, reflects that of the whole city in the 18th and 19th centuries. The decision to build it was taken in 1716 on the strength of the imminent transfer of the Casa de la Contratación, which controlled Spanish trade with the Americas, from Seville to Cádiz. But the cathedral wasn't finished till 1838, by which time not only had neoclassical elements (including the dome, towers and main façade) diluted Vicente Acero's original baroque plan, but also funds had run short, forcing cutbacks in size and quality. It's still a beautiful and impressive construction, perhaps seen to best effect when floodlit at night. The most unusual feature inside the cathedral is the large, circular underground crypt, built of stone excavated from the sea bed. Cádiz-born composer Manuel de Falla is among those buried here.

From a separate entrance on Plaza de la Catedral you can climb up inside the cathedral's **Torre de Poniente** (Western Tower; adult/child/senior €3/2/2; ⏰ 10am-6pm, to 8pm mid-Jun–mid-Sep),

Cádiz's tallest tower, for marvellous views of the old city. Note the many watchtowers built in the 18th century so citizens could keep an eye on shipping movements without stepping outside their front doors.

The cathedral ticket also admits you to the nearby **Museo Catedralicio** (Cathedral Museum; Plaza de Fray Félix; ⏰ 10am-1.30pm & 4.30-7pm Tue-Fri, 10am-12.30pm Sat), with an excavated medieval street and material on the Anglo-Dutch sacking of 1596 alongside assorted art and artisanry.

Plaza de Topete & Around

A short walk northwest from the cathedral, this square is one of Cádiz's liveliest, with bright flower stalls and adjoining the large, animated **Mercado Central** (Central Market). It's still widely known by its old name, Plaza de las Flores (Square of the Flowers). A few blocks further northwest, the **Torre Tavira** (☎ 956 21 29 10; Calle Marqués del Real Tesoro 10; admission €3.50; ⏰ 10am-6pm, to 8pm mid-Jun–mid-Sep) is the highest and most important of the city's old watchtowers, with a dramatic panorama of Cádiz. Its camera obscura projects live, moving images of the city onto a screen (sessions start at half-hourly intervals). Back in the 18th century, Cádiz had no less than 160 watchtowers.

Also nearby is the 18th-century **Hospital de Mujeres** (☎ 956 22 36 47; Calle Hospital de Mujeres 26; admission to chapel €0.80; ⏰ 10am-1.30pm Mon-Sat), a former women's hospital whose chapel is one of the most profusely decorated churches from Cádiz's golden century and contains El Greco's *Extasis de San Francisco* (Ecstasy of St Francis).

A little further northwest you reach the **Museo de las Cortes de Cádiz** (☎ 956 22 17 88; Calle Santa Inés 9; admission free; ⏰ 9am-1pm & 4-7pm Tue-Fri Oct-May, 9am-1pm & 5-7pm Tue-Fri Jun-Sep, 9am-1pm Sat & Sun), full of historical memorabilia focusing on the 1812 Cortes de Cádiz parliament. Pride of place belongs to a large, marvellously detailed model of 18th-century Cádiz, made in mahogany and ivory in the 1770s for Carlos III. Just along the street is the church where the parliament actually met, the **Oratorio de San Felipe Neri** (☎ 956 21 16 12; Plaza de San Felipe Neri; admission €1.20; ⏰ 10am-1pm Mon-Sat). One of Cádiz's finest baroque churches, this has an unusual oval interior and a beautiful dome. A masterly Murillo *Inmaculada* of 1680 has a place of honour in the main retable.

Plaza de Mina & Around

Moving northeast from the Oratorio de San Felipe Neri towards Plaza de Mina you'll cross **Calle Ancha**, where members of the 1812 Cortes would gather in cafés and bars. Still true to its name ('Broad Street'), Calle Ancha is today a pleasant pedestrianised thoroughfare and a fine place to stop for an ice cream (see p173).

Plaza de Mina, one of Cádiz's largest and leafiest squares, is home to the city's excellent major museum, the **Museo de Cádiz** (☎ 956 21 22 81; Plaza de Mina; non-EU citizen €1.50, EU citizen free, Sun free; ⏰ 2.30-8pm Tue, 9am-8pm Wed-Sat, 9.30am-2.30pm Sun). The stars of the ground-floor archaeology section are two Phoenician marble sarcophagi carved in human likeness. There's also some beautiful Phoenician jewellery and Roman glassware, and lots of headless Roman statues – plus Emperor Trajan, with head, from the ruins of the Roman town of Baelo Claudia (see p203). The highlight of the fine arts collection, upstairs, is a group of 21 superb canvases of saints, angels and monks by Francisco de Zurbarán. Also here is the painting that cost Murillo his life, the altarpiece from the chapel of Cádiz's Convento de Capuchinas – the artist died in 1682 from injuries received in a fall from the scaffolding.

The **Oratorio de la Santa Cueva** (☎ 956 22 22 62; Calle Rosario 10; admission €2; ⏰ 10am-1pm & 5-7.30pm Tue-Fri, 10am-1pm Sat & Sun), a short distance southeast of Plaza de Mina, is a 1780s neoclassical church with an unusual contrast between its austere underground Capilla Baja (Lower Chapel) and its richly decorated oval-shaped Capilla Alta (Upper Chapel). Three of the Capilla Alta's eight arches frame paintings by Francisco de Goya.

A few streets east, on Plaza de España, stands Cádiz's elaborate neoclassical monument to the 1812 parliament, the **Monumento a las Cortes Liberales**.

Beaches

Old Cádiz has one short curve of beach, Playa de la Caleta (see Cádiz Coastal Walk, p171), but the modern part of the city is fronted by a superb, wide ocean beach of fine Atlantic sand, **Playa de la Victoria**, beginning about 1.5km beyond the Puertas de Tierra and stretching about 4km back along the peninsula from there. On summer weekends almost the whole city seems to

---

CÁDIZ COASTAL WALK

This circuit takes you right around the Cádiz seaboard from Plaza de Mina to the cathedral – a 4.5km walk that could last anything from 1¼ hours upward. Go one block north from Plaza de Mina to the city's northern seafront, with views across the Bahía de Cádiz to El Puerto de Santa María, then head northwest along the jungly **Alameda** gardens (with two truly gigantic rubber trees) to the **Baluarte de la Candelaria** bastion (occasionally housing art exhibitions). Here turn southwest to the **Parque del Genovés**, laid out, like the Alameda, in the 19th century and with some nicely clipped trees. You might stop for refreshments at the Parador Hotel Atlántico at the southwest end of the park. Continue to the **Castillo de Santa Catalina** (☎ 956 22 63 33; admission free; ⏲ 10.30am-6pm, to 8pm approx May-Aug), a star-shaped fort built to defend the city after the Anglo-Dutch sacking of 1596: inside is a historical exhibit on Cádiz and the sea and a gallery for temporary exhibitions. The sandy beach **Playa de la Caleta** (very crowded in summer) separates Santa Catalina from another fort, the 18th-century **Castillo de San Sebastián**. You can't enter San Sebastián but do walk along the airy 750m causeway to its gate. At low tide you can have a poke around the rock pools along the way. Finally, follow the broad promenade east along **Campo del Sur** to the yellow-domed cathedral.

---

be out here. Where the city ends, the beach continues under the name **Playa de la Cortadura**. Bus No 1 'Plaza España–Cortadura' from Plaza de España will get you to both beaches (€0.80).

COURSES

Cádiz has a few popular language schools.
Gadir Escuela Internacional de Español (☎ /fax 956 26 05 57; www.gadir.net; Calle Pérgolas 5) A couple of blocks southeast of the Puertas de Tierra, offering cultural as well language courses.

Melkart Centro Internacional de Español (☎ /fax 956 22 22 13; www.centromelkart.com; Calle General Menachu 7) In the old city.

SIC (☎ 956 25 27 24; www.spanishincadiz.com; Calle Condesa Villafuente Bermeja 7) About 1km southeast of the Puertas de Tierra.

FESTIVALS & EVENTS

No other Spanish city celebrates **Carnaval** (www.carnavaldecadiz.com in Spanish) with the verve of Cádiz, where it turns into a 10-day singing, dancing and drinking fancy-dress party spanning two weekends (3 to 13 February 2005 and 23 February to 5 March 2006). Everybody dresses up and the fun, abetted by quantities of alcohol, is infectious. Costumed groups called *murgas* tour the city on foot or on floats, dancing, singing satirical ditties or performing sketches (unfortunately most of the *gaditanos'* famed verbal wit will be lost on all but fluent Spanish speakers). In addition to the 300 or so officially recognised *murgas*, who are judged by a panel in the Gran Teatro Falla (p174),

there are also the *ilegales* – any group that fancies taking to the streets and trying to play or sing.

Some of the liveliest scenes are in the working-class Barrio de la Viña, between the Mercado Central and Playa de la Caleta, and along Calle Ancha and Calle Columela where *ilegales* tend to congregate.

Rooms in Cádiz are all booked months in advance for Carnaval. Assuming you haven't managed to snatch a room, you could just go to Cádiz from Seville or anywhere else within striking distance, just for the night. Plenty of people do this – many wearing fancy dress.

SLEEPING

Room rates given here, for July, can almost double during Carnaval. They may also rise in a few places in August, but often go down 20% to 25% outside the summer season.

Budget

Many budget places cluster in the streets just north of Plaza San Juan de Dios.

Hostal Centro Sol (☎ /fax 956 28 31 03; www .hostalcentrosolcadiz.com; Calle Manzanares 7; s/d €40/49) This efficient and friendly *hostal* (a simple guesthouse or small place offering hotel-like accommodation) in an attractive neoclassical house dating from 1848 has plain and smallish rooms, with cable TV and wooden furniture of assorted age. Breakfast is available, and the owners speak French.

Hostal Fantoni (☎ 956 28 27 04; www.hostalfantoni .com; Calle Flamenco 5; d €40, s/d with shared bathroom

€20/30) The friendly, family-run Fantoni is in an 18th-century house with around 15 spotless, white-walled rooms with pretty flower prints. The roof terrace catches a breeze in summer.

Hostal Colón (☎ 956 28 53 51; Calle Marqués de Cádiz 6; r with shared/private bathroom €40/50) The good, bright, reasonably sized rooms, all with firm beds and TV, overlook a quiet street.

Hostal San Francisco (☎ 956 22 18 42; Calle San Francisco 12; r with shared/private bathroom €37/48) Deeper into the old city, the San Francisco has reasonable rooms with TV and pine-veneer furnishings, though they're moderately sized and some have little natural light. Bicycles rent for €6 a day.

Quo Qadis (☎/fax 956 22 19 39; www.quoqadis .com; Calle Diego Arias 1; dm incl breakfast €6-12, d incl breakfast with shared/private bathroom €24/30; ✗) Cádiz's independent youth hostel occupies a revamped old house near the Gran Teatro Falla. It provides basic and sometimes crowded accommodation, but it gets a good clean out between 11am and 5pm each day when the guests have to be out. Vegetarian dinner is served for €3. With a sleeping bag, you can sleep on the roof terrace for €6. The place gets pretty busy in summer and it's advisable to book ahead. The owners rent bikes for €6 a day and organise trips to the beaches and mountains of Cádiz province.

Other acceptable budget options include the following:

Hostal Marqués (☎ 956 28 58 54; Calle Marqués de Cádiz 1; d €30-36, s/d with shared bathroom €18/25)

Pensión Cádiz (☎ 956 28 58 01; Calle Feduchy 20; r with shared/private shower €34/42)

Mid-Range

Parador Hotel Atlántico (☎ 956 22 69 05; www .parador.es; Avenida Duque de Nájera 9; s €63.70-121.90, d €79.60-152.40; P ☒ ☐ ☛) Cádiz's Parador is a hideous brown concrete building but inside it's as comfortable, spacious and attractive as you would expect from this luxury chain. All rooms have a private terrace with sea view of some sort (best at the front). The pool is set in a lawn overlooking the ocean.

Hostal Bahía (☎ 956 25 90 61; hostalbahia@terra.es; Calle Plocia 5; s/d €47.05/64.20; ☒) Handily placed just off Plaza San Juan de Dios, the Bahía's 21 rooms, all exterior, are neat and spotless, with phone and TV.

Hotel Francia y París (☎ 956 21 23 19; www.hotel francia.com in Spanish; Plaza San Francisco 2; s/d €61.70/

77.15; ☒ ☐) This is a bigger hotel (57 rooms) with comfortable but unexciting rooms and little atmosphere.

Hotel Regio (☎ 956 27 93 31; www.hotelregiocadiz .com; Avenida Ana de Viya 11; s/d €52/88; P ☒) A short stroll from Playa de la Victoria, the 42-room Regio is comfy but unimaginative. It has a café, and phones in the rooms.

Top End

Hospedería Las Cortes de Cádiz (☎ 956 21 26 68; www.hotellascortes.com in Spanish; Calle San Francisco 9; s/d incl breakfast €98.45/128.40; P ☒ ☐) This charming new hotel occupies an 1850s mansion centred on an elegant four-storey balustraded atrium. The 36 rooms have attractive period-style furnishings and plenty of modern comforts. Each is named after, and contains a specially commissioned oil painting of, a figure or place associated with the Cortes de Cádiz. Three rooms are adapted for the disabled and the hotel also has a roof terrace, gym and Jacuzzi.

Hotel Playa Victoria (☎ 956 20 51 00; www .palafoxhoteles.com; Glorieta Ingeniero La Cierva 4; s/d from €115.55/166.40; P ☒ ☒ ☛) This is the best of the beach hotels, fronting directly onto Playa de la Victoria, 2.6km from the Puertas de Tierra, with 188 elegant, balconied rooms. Make sure you get an ocean view (one-third of the rooms face inland).

Hotel Tryp La Caleta (☎ 956 27 94 11; Avenida Amílcar Barca 47; s/d €87.75/144.45; P ☒ ☐) Half the 143 rooms face the beach and ocean, 400m west of Hotel Playa Victoria. Ask about weekend and with-breakfast deals.

EATING
Plaza San Juan de Dios

All the cafés and restaurants around this busy square are good for watching *gaditano* life.

Cafetería La Marina (☎ 956 25 55 31; Plaza San Juan de Dios 13; breakfast €3) A friendly spot for breakfast or a drink, cake, croissant or *empanada* (pasty).

La Cigüeña (☎ 956 25 01 79; Calle Plocia 2; mains €12-16; ☽ closed Sun) A few steps off the square, 'The Stork' has a Dutch chef who prepares adventurous and excellent food, such as caramelised duck breast with potato omelette and grape sauce. The table settings look a little formal but staff are friendly and relaxed.

Restaurant El Sardinero (☎ 956 26 33 37; Plaza San Juan de Dios 4; mains €10-15) El Sardinero is the best place on the square for seafood, with plenty of choice and lots of tables out front. Local fish from the bay are pricey, though, at €25-plus.

Las Nieves (Plaza Mendizábal; menú €7; [Y] closed Sun) A couple of blocks into the old town, wood-beamed Las Nieves attracts Cádiz's professional classes for breakfast and a good-value lunch *menú* (set menu).

Plaza San Francisco & Plaza de Mina

Mesón Cumbres Mayores (☎ 956 21 32 70; Calle Zorrilla 4; tapas €1.50-2, mains €5-15) This popular place, hung with dangling hams and garlic, has an excellent tapas bar in the front and a restaurant in the back, both providing delicious fare at reasonable prices. In the bar it's hard to beat the ham and cheese *montaditos* (open sandwiches). In the restaurant, the endive and avocado salad with a Roquefort dressing is a meal in itself: if you can, follow up with *guisos* (stews), seafood or barbecued meats.

Taberna San Francisco Uno (Plaza San Francisco 1; raciones €6.50-10) This cosy bar, with some tables on the plaza, offers a tempting range of meat, fish and stews, plus a good wine list and platters of hams, cheeses, sausages and smoked fish to share.

El Balandro (☎ 956 22 09 92; Alameda Apodaca 22; tapas €3.50; [Y] closed Sun evening & Mon) Find a space at the long U-shaped bar or sit down by the windows overlooking the bay. The Balandro offers a huge range of filling tapas, almost equivalent to restaurant main courses.

Cervecería-Marisquería Aurelio (☎ 956 22 10 31; Calle Zorrilla 1; tapas €1.50-2, raciones €6-10) It's hard to pass up the fresh seafood tapas at this sparklingly white-tiled establishment.

Salón Italiano (☎ 956 22 18 97; cnr Calles Ancha & San José; ice cream €1-4.20) When the heat strikes, head here for many varieties of tasty ice cream.

Plaza de Topete

Freiduría Las Flores (☎ 956 22 61 12; Plaza de Topete 4; seafood per 250g €2.50-4.50) Cádiz specialises in fried fish and seafood and Las Flores, resembling a fancy fish and chip shop, is one of the best places to sample it. You order by weight. To try a range of things together, have a *surtido* (a mixed fry-up).

Barrio de la Viña

El Faro (☎ 956 22 99 16; Calle San Felix 15; mains & raciones €7-15; [X]) Over in the old fishermen's district near Playa La Caleta, El Faro is Cádiz's most famous seafood eatery. Sit in

the restaurant decorated with pretty ceramics, or squeeze up to the adjoining tapas bar. The seafood is excellent in both parts but the bar offerings are less pricey. *Tortillitas de camarones* (prawn fritters) make a good start, then follow your instincts.

Nearby Calle Virgen de la Palma is lined with orange trees and several restaurants and bars serving inexpensive fish and seafood. Stroll by at night!

Playa de la Victoria

There's heaps of choice along Paseo Marítimo facing the beach. Both of the following are between the Playa Victoria and Tryp La Caleta hotels:

Arana Restaurante (☎ 956 20 50 90; Paseo Marítimo 1; mains €10-18; [X]) Arana serves quality Andalucian meat and seafood (entrecôte – rib steak – in sweet Pedro Ximénez wine, monkfish in white-wine sauce) in stylish, modern surroundings.

Arte Serrano (☎ 956 27 72 58; Paseo Marítimo 2; mains €8-12) Specialises in meat from the Andalucian hill country.

DRINKING

For coffee, beer, wine and people-watching take a seat at one of the café-bars on Plaza San Juan de Dios, Plaza San Francisco or Plaza de Mina.

The Plaza San Francisco, Plaza de España and Plaza de Mina area is the hub of the nocturnal bar scene. Things start to get going around 11pm or midnight at most places but can be pretty quiet in the first half of the week, when some late bars don't bother opening.

Cambalache (Calle José del Toro 20; [Y] from 8.30pm Mon-Sat) This long, dim, jazz and blues bar occasionally hosts live music.

Medussa (Calle General Luque 8) Local and foreign students converse above loud music in the dimly red-lit interior or spill out into the street.

The following are other favourite nocturnal hang-outs:

Café de Levante (Calle Rosario 35; [Y] 8pm-1am) Relaxed gay/mixed bar hung with photos of arts and showbiz icons.

Woodstock Bar (☎ 956 21 21 63; cnr Calles Sagasta & Cánovas del Castillo) *'Música, paz y cerveza'*.

Café Poniente (Calle Beato Diego de Cádiz 18; [Y] closed Sun & Mon) Gay/mixed pub with occasional drag shows.

In summer the late-night scene migrates to the Paseo Marítimo along Playa de la Victoria, around and beyond the Hotel Playa Victoria. You'll find lively music bars and throngs of people in the street drinking. Others hang out on the beach. A taxi from the old city (try Plaza de España) to this area costs about €5. Up to about 1.30am you can use bus No 1 from Plaza de España (€0.80).

If your preferred beverage is tea, drop into **La Morería** (Calle San Pedro 5; ☉ from 4pm), a hip Moroccan tearoom serving all manner of infusions in silver pots.

ENTERTAINMENT

There's a great atmosphere in old-city squares such as Plaza de Mina on hot summer nights, with bars and cafés busy till well after midnight, and kids playing football or cruising on bikes or skates. Cádiz also has a lively cultural scene: pick up a programme from one of the tourist offices.

Peña Flamenca La Perla (☎ 956 25 91 01; Calle Carlos Ollero s/n) Cádiz is one of the true homes of flamenco. This atmospheric, cavernlike den of a club was hosting flamenco nights at 10pm on Friday at the time of writing.

Gran Teatro Falla (☎ 956 22 08 28; Plaza de Falla) Cádiz's main theatre, a fine neo-Islamic building in pink brick, stages a busy programme of theatre, dance and music.

Central Lechera (☎ 956 22 06 28; Plaza de Argüelles s/n) This smaller venue plays host to more-adventurous/experimental music, dance and theatre.

If it's time to dance, head out along the northern side of the harbour to the *puerto deportivo* (marina) area at Punta de San Felipe. This is the real late, late zone, with a row of dance bars. Here, **El Malecón** (☎ 956 22 45 19; Paseo Pascual Pery; ☉ from midnight Fri & Sat) is Cádiz's top Latin dance spot.

GETTING THERE & AWAY
Boat
See p179 for details of the passenger ferry across the bay to El Puerto de Santa María.

Bus
Most buses are run by **Comes** (☎ 956 80 70 59) from Plaza de la Hispanidad. Destinations include Algeciras (€8.70, 2½ hours, 10 daily), Algodonales (€8.20, 1¾ hours, five daily), Arcos de la Frontera (€4.80, 1¼ hours, six daily), Barbate (€4.75, one hour, 14 daily),

Córdoba (€18.35, three hours, one or two daily), El Puerto de Santa María (€1.45, 30 to 40 minutes, 23 daily), Granada (€25.95, 4½ hours, four daily), Jerez de la Frontera (€2.55, 40 minutes, 23 daily), Los Caños de Meca (€4.50, 1¼ hours, two daily Monday to Friday) via El Palmar, Málaga (€18.05, four hours, six daily) via Marbella, Ronda (€11.80, two hours, three daily), Seville (€9.50, 1¾ hours, 11 daily), Tarifa (€6.95, 1¾ hours, five daily), Vejer de la Frontera (€4.10, 50 minutes, eight daily) and Zahara de los Atunes (€6.15, two hours, four daily). Frequency of service to some destinations is reduced on Saturday and Sunday.

Los Amarillos runs 11 buses daily (five on Saturday and Sunday) to El Puerto de Santa María (€1.25, 30 to 40 minutes) and Sanlúcar de Barrameda (€2.75, 1¼ hours), and five Monday to Friday (two on Saturday and Sunday) to Arcos de la Frontera (€4, 1¼ hours) and El Bosque (€6.40, two hours), from its stop by the southern end of Avenida Ramón de Carranza. Tickets and information are available at **Viajes Socialtur** (☎ 956 29 08 00; Avenida Ramón de Carranza 31). Take the 12.30pm bus to El Bosque (Monday to Saturday only) for connections to Grazalema.

Car & Motorcycle
The AP4 motorway from Seville to Puerto Real on the eastern side of the Bahía de Cádiz carries a toll of €6. The toll-free alternative, the NIV, is a lot busier and slower. From Puerto Real, a bridge crosses the narrowest part of the bay to join the N340/A48 entering Cádiz from the south.

Train
The **train station** (☎ 956 25 10 01) is just off Plaza de Sevilla, near the Puertas de Tierra. Up to 36 trains run daily to/from El Puerto de Santa María (from €2, 30 to 35 minutes) and Jerez de la Frontera (€2.50 to €2.75, 40 to 50 minutes), nine or more daily to/from Seville (€8.40 to €22.50, 1¾ hours), and four to/from Córdoba (€15.75 to €32, three hours).

GETTING AROUND
There are a few places to park in the old city.
Aparcamiento Nueva Juventud de Trille (per 24hr €4.50) Open-air parking by Parque del Genovés.
Underground car park (Campo del Sur; per 24hr €9)
Underground car park (Paseo de Canalejas; per 24hr €6.50)

THE SHERRY TRIANGLE

North of Cádiz, the towns of Jerez de la Frontera, Sanlúcar de Barrameda and El Puerto de Santa María are best known as the homes of that unique Andalucian wine, sherry. But there's a wealth of other good reasons to visit the 'sherry triangle': beaches, music, horses, history, and trips into the Parque Nacional de Doñana.

EL PUERTO DE SANTA MARÍA

pop 76,500

El Puerto, 10km northeast of Cádiz across the Bahía de Cádiz (22km by road), is easily and enjoyably reached by ferry. Alfonso X conquered the city for the Christians in 1260 and called it Santa María del Puerto. Christopher Columbus was a guest of the knights of El Puerto from 1483 to 1486: it was here that he met Juan de la Cosa, the owner of his 1492 flagship, the *Santa María*, and Columbus' pilot on the great voyage. From the 16th to 18th centuries El Puerto was the base of the Spanish royal galleys. Its heyday came in the 18th century, when it flourished on American trade and earned the name Ciudad de los Cien Palacios (City of the Hundred Palaces). Today its beaches, sherry bodegas (wineries) and tapas bars make it a favourite outing for *gaditanos*, *jerezanos* and others looking for a change of scenery. In summer it's a very lively town.

Orientation & Information

The heart of the town is on the northwest bank of the Río Guadalete, just upstream from its mouth, though development spreads along the beaches to the east and west of the mouth. The ferry *El Vapor* arrives dead centre at the Muelle (Jetty) del Vapor on Plaza de las Galeras Reales. Calle Luna, one of the main streets, runs straight inland from Plaza de las Galeras Reales. The train station is a 10-minute walk northeast of the centre, beside the Jerez road. Some buses stop at the train station, others at the Plaza de Toros (bullring), five blocks south of Calle Luna.

Internet (Calle Palacios 39; per hr €1.80; 11am-2pm & 6-10pm Mon-Fri, 6-10pm Sun)

Post Office (Avenida Aramburu de Mora) Four blocks south of Calle Luna.

Tourist Office (956 54 24 13; www.elpuertosm.es; Calle Luna 22; 10am-2pm & 6-8pm May-Sep, 10am-2pm & 5.30-7.30pm Oct-Apr) Excellent, with plenty of information about water sports, horse riding and other activities.

Sights & Activities

Start your explorations at the historic four-spouted **Fuente de las Galeras Reales** (Fountain of the Royal Galleys), on Plaza de las Galeras Reales. America-bound ships drew their water here. Two blocks southwest, then a block inland, stands the **Castillo San Marcos** (956 85 17 51; Plaza Alfonso El Sabio 3; admission free; 10am-2pm Tue). Heavily restored in the 20th century, the beautiful castle incorporates a mosque and was built by Alfonso X after he took the town in 1260. Visits are by half-hour guided tour: the highlight is the mosque itself, now converted to a church.

Three blocks further inland is the **Fundación Rafael Alberti** (956 85 07 11; Calle Santo Domingo 25; admission €2.50; 11am-4pm Tue-Sun) with interesting exhibits on one of El Puerto's famous sons, Rafael Alberti (1902–99). A poet, painter and communist politician of the Generation of '27 (see p44), Alberti lived in this house as a child.

Nearby, the little **Museo Municipal** (956 54 27 05; Calle Pagador 1; admission free; 10am-2pm Tue-Fri, 10.45am-2pm Sat & Sun) has interesting archaeological and fine art sections, including paintings by Rafael Alberti.

The impressive sandstone **Iglesia Mayor Prioral** (956 85 17 16; 8.30am-12.45pm Mon-Fri, 8.30am-noon Sat, 8.30am-1.45pm Sun, 6.30-8.30pm) dominates Plaza de España. Built between the 15th and 18th centuries, it boasts the lavish Puerta del Sol, a plateresque/baroque portal, facing the plaza, and a huge 17th-century Mexican-made silver retable in the Capilla del Sagrario (to the right of the main altar). If you're interested in bullfighting, detour four blocks southwest from Plaza de España to El Puerto's 19th-century **Plaza de Toros** (admission free; 11am-1.30pm & 6-7.30pm Tue-Sun May-Sep, 11am-1.30pm & 5.30-7pm Tue-Sun Oct-Apr). This is one of Andalucía's most beautiful and important bullrings, with room for 15,000 spectators. It's closed on days before and after bullfights. For details of when bullfights are held, see p179.

A short walk northeast from Plaza de España is the **Casa de los Leones** (House of the Lions; 956 87 52 77; Calle La Placilla 2; admission free; 10am-2pm & 6-8pm), one of the finest of the many baroque mansions that were built in

CÁDIZ PROVINCE

EL PUERTO DE SANTA MARÍA

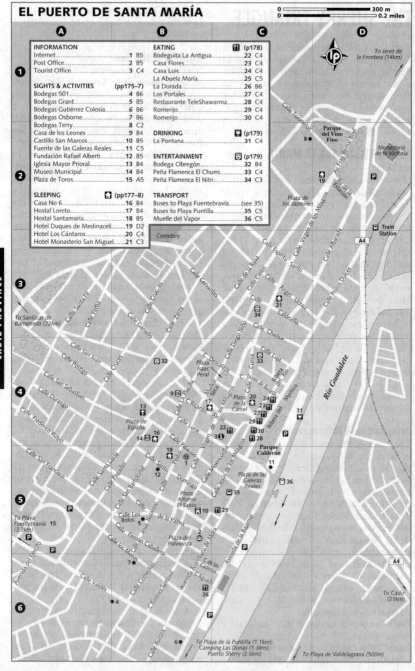

| 0 | 300 m |
| 0 | 0.2 miles |

SACRED BULLS

As you roam the highways of Spain, every now and then you catch sight of the silhouette of a truly gigantic black bull on the horizon. When you get closer to the creature you'll realise it's made of metal and held up by bits of scaffolding. What's it for?

It's not a silent homage to bullfighting erected by the local folk, nor a sign that you're entering a notable bull-breeding area. It's a sherry and brandy advertisement for the Bodegas Osborne company of El Puerto de Santa María. At the last count there were 92 *toros de Osborne*, each weighing up to four tonnes, looming beside roads all over the country.

Why doesn't Osborne put its name on the bulls if it's trying to advertise, you might ask? From 1957, when the first bull was erected on the Madrid–Burgos road, until 1988, it did. Then a new law banned advertising billboards beside main roads, to prevent drivers being distracted. Osborne left the bulls standing but removed its name, which seemed to pacify the authorities, until 1994 when word got about that the law was going to be enforced strictly, meaning no more bulls. This provoked an enormous furore, with intellectuals writing to newspapers about the national heritage, the Andalucian regional government declaring the 21 bulls in Andalucía protected monuments, and Osborne taking the fight to the courts. In 1997 Spain's supreme court decided that the bulls had transcended their original advertising purpose and were now part of the landscape. They still are.

El Puerto's 18th-century heyday. This house was recently restored as holiday apartments: most impressive is its façade but there are interesting information panels in the interior patio.

SHERRY BODEGAS

Phone a day or more ahead to visit either of the best-known sherry wineries, **Bodegas Osborne** (☎ 956 86 91 00; Calle los Moros) and **Bodegas Terry** (☎ 956 85 77 00; Calle Toneleros s/n). These bodegas offer tours (€5) Monday to Friday; Terry includes a visit to its carriage museum. Tours are in Spanish with English translations if necessary (or, all in English if only English speakers are present).

You can visit three other sherry houses without booking:

Bodegas 501 (☎ 956 85 55 11; Calle Valdés 9; admission €4; ☺ 10am-1pm Mon-Fri)

Bodegas Grant (☎ 956 87 04 06; Calle Los Bolos 1; admission €2.10; ☺ tours 12.30pm & 1.30pm Sat)

Bodegas Gutiérrez Colosía (☎ 956 85 28 52; Avenida de la Bajamar; admission €3; ☺ tours 1.30pm Sat)

BEACHES

When you've finished sightseeing you'll probably want to head for the beach. A range of activities from canoeing to windsurfing are possible. The tourist office has a leaflet with details.

Pine-flanked **Playa de la Puntilla** is a half-hour walk southwest of the town centre, or you can get here by bus No 26 (€0.60)

heading southwest on Avenida Aramburu de Mora. **Playa Fuentebravía**, further west, is accessible by bus No 35 (€0.60) from the same stop. Between the two beaches is a swish marina development called, of course, **Puerto Sherry**.

Tours

Free, guided walking tours of the town set off at 11am Saturday (and Tuesday from July to September) from the tourist office.

El Vapor (☎ 629-468014) conducts 1½-hour night cruises (€5) around the bay at 9.45pm on Tuesday, Thursday and Saturday, from 1 July to 7 September.

Festivals & Events

Feria de la Primavera (Spring Fair; early May) Held over four days, this fiesta is deeply influenced by sherry, with around 200,000 half-bottles being drunk.

Campeonato del Mundo de Motociclismo de Jerez (early May) An unofficial motorbike fiesta takes over central El Puerto for the weekend of the Jerez motorcycle Grand Prix (see p188).

Sleeping

Reserve ahead for July and August. Prices drop noticeably out of season.

Hotel Duques de Medinaceli (☎ 956 86 07 77; www.jale.com/dmedinaceli; Plaza de los Jazmines 2; s/d €212/234; P ✗ ⌘) El Puerto's newest top-end hotel, converted from an 18th-century mansion, drips with antiques. It was most recently the home of the Terry Irish sherry family. The 28 rooms are equipped with every comfort.

Hotel Monasterio San Miguel (☎ 956 54 04 40; www.jale.com/monasterio; Calle Virgen de los Milagros 27; s/d from €144/179; P ⊠ ⚍) This stylish and luxurious hotel in a converted 18th-century monastery is El Puerto's second top-end option. A tropical garden, pool, valuable artworks and a gourmet restaurant await your pleasure if your pockets are deep enough.

Casa No 6 (☎ 956 87 70 84; www.casano6.com; Calle San Bartolomé 14; r/f incl breakfast €60/100, 4-person apt €120; P) This is an early-19th-century house beautifully renovated by its lively Spanish-English owners. It provides charming, spacious and spotless rooms with high, wood-beamed ceilings, comfy beds and old-fashioned tiling, all around a lovely pillared patio open to the sky. Two rooftop apartments have outdoor sitting areas.

Hotel Los Cántaros (☎ 956 54 02 40; www.hotelloscantaros.com; Calle Curva 6; s/d €88/105; P ⊠) This classy hotel (named for the 18th-century water jugs found by archaeologists beneath the hotel) has 39 comfortable, well equipped rooms, some with balconies. Its restaurant looks out to a small garden. There is also a lift.

Hostal Loreto (☎ /fax 956 54 24 10; Calle Ganado 17; s/d/tr €48/48/72, with shared bathroom €42/42/60) The homely Loreto is set around a leafy, flower-filled courtyard. All 23 rooms have windows on the street or courtyard.

Hostal Santamaría (☎ 956 85 36 31; Calle Pedro Muñoz Seca 38; s/d €13/28, with shared bathroom €12/25) This friendly guesthouse has 12 good, clean, simple rooms. Its signs simply say 'CH' and 'Camas'.

Camping Las Dunas (☎ 956 87 22 10; www.lasdunascamping.com; camping per adult/tent/car €4/4/3.40) The town's well-equipped and shady camping ground is just behind Playa de la Puntilla.

Eating

El Puerto is an excellent place in which to sample seafood and has some terrific tapas bars.

Romerijo (☎ 956 54 12 54; Ribera del Marisco s/n; 250g seafood from €3) This is a huge El Puerto institution, with crowds flocking to its two facing buildings. One building boils the seafood, the other fries it, and you buy portions in paper cones to take away or eat at the many tables. Everything's on display and you just take your pick and buy by the quarter-kilogram: for example, €3 for chunks of fried *cazon* (dogfish) or €4.80 to €12.50 for various types of boiled prawns.

Casa Flores (☎ 956 54 35 12; Ribera del Río 9; entrées €5-11, mains €14-34) Facing the river, this is a place for more-formal dining. You can choose from a lovely array of entrees including endive leaves with Roquefort cheese, or all manner of shellfish. Oven-baked fish encrusted with salt (€34) tops the price list.

Los Portales (☎ 956 54 21 16; Ribera del Río 13; mains €8.50-15) Another formal place, it's hard to go wrong here for grilled fish and seafood. A local speciality well worth trying is *urta roteña* (sea bream cooked in white wine, tomatoes, peppers and thyme; €12).

Restaurante TeleShawarma (☎ 956 87 64 23; Ribera del Marisco s/n; falafel roll €3; mains €9) Vegetarians will just love this small, simple restaurant next to the large Romerijo seafood complex. The food, authentic Lebanese-Greek, provides a welcome change from the usual fare. The falafel is unbeatable. Meat options include souvlakia.

Calle Misericordia also sports half a dozen varied tapas bars dishing up some of the tastiest morsels in the region.

Bodeguita La Antigua (Calle Misericordia 8; tapas €2.70) La Antigua helpfully provides tapas menus in English and French as well as in Spanish. The *serranito*, a bread roll with pork, fried green pepper and a few chips (€2.70), makes people happy.

Casa Luis (Ribera del Marisco s/n; tapas/raciones €2.50/7; ⏰ 1.30-4pm & 9.30-11pm Tue-Sun) This is a tightly packed little den with just a few tables inside and out, and a bar you can only elbow towards. They come for Luis' innovative tapas, such as *paté de cabracho* (scorpion fish pâté) or *hojaldres* (puff pastries) with cheese and anchovy filling.

Crowds also flock to the tapas bars along the streets south of Plaza de las Galeras Reales.

La Abuela María (☎ 956 85 61 40; Avenida Aramburu de Mora s/n; tapas/media-raciones/raciones/mains €1.80/3.60/6.60/10) 'Granny Maria's' is neat and relatively spacious, with interesting sculptures. Seafood is the speciality: try *bacalao rebozado* (breadcrumbed salted cod).

La Dorada (☎ 956 85 52 14; Avenida de la Bajamar 26; tapas/media-raciones €1.80/5; ⏰ closed Mon) This slightly rougher-and-readier seafood haunt's speciality is *choco a la plancha* (grilled cuttlefish).

Drinking & Entertainment

Youthful music bars cluster around the centre and on the eastern side of town at Playa de Valdelagrana.

La Pontana (Parque Calderón; ☽ from 4pm) Get the real maritime feel at this bar-disco. Floating on the river just north of Plaza de las Galeras Reales, it has views down river and is *the* place to go from about 11pm onwards.

Flamenco happens some weekends at **Peña Flamenca El Nitri** (☎ 956 54 32 37; Calle Diego Niño 1) and **Peña Flamenca El Chumi** (☎ 956 54 00 03; Calle Luja 15). **Bodega Obregón** (Calle Zarza 51), the oldest bar in the city, has flamenco on Sunday from 12.30pm to 3.30pm.

Top matadors fight every Sunday in July and August at El Puerto's **Plaza de Toros** (Bull-ring; ☎ 956 54 15 78; www.justo-ojeda.com; Plaza Elías Ahuja; seats in the sun/shade from €10/21).

Getting There & Away

BOAT

The small passenger ferry *Adriano III,* better known as *El Vapor* or **El Vaporcito** (The Little Steamship; ☎ 956 85 59 06; www.vapordeelpuerto.com in Spanish) sets sail for El Puerto (€3, 45 minutes) from Cádiz's Estación Marítima (passenger port) at 10am, noon, 2pm, 4.30pm and 6.30pm daily from 8 February to 9 December (except nonholiday Mondays from 9 September to 30 May), with an extra trip at 8.30pm from 1 July to 8 September. Trips from El Puerto to Cádiz leave one hour earlier than all the above times, departing from the Muelle del Vapor. The *Adriano III* and its predecessors *Adriano I* and *Adriano II* have provided this vital link between the two cities since 1929.

BUS

Monday to Friday, buses to Cádiz (€1.25 to €1.45, 30 to 40 minutes) depart about half-hourly, 6.45am to 10pm, from the bullring, and at least seven times between 8.30am and 11.30pm from the train station. Weekend services are about half as frequent. For Jerez de la Frontera (€1.05, 20 minutes) there are nine to 15 buses daily from the train station and nine from the bullring Monday to Friday (but only one on Saturday and Sunday). For Sanlúcar de Barrameda (€1.50, 30 minutes) and Chipiona (€2.25, 30 minutes), five to 11 buses daily go from the bullring. For Seville (€7.50, 1½ hours), five buses go daily from the train station.

TRAIN

Up to 36 trains daily travel to/from Jerez (from €1.15, 12 minutes) and Cádiz (from €2, 30 to 35 minutes), and ten or more daily to/from Seville (€7 to €20, one to 1½ hours).

Getting Around

There's plenty of parking along the river-front, especially south of Plaza de las Galeras Reales. Most of it is free, but the semi-supervised area next to the plaza costs €1.60 for 24 hours.

SANLÚCAR DE BARRAMEDA

pop 62,000

The northern tip of the sherry triangle and a flourishing summer resort, Sanlúcar is 23km northwest of El Puerto de Santa María. It has a likable, mellow atmosphere and a fine location on the Guadalquivir estuary looking across to the Parque Nacional de Doñana.

Columbus sailed from Sanlúcar in 1498 on his third voyage to the Caribbean. So, in 1519, did the Portuguese Ferdinand Magellan, seeking – as Columbus had – a westerly route to the Asian spice islands. Magellan succeeded by making the first known voyage around the bottom of South America but was killed in a battle in the Philippines. His Basque pilot Juan Sebastián Elcano completed the first circumnavigation of the globe by returning to Sanlúcar with just one of the five ships, the *Victoria.*

Orientation & Information

Sanlúcar stretches along the southeast side of the Guadalquivir estuary. Calzada del Ejército, running 600m inland from the seafront Paseo Marítimo, is the main avenue (often just called La Calzada) and it has underground parking. A block beyond its inland end is Plaza del Cabildo, the central square. The bus station is on Avenida de la Estación, 100m southwest of the middle of La Calzada.

The old fishing quarter, Bajo de Guía, site of Sanlúcar's best restaurants and boat departures to Doñana, is 750m northeast along the riverfront from La Calzada. There are banks on Calle San Juan, which runs southwest off Plaza del Cabildo.

Centro de Visitantes Bajo de Guía (☎ 956 38 09 22; Bajo de Guía s/n; ☽ 10am-2pm Tue-Sun & 4-6pm holidays & the evening before) Run by the Junta de Andalucía, this visitors centre has info on the Parque

Natural de Doñana (distinct from the Parque Nacional – for the difference, see p148) and other natural spaces in Andalucía.

Centro de Visitantes Fábrica de Hielo (☎ 956 38 16 35; Bajo de Guía s/n; ◷ 9am-7pm or 8pm) This, the original visitors centre, is run by the national parks folk. It has interesting displays and information on the Parque Nacional de Doñana and related topics.

Cibercafe Guadalquivir (Calle Infanta Beatriz; Internet per hr €1.80; ◷ 10am-1am) Central location, by the Hotel Guadalquivir.

Tourist Office (☎ 956 36 61 10; Calzada del Ejército s/n; ◷ 10am-2pm year-round & 4-6pm Oct-Apr, 5-7pm May, 6-8pm Jun-Sep) Towards the inland end of La Calzada, this tourist office has helpful staff with plenty of info to hand out.

Sights & Activities
WALKING TOUR
From Plaza del Cabildo, cross Calle Ancha to Plaza San Roque and head up Calle Bretones to admire the elaborate Gothic façade of **Las Covachas**, a set of 15th-century wine cellars in an outer wall of the Palacio de los Duques de Medina Sidonia (see below). Here, the street becomes Calle Cuesta de Belén and doglegs up to the entrance to the **Palacio de Orleans y Borbon** (admission free; ◷ 10am-1.30pm Mon-Fri). The creation of this beautiful neo-Mudejar palace as a summer home for the aristocratic Montpensier family in the 19th century was what started Sanlúcar's growth as a resort. Today the palace is Sanlúcar's *ayuntamiento* (town hall). Join a free guided tour at 12.30pm Monday, Wednesday and Friday.

From the town hall entrance at the top of Calle Cuesta de Belén, a block to the left along Calle Caballero, is the 15th-century **Iglesia de Nuestra Señora de la O** (Plaza de la Paz; ◷ 9am-1pm Sun, 7.30-8pm Sun-Fri), with a Mudejar façade and ceiling. Next door is the **Palacio de los Duques de Medina Sidonia** (☎ 956 36 01 61; www.fcmedinasidonia.com; Plaza Condes de Niebla 1; admission €3; ◷ 9.30am-2pm Sun), a large and rambling stately home that dates all the way back to the time of Guzmán El Bueno, the 13th-century ancestor of the Duques de Medina Sidonia (see p205 for more on Guzmán). This powerful aristocratic family once owned more of Spain than anyone else. The current incumbent, Luisa Isabel Álvarez de Toledo, has fought long and hard to keep the priceless Medina Sidonia archive in Sanlúcar. The house is bursting

with antique furniture, paintings by famous Spanish artists, even Goya and Zurbarán, and other wonderful decorations. Enjoy yourself at the attached **café** (◷ 9am-2pm & 3.30-9pm) where you'll find classical music, coffee, tea and cakes.

Some 200m further along the street is the 15th-century **Castillo de Santiago** (Plaza del Castillo; ◷ not open), amid buildings of Sanlúcar's biggest sherry company, Barbadillo. Plans to reform the castle and create a cultural centre, concert space, restaurant and shops seem to be on the verge of implementation. Look forward to stunning views from the castle towers when the project is completed. From the castle you can return directly downhill to the town centre.

BEACH
Sanlúcar's good sandy beach runs all along the riverfront and for several kilometres beyond to the southwest.

BODEGAS
Sanlúcar produces a distinctive sherrylike wine, manzanilla. Three bodegas give tours (principally in Spanish, but they can be adapted for the group) for which you don't need to book ahead:

Barbadillo (☎ 956 38 55 00; Calle Luis de Eguilaz 11; tour €3; ◷ noon & 1pm Mon-Sat; in English 11am Tue-Sat; Museo de Manzanilla 11am-3pm Mon-Sat) Near the castle. The museum (admission free), in a 19th-century building, traces the 200-year history of Sanlúcar's unique manzanilla wine and the history of the Barbadillo family, the first wine producers to bottle manzanilla. It also outlines the production process from start to finish.

Bodegas Hidalgo-La Gitana (☎ 956 38 53 04; Calle Banda Playa; tour €3; ◷ 11.30am & 12.30pm)

La Cigarrera (☎ 956 38 12 85; Plaza Madre de Dios; tour €2.50; ◷ 10am-2pm Mon-Sat)

Tours
On any of these trips, except in winter, take mosquito repellent or cover up.

Real Fernando (Centro de Visitantes Fábrica de Hielo; ☎ 956 36 38 13; www.visitasdonana.com; 3½-hr trips adult/child under 13/child under 16 €15.05/6.50/10.50; ◷ 10am Nov-Feb, 10am & 4pm Mar-May & Oct, 10am & 5pm Jun-Sep) This boat makes one or two trips daily on the Guadalquivir from Bajo de Guía. Despite stops in the national park and the Parque Natural de Doñana, these trips are not designed for serious nature enthusiasts. Book two or three days ahead, and a week or more ahead in summer and during holiday periods.

Viajes Doñana (☎ 956 36 25 40; Calle San Juan 20; 3½-hr tour per person €33; ☷ 8.30am & 4.30pm Tue & Fri May–mid-Sep, 8.30am & 2.30pm Tue & Fri mid-Sep–Apr) These tours into the national park go from Bajo de Guía: after the river crossing, the trip is by 4WD vehicle holding about 20 people, visiting much the same spots as the tours from El Acebuche (see p149). Make bookings as far ahead as you can.

Festivals & Events

Feria de la Manzanilla (late May/early June) The Sanlúcar summer begins with a big spring fair.

Music Festivals (July and August) Summer revs up with jazz, flamenco and classical music festivals, and one-off concerts by top Spanish bands.

Carrereras de Caballos (August; www.carrerassanlucar .com) Two horse-race meetings of three or four days every August: unique thoroughbred races on the sands beside the Guadalquivir estuary, held almost every year since 1845.

Sleeping

Book well ahead for a room at holiday times. Budget accommodation is scarce.

Hotel Posada de Palacio (☎ 956 36 48 40; www .posadadepalacio.com; Calle Caballeros 11; s/d/q €85/105/ 149; P ☖ ☐) In the upper part of town, Sanlúcar's most charming lodging is an 18th-century mansion with 27 rooms, a couple of pretty patios and a roof terrace. Furniture is old-style and heavy. The hotel is quite sumptuous (not really suitable for kids).

Hotel Tartaneros (☎ 956 38 53 94; Calle Tartaneros 8; s/d €81/102; P ☖) At the inland end of Calzada del Ejército, this is a century-old industrialist's mansion with solidly comfortable rooms. Prices are a bit steep for what you get.

Hotel Guadalquivir (☎ 956 36 07 42; www.hotel guadalquivir.com in Spanish; Calzada del Ejército 20; s/d €77/97) A large modern hotel, the Guadalquivir is opposite the tourist office. Prices nearly halve from January to March. There's room to move here.

Hostal La Bohemia (☎ 956 36 95 99; Calle Don Claudio 5; s/d €20/38) Pretty, folksy-painted chairs dot the corridors of this little *hostal* off Calle Ancha, 300m northeast of Plaza del Cabildo. Rooms are neat and clean.

Hostal Blanca Paloma (☎ 956 36 36 44; hostal blancapaloma@msn.co; San Roque 15; s/d/tr €15/27/39) Prices at the Blanca Paloma remain steady throughout the whole year. White and orange is the colour scheme of the 10 simple, clean rooms.

Eating

The line of seafood restaurants facing the river at Bajo de Guía are a reason in themselves for visiting Sanlúcar. It's an idyllic experience to watch the sun go down over the Guadalquivir while tucking into the succulent fresh fare and washing it down with a drop of manzanilla. Just wander along and pick a restaurant that suits your pocket. **Restaurante Virgen del Carmen** (Bajo de Guía; fish mains €6-11) is one that's good but not excessively expensive. Decide whether you want your fish *plancha* (grilled) or *frito* (fried), and don't skip the starters: *langostinos* (king prawns) and the juicy *coquines al ajillo* (clams in garlic), both €7, are specialities. A half-bottle of manzanilla costs €4.50. Other popular places along here include Restaurante Poma, Casa Bigote, Casa Juan and Bar Joselito Huerta.

Casa Balbino (Plaza del Cabildo 11; tapas/raciones €1.50/9) Lots of cafés and bars, many serving manzanilla from the barrel, surround Plaza del Cabildo. Casa Balbino has tables on the square where you can enjoy wonderful seafood and other snacks such as *tortillas de camarones* (crisp shrimp fritters). Locals go for the *coctel de bogavante* (lobster cocktail).

Bar El Cura (Calle Amargura 2; meat dishes €4-10, fish dishes €5-21) In an alley between Calle San Juan and Plaza San Roque, El Cura offers imaginative and fairly economical platters that please the lunch-time crowd.

Entertainment

There are some lively music bars on and around Calzada del Ejército and Plaza del Cabildo. Many concerts are held here during the summer.

Getting There & Away

BOAT

Though you can visit Sanlúcar on day-trip boats from Seville (see p107), you are unable to take a one-way ride upriver from Sanlúcar to Seville.

BUS

All buses leave from the bus station on Avenida de la Estación. **Los Amarillos** (☎ 956 38 50 60) runs up to 10 buses daily to/from El Puerto de Santa María (€1.50, 30 minutes) and Cádiz (€2.75, 1¼ hours) and up to 10 to/from Seville (€7.40, 1½ hours). Linesur runs up to 14 buses daily to/from Jerez de

CÁDIZ PROVINCE

la Frontera (€1.50, 30 minutes). Change in Jerez for buses to Arcos de la Frontera and El Bosque.

JEREZ DE LA FRONTERA

pop 191,000 / elevation 55m

Sherry, horses and flamenco – Jerez guarantees to beguile!

The city of Jerez, spread over a low rise in the rolling countryside 36km northeast of Cádiz, is world-famous for its wine – sherry – made from grapes grown on the chalky soil surrounding the town. Many people come here to visit its bodegas, but Jerez (heh-*reth* or, in the Andalucian accent, just heh-*reh*) is also Andalucía's horse capital and, along-

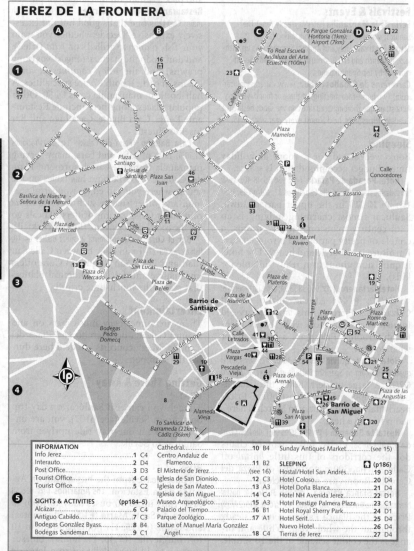

JEREZ DE LA FRONTERA

CÁDIZ PROVINCE

side its affluent upper-crust society, is home to a *gitano* (Roma) community that is one of the hotbeds of flamenco.

For centuries the British have had a taste for sherry: British money launched the development of wineries from the 1830s. Today, Jerez high society is a mixture of Andalucian and British, due to intermarriage among

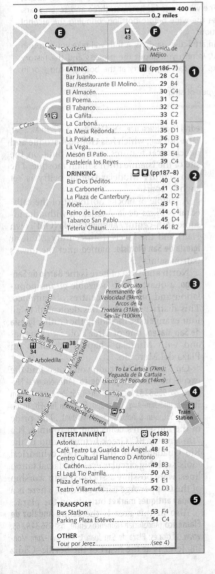

families of wine traders over the past 150 years. Since the 1980s most of the wineries, which were previously owned by about 15 families, have been bought out by multinational companies.

Jerez reeks of money, with fancy shops, well-heeled residents, and old mansions and beautiful churches in its old quarter. It stages fantastic fiestas with sleek horses, beautiful people and flamenco. There are big schemes to revitalise the city's old quarter.

History

The Muslims called the town 'Scheris', from which 'Jerez' and 'sherry' are both derived. The drink was already famed in England in William Shakespeare's time. Jerez had its share of strife during the late 19th century, when anarchism gained ground in Andalucía. One day in 1891, thousands of peasants armed with scythes and sticks marched in and occupied the town for a few hours, succeeding only in bringing about further repression. The sherry industry has provided greater prosperity in more recent times. Jerez *coñac* (brandy), widely drunk in Spain, is also a profitable product – 63 million bottles are produced annually.

Orientation & Information

The centre of Jerez is between the Alameda Cristina and Plaza del Arenal, which are connected by the north–south Calle Larga and its continuation, Calle Lancería (both pedestrianised). The old quarter is west of Calle Larga.

There are plenty of banks and ATMs on and around Calle Larga.

Info Jerez (Calle San Agustín 15; Internet per hr €1.80; 🕐 11am-2pm & 4-10pm Mon-Sat, 3-10pm Sun) Also offers fax service, phonecards and cheap phone rates to many countries, but not Australia or the USA.

Interauto (Calle Bodegas s/n; Internet per hr €1.50; 🕐 10am-10pm) Opposite Hotel Doña Blanca, this cyber-café has speedy connections.

Post office (☎ 956 34 22 95; cnr Calles Cerrón & Medina) Just east of Calle Larga.

Tourist office (www.webjerez.com; 🕐 10am-2pm & 5-7pm Mon-Fri, 9.30am-2pm Sat & Sun mid-Jun–mid-Sep, 9.30am-3pm Mon-Fri, 9.30am-2.30pm Sat & Sun mid-Sep–mid-Jun); Alameda Cristina (☎ 956 33 11 50); Plaza del Arenal (☎ 956 35 96 54) The polite, multilingual staff have mountains of information to give away.

THE SOLERA PROCESS

Once sherry grapes have been harvested, they are pressed and the resulting must is left to ferment. Within a few months a frothy veil of *flor* (yeast) appears on the surface. The wine is then transferred to the bodegas (wineries) in big barrels of American oak.

Wine enters the *solera* process when it is a year old. The barrels, about five-sixths full, are lined up in rows at least three barrels high. The barrels on the bottom layer, called the *solera* (from *suelo*, meaning floor), contain the oldest wine. From these, around three times a year, 10% of the wine is drawn off. This is replaced with the same amount from the barrels in the layer above, which is in turn replaced from the next layer. The wines age for between three and seven years. A small amount of brandy is added to stabilise the wine before bottling, bringing the alcohol content to 16% to 18%, which stops fermentation.

Sherry houses are often beautiful buildings in attractive gardens. A tour will take you through the cellars where the wine is stored and aged, inform you about the process and the history of the sherry producers, and give you a tasting. You can buy sherry at the bodegas too – or in any supermarket.

See p78 for an explanation of the various types of sherry.

Sights & Activities

OLD QUARTER

The obvious place to start a tour of the old town, parts of whose walls survive, is the 11th- and 12th-century Islamic fortress southwest of Plaza del Arenal, the **Alcázar** (☎ 956 31 97 98; Alameda Vieja; admission incl/excl camera obscura €3.30/1.30; ⌚ 10am-8pm Mon-Sat, 10am-3pm Sun mid-Jun–mid-Sep, 10am-6pm mid-Sep–Apr, 10am-8pm May–mid-June). Inside the Alcázar is a beautiful **mezquita** (mosque), converted to a chapel by Alfonso X in 1264; an impressive set of **Baños Árabes** (Arab Baths) and the 18th-century **Palacio Villavicencio**, built over the ruins of the old Islamic palace. Don't miss the gardens, which, with their geometrically laid-out plant beds and tinkling fountains, recreate the ambience of Islamic times.

Top off your visit with a bird's-eye view of Jerez: a **camera obscura** in the palace's tower provides a picturesque live panorama of Jerez accompanied by an interesting 15-minute commentary in Spanish, English, French and German. Camera obscura sessions begin every half-hour until 30 minutes before closing time.

The orange-tree-lined promenade around the Alcázar has good vistas to the west. In the foreground stands a large **statue of Manuel María González Ángel** (1812–87), the founder of Bodegas González Byass (p185). It was this man's uncle, José Ángel, who gave his name to González Byass' famous dry sherry Tio Pepe (*tío* meaning uncle and Pepe being a nickname for José). Behind Señor González is Jerez's mainly 18th-century **cathedral** (admission free; ⌚ 11am-1pm & 6-8pm Mon-Sat, 11am-2pm Sun), which has Gothic, baroque and neoclassical features, and was built on the site of the Islamic town's main mosque. The 15th-century Mudejar-Gothic belfry is set slightly apart.

A couple of blocks northeast of the cathedral is Plaza de la Asunción, with a handsome 16th-century **Antiguo Cabildo** (Old Town Hall) and the lovely 15th-century Mudejar **Iglesia de San Dionisio**, named after the town's patron saint.

North and west of here is the **Barrio de Santiago**, a quarter with a sizable *gitano* population and one of the centres of flamenco. This district has churches dedicated to all four evangelists: including the Gothic **Iglesia de San Mateo**, one of Jerez's oldest churches and with Mudejar chapels, which is on Plaza del Mercado.

On Plaza del Mercado you'll also find the excellent **Museo Arqueológico** (Archaeological Museum; ☎ 956 33 33 16; admission €1.75; ⌚ 10am-2.30pm Tue-Sun mid-Jun–Aug, 10am-2pm & 4-7pm Tue-Fri, 10am-2.30pm Sat, Sun & holidays Sep–mid-Jun). The pride of the museum's collection, in room 4, is a 7th-century-BC Greek helmet found in the Río Guadalete. In room 3, two cylindrical idols, with big circular eyes and facial tattoo lines, were possibly associated with worship of the Copper Age earth goddess. There is a **Sunday antiques market** outside on the plaza.

Also in this area is the **Centro Andaluz de Flamenco** (Andalucian Flamenco Centre; ☎ 956 34 92 65; www.caf.cica.es; Plaza de San Juan 1; ⌚ 9am-2pm Mon-Fri). Jerez is at the heart of the Seville–Cádiz axis where flamenco began and that remains its heartland today. This centre is a museum and school dedicated to the preservation and promotion of the flamenco arts, with print and music libraries holding thousands of works. Flamenco videos are screened each morning that the centre is open.

Southeast of Plaza del Arenal is one of Jerez's loveliest churches, the 16th-century **Iglesia de San Miguel** (Plaza San Miguel; 8pm for Mass) built in Isabelline Gothic style but with a baroque main façade. It features superb stone carving, beautiful stained glass windows and an elaborate retable by Juan Martínez Montañés. It has a distinctive blue-and-white-tiled steeple.

SHERRY BODEGAS

For most bodegas, you need to phone ahead to book your visit. But a few offer tours where you can just turn up. Confirm hours and arrangements in advance with the wineries or tourist offices, which have full details on bodega visits. Most of the wineries do tours in English, and often German, sometimes French, as well as Spanish.

Wineries where you can turn up without booking include:

Bodegas González Byass (☎ 956 35 70 00; www .gonzalezbyass.es; Calle Manuel María González 12; tour €7; 11.30am-2pm & 3.30-5.30pm Mon-Sat, 11.30am-1.30pm Sun) One of the biggest sherry houses, handily located just west of the Alcázar. Tours are in English.

Bodegas Sandeman (☎ 956 15 17 11; www.sandeman .com; Calle Pizarro 10; tour €5; 10.30am-3.30pm Mon-Fri) Sandeman sherries carry the black-caped 'Don' logo. There are three or four tours in English.

REAL ESCUELA ANDALUZA DEL ARTE ECUESTRE

Found in the north of town, the **Real Escuela Andaluza del Arte Ecuestre** (Royal Andalucian School of Equestrian Art; ☎ 956 31 80 08; www.realescuela.org; Avenida Duque de Abrantes) is one of Jerez's great attractions. The school trains horses and riders in dressage and you can watch them being put through their paces in **training sessions** (admission €6; 10am-1pm Mon, Wed & Fri Mar-Jul & Sep-Oct, 10am-1pm Mon & Wed Aug, 10am-1pm Mon, Tue, Wed & Fri Nov-Feb). There's an official **espectáculo** (show; admission €13-21), where the handsome white horses show off their tricks to classical music, at noon on Thursday year-round and noon on Tuesday from March to October (except holidays), plus Fridays in August.

PALACIO DEL TIEMPO & EL MISTERIO DE JEREZ

Close to the equestrian school, the **Palacio del Tiempo & El Misterio de Jerez** (Palace of Time & the Mystery of Jerez; Centro Temático La Atalaya; ☎ 956 18 21 00; www.elmisteriodejerez.org; Calle Cervantes 3; admission Palacio del Tiempo €5.10, El Misterio de Jerez €6, combined ticket €9; 10am-2pm & 6-8pm Tue-Sat, 10am-2pm Sun) combines Jerez's clocks-and-watches museum, revamped with multiple special effects, with a new sherry museum incorporating actors and wraparound images on giant screens.

PARQUE ZOOLÓGICO

Only a couple of kilometres west of the centre, **Parque Zoológico** (Zoo Jerez; ☎ 956 18 23 97; www.zoobotanicojerez.com in Spanish; Calle Taxdirt s/n; adult/child €4.20/2.70; 10am-8pm Tue-Sun Jun-Sep, 10am-6pm Tue-Sun Oct-May) has 1300 animals; well-established gardens; and a recuperation centre for wild animals.

PLAZA DE BELÉN & CIUDAD DE FLAMENCO

The *ayuntamiento* is promoting the ambitious Ciudad de Flamenco (Flamenco City) project, which is intended to revitalise the old quarter and to celebrate, conserve and promote flamenco. The site, Plaza de Belén, is in the centre of the flamenco district Barrio de Santiago, and was also the heart of Islamic Jerez. There will be an auditorium, a library, a flamenco school and a museum, all centred on a garden. The proposed buildings, though modern, will echo the symmetry of the Islamic past with walls and towers having Islamic-style decorations.

Tours

Tour por Jerez (☎ 954 56 06 93; tour €8; tours every 30min Jul & Aug, hourly Sep-Jun) Takes you around the sights in an open-topped double-decker bus, with live commentary. Get off and on as many times as you please in 24 hours. It stops outside the Plaza del Arenal tourist office.

Festivals & Events

Festival de Jerez (late February/early March) The Jerez Festival is a two-week event dedicated to music and dance, particularly flamenco; a good opportunity to see big flamenco names in action. The Teatro Villamarta (p188) is the main venue.

Feria del Caballo (May) One week in the first half of May, Jerez's Horse Fair is one of Andalucía's biggest festivals, with music, dancing and bullfights, as well as all kinds of horse competitions. Colourful parades of horses pass through the Parque González Hontoria fairgrounds in the north of town, the aristocratic-looking male riders decked out in flat-topped hats, frilly white shirts, black trousers and leather chaps, their female *crupera* (sideways pillion) partners in long, frilly, spotted dresses. The Jerez motorcycle Grand Prix (see p188) often coincides with the Feria del Caballo.

Fiestas de Otoño (September) Autumn festivals celebrating the grape harvest for three weeks or so range from flamenco and horse events to the traditional treading of the first grapes on Plaza de la Asunción. They conclude with a massive parade of horses, riders and horse-drawn carriages.

Fiesta de la Bulería (September) Jerez gives its definition to flamenco music, song and dance for one Saturday.

Sleeping

Room rates go sky-high during the Feria del Caballo and you need to book well ahead.

Most budget accommodation clusters around Avenida de Arcos and Calle Medina, east of Calle Larga. You'll find Jerez's top hotels in the north of town along Avenida Álvaro Domecq and the parallel Avenida Duque de Abrantes. Buffet breakfasts cost €6 to €7.

Hotel Prestige Palmera Plaza (☎ 956 03 18 00; www.palmeraplaza.com; Calle Pizarro 1; s/d €192/224; P ❄ ⚠ ☕) At the south end of Avenida Duque de Abrantes, this top luxury option with 48 rooms incorporates the spacious grounds and buildings of a 19th-century bodega. There is plenty of space and light; elegant, modern furnishings complement stylish design features throughout.

Hotel Royal Sherry Park (☎ 956 31 76 14; www.sherryparkhotel.com; Avenida Álvaro Domecq 11; s/d €109/137; P ❄ ⚠ ☕) A long-standing Jerez favourite, this place boasts 170 soundproofed rooms, excellent indoor and outdoor pools, verdant parklike grounds and a restaurant, café and banquet hall. Double rooms are €267 during the Feria del Caballo but only €77 on off-season weekends.

Hotel NH Avenida Jerez (☎ 956 34 74 11; www.nh-hoteles.com; Avenida Álvaro Domecq 10; s/d €95/105; P ❄ ⚠) A comfortable 90-room option. Rooms have all the trappings of the price bracket with décor that is, as the hotel's publicity says, 'modern without strident notes'. Avant-garde artworks add interest.

Hotel Doña Blanca (☎ 956 34 87 61; www.hoteldonablanca.com in Spanish; Calle Bodegas 11; s/d €79/96; P ❄ ⚠) On a quiet side street, this is an excellent 30-room hotel with parquet floors, soothing light-blue paintwork, decent bath-

rooms, satellite TV and safety boxes. Prices go up to €118/164 during May.

Hotel Serit (☎ 956 34 07 00; www.hotelserit.com; Calle Higueras 7; s/d new section €77/96, original section €66/85; P ❄) The revamped Serit has 37 comfy rooms with satellite TV. The more stylish, and expensive, rooms are across the street in a new section. A few ground-floor rooms in the older section are adapted for wheelchair users. Parking is €7 per day.

Tierras de Jerez (☎ 956 34 64 00; www.grouphoteles.com; Calle Corredera 58; s/d €58/91; P ❄ ⚠) This is a welcome recent addition to the Jerez accommodation scene. The 30 rooms are decked out semi-suavely (and have all mod cons including satellite TV and hairdryer). The central location is especially handy. There's a lift and on-site parking (€8.50 per day).

Nuevo Hotel (☎ 956 33 16 00; www.nuevohotel.com; Calle Caballeros 23; s/d €21/35; ❄) In a modernised mansion, Jerez's best budget accommodation provides 27 rooms (nine singles and 18 spacious doubles) all with TV and winter heating. Some facilities are adapted for wheelchair users. Rates rise a few euros during August and the major festivals. A buffet breakfast (€6) is served in the bright dining room. Reservations are essential. Park in the public car park located under Plaza Estévez.

Hotel Coloso (☎ 956 34 90 08; www.elcolosohotel.com; Calle Pedro Alonso 13; s/d €33/52; P) Don't be put off by the gloomy foyer and sometimes grumpy reception. This is a convenient, reasonable place down the street and around the corner from the Nuevo Hotel, and it has parking (€5 per day). Rooms are bright enough and have satellite TV.

Hostal/Hotel San Andrés (☎ 956 34 09 83; www.telefonica.net/web/hotelsanandres in Spanish; Calle Morenos 12; s/d €24/38, with shared bathroom €20/28; ❄) The San Andrés' plant-filled and tiled entrance patio is one of the prettiest you'll see in Jerez. There are two further patios. The clean and fairly comfy hotel rooms have TV and winter heating. The 16 *hostal* rooms are more basic. Rooms with shared bathroom are only available in the *hostal* while rooms with private bathroom are available in both sections.

Eating

Jerez food combines an Islamic heritage and maritime influences with English and French touches. Not surprisingly, sherry flavours many local dishes such as *riñones al jerez* (kidneys braised in sherry) and *rabo de toro* (oxtail stew).

BAKERIES
Pastelería Los Reyes (Calle San Agustín; toast, coffee & orange juice €3.50; ☿ at least 8am-9.30pm) Join the locals for breakfast at this tiny central bakery-cake shop. Choose from a delicious array of cakes and pastries or a variety of breads. Tea addicts are also catered for.

RESTAURANTS & CAFÉS
La Mesa Redonda (☎ 956 34 00 69; Calle Manuel de la Quintana 3; mains €12-15) This small, intimate restaurant is at the bottom of a Soviet-style block of flats. Décor and waitstaff attire are old-fashioned; soft music plays and excellent food prepared in an adventurous manner arrives at the tables. Portions are small.

Mesón El Patio (☎ 956 34 07 36; Calle San Francisco de Paula 7; salads €4, fish raciones €6-10, menú €20; ☿ closed Mon) This place combines a touch of refinement with local conviviality. It has high ceilings, warm tones and a collection of old radios. Above all, the food is terrific. There's a huge choice.

La Carboná (☎ 956 34 74 75; Calle San Francisco de Paula 2; mains €10.50-12.50) This popular, cavernous restaurant with an eccentric *menú* occupies an old bodega. Specialties include grilled meats and fresh fish. Quail with foie gras and rose petals is a quirky option.

La Posada (Calle Arboledilla 2; mains €12) This cosy place straddles both sides of the street and is much sought after for its fine home cooking, though the choice is limited.

Bar/Restaurante El Molino (☎ 956 33 71 86; Plaza Domecq 16; menú €7; ☿ closed Sun night) Tables are outside on the street below the cathedral but traffic noise subsides at lunch-time. The stuffed eggplants with béchamel sauce are a good choice.

La Vega (Plaza Estévez s/n; breakfast €4, raciones €7.50) Get a good glimpse of local life at this bustling café, a fine though noisy spot for breakfast. You can buy *churros* (long thin doughnuts with sugar; €1.50 per 250g) at a kiosk by the adjacent market and bring them here to eat with a coffee or hot chocolate.

TAPAS BARS
Bar Juanito (Pescadería Vieja 8-10; tapas €1.80-2.50; media-raciones €3-6.60) Fine place to sample tapas with a sherry. You can sit or stand at the bar, sit at the tables outside, or take

to the folksy dining room out back. (Pescadería Vieja, a little alley off Plaza del Arenal, catches a refreshing breeze on a hot day.)

El Almacén (Calle Ferros 8; montaditos €1.50, tapas €2-3) Get a table in El Almacén's bodega-like back room, put together a *tabla* (selection of tapas) of pâtés and cheeses or hams and sausages, and soak up the atmosphere.

Further brilliant tapas bars surround quiet little Plaza Rafael Rivero, about 500m north, with tables out under the sky. Head here after 9.30pm or late Sunday morning and don't miss the *montaditos* or *panes* (larger open sandwiches), which cost from €1.50 to €4.50, at **El Poema**. The owner prepares some inspired combinations. Then move a couple of tables away for a bite of ham at **El Tabanco**.

La Cañita (Calle Porvera 11; montaditos €1.50, tapas €1.50-6) is the best of a string of tapas spots just a short walk from Plaza Rafael Rivero – if you've still got room! The *montaditos* (again) are small but delicious: try brie and anchovies.

Drinking
Tetería Chauni (Calle Chancillería 10; tea €1.20-2.50, Arabic sweets €3; ☿ 5.30pm-late Mon-Sat, 3.30-10pm Sun) This youthful tea drinker's haven is modelled on the tearooms of Granada's Albayzín (see p315). Decoration is Moroccan with carpets and cushions on the floor and tiled tables of various heights, with matching chairs. Sip one of a mind-boggling range of teas – black, red, green, herbal, aphrodisiac. Arabic sweets are served as a selection of four.

A small cluster of bars in the narrow streets north of Plaza del Arenal can get lively with a 20s-ish crowd late in the evening: try **Bar Dos Deditos** (Plaza Vargas 1), **Reino de León** (Calle Ferros) and **La Carbonería** (Calle Letrados 7). You might come across some live music at one of these places. On the other side of Plaza del Arenal, the neighbourhood bars along pedestrianised Calle San Pablo can keep going till 2am or so: **Tabanco San Pablo** (Calle San Pablo 12; ☿ closed Sun) is a lively, tavernlike spot with big sherry barrels.

Northeast of the centre, **La Plaza de Canterbury** (Calle N de Cañas), with lots of bars around a central courtyard, attracts a young crowd.

For music bars and dancing, head a little further northeast of La Plaza de Canterbury to Avenida de Méjico and places such as **Moët**. The crowd is young but not as young as the hundreds of teenagers who hang out and drink on the street after midnight here and on nearby Calle Salvatierra (and on Plaza del Arenal).

Entertainment

To find out what's on in Jerez check at the tourist office, visit www.webjerez.com and watch for posters advertising upcoming events. *Diario de Jerez* and *Jerez Información* newspapers have some what's-on information, and the **Teatro Villamarta** (☎ 956 32 95 07; Plaza Romero Martínez) puts out a seasonal programme. Varied live music happens at **Astoria** (Calle Francos), an outdoor concert area, and there are sometimes concerts held in the **Plaza de Toros** (bullring). A hip venue for live music (Latin and other) and theatre is **Café Teatro La Guarida del Ángel** (☎ 956 34 91 52; Calle Porvenir 1; ☺ 8pm-late).

There are several active *peñas flamencas* (flamenco clubs) in the Barrio de Santiago and elsewhere. They usually welcome genuinely interested visitors: ask at the tourist office about upcoming events. They have a list of 16 *peñas flamencas*. **Centro Cultural Flamenco D Antonio Cachón** (☎ 956 34 74 72; Calle Salas 12) hosts authentic flamenco nights.

The **Viernes Flamencos** season sees open-air flamenco performances on August Friday nights at the Astoria: the season culminates in the **Fiesta de la Bulería**, a festival of flamenco song and dance in the Plaza de Toros, one Saturday in September. **El Lagá Tio Parrilla** (☎ 956 33 83 34; Plaza del Mercado) has flamenco performances at 10.30pm and 12.30am Monday to Saturday: it's more tourist-oriented but it can still be pretty gutsy.

Jerez's **Circuito Permanente de Velocidad** (☎ 956 15 11 00; www.circuitodejerez.com; Carretera de Arcos Km 10), on the A382 10km east of town, hosts several motorcycle and car race events through the year including – in April or May – one of the Grand Prix races of the **World Motorcycle Championship**. This is one of Spain's biggest sporting events, with around 150,000 spectators, and Jerez and other nearby towns are swamped by fans and their bikes. Occasionally one of the motor-racing events is a Formula One Grand Prix.

Getting There & Away

AIR

Jerez **airport** (☎ 956 15 00 00), the only one serving Cádiz province, is 7km northeast

of town on the NIV. Budget airline **Ryanair** (www.ryanair.com) flies to/from London Stansted twice daily and three times on Saturday. **Hapag-Lloyd** (☎ 902 48 05 00; www.hlf.de) flies to/from 10 German cities. **Iberia** (☎ 956 15 00 09) has at least two direct flights daily to/from Madrid and one daily to/from Barcelona.

BUS

The **bus station** (☎ 956 34 52 07; Calle Diego Fernández Herrera) is 1km southeast of the centre. **Comes** (☎ 956 34 21 74) has buses for Cádiz (€2.55, 40 minutes, 23 daily), El Puerto de Santa María (€1.05, 20 minutes, up to 19 daily), Barbate (€6.35, 1½ hours, one daily Monday to Friday), Ronda (€8.90, three hours, three daily) via Arcos de la Frontera (€2.15, 45 minutes) with one continuing to Málaga (€16.10, five hours), and Algeciras (€9.20, three hours, three daily) via Tarifa (€8.25, 2½ hours). From June to September, Comes runs daily buses to Los Caños de Meca (€5, 1½ hours). **Los Amarillos** (☎ 956 32 93 47) has more-frequent buses to Arcos and also runs two to seven times daily to El Bosque (€5, 1½ hours) and Ubrique (€7, two hours). There are plenty of buses to Seville (€5.40, 1¼ hours) by **Linesur** (☎ 956 34 10 63) and nine by Comes. Linesur also runs to Sanlúcar de Barrameda (€1.50, 30 minutes) at least seven times daily, and at least six times to Algeciras (€7.35, three hours).

TRAIN

The **train station** (☎ 956 34 23 19; Plaza de la Estación) is 300m east of the bus station. To get there take a taxi from the centre for €3. Jerez is on the Cádiz–El Puerto de Santa María–Seville line with trains to Seville (€5.85 to €19, one to 1¼ hours, nine or more daily), El Puerto de Santa María (€1.15, 12 minutes, up to 36 daily) and Cádiz (€2.50 to €2.75, 40 to 50 minutes, up to 36 daily).

Getting Around

Jerez is not too difficult to get around by car, but you're best off parking and walking, or taking buses to the slightly more distant sights, in order to avoid city centre congestion.

Blue lines on the road indicate meter parking, which you have to pay from 9am to 1.30pm and 5pm to 8pm Monday to Friday, and 9am to 2pm Saturday. There's a two-hour maximum (€2) during these periods.

There's underground parking at **Parking Plaza Estévez** (1hr/24hr €1/11).

AROUND JEREZ DE LA FRONTERA
La Cartuja & Yeguada de la Cartuja – Hierro del Bocado

La Cartuja monastery (☎ 956 15 64 65; gardens ۞ 9.30-11.15am & 12.45-6.30pm Mon-Sat), an architectural gem founded in the 15th century, is set amid lovely gardens beside the A381 towards Medina Sidonia, 9km from central Jerez. The early monks here are credited with breeding the much-prized Spanish thoroughbred horse, also called the Cartujano or Andaluz, which is particularly admired for its grace and gentle temperament. You can look around the gardens and admire the church's impressive baroque façade but not go inside.

Yeguada de la Cartuja – Hierro del Bocado (☎ 956 16 28 09; www.yeguadacartuja.com; Finca Fuente del Suero; adult/child €10/6; ۞ 11am-1pm Sat) is a stud farm dedicated to improving the Cartujano stock, where you can expect to see free-running of colts, demonstrations by a string of mares, and dressage. Book ahead. To get here, turn off the A381 at the 'La Yeguada' sign 5km after La Cartuja, and follow the sideroad for 1.6km to the entrance.

ARCOS & THE SIERRA DE GRAZALEMA

The Sierra de Grazalema in the northeast of Cádiz province is one of Andalucía's most beautiful and greenest mountain areas. Between the park and Jerez de la Frontera is the spectacular old town of Arcos de la Frontera.

ARCOS DE LA FRONTERA
pop 29,000 / elevation 185m

Arcos is 30km east of Jerez along the A382, across (in season) pretty wheat and sunflower fields, vineyards and fruit orchards. The old town could not be more dramatically sited: it stands on a high ridge with sheer precipices dropping away on both sides. It's intriguing to explore its mazelike streets with their medieval street plan, Renaissance palaces and beautiful churches.

History

Arcos has always been prized for its strategic location. In Islamic times it was, for a while during the 11th century, an independent kingdom, until being absorbed by Seville. In 1255 Alfonso X took the town and repopulated it with Castilians and Leonese. Some Muslims stayed, but rebelled in 1261 and were evicted by 1264. In 1440 the town passed to the Ponce de León family, Duques de Arcos, who were active in the conquest of Granada. When the last Duque de Arcos died heirless in 1780, his cousin, the Duquesa de Benavente, took over his land. With her help, agriculture around Arcos diversified and more-profitable cereals, olives, vines and horse breeding replaced sheep farming.

Orientation & Information

From the bus station on Calle Corregidores in the new town, it's a 1.5km walk uphill to the old town, via the leafy Paseo de Andalucía. From Plaza España at the top of Paseo de Andalucía, Paseo de los Boliches and Calle Debajo del Corral (becoming Calle Corredera) both head east up to the old town's main square, Plaza del Cabildo.

Banks and ATMs are on Calle Debajo del Corral and Calle Corredera, down to the west of the old town.

Post office (Paseo de los Boliches 24; ۞ 8am-2pm Mon-Fri, 9am-1pm Sat) West of the old town.

Tourist information kiosk (Paseo de Andalucía; ۞ 10.30am-1.30pm Mon-Sat year-round, 5.30-7pm Mon-Fri mid-Mar–mid-Oct, 5-6.30pm Mon-Fri mid-Oct–mid-Mar) In the new town.

Tourist office (☎ 956 70 22 64; Plaza del Cabildo; ۞ 10am-2pm Mon-Sat year-round, 4-8pm Mon-Sat mid-Mar–mid-Oct, 3.30-7.30pm Mon-Sat mid-Oct–mid-Mar) On the old town's main square.

Sights

Wander around the old town with its narrow cobbled lanes, Renaissance mansions, whitewashed houses and spectacular vistas. **Plaza del Cabildo** is surrounded by fine old buildings and has a vertiginous **mirador** (lookout) with panoramic views of the river and countryside. On the west side of the plaza Arcos' crowning glory, the **Castillo de los Duques**, dating from the 11th century, is privately owned and not open to the public. On the northern side, the **Basílica-Parroquia de Santa María** (admission €1; ۞ 10am-1pm & 4-7pm Mon-Fri, 10am-2pm Sat) was begun on the site of a mosque in the

13th century but not completed until the 18th century. Its western façade is in Gothic style but the tower, built later, is baroque. Inside it has a beautiful carved wooden choir stall. On the eastern side of the square, the **parador** (p190) is a 1960s reconstruction of a 16th-century magistrate's house, the Casa del Corregidor.

Explore the streets east of here, passing by lovely buildings such as the early 16th-century **Convento de la Encarnación** (Calle Marqués de Torresoto), which has a Gothic façade. The **Iglesia de San Pedro** (Calle Núñez de Prado; admission €1; 🕙 10am-1pm & 4-7pm Mon-Sat, 10am-1.30pm Sun) is in 15th-century Gothic style but with an impressive 18th-century baroque façade and bell tower. Inside is an impressive gilded retable. Nearby, the 17th-century **Palacio Mayorazgo** (admission free; 🕙 10am-2pm & 5-8pm Mon-Sat, 11am-2pm Sun), with a Renaissance façade and pretty patios, is now a community building.

Tours

Guided walking tours (€5; one hour) of the old town's monuments start from the tourist office at 10.30am and 5pm Monday to Friday, and 10.30am only on Saturday. Tours of Arcos' pretty patios start from the tourist office at noon and 6.30pm Monday to Friday, and noon only on Saturday.

Festivals & Events

Semana Santa (Holy Week; March/April) These dramatic Easter processions weave through the town's narrow streets; on Easter Sunday there's a hair-raising running of the bulls.

Fiesta de la Virgen de las Nieves (early August) This three-day fiesta includes a top-class flamenco night in Plaza del Cabildo, usually on the 5th.

Feria de San Miguel (around 29 September) Arcos celebrates its patron saint with a four-day *feria* (fair).

Sleeping

Arcos has some charming mid-range and top-end places to stay but there's little budget accommodation up in the old town.

Parador Casa del Corregidor (☎ 956 70 05 00; www.parador.es; Plaza del Cabildo; s/d €97/120; 🔀) Here you'll find combined typical parador luxury and magnificent views. Eight of the 24 rooms have balconies with cliff views.

ARCOS DE LA FRONTERA

INFORMATION		
Post Office	1	B1
Tourist Information Kiosk	2	A1
Tourist Office	3	A2

SIGHTS & ACTIVITIES	(pp189–90)	
Basílica-Parroquia de Santa María	4	A2
Castillo de los Duques	5	A2
Convento de la Encarnación	6	A2
Iglesia de San Pedro	7	D2
Mirador	8	A2
Palacio Mayorazgo	9	D2

SLEEPING	(pp190–1)	
Hostal San Marcos	10	B2
Hotel El Convento	11	B2
Hotel Los Olivos	12	B1
Hotel Real de Veas	13	C1
La Casa Grande	14	D2
La Fonda Hotel	15	B1
Parador Casa del Corregidor	16	A2

EATING	(p191)	
Bar San Marcos	(see 10)	
El Convento	17	B2

Los Faraones	18	B1
Mercado	19	B2
Mesón Los Murales	20	B2
Restaurante-Asador Los Murales	21	A2

ENTERTAINMENT	(pp191–2)	
Carpas de Verano	22	A1
El Burlaero	23	A1

TRANSPORT		
Bus Station	24	A1
Subterranean Car Park	25	A1

La Casa Grande (☎/fax 956 70 39 30; www.lacasa grande.net; Calle Maldonado 10; d €80, ste €87-94; 🖭) This quirky place occupies a gorgeous 18th-century cliff-side mansion that once belonged to flamenco dancer Antonio Ruiz Soler. It has just five very individual rooms and suites but two new doubles with terrace are being prepared. There's a cliff-edge roof terrace. The hearty breakfast costs €7.

Hotel El Convento (☎ 956 70 23 33; www.web dearcos.com/elconvento; Calle Maldonado 2; s/d €55/65, d with terrace €80) Set in a beautiful 17th-century convent just east of Plaza del Cabildo, this hotel has 11 tasteful and varied rooms: try for one with a view. Six of the rooms have terraces. There's a large communal terrace on the cliff edge.

Hotel Los Olivos (☎ 956 70 08 11; losolivos.prof esionales.org; Paseo de los Boliches 30; s/d €45/70; 🅿 🖭) You'll find this friendly, attractive, 19-room hotel, with an interior patio, down the hill from Plaza del Cabildo towards Paseo de Andalucía. Breakfast costs €6.

Hotel Real de Veas (☎ 956 71 73 70; Calle Corredera 12; s/d €48/72) Friendly folk run this converted traditional home on the western edge of the old town. It has a glass-covered patio and a roof terrace with 360-degree views. Rustic wooden furniture, metalwork fittings, green marble washbasins, patterned tiles and gentle colours make for agreeable rooms. Massage is available.

La Fonda Hotel (☎ 956 70 00 57; Calle Corredera 83; s/d €30/50; 🖭) Here, ample-sized rooms with good beds, winter heating, and TV in a renovated 19th-century inn are all yours. The street is noisy, though. The old stables house a restaurant.

Hostal San Marcos (☎ 956 70 07 21; Calle Marqués de Torresoto 6; s/d €25/35; 🖭) A short walk east of Plaza del Cabildo is the San Marcos – a simple place with four pretty little rooms that have either fan or air-con. There's a roof terrace and an economical café downstairs (see Eating, opposite).

Camping Lago de Arcos (☎ 956 70 83 33; Santiscal s/n; camping per adult/tent/car €3.20/3.70/3.80; 🅿 🖭) This first-rate year-round camping ground is in El Santiscal near the Lago de Arcos reservoir northeast of town. The easiest route from the old town is by the A382 and the Carretera El Bosque y Ubrique (A372). Turn left after the bridge across the dam. A local bus runs out here from Arcos, passing through Paseo de Andalucía.

Eating

All of the following are in the old town.

Restaurante-Asador Los Murales (☎ 956 71 79 53; www.restaurantelosmurales.com in Spanish; Calle Marqués de Torresoto; menú €15) This slightly classy spot with mellow music and mellow décor specialises in meat and fish *a la brasa* (grilled; €8 to €14).

El Convento (☎ 956 70 32 33; Calle Marqués de Torresoto 7; mains €8-15, menú €24) In the pillared patio of a 17th-century palace, this is a fancy restaurant turning out old country dishes including herbed lamb, venison steak, and wild asparagus with *jamón ibérico* (ham from the black Iberian breed of pig).

Mesón Los Murales (☎ 956 70 06 07; Calle Boticas 1; mains €5.40-8.40, menú €7.50; 🕑 closed Thu) An inexpensive option with tables outside on Plaza de Boticas. There are a few more restaurants on this street.

Bar San Marcos (☎ 956 70 07 21; Calle Marqués de Torresoto 6; tapas & montaditos €1.50-2.50, platos combinados €4-5, menú €6) A friendly and reliable little place. The dressed-carrot tapas is original and the *platos combinados* (mixed plates) are good value. The owner enjoys flamenco music.

The *mercado* (market) is opposite Mesón Los Murales.

Down towards the new town, **Los Faraones** (☎ 956 70 06 12; Calle Debajo del Corral 8; menú €9), the 'only Egyptian restaurant in Andalucía', serves up reliable fare with a Middle Eastern touch. The set menus (vegetarian and nonvegetarian) are available for lunch and dinner.

There are numerous places to get a snack around Paseo de Andalucía. People enjoy the food a couple of kilometres out of town on the A382 in the Jerez direction at **Venta Mesón La Coruña** (☎ 956 70 25 15; tapas €1-2, raciones & mains €6-10, menú €6).

Drinking & Entertainment

El Burlaero (Avenida Miguel Mancheño) This small, late-night haunt near the northwest end of Paseo de Andalucía features live guitar music and singing from 11pm on Thursday nights.

Arcos' **Jueves Flamencos** are a series of weekly flamenco nights on Thursday at 10.30pm throughout July and August, at various locations in the old town including the small but atmospheric Plaza del Cananeo. From mid-June to late August,

---

DETOUR: ALCALÁ DE LOS GAZULES TO UBRIQUE

This alternative route to the Sierra de Grazalema takes you through the beautiful woodlands of the northern part of the Parque Natural Los Alcornocales. In early summer the roadside wild flowers on some stretches are unbelievable. If you have a whole day on your hands, there is also the opportunity to climb one of the park's most prominent peaks, El Picacho (882m) or Aljibe (1091m).

From Jerez or Cádiz or anywhere down the coast of Cádiz province, make first for the hill town of Alcalá de los Gazules, just off the A381 in the centre of the province, where this route begins. On Plaza San Jorge at the top of the town is the office of the **Consejería de Medio Ambiente** (☎ 956 41 33 07; ☽ 9am-2pm Mon-Fri, 9.30am-noon Sat & Sun), which issues the permits needed to climb Aljibe or El Picacho (just show your passport).

Leave Alcalá northeast along the A375. After about 8km, the rocky sandstone hill El Picacho appears ahead of you, and 11km from Alcalá the joint start of the trails up **El Picacho** and neighbouring **Aljibe** is marked by some rather confusing roadside maps, opposite the entrance to the Área Recreativa El Picacho picnic area. The Picacho walk (about 3km each way; 500m ascent) takes approximately five hours there and back. Aljibe (6km each way; 700m ascent) is about seven hours there and back.

To continue the drive, head on along the A375 towards Ubrique, ignoring turn-offs to other places. The road winds up and down through thick woodlands of cork oak, wild olive, carob and other native trees, with occasional wonderful long-distance panoramas. After 30km, at the Puerto de Mogón de la Víbora pass (595m), turn left down the A373 for the last 9km to **Ubrique**, a white splash against the dramatic backdrop of the Sierra de Grazalema. Ubrique is a busy working town: if you need a smart leather bag, briefcase, wallet, jacket or belt, in any colour you fancy, take a stroll along the main street, Avenida Solís Pascual, which is lined with shops selling these goods, all made locally.

From Ubrique it's a further 26km on to Grazalema village via **Benaocaz** (p196) and **Villaluenga del Rosario**.

---

free concerts of pop, salsa, rock etc happen on Friday nights at the **Carpas de Verano**, an open-air entertainment area on Avenida Duque de Arcos.

Getting There & Away

Departures from the **bus station** (☎ 956 70 49 77) by Los Amarillos and/or Comes from Monday to Friday include buses going to Jerez (€2.15, 45 minutes, 24 daily), Cádiz (€4.80, 1¼ hours, 11 daily), El Puerto de Santa María (€3.50, 1¼ hours, five daily), El Bosque (€2.35, 45 minutes, eight daily), Ronda (€7, two hours, four daily) and Seville (€6.35, two hours, two daily). Fewer buses run at weekends.

Getting Around

You can park on Plaza del Cabildo in the old town and under Paseo de Andalucía in the subterranean car park. A local minibus (€0.80) runs up into the old town from Plaza de España every half-hour from 7.45am to 11.15pm Monday to Friday and from 9.15am to 11.15pm Saturday.

PARQUE NATURAL SIERRA DE GRAZALEMA

The Cordillera Bética – the band of rugged mountain ranges that stretches across much of Andalucía – has beautiful beginnings in the Sierra de Grazalema in northeast Cádiz province. The landscape ranges from pastoral river valleys and white villages to precipitous gorges and rocky summits. It's one of the greenest parts of Andalucía: Grazalema town has the highest measured rainfall in Spain at an average 2153mm a year. Snow is common on the mountains in late January or February.

This is excellent walking country (see p193) and there are plentiful opportunities for other activities, from climbing, caving and canyoning to bird-watching, paragliding and trout fishing. Much of the area is covered in beautiful Mediterranean woodland of evergreen oaks, *acebuche* (wild olive) and *algarrobo* (carob). Broom adds splashes of yellow.

The 517-sq-km Parque Natural Sierra de Grazalema covers not only this corner of

GRAZALEMA WALKS

The Sierra de Grazalema's beautiful scenery makes for great walking, especially in May, June, September and October, when the climatic conditions are best. Equip yourself with the best map you can get, preferably the IGN/Junta de Andalucía *Sierra de Grazalema* (1:50,000), walking guides such as *Walking in Spain* (Lonely Planet) or *Walking in Andalucía* by Guy Hunter-Watts, or the booklet *Eight Walks from Grazalema* by RE Bradshaw. Some of these are sold locally, but also look for them before you come.

The natural park's three major highlight walks – El Torreón, the Pinsapar and the Garganta Verde – are all within the park's 30-sq-km central *área de reserva* (reserve area). To do these walks you need a free permit (each route has a maximum number of people per day) from the park information office in El Bosque (see p194). You can telephone or visit the El Bosque office up to 15 days in advance for this, and if you wish they will forward permits to be collected at the Zahara de la Sierra information office or Grazalema tourist office instead of El Bosque. Staff at any of these offices may or may not speak languages other than Spanish. It's normally only necessary to book ahead for walking on a weekend or public holiday. In July, August and September, when fire risk is high, it's obligatory to go with a guide from an authorised local company, such as Horizon (p195) or Al-qutun (p196).

El Torreón

The usual route up El Torreón (1654m), the highest peak in Cádiz province, starts 100m east of the Km 40 marker on the Grazalema–Benamahoma road, about 8km from Grazalema. It takes about 2½ hours of walking to reach the summit and 1½ hours to get back down. From the summit on a clear day you can see Gibraltar, the Sierra Nevada and the Rif Mountains of Morocco.

Grazalema–Benamahoma via the Pinsapar

This 14km walk takes around six hours and passes through a 3-sq-km *pinsapar*, Spain's best-preserved woodland of the rare and beautiful Spanish fir (*pinsapo* in Spanish).

You walk about 40 minutes up from Grazalema to a point on the Zahara road where a footpath heads off across the northern slopes of the Sierra del Pinar. After an ascent of 300m, this path sticks close to the 1300m contour. The thickest part of the *pinsapar* comes in the middle third of the walk, below the range's precipitous upper slopes. The dark green Spanish fir, a relic of the extensive Mediterranean fir forests of the Tertiary period, survives in significant numbers only in isolated pockets in southwest Andalucía and northern Morocco.

Garganta Verde

The path into this lushly vegetated ravine, more than 100m deep, starts 3.5km from Zahara de la Sierra on the Grazalema road. It passes a viewpoint overlooking a large colony of enormous griffon vultures before the 300m descent to the bottom of the gorge. Then you come back up! It's a beautiful walk. Allow three to four hours' walking if you drive to the start.

Other Walks

These excellent walks are outside the reserve area and require no permit. You'll need a decent guide (human or printed) for the last two:

Benamahoma–Zahara de la Sierra A beautiful trip of 15km (about five hours plus stops) on dirt roads via the Puerto de Albarranes, Laguna del Perezoso and Puerto de Breña.
Salto del Cabrero About two hours' walk southwest from Grazalema, or 1¼ hours north from Benaocaz, this is an impressive fissure in the earth's surface – 100m deep and 500m long.
Casa del Dornajo About two hours' walk southwest from Grazalema, or 1½ hours north from Benaocaz, to a ruined farmstead in a beautiful valley; good chances of seeing ibex.

Note: The Salto del Cabrero and Casa del Dornajo can be combined in one full day's circuit starting from either Grazalema or Benaocaz.

Cádiz province but also extends into north-western Málaga province, where it includes the Cueva de la Pileta near Ronda (p264).

El Bosque

pop 2000 / elevation 385m

El Bosque, 33km east of Arcos across rolling countryside, is prettily situated below the wooded Sierra de Albarracín to the south-east. There's a take-off point for hang-gliders and paragliders in the Sierra de Albarracín, and trout to be fished in local streams.

INFORMATION

The natural park's **Punto de Información El Bosque** (☎ 956 72 70 29; Avenida de la Diputación s/n; 🕙 10am-2pm & 5-7pm Mon-Fri, 9am-2pm & 5-7pm Sat, 9am-2pm Sun) is down a lane off the A372 at the western end of the village (turn off opposite Hotel Las Truchas). A new, improved visitors centre is due to open in 2005 beside the bullring (directly opposite Hotel Las Truchas).

SLEEPING & EATING

Hotel Las Truchas (☎ 956 71 60 61; www.tugasa.com; Avenida Diputación s/n; s/d €34.25/56.20; mains €6-12; P ⊠ ☒) Many of the comfy rooms here have balconies. The lounge, dining and foyer areas are in traditional wood-beamed style; the restaurant has a terrace overlooking the countryside. Try the trout – the local speciality.

Hostal Enrique Calvillo (☎ 956 71 61 05; Avenida Diputación 5; s/d €21/35; ☒) The 30-plus rooms here, near the park information office, are being attractively revamped with wood-beam ceilings, stained-wood furniture and nicely tiled bathrooms. All are due to be completed by 2005.

Albergue Campamento Juvenil El Bosque (☎ 956 71 62 12; Molino de Enmedio s/n; per person incl breakfast under 26 €9.05-13.75, over 26 €12.25-18.35; 🕙 closed approx 20 Dec–8 Jan; ☒) El Bosque's modernised 131-capacity youth hostel is pleasantly sited in a wooded area 800m up a side road from Hotel Las Truchas. Accommodation is in double, triple and quadruple rooms, nearly all with private bathroom, and three rooms are adapted for the disabled.

Mesón El Tabanco (☎ 956 71 60 81; Calle Huelva 1; mains & menú €8-12; 🕙 9am or 10am-1.30am Mon-Sat, 9am-7pm Sun, closed 7-12 Jan & 2nd half Jun) Up in the village centre, El Tabanco serves excellent meat dishes in a sky-lit dining room

decorated with traditional tools of the agriculturalist's trade. Good tapas are available in the adjoining bar.

Benamahoma

pop 400 / elevation 450m

Little Benamahoma, 4km east of El Bosque on the A372 to Grazalema, is known for its market gardens, trout farm and cottage industry of rush-backed chairs. **Camping Los Linares** (☎ 956 71 62 75; www.campingloslinares.com in Spanish; Camino del Nacimiento s/n; camping per adult/tent/car €4/4/3.50, 2-/4-person cabins €28/50; 🕙 daily mid-Jun–mid-Sep, 3pm Fri–noon Sun & holidays mid-Sep–mid-Jun; ☒) is above the Breña del Agua river at the back of the village. The wooden cabins, with bathroom and TV, are a good deal for three or four people on a budget. There is also a restaurant and a swimming pool.

Grazalema

pop 2200 / elevation 825m

From Benamahoma the A372 winds east beneath the Sierra del Pinar and over the Puerto del Boyar pass (1103m) to Grazalema. Take care driving on this road when the mist comes down.

Grazalema is a pretty, picture-postcard village (especially when dusted with snow), nestling into a corner of beautiful mountain country beneath the rock-climbers' crag of Peñón Grande. Its steep cobbled streets are lined by sturdy white houses with black grilles, flowery window boxes and solid, nail-studded doors set in carved stone portals. Local products include pure wool blankets and rugs – the making of which follow centuries-old traditions.

INFORMATION

The village centre is the pretty Plaza de España, where you'll find the **tourist office** (☎ 956 13 22 25; 🕙 10am-2pm & 5-7pm Tue-Sun), with an upstairs shop selling local wool products and other crafts (blankets and rugs start around €55). Two banks on Plaza de España have ATMs.

SIGHTS & ACTIVITIES

Plaza de España is overlooked by the handsome 18th-century **Iglesia de la Aurora**. In the plaza stand two of the Spanish fir trees for which the area is famous (see p193 for details of a walk through a woodland of these rare and beautiful firs).

Horizon (☎/fax 956 13 23 63; www.horizonaventura .com; Calle Corrales Terceros 29), a block off Plaza de España, is an experienced adventure tourism firm that will take you climbing, bungee jumping, caving, canyoning, walking or bird-watching, with English-speaking guides. Prices range from around €13 for a half-day walk to over €30 for some caving and canyoning trips.

Al-hazán (☎ 956 13 22 96; www.al-hazan.net; horse riding 2/6hr €35/90), based about 4km outside town, offers horse rides varying in duration from one hour to one week.

FESTIVALS & EVENTS
Grazalema's **Fiestas del Carmen**, with plenty of late-night music and dance performances, fill several days in mid-July, ending on a Monday with a bull-running through the streets.

SLEEPING
Hotel Peñón Grande (☎/fax 956 13 24 35; Plaza Pequeña 7; s/d €36/52; ✿) This friendly and comfortable hotel just off Plaza de España is only a few years old. The 17 good-sized rooms have an agreeable rustic style, with solid stained-wood furnishings, terracotta tiles and blue and yellow walls.

Casa de las Piedras (☎/fax 956 13 20 14; Calle Las Piedras 32; s/d €34/42.50, with shared bathroom €10/20; mains €6-10) A friendly and good-value *hostal* occupying a fine old village house a short distance up from Plaza de España, with a couple of pleasant patios and a log fire in winter. The rooms are very plain, but clean and comfy, with winter heating. The restaurant serves hearty meals.

La Mejorana (☎/fax 956 13 23 37; www.lamejo rana.net in Spanish; Calle Santa Clara 6; r €54; ✿) This lovely village house has just five fetchingly country-style rooms, with beautiful wrought-iron bedsteads, plus a large lounge, kitchen and leafy garden with pool. Breakfast is available.

Hotel Puerta de la Villa (☎ 956 13 23 76; www .grazalemahotel.com in Spanish; Plaza Pequeña 8; s/d €102.95/128.70; mains €10-16; P ✿ ✿) This top-end hotel has tasteful, comfortable and good-sized rooms, plus amenities such as a gym, classy restaurant and crafts shop. Prices drop significantly outside the high seasons (mid-July to mid-September and early December to early January), and promotional offers can almost halve rates.

Camping Tajo Rodillo (☎ 956 13 24 18; Carretera a El Bosque; camping per adult/tent/car €4/4/3.50, 4-person cabins €65; ✿ daily mid-Jun–mid-Sep, 3pm Fri-noon Sun & holidays mid-Sep–mid-Jun; ✿) Camping ground at the top of the village. It's a small site with a restaurant.

EATING
Mesón El Simancón (☎ 956 13 24 21; Plaza Asomadero; mains €5-12) Set by the main car park, this is one of the best places at which to eat. Well prepared local dishes – ham, beef, quail, venison, *revueltos* (scrambled-egg dishes) – are served in a dining room that's decorated with deer heads.

Restaurante El Pinsapar (☎ 956 13 22 02; Calle Dr Mateos Gago 24; mains €6-11, menú €7-14) A short distance from Plaza de España, the Pinsapar specialises in tasty *carnes a la brasa* (char-grilled meats).

There are plenty more places to eat and drink on Calle Agua, running between Plaza de España and the car park:

Bar La Posadilla (☎ 956 13 20 43; Calle Agua 19; platos combinados €2-4; ✿ closed Thu) Excellent-value budget eating.

Restaurant El Torreón (☎ 956 13 23 13; Calle Agua 44; mains €5-11; ✿ closed Wed)

Zahara de la Sierra
pop 1500 / elevation 550m
Clinging to the sides of a crag topped by a ruined castle, Zahara de la Sierra is the most northerly and most dramatically sited of the natural park's villages. It feels quite otherworldly if you've driven the 18km from Grazalema through heavy mist via the vertiginous 1331m Puerto de los Palomas (Doves' Pass, but with more vultures than doves). A large reservoir spreads below Zahara, to the north and east.

ORIENTATION & INFORMATION
The village centres on Calle San Juan, with a church at each end. Near one end is the natural park's **Punto de Información Zahara de la Sierra** (☎/fax 956 12 31 14; Plaza del Rey 3; ✿ 9am-2pm & 5-7pm Mon-Sat, 9am-2pm Sun). If you have a car to park, follow the one-way street beyond here for 150m.

SIGHTS & ACTIVITIES
Zahara's streets invite investigation, with vistas framed by tall palms or hot-pink bougainvillea in summer, and fruited orange

trees in winter. To climb up to the 12th-century **castle keep**, take the path almost opposite the entrance to the Hotel Arco de la Villa – it's a steady 10- to 20-minute climb. The castle's brief recapture from the Christians by Abu al-Hasan of Granada in a daring night raid in 1481 sparked the last phase of the Christian reconquest of Andalucía, which ended in the fall of Granada in 1492.

The established adventure tourism firm **Al-qutun** (☎ 956 13 78 82; www.al-qutun.com) in Algodonales, 7km north of Zahara, will take you canyoning, paragliding, canoeing, caving, climbing or walking.

SLEEPING & EATING

Hostal Marqués de Zahara (☎ /fax 956 12 30 61; www.marquesdezahara.com; Calle San Juan 3; s/d €30/ 39.60; mains €7-10) This converted mansion in the village centre has 10 comfortable if un-exciting rooms with winter heating, and a restaurant. Rooms with balcony cost a few euros extra.

Hotel Arco de la Villa (☎ 956 12 32 30; www.tugasa .com; Paseo Nazarí s/n; s/d €34.25/56.20; **P** 🐕) The Arco de la Villa is a comfortable, modern hotel with a cliff-top setting. Its 17 rooms, with phone and TV, all enjoy spectacular views.

Hostal Los Tadeos (☎ 956 12 30 86; Paseo de la Fuente s/n; s/d/tr €25/39.50/50; **P** 🐕) Down to-wards the municipal swimming pool on the southwestern edge of the village, the friendly Hostal Los Tadeos has 11 good rooms with nice tiled floors and wooden furniture.

You won't go wrong at either of two neighbouring eateries on Calle San Juan, both with indoor and outdoor tables:

Restaurante Los Naranjos (☎ 956 12 33 14; mains €7-12)

Bar Nuevo (☎ 956 12 31 94; menú €8)

Benaocaz

pop 700 / elevation 790m

The pretty village of Benaocaz, on the A374 Ubrique–Grazalema road amid limestone country in the south of the park, has a couple of reasonable accommodation options and is a starting point for some good walks. There is also good rock-climbing in the area.

The seven-room **Museo Histórico de Benao-caz** (☎ 956 12 55 00; Calle Jabonería 7; admission free;

⏰ 11.30am-1.30pm & 6-8pm Sat & Sun) covers the district's history from the early Stone Age to the 20th century.

Hostal San Antón (☎ 956 12 55 77; Plaza de San Antón s/n; s/d €18/36), at the northern end of Benaocaz, offers five pretty rooms with kitchenette and fireplace. The rooms up-stairs have breezy terraces. The same friendly family also has two comfy six-person apartments, Casa Noelia and Casa Rebeca, for €106 each in a traditional-style village house.

Casa Olivia (☎ 956 12 55 98; Calle Lavadero s/n; mains €5-10; ⏰ lunch daily, dinner Fri & Sat), at the south end of the village, serves up quality local dishes in a dining room that's hung with oil paintings of local scenes.

Getting There & Away

Bus schedules are subject to change. Monday to Friday, **Los Amarillos** (☎ 902 21 03 17) runs up to eight buses daily to El Bosque from Jerez (€5, 1½ hours) and Arcos de la Frontera (€2.35, 45 minutes), and five from Cádiz (€6.40, two hours). On Saturday and Sunday there are just a couple of buses on each route. From Seville (Prado de San Sebastián bus station) there are two daily (€6.30, 1¾ hours) to El Bosque. Most of these buses continue from El Bosque to Ubrique. From El Bosque, buses leave for Grazalema (€1.90, 30 minutes), via Benamahoma, at 6.45am and 3.15pm Monday to Friday and 7.30pm Friday only. Grazalema–El Bosque buses depart at 5.30am Monday to Friday and 7pm Friday.

Los Amarillos also runs buses twice daily from Málaga to Ubrique via Ronda, Grazalema and Benaocaz. Grazalema is 35 minutes from Ronda (€1.95) and 2½ to three hours from Málaga (€9.50). The return buses stop at Benaocaz at 7.35am (8.35am Saturday, Sunday and holidays) and 3.35pm, and then stop off in Grazalema about 25 minutes later.

Comes (in Ronda ☎ 95 287 19 92) operates two buses each way Monday to Friday between Ronda and Zahara de la Sierra (€3, one hour), via Algodonales. Departures from Ronda are at 7am and 1pm, and from Za-hara at 8.15am and 2pm. To travel between Zahara and Seville, Arcos, Jerez or Cádiz, you need to change buses at Algodonales. There's no bus service between Zahara and Grazalema.

COSTA DE LA LUZ

The 90km coast between Cádiz and Tarifa can be windy, and its Atlantic waters are a shade cooler than those of the Mediterranean. But these are small prices to pay for an unspoiled, often wild shore, strung with long, clean, white-sand beaches and just a few small towns and villages. (It's known as the Costa de la Luz – the Coast of Light – due to the brightness that results from many hours of sunlight hitting the white sandy beaches.) Andalucians are well aware of its attractions and they flock down here in their thousands during July and August, bringing a vibrant fiesta atmosphere to the normally quiet coastal settlements.

You will need to book ahead for rooms in these months.

From before Roman times until the advent of 20th-century tourism, this coast was mainly devoted to tuna fishing. Shoals of big tuna, some weighing 300kg, are still intercepted by walls of net several kilometres long as the fish head in from the Atlantic towards their Mediterranean spawning grounds in spring, and again as they head out in July and August. Barbate has the main tuna fleet today.

VEJER DE LA FRONTERA
pop 13,000 / elevation 190m

This old-fashioned white town looms mysteriously atop a rocky hill above the busy A48, 50km southeast from Cádiz and 10km

---

DETOUR: SANCTI PETRI & MEDINA SIDONIA

If you're driving up or down the A48 between Cádiz and Vejer de la Frontera with half a day to spare, two contrasting but equally attractive detours can be made from the Chiclana de la Frontera junction where the A48 meets the A390, 22km southeast of Cádiz.

Sancti Petri

Head west towards the coast from the A48/A390 junction: the road skirts the southern edge of Chiclana. Follow 'Puerto Deportivo' signs, which will lead you to Sancti Petri, a small, historically intriguing fishing village, no longer inhabited but still with fishing boats and, today, a marina. The village has a nautical and water-sports centre and is a fine windsurfing spot. Windsurfing equipment, catamarans and kayaks are available for rent on the beach here (Playa de Sancti Petri). An offshore island, Isla de Sancti Petri, has a ruined, mainly 19th-century **castle**, beneath which are the remains of a Roman temple dedicated to Hercules, originally a temple to the Phoenician god Melkart. You can visit the island daily from 1 July to 15 September with **Cruceros Sancti Petri** (☎ 617-378894; Playa de Sancti Petri; 1hr trip per person €9).

Medina Sidonia

If you head east along the A390, a 19km drive brings you to the interesting hill-top town of **Medina Sidonia**, whose long and turbulent history goes at least as far back as the Phoenician colony of Bulla Assido. Later it fell into the hands of invaders as diverse as the Byzantines and the Normans. After the Christians reconquered the town from the Muslims in 1264, it became a bone of contention between the Castilian monarchy and the powerful Guzmán family (see p205), changing hands repeatedly until 1445 when King Juan II ceded it to Juan Alfonso Guzmán III. Guzmán thus became the Duque de Medina Sidonia, the first of a long and very powerful aristocratic line (one of whom was the notoriously useless commander of the ill-fated Spanish Armada of 1588).

On arrival head up to the top of the hill to the helpful **tourist office** (☎ 956 41 24 04; Plaza de la Iglesia Mayor; ☒ 10am-2pm & 5-6pm Tue-Sun), then make for the main monuments nearby – the remains of the 12th- to 15th-century **castle**; the **Iglesia de Santa María La Coronada** (built in the 16th century when the hierarchy of Cádiz cathedral had retreated here for sanctuary from English and Portuguese raids); and the **Conjunto Romano** (well-preserved sections of Roman street and Roman drains). For a meal descend to the broad Plaza de España where **Restaurante Bar Cádiz** (mains €6-12) serves a wide range of very good Andalucian food.

inland from El Palmar. It's well worth a wander. As with many spots between El Palmar and Tarifa, Vejer is experiencing a foreign influx. Hip boutiques and foreign-run *hostales* are proliferating. There's an art and craft scene here, too.

Orientation

The oldest area of town, still partly walled and with narrow winding streets clearly signifying its Islamic origins, spreads over the highest part of the hill. Just below is the small Plazuela, more or less the heart of town, with the Hotel Convento de San Francisco. Buses stop on Avenida Los Remedios, the road up from the A48, about 500m below the Plazuela.

Information

Bookend English Bookshop (☎ 625-870255; Avenida Juan Relinque 45) New and second-hand books in English; some second-hand books in German.
Post office (Calle Juan Bueno)
Tourist office (☎ 956 45 17 36; www.turismovejer.com; Avenida Los Remedios; 🕙 9.30am-2.30pm & 5-8pm Mon-Fri, 11am-2.30pm & 5.30-8.30pm Sat & Sun mid-Jun–Sep, 9.30am-2.30pm & 4-8pm Mon-Sat, 11am-2pm Sun Apr-mid–Jun & Oct-Dec, 9am-2.30pm Mon-Fri Dec-Mar)

Sights & Activities

Vejer's walls date from the 15th century. Four gateways and a couple of towers survive. Within the 40,000-sq-m walled area, seek out the **Iglesia del Divino Salvador** (☎ 956 45 00 56; 🕙 10.30am-1.30pm Tue & Thu, 10.30am-1.30pm & 6.30-8.30pm Fri-Mon & Wed), whose interior is Mudejar at the altar end and Gothic at the other, and the much-reworked **castle** (🕙 10am-9pm), with great views from its battlements and a small museum that preserves one of the black cloaks, covering everything but the eyes, that Vejer women wore until just a couple of decades ago. Don't miss pretty palm-filled **Plaza de España** and its attractive Seville-tiled fountain, a 10-minute stroll along Calle Marqués de Tamarón (which heads uphill from the Plazuela).

You can rent good mountain bikes (from €12.50 per day) at **Discover Andalucía** (☎ 956 44 75 75; Avenida Los Remedios 45), opposite the bus stop. **Natural Sur** (☎ 956 45 14 19; www.naturalsur .com), a subsidiary of Discover Andalucía, runs activities (€16 to €36) for individuals and small groups. Choose from trekking, kayaking, or biking.

Festivals & Events

Easter Sunday (March/April)There's a Toro Embolao (running of the bulls) at noon and 4pm.
Feria (10-24 August) Music and dancing nightly in Plaza de España with one night devoted entirely to flamenco.

Sleeping

Hotel Convento de San Francisco (☎ 956 45 10 01; www.tugasa.com; Plazuela s/n; s/d €48.50/68.50; **P** 🌐) This restored 17th-century convent has 25 simple but charming rooms and helpful reception staff.

Hotel La Casa del Califa (☎ 956 44 77 30; www .vejer.com/califa; Plaza de España 16; s incl breakfast €52-84, d incl breakfast €66-98; 🌐) This great little place rambling over several floors has 19 peaceful, comfortable rooms with Islamic décor – the ironwork comes from Marrakesh. Artworks are by painters from Algeria, Granada and Morocco.

El Cobijo de Vejer (☎ 956 45 50 23; Calle San Filmo 7; www.elcobijo.com; r incl breakfast €62-78; 🌐) Find this place along the street from the market. Seven rooms and apartments (some self-catering and with terrace and views over the town's rooftops out to sea and beyond to the Moroccan mountains) are set around a pretty tiled patio with a fountain and vines. The breakfast is healthily scrumptious.

Casablanca (☎ 956 44 75 69; www.andaluciacasa blanca.com; Calle Canalejas 8; r €50; 🕙 closed 22 Dec–15 Jan) The friendly Casablanca has four self-catering apartments that are set around a pretty traditional patio.

Hostal Buena Vista (☎ 956 45 09 69; Calle Machado 4; s/d €21/42; **P**) Down a side street near Hostal La Janda, the family-run Buena Vista has spotless, spacious rooms, some with fine views across to the old part of town.

Hostal La Janda (☎ 956 45 01 42; Calle Machado s/n; s/d €20/40; **P**) A simple, friendly place across town from the old walled area.

Eating & Drinking

You're spoilt for choice when it comes to eating out in Vejer.

El Jardín del Califa (☎ 956 44 77 30; Plaza de España 16; mains €7.80-17) At the bottom of the Hotel La Casa del Califa (above) and extending out into the garden, this is Vejer's coolest eatery. The food and décor are Arabic. Choose from couscous, tagines and barbecued meats and don't skip the tasty dips. Sit in the garden and soak up the ambience. Moroccan tiled tables under tall trees, the scent of jasmine, and walls with ancient brickwork set the mood.

Restaurante Trafalgar (☎ 956 44 76 38; Plaza de España 31; mains €10-17) Owned by the same folk as the Casablanca, the Trafalgar provides semiformal dining. Specialties are dishes made from local fish and seafood.

La Bodeguita (☎ 956 45 15 82; Calle Marqués de Tamarón 9; tapas & montaditos €0.90-1) This plain but tastefully decked-out bar has good vibes, breakfast, excellent tapas and snacks, and an extensive music collection. It's just before the arch, Arco de la Segur, on Calle Marqués de Tamarón.

Pastelería Galvin (Calle Altocano 1) Dive into this terrific tea, coffee and cakes haunt just around the corner from the Plazuela.

Bar Joplin (Calle Marqués de Tamarón) Opposite La Bodeguita, this laid-back drinking haunt lives up to its namesake. It's best late on the weekends.

Getting There & Away

The small office of **Comes** (☎ 956 44 71 46; Plazuela) has bus information. Buses run to/from Cádiz (€4.10, 50 minutes) and Barbate (€0.95, 10 minutes) up to 10 times a day. More buses for the same places, plus Tarifa (€3.40, 50 minutes, about 10 daily), Algeciras (€4.75, 1¼ hours, about 10 daily), La Línea de la Concepción (€5.50, 1½ to two hours, seven daily), Málaga (€13.80, 2¾ hours, two daily) and Seville (€10.80, three hours, five daily) stop at La Barca de Vejer, on the A48 at the bottom of the hill. By road it's 4km uphill from La Barca to the town; on foot, there's an obvious 15-minute short cut.

EL PALMAR

pop 800

Sleepy El Palmar, 10km southwest of Vejer de la Frontera, has a lovely 4.8km sweep of white sandy beach, which is good for body surfing, and for board surfing from October to May. Green fields with crops or grazing cows surround the town. El Palmar livens up during Semana Santa and high summer.

The **Nickolas Surfing Co** (☎ 610-676323) rents boards and wetsuits and offers surf lessons (€50, 1½ to two hours) for one or two people. The instructors are good with kids. Phone, or drop by their beach shack opposite El Chancla.

Camping El Palmar (☎ 956 23 21 61; 2 adults, tent & car €39; 🔊) is a well-equipped camping

ground, 900m from the beach down a little dirt track. It has a supermarket.

Right in front of the beach is **Hostal Casa Francisco** (☎ 956 23 22 49; s/d incl breakfast €50/60, d with sea view incl breakfast €80; menú €15). It has a good restaurant and is the best of a handful of *hostales*; it's open for most of the year.

Open all year except for February, **El Chancla** (mains €8), made out of an old tuna preparation factory, is well-frequented for its tasty meat and fresh fish dishes.

Two buses run to/from Cádiz Monday to Friday (€4.10, one hour).

LOS CAÑOS DE MECA

pop 200

Los Caños, once a hippy hideaway, straggles along a series of gorgeous sandy coves beneath a pine-clad hill about 7km southeast of El Palmar and 12km west of Barbate. It maintains its laid-back, off-beat air even during the height of summer when it gets very busy. The informal architecture around here is an eclectic mix of Moroccan, Andalucian, surfer and alternative.

Information

The helpful folk at the Barbate tourist office (p201) can provide information for the whole area.

Sights & Activities

Coming from El Palmar or Vejer, you pass through the separate settlement of Zahora a couple of kilometres short of Los Caños. Then, at the western end of Los Caños, a side road leads out to a lighthouse on a low spit of land, the famous Cabo de Trafalgar. It was off this cape that Spanish naval power was terminated in a few hours one day in 1805 by a British fleet under Admiral Nelson. Wonderful beaches stretch either side of Cabo de Trafalgar. Towards the eastern end of Los Caños, the main street, which is mostly called Avenida Trafalgar, is met by the road from Barbate. The main beach is straight in front of this junction. Nude swimmers head for around the small headland at its eastern end. At the western end there are surfable waves in winter and the best windsurfing zone.

The coast between Los Caños and Barbate is mostly cliffs up to 100m high. The road between the two places runs inland through umbrella pine forest. These cliffs and forest, along with wetlands east and north of Barbate, form the **Parque Natural de la Breña y Marismas de Barbate**. A couple of walking paths start from the road: one goes to Playa de la Hierbabuena just west of Barbate, the other to the Torre del Tajo, a 16th-century cliff-top lookout tower. Another tower, the 18th-century Torre de Meca on the hill behind Los Caños, can be reached from this road: you can also walk up to it from Los Caños.

Activities such as horse riding, surfing and mountain biking can be organised through the Hostal Madreselva (below).

Sleeping

The high-season prices given here are fairly inflated on what you'll pay at other times.

Casas Karen (☎ 956 43 70 67; www.casaskaren.com; Fuente del Madroño 6; r €85-90, q €102-159, 2-person traditional hut per week €480; P) This eccentric place is owned by warm, vibrant, dynamic Karen Abrahams who settled here around 20 years ago. Her large, pretty mimosa- and broom-covered plot has seven or so eclectic buildings, all with kitchen, bathroom, lounge, and outdoor sitting areas and hammock: they range from a converted farmhouse to exotic, thatched *chozas* (traditional huts), built of local materials. Décor is casual Andalucian-Moroccan. Massage is available. Casas Karen is accessed from the main road, 500m east of the Cabo de Trafalgar turning. Look for a whitewashed wall with 'Apartamentos y Bungalows' tiled into it. Follow the road next to the sign for 500m. Turn right for 80m and you'll see a wooden ranch-style fence: you've arrived. Karen also has an apartment on the front line of the beach (€114 for up to four people).

Hostal Madreselva (☎ 956 43 72 55; www.madre selvahotel.com; Avenida Trafalgar 102; s/d €62/74; ste €145; ☼ 27 Mar–30 Sep; P ⯑) This place with friendly management has been artistically transformed by the owner of the Hurricane Hotel near Tarifa. Some of the 18 rooms have small gardens: all, including a newly refurbished apartment with a good-sized patio, have inspired design features. Mountain biking, horse riding and surfing can be arranged.

Casa Meca (☎ 956 43 14 50, 639-613402; www .casameca.com; Avenida Trafalgar s/n; studio d per week €450, 2-bedroom apt per week €640; P) An attractive house with pretty garden and grounds, Casa Meca is 100m east of the Cabo de Trafalgar turning. It comprises three bright apartments with kitchen, bathroom, lounge, views and outdoor sitting areas. Double-glazed windows and central heating make it a good year-round choice.

Hotel Fortuna (☎ 956 43 70 75; www.hotelfortuna .net; Avenida Trafalgar 34; s/d €53/66; P) A short walk east of the Barbate road corner, the Fortuna has excellent rooms with terrace and sea views, safety box and satellite TV.

Hostal Mar de Frente (☎ 956 43 70 25; Avenida Trafalgar 3; s/d €45/80, r with terrace €103.30; P) This totally new place, on several levels right on the cliff edge above the eastern end of the beach, has a youthful management and bright, comfy rooms with satellite TV.

Hostal Alhambra (☎ /fax 956 43 72 16; Carretera Caños de Meca Km 9.5; r €65-80; ☼ closed 25 Dec–14 Jan; P) The friendly Alhambra, opposite Camping Caños de Meca at Zahora, has genuinely Alhambraesque trimmings, a restaurant, and pleasant rooms with attractive furniture and little verandas.

Three medium-sized camping grounds open from April to September and get pretty crowded and noisy in high summer: **Camping Faro de Trafalgar** (☎ 956 43 70 17; 2 adults, tent & car €20.60) Close to the beach 1.7km west from the Barbate road corner in Los Caños village.

Camping Camaleón (☎ 956 43 71 54; Avenida Trafalgar s/n; 2 adults, tent & car €13) Shady sites and near the centre, about 1km west from the Barbate road corner.

Camping Caños de Meca (☎ 956 43 71 20; www .camping-canos-de-meca.com; Carretera Caños de Meca, Km 10; 2 adults, tent & car €18.35) On the main road at Zahora.

Eating

Bar-Restaurante El Caña (Avenida Trafalgar s/n; seafood dishes from €8.50) Super position atop the small cliff above the beach. It's a short distance east from the Barbate road corner, but only open in tourist seasons.

El Pirata (Avenida Trafalgar s/n; seafood media-raciones €5) Overlooking the beach a couple of hundred metres west of El Caña, the Pirata is a good bet whenever the weather is fine. The excellent *revuelto de gambas* (scrambled eggs with prawns) costs €6.60. It's a cosy place for a drink on winter weekend nights.

Restaurante El Capi (Carretera Caños de Meca 276; media-raciones €7, fish mains €10-14) In winter, when little is open in the village, try the Capi, attached to the *hostal* of the same name on the main road at Zahora. Decent tapas and good fish dishes (including home-made fish cakes) are served and there's a welcoming open fire.

Las Dunas (Carril El Faro; tapas €1.80) On the road out to Cabo de Trafalgar this attractive place is another of the few open year-round. Come here for snacks, fresh fruit juices and late breakfasts. The stone building has *choza*-style roofing.

La Pequeña Lulu (Avenida Trafalgar s/n; crepes, salads & seafood raciones €5-6) At the far eastern end of the village backing on to the natural park, this cosy place specialises in crepes. It's open day and night throughout the year.

Drinking & Entertainment

In the main tourist season, good bars include the cool **Los Castillejos** at the eastern end of the village, **Café-Bar Ketama** across the street from El Pirata, and a couple of livelier places with music on the road out to Cabo de Trafalgar such as **Las Dunas** (above), which is really a late-night place with a pool table. **La Pequeña Lulu** (above) often has live music, even some jammin'.

Getting There & Away

Monday to Friday, three buses run to/from Barbate (€0.80, 15 minutes) and two to/from Cádiz (€4.50, 1¼ hours). Extra buses may run from Seville or Cádiz from mid-June to early September.

BARBATE

pop 20,000

A fishing and canning town with a long sandy beach and a big harbour, Barbate becomes a fairly lively resort in summer, but it's mostly a drab place. You might need to use Barbate as a staging post if you're travelling by bus. Or, you might like to get a taste of more ordinary Spanish life than offered by the coastal resorts.

Information

Barbate's **tourist office** (☎ 956 43 39 62; Calle Vázquez Mella s/n; ☼ 8am-3pm & 4.30-7.30pm Mon-Fri, 10am-2pm Sat) is the only one in the Los Caños–Barbate–Zahara de los Atunes area. Coming from the bus station along Avenida del Generalísimo towards the beach, turn left into Calle Agustín Varo about halfway, and follow it nine blocks to Calle Vázquez Mella. The tourist office is one block south

of here. A tourist information kiosk opens at the beach end of Avenida del Generalísimo during July and August. Banks are on Avenida del Generalísimo.

Sleeping

Hotel Chili (☎ 956 45 40 33; www.madreselvahotel.com; cnr Calle Real 1 & Avenida José Antonio; s/d incl breakfast from €69/80; **P** ✖) Austrian-Cuban influences mix here with touches of Morocco and Asia. The piano in the restaurant (below) is certainly Austrian-inspired, but what about the Harley Davidson in the bar? Rooms are straightforward and decorated in subdued colours. The Chili is about 1km along Avenida José Antonio from the roundabout by the bus station.

Hotel Galia (☎ 956 43 33 76; fax 956 43 04 82; Calle Doctor Valencia 5; s/d €35/50; **P** ✖) A few blocks towards the sea from the bus station, the Galia is friendly and the rooms are fine.

Hotel Nuro (☎ 956 43 48 84; Avenida José Antonio s/n; d €30-54; **P** ✖) This is a simple but comfy hotel, with TV in the rooms. It's only 100m from the intersection of Avenida José Antonio with Avenida del Generalísimo and the bus station. One room is adapted for wheelchair users.

Eating

The Barbate food market on Avenida de Andalucía is excellent. There are plenty of seafood eateries with lots of local specialities on Paseo Marítimo.

Café-Bar Estrella Polar (Avenida del Generalísimo 106; salads €3.60, mains €7.80-8.40) Away from the beach, this café-bar offers good portions at fair prices. Try the swordfish, or a platter of mixed fried fish.

El Campero (☎ 956 43 23 00; Avenida de la Constitución 5C; entrées €7.20-11.50, fish mains €15.50-16.50) A few blocks along from the Estrella Polar, head to El Campero if you feel like a splurge. Fish is the house speciality. Try the *urta a la roteña* (bream cooked in white wine with tomatoes, peppers and thyme) or *atún a la plancha* (fresh grilled tuna). *Atún encebollado* (tuna stewed with onions and tomatoes), a tasty local speciality, is also whipped up here.

El Chile (☎ 956 45 40 33; cnr Calle Real 1 & Avenida José Antonio; mains €13) At the Hotel Chili (above), this restaurant offers a changing menu – including fish and seafood choices – accompanied by live piano music on Friday evening and at Sunday lunch.

Getting There & Away

The **Comes bus station** (☎ 956 43 05 94; Avenida del Generalísimo) is more than 1km back from the beach at the northern end of the long main street. Buses run to/from La Barca de Vejer (4km from the town of Vejer de la Frontera; see p199) and Cádiz (€4.75, one hour) up to 14 times daily, Vejer de la Frontera (€0.95, 10 minutes) up to 10 times, and Tarifa (€3.60, 50 minutes) and Algeciras (€5.20, one hour and 20 minutes) once daily. Five buses run Monday to Friday (two on Saturday and Sunday) to/from Zahara de los Atunes (€0.80, 15 minutes).

ZAHARA DE LOS ATUNES

pop 1000

Plonked in the middle of nothing except a broad, 12km-long, west-facing sandy beach, Zahara is an elemental sort of place. At the heart of the village stands the crumbling walls of the old **Almadraba**, once a depot and refuge for the local tuna fishers, who were an infamously rugged lot. Miguel de Cervantes, in *La Ilustre Fregona*, wrote that no-one deserved the name *pícaro* (low-life scoundrel) unless they had spent two seasons at Zahara fishing for tuna. The *pícaros* were evidently good at their job, for records state that in 1541 no fewer than 140,000 tuna were brought into Zahara's Almadraba. Today the tuna industry has dwindled out of sight but Zahara is an increasingly popular, almost fashionable, Spanish summer resort. With a little old-fashioned core of narrow streets, it's altogether a fine spot to let the sun, sea, wind and, in summer, a spot of lively nightlife – batter your senses.

Information

There's a tourist **information kiosk** (☎ 956 44 95 25; ☺ noon-6pm Mon-Fri, noon-5pm Sat Semana Santa–mid-Sep) on the sands near the Almadraba. Unicaja and Caja Rural, both on Calle María Luisa, opposite Plaza de Tamarón, have ATMs.

Sleeping

Hotel Gran Sol (☎ 956 43 93 09; www.gransolhotel.com; Avenida de la Playa s/n; s/d incl breakfast €101/110, d with sea view incl breakfast €121; P ☒ ☒) Sample just how 'elemental' Zahara is at the Gran Sol, which occupies the prime beach spot right by the sands, facing the old Almadraba walls on one side and the ocean on the other. It has

large, comfortable rooms with all the trims. The hotel has a couple of dining areas – the terrace restaurant (below), almost on the sands, has stupendous sea views.

Hotel Doña Lola (☎ 956 43 90 09; Plaza Thompson 1; s/d €90/115; P ☒ ☒) Near the entrance to Zahara, but only two minutes to the beach, this is a modern place in lovely large grounds, with good rooms decorated in an attractive old-fashioned style.

Hotel Nicolás (☎ 956 43 92 74; www.hotel-nicolas .tuweb.net in Spanish; Calle María Luisa 13; s/d €39.10/51.10, with half-board €51/80.10; P ☒) This friendly hotel has just 11 simple but attractive rooms with TV, bathroom, winter heating and a restaurant (below). Half-board (bed, breakfast and either lunch or dinner) is obligatory in July and August.

Hostal Monte Mar (☎ 956 43 90 47; Calle Bullón 17; s/d €25/48; P) This cruisy place right on the sands at the northern tip of the village may not have the best beds in town but at least it may have a room when everywhere else is full in July and August.

Camping Bahía de la Plata (☎ 956 43 90 40; Avenida de las Palmeras; 2 adults, tent & car €16.35, q bungalow €84.15) This is a good treed camping ground fronting the beach at the southern end of Zahara.

Eating

Most restaurants can be found on or near Plaza de Tamarón behind Hotel Doña Lola, and most offer similar lists of fish, seafood, salads, meats and sometimes pizzas.

Patio la Plazoleta (Plaza de Tamarón; fish dishes €9, pizzas €10) This open-air restaurant with an old fishing boat in the centre is a good choice: try the *pez limón a la plancha* (grilled tuna with lemon and vegetables), or a pizza.

Café-Bar Casa Juanita (Calle Sagasta) Off the main drag on a little pedestrian street that faces Plaza de Tamarón, this good place has a long tapas list with lots of fishy things. It's not a bad spot for breakfast.

Two of the hotels (see above) have eating options:

Hotel Nicolás (Calle María Luisa 13; mains €6.50-11) This family-run establishment offers tapas, starters, *raciones* (meal-sized servings of tapas) and main meals. Fish and seafood feature. Enjoy baked fish smothered in salt crystals (€11) or a seafood cocktail (€7.50).

Hotel Gran Sol (Avenida de la Playa s/n; paella for 2 €25) From the terrace restaurant, gaze out to sea or check out the old Almadraba on the sands while you share a paella. Or you could sample a Cádiz-style fish fry-up (€12) instead.

Drinking & Entertainment

In July and August a line of tents and makeshift shacks along the beach south of the Almadraba serves as bars, discos and *teterías* (Arabian-style tearooms). They get busy from about midnight, and some have live flamenco or other music.

Chiringuito La Gata (Playa Zahara de los Atunes) Mix with Spain's artists and musicians who holiday in Zahara. The beach-front location makes for a perfect place to watch the sun go down and later there's live music. You can eat here during the day.

Getting There & Away

Comes runs up to five buses daily to/from Barbate (€0.80, 15 minutes), up to four buses to/from Cádiz (€6.15, two hours) via Barbate, and one each Monday to Friday to/from Tarifa (€2.85, 45 minutes). There are more buses from mid-June to September.

BOLONIA

pop 125

This tiny village, 10km down the coast from Zahara and about 20km northwest of Tarifa, has a fine white-sand beach (good for windsurfing), several restaurants and small *hostales*, lots of cockerels, and the ruins of the Roman town of **Baelo Claudia** (☎ 956 68 85 30; non-EU citizen €1.50, EU citizen free; 10am-7pm Tue-Sat Mar-May & Oct, 10am-8pm Tue-Sat Jun-Sep, 10am-6pm Tue-Sat Nov-Feb, 10am-2pm Sun year-round). The ruins include substantial remains of a theatre, a paved forum surrounded by remains of temples and other buildings, and the remains of the workshops that turned out the products that made Baelo Claudia famous in the Roman world: salted fish and *garum* paste (a spicy seasoning derived from fish). The place flourished under Claudius from AD 41 to 54 but went into economic decline after an earthquake in the 2nd century.

West beyond the ruins is a big **dune** that you can climb up. The sandstone crag **San Bartolo** (or San Bartolomé) looming just east of Bolonia is the biggest magnet for rock climbers in the area. Bolonia shows a few signs of growing prosperity – part of the main street has been paved, street lights

have been erected and a few palms have been planted.

Sleeping

The following places are open year-round. Around four others open seasonally.

Hostal Lola (☎ 956 68 85 36; www.hostallola.com; El Lentiscal 26; r with shared/private bathroom €40/50; P) Lola's gets better every year. The latest designer washbasins have been installed in the shared bathroom area and there's lots of cheerful paint work: eight rooms share three bathrooms. The pretty garden is flower-filled and orderly. The 16 rooms are simple but attractive. There's a little Moroccan-inspired sitting area, too. To get here follow the signs on giant surfboards to beyond Hostal Miramar.

Hostal Bellavista (☎ 956 68 85 53; s/d €40/45; P) A reasonable place in the centre of the village. Some rooms have terrace and plum sea views. There are also apartments.

La Hormiga Voladora (☎ 956 68 85 62; El Lentiscal 15-16; r €48, with terrace €60; P) A newish place right on the seafront, this is a sound option.

Hostal Miramar (☎ 956 68 42 04; r €42, 2-bedroom q €73; P) This place has fine views and is run by friendly folk from Tarifa. It's not luxurious but will do.

Eating

In summer there are three or four open-air restaurants on the beach at the eastern end of the village. Of these, **Chiringuito Los Troncos** (mains around €10; ☼ Apr-Oct) gets the thumbs up for its fresh vegetables, fish, seafood and meats. In the village on the main drag, try the seafood at **Restaurante Marisma** (mains €4.50-11; ☼ daily Semana Santa–Oct, weekends year-round), with tables outside, or at the popular, slightly more upmarket **Bar Restaurante Las Rejas** (salad €4, paella per person €8; ☼ year-round) where the ever-helpful waitstaff will suggest the day's best tasty options.

Getting There & Away

The only road to Bolonia heads west off the N340, 15km from Tarifa. In July and August there is usually some sort of bus service between Tarifa and Bolonia (see p211 for details). Otherwise, without wheels it's a 7km hilly walk from the main road. You can walk 8km along the coast from Ensenada de Valdevaqueros via Punta Paloma (see p207).

SURFERS' PARADISE

What better way to start the day than slipping on a wet suit, grabbing your board and hitting the waves for a day of frolicking in the elements. No need for alternative therapies. This is the therapy. Age is really no barrier although this is a big scene for the young and beautiful. Then there's the après-surf...

The Atlantic coast of Cádiz province provides Spain's, and arguably Europe's, finest conditions for windsurfing and kitesurfing. Most of the action is around Tarifa, which has a cool international scene to go with it, but there are other spots, too.

Windsurfing

The most popular strip is along the coast between Tarifa and Punta Paloma, 10km to the northwest. The best spots depend on wind and tide conditions. El Porro, on the bay Ensenada de Valdevaqueros, is one of the most popular, as it has easy parking and plenty of space to set up. Other popular take-off points are the Río Jara, about 3km northwest from Tarifa, and Arte-Vida, Hurricane, and Hotel Valdevaqueros, in front of the respective hotels (which are out of town on the N340; see p208).

Slalom is the more common form of sailboarding here, but wave riders get their chance when the *poniente* (west wind from the Atlantic) is blowing, especially in spring and autumn and during full moon. The best waves for wave-riding are actually found up the coast at Los Caños de Meca (p199), though new winds are less reliable here.

You can buy new and second-hand windsurfing gear in Tarifa at the surf shops along Calle Batalla del Salado. For board rental and classes, head to places up the coast such as **Club Mistral** (at Hurricane Hotel ☎ 956 68 49 19, at Hotel Valdevaqueros ☎ 956 23 67 05) or **Spin Out** (☎ 956 23 63 52), which is on the beach in front of Camping Torre de la Peña II, near El Porro. At Spin Out board, sail and wet-suit rental costs per hour/day €34/66, and a six-hour beginner's course is €150.

Competitions are held year-round; the PWA (Professional Windsurfing Association) has an international competition at Easter.

Other spots with good winds and equipment rentals, further up the coast, are Sancti Petri (p197) and El Puerto de Santa María (p177). At Sancti Petri you can choose between the river mouth, the open ocean and a lagoon.

Kitesurfing

This exciting and colourful sport has taken the Tarifa coast by storm, but kites give way to sails when the wind really gets up. Kitesurf rental is available from the same places as windsurfing gear. This is a sport where beginners definitely need instruction: Spin Out charges €69 for a two-hour introduction to kitesurfing and €207 for three two-hour sessions. Tarifa has hosted international kitesurfing competitions.

Surfing

There's a bit of a board-riding scene in Tarifa but it's better for bodyboarding. Between October and May there can be surfable waves at Los Caños de Meca (p199) and – usually better – El Palmar (p199).

For introductory information about these sports see p61.

TARIFA

pop 16,500

Tarifa is an attractive, laid-back town even during the summer frenzy, although this could be set to change with the arrival of glitzy shop fronts and steady development. Two to three decades ago it was relatively unknown, but it is now a mecca for windsurfers, and more recently, kitesurfers. A hip international scene with an eclectic bunch of restaurants, bars and places to stay has grown up around the surf crowd. The beaches have clean, white sand and good waves, and inland the country is green and rolling, though it can be chilly and wet in winter. The old town merits investigation, with its pretty, narrow streets, whitewashed houses and flowers cascading from balconies with fancy ironwork and window boxes. Tarifa's castle is striking, too.

Tarifa has a thriving art scene that feeds on the natural beauty and the crazy population mix.

The only negative – though not for surfers or the hundreds of modern windmills on the hill-tops inland – is the wind on which Tarifa's new prosperity is based. For much of the year, either the *levante* (easterly) or *poniente* (westerly) is blowing, which is ruinous for a relaxed sit on the beach. Mind you, Tarifa's famous winds have moderated over the last couple of years. The windmills are a mainly EU-funded experiment, recently expanded, feeding power into Spain's national grid.

History

Tarifa may be as old as Phoenician Cádiz and was definitely a Roman settlement, but it takes its name from Tarif ibn Malik who led a Muslim raid in AD 710, the year before the main Islamic invasion of the peninsula. Muslims built the castle in the 10th century as fortification against Norse and African raids. Pirates in the area at this time are said to have extracted a fee from ships wishing to pass safely from the Atlantic through the Strait of Gibraltar to the Mediterranean. This may be the origin of the Spanish word *tarifa* and its English equivalent, tariff. Christians took Tarifa in 1292 but it was not secure until Algeciras was won in 1344. Later, Tarifa was active in the colonisation of the Americas: many of its people left for Peru in the 16th and 17th centuries.

Orientation

Two roads lead into Tarifa from the N340. The one from the northwest becomes Calle Batalla del Salado, which ends at east–west Avenida de Andalucía, where the Puerta de Jerez leads through the walls into the old town. The one from the east becomes Calle Amador de los Ríos, which also meets Avenida de Andalucía at the Puerta de Jerez.

The main street of the old town is Calle Sancho IV El Bravo, with the Iglesia de San Mateo at its eastern end.

To the southwest of the town protrudes the **Isla de las Palomas**, a military-occupied promontory that is the southernmost point of continental Europe, with the Strait of Gibraltar to the south and east and the Atlantic Ocean to the west. Africa is only 14km across the strait.

Information

There are banks and ATMs on Calle Sancho IV El Bravo and Calle Batalla del Salado, the main shopping street. Useful information for visitors can be found at www.tarifainfo .com and www.tarifa.net.

Al Sur (Calle Batalla del Salado) International newspapers and a good range of surfing mags. Opposite Puerta de Jerez.

Centro de Salud (Health Centre; ☎ 956 68 15 15/35; Calle Amador de los Ríos)

Lavandería Acuario (Calle Colón 14; 4kg wash €4, 4kg wash, dry and fold €7-8; ☉ 10.15am-1.30pm & 7.30-9pm Mon-Fri)

Pandora's Papelería (Calle Sancho IV El Bravo; Internet per hr €3; ☉ 10am-2pm and 5-9pm)

Planet (Calle Santísima Trinidad; Internet per 15 min €0.75; ☉ 10.30am-2.30pm & 5.30-10pm Mon-Sat, 5.30-10pm Sun)

Policía Local (Local Police; ☎ 956 61 41 86; Plaza de Santa María)

Post office (☎ 956 68 42 37; Calle Coronel Moscardó 9)

Tourist office (☎ 956 68 09 93; www.tarifaweb.com in Spanish; ☉ 9am-3pm) Near the top end of the palm-lined Paseo de la Alameda.

Sights & Activities

Tarifa is easy to enjoy. Stroll through the tangled streets of the old town to the castle walls, check out the castle, stop in at the busy port and sample the beaches.

The Mudejar **Puerta de Jerez** was built after the Reconquista. Look in at the bustling, neo-Mudejar **market** (Calle Colón) before winding your way to the heart of the old town and the mainly 15th-century **Iglesia de San Mateo**. The streets south of the church are little-changed since Islamic times. Climb the stairs at the end of Calle Coronel Moscardó and go left on Calle Aljaranda to reach the **Mirador El Estrecho** atop part of the castle walls, with spectacular views across to Africa.

The **Castillo de Guzmán** (Calle Guzmán; admission €1.80; ☉ 11am-2pm & 6-8pm Tue-Sat, afternoon hours 5-7pm Apr-Jun, 4-6pm Oct-Mar) extends west from here but is entered at its far end on Calle Guzmán. Tickets are sold in the stationery shop across the street from the

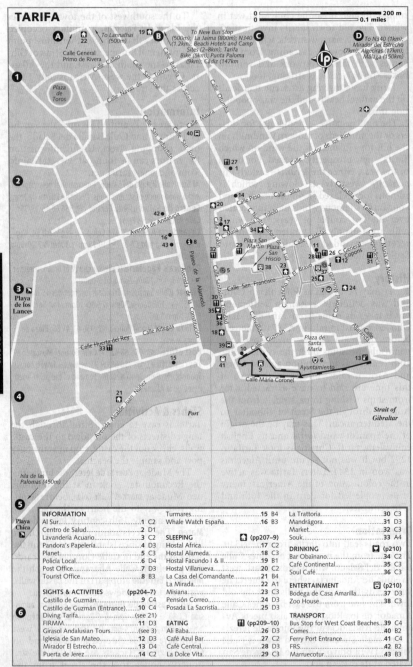

TARIFA

0 — 200 m
0 — 0.1 miles

To Lannathai
(500m)

To New Bus Stop
(500m); La Jaima (800m); N340
(1.2km); Beach Hotels and Camp
Sites (2–8km); Tarifa
Bike (5km); Punta Paloma
(9km); Cádiz (147km)

To N340 (1km);
Mirador del Estrecho
(7km); Algeciras (17km);
Málaga (150km)

Calle General
Primo de Rivera

Plaza
de
Toros

Calle Callao

Calle San Tolosa

Calle Batalla del Salado

Calle Olumba

Calle Navas de Tolosa

Calle Maura

Calle Amador de los Ríos

Calle San Sebastián

Calle San José

Avenida de Andalucía

Plaza
de los
Lances

Calle Colón

Calle Santísima Trinidad

Paseo de la Alameda

Avenida de la Constitución

Calle Huerta del Rey

Calle Artegas

Avenida Alcalde Juan Núñez

Calle Peso

Calle Silos

C Nuestra Señora de la Luz

Calle María Antonia de Toledo

Plaza San
Martín

Plaza
San
Hiscio

Calle San Francisco

Calle Castelar

C General
Copons

C María de Molina

Sancho IV El Bravo

Calzadilla de Téllez

Chinchorreras

Calle Aljaranda

Calle Guzmán

Cilvidos

Plaza de
Santa
María

Ayuntamiento

Calle María Coronel

Port

Strait of
Gibraltar

Isla de las
Palomas (450m)

Playa
Chica

Playa
Chica

CÁDIZ PROVINCE

INFORMATION	
Al Sur	1 C2
Centro de Salud	2 D1
Lavandería Acuario	3 C2
Pandora's Papelería	4 D3
Planet	5 C3
Policía Local	6 D4
Post Office	7 D3
Tourist Office	8 B3

SIGHTS & ACTIVITIES	(pp204–7)
Castillo de Guzmán	9 C4
Castillo de Guzmán (Entrance)	10 C4
Diving Tarifa	(see 21)
FIRMM	11 D3
Girasol Andalusian Tours	(see 3)
Iglesia de San Mateo	12 D3
Mirador El Estrecho	13 D4
Puerta de Jerez	14 C2

Turmares	15 B4
Whale Watch España	16 B3

SLEEPING	(pp207–9)
Hostal Africa	17 C2
Hostal Alameda	18 C3
Hostal Facundo I & II	19 B1
Hostal Villanueva	20 C2
La Casa del Comandante	21 B4
La Mirada	22 A1
Misiana	23 C3
Pensión Correo	24 D3
Posada La Sacristía	25 D3

EATING	(pp209–10)
Ali Baba	26 D3
Café Azul Bar	27 C2
Café Central	28 C3
La Dolce Vita	29 C3

La Trattoria	30 C3
Mandrágora	31 D3
Market	32 C3
Souk	33 A4

DRINKING	(p210)
Bar Obaïnano	34 C2
Café Continental	35 C3
Soul Café	36 C3

ENTERTAINMENT	(p210)
Bodega de Casa Amarilla	37 D3
Zoo House	38 C3

TRANSPORT	
Bus Stop for West Coast Beaches	39 C4
Comes	40 B2
Ferry Port Entrance	41 C4
FRS	42 B2
Marruecotur	43 B3

castle entrance. The castle is named after the Reconquista hero Guzmán El Bueno. In 1294 Merenid attackers from Morocco kidnapped Guzmán's son and threatened to kill the son unless Guzmán relinquished the castle to them. Instead of handing over the castle, Guzmán threw down his own dagger for his son to be killed, a supreme gesture of defiance and sacrifice. Guzmán's descendants became the Duques de Medina Sidonia, who ran much of Cádiz province as a private fiefdom for a long time and remained Spain's largest landowners well into the 20th century.

The imposing fortress was originally built in AD 960 under the orders of the Cordoban caliph, Abd ar-Rahman III. You can walk along the parapets and stand atop the 13th-century Torre de Guzmán El Bueno for 360-degree views. Inside is a small museum with bits of information about the castle, various statues and busts of Guzmán El Bueno and photos and memorabilia from Tarifa's past.

BEACHES

The popular town beach is the sheltered but extremely small **Playa Chica**, on the isthmus leading out to the Isla de las Palomas. From here **Playa de los Lances** stretches 10km northwest to the huge sand dune at Ensenada de Valdevaqueros.

DIVING

For general information on diving in Andalucía, see p61. Diving is generally done from boats around the Isla de las Palomas, which has a military base. Shipwrecks, corals, dolphins, octopuses and more await you. There are a couple of dive companies located in Tarifa – try **Tarifa Diving** (☎ 639-186070; www.tarifadiving.com in Spanish; Calle Alcalde Juan Núñez 8). Based at La Casa del Comandante (p208), Tarifa Diving offers Discover Scuba Diving courses (€75, three hours). One-tank dives with equipment rental and guide cost €60.

HORSE RIDING

Both these stables out of town on Playa de los Lances rent horses with excellent English-speaking guides. An hour's ride along the beach costs €25. Four- to five-hour rides, incorporating beach and inland routes, cost €60 to €80.

Aventura Ecuestre (☎ 956 23 66 32) At Hotel Dos Mares (p208), about 4.5km from Tarifa.
Club Hípica (☎ 956 68 90 92) At Hurricane Hotel (p208), 6km from Tarifa.

WHALE WATCHING

This is great fun! At least three groups run two- to three-hour biologist-led boat trips to track and watch dolphins and whales (mostly adult/child under 14 for €27/18). In all but the Turmares boat, expect to get wet if the sea is rough.

FIRMM (Foundation for Information and Research on Marine Animals; ☎ 956 62 70 08, 619-459441; www .firmm.org; Calle Pedro Cortés 4) Next to Café Central. Uses every trip to record data.
Turmares (☎ 956 68 07 41, 696-448349; www .turmares.com; Avenida Alcalde Juan Núñez 3; dolphin & whale watching adult/child under 14 €25/15, killer-whale watching €40/20) This company has the largest boat (with a glass bottom).
Whale Watch España (☎ 956 68 22 47, 639-476544; www.whalewatchtarifa.org in Spanish; Avenida de la Constitución 6) Meeting point at Café Continental on Paseo de la Alameda.

ROCK CLIMBING, TREKKING & MOUNTAIN BIKING

Girasol Andalusian Tours (☎ 615-456506; www.girasol -adventure.com; Calle Colón 12; orientation rock climbing €28, 6hr trekking €40, bike trips €20-40) Rock-climbing orientation, courses at all levels and climbs on San Bartolo, near Bolonia.
Tarifa Bike (☎ 696-973656; Apartamentos Las Flores, Carretera N340 Km 77.1; rental 2hr/day €8/16) Good mountain bike rental and guided tours (in English).

Sleeping

You can stay in the old town or on and around Calle Batalla del Salado. Plenty more places are dotted along the beach and the inland side of the N340 within 10km northwest of Tarifa, but none are cheap. Rooms can be tight in summer and when there are windsurfing and kitesurfing competitions. Phone ahead in August. Prices given here are for August: expect reductions of 25% to 40% at most places for much of the rest of the year.

IN TOWN

Posada La Sacristía (☎ 956 68 17 59; www.lasacristia .net; San Donato 8; r incl breakfast €115-135) Tarifa's newest central accommodation is in an elegantly renovated 17th-century town house with rooftop views. Attention to detail is impressive. The eight rooms, on several levels around a central courtyard, are painted a fresh white and furnishings are mainly neutral. Beds are large.

Misiana (☎ 956 62 70 83; www.misiana.com in Spanish; Calle Sancho IV El Bravo; s/d incl breakfast €86/112) This place has seen a few incarnations. The current comfortable hotel is mod, almost futuristic in design and colours. Rooms on one floor are painted lilac and silver: red and turquoise rooms and rooms with big views are available, too. All have fan and satellite TV.

Hostal Alameda (☎ 956 68 11 81; www.hostal alameda.com; Paseo de la Alameda 4; s/d €30/50; ❄) This excellent-value place is on the edge of the old town in front of the port. Rooms are cosy, with winter heating and satellite TV. Some have sea views: others look out over the Alameda or Tarifa's pretty roof line.

Hostal Africa (☎ 956 68 02 20, 606-914294; hostal _africa@hotmail.com; Calle María Antonia Toledo 12; s/d €30/45, with shared bathroom €25/35) This revamped old house close to the market is conveniently located and run by hospitable, well-travelled owners who know what travellers need. Rooms are bright and attractive and an expansive roof terrace with views of Africa can be enjoyed. Storage for boards and bicycles is available.

La Mirada (☎ 956 68 06 26; Calle San Sebastián 41; www.hotel-lamirada.com; s/d €42/66; Ⓟ) This hotel right on Playa de los Lances, though still in the town, is excellent value. Of the 24 good spacious rooms, 14 have sea views but all guests can savour the views along the coast and across the strait to Africa from the hotel's large terrace. Wheelchair users are accommodated.

La Casa del Comandante (☎ /fax 956 68 19 25; www.tarifadiving.com/casadelcomandante; Calle Alcalde Juan Núñez 8; s/d without view €60/73, with view €73/85, cabaña €54/60; Ⓟ) Opposite the port, this place has a distinctive glassed-in terrace restaurant (starters €5, fish dishes €14) and nine colourful, smart rooms with good beds, plus a couple of *cabañas* (cabins).

Hostal Villanueva (☎ 956 68 41 49; Avenida de Andalucía 11; s/d €40/75) Built into the old city walls a few doors west of the Puerta de Jerez, this *hostal* has good, clean, no-nonsense rooms, some with TV and some with views of the castle. There's a terrace and the genial owner speaks French.

Pensión Correo (☎ 956 68 02 06; Calle Coronel Moscardó 8; per person €15-22.50) This good budget choice in the old post office has amiable Italian-Spanish owners. The brightly painted rooms, some with bathroom, are not flash, but comfy enough. The top-floor double sports gorgeous views and its own little terrace.

Hostal Facundo I & II (☎ 956 68 42 98; hotelfacundo@ terra.es; Calle Batalla del Salado 47; r €65, s/d with shared bathroom €40/55; Ⓟ) The Facundo is gradually having a much-needed makeover, including new mattresses. It's long been geared to windsurfers with a storage place for boards and is popular for its prices, which nose-dive out of peak season. Rooms vary: the best open right on to the street. Newly added are a communal kitchen and lounge with television.

ALONG THE COAST

All these places are on, or just off, the N340, northwest of Tarifa.

Hurricane Hotel (☎ 956 68 49 19; www.hurricane hotel.com; r incl breakfast land/ocean side €133/150; Ⓟ ❄ ☇) Six kilometres out of Tarifa, this hip Moroccan-style hotel is the place to go if you're feeling flush. Set in semitropical beachside gardens, it has around 30 large, comfy rooms, two pools (one heated), two restaurants (see p210) and a health club. It also has the famous Club Mistral windsurfing and kitesurfing school with board rental next door, and Club Hípica, a horse-riding school (see p207). The scrumptious buffet breakfast has all manner of home-made goodies. The Hurricane's owners are the creative energy behind the refitting of several hotels along this road.

Hotel Dos Mares (☎ 956 68 40 35; www.dosmares hotel.com in Spanish; s/d inside incl breakfast €107/135, bungalow incl breakfast from €102/127; Ⓟ ❄ ☇) This excellent choice is right on the beach about 4.5km from Tarifa. Its eclectic architecture has a mainly Islamic theme. You can stay in the main building (seven rooms), or go for one of 29 bungalows in the gardens or on the beachfront. The bar with tremendous views out to Africa is a popular hangout. The hotel has its own well-run stables, too (see p207).

Hotel Valdevaqueros (☎ 956 23 67 05; www.hurri canehotel.com; r €86, 3-/4-person apt incl breakfast €112; ☽ Mar-Nov; Ⓟ) This attractive old farmhouse, 20m from the beach at Valdevaqueros, has a suitably rustic exterior. Owned by the Hurricane Hotel folk, it has a few trademark design features such as careful and creative renovation and decoration using natural and ethnic materials, plus a beautiful garden. The bar area, featuring mosaic work, extends outside to covered areas with loads of plants. Just off the N340, opposite 100% Fun (below), a metallic sign with horse and cow heads arches over the beginning of a longish, bumpy driveway to the *cortijo* (farmhouse).

Hotel Arte-Vida (☎ 956 68 52 46; www.hotelarte vida.com; N340 Km 79.3; s/d incl breakfast €118/139; **P**) The Arte-Vida, 5km from the town centre, has a garden with lawn opening onto the beach, an excellent restaurant (p210) with stunning views, and attractive, medium-sized rooms. Décor is oriental minimalist (lots of white, cane and bamboo).

100% Fun (☎ 956 68 03 30; www.tarifa.net/100fun; r incl breakfast €85-102; **P** **≋**) 100% Fun is a part-Australian-owned hotel on the N340 just short of Punta Paloma. The thatched-roof Tex-Mex restaurant and some of the rooms are set in pretty tropical gardens adorned with totem poles. Eleven rooms share a large patio, each room with its own flower-shaded veranda. There's also an excellent surf shop.

Hotel Tres Mares (☎ 956 68 06 65; www.tresmares hotel.com in Spanish; N-340 Km 76; s/d €83/102; ☼ Mar-Nov; **P** **≋**) This has the same owners as the Dos Mares but it's a few kilometres further out of Tarifa, next door to 100% Fun. Rooms have sea views and are on two levels of an uninteresting '70s-style brown-painted block. What's distinctive here are the extensive large grounds with wooden oriental furniture, a wooden elephant, a Moroccan tent, hammocks and a bar-restaurant. There is certainly room to chill.

Hotel Punta Sur (☎ 956 68 43 26; www.hotelpuntasur .com in Spanish; N340 Km 77; s/d €103/136; **P** **≋**) With a logo of a surfer riding a wave, the Punta Sur, near the Pharmacy on the N340, is another Hurricane Hotel project: here the team has waved its magic wand and worked design miracles on what was an ordinary roadside hotel. A restaurant, the reception and a billiard table are in a huge open space that has been decorated with flights of fantasy combining modern, futuristic, Gaudiesque and Moroccan influences. The comfortable, eccentrically decorated rooms are set in big gardens with a tennis court.

Hostal Oasis (☎ 956 68 50 65; r €42, 2-person bungalow €60) The Oasis is set in substantial grounds about 8km out of Tarifa, and its 11 clean bungalows, set around the large lawn, have equipped kitchens. They're better than the rooms in the main block.

OTB (☎ 661-030446; www.otb-tarifa.com; N340 Km 81; dm €12, r per person €15; ☼ Mar-Nov; **P** **≋**) This Italian-run place, geared to backpackers, offers dorm accommodation, doubles and quads, kitchen use, television, and laundry facilities. It's located about 1km out of town towards Cádiz.

There are six year-round **camping grounds** (www.campingsdetarifa.com) with room for more than 4000 campers, on or near the beach between Tarifa and Punta Paloma, 10km northwest from Tarifa along the N340. They charge from €16 to €32 for two people with a tent and car. The two Torre de la Peña sites are more modern than the others.

Eating
Tarifa brims with eateries. International residents and visitors guarantee plenty of variety.

IN TOWN
Make your way to Calle Sancho IV El Bravo for takeaways.

Ali Baba (Calle Sancho IV El Bravo) The popular Ali Baba, with benches and stand-up tables outside, serves cheap, filling and tasty Arabic food made with lovely fresh ingredients. Vegetarians can enjoy excellent falafel for €2.50; carnivores pay €3 for the kebabs.

Café Central (Calle Sancho IV El Bravo 8; breakfast €2.50-3.40) This café is the prime location for people-watching, delicious *churros con chocolate* (fingers of doughnut dipped into a cup of hot chocolate) and a large range of breakfasts and teas.

La Trattoria (☎ 956 68 22 25; Paseo de la Alameda; pasta & pizza €5.50-9, mains €9.50-13) Italian restaurants are proliferating in Tarifa. A good location, generally great food and always top-rate service make this one of the best.

Souk (☎ 956 68 07 08; Huerta del Rey 11; entrées €4-6, mains €9-12; ☼ closed Tue) Dripping with Moroccan decorations, the dimly lit Souk has terrific Moroccan- and Asian-inspired food. *Thai rojo de verduras* (Thai vegetables in coconut) goes down well after the *hojaldre de espinacas* (spicy spinach and feta pastry). There are tagines and couscous, too.

Mandrágora (☎ 956 68 12 91; Calle Independencia 3; mains €9-15; ☿ dinner only, closed Sun) Behind Iglesia San Mateo, this intimate place serves Andalucian-Arabic food. Delicious options include lamb with plums and almonds, and prawns with *nora* (Andalucian sweet pepper) sauce.

Misiana (☎ 956 62 70 83; www.misiana.com in Spanish; Calle Sancho IV El Bravo; tapas €2.20-5) This hip, loungy place at the hotel Misiana (p208) has wooden tables outside on the street, eye-catching décor and waitstaff in long aprons. It offers an eclectic *menú* of tasty morsels. You might try yogurt and fruit (€1.80 to €2.80) or scrambled eggs and omelettes (around €3) for breakfast, and perhaps curried almonds or fingers of salmon with a yogurt and mustard dressing for lunch.

Café Azul Bar (Calle Batalla del Salado; breakfast €4-7; ☿ Apr-Oct) This eccentric place prepares the best breakfasts in town. Don't pass up the large muesli, fruit salad and yogurt. There's good coffee, excellent juices and sometimes Thai food at lunch time.

La Dolce Vita (Plaza San Martín; breakfast €2.50; ☿ Mar-Nov) This little place with tables on the square has alternative vibes. It offers lassis, teas, a variety of breakfasts (named after different nationalities), quiches, ice creams and cocktails.

Lannathai (☎ 956 68 14 13; Calle Pintor GP Villalta 60; mains €8-12; ☿ closed Wed) Looking out over Playa de los Lances about 1km from the centre, Lannathai is run by a Thai-German couple. Furniture and decorations are Thai and some are for sale. Thai owner and cook Sujinda grows some of her own special ingredients.

ALONG THE COAST

Most of the hotels and *hostales* up here have restaurants.

Miramar (☎ 956 68 52 46; www.hotelartevida .com; N340 Km 79.3; mains €8-15) This restaurant at Hotel Arte-Vida (p209) lives up to its name with expansive ocean views looking out to Africa. The chefs here whip up a range of pastas and some international meat dishes plus fresh local seafood and fish.

Terrace Restaurant (☎ 956 68 49 19; www.hurri canehotel.com; lunch mains €7-10, dinner mains €10-18) This casual restaurant at the Hurricane Hotel (p208) is good for an economical lunch (various salads, chicken, local fish and seafood). In the evenings the hotel's inside restaurant prepares creative meals, including very good

salads (€7 to €8; try salmon, avocado and grapefruit), and main dishes such as lamb chops with garlic and rosemary.

Hotel Valdevaqueros (☎ 956 23 67 05; www.hurri canehotel.com; mains €7-10; ☿ Mar-Nov) The Hurricane's relative (see p208), this place fills windsurfer stomachs with large plates of chicken, salad, bread and condiments.

Chiringuito Tangana (mains €4-7.50; ☿ noon-7pm) Nearby, next to Spin Out on the beach, this place serves up pies, lasagne, savoury pastries and *bocadillos* (filled rolls). Chill to the beat on the grass or relax on the Moroccan carpets on the floor of the glassed-in patio.

Drinking & Entertainment

Soul Café (Calle Santísima Trinidad 9) This hip, popular bar is run by travel-loving Italians. You may hear guest DJs from Milan spin their favourites. Stop by after 11pm, but not in winter when the owners are travelling.

Bodega de Casa Amarilla (Calle Sancho IV El Bravo 9) A convivial *típico* (typical) bar-restaurant run by the Café Central (p209) family, it sometimes has live flamenco.

Bar Obaïnano (Calle Nuestra Señora de la Luz) Serves fresh juices and exotic cocktails with cheerful background music. Shows surfing footage. It's popular with French travellers.

Misiana (☎ 956 62 70 83; www.misiana.com in Spanish; Calle Sancho IV El Bravo) One of *the* places to be seen in Tarifa, the futuristic bar with blue neon lighting at the Misiana (p208) hotel has weekly live music, sometimes flamenco, at least in the summer season.

Café Continental (Paseo de la Alameda) This good tapas, drinks and coffee stop has low-key local live music on summer weekend nights.

La Jaima (Playa de los Lances) In summer, this Moroccan tent arrangement pops up on the beach near the edge of town. From 7pm to 10pm it's an Islamic-style tearoom but, come midnight, disco sounds take over.

Zoo House (formerly Tanakas; Plaza de San Hiscio) This central disco plays house music. An upstairs bar with tapas draws a bit of an older crowd.

Getting There & Away
BOAT

FRS (☎ 956 68 18 30; www.frs.es; Avenida Andalucía) runs a fast ferry between Tarifa and Tangier in Morocco (passenger/car/motorcycle €24.50/73/23, 35 minutes one-way) up to four times daily, with possibly more sailings in

July and August. There are two daily sailings from Tarifa at 9am and 11.30am (Spanish time) and from Tangier at 5pm and 7.30pm (Moroccan time). Get details of the service at the port, at FRS or at **Marruecotur** (☎ 956 68 18 21; Avenida de la Constitución 5/6).

Tarifa is in the process of being upgraded to a full Schengen port, meaning that travellers of all nationalities will be able to pass through it. In practice in 2004, Tarifa operated as a Schengen port except for the months of July and August, during which time travellers without EU residence documents or passports were not permitted to use the ferries entering or leaving Spain at Tarifa. For the latest information check with FRS or the tourist office.

BUS
From its base, 1½ blocks north of Avenida de Andalucía, **Comes** (☎ 956 68 40 38, 956 65 57 55; Calle Batalla del Salado) runs five or more buses daily to Cádiz (€6.95, 1¾ hours), Algeciras (€1.55, 30 minutes), and La Línea de la Concepción (€3.25, 45 minutes), three to Jerez de la Frontera (€8.25, 2½ hours), four to Seville (€14, three hours), two to Málaga (€10.80, two hours) and six to Barbate (€3.60, 50 minutes). There is one bus daily Monday to Friday to Zahara de los Atunes (€2.85, 45 minutes).

The office has *consigna automática* (secure locker) luggage storage. Note, buses are projected to use a new stop opposite the petrol station at the north end of Calle Batalla del Salado. When this stop is up and running, the Comes office will be next door to it.

CAR & MOTORCYCLE
Stop at the Mirador del Estrecho, about 7km out of Tarifa on the N340 towards Algeciras, to take in magnificent views of the Strait of Gibraltar, the Mediterranean, the Atlantic and two continents. Beware of the frequent police speed trap in the 50km/h zone at Pelayo, a few kilometres further east.

Getting Around
In July and August local buses run every 90 minutes from Tarifa up the west coast to Punta Paloma. Some go on to Bolonia. The tourist office will have details. There's a stop at the bottom of the Paseo de la Alameda. The main stop will soon be next to the petrol station at the north end of Calle Batalla

del Salado. A timetable and prices should be posted here. Taxis (around €13) line up on Avenida de Andalucía near the Puerta de Jerez. For bicycle hire see p207.

THE SOUTHEAST

PARQUE NATURAL LOS ALCORNOCALES
This large (1700 sq km) and beautiful natural park stretches 75km north almost from the Strait of Gibraltar to the border of the Parque Natural Sierra de Grazalema. It's a jumble of sometimes rolling, sometimes rugged hills of medium height, much of it covered in Spain's most extensive *alcornocales* (cork oak woodlands).

Los Alcornocales is rich in archaeological, historical and natural interest, but is little visited because it's well off the beaten track and sparsely populated. There are plenty of walks and opportunities for other activities in the park, but you need your own wheels to make the most of it (see p192). The park has several visitors centres and information offices, including:

Centro de Visitantes Cortes de la Frontera (☎ 952 15 43 45; Avenida de la Democracia s/n, Cortes de la Frontera; ☺ 10am-2pm Thu all year, 10am-2pm & 6-8pm Fri-Sun Apr-Sep, 10am-2pm & 4-6pm Fri-Sun Oct-Mar)

Centro de Visitantes Huerta Grande (☎ 956 67 91 61; N340 Km 96, Pelayo; ☺ 10am-2pm Thu all year, 10am-2pm & 6-8pm Fri-Sun Apr-Sep, 10am-2pm & 4-6pm Fri-Sun Oct-Mar) On the Tarifa–Algeciras road.

Punto de Información Castillo de Castellar (☎ 956 23 68 87; Taraguilla, Castellar de la Frontera; ☺ 11am-2pm & 5-6pm Wed-Sun May-Sep, 10am-2pm & 3-5pm Wed-Sun Oct-Apr)

Punto de Información Jimena de la Frontera (☎ 956 64 05 69; Calle Misericordia s/n, Jimena de la Frontera; ☺ 11am-1pm & 4-6pm Mon-Fri, 10am-1pm & 4-7pm Sat & Sun)

One good base is **Jimena de la Frontera**, a small town on the A369 Algeciras–Ronda road on the park's eastern boundary. It's crowned by a fine Islamic castle, has a handful of *hostales* and is served by train and bus from Algeciras and Ronda.

The CA3331 heading northwest leads to **La Sauceda**, an abandoned village that's now the site of a recreational area and field education centre. The La Sauceda area is beautiful country that was once a den of bandits and smugglers, and even guerrillas during

HIGH-FLIERS OVER THE STRAIT OF GIBRALTAR

Keen bird-watchers mustn't miss the Strait of Gibraltar, a key point of passage for migrating birds between Africa and Europe. In general, northward migrations occur between mid-February and early June, and southbound flights between late July and early November. When a westerly wind is blowing, Gibraltar itself is usually a good spot for seeing the birds. When the wind is calm or easterly, the Tarifa area (including the Mirador del Estrecho lookout 7km east of the town) is usually better.

Soaring birds such as raptors, storks and vultures cross at the strait because they rely on thermals and updraughts, which don't happen over wider expanses of water. White storks sometimes congregate in flocks of up to 3000 to cross the strait (January and February northbound, July and August southbound). There are just two places where the seas are narrow enough for the stork to get into Europe by this method. One is the Bosphorus (the strait between the Black Sea and the Sea of Marmara) and the other is right here at the Strait of Gibraltar.

the Spanish Civil War (when the village was bombed by Francisco Franco's planes). It's the starting point for an alternative route up Aljibe, the park's highest peak (see p192).

ALGECIRAS

pop 109,000

Algeciras, the major port linking Spain with Africa, is also an industrial town, a big fishing port and a drug smuggling centre. Though it's unattractive and polluted, it's not without interest. Proximity to Africa gives the port an air of excitement and the gentrification of the town centre makes it quite pleasant to walk around. A few pretty old buildings with wrought-iron balconies remain and there are some good restaurants. During the summer the port is hectic with hundreds of thousands of Moroccans who have been working in Europe and are on the way home for summer holidays.

History

Algeciras was an important Roman port. Alfonso XI of Castilla wrested it from the

Merenids of Morocco in 1344 but later Mohammed V of Granada razed it to the ground. In 1704, Algeciras was repopulated by many of those who left Gibraltar after the latter was taken by the British. During the Franco era, industry was developed.

Orientation

Algeciras is on the western side of the Bahía de Algeciras, opposite Gibraltar. Avenida Virgen del Carmen runs north to south along the seafront, becoming Avenida de la Marina around the entrance to the port. From here Calle Juan de la Cierva (becoming Calle San Bernardo) runs inland beside a disused rail track to the Comes bus station (350m) and the train station (400m). The central square, Plaza Alta, is a couple of blocks inland from Avenida Virgen del Carmen. Plaza Palma, with a bustling daily market (except Sunday), is one block west of Avenida de la Marina.

Information

Exchange rates for buying dirham (the Moroccan currency) are better at the banks than at travel agencies. There are banks and ATMs on Avenida Virgen del Carmen and around Plaza Alta, plus a couple of ATMs inside the port.

In the port, luggage storage (€1.80 to €2.50) is available from 8am to 9pm. If you have valuables there are lockers nearby (€2.40). Both the Comes and the smaller Portillo/Alsina Graells bus stations also have luggage storage.

Hospital Punta de Europa (☎ 956 02 50 50; Carretera de Getares s/n) About 3km west of the centre.

Policía Nacional (☎ 956 66 04 00; Avenida de las Fuerzas Armadas 6) Next to Parque de María Cristina, northwest of the town centre.

Post office (☎ 956 58 74 05; Calle José Antonio) Just south of Plaza Alta.

Tourist office (☎ 956 57 26 36; Calle Juan de la Cierva s/n; 🕑 9am-2pm Mon-Fri) A block inland from Avenida de la Marina. Friendly English-speaking staff. Useful message board.

Dangers & Annoyances

Be alert in the port, bus terminal and market and walk purposefully when moving between the Comes and Portillo bus stations in the evening. If you want to leave your vehicle in Algeciras, your most secure bet is the multistorey car park inside the port (per 24 hours €25).

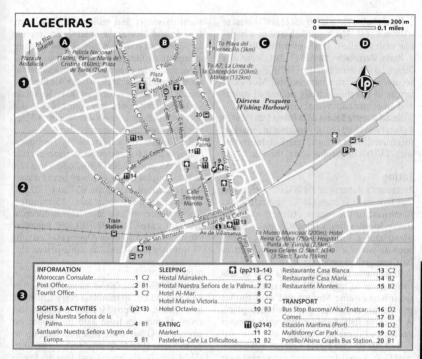

ALGECIRAS

INFORMATION			SLEEPING	(pp213–14)	Restaurante Casa Blanca.............**13** C2
Moroccan Consulate......................**1** C2			Hostal Marrakech..........................**6** C2		Restaurante Casa María.................**14** B2
Post Office....................................**2** B1			Hostal Nuestra Señora de la Palma..**7** B2		Restaurante Montes.......................**15** B2
Tourist Office................................**3** C2			Hotel Al-Mar.................................**8** C2		
			Hotel Marina Victoria....................**9** C2		TRANSPORT
SIGHTS & ACTIVITIES	(p213)		Hotel Octavio...............................**10** B3		Bus Stop Bacoma/Alsa/Enatcar......**16** D2
Iglesia Nuestra Señora de la					Comes..**17** B3
Palma...**4** B1			EATING	(p214)	Estación Marítima (Port)................**18** D2
Santuario Nuestra Señora Virgen de			Market..**11** B2		Multistorey Car Park.....................**19** D2
Europa.......................................**5** B1			Pastelería-Cafe La Dificultosa.........**12** B2		Portillo/Alsina Graells Bus Station..**20** B1

Sights & Activities

Wander up to palm-fringed Plaza Alta, which has a lovely tiled fountain. On its western side is the 18th-century **Iglesia Nuestra Señora de la Palma** and on its eastern side the 17th-century **Santuario Nuestra Señora Virgen de Europa**, both worth a look. Some of the houses on the streets around here are fetchingly tumbledown.

Leafy **Parque de María Cristina**, a few blocks to the north, also provides a change from the hustle and bustle of the port. The **Museo Municipal** (Calle Nicaragua), just south of the main tourist office, is reasonably interesting. If you've got your own wheels, check out the town's two beaches – **Playa Getares** (to the south) and **Playa del Rinconcillo** (to the north), which have reasonable sand and are kept quite clean.

Festivals & Events

Feria (around 19 June) The town's nine-day fair.
Fiesta del Virgen de la Palma (15 August) The town honours its patroness with a maritime pilgrimage. (Spanish maritime pilgrimages are fun-filled occasions and a pretty sight.)

Sleeping

There's loads of budget accommodation in the streets behind Avenida de la Marina, but market traffic in the small hours makes sleep difficult. Some places are also grotty.

Hotel Reina Cristina (☎ 956 60 26 22; www.reinacristina.com in Spanish; Paseo de la Conferencia s/n; s/d €77/116; P ⊠ ⊠) If you can afford it, make your way south from the port to this colonial-style hotel with 188 olde-worlde rooms, and two swimming pools set amid tropical gardens. Stories of it being a haunt of spies in WWII intrigue: apparently they observed sea traffic in the Strait of Gibraltar from here.

Hotel Octavio (☎ 956 65 27 00; www.husa.es; Calle San Bernardo 1; s/d €100/125; P ⊠) Public spaces at the Octavio are a bit frayed around the edges. Still, the 74 spacious rooms, with satellite TV, hairdryer etc, are a huge step up from most other places to stay in town.

Hotel Al-Mar (☎ 956 65 46 61; Avenida de la Marina 2-3; s/d €46/81; P ⊠) Two oversized Moroccan lamps decorate the foyer of this comfortable mid-range place, which is handy for the port. There are 192 rooms, some with sea views.

Hotel Marina Victoria (☎ 956 63 28 65; Avenida de la Marina 7; r €47; 🕃) A solid choice in a high-rise with excellent views over the port.

Hostal Marrakech (☎ 956 57 34 74; Calle Juan de la Cierva 5; s/d with shared bathroom €18/25) This clean, secure place is run by a helpful Moroccan family. It has thoughtfully decorated rooms and an exotic communal lounge with TV.

Hostal Nuestra Señora de la Palma (☎ 956 63 24 81; Plaza Palma 12; s/d €20/28) Fronting the market, this friendly *hostal* has 25 comfortable rooms with TV. It's in earplug zone, though.

Eating

Restaurante Montes (☎ 956 65 42 07; Calle Juan Morrison 27; menú €7.50, mains €10-18) Several blocks northwest of the tourist office, the slightly flashy Montes has a hugely popular lunch *menú* and a long list of delicious dishes such as *pargo a la espalda* (bream split in half and grilled on its back).

Restaurante Casa María (☎ 956 65 47 02; Calle Emilio Castelar 53; menú €7.50) Down the street from Restaurante Montes and with similar prices, this is another popular lunch place. À la carte fish dishes come with various sauces and there are steaks.

Restaurante Casa Blanca (Calle Juan de la Cierva 1; menú €7.50) A well-frequented restaurant near the tourist office with a good-value *menú* and nice fresh tapas.

The city market has a wonderful array of fresh fruit, vegetables, hams and cheese. Nearby, **Pastelería-Cafe La Dificultosa** (Calle José Santacana; breakfast €2) is the place to breakfast or take a coffee break.

Plaza Alta has a couple of sidewalk cafés and restaurants. Tea on the terrace at the Hotel Reina Cristina (p213) is relaxing.

Entertainment

In the summer, flamenco, rock and classical music concerts happen at some of the more attractive spots in town – Parque de María Cristina and the Plaza de Toros. The tourist office has a list of events.

Getting There & Away

The daily paper *Europa Sur* has up-to-date transport arrival and departure details.

BOAT

Trasmediterránea (☎ 956 58 34 00, 902 45 46 45; www .trasmediterranea.es), **EuroFerrys** (☎ 956 65 11 78; www .euroferrys.com) and other companies operate frequent passenger and vehicle ferries to/from Tangier and Ceuta, the Spanish enclave on the Moroccan coast. Usually at least 16 daily sailings go to Tangier and the same to Ceuta. From mid-June to September ferries operate almost around the clock to cater for the Moroccan migration – you may have to queue for up to three hours. Buy your ticket in the port or at the agencies on Avenida de la Marina: prices are the same everywhere.

To Tangier, on a ferry taking 2½ hours, one-way fares for passenger/car/motorcycle over 500cc are €25.30/78.80/27.30. On a fast ferry taking 1¼ hours, one-way fares for passenger/car/motorcycle are €27.20/67/22.30.

To Ceuta, a fast ferry takes 35 minutes. One-way fares for passenger/car/motorcycle over 500cc are €21.40/62.70/13.40. **Buquebus** (☎ 902 41 42 42) also does Algeciras–Ceuta in 35 minutes for almost the same price.

BUS

Comes (☎ 956 65 34 56; Calle San Bernardo) buses go to La Línea (€1.60, 30 minutes) every half-hour from 7am to 9.30pm Monday to Friday, and every 45 minutes from 8am to 7.30pm on weekends. Other daily buses include up to 12 to Tarifa (€1.55, 30 minutes), up to 10 to Cádiz (€8.70, 2½ hours) and four to Seville (€13.35 to €14.75, 3½ hours). There's one bus daily Monday to Friday to Jimena de la Frontera (plus one on Saturday; €3, 30 minutes), Zahara de los Atunes (€4.40, one hour), Barbate (€5.20, 1¼ hours) and Ronda (€8, 1½ hours). **Daibus** (☎ 956 65 34 56; www.daibus .es in Spanish) runs four daily buses to Madrid (€23.55, eight to nine hours) starting from the port then dropping in at the Comes station.

Portillo & Alsina Graells (☎ 956 65 10 55; Avenida Virgen del Carmen 15) operates five direct buses daily to Málaga (€9.30, 1¾ hours), four to Granada (€17.60, 3½ hours) and two to Jaén (€3.65, five hours). Several more buses daily to Málaga (€9.05, three hours) stop at towns en route.

Bacoma/Alsa/Enatcar (☎ 902 42 22 42; www.alsa .es), inside the port, runs up to four services daily to Murcia, Alicante, Valencia and Barcelona. This company also runs daily buses to Portugal and thrice-weekly buses to France, Germany and Holland.

TRAIN

From the **station** (☎ 956 63 02 02), adjacent to Calle San Bernardo, two direct trains run daily to/from Madrid (€35 to €52.50, six or 11 hours) and three to/from Granada (€15.75, four to 4½ hours). All trains pass through Ronda (€5.85 to €15.50, 1¾ hours) and Bobadilla (€9.65 to €27.50, 2¾ hours) taking in some spectacular scenery en route. At Bobadilla you can change for Málaga, Córdoba and Seville plus more trains to Granada and Madrid.

LA LÍNEA DE LA CONCEPCIÓN
pop 62,000

La Línea, 20km east of Algeciras, around the bay, is the unavoidable stepping stone to Gibraltar. The city was built in 1870 in response to the British expansion around the rock of Gibraltar.

Orientation & Information

A left turn as you exit La Línea's bus station will bring you out on Avenida 20 de Abril, which runs the 300m or so between the town's main square, Plaza de la Constitución, and the Gibraltar border.

Municipal tourist office (☎ 956 17 19 98; Avenida Príncipe Felipe s/n; ✆ 9am-8pm Mon-Fri, 9am-2pm Sat) At the end of Avenida 20 de Abril facing the border.

Regional tourist office (☎ 956 76 99 50; ✆ 9am-3pm Mon-Fri, 10am-1pm Sat) On the corner of the main square.

Sights & Activities

La Línea's city centre has been improved and it has a couple of museums that are worth visiting. The **Museo del Istmo** (Plaza de la Constitución; ✆ 10am-2pm & 5-9pm Mon-Sat, 10am-1pm Sun) has archaeological finds, paintings, sculptures and changing exhibitions. **Museo Cruz Herrera** (Calle Doctor Villar; ✆ 10am-2pm & 5-9pm Mon-Sat, 10am-1pm Sun), opposite the palm-lined Plaza Fariñas, exhibits the work of José Cruz Herrera, a successful early-20th-century painter from La Línea. His subjects were often beautiful Andalucian women and he lived and worked for a time in Morocco, which is reflected in his paintings.

You can also visit WWII bunkers opposite Gibraltar.

Sleeping & Eating

La Línea has around four mid-range to top-end options. Cheaper rooms can be had around Plaza de la Constitución.

Hotel Quercus (☎ 956 79 21 59; www.quercusalcaidesa.com; Urbanización La Alcaidesa; s/d €100/150; P ⊠) Near the golf course, this elegantly decked-

out hotel with just nine rooms will suit those who enjoy an intimate setting.

Hostal La Campana (☎ 956 17 30 59; Calle Carboneros 3; s/d €39/46) This friendly *hostal* just off the western side of Plaza de la Constitución has decent rooms with fan and TV. Its restaurant does a three-course *menú* (€6.50).

Pensión Carlos II (☎ 956 66 21 35; Calle Méndez Núñez 12; s/d €32/36; ⊠) This *hostal* has decent rooms with satellite TV. It's near the Iglesia de la Inmaculada, about a five-minute walk from the main plaza.

Pensión Florida (☎ 956 17 13 00; Calle Sol 37; s/d €18/36) A little north of the Campana and Carlos II, this is another friendly central place and it has a restaurant.

Cafetería Okay (Calle Real 23) Just off the northwestern corner of Plaza de la Constitución, this place has a good bakery and does breakfasts (coffee and toasted roll for €3).

Later in the day, check out Plaza del Pintor Cruz Herrera, with a pretty tiled fountain, orange trees, and more places to eat and drink.

Getting There & Away
BUS

Comes (☎ 956 17 00 93) buses run about every 30 minutes to/from Algeciras (€1.60, 30 minutes) every half-hour from 7am to 9.30pm Monday to Friday, and every 45 minutes from 8am to 7.30pm on weekends. There are six daily buses to Tarifa (€3.25, 45 minutes), four to Cádiz (€10.30, 2½ hours), three to Seville (€18.40, four hours), and two to Granada (€16, four hours). A bus runs to Jimena de la Frontera (€3.60, 45 minutes) at 3pm Monday to Friday. Portillo buses go to Málaga (€9.40, 2½ hours, four daily) and Estepona (€3.20, one hour, eight daily).

CAR & MOTORCYCLE

Owing to the usually long vehicle queues at the Gibraltar border, many visitors to Gibraltar opt to park in La Línea and then walk across the border. Parking meters in La Línea cost €0.90 for one hour or €4.50 for six hours and are free from 10.30pm until 9am Monday to Friday and from 2pm Saturday until 9am Monday. Meters are plentiful on Avenida Príncipe Felipe opposite the frontier. The underground Parking Fo Cona, just off Avenida 20 de Abril, charges per hour/day €1/6.30. Parking on the street in La Línea is fine but do not leave any items visible.

Gibraltar

CONTENTS

Looming like the prow of some great ship off Spain's most southerly coast, the British colony of Gibraltar is a fascinating mix of curiosities, not least for its perfectly preserved atmosphere of 1960s little England – all sticky rock and five-figure phone numbers. However, despite all the red letter boxes and bobbies on the beat, this tiny handkerchief of land (it is only 5km long and 1.6km wide) is a cultural cocktail of British, Jewish, Genoese, north African, Portuguese, Spanish, Maltese and Indian elements which have made Gibraltar fantastically prosperous over the last 300 years.

Naturally, the main sight is the awesome Rock; a vast limestone ridge that rises to 426m, with sheer cliffs on its northern and eastern sides. For the ancient Greeks and Romans this was one of the two Pillars of Hercules, split from the other pillar, the coastal mountain Jebel Musa in Morocco, 25km south, in the course of his arduous Twelve Labours. The two promontories marked the edge of the ancient world and the stormy seas of the Strait of Gibraltar provided the gateway to the Mediterranean.

This strategic position has made Gibraltar an irresistible proposition to everyone from Julius Caesar to Franco, and continues to make it a bone of contention between the Spanish and British governments. However, more recent years have seen an increasingly relaxed spirit on both sides of the border just in time for the massive party in August 2004, which celebrated 300 glorious years of stiff upper lip.

HIGHLIGHTS

- Watching **dolphins** (p224) in the Bahía de Algeciras
- Meeting Gibraltar's oldest inhabitants at the **Apes' Den** (p223)
- Exploring one of the best defence systems in the world in the caves, paths and old military installations of the **Upper Rock Nature Reserve** (p222)
- Gliding to the top of the Rock in the **cable car** (p223) for a bird's-eye view of the Bahía de Algeciras
- **Diving** (p224) among sea wrecks and discovering the marvellous underwater world of the Rock
- Losing yourself in time and place in **Gibraltar town's** (p223) hidden corners

Gibraltar Town ★
Upper Rock Nature Reserve ★
Bahía de Algeciras ★
Cable Car ★
Apes' Den ★
Diving ★

POPULATION:	GIBRALTAR AVERAGE DAILY HIGH:	ALTITUDE RANGE:
28,600	JAN/AUG 15°C/24°C	0m–426m

HISTORY

Almost every square metre of Gibraltar can tell a tale as far back as the days of the last Neanderthals as skulls discovered in 1848 and 1928 testify. The skull discovered in 1848 was that of a female; a find that predated the discovery of a male skull in Germany's Neander Valley by eight years. (The latter discovery inspired the anthropological term 'Neanderthal man', although 'Gibraltar woman' surely had the fairer claim.)

Phoenicians and ancient Greeks left traces here, but Gibraltar really entered the history books in AD 711 when Tariq ibn Ziyad, the Muslim governor of Tangier, made it the initial bridgehead for the Islamic invasion of the Iberian Peninsula, landing with an army of some 10,000 men. The name Gibraltar is derived from Jebel Tariq (Tariq's Mountain).

The Almohad Muslims founded a town here in 1159 and were subsequently usurped by the Castilians in 1462. Then in 1704 an Anglo-Dutch fleet captured Gibraltar during the War of the Spanish Succession. Spain ceded the Rock of Gibraltar to Britain by the Treaty of Utrecht in 1713, but didn't give up military attempts to regain it until the failure of the Great Siege of 1779–83. In the aftermath of the capture of the Rock most of the resident Spanish population fled and settled in what is now called the Campo de Gibraltar, the area around the Bahía de Algeciras (or the Bay of Gibraltar), incorporating towns such as San Roque, Algeciras and La Línea de la Concepción.

Subsequently, Britain developed Gibraltar into an important naval base, and during WWII Gibraltar became a base for allied landings in north Africa. The British garrison was withdrawn in the early 1990s but the British navy continues to use Gibraltar's facilities. The constant shipping services and the free-port status only strengthened the relationship between the local population and Britain and continues to attract investment today.

In 1969 when Franco closed the Spain–Gibraltar border (infuriated by a referendum in which the Gibraltarians voted by 12,138 to 44 to remain under British sovereignty) the result was the complete severing of cross-border relationships and the seemingly irrevocable polarisation of attitudes and sentiments in Gibraltar and Spain. The same year a new constitution committed Britain to respecting Gibraltarians' wishes over sovereignty, and gave Gibraltar domestic self-government and its own parliament, the House of Assembly. In 1985, just prior to Spain joining the EC (now the EU) in 1986, the border was opened after 16 long years bringing a breath of fresh air to the Rock.

GOVERNMENT & POLITICS

Gibraltar's last two elections (2000 and 2004) have been won by the centre-right Gibraltar Social Democrat Party, led by Peter Caruana. The main opposition is the Gibraltar Socialist Labour Party, led by Joe Bossano. Caruana has shown himself willing to talk with Spain about Gibraltar's future, but fiercely opposes any concessions over sovereignty.

When Spain wants to exert pressure on Gibraltar, it employs such methods as extra-thorough customs and immigration procedures, which cause hours-long delays at the border. Spain has proposed a period of joint British-Spanish sovereignty leading to Gibraltar eventually becoming the 18th Spanish region, with greater autonomy than any of the others.

Tourism, the port and financial services are the mainstays of Gibraltar's economy. Spanish police complain that Gibraltar, with more than 70,000 domiciled companies, is a centre for the laundering of illicit money from organised crime and tax evasion elsewhere in Europe. Much of this money, it's said, is invested in property in southern Spain. Caruana does not deny that Gibraltar is a tax haven but says it is a well-supervised one. Another problem, cigarette smuggling from Gibraltar into Spain, seems to have diminished under the Caruana government.

Successive British governments have refused to give way over Gibraltar's sovereignty, but in March 2002, for the European Council's Barcelona Summit, Spain and Britain came to a broad agreement about sharing sovereignty. The agreement, which was presented at the summit, was backed by the 15 member states of the EU. Gibraltar reacted angrily at what it saw as Europewide support for a nonrepresentative deal

SMUGGLERS' COVE

Once a den of smugglers who supplied the mountain bandits of Ronda with contraband, Gibraltar remains something of a renegade fiscal enclave – another bone of contention for the Spanish government. With cheap electronics, chocolates, perfume, alcohol and cigarettes (which are half the price of those in Spain) due to its VAT-free status, smuggling continues apace. To try and combat the lucrative illegal trade of cigarettes, checks at the border can be very lengthy and customs police are constantly rotated in an attempt to confuse and thwart any underhand deals.

Spain endlessly complains to the British government about the smuggling in Gibraltar as well as the money-laundering through its 75,000 'off-shore' financial institutions (over double the population), which are thought to be the repository of Russian mafia money. Certainly, Gibraltar, with its three marinas, is the richest town in the area, and has much to lose should Spanish sovereignty (and the nemesis of VAT) put an end to these lucrative shenanigans.

over Gibraltar allegedly being set up by Britain's prime minister Tony Blair and his Spanish counterpart José María Aznar. Gibraltarians saw the deal as Britain offering Spain 'in-principle' sovereignty concessions that breached the 1969 constitutional commitment.

In response, an estimated 20,000 Gibraltarians answered Peter Caruana's call to take to the streets on 18 March 2002 in a peaceful but passionate demonstration of their fierce commitment to retaining their British nationality. The rallying cry was: 'No in-principle concessions against our wishes. Yes to reasonable dialogue.' By mid-2002 it appeared that a Britain-Spain deal was foundering in any case, over the issue of control of Gibraltar's naval base and military airfield.

In early September 2002 the government of Gibraltar announced the staging, on 7 November 2002, of a referendum that would ask its people whether Britain should share its sovereignty with Spain over Gibraltar. The result of the referendum was a resounding rejection of the idea by the people of Gibraltar.

Britain and Spain both said that they would not recognise the referendum. The British government reiterated its position that it would not relinquish Gibraltar's status against local wishes, but insisted that it would not recognise as legitimate any referendum not called by the UK government.

As Gibraltar celebrated 300 years of British rule in 2004 it is certainly true that most Gibraltarians no longer view Britain as the mother country, although they still adore British traditions and their own peculiar way of life. The resolution of this remarkable territorial anomaly probably lies in a political-economic compromise; one that brings mutual benefits to Gibraltar and Spain while satisfying the passionate desire of Gibraltarians to retain British citizenship under British sovereignty and the territorial sensitivity of the Spanish.

POPULATION

Of Gibraltar's civilian population, about 77% are classed as Gibraltarians, 14% as British and 9% as other nationalities. The Gibraltarians are of mixed Genoese, Jewish, Portuguese, Spanish, Maltese, Indian and British ancestry, the Genoese element coming from Genoese ship repairers brought here by the British in the 18th century. A substantial percentage of those of other nationalities are Moroccans, many of whom are on short-term work contracts.

LANGUAGE

Gibraltarians speak English, Spanish and a curiously accented, singsong mix of the two, slipping back and forth from one to the other, often in mid-sentence. Signs are in English.

ORIENTATION

To reach Gibraltar by land you must pass through the Spanish frontier town of La Línea de la Concepción (p215). Just south of the border, the road crosses the runway of Gibraltar airport, which stretches east to west across the neck of the peninsula. The town and harbours of Gibraltar lie along the Rock's less-steep western side, facing the Bahía de Algeciras.

GIBRALTAR

GIBRALTAR

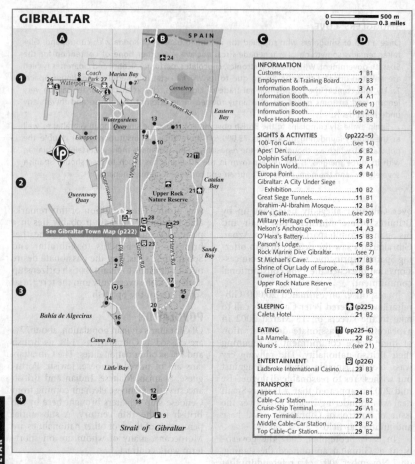

0 ————— 500 m
0 ————— 0.3 miles

INFORMATION	
Customs	1 B1
Employment & Training Board	2 B3
Information Booth	3 A1
Information Booth	4 A1
Information Booth	(see 1)
Information Booth	(see 24)
Police Headquarters	5 B3

SIGHTS & ACTIVITIES	(pp222–5)
100-Ton Gun	(see 14)
Apes' Den	6 B2
Dolphin Safari	7 B1
Dolphin World	8 A1
Europa Point	9 B4
Gibraltar: A City Under Siege Exhibition	10 B2
Great Siege Tunnels	11 B1
Ibrahim-Al-Ibrahim Mosque	12 B4
Jew's Gate	(see 20)
Military Heritage Centre	13 B1
Nelson's Anchorage	14 A3
O'Hara's Battery	15 B3
Parson's Lodge	16 B3
Rock Marine Dive Gibraltar	(see 7)
St Michael's Cave	17 B3
Shrine of Our Lady of Europe	18 B4
Tower of Homage	19 B2
Upper Rock Nature Reserve (Entrance)	20 B3

SLEEPING	(p225)
Caleta Hotel	21 B2

EATING	(pp225–6)
La Mamela	22 B2
Nuno's	(see 21)

ENTERTAINMENT	(p226)
Ladbroke International Casino	23 B3

TRANSPORT	
Airport	24 B1
Cable-Car Station	25 B2
Cruise-Ship Terminal	26 A1
Ferry Terminal	27 A1
Middle Cable-Car Station	28 B2
Top Cable-Car Station	29 B2

INFORMATION

Bookshops

Good places to stock up on English-language reading material include the following:

Bell Books (Map p222; ☎ 76707; 11 Bell Lane)

Gibraltar Bookshop (Map p222; ☎ 71894; 300 Main St)

Electricity

Electric current is the same as in Britain – 220V or 240V, with plugs of three flat pins.

Emergency

The police wear British uniforms.

Emergency (☎ 199) For the police or an ambulance.

Police Headquarters (Map p220; ☎ 72500; Rosia Rd) In the south of the town at New Mole House.

Police Station (Map p222; ☎ 72500; 120 Irish Town)

Foreign Consulates

Eleven countries, mostly European, have consulates in Gibraltar. Tourist offices will be able to provide you with lists of these.

Internet Access

General Internet Business Centre (Map p222; ☎ 44227; 36 Governor's St; ☻ 10am-10pm Tue-Sat, noon-9pm Sun & Mon) Charges £3 an hour, although you can spread the time over 15 days.

Internet Resources

For useful Gibraltar-specific websites try the following:

www.gibraltar.gi

www.gibraltar.gov.uk Maintained by the government of Gibraltar.

Medical Services

Health Centre (Map p222; ☎ 72355, 77003; Grand Casemates Square) Offers 24-hour emergency facilities.
St Bernard's Hospital (Map p222; ☎ 79700; Hospital Hill) Also offers 24-hour emergency facilities.

Money

The currencies in Gibraltar are the Gibraltar pound and the pound sterling, which are interchangeable. You can use euros (except in payphones and post offices) but you'll get a better value if you convert them into pounds. Exchange rates for buying euros are a bit better here than in Spain. You can't use Gibraltar money outside Gibraltar, so it's worth requesting change in British coins and changing any unspent Gibraltar pounds before you leave.

Banks are open between 9am and 3.30pm Monday to Friday. There are several (with ATMs) on Main St. There are also exchange offices, which are open longer hours.

Post

Main post office (Map p222; 104 Main St; ◷ 9am-2.15pm Mon-Fri & 10am-1pm Sat mid-Jun–mid-Sep, 9am-4.30pm Mon-Fri & 10am-1pm Sat mid-Sep–mid-Jun).

Telephone

To phone Gibraltar from Spain, precede the five-digit local number with the code ☎ 9567; from other countries dial the international access code, then ☎ 350 (Gibraltar's country code) and the local number. Mobile phone numbers are all eight-digit numbers beginning with a ☎ 5.

In Gibraltar you can make international as well as local calls from street payphones. To make a call to Spain, just dial the nine-digit number. To make a call to any other country, dial the international access code (☎ 00), followed by the country code, area code and number.

Tourist Information

Gibraltar Tourist Board (Map p222; ☎ 45000, 74950; www.gibraltar.gov.uk; Duke of Kent House, Cathedral Square; ◷ 9am-5.30pm Mon-Fri) Very helpful with plenty of free information sheets and brochures.
Information booths airport (Map p220; ☎ 73026; ◷ Mon-Fri, for lunchtime flights only); coach park (Map p220; ☎ 78198; Waterport Wharf Rd; ◷ 9am-4.30pm Mon-Fri, 10am-3pm Sat); cruise-ship terminal (Map p220; ☎ 47670; ◷ only when a cruise liner is in port); customs (Map p220; ☎ 50762; Frontier; ◷ 9am-4.30pm Mon-Fri & 10am-3pm Sat)
Tourist office (Map p222; ☎ 74982; Grand Casemates Square; ◷ 9am-5.30pm Mon-Fri, 10am-3pm Sat, 10am-1pm Sun & public holidays)

Work

Work is not easy to find in Gibraltar, but information on job opportunities can be obtained from the **Employment & Training Board** (Map p220; ☎ 74999; Rosia Rd). Except for Palma de Mallorca, Gibraltar is better than anywhere else in Spain for picking up unpaid

GIBRALTAR

GIBRALTAR TOWN
0 — 50 m

yacht berths on boats heading to the Canary Islands, Madeira and even the West Indies. Ask around at Marina Bay harbour.

SIGHTS
The Rock of Gibraltar   Map p220

Naturally, the main sight in Gibraltar is the Rock, a huge pinnacle of limestone, with sheer sides rising some 426m. Most of the upper parts of the Rock, starting just above the town, are a nature reserve with spectacular views. Tickets for the **Upper Rock Nature Reserve** (adult/child/vehicle £7/4/1.50, pedestrians excluding attractions £0.50; 9.30am-7pm, last visit 6.30pm) include entry to St Michael's Cave, the Apes' Den, the Great Siege Tunnels, the Military Heritage Centre, the Tower of Homage and the 'Gibraltar: A City Under Siege' exhibition. The upper Rock is home to 600 plant species and is ideal for observing the migrations of birds between Europe and Africa (see High-Fliers over the Strait of Gibraltar, p212).

The Rock's most famous inhabitants are the Barbary apes, the only wild primates in Europe. Some of these hang around the **Apes' Den** near the middle cable-car station; others can often be seen at the top cable-car station and the Great Siege Tunnels. Legend has it that when the apes (which may have been introduced from north Africa in the 18th century) disappear from Gibraltar, so will the British. When numbers were at a low ebb during WWII, the British brought in simian reinforcements from Africa. Recently, however, their numbers have been increasing rapidly and a range of control measures from contraceptive implants to 'repatriation' to north Africa have been considered. Summer is the ideal time to see their newborns, but keep a safe distance to avoid their sharp teeth and short tempers for which they are well known. For those who are nervous around animals or with very small children it may be worth considering a guided tour as the official guides know the moods and habits of the apes.

To reach the Apes' Den and the upper Rock take the **cable car** (see p227). At the top station there are breathtaking views over the Bahía de Algeciras and across the Strait of Gibraltar to Morocco if the weather is clear. You can also look down the sheer precipices of the Rock's eastern side to the biggest of the old water catchments, which channelled rain into underground reservoirs.

About 15 minutes' walk south down St Michael's Rd from the top cable-car station, O'Hara's Rd leads up to the left to **O'Hara's Battery**, an emplacement of big guns on the Rock's summit. Just by the gate is the Mediterranean Steps (see p224). A few minutes farther down (or 20 minutes up from the Apes' Den) is the extraordinary **St Michael's Cave** (St Michael's Rd; admission £2; 9.30am-7pm), a huge natural grotto full of stalagmites and stalactites. In the past, people thought the cave was a possible subterranean link with Africa, needless to say its size is impressive. Today, apart from attracting tourists in droves, it's used for concerts, plays and even fashion shows. For a more extensive guided tour into the lower caves, which end at an underground lake, contact the tourist office (p221).

About 30 minutes' walk north (downhill) from the top cable-car station is Princess

Caroline's Battery, housing the **Military Heritage Centre**. From here one road leads down to the Princess Royal Battery – more gun emplacements – while another leads up to the **Great Siege Tunnels** (or Upper Galleries), a complex defence system hewn out of the Rock by the British during the siege of 1779–83 to provide gun emplacements. They constitute only a tiny proportion of more than 70km of tunnels and galleries in the Rock, most of which are off limits to the public.

On Willis' Rd, the way down to the town from Princess Caroline's Battery, you'll find the **'Gibraltar: A City Under Siege' exhibition**, in the first British building on the Rock (originally an ammunition store), and the **Tower of Homage**, the remains of Gibraltar's Islamic castle built in 1333. The tower is currently undergoing extensive renovations and at the time of writing there was no date set for its opening (check with the tourist office for up-to-date information).

Gibraltar Town

Map p222

Gibraltar's town centre generates an engaging mid-morning Mediterranean buzz, although there is an emphatically British flavour about the shops, pubs and restaurants that line either side of the pedestrianised Main St. A Spanish lilt in the air and the fairly regular sight of Moroccans in traditional dress are reminders that this little slice of Blighty is still part of Mediterranean Europe and was a Muslim stronghold for over seven centuries and a Spanish one for 240 years.

Nowadays, the entire Rock reflects 300 years of British military and bureaucratic administration, literally bristling with the often antique remnants of British fortifications, gates and gun emplacements. The *Guided Tour of Gibraltar* booklet by TJ Finlayson is rewarding if you want to delve into details of the British heritage. It's available from the Gibraltar Museum for £2.

To get acquainted with Gibraltar's cultural melange and volatile history visit the **Gibraltar Museum** (☎ 74289; Bomb House Lane; adult/ child under 12 £2/1; ⏰ 10am-6pm Mon-Fri, 10am-2pm Sat) which contains an extensive, if in some cases odd, assortment of historical, architectural and military displays dating back to prehistoric times. Highlights include a well-preserved 14th-century Arab bathhouse and a copy of the 100,000-year-old female skull discovered in Forbes Quarry on the Rock's

GIBRALTAR

THE MEDITERRANEAN STEPS

For the fit and agile, one of the best ways to climb the upper Rock is via the Mediterranean Steps (Map p220). A terrific two-hour clamber up the Rock's eastern face along paths that zigzag between limestone cliffs and through a lushly vegetated landscape that smacks of a semiwild Islamic garden, and a bird reserve. The views are stupendous. The paths are linked by sections of steps and the final, upper section leads to O'Hara's Battery, the Rock's highest point. The Mediterranean Steps date from the late-18th century and connect a series of now-ruined gun placements. The intermittent flights of steps are broken in places, but not dangerously so, although a descent of the route from O'Hara's Battery can be uncomfortable and is not recommended (take the cable car or walk back down the road). The way up is the better option; it is more strenuous, but it is not daunting for an average fit person and nowhere is the route exposed, nor does it traverse dangerous ground. The Mediterranean Steps path starts at Jew's Gate, the entrance to the Upper Rock Nature Reserve. Jew's Gate can be reached on foot, or by taxi, up Engineer Rd. There is a tumbledown sign, indicating the start of the path, down to the left of the single-storey building behind Jew's Gate. The route is not overly difficult to follow, but you'd be advised to obtain a print-out from the tourist office that gives simple directions and that describes some of the wildlife along the way.

northern face in 1848 (the original is now in the Natural History Museum in London).

A more poignant lesson in history can be found in the atmospherically overgrown **Trafalgar Cemetery** (Prince Edward's Rd; ☾ 9am-7pm), just south of Southport Gate. The graves are those of British sailors who died at Gibraltar after the Battle of Trafalgar (1805). Further south, **Nelson's Anchorage** (Rosia Rd; admission £1; ☾ 9.30am-5.15pm Mon-Sat) pinpoints the site where Nelson's body was brought ashore from HMS *Victory* – preserved in a rum barrel, so legend says. A 100-tonne Victorian supergun, made in Britain in 1870, commemorates the spot. A little further south is **Parson's Lodge** (Rosia Rd; adult/child £1/0.50; ☾ 10am-6pm Mon-Fri), a gun battery atop a 40m cliff. Beneath the gun emplacements is a labyrinth of tunnels with former ammunition stores and living quarters.

History aside, take some time to meander through the **Alameda Botanical Gardens** (Europa Rd; admission free; ☾ 8am-sunset), the lushly overgrown scene of Molly Bloom's famous deflowering in James Joyce's *Ulysses*.

Europa Point   Map p220

The southern tip of Gibraltar is known as **Europa Point**, the location of Gibraltar's first lighthouse, sacked by the infamous corsair (pirate), Barbarossa. It is also the site of the Christian **Shrine of Our Lady of Europe** (☎ 71230; ☾ 10am-1pm & 2-7pm Mon-Fri, 11am-1pm & 2-7pm Sat & Sun), whose 15th-century statue of the Virgin and Child was miraculously unscathed

during the pirate's devastating attack. Nearby, a symbol of the racial and religious symbiosis of Gibraltar's past and, to some degree its present, is the **Ibrahim-Al-Ibrahim Mosque** (☎ 47694), opened in 1997. It was built at the behest of King Fahd of Saudi Arabia to cater for all the Moroccans working on the Rock and is said to be the largest mosque in a non-Islamic country. Phone for visiting hours.

ACTIVITIES
Dolphin Watching

The Bahía de Algeciras has a sizable year-round population of dolphins and at least six boats run dolphin-watching trips. From about April to September most boats make two or more daily trips; at other times of year there's usually at least one in daily operation. Most of the boats go from Watergardens Quay or the adjacent Marina Bay, northwest of the town centre. Trips last about 2½ hours and the cost per adult is around £20. Children go for half price. You'll be unlucky if you don't get plenty of close-up dolphin contact, and you may even come across whales. Two possibilities for trips are **Dolphin World** (Map p220; ☎ 54481000; Ferry Terminal, Waterport; adult/child under 12 £20/10) and **Dolphin Safari** (Map p220; ☎ 71914; Marina Bay; adult/child under 12 £20/10) – both take bookings by prior arrangement.

Diving

Around the Rock there is also some surprisingly good (and reasonably priced) diving.

The rock has its own unique sea life and underwater landscape, with many wrecks. **Rock Marine Dive Gibraltar** (Map p220; ☎ 73147; The Square, Marina Bay) runs a variety of dives from £17.50 to £25, including an exciting night dive.

Beaches
To escape from the town for a spot of sunbathing take bus No 4 from Line Wall Rd (every 15 minutes) to **Catalan Bay**, a tiny fishing village on the eastern side of the Rock.

TOURS
Taxi drivers will take you on a 1½-hour 'Official Rock Tour' of Gibraltar's main sights for £7 per person (minimum four people) plus the cost of admission to the Upper Rock Nature Reserve. Most drivers are knowledgeable. Many travel agents run tours of the same sights for £11 to £12.50.

Bland Travel (Map p222; ☎ 77012; 81 Irish Town), **Parodytur** (Map p222; ☎ 76070; Cathedral Square) and **Exchange Travel** (Map p222; ☎ 76151; 241 Main St) offer guided day trips to Tangier for £48 including lunch.

SLEEPING
Caleta Hotel (Map p220; ☎ 76501; www.caletahotel.com; Sir Herbert Miles Road; d without/with sea view £74/81; P ⊠ ⬜ ⬛) Gibraltar's best four-star hotel in a wonderful location overlooking Catalan Bay (five minutes from town). On the edge of a rocky outcrop the cascading terraces have panoramic sea views, and a host of gym and spa facilities make this a truly luxurious option.

Rock Hotel (Map p222; ☎ 73000; www.rockhotelgibraltar.com; 3 Europa Rd; d without/with balcony £165/175; P ⊠ ⬛) Built by the Marquis of Bute in 1932 this institution has hosted the likes of Winston Churchill and Noel Coward. The Rock Hotel was recently modernised and the lavish service includes bathrobes, CD players and free parking.

Bristol Hotel (Map p222; ☎ 76800; www.gibraltar.gi/bristolhotel; 10 Cathedral Square; s/d without sea views £49/64, s/d with sea views £53/69; P ⊠ ⬛) This hotel, with its attractive walled garden and swimming pool, is centrally located. Many of the 60 recently refurbished rooms have lovely sea views. Parking is available but you must request it when booking your room.

Cannon Hotel (Map p222; ☎ 51711; www.cannonhotel.gi; 9 Cannon Lane; s/d with shared bathroom incl breakfast £24.50/36.50, d with private bathroom incl break-

fast £45) An attractive small hotel with 18 rooms right in the main shopping centre of Gibraltar town. Rooms are modestly kitted out with pine furnishings and some overlook an attractive patio. A great location within walking distance of all the major sights and good value-for-money.

Eliott Hotel (Map p222; ☎ 70500; www.gibraltar.gi/eliotthotel; 2 Governor's Parade; d £165-220, ste £200-420; P ⊠ ⬛) Located in a leafy square the Eliott is a slightly characterless four-star option but has a range of facilities such as a gym and rooftop pool. Free parking is also available.

Queen's Hotel (Map p222; ☎ 74000; www.queenshotel.gi; 1 Boyd St; s/d incl breakfast £40/60; P ⊠) A large, pink, modern monstrosity, Queen's hotel is not the most attractive sight. However, it does offer good discounts of 20% to students and travellers under the age of 25.

Emile Youth Hostel (Map p222; ☎ 51106, 57686000; fax 78581; Montagu Bastion, Line Wall Rd; dm/s/d £15/17/30) This hostel is full of old seamen and louche expatriates, making it an unattractive proposition for lone women travellers. However, it is cheap and has 43 places in single- to eight-person rooms. Conditions are basic, and the eight-person dorms are cramped.

If you feel daunted by Gibraltar's prices, there are some economical options in the Spanish frontier town of La Línea de la Concepción (p215).

EATING
Most of the many pubs in town do typical British pub meals.

Nuno's (Map p220; ☎ 76501; Caleta Hotel, Sir Herbert Miles Road; mains £13-16) A top-class Italian restaurant in the Caleta Hotel with fabulous terrace views. The extensive wine list is accompanied by delicious home-made pastas for a stylish and romantic evening meal.

Claus on the Rock (Map p222; ☎ 48686; 14 Queensway Quay; mains £7.50-14; ☾ closed Sun) Situated on the latest marina development, the posh Queensway Quay, this stylish restaurant has a wonderful array of international cuisine – a welcome relief from pub grub. The menu includes dishes with a range of influences from the Caribbean to the Middle East.

La Mamela (Map p220; ☎ 72373; Catalan Bay; mains £9.50-16) An excellent and atmospheric fish eatery located right on Catalan Bay at the southern end of the beach. Dust the sand off your feet and sit down to a range of hearty paellas and fish stews.

Clipper (Map p222; ☎ 79791; 78B Irish Town; roast £5.95) One of the best and busiest bars, all varnished wood with full-on footy and a cracking Sunday roast. The occasional live-music session at the weekend livens things up further.

House of Sacarello (Map p222; ☎ 70625; 57 Irish Town; daily specials £5.50-6.10; ☺ closed Sun) A chic place with a good range of vegetarian options and some tasty home-made soups for around £2. You can linger over afternoon tea for two (£7.75) between 3pm and 7.30pm.

Cannon Bar (Map p222; ☎ 77288; 27 Cannon Lane; mains around £4.75) Justifiably famous for some of the best fish and chips in town, and in big portions. It also does steak-and-kidney pie and salads for about the same price.

Star Bar (Map p222; ☎ 75924; 12 Parliament Lane; breakfast £4.25; ☺ 24hr) Gibraltar's oldest bar, if the house advertising is to be believed, the Star Bar is still one of its best having won the Golden Egg Award five years in a row. Open all day every day this is a fail-safe option.

Three Roses Bar (Map p222; ☎ 51614; 60 Governor's St; breakfast £3.50, mains £2.90-6.50; ☺ 11am-late) Three Roses does a hefty breakfast of two eggs, sausage, bacon, fried bread, beans, tomato and mushrooms – but it's not for early risers. This is Gibraltar's unofficial 'Scottish Embassy', with Scottish dishes a speciality.

Figaro (Map p222; 9 Market Lane; mains £4-8) More commonly referred to as 'The Tea Room', this neat café-cum-restaurant serves up traditional scones with jam and cream, and it does some good lunchtime specials too.

At Marina Bay, a little out of the centre, there's a line of pleasant waterside cafés and restaurants.

ENTERTAINMENT

Several of Gibraltar's pubs put on live music from pop to rock, jazz to folk. Alternatively, **UnderGround** (Map p222; ☎ 40651; 8 West Place of Arms) has two dance floors and an open-air terrace. Concerts and other performances are staged in the atmospheric venue of **St Michael's Cave** (check with the tourist offices for details). The **Ladbroke International Casino** (Map p220; ☎ 76666; 7 Europa Rd) offers casino gaming and slot machines, and also has live entertainment, a disco and restaurant.

No membership or passport is needed and smart casual wear is accepted.

SHOPPING

Gibraltar has lots of British high-street chain stores, such as Marks & Spencer, Mothercare and the Body Shop (all on Main St) and Safeway (in the Europort development at the northern end of the main harbour). **Gibraltar Crystal** (Map p222; ☎ 50136; Grand Casemates Square) produces fine glassware on its premises and there are free demonstrations. Shops are normally open 9am to 7.30pm Monday to Friday and until 1pm Saturday.

GETTING THERE & AWAY

The border is open 24 hours daily. Give yourself ample time if you are heading out of Gibraltar to catch a bus from La Línea. Vehicles and pedestrians are delayed from crossing the airport runway for a minimum of five minutes when flights are landing or taking off – there are two to three flights a day. You may also be delayed passing through Spanish customs, where bag searches are usually perfunctory, but may be time-consuming.

Air

At the time of writing, the only flights into and out of Gibraltar are to/from the UK.

GB Airways (☎ 79300; www.gbairways.com) flies daily to/from London. Return fares from London range between UK£76 and UK£205, depending on the season and special offers.

Monarch Airlines (☎ 47477; www.flymonarch.com) flies daily to/from Luton London. Return fares range between UK£94 and UK£235.

In Gibraltar the airline offices are at the airport; alternatively, book through travel agents.

Boat

At the time of writing there is only one ferry (adult one-way/return £18/30, child one-way/return £9/15, car one-way/return £46/92, 80 minutes) a week between Gibraltar and Tangier (Morocco) departing Gibraltar at 6pm on Friday. The ferry leaves from the terminal in front of the coach park. In Gibraltar, you can buy tickets for the ferry at **Turner & Co** (Map p222; ☎ 78305; turner@ gibnynex.gi; 65 Irish Town). Booking ahead is advised. Ferries to and from Tangier are more frequent from Algeciras (p214).

For information on the Gibraltar–Tangier and Algeciras–Tangier ferries, see the website www.frs.es.

Bus

Buses from Spain do not terminate within Gibraltar itself, but the bus station in La Línea de la Concepción (p215) is only a short walk from the border, from where there are frequent buses into Gibraltar's town centre (see below).

GETTING AROUND

The 1.5km walk from the border to the town centre is entertaining, not least because it crosses the airport runway. A left turn (south) off Corral Rd will take you through the pedestrian-only Landport Tunnel (once the only land entry through Gibraltar's walls) into Grand Casemates Square and on to Main St.

All of Gibraltar can be covered on foot and much of it (including the upper Rock) by car or motorcycle, but there are other options worth considering.

Bus

Buses No 3, 9 and 10 go from the border into town about every 15 minutes on weekdays, and every 30 minutes on Saturday and Sunday. Bus No 9 goes to Market Place (Grand Casemates Gate). It runs between 7.15am and 8.30pm Monday to Saturday and from 9am to 8.45pm on Sunday. Bus No 3 goes to Cathedral Square and the lower cable-car station and then on to Europa Point. It runs between 6.30am and 9pm Monday to Saturday and from 7.30am to 9pm on Sunday. Bus No 10 goes from the border to Europort (with a stop at the Safeway supermarket), then via Queens Way to Reclamation Rd

near the town centre. Bus No 4 connects Catalan Bay on the Rock's eastern side with the centre and Europort. All buses cost adult/child/senior 60p/40p/30p per trip.

Cable Car

An obvious way to explore Gibraltar is via the **cable car** (Map p220; Red Sands Rd; adult one-way/return £6/7.50, child one-way/return £3.50/4; ☯ 9.30am-5.15pm Mon-Sat). Tickets at the prices shown do not include admission to the attractions on the upper Rock (see p222 for details). For the Apes' Den, disembark at the middle station. You can get back on to go up to the top station. The operation of the cable car may be halted during periods of bad weather, especially if wind speeds are very high. The cable car runs every few minutes, with the last cable car going down at 4.45pm.

Car & Motorcycle

Gibraltar's streets are congested and parking can be difficult. Vehicle queues at the border often make it less time-consuming to park in La Línea, then walk across the border. To take a car into Gibraltar you need an insurance certificate, registration document, nationality plate and a valid driving licence. You do not have to pay any fee: some people driving into Gibraltar have been cheated of a dozen or so euros by con artists claiming you need to pay to take a vehicle across the border. In Gibraltar, driving is on the right, as in Spain. At the time of writing petrol in Gibraltar was around 10% cheaper than in Spain. There are car parks on Line Wall Rd and Reclamation Rd (see Map p222), and at the Airport Car Park on Winston Churchill Ave; the hourly charge at these car parks is about 60p.

Málaga Province

At the end of the 19th century the province of Málaga was a beehive of activity. It was the dawn of a new era: of change and uncertainty, of opportunity and brigandage, of romance and hard-nosed business. The city of Málaga was filled with patrons and industrialists, bohemians and artists, and bullfighters hungry for fame. The province and city readily embraced the modern age, an age that gave birth to its most famous modernist son, Pablo Ruiz Picasso.

Nearly 14 million tourists now pass through Málaga province every year – an astonishing figure. What is even more surprising is the unjaded and urbane good humour of the local inhabitants, who, despite the obvious pressures, still manage to offer travellers excellent service and good facilities with a friendly and unpretentious attitude. Málaga may not have the historical legacies of Seville, Córdoba and Granada but it is a vibrant and self-confident province. It has a fun-loving coast and an intriguing interior full of charming white-walled villages and dramatic mountain ranges. It's in these mountains that you can indulge in almost any kind of outdoor activity, from horse riding and hiking to speleology and kayaking.

Over the four years from 2000 to 2004, property prices in the province rose by a staggering 80% due to the rising number of expatriates who arrive year after year – Málaga now contributes the most, financially, to the regional government of Andalucía. It seems that the enduring appeal of the sunshine coast remains undimmed and unapologetic.

HIGHLIGHTS

- Soaking up the vibrant street life of Málaga and catching the Costa del Sol's most ebullient festivals, the **Feria de Málaga** (p238), the **Feria de San Bernabé** (p253) and the **Día de la Virgen del Carmen** (p248)

- Stepping back in time in Málaga's **Castillo de Gibralfaro** (p235) or getting up close and personal with the stunning Picasso collection at the new **Museo Picasso** (p235)

- Getting to grips with the history of bullfighting, brought to life in Ronda's **Feria de Pedro Romero** (p261)

- Scaling the spectacular limestone gorges of **El Chorro** (p265) or wild-water kayaking down the **Río Genil** (p266)

- Exploring the rolling countryside of **La Axarquía** (p270)

- Coasting along with the kids in the unashamed good-time resorts of the **Costa del Sol** (p244)

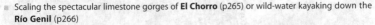

POPULATION:	MÁLAGA AVERAGE DAILY HIGH:	ALTITUDE RANGE:
1.3 MILLION	JAN/AUG 13°C/26°C	0m–2069m

MÁLAGA PROVINCE

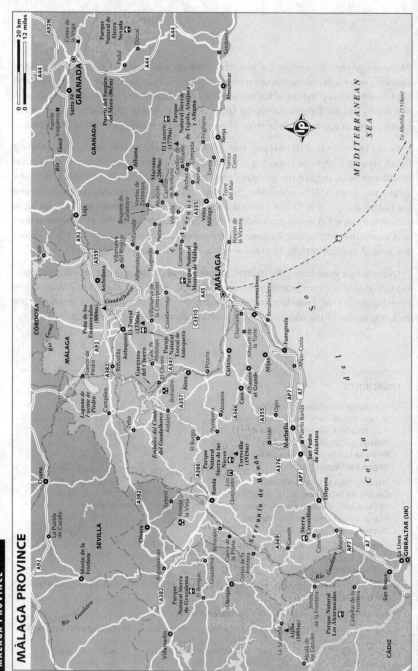

MÁLAGA

pop 547,000

Compared with the adjoining Costa del Sol, Málaga is a world apart. It is a briskly modern yet historic city that still retains the atmosphere and swagger of a Mediterranean port. Forget the concrete and commonplace of the city's peripheries – its centre pulses with colourful life. With a backdrop of the blue Mediterranean, the city offers a pleasant mix of wide, leafy boulevards, a handful of impressive monuments and a charming historic centre.

Málaga is a late starter to the idea of sprucing itself up for tourists, but things are changing. A major new museum devoted to Málaga-born Pablo Picasso opened in 2003, as did a new museum of contemporary art, and the young and the enterprising are starting up small businesses all over the place. *Malagueños* (residents of Málaga) are open and sociable people and they like to party – as a result the city stays open very late, with some healthy nightlife kicking off at around 10pm.

ORIENTATION

The eastern and western halves of the city are neatly separated from each other by the Río Guadalmedina. Málaga's central axis, crossing the river west to east heading into town, is the Avenida de Andalucía, which becomes the Alameda Principal and finally the landscaped Paseo del Parque (ending up in the upmarket district of La Malagueta). From La Malagueta, Avenida Pries takes you, with several changes to its name, out to the eastern beaches of Pedregalejo and El Palo.

Rising up above the eastern half of Paseo del Parque, the Alcazaba and Castillo de Gibralfaro dominate the city and overlook the *casco antiguo* (old town) with its narrow, winding streets. The main streets leading north into the old town are Calle Marqués de Larios, ending at Plaza de la Constitución, and Calle Molina Lario.

The modern shopping district stretches between Calles Marqués de Larios and Puerta del Mar.

The airport is 9km from the city centre – for details on getting to/from the airport, see p243.

INFORMATION

Bookshops

Librería Alameda (Map pp232-3; Alameda Principal 16) One of Málaga's largest bookshops, stocking English and French titles. It also has a good travel section.

Emergency

Policía Local (Local Police; Map pp232-3; ☎ 952 12 65 00; Avenida de la Rosaleda 19)
Policía Nacional (National Police; Map pp232-3; ☎ 952 31 71 00; Plaza de Manuel Azaña) The main police station.

Internet Access

N@veg@web (Map p234; Calle Molina Lario 11; per hr €1.50; ☒ 4-10pm) A large, conveniently located Internet café.
Pasatiempos (Map pp232-3; Plaza de la Merced 20; per hr €1-2 depending on time of day; ☒ 10am-11pm) Plenty of computers, and friendly staff.

Left Luggage

There are baggage lockers at the main **bus station** (Map pp232-3; Paseo de los Tilos) and **train station** (Map pp232-3; Explanada de la Estación), open from 8am to 8pm Monday to Friday and charging €3 per day.

Media

The Costa del Sol is flooded with free English-language magazines loaded down with property ads. Generally more worthwhile is *Sur in English,* a free weekly English-language digest of Málaga's daily newspaper *Sur.*

Roam the FM wavelengths between about 97MHz and 105MHz in Málaga province and you'll run into half a dozen Costa-based English-language radio stations.

Medical Services

Farmacia Caffarena (Map p234; ☎ 952 21 28 58; Alameda Principal 2) A centrally located, convenient 24-hour pharmacy.
Hospital Carlos Haya (Map pp232-3; ☎ 952 39 04 00; Avenida de Carlos Haya) The main city hospital is 2km west of the city centre.

Money

There are plenty of banks with ATMs on Calle Puerta del Mar and Calle Marqués de Larios, as well as in the airport's arrivals' hall.

Post

Post office (Map pp232-3; Avenida de Andalucía 1; ☒ 8.30am-8.30pm Mon-Fri, 8.30am-2pm Sat) This main office is in a fairly central location.

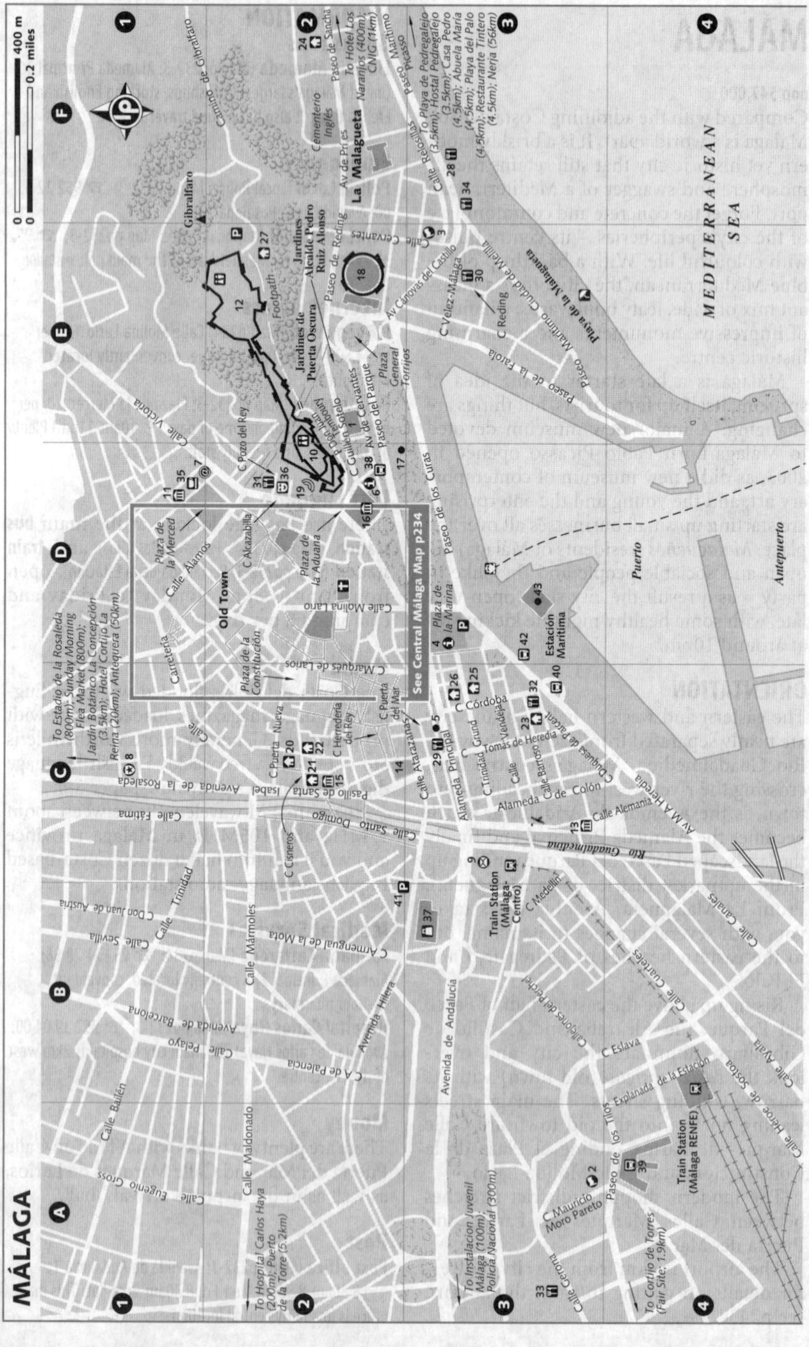

MÁLAGA

Map legend / labels

- 400 m
- 0.2 miles

MEDITERRANEAN SEA

F Gibralfaro

Camino de Gibralfaro

24
2 To Hotel Los
Paseo de Sancha
Naranjos (400m);
CNG (1km)

Av de Pries
Cementerio
Inglés
Paseo Marítimo

Plaza de Portugalete
(3.5km); Hostal Pedregalejo
(3.5km); Abuela María
(4.5km); Casa Pedro
(4.5km); Playa del Palo
(4.5km); Restaurante Tintero
(4.5km); Nerja (56km)

La Malagueta
Paseo de Reding
Calle Reding

C Reding

C Vélez-Málaga

Playa de la Malagueta

Paseo Marítimo Ciudad de Melilla

Paseo de la Farola

3
28
34
30

E

P
27
12

Jardines de
Puerta Oscura

Jardines de
Alcalde Pedro
Ruiz Alonso

Footpath

Paseo de Reding

Paseo del Parque

18

Plaza
General
Torrijos

Av Cánovas del Castillo

C Guillén Sotelo
Av de Cervantes

Calle Victoria
C Peña
Calle Refino

31 36
35
11

Plaza de
la Merced

C Álamos

C Alcazabilla

Av de Cervantes

Paseo de los Curas

10
38
19
6
16
17

D
Old Town

Calle Álamos

Plaza de
la Aduana

See Central Málaga Map p234

Carretería

Plaza de la
Constitución

Calle Molina Lario

Calle Granada

Paseo de la Farola

Puerto

Antepuerto

To Estadio de la Rosaleda
(800m); Sunday Morning
Flea Market (800m);
Jardín Botánico La Concepción
(3.5km); Hotel Conijo La
Reina (2.0km); Antequera (50km)

C Cisneros
Plaza de la
Constitución

C Marqués de Larios

Plaza de
la Marina

4

P

43

C
Calle Fátima

Pasillo de Santa
Isabel

Avenida de la Rosaleda

C Puerta Nueva

C Herrería del Rey

14

C Puerta
del Mar

C Alarcón Luján

Alameda Principal

C Trinidad Grund

Calle Córdoba

5
26
25
29

42
40

Estación
Marítima

C Pelayo
Avenida de Barcelona

C Capuchinos
Calle Santo Domingo

Calle Trinidad

Avenida Fuente

21
8
15

20

C Tomás de Heredia

Alameda O de Colón

23
32

Calle Alemania

AV M A Heredia

B
Calle Balién

Calle Maldonado

C A de Palencia

Amenqual de la Mota

Río Guadalmedina

Calle Camas

Calle Eslava

Calle Guerreros

Calle Canales

9

Train Station
(Málaga
Centro)

C Medellín

13

A
Eugenio Gross

Calle Maldonado

Avenida de Andalucía

C Mauricio
Moro Pareto

2

Paseo de los 1105

Explanada de la Estación

Train Station
(Málaga RENFE)

39

C Cuarteles

Calle Héroe de Sostoa

Calle Ayala

To Hospital Carlos Haya
(200m); Puerto
de la Torre (5.2km)

To Instalación Juvenil
Málaga (700m);
Policía Nacional (900m)

33

To Cortijo de Torres
(Fair Site; 1.9km)

1   **2**   **3**   **4**

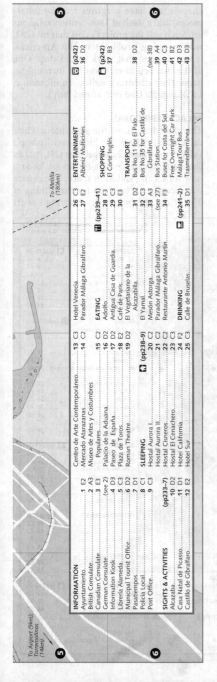

To Airport (9km);
Torremolinos
(14km)

To Melilla
(180km)

Telephone

Telephone calls are easily made from phone booths dotted around the city, and cards can be purchased from cigarette shops and newsagents.

Tourist Information

Municipal tourist office (Map pp232–3; ☎ 952 13 47 30; Avenida de Cervantes 1, www.malagaturismo.com in Spanish; ☽ 9am-2.30pm & 4-7pm Mon-Fri, 9.30am-1.30pm Sat & Sun) Offers a range of city maps and booklets, including the monthly *¿Qué Hacer?*, which gives a day-by-day account of events in the province. It also operates a large information kiosk in the Plaza de la Marina, as well as smaller offices at the main bus station and on Plaza de la Merced.

Regional tourist office (Map p234; ☎ 952 21 34 45; Pasaje de Chinitas 4; www.andalucia.org; ☽ 9am-8pm Mon-Fri, 10am-2pm Sat & Sun) On an alley off Plaza de la Constitución. Provides a range of information (such as on hiking and cycling) as well as maps of the regional cities (€0.60 each). The staff speak numerous languages. It also operates a second office at the airport.

DANGERS & ANNOYANCES

Take care of your valuables at all times and watch bags, especially when you're seated at café terraces (on Plaza de la Merced, in particular) and the bus station; there are some sharp teams of snatchers around. Night-time Málaga is generally safe, but avoid the darker and quieter side-streets. The teenage craze for drinking in the plaza hits Málaga in locations such as Plaza de la Merced. The downside is more mess than mayhem. Remove all valuables and bags when leaving cars parked overnight, and if possible use the guarded car parks around the city centre.

SIGHTS

Málaga's major cultural sights are clustered in or near the city's charming old town, which is situated beneath the Alcazaba and the Castillo de Gibralfaro. However, many visitors take an additional day or two to head out to the beaches on the eastern edge of the city.

Old Town

Essentially a Renaissance city with its wide boulevards and decorative façades, Málaga bears the stamp of Fernando and Isabel's ambitious transformation of Islamic Andalucía as they united Spain under a single rule in the 15th century.

MALAGA PROVINCE

CATHEDRAL

Málaga's **cathedral** (Map pp232-3; 952 21 59 17; Calle Molino Lario, enter from Calle Cister; cathedral & museum admission €3; 🕙 10am-6.45pm Mon-Sat, closed holidays), which took 200 years to complete, was plagued by over-ambition, and the initial proposal for a new cathedral had to be shelved. Instead, a series of architects (five in total) set about transforming the original mosque – of this, only the **Patio de los Naranjos** survives; a small courtyard of fragrant orange trees where the ablutions fountain used to be.

Inside, it is easy to see why the epic project took so long. The fabulous domed ceiling soars 40m into the air, while the vast colonnaded nave houses an enormous cedar-wood choir. Aisles give access to 15 chapels that have gorgeous *retablos* (altarpieces) and a stash of 18th-century religious art. Such was the project's cost that by 1782, with pressing problems in the Americas, it was decided that work would stop. One of the two bell towers was left incomplete, hence the cathedral's well-worn nickname, *La Manquita* (the one-armed lady).

PALACIO EPISCOPAL

The cathedral fronts the sumptuous Plaza del Obispo, where the blood-red Bishop's Palace, the **Palacio Episcopal** (Map p234; Plaza del Obispo; admission free; 🕙 10am-2pm & 6-9pm Tue-Sun), now forms an exhibition space. The square was recently the location for the filming of *The Bridge of San Luis Rey*, starring Robert

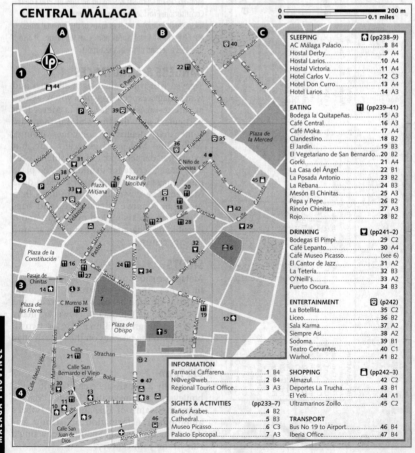

CENTRAL MÁLAGA

0 — 200 m
0 — 0.1 miles

SLEEPING	(pp238–9)
AC Málaga Palacio	**8** B4
Hostal Derby	**9** A4
Hostal Larios	**10** A4
Hostal Victoria	**11** A4
Hotel Carlos V	**12** C3
Hotel Don Curro	**13** A4
Hotel Larios	**14** A3

EATING	(pp239–41)
Bodega la Quitapeñas	**15** A3
Café Central	**16** A3
Café Moka	**17** A4
Clandestino	**18** B2
El Jardín	**19** B3
El Vegetariano de San Bernardo	**20** B2
Gorki	**21** A4
La Casa del Ángel	**22** B1
La Posada Antonio	**23** B2
La Rebana	**24** B3
Mesón El Chinitas	**25** A3
Pepa y Pepe	**26** B2
Rincón Chinitas	**27** A3
Rojo	**28** B2

DRINKING	(pp241–2)
Bodegas El Pimpi	**29** C2
Café Lepanto	**30** A4
Café Museo Picasso	(see 6)
El Cantor de Jazz	**31** A2
La Tetería	**32** B3
O'Neill's	**33** A2
Puerto Oscura	**34** B3

ENTERTAINMENT	(p242)
La Botellita	**35** C2
Liceo	**36** B2
Sala Karma	**37** A2
Siempre Así	**38** A2
Sodoma	**39** B1
Teatro Cervantes	**40** C1
Warhol	**41** B2

INFORMATION		
Farmacia Caffarena	**1**	B4
N@veg@web	**2**	B4
Regional Tourist Office	**3**	A3

SIGHTS & ACTIVITIES	(pp233–7)	
Baños Árabes	**4**	B2
Cathedral	**5**	B3
Museo Picasso	**6**	C3
Palacio Episcopal	**7**	A3

SHOPPING	(pp242–3)
Almazul	**42** C2
Deportes La Trucha	**43** B1
El Yeti	**44** A1
Ultramarinos Zoíllo	**45** C2

TRANSPORT	
Bus No 19 to Airport	**46** B4
Iberia Office	**47** B4

RETURN OF THE NATIVE

Perhaps it is the luminosity of Málaga's light or the severe, angular shapes of the region's dozens of pueblos (villages), but Picasso believed that 'to be a cubist one has to have been born in Málaga'. Banned from Spain by General Francisco Franco for his 'degenerate' art, Picasso lived much of his life in France, claiming he would never return to Spain as long as Franco was in power. But his passion for Málaga never faded. When the idea for a Picasso museum was first mooted in 1954, the town council asked him to send a few paintings from Paris. He declared: 'I will not send one or two examples. I will send lorry-loads of paintings.' And so some 50 years later with the spectacular opening of the Museo Picasso, some 200 paintings, drawings, sculptures, ceramics and engravings (many of which had been stored in a bank vault in Madrid) have finally been exhibited. They chart practically every phase of his career from cubism to modernism.

Surrounded and influenced by women all of his life, from his mother, sisters, grandmother and aunts to a string of beautiful muses – most famously Olga Kokhlova, Dora Maar, Francoise Gilot and Jacqueline Roque – women create the most obvious theme in the new museum. There are famous works such as *Olga Kokhlova with Mantilla* (1917), *Woman with Raised Arms* (1939) and *Jacqueline Sitting* (1954), with each woman evoking a different stylistic response from the artist.

As ever, there are also doves in the paintings. It is said that doves and pigeons reminded him of his early childhood, when they scratched on the windowsill in the Plaza de la Merced in Málaga. For a wonderful account of Picasso's life, get hold of John Richardson's two-volume *A Life of Picasso*, which won the Whitbread Book of the Year in 1991.

de Niro, where it provided an atmospheric location for Inquisition burnings.

HOMAGE TO PICASSO

From the cathedral a short walk up Calle San Agustín will bring you to the new holy grail of Málaga's tourist scene, the **Museo Picasso** (Map p234; ☎ 902 44 33 77; www.museopicasso malaga.org; Palacio de Buenavista, Calle San Agustín 8; permanent collection €6, temporary exhibition €4.50, combined ticket €8, concession 50% for students under 26 and senior citizens; ⏲ 10am-8pm Tue-Thu & Sun, 10am-9pm Fri & Sat). It has an enviable collection of 204 works, donated and lent to the museum by Christine Ruiz-Picasso (wife of Paul, Picasso's eldest son) and Bernard Ruiz-Picasso (his grandson). With about 600,000 visitors expected in 2004 the museum is set to make waves on an international scale, and many anticipate Málaga's cultural and economic revival with the museum's opening.

The regional government of Andalucía has also invested some €66 million in the restoration of the 16th-century **Palacio de los Condes de Buenavista** in which the museum is housed, with fabulous results (although the lack of any English explanations throughout the exhibits is a serious oversight). Be sure not to miss the atmospherically preserved **archaeological remains** in the museum's basement, nor the fantastic Café Museo Picasso (see p242).

For a more-intimate insight into the painter's humble childhood, the **Casa Natal de Picasso** (Map pp232-3; ☎ 952 06 02 15; Plaza de la Merced 15; admission free; ⏲ 10am-2pm & 5-8pm Mon-Sat, 10am-2pm Sun), the house where Picasso was born in 1881, now acts as a Foundation for study. The house also has a small exhibition of personal memorabilia. Ironically, the Picasso family had to move from this house, which was too expensive, to the cheaper number 17.

Castle Complex
CASTILLO DE GIBRALFARO

One remnant of Málaga's Islamic past is the craggy ramparts of the **Castillo de Gibralfaro** (Map pp232-3; ☎ 952 22 51 06; admission €1.80; ⏲ 9am-8.30pm Apr-Sep, 9am-6pm Oct-Mar), spectacularly located high on the hill overlooking the city. Originally built by Abd ar-Rahman I, the 8th-century Cordoban emir, and later rebuilt in the 14th century when Málaga was the main port for the Emirate of Granada, the castle originally acted as a lighthouse (its name means Beacon Hill) and a military barracks.

Nothing much remains of the interior of the castle, but the airy walkway around the ramparts affords the best views over Málaga. There is also a military **museum**, which includes a small-scale model of the entire castle complex and the lower residence, the Alcazaba. The model clearly shows the 14th-century curtain wall that connected the two sites and which is currently being restored. As the walk up to the castle and around the ramparts takes a full morning, lunch or a drink on the panoramic terrace of the nearby Parador Málaga Gibralfaro (p240) is a good way to finish up.

The best way to reach the castle is walking via the scenic Paseo Don Juan de Temboury, to the south of the Alcazaba. The road winds pleasantly (and steeply) through lushly gardened terraces with viewpoints over the city. Alternatively you can drive up the Camino de Gibralfaro or take bus No 35 from Avenida de Cervantes.

ALCAZABA

In the shadow of the Gibralfaro, the 11th-century **Alcazaba** (Map pp232-3; ☎ 952 22 51 06; Calle Alcazabilla; admission Alcazaba €1.80, admission Alcazaba & Castillo de Gibralfaro €3; ☒ 9.30am-8pm Tue-Sun Apr-Sep, 8.30am-7pm Tue-Sun Oct-Mar) was the sumptuous palace-fortress of the Muslim governors. Its multifaceted construction, meandering waterways and leafy terraces, with their rising sequence of viewpoints, are a pleasure to visit in the summer heat. Just below the palace, new excavations continue to unearth a small **Roman theatre**, which is eventually intended for outdoor events.

For immediate access to the Alcazaba from Calle Guillén Sotelo (behind the municipal tourist office), take the lift, which brings you out in the heart of the palace.

Around the Alameda Principal

The Alameda Principal, now a busy thoroughfare, was created in the late 18th century as a boulevard on what were then the sands of the Guadalmedina estuary. It's adorned with old trees from the Americas and lined with 18th- and 19th-century buildings.

The **Paseo del Parque**, a palm-lined extension of the Alameda, was created in the 1890s on land reclaimed from the sea. The garden along its southern side, **Paseo de España** (Map p232-3), is full of exotic tropical plants, making a pleasant refuge from the bustle of the city. On the northern side is the grand **Palacio de la Aduana** (Map pp232-3; Paseo del Parque; admission free; ☒ 3-8pm Tue, 9am-8pm Wed-Fri, 9am-3pm Sat & Sun), which now houses a temporary exhibition of works from the **Museo de Málaga** (originally housed in the

Picasso museum). The collection includes fine works by great artists such as Francisco de Zurbarán, Bartolomé Esteban Murillo, Jusepe de Ribera and Pedro de Mena.

To the north of the Alameda, in what is now the commercial district, you will find the neo-Islamic **Mercado Atarazanas** (Map pp232-3; Calle Atarazanas), entered through its huge horseshoe-shaped arch. The daily market in here is pleasantly noisy and animated and there is a whole host of food on sale. You can choose from swaying legs of ham and rolls of sausages to cheese, fruit, fish and sweets – but watch out for old señoras with their wheely-shopping-trolleys, as some are fantastically bad-tempered. Nearby are plenty of cafés on pedestrian Calle Herredería del Rey.

If you strike out south of the Alameda you will find a new museum on the Málaga circuit, the funky **Centro de Arte Contemporáneo** (Map pp232-3; ☎ 952 12 00 55; Calle Alemania; admission free; ☒ 10am-8pm Tue-Sun), which is housed in a skilfully converted 1930s wholesale market on the river estuary. The bizarre triangular floor plan of the building have been retained, with its cubist lines and shapes displaying the modern art brilliantly. Painted entirely white, windows and all, the museum exhibits works by well-known 20th-century artists and collectors such as Roy Lichtenstein, Gerhard Richter and Miquel Barceló. For a good introduction to the museum, ask about the free half-hour guided tours.

La Malagueta & the Beaches

At the end of the Paseo del Parque lies the district of La Malagueta, an exclusive residential area. Situated on a spit of land protruding into the sea, apartments here have frontline sea views, and some of Málaga's best restaurants are found near the local **Playa de la Malagueta** (the beach closest to the city centre). Take a walk along the beach before settling down to a full-on fish lunch at Adolfo (p240) and a visit to the museum of the **Plaza de Toros** (Map pp232-3; Paseo de Reding; museum €1.80; ☒ 10am-1pm & 5-8pm Mon-Fri). The museum is OK if you want to see some stuff on bullfighting, but the museum in Ronda (p259) is much better. Málaga's bullring is much more a working bullring and is the busiest on the *costa* (coast). The main bullfighting festival takes place at the plaza during the Feria de Málaga in August.

The festival has an 11-day programme, the longest of its kind in the province. Tickets for the fights, depending on where you sit, can cost from €12 to €50.

East of Playa de la Malagueta, sandy beaches continue to line most of the waterfront for several kilometres. Next along from Playa de la Malagueta are two man-made beaches, **Playa de Pedregalejo** and **Playa del Palo**, El Palo being the city's original, salt-of-the-earth fishing neighbourhood. This is a great place to bring children and an even better place to while away an afternoon with a cold beer and a plate of fantastic, sizzling seafood. To top it off, the efforts of the city council have resulted in a huge clean-up of the beach and water. To reach either beach take bus No 11 from Paseo del Parque.

Jardín Botánico La Concepción
Four kilometres north of the city centre is the large tropical **Jardín Botánico La Concepción** (Map pp232-3; ☎ 952 25 21 48; adult/child €2.80/1.40; ☺ 10am-4pm Tue-Sun Oct-Mar, 10am-6.30pm Apr-Sep, closed 25 Dec-1 Jan). Dating from the mid-19th century, the gardens are the brainchild of a local aristocratic couple, Amalia Heredia Livermore and Jorge Loring Oyarzabal. They decided to recreate a tropical forest near the shores of the Mediterranean. Visits are by 90-minute guided tour in English and wend their way through some of the 5000 tropical plants, waterfalls and lakes.

By car, take the A45 Antequera road north from the Málaga ring road (A7) to Km 166 and follow the signs 'Jardín Botánico'. On Saturday, Sunday and holidays the No 61 bus leaves Málaga's Alameda Principal for the gardens hourly from 11am. Alternatively, the MalagaTour bus (p237) also makes a stop here.

ACTIVITIES
Málaga is a busy city with few activities on offer. However, one of the latest – and most welcome – additions is the newly opened **Baños Árabes** (Arab Baths; Map p234; ☎ 952 21 23 27; Calle Tomás de Cózar 13; bath without/with massage €21/50; ☺ 10am-10pm, women only 3-10pm Tue, men only 3-10pm Thu) is a perfect place to sit back and sweat it out amid the steamy semidarkness. It is advisable to book in advance and specialist massages, including Ayurvedic and aromatherapy treatments, are by appointment only.

COURSES
The **Universidad de Málaga** (Map pp232-3; ☎ 952 27 82 11; fax 952 27 97 12; Avenida de Andalucía 24, 29007 Málaga) runs very popular language courses for foreigners. Four-week intensive Spanish-language courses cost €508. For information, write to the Cursos de Español para Extranjeros, Inés Carrasco Cantos (Directora). There are at least 20 private language schools in Málaga; the main tourist offices have contact lists.

MÁLAGA FOR CHILDREN
Málaga for kids is not so different from Málaga for adults, but that is not to say that the city isn't child-friendly. It has a easily navigable, compact centre, lots of child-friendly eateries and miles of popular beaches.

Of the sights, children will particularly like the craggy ramparts of the **Castillo de Gibralfaro** (p235) – a good morning's entertainment. The most suitable museum is the **Museo de Artes y Costumbres Populares** (Map pp232-3; ☎ 952 21 71 37; Pasillo de Santa Isabel 10; adult/child €2/free; ☺ 10am-1.30pm & 4-7pm Mon-Fri, 10am-1.30pm Sat), which focuses on everyday rural life with all the requisite farming and fishing regalia. Note the glass cabinets containing painted *barros* (clay figures) of characters from local folklore.

Of course a day spent on the **beaches** (p236), eating fish from *chiringuitos* (open-air, makeshift shacks serving seafood), will be the most popular option, and lots of fun can be had when tucking into tapas without the niceties of knives and forks (see The Tapas Trail, p241). Another good day out is a trip to the **Jardín Botánico La Concepción** (p237), a great place for a discreet picnic among the tropical fauna, and older children will have great fun experiencing the steamy darkness of the **Baños Árabes** (opposite).

Cheaper than the Costa del Sol, Málaga is also a great base from which to enjoy many of the treats of the *costa* without the expense. A frequent and efficient bus service (see p244) links the city with the towns of the Costa del Sol enabling easy day trips to all the large adventure parks and aquariums (see Kid's Costa, p248).

TOURS
To pick up the child-friendly, open-topped **MalagaTour** (Map pp232-3; ☎ 902101081; www.citysight seeing-spain.com; adult/child €12/5.50; ☺ 9.30am-7pm

at half-hourly intervals) bus ride head for Avenida Manuel Agustín Heredia or the eastern-most end of the Paseo del Parque. This hop-on-hop-off tour does a complete circuit of the city with stops at all the major points of interest. It is a great way to see the city – especially with small children – and tickets (valid for 24 hours) include a multilingual audio guide.

FESTIVALS & EVENTS

There are a whole host of festivals taking place throughout the year in Málaga province, and the booklet ¿Qué Hacer?, available from the municipal tourist office, will give you a blow-by-blow account. The following are the city's main events:

Semana Santa (Holy Week) Each night from Palm Sunday to Good Friday, six or seven cofradías (brotherhoods) bear their holy images for several hours through the city, watched by big crowds. A good place to watch from is along Alameda Principal.

Costa Pop (one night in late May) Previously called World Dance Costa del Sol, this massive all-night concert is attended by 100,000 or more fans and performed by top Spanish and Latin pop stars.

Feria de Málaga (mid-August) Málaga's nine-day feria (fair), launched by a huge fireworks display on the opening Friday, is the most ebullient of Andalucía's summer ferias. During the day the city thrives with music and dancing. Head for Plaza Uncibay, Plaza de la Constitución, Plaza Mitjana or Calle Marqués de Larios to be in the thick of it. At night the fun switches to large fairgrounds and nightly rock and flamenco shows at Cortijo de Torres, 4km southwest of the city centre. Special buses run from all over the city.

Fiesta Mayor de Verdiales (28 December) Thousands congregate for a grand gathering of verdiales folk groups at Puerto de la Torre. They perform an exhilarating brand of music and dance unique to the Málaga area. Bus No 21 from Alameda Principal goes to Puerto de la Torre.

SLEEPING

Málaga has a fairly limited selection of hotels, partly due to the lack of tourists. Off-peak, most places reduce prices significantly. Many of the top-end hotels have a weekly versus weekend pricing system with weekend rates being considerably cheaper.

Budget

True budget rooms are not particularly appealing – and don't expect any extras. Breakfast is not included in the price of the room and many places don't serve food at all.

Hostal Derby (Map p234; ☎ 952 22 13 01; Calle San Juan de Dios 1; s/d €27/40) A good-value hostal (a simple guesthouse or small place offering hotel-like accommodation) with spacious rooms with big windows, some of which overlook the harbour. It shares a building with various offices so don't be surprised to see an office block.

Hostal Aurora II (Map pp232-3; ☎ 952 22 40 04; Calle Cisneros 5; s/d €20/36) Set in a renovated house with good-sized rooms, and a relatively new addition to the scene, the Aurora II is an upmarket version of **Hostal Aurora I** (Map pp232-3; ☎ 95 222 40 04; Calle Muro Puerta Nueva; s/d €20/36), which is just off Calle Puerta Nueva.

Hostal El Cenachero (Map pp232-3; ☎ 952 22 40 88; Calle Barroso 5; s/d €29/46) This modest family-run hostal is close to the harbour. Cheerful and friendly, the hostal has pleasant rooms that are simply furnished and carpeted and come with showers. No meals are served.

Hostal Pedregalejo (Map pp232-3; ☎ 952 29 32 18; hosped@spa.es; Calle Conde de las Navas 9; s/d €41/58) Located near the beach, about 4km east of the city centre, this hostal is family-run and has attractive rooms and little coffee shop where you can buy breakfast. The only drawback is the hike into town.

Instalacion Juvenil Málaga (Map pp232-3; ☎ 952 30 85 00; www.inturjoven.com; Plaza Pío XII No 6; B&B under 26 low/high season €9.05/13.75, over 26 low/high season €12.25/18.35) Málaga's youth hostel has 110 places, most in modern double rooms and many with bathroom. There is also a communal sun terrace. The hostel is 1.5km west of the centre, and bus No 18 along Avenida de Andalucía from the Alameda Principal goes most of the way.

In the high season, when most places are full, you may also want to consider the centrally located **Hostal Larios** (Map p234; ☎ 952 22 54 90; Calle Marqués de Larios 9; s/d €35/45; ✄) or **Hostal Cisneros** (Map pp232-3; ☎ 952 21 26 33; Calle Cisneros 7; s/d €24/48).

Mid-Range

Hotel Don Curro (Map p234; ☎ 952 22 72 00; www .hoteldoncurro.com; Calle Sancha de Lara 7; s/d €65/92; P ✄) The busy Don Curro is a favourite with intense-looking businessmen and although it has a corporate air, the hotel is efficient, comfortable and central. It's also conveniently positioned for getting in and out of town. Rooms are well-appointed and spacious.

Hostal Victoria (Map p234; ☎ 952 22 42 23; Calle Sancha de Lara 3; d low/high season €50/80; ✕) The Victoria is enduringly popular, due to its central location and friendly staff. The clean and comfortable rooms are a cut above most other *hostales* and have a bath in the bathrooms.

Hotel Venecia (Map pp232-3; ☎ 952 21 36 36; fax 952 21 36 37; Alameda Principal 9; s/d €58/72; ✕) Located on the southern side of the Alameda, Hotel Venecia has 40 very comfortable rooms, and helpful English-speaking staff.

Hotel Carlos V (Map p234; ☎ 952 21 51 20; fax 952 21 51 29; Calle Císter 10; s/d €29.95/62.36; ✕) Due to its location, tucked behind the cathedral in a windy old street, Hotel Carlos V is enduringly popular. Although slightly gloomy inside, the basic rooms are clean.

Hotel Sur (Map pp232-3; ☎ 952 22 48 03; www.hotelsur.com; Calle Trinidad Grund 13; s/d €60/69; P ✕) Just south of the Alameda, this is another reasonable option. Despite its rather grandiose entrance hall, the rooms are beginning to look a bit worn, but it's relaxed and quiet and has the benefit of onsite parking.

Hotel Los Naranjos (Map pp232-3; ☎ 952 22 43 16 17; www.hotel-losnaranjos.com; Paseo de Sancha 35; s/d €67.50/98.50; P ✕) This rather garish-red hotel has clean, if uninspiring rooms, just east of the bullring on the way to the beaches. Front-facing rooms have small balconies, some of which catch glimpses of the sea.

Hotel California (Map pp232-3; ☎ 952 21 51 65; california@spa.es; Paseo de Sancha 17; s/d €54/78; P ✕) One kilometre east of the city centre and close to the beach. A lovely flowery entrance is a good start to the 28 good-sized rooms. Breakfast is also available.

Top End

AC Málaga Palacio (Map p234; ☎ 952 21 51 85; www.ac-hotels.com; Calle Cortina del Muelle 1; d low/high season €122/180; P ✕ ✕) This 15-storey, sleek hotel has sensational views over the busy seafront. Smart, modern design and excellent facilities also make it the best of Málaga's luxury options. It has a rooftop pool and fully fitted-out gym.

Hotel Cortijo La Reina (Map pp232-3; ☎ 951 01 40 00; www.hotelcortijolareina.com; Carretera Málaga-Colmenar; s/d €90/120; P ✕ ✕) This Andalucian-style *cortijo* (country property) is located 30 minutes' drive north of Málaga. At an elevation of 800m it enjoys beautiful views over the valleys, and rooms are sumptuously decor-

ated with four-poster beds and lots of swishy fabrics. Some facilities are adapted for wheelchair users. It makes a great base from which to explore the Parque Natural Montes de Málaga.

Hotel Larios (Map p234; ☎ 952 22 22 00; www.hotel-larios.com; Calle Marqués de Larios 2; d weekday/weekend €144/115; ✕) This quaint, boutique Art Deco hotel occupies a huge corner of Plaza de la Constitución. With all the deep purple, dark reds and browns the hotel certainly has a faded verve, but the rather high-handed service could do with an overhaul.

Parador Málaga Gibralfaro (Map pp232-3; ☎ 952 22 19 02; www.parador.es in Spanish; s/d €99/124; P ✕ ✕) With an unbeatable location perched on the Gibralfaro, Málaga's parador is a real winner. Rooms have spectacular views from their terraces, and you can dine at the excellent terrace restaurant (p240) even if you are not a guest at the hotel.

EATING

A speciality of Málaga is fish fried quickly in olive oil. *Fritura malagueño* consists of fried fish, anchovies and squid. Cold soups are popular: as well as gazpacho (chilled soup of blended tomatoes, peppers, cucumber, garlic, breadcrumbs, lemon and oil) and *sopa de ajo* (garlic soup), try *sopa de almendra con uvas* (almond soup with grapes). Ham is a requisite in most tapas combinations. Málaga's restaurants are well priced and a good standard due to the largely local clientele.

La Casa del Ángel (Map p234; ☎ 952 60 87 50; Calle Madre de Dios 29; mains €14-16; ✕ 8pm-late) An extraordinary restaurant filled with the owners' considerable art collection. The brainchild of Ángel Garó, the interior is a series of unusual features: Renaissance arches, beamed and frescoed ceilings, antique tiled floors and heart-warming orange and ochre paint washes. The cuisine is equally sumptuous: a combination of Andalucian, Arab and International tastes. The restaurant's intimate Salón Cervantes, with its heavy red curtains and double French windows overlooking the Teatro Cervantes, is the place to eat. Reservations are required.

Café de Paris (Map pp232-3; ☎ 952 22 50 43; Calle Velez-Málaga 8; menu de Mercado €38; ✕ 1-5pm & 9-12.30am Tue-Sat) An excellent, long-standing favourite in up-market La Malagueta, presided over by Michelin-starred José Carlos García. The heavy *fin-de-siecle* Parisian décor encourages long, somnolent lunches. Reservations are required.

Parador Málaga Gibralfaro (Map pp232-3; ☎ 952 22 19 02; www.parador.es in Spanish; menú €24) Nestled among pine trees and overlooking the Alcazaba, harbour and bay, the terrace restaurant of the parador is a fantastic dining experience and very romantic in the evenings. The menu is a tour-de-force of Andalucian gastronomy specialising in the popular *fritura de pescaítos a la malagueña* (small, fried fish of Málaga). The inside dining room is a formal affair of beamed ceilings, high-backed chairs and heavy tablecloths – a real treat of any visit to Málaga.

Rojo (Map p234; ☎ 952 22 74 86; Calle Granada 44; mains €20; ⏰ 8.30-12.30am Tue-Sat) A new contender on the Málaga restaurant scene and slap bang in the middle of the old town. Red banquettes line the walls, contrasting sharply with white tablecloths. Rojo attracts a youngish professional crowd with its simple but excellent menu. Reservations are recommended.

Clandestino (Map p234; ☎ 952 21 93 90; Calle Niño de Guevara 3; mains €8; ⏰ 1pm-1am) A trendy backstreet joint serving up top meals to hip, house beats. Hedonistic diners can finish up with a dreamy Doña Blanca ice cream (€2.70).

Mesón Astorga (Map pp232-3; ☎ 952 34 68 32; Calle Gerona 11; mains €15-20; ⏰ 1-5pm & 8.30pm-12.30am Mon-Sat) The excellent meat and fish dishes here have earned this lively little restaurant a well-deserved reputation. It is also one of the few good options in the west of the city near the train station.

El Yamal (Map pp232-3; ☎ 952 21 20 46; Calle Blasco de Garay 7; mains €8; ⏰ 1-5pm) Serves excellent Moroccan food in traditional *tajines* (earthenware dishes with pointed lids). Choose from fish, chicken or couscous with vegetables and soak up the relaxed atmosphere.

Café Central (Map p234; Plaza de la Constitución; platos €6-8.50) An extremely popular café on the main pedestrian square. A cold beer and plate of *rosada frita* (fried hake) is a lunchtime must. Choose your table carefully (somewhere in the middle) or you may be plagued by various musical impresarios determined to serenade you.

El Jardín (Map p234; ☎ 952 22 04 19; Calle Cañón 1; platos combinados €4.20-7.50; ⏰ 9am-midnight Mon-Thu, 9am-2pm & 5pm-midnight Fri & Sat, 5pm-midnight Sun) Next to the palm-filled gardens of the cathedral, this busy Viennese-style café fills up quick on the weekends (due to live music acts). Lots of mock-gold leaf and fancy furniture.

Café Moka (Map p234; ☎ 952 21 40 02; Calle San Bernardo El Viejo 2; breakfast €1.60) Just off the main drag, tucked behind Hotel Don Curro, this busy little retro café caters to a mainly Spanish crowd. It is a great place for breakfast, but fills up quickly both for breakfast (around 10am) and late lunch (3pm).

Seafood

Restaurante Antonio Martín (Map pp232-3; ☎ 952 22 73 98; Playa de la Malagueta; mains €7-14; ⏰ 1-5pm & 9pm-12.30am daily Mar-Oct, Mon-Sat Nov-Apr) Right on the beach with a large sea-view terrace, Antonio Martín rustles up some of the best fish in town. Celebrities and matadors are rumoured to hang out here. Reservations are recommended.

Adolfo (Map pp232-3; ☎ 952 60 19 14; Paseo Marítimo Picasso 12; 2-course meal €21; ⏰ 1.30-5pm & 8.30pm-1am Mon-Sat) Another classy place in the well-heeled La Malagueta area. It does a range of imaginative Mediterranean seafood dishes including tasty *patas de cangrejo* (crab claws). Reservations are required.

Abuela María (Map pp232-3; ☎ 952 29 96 87; Calle Salvador Allende 15; mains €20; ⏰ 1-5pm & 9pm-12.30am) At the El Palo end of town, this fusion restaurant is a real gem that's highly rated by locals. Chef Juan Manuel Rodríguez spent two years working with Martín Berasategui, presiding genius of the New Spanish Food.

Mesón El Chinitas (Map p234; ☎ 952 21 09 72, 952 22 64 40; Calle Moreno Monroy 4-6; mains €8.40-15; ⏰ noon-midnight) Appeals to diners who don't mind being eyeballed by cheesy portraits. The *menú* (set menu) offers a range of mainly fish dishes, including the sweet Picasso sole, sprinkled with cubed fruit.

Other recommended seafront eateries at El Palo are **Casa Pedro** (Map pp232-3; ☎ 952 29 00 13; Quitapenas 121, Paseo Marítimo Picasso; mains €20; ⏰ 1-5pm & 8.30pm-12.30am), and **Restaurante Tintero** (Map pp232-3; ☎ 607-607586; Carretera Almería 99; plates €4; ⏰ 12.30pm-1am), where plates of seafood are brought out by the waiters and you shout out for what you want. Shout loud if you want it sizzling hot.

Vegetarian

El Vegetariano de la Alcazabilla (Map pp232-3; ☎ 952 21 48 58; Calle Pozo del Rey 5; mains €6-8; ⏰ 1.30-4pm & 9-11pm Mon-Sat) Manages to jug-

THE TAPAS TRAIL

The pleasures of Málaga are essentially gentle, undemanding, easy to arrange and cheap. One of the best is a slow crawl around the city's numerous tapas bars and old bodegas (traditional wine bars). In summer these bars are open nearly all the time, late-morning to midnight, and beyond.

Antigua Casa de Guardia (Map pp232-3; ☎ 952 21 46 80; Alameda Principal; tapas €1-1.50, raciones €4-6, wine by the glass €0.80) This venerable old tavern has been serving Málaga's sweet dessert wines since 1840. Try the dark brown, sherry-like *seco* (dry) or the romantically named *Lágrima Trasañejo* (Very Old Tears), complemented by a plate of monster prawns.

Gorki (Map p234; ☎ 952 22 14 66; Calle Strachan 6; platos €5-7) A popular upmarket tapas bar with pavement tables and an interior full of wine barrel tables and stools. It serves an extensive list of Spanish wines, and tangy cheeses such as *manchego*. Try the belly-warming *judias liebre* (hare stew with white beans).

La Rebana (Map p234; Calle Molina Lario 5; tapas €2.10, raciones €4.50) A great, noisy tapas bar opposite Puerto Oscura, great for drinks before or after dining at Le Rebana. The dark wooden interior (with its wrought-iron gallery) creates an atmospheric ambience.

La Posada Antonio (Map p234; Calle Granada 33; tapas €1.80, mains €8-16) A very popular place with locals where you will be hard pressed to find a table after 11pm, despite its barnlike proportions. Great for greasy meat in tremendous proportions; the filling *paletilla cordero* (shoulder of lamb) will set you back €12.60.

Rincón Chinitas (Map p234; Pasaje de Chinitas; tapas €2.10, raciones €4.50) Little more than a hole in the wall, this small tapas bar manages to fry up hefty *raciones* (meal-sized servings of tapas). The delectable shrimp fritters are worth nudging your way in for.

Bodega la Quitapeñas (Map p234; ☎ 952 29 01 29; Calle Sánchez Pastor 2; tapas €2.10) Just around the corner from Chinitas is la Quitapeñas, a tiny, dingy drinking bar where heavily smoking young *malagueños* (Málaga locals) set the world to rights.

Pepa y Pepe (Map p234; Calle Calderería; tapas €1.10-1.50, raciones €3.60-4.10) A snug tapas bar that brims with diners chomping their way through *calamares fritos* (battered squid) and fried green peppers.

gle friendly service and good food, while keeping a laid-back vibe. Leave your mark: add to the graffiti on the yellow walls.

El Vegetariano de San Bernardo (Map p234; ☎ 952 22 95 87; Calle Niño de Guevara; mains €6-8; ☼ 1.30-4pm & 9-11pm Mon-Sat) Tucked away off Calle Granada is the more central sibling of El Vegetariano de la Alcazabilla.

DRINKING
Bars

The best places to look for bars are Plaza de la Merced in the northeast to Calle Carretería in the northwest, Plaza Mitjana (officially called Plaza del Marqués Vado Maestre) and Plaza de Uncibay.

Bodegas El Pimpi (Map p234; ☎ 952 22 89 90; Calle Granada 62; ☼ 7pm-2am) A Málaga institution with a warren of rooms and mini-patios. The huge wine casks are signed by stars (even Tony Blair!) and walls are lined with celebrity pictures and bullfighting posters. It attracts a fun-loving crowd with its sweet wine and thumping music.

Puerto Oscura (Map p234; Calle Molina Lario 5; cocktails €4; ☼ 6pm-very late) An elegant and intimate cocktail lounge with plush velvet seats and secret alcoves – a great way to start the evening. It stays open until 5am on busy summer nights and sometimes puts on live music acts. Relatively smart clothes are the order of the day.

El Cantor de Jazz (Map p234; ☎ 952 22 28 54; Calle Lazcano 7; cocktails €4; ☼ 7pm-2am Tue-Sat) Buffed wooden floors, great jazz portraits and a piano that's longing to be played (there's occasional jazz on Thursday nights).

Calle de Bruselas (Map pp232-3; ☎ 952 60 39 48; Plaza de la Merced 16; ☼ 11am-2am) Retro, Belgian bar appealing to a bohemian crowd. During the day it caters to the coffee scene with pavement tables out in the plaza, then at night the dark little bar comes to life with live music shows.

O'Neill's (Map p234; ☎ 952 60 14 60; Calle Luis de Velázquez 3; ☼ noon-late) A spit-and-sawdust bar that likes to prove how Irish it is by playing nonstop U2. Very busy with a noisy

MÁLAGA PROVINCE

mixed crowd of Spaniards, expats and tourists, with friendly bar staff.

Cafés

Café Museo Picasso (Map p234; ☎ 952 22 50 43; Palacio de Buenavista, Calle San Agustín 8; coffee €1.20, cakes €2.50) Simply excellent, serving the best rich, dark coffee in town, and run by Málaga's most dynamic young chef, José Carlos García (of Cafe de Paris). The cakes are exquisite and the beautiful secluded little patio at the back of the museum is alone worth a trip here.

Café Lepanto (Map p234; Calle Marqués de Larios 7; ice cream €2.80) A noisy local favourite right on the pedestrianised Calle Marqués de Larios, the Regent St of Málaga. As Málaga's poshest *confitería* (sweet shop) it serves up a whole host of delicious *pasteles* (pastries and cakes), ice creams, sweets, chocolates, coffees and drinks to manicured *malagueños*.

La Tetería (Map p234; Calle San Agustín 9; speciality tea €1.85; ☉ 4pm-midnight) Serves heaps of aromatic and classic teas, herbal infusions, coffees and juices, with teas ranging from peppermint to '*antidepresivo*', depending on how you feel. Sit outside and marvel at the beautiful church opposite.

ENTERTAINMENT

Party-seeking holiday-makers generally ignore Málaga and head along the coast, which means the bars and clubs in Málaga are left for discerning locals. The back pages of *Sur* newspaper, and its Friday 'Evasión' section, are useful for what's-on information, as is monthly *¿Qué Hacer?* (free from tourist offices).

Nightclubs

On hot weekends, the web of narrow old streets north of Plaza de la Constitución comes alive; mid-week, the place is dead.

Sala Karma (Map p234; ☎ 952 22 05 03; Calle Luis de Velázquez 5; ☉ 11pm-3am Thu-Sat) Low lighting and higher prices befit the older, classier clientele. There's space for a quick shimmy on the dance floor, too.

Siempre Asi (Map p234; Calle Convalecientes 5; ☉ 11pm-3.30am Thu-Sat) Plays flamenco, rumba and rocky Latino to a slightly pretentious 25-to-40-year-old crowd.

Liceo (Map p234; Calle Beatas 21; ☉ 7pm-3am Thu-Sat) A grand old mansion turned young music bar, which buzzes with a student crowd after

midnight. Go up the winding staircase and you'll find more rooms to duck into.

La Botellita (Map p234; Calle Álamos 36; ☉ 10pm-3am Thu-Sat) Just off Plaza de la Merced, Botellita is chock-a-block with miniature bottles of spirits. Spanish music attracts a young and invariably tipsy crowd.

Warhol (Map p234; Calle Niño de Guevara; ☉ 11pm-late Thu-Sat) A stylish haunt for choosy gay clubbers who want funky house beats mixed by dreadlocked DJs. Another recommended gay venue is **Sodoma** (Map p234; Calle Juan de Padilla 15; ☉ 11pm-late Thu-Sat), which whips up a house-music storm.

Theatre

Teatro Cervantes (Map p234; ☎ 952 22 41 00 tickets, www.teatrocervantes.com in Spanish; Calle Ramos Marín s/n) Housed in a palatial building, the revamped and reopened Cervantes has a good programme of music, dance and theatre.

Cinemas

Posters and *Sur* newspaper list the current movies at Málaga's cinemas. On Wednesday night all cinema tickets are half-price.

Albéniz Multicines (Map pp232-3; ☎ 952 21 58 98; Calle Alcazabilla 4) The home of the large Cinemateca Municipal (Municipal Cinema), showing international films with Spanish subtitles at 10pm most nights.

Sport

Málaga football club went bankrupt and ceased to exist around 1990 but, after being reborn in the early '90s, it now occupies a fair mid-table position in Spain's Primera Liga. The club plays at the **Estadio de la Rosaleda**, beside the Río Guadalmedina, 2km north of the city centre, and the main season runs from September to the end of May.

SHOPPING

El Corte Inglés (Map pp232-3; Avenida de Andalucía) Málaga's branch of this department store, situated on the western continuation of Alameda Principal, is chock-full of goodies ranging from chocolate spread to tailored suits.

For hand-crafted Andalucian ceramics try **Almazul** (Map p234; off Calle San Agustín) and for some tasty *malagueño* treats (and for late-night desperation shopping) look no further than the deli, **Ultramarinos Zoillo** (Map p234; Calle Granada 65). There is a Sunday morning **flea**

MÁLAGA PROVINCE

market (Map pp232-3; Paseo de los Martiricos) near the Estadio de la Rosaleda.

For camping essentials, **El Yeti** (Map p234; Calle Carreteria 71) and **Deportes La Trucha** (Map p234; Calle Carreteria 100) have a wide range of general and specialist camping and climbing equipment.

GETTING THERE & AWAY
Air
Málaga's busy **airport** (Map pp232-3; ☎ 952 04 88 38), the main international gateway to Andalucía, is 9km southwest of the city centre and is host to a rash of budget airlines. Most airline offices are at the airport but **Iberia** (Map p234; ☎ 902 40 05 00; www.iberia.es; Calle Molina Lario 13) has one in the city centre.

See p414 for information on international flights. Domestically, Iberia and Spanair both fly daily nonstop to/from Madrid and Barcelona; Air Europa also flies daily nonstop to/from Madrid. Iberia (or its subsidiary, Air Nostrum) has further nonstop flights to/from Melilla, Valencia, Bilbao, Santiago de Compostela and Palma de Mallorca. Air Europa serves Bilbao and Palma, and Spanair serves several cities with a transfer at Madrid or Barcelona.

Boat
Trasmediterránea (Map pp232-3; ☎ 952 06 12 18, 902 45 46 45; www.trasmediterranea.com; Estación Marítima, Local E1) operates a ferry (except Sunday mid-September to mid-June) to/from Melilla (passenger/car €29/150, 7½ hours, one daily).

Bus
The **bus station** (Map pp232-3; ☎ 952 35 00 61; Paseo de los Tilos) is 1km southwest of the city centre. Frequent buses run along the coast and several go daily to inland towns including Antequera (€4.55, 50 minutes, 12 daily), Nerja (€3.15, one hour, 17 daily) and Ronda (€8.40, 14 daily). Other destinations include Seville (€13.05, 2½ hours, 12 buses daily), Córdoba (€10.45, 2½ hours, five daily), Granada (€8.30, 1½ hours, 16 daily) and Madrid (€17.95, six hours, seven daily). There are also buses to Germany, Portugal, France and Morocco. There is a rather spartan café and adequate toilet facilities at the station.

For the Costa del Sol, regular buses leave Avenida Manuel Agustín Heredia (Map pp232–3) for Torremolinos (€0.90, 30 minutes), Benalmádena Costa (€1.30) and Fuengirola (€2.10, one hour).

Car
Numerous international (including Avis and Hertz) and local agencies have desks at the airport. You'll find them down a ramp in the luggage-carousel hall, and out the side of the arrivals hall.

Train
The **Málaga-Renfe train station** (Map p232-3; ☎ 952 36 02 02; www.renfe.com; Explanada de la Estación) is around the corner from the bus station. Regular trains run daily to and from Córdoba (tourist class €14 to €19.50, first class up to €23, 2½ hours) and Seville (€13.15, 2½ hours, five daily). For Granada (€12, 2½ hours) there are no direct trains, but you can get there with a transfer at Bobadilla. For Ronda (€7.90, 1½ to two hours), too, you usually change at Bobadilla.

Fast Talgo 200s go to/from Madrid (€47 to €79, 4½ hours, four daily). A slower, cheaper Intercity train leaves late morning for Madrid (€35, 6½ hours). There are also trains for Valencia (€45.50, 8½ to 9½ hours, two daily) and Barcelona (€44 to €121, 13 hours, two daily).

GETTING AROUND
To/From the Airport
A taxi from the airport to the city centre costs around €10 to €11.

Bus No 19 to the city centre (€1) leaves from the 'City Bus' stop outside the arrivals hall, about every half-hour from 7am to midnight, stopping at Málaga's main train and bus stations en route. Going out to the airport, you can catch the bus at the western end of Paseo del Parque, and from outside the stations, about every half-hour from 6.30am to 11.30pm. The journey takes around 20 minutes.

The Aeropuerto train station, on the Málaga–Fuengirola line, is a five-minute walk from the airport terminal: follow signs from the departures hall. Trains run about every half-hour from 7am to 11.45pm to the Málaga-Renfe station (€1.20, 11 minutes) and the Málaga-Centro station beside the Río Guadalmedina. Departures from the city to the airport and beyond are about every half-hour from 5.45am to 10.30pm.

Bus
Useful buses around town (€0.90 for all trips around the centre) include No 11 to El Palo,

No 34 to El Pedregalejo and El Palo and No 35 to Castillo de Gibralfaro, all departing from Avenida de Cervantes. The Malaga-Tour (p237) bus is also a useful option.

Car

Convenient car parks such as on Plaza de la Marina tend to be expensive (per hour €1.35, 24 hours €21.35). Side-street parking, off the south side of Alameda Principal, for example, is metered (€1.55 per 90 minutes). Vacant lots are much cheaper (pay €1 to the attendant); there is a large **car park** (Map pp232–3) behind El Corte Inglés, which is free overnight, but it is not secure and vehicles here are prone to break-ins.

Taxi

Fares within the city centre, including to the train and bus stations, are around €3.50. Expect to pay €5 to the Castillo de Gibralfaro.

COSTA DEL SOL

The Costa del Sol stretches along the Málaga seaboard like a wall of wedding cakes. Its recipe for success is the certainty (more or less) of sunshine, convenient beaches, warm sea, cheap package deals and plenty of nightlife and entertainment.

Until the 1950s, the resorts were fishing villages but there's little to show for that now. Launched as a Francoist development drive for impoverished Andalucía, the Costa del Sol is an eye-stinging example of how to fill, without exception, all open spaces. And with nearly 40 golf clubs, several busy marinas, numerous riding schools and a host of beaches offering every imaginable water sport, the Costa attracts an ever-increasing following of pleasure seekers who continue to swell the boom year in, year out.

Getting There & Around

A convenient train service links Málaga and its airport with Torremolinos (€1.20), Arroyo de la Miel (€1.20) and Fuengirola (€1.90). Plenty of buses link coastal towns with Málaga – from Torremolinos (€0.90), from Benalmádena Costa (€1.30) and from Fuengirola (€2.10).

The AP7 Autopista del Sol, bypassing Fuengirola, Marbella, San Pedro de Alcántara and Estepona, makes moving along the Costa del Sol a lot easier for those willing to pay its tolls (€11.20 Málaga–Estepona during Easter and from June to September; €6.90 during October to May).

Many places use Km numbers to pinpoint their location. These numbers rise from west to east. Along the (toll-free) A7, which runs parallel to the AP7, Estepona is at Km 155 and central Marbella at Km 181. Km markers aside, undoubtedly the most useful sign on the A7 is 'Cambio de Sentido',

---

FROM RAGS TO RICHES

I have collected *esparto* [a type of grass] in all the mountains along the coast; in Nerja, in Mijas, in Casares. One has to be born to work in the mountains. Collecting esparto sounds easy, but it isn't. The mountain changes every year. It is full of cracks and holes that are covered in weeks; one must know how to walk there. I have travelled as far as Granada and Córdoba to collect *esparto*. On these trips you had to sleep under trees in the mountain, even at Christmas time, when it was far too cold for this. In the end we managed to save around 300 or 400 pesetas. This we made by going hungry.

Carmen Escalona

This extraordinary account of poverty and physical hardship, given by Carmen Escalona in the folk museum in Mijas (see p249) provides an insight into the rural life of Andalucía of only 40 years ago. Carmen's intimate descriptions powerfully illustrate the common poverty of a poor Spanish backwater where landed aristocrats and the church grew wealthy on the rich land while the majority of working people barely managed to survive. The picture also sheds light on the traditional popularity of the socialist Republican movement in the south. Nowadays, it is difficult to reconcile this humble lifestyle (and indeed difficult to believe that Carmen's family home was fitted with electricity only last year) with the conspicuous excesses of the *costas* (coasts).

indicating that you can change direction to get back to a turning you might have missed. Do not let impatient drivers behind push you into going too fast for comfort. Go steadily and you should not have any problems, but in general, beware of other motorists and watch out for cats, dogs and footloose drunks.

Bargain rental cars (€130 to €150 a week, all inclusive) are available from local firms in all the resorts.

TORREMOLINOS & BENALMÁDENA

Torremolinos pop 51,000
Benalmádena pop 40,000

Britain's Blackpool would kill for what the *costa* capitals have, as far as sunshine goes. This concrete high-rise jungle, beginning 5km southwest of Málaga airport, is designed to squeeze as many paying customers as possible into the smallest available space. Even in winter, pedestrian traffic blocks the narrow lanes behind the main beaches, with holiday-makers scouring endless souvenir shops and real-estate agents.

After leading the Costa del Sol's mass tourist boom of the 1950s and '60s, Torremolinos (Torrie) lost ground to other resorts but is trying hard to spruce itself up. A pleasant seafront walk, the Paseo Marítimo, now extends for nearly 7km and has given a degree of cohesion and character to the resort.

Seven kilometres southwest of Torremolinos is the tamer Benalmádena, split into three distinctive areas: Benalmádena Costa, Benalmádena Pueblo and Arroyo de la Miel (a lively suburb of restaurants and shops).

A clear few steps above Torremolinos, Benalmádena Pueblo still retains an attractive historic centre of cobbled alleys and flower-filled balconies around it's attractive central square Plaza de España. Situated above the coast on a hillside it affords great views of the coast and is usually a touch cooler in summer. Down on the *costa*, the marina is fast becoming the most lively nightspot in the area with some classy restaurants and bars.

Orientation

The main road through Torremolinos from the northeast (the direction of the airport and Málaga) is called Calle Hoyo, becoming Avenida Palma de Mallorca after it passes

through Plaza Costa del Sol. Calle San Miguel runs most of the 500m from Plaza Costa del Sol down to the central beach; Calle San Miguel is the main pedestrian artery, running down to Playa del Bajondillo. The bus station is on Calle Hoyo and the train station is on Avenida Jesús Santos Rein, a pedestrian street intersecting Calle San Miguel 200m from Plaza Costa del Sol. Southwest of Playa del Bajondillo, around a small point, is Playa de la Carihuela, once the fishing quarter, backed by generally lower-rise buildings.

The southwestern end of Torremolinos merges with Benalmádena Costa, the seafront area of Benalmádena. About 2km uphill from here is the part of Benalmádena called Arroyo de la Miel, with Benalmádena Pueblo to its west.

Information

BOOKSHOPS
George's Secondhand Bookshop (Calle San Miguel 26, Torremolinos) This place has plenty of used paperbacks – great if you're not working off that hangover on the beach.

EMERGENCY
Policía Local (☎ 952 38 14 22; Calle Rafael Quintana 28, Torremolinos)
Policía Nacional (☎ 952 38 99 95; Calle Skal 12, Torremolinos) The main police station.

INTERNET ACCESS
Cyber Café (☎ 952 05 86 87; Avenida Los Manantiales 4, Torremolinos; per 30min €1; 🕑 9am-10pm)
Miramar (☎ 952 57 75 75; Avenida del Puerto, Benalmádena Costa, Benalmádena; per 30min €1.80; 🕑 11am-11pm Mon-Fri, 2-6pm Sat & Sun) Scenically sited overlooking the harbour, a great place to chill out while emailing home.

MEDICAL SERVICES
Red Cross Emergencies (☎ 952 37 37 27; Calle María Barrabino 16, Torremolinos)
Sanatorio Marítimo (☎ 952 38 18 55; Calle del Sanatorio 5, Torremolinos) The main hospital in Torremolinos.

MONEY
All the resorts have plenty of banks with ATMs, concentrated on the main pedestrianised shopping streets.

POST
Post office Benalmádena (Avenida Antonio Machado 20; 🕑 8.30am-8.30pm Mon-Fri, 8.30am-2pm Sat); Torremolinos

(Avenida Palma de Mallorca 23; ⌚ 8.30am-8.30pm Mon-Fri, 8.30am-2pm Sat)

TOURIST INFORMATION

Benalmádena tourist office (☎ 952 44 24 94; www .benalmadena.com in Spanish; Avenida Antonio Machado 10, Torremolinos; ⌚ 9.30am-2.30pm) On the main road from Torremolinos.

Torremolinos tourist office (☎ 952 37 95 12; www .ayto-torremolinos.org in Spanish; Plaza Pablo Picasso; ⌚ 9am-1.30pm Mon-Fri) Offers a selection of leaflets on the surrounding amusement parks as well as news of monthly events. There are also numerous information booths dotted around the town and near the beach.

Sights & Activities

Bars and beaches – that says it all. 'Torrie' is still a good-time resort where people come to party hard on the neon-lit **Calle San Miguel** and soak up the sun on the wide, sandy beaches. With the exception of the lonely **Torre de los Molinos** (Tower of the Mills), a 14th-century Arab watchtower, there is precious little to see. Torrie is a 'doing' – not a 'seeing' – place, and along with the rest of the Costa del Sol specialises in **theme parks** (see Kid's Costa, p248), **water sports** and a host of largely free music and dance **festivals** that run throughout the summer months (check with the tourist office for details).

However, people never seem to tire of the good old seafront promenade, which in the case of Torremolinos runs several kilometres west from **Playa de Bajondillo**. It extends to the more-upmarket **La Carihuela**, the original fishing village that used to serve Málaga and that preserves something of its humble past, not least in a good selection of fish restaurants.

Further west, the prettier and less garish **Benalmádena Pueblo**, with its geranium-filled balconies and narrow streets, is a welcome relief from the unrelenting party atmosphere along the coast. A small municipal museum, the **Museo Arqueológico** (☎ 952 44 85 93; Avenida Juan Peralta 49; admission free; ⌚ 10am-2pm & 4-7pm Mon-Fri) exhibits artefacts from the Bronze and Middle Ages. There is a magnificent view of the coast from the tiny church at the top of the village. At Benalmádena Costa there is a **cable car** (☎ 952 19 04 82; www.teleferico-benalmadena.com in Spanish; Esplanade Tívoli s/n; adult/child round-trip €10/7; ⌚ 10.30am-late Mar-Oct) that transports you up into the hills from where you can walk down two marked pathways. To make an outing of it,

go up in the cable car (enjoying the views), have a wander around the pueblo (village) and enjoy a good lunch before heading back down to the coast in the afternoon.

Boat cruises to Fuengirola and Málaga (three to four daily to either destination) leave from the Puerto Deportivo at Benalmádena. To reserve a ticket contact **Costasol Cruceros** (☎ 952 44 48 81; round-trip €11).

Festivals & Events

Torremolinos hosts an exhaustive list of festivals, including the Championship Ballroom Dance Contest, Carnival, the Verdiales (folk-dancing) festival, Holy Week, Crosses of May and the Day of the Tourist(!). However, the most important event is the **La Romería de San Miguel** (29 September). It's a colourful parade of *gitano* (Roma people) caravans, Andalucian horses and flamenco dancers who wend their way through the streets of Torremolinos to the forest behind the town for a night of barbecues, drinking and dancing.

Sleeping

There are a huge numbers of rooms at almost every price. However, to avoid a weary trudge from one *completo* (full) sign to another, you are strongly advised to book ahead during the high season of July, August and, in some places, September. Outside these peak months, room rates often drop sharply. The Costa has about 15 camping grounds (ask at the tourist offices for details).

La Fonda Benalmádena (☎ /fax 952 56 82 73; www .123casa.com/hotels/benalmadendahotellafonda.htm; Calle Santo Domingo 7, Benalmádena Pueblo, Benalmádena ; s/d €60/82; ✖ ✉) La Fonda is a charming place, with large rooms built around Islamic-style patios (which feature fountains). The restaurant (p247) that forms part of a catering school that serves excellent but very moderately priced food.

Hotel Miami (☎ 952 38 52 55; www.residencia-miami .com; Calle Aladino 14, Torremolinos; d €37/57; ✖ ✉) A lovely Andalucian-style villa built in the 1950s by Manolo Blascos (Picasso's cousin) for flamenco dancer Lola Medina. Only 100m from La Carihuela beach, this small hotel has tastefully decorated rooms and is set in the midst of a tropical garden with a wonderful pool.

Hotel Tarik (☎ 952 38 23 00; www.hoteltarik.com; Paseo Marítimo 49, Torremolinos; s/d €55/85; Ⓟ ✖ ✉)

A large, Andalucian-style hotel located right on the seafront behind a swathe of sandy beach. Communal areas are attractively decorated with Moroccan zellij tilework and there is a large secluded pool. Bedrooms have less character but are extremely comfortable with all modern facilities.

Hostal Flor Blanco (☎ 952 38 20 71; Pasaje de la Carihuela 4, Torremolinos; d €40; ⊠) Just metres from the beach in La Carihuela (which is about 1.5km southwest of central Torremolinos), the small and friendly Flor Blanco has seaview rooms. However, as it has only 12 rooms you should book in advance.

Red Parrot (☎ 952 37 54 45; www.theredparrot.net; Avenida Los Manantiales 4, Torremolinos; s/d €36/42; ⊠) Newly refurbished (rooms are now different from those shown on the website) and centrally located, the Red Parrot offers comfortable balconied rooms (with ceiling fans) around an internal patio.

Hotel El Pozo (☎ 952 38 06 22; Calle Casablanca 2, Torremolinos; s/d €32/62; ⊠) Made famous in a 2002 edition of the TV show *Eastenders*, Hotel El Pozo has 28 spacious rooms and is located in the centre of Torremolinos.

Eating

British pit stops pop up everywhere, but there are an abundance of seafood eateries strewn along palm-lined Playa del Bajondillo in Torremolinos. However, the best fish restaurants, as well as the core of the nightlife, tend to centre on La Carihuela and Benalmádena Costa.

Restaurant El Roqueo (☎ 952 38 49 46; Calle Carmen 35, Torremolinos; mains €18) With its wide terrace, El Roqueo has the atmosphere of a beach-side diner, but it's much classier than that. It's bustling and friendly and you can't beat the simple but delicious *dorada la plancha* (grilled bream).

Casa Juan (☎ 952 38 41 06; Calle San Gine's 20, Torremolinos; mains €4.50-15) One of a string of first-rate seafood eateries in La Carihuela, this place does fantastic fish, *malagueño* style. Crack apart a plump lobster or try fish with rice.

Casa Gauquín (☎ 952 38 45 30; Calle Carmen 37, Torremolinos; mains €4.50-15) A relative of Casa Juan, Casa Gauquín concocts good fish dishes and offers both tapas and a more pricey à la carte menu, which is best enjoyed on the terrace.

El Bodegón del Muro (☎ 952 56 85 87; Calle Santo Domingo 23, Benalmádena Pueblo, Benalmádena; mains €15-15) A great place to stop for a leisurely lunch after exploring the winding streets of the pueblo. A touch above most other restaurants, the *menú* is imaginative and the restaurant enjoys spectacular views over the coast.

Restaurant La Fonda (☎ /fax 952 56 82 73; www .123casa.com/hotels/benalmadendahotellafonda.htm; Calle Santo Domingo 7, Benalmádena Pueblo, Benalmádena; mains €7.50-16) The restaurant at La Fonda (p246) hotel is excellent, and has a great location near the central Plaza de España in the pueblo. It has a fantastic terrace and a lovely plant-filled patio.

Bodega Quitapeñas (Cuesta del Tajo, Torremolinos) Tucked away near the tower this busy tapas bar has a small terrace, and is popular with Spaniards for its delicious range of seafood tapas and *raciones* (meal-sized servings of tapas; €4.50 to €6). A similar place is **Bar La Bodega** (Calle San Miguel 40, Torremolinos).

Entertainment

Torremolinos' clubbing vibe has waned, with the thrust of the action moving westwards to Benalmádena Costa's Puerto Deportivo (marina) area, where there are some classy (and touristy) bars. However, Torrie still has some big venues as well as a thriving gay scene that concentrates on Calle Nogalera, off Avenida Jesús Santos Rein. There is also a huge gay rave in August.

Atrevete (Avenida Salvador Allende; ◔ 8pm-5am) A sexy salsa club in La Carihuela with two cosy dance floors on which the clientele can bump and grind.

Fun Beach (☎ 952 05 23 97; Avenida Palma de Mallorca 7; ◔ 8pm-6am) Reputedly the largest club in Europe, Fun Beach has eight huge, packed dance floors in which to lose yourself.

Discoteca Palladium (☎ 952 38 42 89; Avenida Palma de Mallorca 36; admission €8; ◔ 10pm-7am mid-Mar–mid-Oct) A huge club with a fancy swimming pool, balloons and foam parties, spinning out some thumping tunes. Frenetic but fun.

Disco Kiu (Plaza Sol y Mar, Benalmádena Costa) Another popular giant, which has foam parties for added excitement. Dress codes aren't strict but men generally wear collared shirts.

Getting There & Away

From Avenida Palma de Mallorca, at the corner of Calle Antonio Girón, local buses run from Torremolinos to Benalmádena Costa (€0.80, 15 minutes, every 15 minutes), Málaga (€0.90, 30 minutes, every 15 minutes), Benalmádena Pueblo (€0.80, 40 minutes, every

MÁLAGA PROVINCE

30 minutes) and Fuengirola (€1, 30 minutes, every 30 minutes). Buses also run from Málaga to Benalmádena (€1.30, 40 minutes, every 30 minutes).

From the **bus station** (☎ 952 38 24 19; Calle Hoyo, Torremolinos), buses run to Marbella (€2.90, one hour, 14 daily) and to Ronda, Estepona, Algeciras, Tarifa, Cádiz and Granada.

Trains run to Torremolinos, about every half-hour from 5.30am to 10.30pm, from Málaga city (€1, 20 minutes) and the airport (€0.85, 10 minutes). These then continue on from Torremolinos to Benalmádena–Arroyo de la Miel and Fuengirola (€1, 20 minutes).

FUENGIROLA

pop 57,000

Fuengirola, a beach resort 18km down the coast from Torremolinos, has more of a family-holiday scene but is even more densely packed than Torremolinos. Its sometimes drab buildings rather overpower the waterfront and beaches.

Orientation & Information

The narrow streets in the few blocks between the beach and Avenida Matías Sáenz de Tejada (the street on which the bus station is located) constitute what's left of the old town, with Plaza de la Constitución at its heart. The train station is a block inland from the bus station, on Avenida Jesús Santos Rein.

The **tourist office** (☎ 952 46 74 57; Avenida Jesús Santos Rein 6; ☉ 9.30am-2pm & 4.30-7pm Mon-Fri, 10am-1pm Sat) is just along from the train station.

Sights & Activities

One great evening to be had is at the **Hipódromo Costa del Sol** (☎ 952 59 27 00; admission race days €5, otherwise free; ☉ 10pm-2am Sat Jul-Sep, 11.30am-4pm Sun Oct-Jun), which is Andalucía's leading horse racetrack. You'll find it at Urbanización El Chaparral, off the A7 at the southwestern end of Fuengirola. Another worthwhile day out is at Fuengirola's **street market** (Avenida Jesús Santos Rein), held in the fairground. It is held every Tuesday and is the biggest on the Costa.

Festivals & Events

The biggest festival in Fuengirola is the **Día de la Virgen del Carmen** (16 July), in which 120 bearers carry a heavy platform (which supports a lavish effigy of the Virgin) in a two-hour procession from Los Boliches church into the sea.

Sleeping

While there are simply dozens of hotels in Fuengirola, the following are a few of the most appealing.

KID'S COSTA

There is a growing number of attractions along the coast that cater for children of all ages. The oldest and biggest amusement park is **Tivoli World** (☎ 952 57 70 16; www.tivolicostadelsol.com; Avenida de Tivoli; admission €4.50; ☉ 11am-9pm Jan-Mar; 4pm-1am Apr-May & mid-Sep–Oct; 5pm-2am Jun & early-Sep; 6pm-2.30am Jul & Aug, 11am-9pm Sun Nov & Dec). As well as multifarious rides and slides (for which you pay extra to the admission price), it stages daily dance, musical and children's events. It's five minutes' walk from Benalmádena–Arroyo de la Miel train station. For children, consider the good-value 'Supertivolino' ticket for €15, which covers admission and unlimited use on more than 30 rides.

Alternatively, just off the A7 in Torremolinos is the ever-popular **Aquapark** (☎ 952 46 04 04; Calle Cuba 10; adult/child €12.60/8.40; ☉ 10am-6pm May, Jun & Sep, 10am-7pm Jul & Aug) with its chutes and slides, and the similar but cheaper **Parque Acuático Mijas** (☎ 952 46 04 09; www.aquamijas.com; adult/child €13.50/8; ☉ 10.30am-5.30pm May, 10am-6pm Jun, 10am-7pm Jul & Aug, 10am-8pm Sep), beside the A7 Fuengirola bypass, which also has a separate mini-park for toddlers.

Another watery hit is Benalmádena's well-organised **SeaLife** (☎ 952 56 01 50; www.sealife.es in Spanish; Puerto Deportivo; adult/child €8/6.60; ☉ 10am-8pm Jun, 10am-midnight Jul & Aug, 10am-6pm Sep-May), with organised games and shark-feeding of Europe's largest shark collection.

For older kids, try **Quad Bike Rentals** (☎ 676-771120; www.rentaquad.com; Carretera de Coín s/n; adult/child €50/40; ☉ 10am-sunset), in Fuengirola Port, with hourly and day-long trail options, or even **Jardín de las Águilas Falconry Centre** (☎ 952 56 82 39; Castillo de las Aguilas; adult/child €5.80/4; shows ☉ 1pm, 7pm & 8pm Jun-Sep, 1pm & 5pm Oct-May) at Benalmádena Pueblo. Concessions usually apply to children aged between four and 12, with younger tots getting in for free.

Hostal Italia (☎ 952 47 41 93; fax 95 246 19 09; Calle de la Cruz 1; s/d €40/53; ✖) A good, friendly budget option in the heart of things, a couple of blocks from the beach. The rooms are all clean and comfortable.

Hotel Puerto (☎ 952 66 45 03; Calle Marbella 34; s/d €42/59; ✖ ✍) A towering three-star hotel on Fuengirola's beach. Balconies have great sea views and there's a rooftop pool.

Las Islas (☎ 952 47 55 98; Calle Canela 12, Torreblanca del Sol; d €75; ✖ ✍) Just east of Fuengirola, Las Islas is a haven of taste and calm run by the exceptionally friendly Ghislaine and Hardy Honig. Twelve comfortable guest rooms are spread throughout lush tropical gardens and there is an excellent restaurant.

Eating

Calle Moncayo and Calle de la Cruz, a block back from the Paseo Marítimo, are awash with mediocre international eateries. The Paseo Marítimo itself and the Puerto Deportivo (marina) have further strings of bargain eateries.

Lizzaran (☎ 952 47 38 29; Avenida Jesús Santos Rein 1; raciones €4-15) A welcome Spanish relief from the overwhelming number of Chinese and Italian eateries in Fuengirola. Tuck into salty sardine or ham *pinxos* (bread with toppings).

Restaurante Portofino (☎ 952 47 06 43; Paseo Marítimo 29; mains €10.50-30) One of Fuengirola's better offerings, this restaurant has an international menu that features a host of classic fish dishes. Specialities include all manner of fried fish, sole with spinach and excellent shellfish.

Cafetería Costa del Sol (☎ 952 47 17 09; Calle Marbella 3; rosquillas €2.10) Cheerful breakfast spot with a bright, striped awning. It turns out hot, tasty ham and cheese *rosquillas* (toasted rolls).

Drinking & Entertainment

Plenty of tacky disco-pubs line Paseo Marítimo, and a cluster of music bars and discos can be found opposite the Puerto Deportivo. A few hip bars also dot the town.

Cotton Club (Avenida Condes San Isidro 9) Attracts a chilled bunch who are wised-up to the laid-back vibe of this excellent bar. It has jam sessions on Thursday night, and some comedy evenings, too.

Irish Times and Cafetería La Plaza are bars at opposite ends of Plaza de la Constitución. Both fill up with lively, mainly Spanish crowds in the evening. The Irish Times' patio is great on a hot night.

Getting There & Away

From the **bus station** (☎ 952 47 50 66) frequent buses run to Torremolinos (€1, 30 minutes), Málaga (€2.10, one hour), Marbella (€2.05, one hour) and Mijas (€0.90, 25 minutes).

Fuengirola is served by the same trains as Torremolinos, costing €2 from Málaga and the airport.

MIJAS

pop 52,000 / elevation 428m

The story of Mijas encapsulates the story of the Costa del Sol. Originally a humble pueblo, it is now the richest town in the province and the second-largest pueblo on the coast. Since finding favour with discerning bohemian artists and writers in the 1950s and '60s, Mijas has sprawled across the surrounding hills yet managed to retain the original pueblo's picturesque charm. Much like Capri, the effect is somewhat spoiled by the hordes of day-tripping package tourists that pile into the town in summer, but in winter it is blissfully quiet making it possible to appreciate its easy charms.

Information

For information on sights, activities and events in and around Mijas drop in to the helpful **tourist office** (☎ 952 48 58 20; www.mijas .es; Plaza Virgen de la Peña s/n; ☼ 9am-2pm & 4-7pm Mon-Fri Oct-Mar, 9am-2pm & 5-8pm Mon-Fri Apr-Sep, 10am-2pm Sat year-round).

Sights & Activities

Mijas is home to the most interesting 'folk' museum on the *costa*, the **Casa Museo de Mijas** (☎ 952 59 03 80; Calle Málaga; admission free; ☼ 10am-2pm & 4-7pm Sep-Mar, 5-8pm Apr-Jun, 6-9pm Jul-Aug). It was created and is still run by Carmen Escalona, who specialises in crafting folk-themed models. The small models are dotted around the museum, and in light of the explanations and artefacts, show perfectly the style and mode of living of some 40 years ago. It is a great place for children. The museum is on the left-hand side just before you enter the main plaza.

Mijas also has a square **Plaza de Toros** (☎ 952 48 52 48; fights €45-85; ☼ 10am-2pm), presumably an attempt to recreate the original arena of the bullfight that was the main 'square' of the town.

It also has an interesting grotto of the **Virgen de la Peña**, where the Virgin is said to have appeared to two shepherds in 1586. Situated on the cliff edge in an ornamental garden, the spot has wonderful views and is the start of a **panoramic pathway** that wends its way around the vertical edges of the town. The annual village procession is on 8 September, when the effigy of the Virgin is carried 2km up to the **Ermita del Calvario**, a tiny chapel built by Carmelite brothers. Black-iron crosses mark a short walking trail that leads through the forest up to the Hermitage. Alternatively, you can take one of the donkey taxis from the town centre for €7.

Mijas is a noted area for **rock climbing** (particularly in winter) with around 100 grade V–7 climbs.

Sleeping

Mijas is well supplied with quality, top-end hotels such as the sumptuous, Andalucian-style, **Hotel Mijas** (☎ 952 48 58 00; Plaza de la Constitución; s/d €92/113; P ⓧ ⓡ), which has excellent facilities including horse riding, tennis and hydromassage, and the slick **Beach House** (☎ /fax 952 49 45 40; www.beachhouse .nu; Urbanisation El Chaparral; d €125/140, d with sea view €175; P ⓡ).

However, there are also a couple of mid-range gems: from the tidy **Casa El Escudo de Mijas** (☎ 952 59 11 00; www.el-escudo.com; Calle Trocha de los Pescadores 7; s low/high €40/70, d low/high €50/80) with its pretty colourwashes, wrought iron furnishings and tiled bathrooms, to the two excellent B&Bs, **Finca Blake** (☎ /fax 952 59 04 01; www.fincablake.com; Carretera de Mijas, Km 2; d €78-90) and **Casa Kay** (☎ /fax 952 48 57 91; www.anit.es/casa kay; Urbanisation Las Lomas de Mijas; s/d €35/70; P ⓡ). For details of how to reach them check out the websites.

Budget travellers should check out the **Hostal La Posada** (☎ 952 48 53 10; Calle Coin 47; d €37; ⓧ), a friendly and moderately priced option.

Eating

Mijas has dozens of restaurants from which you can choose, the most notable being the Basque-style **El Mirlo Blanco** (☎ 952 48 57 00; Paseo Marítimo 29; mains €16-35) and the haute-Med **El Padrastro** (☎ 952 48 50 00; Paseo del Compás; mains €15-30). Padastro is perched on a cliff above the Plaza Virgen de la Peña, with suitably spectacular views.

Getting There & Away

Frequent buses run from Fuengirola (€0.90, 25 minutes).

MARBELLA

pop 116,000

Marbella is the supermodel on the Costa catwalk, always on show, but still managing to strut with style. From the 1950s to the '80s Marbella was the destination de jour for oil-rich Arabs, film and fashion followers and brokers and barons, who flocked to the sunshine coast to build their luxury pieds-à-terre and be seen amid shoals of glamour groupies.

During the '80s the rapid and unsightly growth of suburbs took some of the shine off the 'rich and famous' tag. Tourist numbers began a steady decline, and it wasn't until the beginning of the 1990s when Jesús Gil y Gil, a flamboyant right-wing businessman, became mayor that Marbella began to see something of a renaissance. Gil immediately set about restoring Marbella's image and, with notoriously heavy-handed policing methods, rid the streets of petty criminals, prostitutes and drug addicts. Gil also encouraged property development and courted the wealthy and famous, including the Costa's recent wave of nouveaux-riches. He was re-elected mayor in 1995 and 1999, but was then banned from holding public office, amid a growing mountain of lawsuits accusing him of a welter of misdeeds. These included the alleged illegal diversion of €27 million of Marbella council money to the Atlético Madrid football team (of which he was president).

In April 2002 Gil was finally jailed, only to make bail a few days later. He then resigned as mayor of Marbella, and with an army of lawyers defiantly defended himself against lawsuits until his death on 14 May 2004.

In Marbella, however, to the innocent eye, all's right with the world. The beaches are clean, and although the celebrity circus around the nearby Puerto Banús waterfront is generally B-list verging on XYZ, the tourists have returned, the sun shines, and Marbella retains its appeal even for the most jaded.

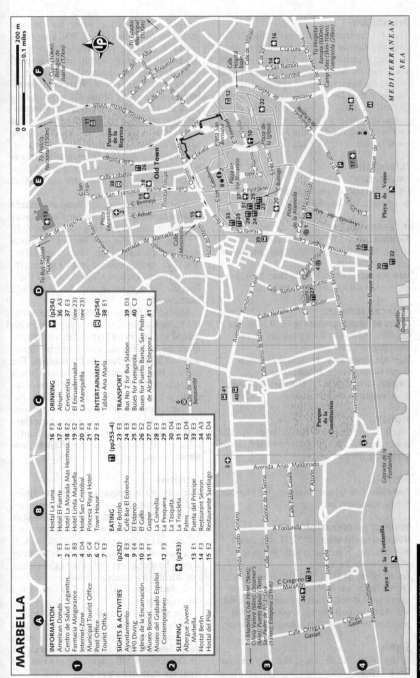

MARBELLA

INFORMATION
American Donats	1	E3
Centro de Salud Leganitos	2	E1
Farmacia Mingorance	3	B3
Internet-Zone	4	D4
Municipal Tourist Office	5	C4
Post Office	6	C2
Tourist Office	7	E3

SIGHTS & ACTIVITIES (p252)
Ayuntamiento	8	E3
H²O Diving	9	E4
Iglesia de la Encarnación	10	E3
Museo Bonsai	11	F1
Museo del Grabado Español		
Contemporáneo	12	F3

SLEEPING (p253)
Albergue Juvenil		
Marbella	13	E1
Hostal Berlín	14	F3
Hostal del Pilar	15	E2
Hostal La Luna	16	F3
Hotel El Fuerte	17	E4
Hotel La Morada Mas Hermosa	18	E2
Hotel Linda Marbella	19	E2
Hotel San Cristóbal	20	E3
Princesa Playa Hotel	21	F4
Town House	22	F3

EATING (pp253–4)
Bar Botolo	23	E3
Café Bar El Estrecho	24	E3
El Estanco	25	E3
El Gallo	26	E2
Gaspar	27	D3
La Comedia	28	E3
La Pesquera	29	E3
La Tasquita	30	D4
La Triciclета	31	E3
Palms	32	D4
Puerta del Príncipe	33	E3
Restaurant Sémon	34	A3
Restaurante Santiago	35	D4

DRINKING (p254)
Atrium	36	A3
Cervecerías	37	E3
El Encuadernador	(see 23)	
La Marejadilla	(see 23)	

ENTERTAINMENT (p254)
Tablao Ana María	38	E1

TRANSPORT
Bus No 2 for Bus Station	39	D3
Buses for Fuengirola	40	C3
Buses for Puerto Banús, San Pedro		
de Alcántara, Estepona	41	C3

Orientation

The A7 through town goes by the names Avenida Ramón y Cajal and (further west) Avenida Ricardo Soriano. Driving in the old town can be something of nightmare due to the tortuous one-way system (see the Marbella map for details). The old town is centred on Plaza de los Naranjos, north of Avenida Ramón y Cajal. The bus station is on the northern side of the Marbella bypass, about 1.2km north of Plaza de los Naranjos.

Information

EMERGENCY

Policía Nacional (National Police; ☎ 091; Avenida Doctor Viñals) The main police station, north of the town.

INTERNET ACCESS

American Donats (☎ 952 86 42 62; Calle Carlos Mackintosh; per 30min €1; ☼ 9am-10pm) Funky Internet café close to the beach.

Internet-Zone (Calle Padre Enrique Cantos 4; per 30min €1; ☼ 10am-midnight) Off Avenida Miguel Cano.

MEDICAL SERVICES

Centro de Salud Leganitos (☎ 952 77 21 84; Plaza Leganitos; ☼ 8am-5pm Mon-Fri, 9am-5pm Sat) For emergency medical attention.

Farmacia Mingorance (☎ 952 77 50 86; Avenida Ricardo Soriano 44) Large, 24-hour pharmacy.

Hospital Europa (☎ 952 77 42 00; Avenida de Severo Ochoa) Hospital 1km east of the centre.

MONEY

There are plenty of banks with ATMs, concentrated on the main pedestrianised shopping streets.

POST

Post office (Calle de Jacinto Benavente; ☼ 8.30am-8pm Mon-Fri, 8.30am-2pm Sat)

TOURIST INFORMATION

Municipal tourist office (☎ 952 77 14 42; Glorieta de la Fontanilla; ☼ 9am-8pm or 9pm) The main tourist office, situated on the seafront.

Tourist office (☎ 952 82 35 50; Plaza de los Naranjos; ☼ 9am-8pm or 9pm) Helpful office stuffed with information on Marbella. Stocks the *Verano Cultural* leaflet with information about what's on as well as bi-monthly publication, *Marbella Día y Noche* (www.guiamarbella.com).

Sights

Away from the beaches, the picturesque **Casco Antiguo** (old town) is chocolate-box perfect, with pristine white houses and geranium-filled balconies. You can easily spend a relaxing morning exploring its delightful alleyways that are crammed with designer boutiques. At the heart of its pleasant web is pretty **Plaza de los Naranjos**, the focal point of the old town dating back to 1485. The 16th-century **ayuntamiento** (town hall) is on its northern side and the fountain opposite was placed in the square in 1504 by the first Christian mayor. Nearby is the **Iglesia de la Encarnación** (Plaza de la Iglesia; admission free; ☼ hours of service), begun in the 16th century and later remodelled in Baroque style.

A little further east, the **Museo del Grabado Español Contemporáneo** (Museum of Contemporary Spanish Prints; Calle Hospital Bazán s/n; admission €2.50; ☼ 10am-2pm & 5.30-8.30pm Mon-Sat), exhibits work by Picasso, Joan Miró and Salvador Dalí, among others. Just to the north, along streets such as Calle Arte and Calle Portada, are the remains of Marbella's old **Islamic walls**.

Marbella's real designer alley is the Avenida Ramón y Cajal, which is peppered with crazed sculptures by Dalí. Cross over to the Plaza de la Alameda and a marble walkway will lead you down to the beaches. The central **Playa de Venus**, immediately below Avenida del Mar and east of the Puerto Deportivo, is a fairly standard Costa beach. For a longer, broader and usually less crowded stretch of sand, walk to the 800m-long **Playa de la Fontanilla**, west of Glorieta de la Fontanilla, or, even better, the 2km **Playa de Casablanca** beyond Playa de la Fontanilla.

Activities

Marbella is a fun place in which to holiday and offers a whole manner of well-organised activities. **H₂O Diving** (☎ 952 77 82 49, 60 936 00 45; Paseo Marítimo; ☼ 10am-2pm & 5-8pm Apr-Sep) runs official PADI diving courses (€420) as well as a host of other activities such as water skiing, boat charters and some exhilarating kite surfing (depends on wind conditions). Call ahead to arrange activities out of the summer season.

The watery Parque de la Represa in the northeast of the old town has a nice play area for young children. It also has the charming **Museo Bonsai** (☎ 952 86 29 26; adult/child €3/1.50; ☼ 10am-1.30pm & 4.30-7.30pm), devoted to the Japanese miniature-tree art.

Festivals & Events

Feria de San Bernabé (11 June) A spectacular week-long celebration commemorating the patron saint of Marbella.

Castillo de Cante Flamenco (August) Commencing on the first or second Saturday of August, this festival takes place in Ojén, 10km northwest of the town, and is a good opportunity to see some big flamenco names.

Sleeping

BUDGET

The high demand for accommodation in Marbella has not led to the opening of charming B&Bs and small hotels. Instead, the choice ranges from some basic old-town *hostales* to super-deluxe monsters gobbling up the seafront.

Hostal del Pilar (☎ 952829936; hostal@marbella-scene .com; Calle Mesoncillo 4; d €40) A popular and friendly British-run place off Calle Peral. Prices depend on the season, and there's a bar with a pool table; a roof terrace for sunbathing and a log fire for the cooler months.

Hostal Berlin (☎ 952 82 13 10; fax 952 82 66 77; Calle San Ramón; s/d/tr €35/45/60; 🐱 🖳) An extremely friendly *hostal* with good facilities, close to the beach. There is a cafe-bar that also serves breakfast for €2.50 and the super-helpful owner will even collect you from the bus station miles away at the top of town. For stays over four days discounts are negotiable.

Albergue Juvenil Marbella (☎ 952 77 14 91; fax 952 86 32 27; Calle Trapiche 2; dm under/over 26 €14/18.40, d €25.70) Marbella's huge modern hostel has about 140 beds in rooms that hold one to four people (half have bathrooms). It is by far the cheapest place to stay in town and is fairly central.

Calle San Ramón and the parallel Calle San Cristóbal are full of small *hostales* that offer suitable budget accommodation. Another good spot is the delightful **Hostal La Luna** (☎ 952 82 57 78; Calle La Luna 7; d €52) where balconied rooms (with fans) overlook an internal patio.

MID-RANGE

Above the *hostal* bracket you'll normally pay €70 or more for a double in summer.

Town House (☎ 952 90 17 91; www.townhouse .nu; Calle Alderete 7; d low/high €95/120; 🐱) A superb, intimate hotel done out in uber-chic furnishings, and a snip at the price. A traditional town house its nine rooms are arranged over four floors and there is a fabulous roof terrace to chill out on. Book early, for style at the right price.

Hotel La Morada Mas Hermosa (☎ 952 92 44 67; www.lamoradamashermosa.com; Calle Montenebros 16A; s/d €68/85; 🐱) A small, character-filled hotel in Marbella's old town. Quaintly decorated with wrought-iron beds and white linen, the hotel's five double rooms are in major demand (even off-season), so advance bookings are recommended.

Hotel San Cristóbal (☎ 952 77 12 50; www.hotel sancristobal.com; Avenida Ramón y Cajal 3; s/d €58/90; 🐱) This is one of the less pricey of the upmarket hotels but with all the requisite facilities; you'll probably be better off with a room at the back or side, away from the noisy avenue.

Hotel Linda Marbella (☎ 952 85 71 71; linda marbellasl@terra.es; Calle Ancha 21; s/d €50/80; 🐱) This reliable, centrally located hotel has basic rooms – the aqua and peach paint job takes some getting used to.

TOP END

Princesa Playa Hotel (☎ 902 11 77 51; www.princesa playa.com; Avenida Duque de Ahumada s/n; studios €82/127, apt low/high season €94/160; 🅿 🐱 🖳) With great sea views, this aparthotel (hotel with apartments rather than rooms) represents great value for money on the seafront.

Hotel El Fuerte (☎ 952 86 15 00; www.hotel-el fuerte.es; Avenida El Fuerte s/n; d low/high season €125/170; 🅿 🐱 🖳) A huge 263-room complex with a whole host of facilities including a gym, gardens, tennis courts and sauna. There's also access to the beach. Many of the rooms have sea views, for which you will pay a premium price.

Marbella Club Hotel (☎ 952 82 22 11; www.marbella club.com; Carretera de Cádiz 178; d low/high season €250/425; 🅿 🐱 🖳) This was one of the original super-deluxe and super-discreet hotels that spearheaded the luxury tourism boom. Situated to the west of Marbella in its own gorgeous gardens, the club has every conceivable luxe facility, plus a beautifully landscaped golf course (green fee €110). Some facilities are adapted for wheelchair users.

Eating

Dining in Marbella doesn't necessarily mean chichi interiors and bikini-size portions. There are some authentic tapas bars and a few trendy restaurants that do delicious, good-value cuisine.

Restaurant Sémon (☎ 952 77 77 96; Calle Gregorio Marañón s/n; buffet €20; 10.30am-4pm) A fantastic Catalan delicatessen-cum-restaurant, and a good place for lunch. The buffet is delicious, but if you can't stretch that far this is also a great place for a late-morning coffee accompanied by a tasty selection of handmade biscuits or cakes. It is popular so reservations in the summer are essential.

La Tricicleta (☎ 952 85 76 86; Calle San Lázaro; mains €14-20; 7.30pm-midnight Mon-Sat Feb-Dec) Located in an alley, La Tricicleta has a rustic downstairs dining area and a showy roof terrace. Dine on duck breast with a five-pepper sauce flambéed with Jerez brandy and you'll see why this eatery is a cracking choice. It is also a good place for vegetarians.

La Comedia (☎ 952 77 64 78; Calle San Lázaro; mains €15-25; 7.30pm-midnight Tue-Sun) A hip place run by a Swedish duo. The minimal décor and international menu have earned it positive reviews and a faithful following.

Gaspar (☎ 952 77 00 78; Calle Notario Luis Oliver 19; mains €20) A good-value, family-run restaurant just off the seafront. Food ranges from *raciones* to full-blown meals. The restaurant also has a quaint small library and a comprehensive wine list.

Restaurante Santiago (☎ 952 77 00 78; Paseo Marítimo 5; 2-course meal €25) One of Marbella's well-established quality restaurants situated on the seafront, offering gourmet seafood dishes in elegant surrounds. Sit on the terrace and survey the palms on Playa de Venus.

Puerta del Príncipe (☎ 952 77 49 64; Plaza de la Victoria; mains €10-25; 10.30am-1.30pm) This successful chain restaurant is always packed on account of its good-value steak menu. If the huge stuffed bull in the entrance doesn't call forth the vegetarian in you, then go for the sizzling Chateaubriand (for two), which is finished off at your table on a steaming-hot clay plate.

La Pesquera (☎ 952 77 53 02; Plaza de la Victoria; mains €10-35; 10.30am-1.30pm) The fish-fancier's version of the steakhouse next door.

El Gallo (☎ 952 82 79 98; Calle Lobatos 44; mains €4-8; 1-4.30pm & 7-11pm Wed-Mon) Situated in the picturesque streets of old Marbella, El Gallo is a real local adventure. Come here for traditional Andalucian food – fish dishes are delicious.

Café Bar El Estrecho (Calle San Lázaro 12; tapas €1.10), **El Estanco** (☎ 952 92 40 11; Calle Buitrago 24; tapas/raciones €1.50/8) and **Bar Botolo** (☎ 952 82 69 50; Calle San Lázaro; tapas €1.80) are three good spots for varied tapas and strong, viscous coffee. If they're busy, just elbow your way in.

The seafront Paseo Marítimo is lined with restaurants. Playa de Venus also has a throng of eateries on the sand. If you can cope with the skinny bronzed bodies then head for **Palms** (salads from €6), or **La Tasquita** (mains €8-10), which serves fried and grilled seafood.

Drinking

Marbella's notorious Puerto Deportivo, the site of many a drinking den, was due to reopen in late 2004 after large-scale renovations. Alternatively, Calle Pantaleón in the old town has a string of *cervecerías* (beer bars). Posey drinkers head for Calle Camilo José Cela and Calle Gregorio Marañón.

El Encuadernador (☎ 952 86 58 92; Calle San Lázaro 3) Tucked away in the narrowest alley in the old town, the Encuadernador, meaning 'The Bookbinder', fosters a loyal following with its authentic beer-den feel. It is a good place to start the evening with a few drinks before nipping across the alley to La Comedia and then onto a club.

La Marejadilla (Calle San Lázaro) Rubbing shoulders with El Encuadernador, this bar is just right for a follow-up round of drinks to keep spirits soaring.

Atrium (☎ 952 82 85 89; Calle Gregorio Marañón 11) Located in an upmarket residential suburb just behind the beach, the somewhat snooty Atrium is the choice of well-heeled *marbellíes* (Marbella locals) who come here for chilled late-night drinks.

Entertainment

The big-name serious clubs cluster around the vanity fair of Puerto Banús – see p255 for information on these.

Tablao Ana María (☎ 952 77 56 46; Plaza Santo Cristo 4/5; admission €19; 8.30-late Tue-Sun Jan-Oct) As far as flamenco goes on the Costa del Sol, Ana María's is a relatively good-value, authentic show run by the veteran star herself. Reservations are essential.

Shopping

If you've come here for sequinned swimwear, you're in luck. The winding streets of the old town are full of glittering, designer-label boutiques, enticing craft shops and fancy antique showrooms. A lively street market takes place on Monday mornings around

MÁLAGA PROVINCE

DANCING QUEEN

Olivia Valere (☎ 95 282 88 61; www.olivia valere.com; Carretera de Istán; admission Sep-Jul/Aug €30/42 ; ☽ midnight-6.30am) If there is a nightclub that epitomises what the hype about Marbella is all about, Olivia Valere is it. Modelled on Granada's Alhambra (p305), the exterior hides an *Arabian Nights'* fantasy of interlinking courtyard dance floors, splashing fountains, gold columns and darkly beautiful bars. Its exclusive restaurant is **Babilonia** (mains €18-30; ☽ 8.30pm-3am), which serves an exquisite international menu. It is hard to overrate the extravagant experience and it should be on everyone's Marbella itinerary.

---

the Estadio Municipal football ground, east of the old town.

Getting There & Away

Buses to Fuengirola (€2.05, one hour), Puerto Banús (€0.95, 20 minutes) and Estepona (€1.85, one hour), leave about every 30 minutes from Avenida Ricardo Soriano. Services from the **bus station** (☎ 952 76 44 00) in the north of town include frequent buses to Málaga (direct €4.30, 45 minutes), and a few a day to Ronda (€4.25, 1½ hours), Ojén (€0.90, 30 minutes), Seville (€13.25, 3¾ hours), Granada (direct €12.35, 2¾ hours), Córdoba (€14.60, five hours), Algeciras (direct €5.30, one hour) and Cádiz (direct €13.80, 2½ hours).

Getting Around

From the bus station, bus No 7 (€0.85) runs to the **Fuengirola/Estepona bus stop** (Avenida Ricardo Soriano) near the town centre. Returning from the centre to the bus station, take No 2 from Avenida Ramón y Cajal (corner Calle Huerta Chica). To walk from the bus station to the centre, cross the bridge over the bypass and carry straight on down Calle de Trapiche, which leads down to the Albergue Juvenil Marbella, then cross Calle Salvador Rueda and continue down Calle Bermeja.

AROUND MARBELLA
Ojén & Around

Eight kilometres north of Marbella, among eucalyptus and citrus groves, the tiny pueblo of **Ojén** is a good place to start exploring the hill country behind the *costa*. The invit-

ing hotel-restaurant **Refugio de Juanar** (☎ 952 88 10 00; www.juanar.com; Sierra Blanca s/n, Ojén; d low/ high season €95/108; **P** ☒ ☒), located 12km north of Marbella off the A355, is a great place to start. This pretty country house nestles amid the chestnut and *pinsapo* trees on the site of the old Larios' hunting lodge. The excellent restaurant specialises in game and is a great spot for lunch before heading out on walking trails. Some facilities are adapted for wheelchair users.

The trails are clearly marked, and the hotel can provide you with a good map. A gentle 3km hike uphill to 3000m will take you to the **mirador** (viewing point), which looks off out over the coast and, on a clear day, as far as Africa. Keen hikers can follow trails back towards Ojén or west to the village of Istán. Afterwards, you may also want to stop off at the **Museo del Vino Málaga** (☎ 952 88 14 53; Calle Carrera 39, Ojén; admission free; ☽ 11am-3pm & 6-10pm Jul-Oct, 11am-8pm Nov-Jun), where you can taste and buy some of Málaga's finest wine in its oldest distillery.

Puerto Banús

The coastal strip west of Marbella is known as **La Milla d'Oro** (the Golden Mile) because of its number of super-luxury properties – including the Marbella Club Hotel (p253) and King Fahd of Saudi Arabia's Mar Mar estate. Along this strip, a mere 7km from Marbella, you will find **Puerto Banús**, one of Spain's first village-style port developments. It has the flashiest marina on the Costa del Sol, attracting huge floating gin palaces. The marina's main entrance has security gates to prevent access by unauthorised cars.

By the control tower at the western end of the harbour – where the swankiest boats tie up – is the **Aquarium de Puerto Banús** (☎ 952 81 87 67; adult/child €4.80/3.60; ☽ 11am-6pm). While open most of the year, it may shut Monday to Friday in winter. As an optional extra, you can take a dive in the aquarium's tanks with rays, lobsters and small sharks.

The western end of the Puerto Banús marina has a few fancy bars: **Salduba Pub** (☎ 952 81 10 92; Calle de Ribera) and **Sinatra Bar** (Calle de Ribera) are two of the most popular.

Dreamer's (☎ 952 81 20 80; www.dreamers-disco.com; Carretera de Cádiz 175, Río Verde), on the eastern outskirts of Puerto Banús, brings house music lovers a taste of paradise. With a mix of tribal house, vocal house, light shows, bongo beats and an ever-changing menu of DJs you'll be hard pushed to find somewhere better to let your hair down.

Estepona

pop 48,000

Estepona has controlled its development relatively carefully and remains a pleasant town with a long seafront promenade overlooking the wide sandy **Playa de la Rada**. The huge, safe sandy beach, clean water and relaxed atmosphere make this an excellent base for families and there is a great play area on the beach for children. The beaches around Estepona are also popular surf spots for beginners.

INFORMATION

The **tourist office** (☎ 952 80 09 13; www.infoestepona.com; Avenida San Lorenzo 1; ☒ 9am-6pm Mon-Fri, 9am-1.30pm Sat) is in the town centre.

SIGHTS & ACTIVITIES

The nearby safari park, **Selwo Aventura** (☎ 952 79 21 50; www.selwo.es; adult/child €18/12; ☒ 10am-6pm Oct-May, 10am-8pm Jun-Sep), 6km east of Estepona, has over 200 exotic animal species. You can tour the park by 4WD or on foot. To get here from Estepona, a taxi is best. A direct daily bus runs from Málaga via Torremolinos, Fuengirola and Marbella (phone Selwo for information).

For adult adventure, the **Happy Divers Club** (☎ 952 88 90 00; www.happy-divers-marbella.com; Atalaya Park Hotel, Carretera de Cádiz) organises week-long sailing and diving packages, while **Adventure-bound Spain** (☎ 952 79 18 57; www.adventurebound spain.com; Apartado de Correo 638) runs some great mountain-biking and trekking excursions.

Behind the beach, Estepona's focal point is the **Plaza de las Flores**, a pretty square lined with cafés reminiscent of the *casco antiguo* in Marbella. A sizable fishing fleet and a large marina share the port beyond the lighthouse at the western end of town, and a lively **fish market** takes place every morning, although it's pretty much over by 7am. The **covered market** (Calle Castillo) is also worth a visit.

SLEEPING & EATING

Centrally located accommodation in Estepona is limited. Except for Hotel El Molino, the following hotels are centrally located.

Hotel El Molino (☎ 952 79 10 85; www.estepona -molino.com; Camino la Lobilla; s/d €53/73.80; **P** ☒) The gorgeous El Molino is an oasis of calm amid the *costa* madness. The hacienda-style house is surrounded by luxuriant plantings and the beach is just down the road. Children are welcome and babysitting can be arranged, which is worth it if you fancy a romantic dinner under the stars (€28). The price includes B&B and some great in-room facilities such as a video and stereo. This is one place on the *costa* you won't be itching to leave.

Hotel Aguamarina (☎ 952 80 61 55; fax 95 280 45 98; Avenida San Lorenzo 32, s/d incl breakfast €54.50/ 76.50; ☒) The recently modernised Aguamarina has comfortable rooms, but the aquamarine paint-job on the exterior is a shock to the system.

Hostal Pilar (☎ 952 80 00 18; pilarhos@anit.es; Plaza de las Flores 22; s/d €25/45; ☒) An old-fashioned, friendly *hostal*, nicely located on the leafy Plaza de las Flores.

Pensión La Malagueña (☎ 952 80 00 11; Calle Castillo 1; s/d €25/49) Just around the corner from the Pilar, La Malagueña also offers comfortable rooms, with fans.

Plaza Las Flores is a student hang-out that's home to a few tapas bars and restaurants. Nightlife focuses on the marina, which has a flush of popular bars including **Christopher Columbus** (☎ 952 80 56 25; Puerto Deportivo).

GETTING THERE & AWAY

The **bus station** (☎ 952 80 02 49; Avenida de España) is 400m west, on the seafront. Buses run to Fuengirola, Torremolinos and Málaga (€5.80, two hours, 11 daily). Buses run every half-hour between 6.40am and 10.30pm to Marbella (€1.85, one hour). There are also services running to Algeciras (€2.95, one hour, 10 daily) and Cádiz (€11.10, 3½ hours, two daily).

THE INTERIOR

The mountainous interior of Málaga province is an area of raw beauty and romantic *pueblos blancos* (white villages) sprinkled across craggy landscapes. Beyond the mountains, the verdant countryside opens out into a wide chequerboard of floodplains. It's all a far cry from the tourist-clogged coast.

RONDA

pop 35,000 / elevation 744m

Perched on an inland plateau riven by the 100m fissure of El Tajo gorge, Ronda has the most dramatic location of all the *pueblos blancos* and gets its name, which means 'surrounded by mountains', from the encircling Serranía de Ronda. Established in the 9th century BC, Ronda is also one of Spain's oldest towns. Its existing old town, La Ciudad (the City), largely dates back to Islamic times, when it was an important cultural centre filled with mosques and palaces. Its wealth as a trading depot made it an attractive prospect for bandits and profiteers and the town has a colourful and romantic past in Spanish folklore.

Ronda was a favourite with the Romantics of the late 19th century, and has attracted an array of international artists and writers, such as David Wilkie, Alexander Dumas, Rainer Maria Rilke, Ernest Hemingway and Orson Welles, who flocked to admire it. Nowadays, Ronda has a lot to live up to, and at just an hour inland from the Costa del Sol it attracts a weight of day-trippers, who nearly double its population in summer. The best time to enjoy the town with some ease is in the honeyed light of evening, or in the early spring and late autumn when the tourist season has lost its sting.

Orientation

La Ciudad stands on the southern side of El Tajo gorge. Following the Reconquista (Christian reconquest) in 1485, new taxes were imposed on La Ciudad that forced the residents to set up the newer town, El Mercadillo (the Market), to the north. Three bridges cross the gorge, the main one being the Puente Nuevo linking Plaza de España with Calle de Armiñán. Both parts of town come to an abrupt end on their western sides with cliffs plunging away to the valley of the Río Guadalevín far below. Places of interest are mainly concentrated in La Ciudad while most places to stay and eat, along with the bus and train stations, are in El Mercadillo.

Information
BOOKSHOPS
Comansur (☎ 952 87 86 67; Calle Lauria 30) Sells 1:50,000 SGE maps of the region.

EMERGENCY
Policía Local (; ☎ 952 87 13 69; Plaza Duquesa de Parcent s/n) The station is located in the *ayuntamiento*.
Policía Nacional (☎ 952 87 10 01; Avenida de Jaén s/n)

INTERNET ACCESS
Central Cibercafé (☎ 952 87 98 39; Calle Los Remedios 26; per 30min €1.50; ☺ 4pm-late) A popular drinking bar and Internet café with six fast computers.

MEDICAL SERVICES
Hospital General Básico (☎ 95 287 15 41; El Burgo Rd) 1km from the town centre, along the El Burgo road.

MONEY
Banks and ATMs are mainly on Calle Virgen de la Paz (opposite the bullring) and Plaza Carmen Abela.

POST
Post office (Calle Virgen de la Paz 18-20; ☺ 9am-8pm Mon-Fri, 9am-2pm Sat)

TOURIST INFORMATION
Municipal tourist office (☎ 952 18 71 19; turismo@ronda-e.com; Paseo de Blas Infante; ☺ 9.30am-6.30pm Mon-Fri, 10am-2pm & 3-6.30pm Sat & Sun) Helpful and friendly staff with a wealth of information on the town and region.
Regional tourist office (☎ 649-965338; www.andalucia.org; Plaza de España 1; ☺ 9am-7pm Mon-Fri, 10am-2pm Sat) Located on the main square.

Sights
LA CIUDAD
Straddling the dramatic gorge and the Río Guadalevín (deep river) is Ronda's most recognisable sight, the towering **Puente Nuevo**, best viewed from the Camino de los Molinos, which runs along the bottom of the gorge. The bridge separates the old and new towns, the former surrounded by massive fortress walls pierced by two ancient gates: the Islamic Puerta de Almocábar, which in the 13th century was the main gateway to the castle; and the 16th-century Puerta de Carlos V. Inside, the Islamic layout remains intact, a maze of narrow streets take their character from the Renaissance mansions of powerful families, whose predecessors accompanied Fernando el Católico in the taking of the city in 1485.

Nearly all of the mansions still bear the crest of each family, as does the **Palacio de Mondragón** (☎ 952 87 84 50; Plaza Mondragón; adult/concession €2/1; ☺ 10am-6pm Mon-Fri, 10am-3pm Sat, Sun & holidays). Built for Abomelic, ruler of Ronda in 1314, the palace retains its internal courtyards and fountains, the most impressive of these being the Patio Mudejar, from which a

RONDA

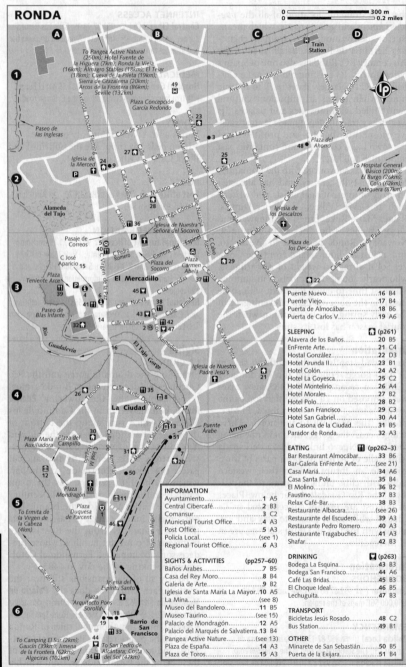

INFORMATION

Ayuntamiento	**1** A5
Central Cibercafé	**2** B3
Comansur	**3** C2
Municipal Tourist Office	**4** A3
Post Office	**5** A3
Policía Local	(see 1)
Regional Tourist Office	**6** A3

SIGHTS & ACTIVITIES (pp257–60)

Baños Árabes	**7** B5
Casa del Rey Moro	**8** B4
Galería de Arte	**9** A5
Iglesia de Santa María La Mayor	**10** A5
La Mina	(see 8)
Museo del Bandolero	**11** B5
Museo Taurino	(see 15)
Palacio de Mondragón	**12** A5
Palacio del Marqués de Salvatierra	**13** B4
Pangea Active Nature	(see 13)
Plaza de España	**14** A5
Plaza de Toros	**15** A3

Puente Nuevo	**16** B4
Puente Viejo	**17** B4
Puerta de Almocábar	**18** B6
Puerta de Carlos V	**19** A6

SLEEPING (p261)

Alavera de los Baños	**20** B5
EnFrente Arte	**21** C4
Hostal González	**22** D3
Hotel Arunda II	**23** B1
Hotel Colón	**24** A2
Hotel La Goyesca	**25** C2
Hotel Montelirio	**26** A4
Hotel Morales	**27** B2
Hotel Polo	**28** B2
Hotel San Francisco	**29** C3
Hotel San Gabriel	**30** A4
La Casona de la Ciudad	**31** B5
Parador de Ronda	**32** A3

EATING (pp262–3)

Bar Restaurant Almocábar	**33** B6
Bar-Galería EnFrente Arte	(see 21)
Casa Mariá	**34** A6
Casa Santa Pola	**35** B4
El Molino	**36** B2
Faustino	**37** B3
Relax Café-Bar	**38** B3
Restaurante Albacara	(see 26)
Restaurante del Escudero	**39** A3
Restaurante Pedro Romero	**40** A3
Restaurante Tragabuches	**41** A3
Shafar	**42** B3

DRINKING (p263)

Bodega La Esquina	**43** B3
Bodega San Francisco	**44** A6
Café Las Bridas	**45** B3
El Choque Ideal	**46** B5
Lechuguita	**47** B3

TRANSPORT

Bicicletas Jesús Rosado	**48** C2
Bus Station	**49** B1

OTHER

Minarete de San Sebastián	**50** B5
Puerta de la Exijara	**51** B4

MÁLAGA PROVINCE

horseshoe arch leads into a cliff-top garden with splendid views.

A minute's walk southeast from the Palacio de Mondragón is the city's original mosque, now the ornate **Iglesia de Santa María La Mayor** (☎ 952 87 22 46; Plaza Duquesa de Parcent; admission €2; 🕑 10am-6pm Nov-Mar, 10am-8pm Apr-Oct). Just inside the church entrance is an arch covered with Arabic inscriptions, which was part of the mosque's mihrab (prayer niche indicating the direction of Mecca). The church has been declared a national monument, and its interior is an orgy of decorative styles and ornamentation. A huge central cedar choirstall divides the church into two sections: aristocrats to the front, everyone else at the back.

Just opposite the church, the amusing **Museo del Bandolero** (☎ 952 87 77 85; Calle de Armiñán 65; admission €2.70; 🕑 10am-6pm Oct-Mar, 10am-8pm Apr-Sep) is dedicated to the banditry for which central Andalucía was once renowned. Old prints reflect that when the youthful *bandoleros* (bandits) were not being shot, hanged or garrotted by the authorities they were stabbing each other in the back, literally as much as figuratively.

Taking the narrow Calle Marqués de Salvatierra will bring you to the small **Puente Viejo** (Old Bridge), with views down onto the river as it rushes into the gorge. Just before you reach it you will pass the **Palacio del Marqués de Salvatierra**, a huge mansion that required the demolition of 42 houses for it to be built. Owned by the descendants of the Marqués de Moctezuma, the Governor of South America, the palace is decorated on its portal with carvings of native American Indians. The palace and all its antiques are sometimes open to the public (ask at the tourist office).

For a more dramatic view of the river and gorge, leave Puente Viejo and head back along Calle Marqués de Salvatierra, turning right up Calle Santo Domingo to the **Casa del Rey Moro** (☎ 952 18 72 00; Calle Santo Domingo 17; adult/child €4/2; 🕑 10am-7pm). Here, terraced gardens give access to **La Mina**, an Islamic stairway of over 300 steps that are cut into the rock all the way down to the river at the bottom of the gorge. These steps enabled Ronda to maintain water supplies when it was under attack. It was also the point where Christian troops forced entry in 1485. The steps are not well-lit and are steep and wet

in places. Care should be taken, even by the fit and able. Also backing on to the river are the almost intact, atmospheric 13th- and 14th-century **Baños Árabes** (Arab Baths; ☎ 952 87 08 18; Hoyo San Miguel; admission €2; 🕑 10am-6pm Mon-Fri, 10am-3pm Sat & Sun).

To walk down into the gorge (a good morning's walk), take the path from Plaza del Campillo. It is steep and long but is well worth the effort, and in springtime the valley below is carpeted in flowers. Further afield is the **Ermita de la Virgen de la Cabeza** (ask at the tourist office for details of this walk).

EL MERCADILLO

Directly across the Puente Nuevo is the main square, **Plaza de España**, made famous by Hemingway in his novel, *For Whom the Bell Tolls*. Chapter 10 tells how early in the Civil War the 'fascists' of a small town were rounded up in the *ayuntamiento* (town hall), clubbed and made to walk the gauntlet between two lines of townspeople before being thrown off the cliff. The infamous scene of this barbarity, the *ayuntamiento*, is now Ronda's Parador (p261).

Nearby, Ronda's elegant **Plaza de Toros** (☎ 952 87 41 32; Calle Virgen de la Paz s/n; admission €5; 🕑 10am-6pm Oct-Mar, 10am-8pm Apr-Sep) is a mecca for bullfighting aficionados. At nearly 200 years of age it is one of the oldest and most revered bullrings in Spain. It has also been the site of some of the most important events in bullfighting history (see the boxed text, p260). Built by Martín Aldehuela, the bullring is universally admired for its soft sandstone hues and galleried arches. At 66m in diameter it is also the largest and, therefore, most dangerous bullring, yet it only seats 5000 spectators – a tiny number compared with the huge 50,000-seater bullring in Mexico. In July the ring is used for a series of fabulous concerts, and opera (ask at the tourist office for details).

The on-site **Museo Taurino**, recently renovated and expanded, is crammed with memorabilia such as blood-spattered costumes worn by Pedro Romero and 1990's star Jesulín de Ubrique. It also includes photos of famous fans such as Orson Welles and Ernest Hemingway, whose novel *Death in the Afternoon*, provides in-depth insight into the fear and tension of the bullring.

Behind the Plaza de Toros, spectacular cliff-top views open out from **Paseo de Blas**

RONDA'S FIGHTING ROMEROS

Ronda can bullishly claim to be the home of bullfighting – and it does. It proudly boasts the equestrian school, known as the Maestranza, where the Spanish aristocracy learned to ride and fight. They did this by challenging bulls in an arena, and thus was born the first bullfight.

Legend has it that one of these fights went awry when a nobleman fell from his horse and risked being gored to death. Without a moment's hesitation local hero, Francisco Romero (b 1698), leapt into the ring and distracted the bull by waving his hat. By the next generation Francisco's son, Juan, had added the *cuadrilla* (the matador's supporting team), consisting of two to three banderilleros (who work on foot) and two to three picadors (men mounted on horseback with pike poles). This married both the habits of the aristocracy (who previously conducted fights on horseback) and the common, dangerous bullfights which took place during fiestas in the main square of each town.

However, ultimately it was the famous Pedro Romero (1754–1839), whose distinguished career saw the death of over 5,000 bulls, who invented the rules and graceful balletlike movements of the modern bullfight, still known as the Escuela Rondeña (Ronda School). In particular he introduced the use of the *muleta* (a variation on his grandfather's hat), a red cape used to attract the bull's attention.

More recently, in 1932, Ronda also gave birth to Spain's greatest bullfighter, the charismatic Antonio Ordóñez, who made his debut at 19 in Madrid's Las Ventas and who was later immortalised by Hemingway in *The Dangerous Summer*.

It was the Ordóñez family that inaugurated the *Goyesca* corrida, held each year in early September in honour of Pedro Romero, and which attracts Spain's best matadors. During the bullfights, the matadors wear the stiff, ornate 19th-century costume which Goya depicted in his paintings of Romero. Out of the three days of fights the most popular is on Saturday, for which you will need to book tickets at least two months in advance. Tickets range in price from €65 *sol* (sun) to €110 *sombra* (shadow).

Infante and the leafy **Alameda del Tajo** park nearby. The park has a good play area for younger children.

BARRIO DE SAN FRANCISCO

Outside La Ciudad's city walls is the **Barrio de San Francisco**, the original Muslim cemetery of the city. A small market was established here in the 15th century, when traders refused to enter the city in order to avoid paying hefty taxes. Some inns and taverns were built and thus began a new quarter. The barrio still has a reputation for down-to-earth tapas bars.

Activities

Ronda is a hub for outdoor activities, and many villa rentals offer a host of on-sight activities (see the boxed text on p262). In Ronda itself, the activity company **Pangea Active Nature** (☎ 952 87 34 96; www.pangea-ronda .com; Calle Dolores Ibarruri 4) offers a range of activities from guided hikes, mountain biking, kayaking and multi-adventure circuits to 4WD expeditions. Excursions range from one-day caving (per person €69), to five days' hiking (per person €495) or seven days' biking (per person €695) with prices

including half-board accommodation. For good guided horse treks contact **Almagro Stables** (☎ 952 18 40 53, 660-458890; Calle Nacimiento 38, Montecorto). Two-hour treks cost €35, or €60 for half a day with a picnic lunch.

Ronda has traditionally been a haven for artists and that is no less true today than it was in the past. A good place for art courses is **Galería de Arte** (☎ 952 19 04 90; www.ronda-art .com; Calle Pozo 11). It is also a great place to purchase the work of contemporary local artists and both Monica and Andrew, who run the gallery, are happy to fill you in on any background information or to arrange the shipping of pieces back home.

Tours

For a lively and engaging guided tour of Ronda, contact the bubbly **Teresa Montero Verdú** (☎ 952 87 21 02, 609-879406), locally born and full of enthusiastically delivered information. A day tour for two people costs €80.

Festivals & Events

Corpus Cristi (Thursday after Trinity) There are bullfights and festivities after the 900kg Station of the Cross is carried 6km through the town.

Feria de Pedro Romero (first two weeks of September) An orgy of partying, including the important flamenco Festival de Cante Grande. Culminates in the Corridas Goyesca (bullfights in honour of legendary bullfighter Pedro Romero – see p260).

Sleeping
BUDGET
Ronda has some of the best character-filled accommodation in the province.

Hotel San Francisco (☎ /fax 952 87 32 99; Calle María Cabrera 18; s/d €25/45; ✱) Possibly the best budget option in Ronda, offering a warm welcome. The *hostal* has recently been refurbished and upgraded to a hotel with facilities to match. The price also includes breakfast.

Hotel Morales (☎ 952 87 15 38; fax 952 18 70 02; Calle de Sevilla 51; s/d €21/39; ✱) A friendly, small hotel with 18 pleasant rooms. Its walls are decked with maps of the area, it has a room for bicycles, and the staff are full of information on the town and nearby natural parks.

Hotel Colón (☎ 952 87 43 78; hotelcolon@ronda .net; Calle Pozo; s/d €34.50/43; ✱) A good budget option with spick-and-span rooms. Ask for a room with a roof terrace.

Hostal González (☎ 952 87 14 45; Calle San Vicente de Paúl 3; s/d €10/16) A really good-value *hostal* with six double bedrooms and shared bathrooms. It is run by a friendly old couple and has been recommended by LP readers.

Hotel Arunda II (☎ 952 87 25 19; Calle José María Castelló Madrid 10; s/d €25/43; P ✱) Convenient for both the bus and the train station, the Arunda offers good rooms and the major bonus of parking in its own garage. Price includes breakfast and taxes.

MID-RANGE
Hotel San Gabriel (☎ 952 19 03 92; www.hotelsan gabriel.com; Calle José M Holgado 19; s/d 68/82; ✱) A charming, historic hotel filled with antiques and photographs that offer an insight into Ronda's history – bullfighting, celebrities and all. Ferns hang down the huge mahogany staircase, there is a billiard room, a cosy living room stacked with books and a super cinema with 10 velvet-covered seats rescued from Ronda's theatre. Members of the Pérez family run the hotel and are delightful and discreet hosts.

Alavera de los Baños (☎ 952 87 91 43; www.andalucia .com/alavera; Hoyo San Miguel s/n; s/d €50/85; ✱ ⎙) Taking its cue from the Arab baths next door the Alavera de los Baños continues the Hispano-Islamic theme throughout, with oriental décor and tasty north African–inspired cuisine (much of it excellent vegetarian food). Ask for a room on the terrace, as they open out onto a small, lush garden.

Hotel Polo (☎ 952 87 24 47; hpolo@ronda.net; Calle Mariano Soubirón 8; s/d 50/80; P ✱) A charming family-run hotel in a graceful 19th-century building. Inside all is light and airy, with elegant high-ceilinged rooms, many with balconied French windows, and attractively furnished communal areas such as the colonial style lounge. A hearty Spanish menu and much needed parking are added bonuses.

Hotel La Goyesca (☎ 952 19 00 49; www.ronda .net/usuar/hotelgoyesca; Calle Infantes 39; s/d €48/67.50) A small hotel arranged around a flowery, geranium-filled courtyard. The owners do their utmost to make you feel at home, creating at atmosphere of tranquillity in the midst of a very busy town.

EnFrente Arte (☎ 952 87 90 88; www.enfrentearte .com; Calle Real 40; s/d €45/90; ✱ ⎙ ⎙) EnFrente offers a huge range of facilities and funky modern décor. A bar, recreation room, pool, flowery patio, sauna, film room and fantastic views out to the Parque Natural Sierra de la Nieves makes this a great new addition to the scene. What's more, the price of your room includes all drinks, breakfast and a buffet lunch.

La Casona de la Ciudad (☎ 952 87 95 95; www .lacasonadelaciudad.com; Calle Marqués de Salvatierra 5; d €91; P ✱ ⎙ ⎙) Another handsome old-town hotel, full of fine antique furnishings and paintings. It has large, beautifully decorated rooms and a good range of facilities.

TOP END
Hotel Montelirio (☎ 952 87 38 55; www.hotelmontelirio .com; Calle Tenorio 8; s/d €100/150; ✱ ⎙) Hugging El Tajo gorge, the new Montelirio has magical views. The converted *palacio* (palace) has been sensitively refurbished, with sumptuous suites. The lounge retains its gorgeous Mudejar ceiling and opens out onto a terrace complete with plunge pool. There is also a fantastic restaurant (see p262).

Parador de Ronda (☎ 952 87 75 00; ronda@parador .es; Plaza de España s/n; s/d €96/120; P ✱ ⎙ ⎙) Also on the gorge, although set back behind a wide terrace, the Ronda Parador is another luxurious option with well-appointed rooms and excellent services.

MÁLAGA PROVINCE

RURAL RONDA

The beautiful countryside surrounding Ronda has attracted a large number of enterprising individuals who have converted traditional houses into gorgeous rural accommodation. If you have your own car it is most certainly worth staying in one of these *cortijos* (country properties) that often offer a host of extras such as guided walks, horse riding and traditional cuisine. The regional website, **www.serraniaronda.org**, has information on rural accommodation, or you could try **www.rusticblue.com**. We recommend the following places:

First up, the Condé Nast *Traveller* favourite, **Hotel Fuente de la Higuera** (☎ 952 11 43 55; www .hotellafuente.com; Partido de los Frontones, Ronda; d/deluxe site €135/260; P 🔀 🔊), a chic colonial villa, with a contemporary interior, that overlooks vast olive groves. Some facilities are adapted for wheelchair users.

Walking and riding enthusiasts can't do any better than at **El Tejar** (☎ 952 18 40 53; eltejar@mercuryin .es; Calle Nacimiento 38, Montecorto; Oct-Apr d €65, May-Sep whole house per week €720; P 🔀 🔊). Here, experienced walker Guy Hunter-Watts, author of *Walking in Andalucía*, can expertly guide you through the surrounding countryside, while his partner Emma supervises horse treks for Almagro Stables. During summer you have to book the whole place.

For sheer indulgence, cosmopolitan atmosphere and out of this world views, opt for **El Nobo** (☎ 952 15 13 03; www.elnobo.co.uk; Apartado 46, Gaucín; d €115, 4-person villa per week €1400; P 🔀 🔊) or **Hotel Casablanca** (☎ /fax 952 15 10 19; Calle Teodoro de Molina 12, Gaucín; s/d €48/96; P 🔀 🔊), both of which offer day trips to Tangiers.

A truly gourmet indulgence can be found at the welcoming and convivial **La Almuña** (☎ 952 15 12 00; fax 95 215 13 43; Apartado 20, Gaucín; s/d €55/110; P 🔀 🔊), which serves up local, home-grown produce.

Eating

Typical Ronda food is hearty mountain fare, with an emphasis on stews (called *cocido*, *estofado* or *cazuela*), *trucha* (trout), game such as *conejo* (rabbit), *perdiz* (partridge), *codorniz* (quail) and *toro* (oxtail).

Restaurante Albacara (☎ 952 16 11 84; Calle Tenorio 8; mains €25-30) Probably Ronda's best restaurant, the new Albacara is situated in the old stables of the Montelirio house and teeters on the edge of the gorge. It serves up a sumptuous menu and has an extensive wine list.

Restaurante Tragabuches (☎ 952 19 02 91; Calle José Aparicio 1; mains €15-20; 🕑 1.30-3.30pm Tue-Sun, 8-10.30pm Tue-Sat) A complete change from the ubiquitous 'rustic' restaurant, Tragabuches is modern and sleek with an innovative menu to match. Michelin-starred in 1998, chef Daniel García continues to send out *cocina creativa*, such pork trotters with squid and sunflower seeds.

Bar Restaurant Almocábar (☎ 952 87 59 77; Calle Ruedo Alameda 5; mains €6-14; 🕑 1.30-5pm & 8pm-1am Wed-Mon) Located in the Barrio San Francisco, Almocábar is an excellent authentic tapas bar, little touched by the tourist hordes at the top of town. In the evening you will be hard pressed to get in, such is its reputation. Reservations are recommended

for the restaurant but you can just drop in to the good and popular bar.

Casa Santa Pola (☎ 952 87 92 08; Calle Santo Domingo 3; menú/mains €15/30) An atmospheric restaurant over three floors of an old aristocratic house. At night each of the small dining rooms is intimate and candlelit and during the day there are good views over the Tajo. The roast lamb cutlets are a must and on Friday and Saturday evening there is also flamenco.

Restaurante del Escudero (☎ 952 87 13 67; Paseo de Blas Infante 1; menú €15; 🕑 1.30-3.30pm Tue-Sun, 8-10.30pm Tue-Sat) This is Tragabuches' sister restaurant, situated in an attractive garden near the Plaza de Toros. A good menú and more-reasonable prices than Tragabuches; the garden makes it popular in the summer.

Restaurante Pedro Romero (☎ 952 87 11 10; Calle Virgen de la Paz 18; mains €9-15) Found opposite the bullring, this celebrated eatery dedicated to bullfighting turns out classic *rondeño* dishes (dishes from Ronda). This is the good place to try the *rabo de toro* (oxtail stew).

Casa María (☎ 952 87 62 12; Calle Ruedo Alameda 27; raciones €6-15; 🕑 1-5pm & 7.30pm-1am Tue-Sun) Although it doesn't draw the crowds in quite the same way as the nearby Almocábar, Casa María is still worth the trip to the Barrio. The fresh seafood is great value for money and when things get going there is a wonderfully unpretentious atmosphere.

Relax Café-Bar (☎ 952 87 72 07; Calle Los Remedios 27; pastas & bakes €5.50; ☼ 1-4pm & 8pm-midnight Mon-Fri) An oasis of good vegetarian food in meat-hungry Ronda. It is run by two friendly Englishwomen, who do a terrific range of tasty dishes including salads, soups, Mexican dishes and sandwiches with imaginative fillings.

Shafar (Calle Ermita 2; ☼ 8pm-midnight) A tiny, one-room hole-in-the wall. Shafar serves up tasty takeaway *shwarmas* (grilled meat in bread) for €2. Great for a late night snack after a few drinks (especially the unconventional curry *shwarma*!)

Faustino (☎ 952 19 03 07; Calle Santa Cecilia; raciones €4.50-8; ☼ 11am-1am Tue-Sun) A traditional, boisterous, male-orientated tapas bar in the centre of town. Heavy on meat and machismo.

El Molino (☎ 952 87 52 49; Calle Molino 6; menú €9) Popular for its pizzas, pasta and varied breakfasts including *desayuno americano* (American breakfast) – a gut-busting dish at €7.20. There are also Internet screens upstairs.

Drinking & Entertainment

El Choque Ideal (☎ 952 16 19 18; www.elchoqueideal .com; Espíritu Santo 9; ☼ 9.30am-3am Feb-Oct, 1pm-1am Nov-Jan) A great new café with fantastic views. It puts on a host of events from films out on the terrace to live bands.

A modest nightlife zone centres on Calle Los Remedios with the ever-popular tapas bars of **Bodega La Esquina** (Calle Los Remedios 22), **Lechuguita** (Calle Los Remedios 25) and **Café Las Bridas** (Calle Los Remedios 18), which sometimes puts on live flamenco or rock. **Relax Café-Bar** (☎ 952 87 72 07; Calle Los Remedios 27; ☼ 1-4pm & 8pm-midnight Mon-Fri) also has a good evening atmosphere, as does **Bar-Galería EnFrente Arte** (☎ 952 87 90 88; www.enfrentearte.com; Calle Real 40), which often stages live music. Down in the Barrio San Francisco is the heaving **Bodega San Francisco** (Calle Ruedo Alameda) – if you can squeeze in the door.

Getting There & Away
BUS
The bus station is at Plaza Concepción García Redondo 2. **Comes** (☎ 952 87 19 92) has buses to Arcos de la Frontera (€7, two hours), Jerez de la Frontera (€8.90, three hours) and Cádiz (€11.80, two hours) up to five times daily; Gaucín, Jimena de la Frontera and Algeciras

(€8, 1½ hours, one daily). **Los Amarillos** (☎ 952 18 70 61) goes to Seville (€8.40, 2½ hours, five daily) via Algodonales; Grazalema (€1.95, 35 minutes, two daily); and Málaga (€7.90, two hours, four daily), via Ardales. **Portillo** (☎ 952 87 22 62) runs to Málaga (€7.85, 1½ hours, four daily), via San Pedro de Alcántara and Marbella.

TRAIN
Ronda's **train station** (☎ 952 87 16 73; Avenida de Andalucía) is on the scenic line between Bobadilla and Algeciras. Trains run to Algeciras (€5.85, direct €15.50, 1¾ hours, six daily) via Gaucín and Jimena de la Frontera. This train ride is incredibly scenic and worth taking just for the views. Other trains depart for Granada (€10.50, three hours, three daily) via Antequera; Málaga (€7.90, 1½ to two hours, one daily Monday to Saturday); Córdoba (€16 to €20.50, 2½ hours, two daily); and Madrid (by day €49.50, 4½ hours; overnight €32, nine hours). For Seville change at Bobadilla or Antequera.

Getting Around
BICYCLE
For bicycle rental, **Bicicletas Jesús Rosado** (☎ /fax 95 287 02 21, ☎ 637-457756; jrosado@ronda.net; 87 Plaza del Ahorro 1) rents out well-equipped mountain bikes for €2.40 an hour or €9 a day.

BUS
It's less than 1km from the train station to most accommodation. Every 30 minutes, town minibuses run to Plaza de España from Avenida Martínez Astein (across the road from the train station), but it's not too far to walk to the centre of town.

CAR & MOTORCYCLE
Parking in Ronda is, inevitably, difficult. There are a number of underground car parks and some hotels have parking deals for guests. Parking charges are about €1 per hour, €12 for 12 to 24 hours. Taxis are found in Plaza Carmen Abela.

AROUND RONDA
Serranía de Ronda
Curving around the south and southeast of the town, the **Serranía de Ronda** may not be the highest or deepest or most dramatic mountain range in Andalucía, but it's certainly among the prettiest. Any of the roads

through them between Ronda and southern Cádiz province, Gibraltar or the Costa del Sol, makes a picturesque route. **Cortés de la Frontera**, overlooking the Guadiaro valley, and **Gaucín**, looking across the Genal valley to the Sierra Crestellina, are among the most beautiful spots to stop.

To the west of the Serranía de Ronda stretches the wilder **Sierra de Grazalema** (p192) and **Los Alcornocales** (p211) natural parks. There are plenty of walking and cycling possibilities and Ronda's tourist office can provide details of these as well as maps.

Ronda la Vieja

To the north (located off the A376) is the relatively undisturbed site of **Acinipo** at **Ronda la Vieja** (☎ 630-429949; admission free; ☽ 10am-5pm or 6pm Tue-Sun), with its partially reconstructed theatre. Although completely ruinous, with the exception of the theatre, it is a wonderfully wild site with fantastic views of the surrounding countryside and you can happily while away a few hours wandering through the fallen stones trying to guess the location of various baths and forums.

Cueva de la Pileta

Twenty kilometres southwest of Ronda la Vieja are some of Andalucía's most ancient caves, the **Cueva de la Pileta** (☎ 952 16 73 43; adult/child/student €6.50/2.50/3; hourly tours ☽ 10am-1pm & 4-6pm, call for details). The guided tour by candlelight into the dark belly of the cave reveals Palaeolithic paintings of horses, goats and fish from 20,000 to 25,000 years ago. Beautiful stalactites and stalagmites add to the effect. The guided tour is given by a member of the Bullón family who discovered the paintings in 1905 (the family speaks some English). The maximum group size is 25, so if you come on a busy day you may have to wait for a place.

Benaoján village is the nearest that you can get to the Cueva de la Pileta by public transport. There is only one place to stay in Benaoján, but it is the beautiful converted water mill of **Molino del Santo** (☎ 952 16 71 51; www.molinodelsanto.com; Barriada Estación s/n; d B&B/half-board €76/99; ☽ mid-Feb–mid-Nov), which also puts on a fantastic lunch menu.

The caves are 4km south of Benaoján, about 250m off the Benaoján-Cortes de la Frontera road – there is no transport to the caves, only a bus to Benaoján, so you will

need your own car to get here. The turn-off is signposted. Benaoján is served by two Los Amarillos buses (from Monday to Friday) and up to four daily trains to/from Ronda. Walking trails link Benaoján with Ronda and villages in the Guadiaro valley.

Parque Natural Sierra de las Nieves

Southeast of Ronda lies the 180-sq-km **Parque Natural Sierra de las Nieves**, noted for its rare Spanish fir, the *pinsapo*, and fauna including some 1000 ibex and various species of eagle. The *nieve* (snow) after which the mountains are named usually falls between January and March. El Burgo, a remote but attractive village 10km north of Yunquera on the A366, makes a good base for visiting the east and northeast of the park. Information is available from Yunquera's **tourist office** (☎ 952 48 25 01; Calle del Pozo 17; ☽ 8am-3pm Tue-Fri), or the **ayuntamiento** (☎ 952 16 00 02) in El Burgo.

Camping Conejeras (☎ 619-180012; 1 person, tent & car €7.25; ☽ Oct-Jun, Sat & Sun Jul-Sep), 800m off the A376 on the road to Los Quejigales, and **Camping Pinsapo Azul** (☎ 952 48 27 54; Yunquera 29410; 1 person, tent & car €7.80; ☽ Apr-Oct; ☒) at Yunquera are both pleasant sites. In El Burgo the delightful small hotel **Posada del Canónigo** (☎ 952 16 01 85; Calle Mesones 24; s/d €37.30/52) is housed in a restored mansion with its own good restaurant. The management can help with walking routes and can organise horse riding.

DETOUR: TORRECILLA

The most rewarding walk in the Sierra de las Nieves is the ascent of **Torrecilla** (1919m), the highest peak in western Andalucía. Start at 'Área Recreativa Los Quejigales', which is 10km east by unpaved road from the A376 Ronda–San Pedro de Alcántara road. The turn-off, 12km from Ronda, is marked by 'Parque Natural Sierra de las Nieves' signs. From Los Quejigales you have a steepish 470m ascent by the **Cañada de los Cuernos** gully, with its tranquil Spanish fir woods, to the high pass of **Puerto de los Pilones**. After a fairly level section, the final steep 230m to the summit rewards you with marvellous views. The walk takes about five hours in total. The IGN/Junta de Andalucía *Parque Natural Sierra de las Nieves* map (1:50,000) shows the relevant path and other hikes.

Festival-goers (p406)

ROBIN CHAPMAN

GERRY REILLY

Flamenco dancer, Noche del Vino (Night of
the Wine; p271), Cómpeta, Málaga province

Whitewashed house, Málaga province (p229)

DAVID TOMLINSON

ANDERS BLOMQVIST

Rock climbing, El Chorro Gorge (p265), Málaga province

JEFF GREENBERG

Fishing boats, Benalmádena (p245), Costa del Sol, Málaga province

Marina, Puerto Banús (p255), Costa del Sol, Málaga province

NEIL SETC

To tap into the new wave of spiritual tourism in beautiful surroundings, check into the converted mill of **Molino del Rey** (☎ 952 48 00 09; www.molinodelrey.info/ihome.htm; Valle de Jorox, E-29567, Alozaina; 1-week course per person €640; **P** **☻**), where teachers from London's popular Triyoga centre bring their groups for hatha and ashtanga yoga. The mill overlooks the Sierra de las Nieves park and features a yoga room, meditation caves and a good vegetarian restaurant.

Buses between Málaga and Ronda (€7.50, 2½ hours, two to three daily) through Yunquera and El Burgo are run by **Sierra de las Nieves** (☎ 952 87 54 35).

ARDALES & EL CHORRO

Ardales pop 2700 / elevation 450m
El Chorro pop 100 / elevation 200m

Fifty kilometres northwest of Málaga, the Río Guadalhorce carves its way through the awesome Garganta del Chorro (El Chorro Gorge). Also called the Desfiladero de los Gaitanes, the gorge is about 4km long, as much as 400m deep, and sometimes just 10m wide. Its sometimes sheer walls, and other rock faces nearby, are the biggest magnet for rock climbers in Andalucía, with hundreds of bolted climbs snaking their way up the limestone cliffs.

Along the gorge runs the main railway into Málaga (with the aid of 12 tunnels and six bridges) and a path called the Camino (or Caminito) del Rey (the King's Path), so named because Alfonso XIII walked on it when he opened the Guadalhorce hydroelectric dam in 1921. For long stretches the path becomes a concrete catwalk 100m above the river, clinging to the gorge walls. It has been officially closed since 1992 and, by 2000, gaping holes in its concrete floor had made it impassable for all but skilled rock climbers. You *can* view much of the gorge and the path by walking along the railway.

The pleasant, quiet town of Ardales is the main centre of the area and is a good base for exploring further afield. However, most people aim for the climbing mecca of El Chorro, a tiny settlement in the midst of a spectacular and surreal landscape of soaring limestone crags.

Sights & Activities

Six kilometres from Ardales is the large Parque Ardales camping ground, situated on the picturesque **Embalse del Conde del Guadalhorce** – a huge reservoir that dominates the landscape and is noted for its carp fishing.

In Ardales itself are two small museums largely concerned with the **Cueva de Ardales**, a Palaeolithic cave complex similar to the Cueva de la Pileta. For two-hour guided visits costing €4.80 to the Cueva de Ardales (possible between May and October), contact the **ayuntamiento** (☎ 952 45 80 87) a week or two in advance. The caves contain 60 Palaeolithic paintings and carvings of animals, done between about 18,000 BC and 14,000 BC, and traces of later occupation and burials from about 8000 BC to after 3000 BC.

You can also get information on the caves at the **Museo de la Historia y las Tradiciones** (☎ 952 45 80 46; A357; admission €1.20; ☘ 10.30am-2pm & 5-8pm Tue-Sun), which also has an exhibit of Roman and Islamic artefacts. Adjoining the central Plaza de San Isidro is the **Museo Municipal Cueva de Ardales** (Plaza Ayuntamiento; admission €0.70; ☘ 10.30am-2pm & 4-6pm Tue-Sun Nov-May, 10.30am-2pm & 5-7pm Tue-Sun Jun-Oct), which has copies of the prehistoric rock paintings and carvings.

Most of the activity in the area centres on the thriving hamlet of El Chorro, amid spectacular scenery. **Aventur El Chorro** (☎ 649-249444), near the train station, rents out mountain bikes for about €1.80 per hour and can arrange organised climbs. **Camping El Chorro** (closed for refurbishment at the time of writing) rents out bikes for about the same price as Aventur El Chorro. The best place for organised activities, great company and a host of organised activities is the **Finca La Campana** (see Thrills & Spills, p266).

Nine kilometres east of El Chorro is the Valle de Abdalajís, Andalucía's paragliding capital. Tuition is offered by the **Club-Escuela de Parapente** (☎ 952 48 91 80; Calle Sevilla 4, Valle de Abdalajís).

Sleeping & Eating

Apartamentos La Garganta (☎ 952 49 51 19 inform acion@lagarganta.com; 5-person apt €72; ☻ ☻) The best option actually in El Chorro, this converted flour mill has small apartments and a good restaurant.

Pensión Estación (☎ 952 49 50 04; s/d €21/24) Found at El Chorro station, this *pensión* (guesthouse) has four clean rooms, and Restaurante Estación (also called Bar Isabel), a renowned climbers' gathering spot, serves *platos combinados* (combined plates) from €3.50 to €4.50.

Camping El Chorro (☎ /fax 952 49 52 95; camping per adult/child €3.20/2, tent €1.75-3) Set among eucalyptus trees 350m towards the gorge from the village. It has room for 150 people but was closed for refurbishment at the time of writing. The **Albergue** (adult incl breakfast €9.60) is further along the wooded slopes from Camping El Chorro and is approached by going left at the entrance gate. It has clean and smart rooms.

Parque Ardales (☎ 952 11 24 01; 2 people, tent & car €9, 4-person apt €64) Situated on the banks of the Embalse del Conde del Guadalhorce, the park has a large, appealing, shady camping ground, and apartments.

La Posada del Conde (☎ 952 11 24 11; Pantano del Chorro; s/d €48/64) Situated across the dam from Ardales, the new La Posada has lovely rooms overlooking the reservoir. It also has a very good restaurant that offers varied delicious grilled meats for around €14 to €16.

Pensión Bobastro (☎ 952 45 91 50; Plaza de San Isidro 13; s/d €12/24) In the centre of Ardales, Bobastro has spotless, comfy rooms with shared bathrooms. It's a lot like living with a local extended family.

There is nowhere to eat in El Chorro with the exception of Restaurante Estación and

La Garganta, however, there is a small supermarket in town catering for the camping ground. The restaurants along the reservoir beyond Parque Ardales are popular on the weekends. In Ardales itself there are a handful of places, including the hotel restaurants mentioned previously.

Bar El Casino (Plaza de San Isidro; raciones €4-6) One of the town's main bars – try the delicious *huevos con bechamel* (hard-boiled eggs in béchamel sauce) or *pimientos rellenos de ternera* (veal-stuffed peppers): both are rolled in breadcrumbs then deep-fried.

Bar El Mellizo (Plaza de San Isidro; tapas €0.90) A central and popular meeting place for locals that's always full and has a great atmosphere.

Getting There & Away

Los Amarillos buses run from Málaga to Ronda (€8.40, 14 daily) and vice versa, with four services going via Ardales, but there's no bus service to El Chorro.

Trains run to El Chorro from Málaga (€3.30, 45 minutes, three daily), except on Sunday and holidays. You can also reach El Chorro from Ronda (€4.80, 70 minutes, one daily except Sunday and holidays) or Seville. Only from Ronda (except Friday, Sunday and holidays) do schedules allow a

---

THRILLS & SPILLS

The **Finca La Campana** (☎ /fax 952 11 20 19; www.el-chorro.com; bunks €10, d €24, 2–8-person apt €34-80; 🛏 🐾) just outside El Chorro is more than a great place to stay, it is a club for like-minded adrenalin junkies. It has a cultlike following and is run by experienced climbers Jean-Bernard and Christine Hofer.

The Finca offers a huge range of activities and supervised climbing courses for all levels from beginners through to push-the-grade courses (€40 per person in groups of two or four). Its grouped climb along the Camino del Rey is a real adrenalin rush. The crumbling walkway can only be accessed by a thrilling abseil and the climb then follows the river to El Chorro, with spectacular views all the way. The climb takes about five hours and is worth every penny of the €40.

Not satisfied with the hundreds of climbs around El Chorro, why not try some wild-water kayaking? The wild-water season starts in June and ends in September, throughout which time the **Río Genil**, known locally as Amazonas, is full of swirling water. The grade-two trip covers manoeuvring in running water, taking eddies and crossing the river, and for more advanced levels there is a faster grade-four trip (one-/two-day course €60/100).

Just outside El Chorro, the underground Aguilas cave system provides another opportunity to test nerve and verve. A 70m abseil brings you to a beautiful system of tunnels full of amazing rock formations. The demanding, full-day trip includes diving through two siphons (per person €50).

If your nerves are frayed by this point, rent a mountain bike for €10 (including helmet, repair kit and map) and explore some of the delightful countryside. Or, you could just relax by the pool!

To reach the Finca follow the signs from behind Apartamentos La Garganta in El Chorro. During the climbing season (October to March) the Finca is very busy, so book ahead.

DETOUR: BOBASTRO

Back in the 9th century, the rugged El Chorro area was the redoubt of a kind of Andalucian Robin Hood, Omar ibn Hafsun, who resisted the armies of Córdoba for nearly 40 years from the hill fortress of **Bobastro**. At one stage he controlled territory all the way from Cartagena to the Strait of Gibraltar.

Legend has it that Ibn Hafsun converted to Christianity (thus becoming a Mozarab) and built the **Iglesia Mozárabe** where he was then buried in AD 917. When Bobastro was finally conquered by Córdoba in 927, Ibn Hafsun's remains were taken away for posthumous crucifixion outside Córdoba's *mezquita* (mosque).

Although the small church is now only a ruin, the drive and walk to get to it are delightful. From El Chorro follow the road up the valley from the western side of the dam, and after 3km take the signposted Bobastro turn-off. Nearly 3km up, an 'Iglesia Mozárabe' sign indicates the 500m footpath to the remains of the church. The views are magnificent and you can take refreshments at **Bar La Mesa** (☼ Jun-Sep), a further 2.5km up the road, where you'll get 360-degree views of the surrounding countryside.

round trip in one day. Timetables change from time to time, however.

To reach El Chorro, drivers from Málaga can branch off the A357 onto the A343 Antequera road near Pizarra. About 4km north of Pizarra, turn left for Álora and El Chorro. The road passes narrowly between houses, and you eventually hit a pot-holed road that takes you to El Chorro. Another approach from Málaga is to continue on the A357 to the Ardales junction. Turn right here along the MA444 with the reservoir on your left, then in about 5km turn off right, signed to El Chorro. Also from Ardales, a partly unpaved road leads 20km southwest along the remote Turón valley to El Burgo (see p264).

ANTEQUERA

pop 42,000 / elevation 577m

The sleepy provincial town of Antequera, a mass of red-tiled roofs punctuated by some 30 church spires, hides one of the richest historical legacies in Andalucía.

The area's Neolithic and Bronze Age inhabitants erected some of Europe's largest and oldest dolmens (burial chambers built with huge slabs of rock), around 2500 BC to 1800 BC. Since then, Antequera has had a long and illustrious history spanning the three major influences in the region – Roman, Islamic and Spanish – due to its strategic location. The scattered remains of each of these civilisations are dotted around the town in a rich tapestry of architectural gems, whose highlight is the opulent Spanish Baroque style that gives the town its character. The commercial momentum that contributed to Antequera's importance also led to the town's cultural 'golden age' during the 16th and 17th centuries, when it became a centre for the Spanish humanist movement. Nowadays the civic authorities are working hard to restore and maintain the town's unique historic character.

Orientation

The substantial remains of a hill-top Muslim-built castle, the Alcazaba, dominate the town. Down to the northwest is Plaza de San Sebastián, from which the main street, Calle Infante Don Fernando, runs northwest.

Information

There are plenty of banks and ATMs along Calle Infante Don Fernando.

Antakira (Calle Barrero 20; per hr €1.80; ☼ 10.30am-2pm & 4.30pm-1am Mon-Thu, to 2am Fri, 11am-3pm & 4.30pm-2am Sat, 4.30pm-1am Sun) Internet access.

Hospital General Básico (☎ 952 84 40 01; Calle Infante Fernando 67)

Librería and Papelería (Infante Don Fernando 15) Sells maps and local books.

Municipal tourist office (☎ 952 70 25 05; www.turismoantequera.com; Plaza de San Sebastián 7; ☼ 10am-2pm & 5-8pm Mon-Sat, 10am-2pm Sun) Friendly staff with limited information.

Policía Local (☎ 95 284 20 00; Carretera Málaga s/n)

Policía Nacional (☎ 95 284 12 89; Calle San Bartolomé 8)

Post Office (Calle Nájera 26; ☼ 9am-8pm Mon-Fri, 9am-2pm Sat)

Sights

Favoured by the Granada emirs of Islamic times, Antequera is overlooked by an **Alcazaba**, which gives the best views of the town. The main approach to the hill-top is from Plaza de San Sebastián, up the stepped Cuesta de San Judas and then through an impressive archway, the **Arco de los Gigantes**, built in 1585 and incorporating stones with Roman inscriptions. Not a huge amount remains of the Alcazaba itself, but it has been turned into a pine-scented, terraced garden and you can visit the **Torre del Homenaje** (admission free) – this was closed at the time of writing, so ask at the tourist office for details of re-opening. There are great views from this high ground, especially towards the northeast and the **Peña de los Enamorados** (Rock of the Lovers).

Just below the Alcazaba is the large 16th-century **Colegiata de Santa María la Mayor** (Plaza Santa María; admission free; ☯ 10am-2pm & 4.30-6.30pm Tue-Fri, 10.30am-2pm Sat, 11.30am-2pm Sun). This church-cum-college played an important part in Andalucía's 16th-century humanist movement, and boasts a beautiful Renaissance façade, lovely fluted stone columns inside, and a Mudejar *artesonado* (a ceiling of interlaced beams with decorative insertions). It also plays host to some excellent musical events.

In the town below, the pride of the **Museo Municipal** (Plaza del Coso Viejo; hourly tours €3; ☯ 10am-1.30pm Tue-Sat, 11am-1.30pm Sun) is the elegant and athletic 1.4m bronze statue of a boy, *Efebo*. Discovered on a local farm in the 1950s, it is possibly the finest example of Roman sculpture found in Spain. The museum also displays some pieces from a Roman villa in Antequera, where a superb group of mosaics was discovered in 1998.

The **Museo Conventual de las Descalzas** (Plaza de las Descalzas; compulsory guided tour €2.40; ☯ 10am-1.30pm & 5-6.30pm Tue-Fri, 10am-noon Sat & Sun) in the 17th-century convent of the Carmelitas Descalzas (Barefoot Carmelites), approximately 150m east of the Museo Municipal. It displays highlights of Antequera's rich religious-art heritage. Outstanding works include a painting by Lucas Giordano of St Teresa of Ávila (the 16th-century founder of the Carmelitas Descalzas), a bust of the Dolorosa by Pedro de Mena and a *Virgen de Belén* sculpture by La Roldana.

Only the most jaded would fail to be impressed by the **Iglesia del Carmen** (Plaza del Carmen; admission €1.30; ☯ 10am-2pm & 4-7pm Mon-Sat, 10am-2pm Sun) and its marvellous 18th-century Churrigueresque retable. Carved in red pine (unpainted) by *antequerano* (Antequero local) Antonio Primo, it's spangled with statues of angels by Diego Márquez y Vega,

and saints, popes and bishops by José de Medina.

The **Dolmen de Menga** and the **Dolmen de Viera** (admission free; ☯ 9am-3.30pm Tue, 9am-3pm Wed-Sat, 9.30am-2.30pm Sun), both from around 2500 BC, are a kilometre from the town centre in a small, wooded park beside the road that leads northeast to the A45. Head down Calle Encarnación from the central Plaza de San Sebastián and follow the signs. Prehistoric people of the Copper Age transported dozens of huge slabs from nearby hills to construct these burial chambers. The stone frames were covered with mounds of earth.

The engineering implications for the time are astonishing. Menga, the larger, is 25m long, 4m high and composed of 32 slabs, the largest of which weighs 180 tonnes. In midsummer the sun rising behind the Peña de los Enamorados to the northeast shines directly into the chamber mouth. A third chamber, the **Dolmen del Romeral** (admission free; ☯ 9am-3.30pm Tue, 9am-3pm Wed-Sat, 9.30am-2.30pm Sun), is further out of town. It is of later construction (around 1800 BC) and features much use of small stones for its walls. To get there, continue 2.5km past Menga and Viera through an industrial estate, then turn left following 'Córdoba, Seville' signs. After 500m, turn left at a roundabout and follow 'Dólmen del Romeral' signs for 200m.

Festivals & Events
The **Real Feria de Agosto** (held in mid-August) celebrates the harvest with bullfights, dancing and street parades.

Sleeping
La Posada del Torcal (☎ 952 03 11 77; Villanueva de la Concepcion; d low/high season €120/180; ⓟ ⓧ ⓡ) Outside Antequera close to El Torcal, this fantastic hill-top *cortijo* is surrounded by wonderful panoramic views. It offers luxurious rooms and facilities including tennis courts, riding treks and a pool with a view.

Parador de Antequera (☎ 952 84 02 61; antequera@ parador.es; Paseo García del Olmo s/n; s/d €70/88; ⓟ ⓧ) Located in a quiet area north of the bullring and near the bus station. The Parador is comfortably furnished and set in pleasant gardens with a good view.

Hotel San Sebastián (☎ /fax 952 84 42 39; Plaza de San Sebastián 5; s/d €25/39; ⓧ) Nicely refurbished, and you can't get much more central. The San Sebastián has rather a schizophrenic bar-restaurant downstairs (rustic Spain with game machines and constant pop music) that serves up good fish.

Hotel Colón (☎ 952 84 00 10; www.castelcolon.com; Calle Infante Don Fernando 31; s/d €25/40; P ⊗ ⊡) A rambling place with rooms arranged around a flowery inner courtyard. Prices rise in August, at Easter and at Christmas.

Hotel Castilla (☎ 952 84 30 90; www.hotelcastilla deantequera.com in Spanish; Calle Infante Don Fernando 40; s/d €25/39; ⊗) Adequate, clean rooms with TV. The hotel also has a very lively bar downstairs that's great for tapas.

Hostal Manzanito (☎ 952 84 00 14; Calle Calzada 25; s/d €20.50/28) A friendly place 400m northeast of Plaza de San Sebastián, near the market. It has comfy, ordinary rooms plus a couple of small singles.

Camas El Gallo (☎ 952 84 21 04; Calle Nueva 2; s/d €18/35) A good central option with adequate clean rooms. The downstairs restaurant is also well regarded.

Eating

Local specialities you'll encounter on almost every Antequera menu include *porra antequerana*, a cold dip that's similar to gazpacho (before the water is added); *bienmesabe* (literally 'tastes good to me'), a sponge dessert; and *angelorum*, a dessert incorporating meringue, sponge and egg yolk. Antequera is also one of the world capitals of the breakfast *mollete* (soft bread roll).

Restaurante La Espuela (Calle San Agustín 1; ⊗ 1-4pm & 8-11pm Tue-Sun; mains €6-14) Found in a gorgeous cul-de-sac off Calle Infante Don Fernando, La Espuela offers traditional dishes such as wild boar, venison and oxtail, along with a fine selection of Antequera specialities.

Restaurante La Espuela Plaza (☎ 952 70 30 31; Calle Infante Don Fernando; mains €5-12) A long-established Antequera favourite in the bullring at the northwestern end of Calle Infante Don Fernando. It offers similar fare and prices to La Espuela.

Bar Castilla (☎ 952 84 30 90; Calle Infante Don Fernando 40; platos combinados €4) A very busy and popular bar-cum-restaurant serving good-value tapas and meals. Generous helpings of chicken or pork with chips.

El Angelote (☎ 952 70 34 65; Plaza Cosa Viejo; mains €5-15; ⊗ noon-5pm & 7-11pm Tue-Sun) Located on the attractive Plaza Cosa Viejo (perfect after a visit to the museum), this dark little tapas

bar has a sumptuous meaty menu of Anterqueran dishes.

Getting There & Around

The **bus station** (Calle Sagrado Corazón de Jesús) is 1km north of the centre. **Automóviles Casado** (☎ 952 84 19 57) runs buses to Málaga (€4.55, 50 minutes, 12 daily). **Alsina Graells** (☎ 952 84 13 65) runs buses to Seville (Prado de San Sebastián; €9.90, 2 hours, six daily), Granada (€6.20, 1½ hours, five daily), Córdoba (€7.45, 1½ hours, three daily) and Almería (€16.15, 4½ hours, five daily). For information contact **Antequera bus station** (☎ 952 84 32 26).

The **train station** (☎ 952 84 32 26; Avenida de la Estación) is 1.5km north of the centre. Two to four trains a day run to/from Granada (€5.85 to €6.55, 1½ hours, six daily), Seville (€10.60, 1¾ hours, three daily), and Ronda (€4.95, 1¼ hours, three daily). For Málaga or Córdoba, change at Bobadilla (€1.40, 15 minutes, three daily).

Antequera can be a traffic nightmare and a team of formidable traffic wardens keep a tight grip on things. Buy tickets from them at street-side parking spots, (per hour €0.60). There is underground parking in Calle Diego Ponce north of Plaza de San Sebastián (per hour €1 or 12 to 24 hours €12). Taxis wait half-way along Calle Infante Don Fernando, or you can call ☎ 952 84 10 08.

AROUND ANTEQUERA
Paraje Natural Torcal de Antequera

South of Antequera are the weird and wonderful rock formations of the **Paraje Natural Torcal de Antequera**. A 12-sq-km area of gnarled, serrated and pillared limestone, it formed as a sea bed 150 million years ago and now rises to 1336m (El Torcal). For maps and general information about the park, including an audio-visual presentation on its geology, go to the **Centro de Recepción** (☎ 952 03 13 89; ⊗ 10am-2pm & 3-5pm Nov-May, 10am-2pm & 4-6pm Jun-Oct). Casual visitors are only allowed to follow a single marked walking trail, the 1.5km 'Ruta Verde', which starts and ends near the visitors centre. For more-dramatic views take a guided tour along the restricted 'red' and 'yellow' routes – for these you should ring ahead for a guide or ask at Antequera's tourist office.

To get to here you will need your own car or a taxi (you cannot do a return trip on the bus). From Antequera follow the C3310 towards Villanueva de la Concepción. Twelve kilometres from Antequera a turn uphill to the right leads 4km to the visitors centre. A return taxi costs €18, with one hour at El Torcal. It's best to get the tourist office to arrange a taxi for you.

Laguna de Fuente de Piedra

About 20km northwest of Antequera is the **Laguna de Fuente de Piedra**. When it's not dried up by drought, this is Andalucía's biggest natural lake and one of Europe's two main breeding grounds for the greater flamingo (the other is in the Camargue region of southwest France). After a wet winter as many as 20,000 pairs of flamingos will breed at the lake. The birds arrive in January or February, with the chicks hatching in April and May. The flamingos stay till about August, when the lake, which is rarely more than 1m deep, no longer contains enough water to support them. They share the lake with thousands of other birds of some 170 species.

The **Centro de Información Fuente de Piedra** (☎ 952 11 17 15; ◷ 10am-2pm & 4-6pm) is at the lakeside. It gives advice on the best spots for bird-watching. It also sells a range of good maps and hires binoculars (an essential) at €1.45 for 45 minutes.

Nearby, the well-regarded **Caserío de San Benito** (☎ 952 11 11 03; Carretera Córdoba-Málaga Km 108; mains €5-14; ◷ noon-5pm & 8pm-midnight Tue-Sun) is a good place to stop for a quality lunch. A beautifully converted farmhouse, San Benito is stuffed with antiques and serves up exquisitely prepared traditional dishes.

Buses run between Antequera and Fuente de Piedra village (€0.90, four daily). By car, take the A354 for Seville, then head northwest along the A92 *autovía* (toll-free motorway) until the signed turn-off.

EAST OF MÁLAGA

The coast east of Málaga, sometimes described as the Costa del Sol Oriental, is less developed than the coast west of the city. The suburban sprawl of Málaga extends east into a series of unmemorable and unremarkable seaside towns – Rincón de la Victoria, Torre del Mar, Torrox Costa – which pass in a blur amid huge plastic greenhouses before culminating in the almost wholly British town of Nerja.

The area's main redeeming feature is the rugged region of La Axarquía, an interior of mountainous villages straddling the border of Granada province. The area is full of great walks, which, unlike the northwest of the province around Ronda, remain largely undiscovered. A 406-sq-km area of these mountains was declared the Parque Natural Sierras de Tejeda, Almijara y Alhama in 1999.

LA AXARQUÍA

The Axarquía region is riven by deep valleys lined with terraces and irrigation channels that date back to Islamic rule – nearly all the villages dotted around the olive-, almond- and vine-planted hillsides date from this era. The wild, inaccessible landscapes, especially around the Sierra de Tejeda, made it a stronghold of *bandoleros* who roamed the mountains without fear or favour. Nowadays, its chief attractions include fantastic scenery; pretty white villages; strong, sweet, local wine made from sun-dried grapes; and good walking in spring and autumn.

The 'capital' of La Axarquía, **Vélez Málaga**, 4km north of Torre del Mar, is a busy but unspectacular town, although its restored hilltop castle is worth a look. From Vélez the A335 heads north past the Embalse de la Viñuela reservoir and up through the **Boquete de Zafarraya** (a dramatic cleft in the mountains) towards Granada. One bus a day makes its way over this road between Torre del Mar and Granada, each way.

Some of the most dramatic La Axarquía scenery is up around the highest villages, **Alfarnate** (925m) and **Alfarnatejo** (858m), with towering, rugged crags such as Tajo de Gomer and Tajo de Doña Ana rising to their south.

To sample one of Andalucía's oldest inns, dating from 1690, head north from Alfarnate along the Loja road. Just outside town you will find **Venta de Alfarnate** (☎ 952 75 93 88; Antigua Carretera de Málaga-Granada; mains €7.20-15; ◷ 11am-7pm Tue-Thu & Sun, 11am-midnight Fri & Sat). It displays mementos of past visitors including some of the bandits who used to roam these hills. Foodwise, it's renowned for *huevos a la bestia,* a kind of hill-country mixed grill of fried eggs and assorted pork products (€9).

You can pick up information on La Axarquía at the tourist offices in Málaga, Nerja,

Torre del Mar or Cómpeta. Prospective walkers should ask for the leaflet on walks in the Parque Natural Sierras de Tejeda, Almijara y Alhama. **Rural Andalus** (☎ 952 27 62 29) – see p399 – and the website **Rustic Blue** (www.rusticblue.com) have details of numerous self-catering houses and apartments, covering all budgets.

The best maps for walkers are *Mapa Topográfico de Sierra Tejeda* and *Mapa Topográfico de Sierra Almijara* by Miguel Ángel Torres Delgado, both at 1:25,000. Useful guides include *25 Walks in and around Cómpeta & Canillas de Albaida* by Albert and Dini Kraaijenzank and the Spanish walking guide *Sendas y Caminos por los Campos de la Axarquía* (Interguías Clave).

Comares

pop 1300

Comares sits like a snowdrift atop its lofty hill. You see it for mile after mile before a final twist in an endlessly winding road lands you below the hanging garden of its cliff. From a little car park you can climb steep, winding steps to the village. Look for ceramic footprints underfoot and simply follow them through a web of narrow, twisting lanes past the Iglesia de la Encarnación and eventually to the ruins of Comares' castle and a remarkable summit cemetery. The village has a history of rebellion, having been a stronghold of Omar ibn Hafsun (see p267), but today there is a tangible sense of contented isolation. The views across the Axarquía are stunning.

For accommodation your best bet is **Mirador de la Axarquía** (☎ 952 50 92 09; Calle Encinillas s/n; d €40), in towards the village. It has good-value, studio-style rooms and a friendly bar-restaurant that serves up tasty grills (€6) on its stunning terrace. You could also try **Hotel Atalaya** (☎ 952 50 92 08; Calle Encinillas 4; s/d €24/42) at the entrance to the village. It has a restaurant that serves mainly meat dishes from €4.25 to €9.60.

There are a couple of friendly bars at the heart of the village and the ceramic footprints will lead you eventually to the **Centro de Medicina Natural** (Calle Agua), where there's a little café offering delicious vegetarian snacks (€3 to €6).

On weekdays only a bus leaves Málaga for Comares at 6pm and returns at 7am the next morning (€1.90).

Cómpeta

pop 3200 / elevation 625m

The highest mountains in the area stretch east from the Boquete de Zafarraya. The village of Cómpeta is one of the best bases for a stay in La Axarquía. It has some of the area's best local wine, and the popular **Noche del Vino** (Night of the Wine) on 15 August features a programme of flamenco and Sevillana music and dance in the central Plaza Almijara, and limitless free wine.

At the foot of the central part of the village is a new **tourist office** (☎ 951 51 60 60; Avenida de la Constitución; ☻ 10am-2pm Wed-Sun), with a car park nearby. **Marco Polo** (Calle José Antonio 3), just off Plaza Almijara, sells books in English and several other languages as well as a good selection of maps and Spanish walking guides.

The tourist office has a good selection of information on activities in the area, including horse riding at **Los Caballos del Mosquín** (☎ 608-658108; www.caballos-mosquin.com), which is 2km from Cómpeta, just above the nearby village of Canillas de Albaida. There are also Spanish classes to be had at **Santa Clara Academia de Idiomas** (☎ 952 55 36 66; www.santaclara-idiomas.com; Calle Andalucía 6). Prices are available on the website.

Rooms and houses are available to rent on the website **Cómpeta Direct** (www.competadirect.com) or you could try the delightful **Las Tres Abejas** (☎ 952 55 33 75; www.lastresabejas.com; Calle Panaderos 43; B&B s/d €35/45), about 150m uphill from Plaza Almijara. The main, three-star hotel in Cómpeta is **Hotel Balcón de Cómpeta** (☎ 952 55 35 35; www.hotel-competa.com; Calle San Antonio 75; d low/high season €56.80/63.10; ☒ ☒), which has comfortable rooms with balconies, a good restaurant, bar and a tennis court.

For very good Spanish food don't miss **El Pilón** (Calle Laberinto; mains €9-15) or the excellent **Museo del Vino** (Avenida Constitución; raciones €6), which serves ham, cheese and sausage *raciones* and wine from the barrel. It's also something of an Aladdin's Cave of regional crafts and produce. For good meat grills try next door at **Restaurante Asador Museo del Vino** (Avenida Constitución; mains €6-15). Another excellent restaurant, with views to the distant sea from its terrace, is **Cortijo Paco** (☎ 952 55 36 47; Avenida Canillas 6; mains €9-15).

Three buses run from Málaga to Cómpeta via Torre del Mar.

DETOUR: EL LUCERO

Perhaps the most exhilarating walk in the La Axarquía region is up the dramatically peaked **El Lucero** (1779m). From its summit on a clear day there are stupendous views as far as Granada in one direction and Morocco in the other. This is a full, demanding day's walking, with an ascent of 1150m from Cómpeta: start by climbing left along the track above Cómpeta football pitch. About 1½ hours from Cómpeta you pass below and west of a fire observation hut on the La Mina hill. Four hundred metres past the turning to the hut, turn right through a gap in the rock (which is not signed, but fairly obvious). This path leads in about one hour to **Puerto Blanquillo** (1200m), from which a path climbs 200m to the **Puerto de Cómpeta**.

One kilometre down from the latter pass, past a quarry, the summit path (1½ hours) diverges to the right across a stream bed, marked by a sign board and map. El Lucero is topped by the ruins of a Guardia Civil post that was built after the Civil War to watch for anti-Franco rebels.

It's possible to drive as far up as Puerto Blanquillo on a rough mountain track from Canillas de Albaida, a village 2km northwest of Cómpeta.

NERJA

pop 18,000

Fifty-six kilometres east of Málaga with the Sierra de Tejuda, Almijara and Alhaina rising close behind it, Nerja is older and more charming than the other east-coast towns of Rincón de la Victoria, Torre del Mar and Torre Costa. However, tourism development has pushed it far beyond its old confines. Made famous in the '80s by the TV series *Verano Azul* (Blue Summer), a kind of Spanish *Neighbours*, the town retains a perpetual holiday atmosphere and is increasingly popular with package and independent holiday-makers.

Orientation

Buses stop on the main road at the north edge of the town centre. Just below the bus stop is Plaza Cantarero. From here it is just over 500m to the Balcón de Europa and the tourist office – just head straight down Calle Pintada.

Information

There are plenty of ATMs dotted around the town.

DiGi Iberica (Calle San Miguel 243; per 30min €1; ۞ 10.30am-5.30pm Mon-Fri, 11.15am-6.30pm Sat, 6-10pm Sun) Internet access.

Hospital Comarcal de la Axarquía (☎ 952 54 16 00; Calle El Tomillar, Torre del Mar) There is no hospital in Nerja. The main hospital for the region is in Torre del Mar.

Med Webc@fe (Calle Málaga; per 15min €0.90; ۞ 10am-midnight) Internet access.

Municipal tourist office (☎ 952 52 15 31; www.nerja .org; Puerta del Mar; ۞ 10am-2pm & 5.30-8.30pm Mon-Sat, 10am-2pm Sun) Has plenty of useful leaflets.

Nerja Book Centre (Calle Granada 30) Has second-hand books in English and also stocks videos for rent.

Policía Local (☎ 952 52 15 45; Calle Carmen 1) Located in the *ayuntamiento*.

Post office (Calle Cristo 6; ۞ 9am-8pm Mon-Fri, 9am-2pm Sat) A short distance north of the tourist office.

WH Smiffs (Calle Almirante Ferrandíz) Bookshop, in a small arcade along from the post office.

Sights & Activities

The town centres on the delightful **Balcón de Europa**, a lookout built on the base of an old fort that juts out over the deep, blue water. From the Balcón a walkway, the **Paseo de los Carabineros** (currently closed for safety reasons) winds its way to **Playa Burriana**, Nerja's biggest and best beach.

There are no real sights within Nerja, but there are lively markets on Tuesday and Sunday morning along Calle Almirante Ferrandíz. There is also a host of activities on offer from outlets such as **Club Nautique Nerja** (☎ 952 52 46 54; Avenida Castilla Pérez 2), which runs diving courses (guided dive/Open Water PADI course €40/360), rents out mountain bikes (one day/week €15/75) and scooters (one day/week €27/139) as well as arranging horse treks (two hours €40) and guided walks. You could also try **Scuba Nerja** (☎ 952 52 72 51; Playa Burriana), on the beach, which runs dives for similar prices as Club Nautique Nerja.

Sleeping

For the summer period, rooms in the better hotels tend to be booked at least two months in advance. Nerja has a number of apartments to let; inquire at the tourist office.

NERJA

0 ————— 300 m
0 ————— 0.2 miles

INFORMATION	
DiGi Iberica	1 C1
Med Webc@fe	2 A3
Municipal Tourist Office	3 C3
Nerja Book Centre	4 B2
Policía Local	5 B3
Post Office	6 C3
WH Smiffs	7 C2

SIGHTS & ACTIVITIES	(p272)
Club Nautique Nerja	8 B2

SLEEPING	(pp272–3)
Hostal Alhambra	9 A2
Hostal Lorca	10 C1
Hostal Marazul	11 A3
Hostal Mena	12 B3
Hotel Carabeo	13 C3
Hotel Marissal	14 C2
Hotel Nerja Princess	15 C2
Hotel Plaza Cavana	16 B2

EATING	(p274)
A Taste of India	17 C2
Casa Luque	18 C3
Osteria di Mamma Rosa	19 A2
Restaurant el Puente	20 A1

ENTERTAINMENT	(p274)
Centro Cultural Villa de Nerja	21 B2
Shambles Bar	22 A2

TRANSPORT	
Bus Stop	23 C1
Underground Car Park	24 B3

Hotel Nerja Princess (☎ 952 52 89 86; www.hotel np.com; Calle Los Huertos 46; s/d €61/90; P ⊠ ☒) Located right in the heart of the old town is this excellent small hotel, with the fabulous bonus of a big pool. Balconied rooms look out over the picturesque streets and are well-equipped with all mod-cons and comfortable furnishings.

Hotel Carabeo (☎ 952 52 54 44; www.hotelcarabeo .com; Calle Carabeo 34; d/ste incl breakfast €66/185; P ⊠ ☒) Full of stylish antiques, this small, family-run, seafront hotel is set above manicured terraced gardens. There is also a good restaurant and the pool is on a terrace overlooking the sea.

Hostal Marissal (☎ 952 52 01 99; www.marissal .net; Balcón de Europa; d low/high season €45/60; ⊠) With sea views and looking out over the Balcón de Europa, this lovely new *hostal* has been recommended by LP readers. It offers great value, comfortable rooms and a good restaurant.

Hostal Lorca (☎ 952 52 34 26; hostallorca@teleline .es; Calle Méndez Núñez 20; d €47; ☒) A charming place with comfy, spotless rooms. It's run by a friendly Dutch couple who have lots

of local information, including details of walking routes.

Hotel Plaza Cavana (☎ /fax 952 52 40 00; Plaza Cavana 10; s/d €77/107; P ⊠ ☒) With a *Love Boat* interior of mint greens and peach this is probably the smartest hotel in the centre of town with excellent facilities and much-needed parking space.

Hotel Paraíso del Mar (☎ 952 52 16 21; Calle Prolongación de Carabeo; d low/high season €60/94; P ⊠ ☒) To the east of Nerja along one of the better beaches, Playa Carabeo, the Paraíso del Mar has great sea views and private access to the beach. The hotel also has a range of spa facilities.

Hostal Mena (☎ 952 52 05 41; Calle El Barrio 15; s/d €23/36.50) A short distance west of the tourist office, this *hostal* has immaculate rooms (some with sea views) and a pleasant garden.

In summer, when things get very busy you could also try the pleasant **Hostal Alhambra** (☎ 95 252 21 74; hmarazul@tiscali.es; Calle Antonio Millón 12; s/d €32/44) or **Hostal Marazul** (☎ 952 52 41 91; Avenida del Mediterráneo; d low/high season €40/47; ☒).

Eating

Merendero Ayo (☎ 952 52 12 53; Playa Burriana; mains €5-9) An open-air place at Nerja's best beach, where you can enjoy a plate of paella cooked on the spot in great sizzling pans over an open fire – and you can go back for a free second helping. It is run by Ayo, the man famed for the discovery of the Cueva de Nerja cave complex.

El Ancladero (☎ 952 52 19 55; Playa El Capistrano; mains €7-12) A fantastic restaurant perched on a cliff above a lovely beach. There is a good range of seafood and on Saturday nights it stages flamenco. Worth coming for a lazy afternoon.

Casa Luque (Plaza Cavana 2; mains €10) The attractive and pretentious Casa Luque has a prime position on the picturesque Plaza Cavana. It also has a wonderful panoramic terrace, an elegant haute-Med menu and a lot more character than most Nerja eateries.

A Taste of India (☎ 952 50 00 43; Calle Carabeo 51; mains €10-12) Maybe not the most obvious Spanish choice, but this is a fantastic Goan Indian restaurant that serves delicious coconut curry cooked on the spot.

Osteria di Mamma Rosa (☎ 952 52 12 62; Edificio Corona, Calle Chaparil; mains €8-14) Going strong for 20 years, Mamma Rosa still turns out good local cooking with some delicious starters and home-made desserts.

Restaurant el Puente (Calle Carretera 4; raciones €4) A great place despite being awkwardly placed on the west side of town where the Málaga road crosses a bridge over the Río Chillar. The food makes up for the location, with tapas for €1 and big helpings of everything.

Entertainment

The **Centro Cultural Villa de Nerja** (☎ 952 52 38 63; Calle Granada 45) runs an ambitious annual programme of classical music, theatre, jazz and flamenco, featuring international artists. It also has a film programme of top current releases, in Spanish.

Nightlife is focused on the aptly named Tutti-Frutti Plaza, which is disco-central, and the adjoining Calle Antonio Millón. Just up the road is the self-proclaimed 'Nerja's biggest', the **Shambles Bar** (Calle Antonio Millón) – which is how you may well end up at the end of the night. Things hot up after midnight.

Getting There & Around

Alsina Graells (☎ 952 52 15 04; A7) runs buses to/from Málaga (€3.15, one hour, 17 daily), Almuñécar (€2.10, 30 minutes, eight daily), Almería (€12.50, 2½ hours, five daily) and Granada (€14.25, 1½ hours, three daily). Nerja's streets are very narrow – for drivers who end up in the heart of the town, there is an **underground car park** (1/24hr €0.90/21.60) off Calle La Cruz.

AROUND NERJA

East of Nerja, the coast becomes more rugged and with your own wheels you can head out to some good beaches reached by tracks down from the A7. **Playa de Cantarriján**, just over the border in Granada province, and **Playa del Cañuelo**, immediately before the border, are two of the best, with a couple of summer-only restaurants.

Nerja's really big tourist attraction, the **Cueva de Nerja** (☎ 952 52 95 20; adult/child €5/2.50; ☼ 10am-2pm & 4-6.30pm), lies 3km east just off the A7, and is extremely busy in summer. The enormous 4km-long cave complex, hollowed out by water around five million years ago and once inhabited by Stone Age hunters, is full of spooky stalactites and stalagmites. Don't miss the huge central column in Cataclysm Hall, which, at 32m, is the largest in the world. Every July, Spanish and international ballet and music stars perform in the cave as part of the **Festival Cueva de Nerja**. You need to ask at Nerja tourist office for programme details.

Seven kilometres north of Nerja and linked to it by several buses daily (except Sunday) is the pretty village of **Frigiliana**, some say the prettiest village in La Axarquía. The **tourist office** (☎ 952 53 42 40; www.frigiliana.com; Plaza del Ingenio) runs guided tours (per person €5; at 10.15am and 12.30pm) from outside the office. El Fuerte, the hill that climbs above the village, was the scene of the final bloody defeat of the Moriscos of La Axarquía in their 1569 rebellion, and where they reputedly plunged to their death rather than be killed or captured by the Spanish. You can walk up here if you follow the streets to the top of the town and then continue along the dusty track.

T. ALSINA GRAELLS SUR S.A.
Servicios de:

GRANADA - ALMUÑECAR - T. DEL MAR

SALIDAS DESDE	LMXJVS (LABORABLES)	DIARIO	DIARIO	DIARIO	DIARIO	DIARIO	DIARIO	DIARIO	DIARIO	DIARIO	DIARIO	DIARIO	DIARIO	DIARIO	DIARIO
GRANADA	7:00	09:00	10:00	10:30	11:00	11:30	12:00	13:00	14:30	15:30	16:00	17:00	19:00	20:00	21:00
SALOBREÑA	8:20	09:55	10:55	11:40	12:00	12:30	12:55	14:00	15:30	****	16:55	17:50	****	19:55	20:55	21:55
ALMUÑECAR	8:40	10:30	11:30	12:00	12:45	13:15	14:20	15:45	****	17:30	18:30	19:30	20:20	21:15	22:15
HERRADURA	8:50	10:40	11:45		13:00		14:30			17:40		19:40			
NERJA	9:15	11:05	12:20		13:20		14:50			18:00		20:00			
T. DEL MAR	11:40		13:45							18:20					

T. DEL MAR - ALMUÑECAR - GRANADA

SALIDAS DESDE	LMXJVS (LABORABLES)	DOMINGOS Y FESTIVOS	LMXJVS (LABORABLES)	DIARIO	DIARIO	DIARIO	DIARIO	DIARIO	DIARIO	DIARIO	DIARIO	LMXJVS (LABORABLES)	DIARIO	DIARIO	DIARIO	DIARIO
T. DEL MAR			08.10													
NERJA	06.30	****	****		9.45			14.30	15.45	16.00		16.15	17.45	18.00	19.15	
HERRADURA	06.50	****	****		10.00			14.50	16.00	17.05			18.35	19.35	
ALMUÑECAR	06.30	07.00	07.15	08.00	9:00	10:30	13:00	14:00	15:15	16:30	17:30	19:00	20:00	21:00
SALOBREÑA	06.45	07.15	****	08.15	9:15	10:45	13:15	14:15	15:30	16:45	17:45	19:15	20:20	20:20	21:15
GRANADA	08.00	08.30	09.00	11.00	9.20	10:30	12:00	14:30	15:30	16:45	18:00	19:00	20:30	20:30	21:30	21:30	22:30

LOS HORARIOS DE POBLACIONES INTERMEDIAS SON DE PASO APROXIMADO
SALIDAS, LLEGADAS, INFORMACION Y DESPACHO DE BILLETES:
GRANADA: Ctra de Jaén, s/n Tlf 958185480   ALMUÑECAR: Estación Autobuses Tlf 9588807704
SALOBREÑA: Av.Mayor Zaragoza Tlf 958612521   T. DEL MAR: Estación Autobuses Tlf 952540936
LOS HORARIOS CONTENIDOS EN ESTE FOLLETO, SOLAMENTE SON A TITULO INFORMATIVO Y PUEDEN SER SUSCEPTIBLES DE MODIFICACIÓN PREVIO AVISO EN LAS
TAQUILLAS DE LA EMPRESA

Córdoba
Province

With an opulent Islamic heritage that's almost overwhelming, Córdoba province manages to blend oriental romanticism with a healthy dose of modern commercial reality. Its fascinating past as the capital of the Al-Andalus region (the Islamic-ruled parts of medieval Spain), with its splendid court and powerful, cultured caliphs, is still an intoxicating draw for travellers who – like Washington Irving, Richard Ford and Théophile Gautierto – wish to witness and be part of this legendary landscape.

Córdoba's greatest monument and the sight that everyone flocks to see is the Mezquita, one of the world's architectural wonders, the most striking example of Islamic arts in the West and also one of lasting importance because of its technical and aesthetic innovations. Ironically, despite the failure of the Muslims to hold the Iberian peninsula, Islamic culture continues to inform and influence much of everyday life in Andalucía. The last decade has seen a huge return to this past, with the opening of numerous Arabian-style tearooms, Islamic-inspired restaurants and hotels, and even an increase in Muslim migrants from North Africa.

Outside Córdoba a sea of olive trees encircles the city and a fascinating patchwork of small towns – from introverted Islamic mazes to extravagant baroque showpieces – make for some interesting excursions throughout the province. Characterised by high mountains and flat plains, the province also produces some of the best wine, oil, cheese and pork products in Andalucía.

HIGHLIGHTS

- Marvelling at Córdoba city's **Mezquita** (p279), a jewel of Islamic architecture

- Getting lost in the labyrinthine alleys of Córdoba's **Judería** (p284) and enjoying the flowers of the city's secret patios, at their best during the **Cruces de Mayo** (p286) festival

- Sweating it out in Córdoba's sumptuous **Hammam Baños Árabes** (p286) and following it up with a glass of mint tea

- Wandering through the ruins and conjuring up the medieval wonders of the **Medina Azahara** (p283)

- Heading for **Priego de Córdoba** (p296) and its extravagant baroque architecture

- Taking the high road into the beautiful mountains of the **Parque Natural Sierras Subbéticas** (p294) or the wooded hills of **Parque Natural Sierra de Hornachuelos** (p293)

| POPULATION: 1.14 MILLION | CÓRDOBA AVERAGE DAILY HIGH: JAN/AUG 11°C/27°C | ALTITUDE RANGE: 55m–1570m |

CÓRDOBA PROVINCE

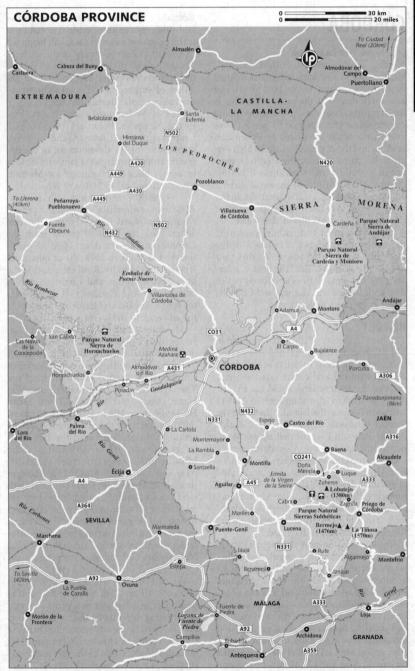

0 _____ 30 km
0 _____ 20 miles

To Ciudad
Real (20km)

Castuera

Cabeza del Buey

Almadén

Almodóvar del
Campo

Puertollano

EXTREMADURA

**CASTILLA-
LA MANCHA**

Belalcázar

Santa
Eufemia

Hinojosa
del Duque

N502

LOS PEDROCHES

A420

N420

A449

A430

Pozoblanco

To Llerena
(40km)

Peñarroya-
Pueblonuevo

A449

N502

Villanueva
de Córdoba

SIERRA

MORENA

Cardeña

Parque Natural
Sierra de
Andújar

Fuente
Obejuna

N432

Río Guadiato

Parque Natural
Sierra de
Cardeña y Montoro

Río Bembezar

Embalse de
Puente Nuevo

Villaviciosa de
Córdoba

Adamuz

Montoro

Andújar

Las Navas
de la
Concepción

San Calixto

Parque Natural
Sierra de
Hornachuelos

CO31

A4

El Carpio

Bujalance

Porcuna

A306

Hornachuelos

Medina
Azahara

Almodóvar
del Río

A431

CÓRDOBA

To Torredonjimeno
(8km)

Posadas

Guadalquivir

JAÉN

Río

Palma
del Río

N432

Espejo

Castro del Río

Lora
del Río

La Carlota

A316

Río Genil

Montemayor

Baena

Alcaudete

Écija

La Rambla

CO241

Doña
Mencía

Luque

A333

Santaella

Montilla

Ermita
de la Virgen
de la Sierra

Zuheros

▲Lobatejo
(1380m)

A364

SEVILLA

A45

Aguilar

Cabra

Zagrilla

Priego de
Córdoba

Marinaleda

Moriles

Parque Natural
Sierras Subbéticas

Marchena

Puente-Genil

Lucena

Bermejo▲
(1476m)

▲ La Tiñosa
(1570m)

Río Corbones

Jauja

Rute

Algarinejo

Montefrío

To Seville
(42km)

Estepa

Benamejí

Iznájar

A92

Osuna

Río

Genil

La Puebla
de Cazalla

MÁLAGA

A333

Loja

Morón de la
Frontera

Fuente de
Piedra

Laguna de
Fuente de
Piedra

A92

Archidona

GRANADA

Campillos

Bobadilla

A359

Antequera

CÓRDOBA

pop 319,000 / elevation 110m

Nestling on a curve of the Río Guadalquivir, the city of Córdoba dominates a small rural province, and seems both provincial and sophisticated at the same time. This is unsurprising, considering the surrounding countryside is characterised by ancient olive groves (whose oil was prized by Phoenician traders) and the city itself is famous for a single architectural treasure, the Mezquita, symbol of a worldly and sophisticated Islamic culture. The labyrinthine medieval quarter adjoining the Mezquita is what fascinates most visitors, and the winding, flower-filled alleys provide endless pleasurable walks.

The city is quiet and withdrawn during the winter months, but it bursts into life from mid-April to mid-June. At this time of year the skies are blue, the heat is tolerable, the city's many trees and lovely patios drip with foliage and blooms, and Córdoba stages most of its major fiestas.

HISTORY

The Roman colony of Corduba, founded in 152 BC, became the capital of Baetica province, covering most of today's Andalucía. This Roman cultural centre was the birthplace of the writers Seneca and Lucan.

Córdoba fell to Islamic invaders in AD 711 and soon became the Islamic capital on the Iberian Peninsula. It was here in 756 that Abd ar-Rahman I set himself up as the independent emir of the Al-Andalus region, founding the Omayyad dynasty. Córdoba's – and Al-Andalus' – heyday came under Abd ar-Rahman III (912–61), who in 929 named himself caliph (the title of the Muslim successors of Mohammed), sealing Al-Andalus' long-standing de facto independence from the Abbasid caliphs in Baghdad.

Córdoba was by now the biggest city in Western Europe, with a population somewhere between 100,000 and 500,000. Its economy flourished on the agriculture from its irrigated hinterland and the products of its skilled artisans – leatherwork and metalwork, textiles, glazed tiles and more. It had dazzling mosques, patios, gardens and fountains, plus aqueducts and public baths. Abd ar-Rahman III's court was frequented by Jewish, Arab and Christian scholars, and

Córdoba's university, library, observatories and other institutions made it a centre of learning whose influence was still being felt in Christian Europe many centuries later. Abulcasis (936–1013), author of a 30-volume medical encyclopedia and considered the father of surgery, was the area's most remarkable scholar during this age.

One of Mohammed's arm bones, kept in the Mezquita, became a psychological weapon against the Christians and was partly responsible for the development of the opposing cult of Santiago (St James). Córdoba became a place of pilgrimage for Muslims who could not get to Mecca or Jerusalem.

Towards the end of the 10th century, Al-Mansur (Almanzor), a ruthless general whose northward raids terrified Christian Spain, took the reins of power from the caliphs. But after the death of Al-Mansur's son Abd al-Malik in 1008, the caliphate descended into anarchy. Rival claimants to the title, Berber troops and Christian armies from Castile and Catalonia all fought over the spoils. The Berbers terrorised and looted the city and, in 1031, Omayyad rule ended.

Al-Andalus collapsed into dozens of *taifas* (petty kingdoms). Córdoba became part of the Sevilla *taifa* in 1069 (and has been overshadowed by that city ever since). But Córdoba's intellectual traditions lived on. The 11th-century philosopher-poets Ibn Hazm (who wrote in Arabic) and Judah Ha-Levi (who wrote in Hebrew) both spent important parts of their lives here. Twelfth-century Córdoba produced the two most celebrated scholars of Al-Andalus – the Muslim philosopher Averroës (1126–98; p43) and the Jewish Moses ben Maimon (known as Maimónides; 1135–1204). Both were men of multifarious talents, best remembered for their philosophical efforts to harmonise religious faith with Aristotelian reason. But while Averroës held high office under the Almohads in Córdoba and Sevilla, Maimónides fled Almohad intolerance and spent most of his career in Egypt.

When Córdoba was taken by Castile's Fernando III in 1236, much of its population fled. Córdoba became a provincial city of shrinking importance and its decline was only reversed by the arrival of industry in the late 19th century. However, Christian Córdoba did produce one of the greatest Spanish poets, Luis de Góngora (1561–1627).

ORIENTATION

The medieval city is immediately north of the Guadalquivir. It's a warren of narrow streets surrounding the Mezquita, which is just a block from the river. Within the medieval city, the area northwest of the Mezquita was the Judería (Jewish quarter), the Muslim quarter was north and east of the Mezquita, and the Mozarabic (Christian) quarter was further to the northeast.

The main square of Córdoba is Plaza de las Tendillas, 500m north of the Mezquita, with the main shopping streets to the plaza's north and west. The train and bus stations are 1km northwest of Plaza de las Tendillas.

INFORMATION
Bookshops

Luque Libros (☎ 957 47 30 34; Calle José Cruz Conde 19) Sells city and Michelin maps at about half the price of those from the tourist shops near the Mezquita. It also sells CNIG and SGE maps and Editorial Alpina maps.

Emergency

Ambulance (☎ 957 21 79 03, 957 29 55 70)
Policía Nacional (National Police; ☎ 95 747 75 00; Avenida Doctor Fleming 2) The main police station.

Internet Access

Ch@t (Calle Claudio Marcelo 15; per hr €1.80; ☻ 10am-1pm & 5-9.30pm Mon-Fri, 10am-2pm Sat) Large and efficient Internet room in the modern part of town.
Mundo Digital (Calle del Osario 9; ☻ 10am-2pm & 5-10pm Mon-Fri, 11am-2pm & 5-10pm Sat & Sun) Has similar prices to those of Ch@t.
Pilar del Potro (Calle Lucano 12; per 30min €1; ☻ 10am-1pm & 5-10pm) Convenient Internet room in Hostal Pilar.

Left Luggage

There is a baggage deposit facility at the main **bus station** (per day €3; ☻ 8am-8pm Mon-Fri) in the form of lockers. There are also lockers at the main train station, which operate similar hours.

Medical Services

Hospital Cruz Roja (Red Cross Hospital; ☎ 957 29 34 11; Avenida Doctor Fleming s/n) The most central hospital.
Hospital Reina Sofía (☎ 957 21 70 00; Avenida de Menéndez Pidal s/n) Located nearly 2km southwest of the Mezquita.

Money

Most banks and ATMs are in the newer part of the centre, around Plaza de las Tendillas

> **OPENING HOURS**
>
> Opening hours for Córdoba's sights change frequently, so check with the tourist offices for updated times. Most places except the Mezquita close on Monday. Closing times are generally an hour or two earlier in winter than summer.

and Avenida del Gran Capitán. The bus and train stations also have ATMs.

Post

Post office (Calle José Cruz Conde 15; ☻ 8.30am-8.30pm Mon-Fri, 9am-2pm Sat)

Tourist Information

Information booth (☻ 10am-2pm & 4.30-8pm Mon-Fri) A kiosk at the train station.
Municipal tourist office (☎ 957 20 05 22; Plaza de Judá Leví; ☻ 8.30am-2.30pm Mon-Fri) A block further west of the regional tourist office.
Regional tourist office (☎ 957 47 12 35; Calle de Torrijos 10; ☻ 9.30am-8pm Mon-Sat, 10am-2pm Sun Apr-Jul, ☻ 9.30am-7pm Mon-Sat, 10am-2pm Sun Aug-Mar) Located in a 16th-century chapel facing the western side of the Mezquita.

SIGHTS & ACTIVITIES

All of Córdoba's sights can be found in a compact area on the north side of the Río Guadalquivir, with the main tourist activity concentrated around the Mezquita and the adjacent Judería. Directly north of the Mezquita is Plaza Tendillas and the busy commercial sector where shops and businesses cluster.

Most people take a good half day to enjoy the grand mosque, and another day or two to explore the city's museums and palaces, which are all a short walk to the northeast. Another not-to-be-missed day trip is to the ruins of the palace-city, Medina Azahara, located 8km west of Córdoba.

Mezquita

Along with the Alhambra in Granada (p305), Córdoba's **Mezquita** (Mosque; ☎ 957 47 05 12; adult/child €6.50/3.25, ☻ 10am-7pm Mon-Sat Apr-Oct, 10am-6pm Mon-Sat Nov-Mar, 9-10.45am & 1.30-6.30pm Sun; Masses at 11am, noon & 1pm) represents the ideal of Islamic Andalucía that travellers flock in their thousands to see; an ideal that glorifies a 'perfect' medieval past. The

CÓRDOBA

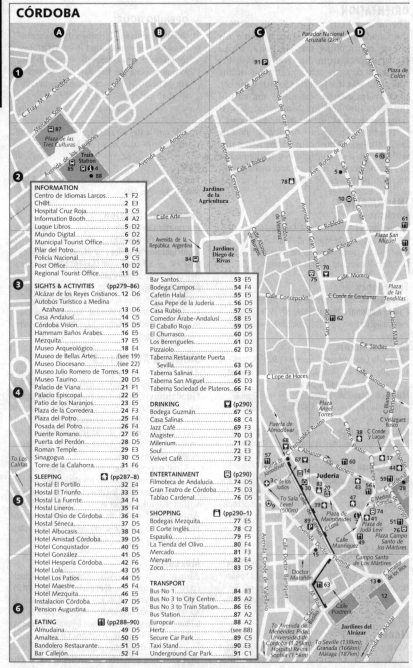

INFORMATION

Centro de Idiomas Larcos	1	F2
Ch@t	2	E3
Hospital Cruz Roja	3	C5
Information Booth	4	A2
Luque Libros	5	D2
Mundo Digital	6	D2
Municipal Tourist Office	7	D5
Pilar del Potro	8	F4
Policía Nacional	9	C5
Post Office	10	D2
Regional Tourist Office	11	E5

SIGHTS & ACTIVITIES   (pp279–86)

Alcázar de los Reyes Cristianos	12	D6
Autobús Turístico a Medina Azahara	13	D6
Casa Andalusí	14	C5
Córdoba Vision	15	D5
Hammam Baños Árabes	16	E5
Mezquita	17	E5
Museo Arqueológico	18	E4
Museo de Bellas Artes	(see 19)	
Museo Diocesano	(see 22)	
Museo Julio Romero de Torres	19	F4
Museo Taurino	20	D5
Palacio de Viana	21	F1
Palacio Episcopal	22	E5
Patio de los Naranjos	23	E5
Plaza de la Corredera	24	F3
Plaza del Potro	25	F4
Posada del Potro	26	F4
Puente Romano	27	E6
Puerta del Perdón	28	D5
Roman Temple	29	E3
Sinagogua	30	C5
Torre de la Calahorra	31	F6

SLEEPING   (pp287–8)

Hostal El Portillo	32	E4
Hostal El Triunfo	33	E5
Hostal La Fuente	34	F4
Hostal Lineros	35	F4
Hostal Osio de Córdoba	36	E4
Hostal Séneca	37	D5
Hotel Albucasis	38	D4
Hotel Amistad Córdoba	39	D5
Hotel Conquistador	40	E5
Hotel González	41	D5
Hotel Hespería Córdoba	42	F6
Hotel Lola	43	D5
Hotel Los Patios	44	D5
Hotel Maestre	45	F4
Hotel Mezquita	46	E5
Instalacion Córdoba	47	E5
Pension Augustina	48	E5

EATING   (pp288–90)

Almudaina	49	E5
Amaltea	50	E5
Bandolero Restaurante	51	D5
Bar Callejón	52	F4
Bar Santos	53	E5
Bodega Campos	54	F4
Cafetín Halal	55	E5
Casa Pepe de la Judería	56	D5
Casa Rubio	57	C5
Comedor Árabe-Andalusí	58	E5
El Caballo Rojo	59	D5
El Churrasco	60	D5
Los Berengueles	61	D2
Pizzaiolo	62	D3
Taberna Restaurante Puerta Sevilla	63	D6
Taberna Salinas	64	F3
Taberna San Miguel	65	E3
Taberna Sociedad de Plateros	66	D3

DRINKING   (p290)

Bodega Guzmán	67	C5
Casa Salinas	68	C4
Jazz Café	69	F3
Magister	70	D3
Milenium	71	E2
Soul	72	E3
Velvet Café	73	E2

ENTERTAINMENT   (p290)

Filmoteca de Andalucía	74	D5
Gran Teatro de Córdoba	75	D3
Tablao Cardenal	76	D5

SHOPPING   (pp290–1)

Bodegas Mezquita	77	E5
El Corte Inglés	78	C2
Espauliú	79	F5
La Tienda del Olivo	80	F4
Mercado	81	F3
Meryan	82	E4
Zoco	83	D5

TRANSPORT

Bus No 1	84	B3
Bus No 3 to City Centre	85	A2
Bus No 3 to Train Station	86	E6
Bus Station	87	A2
Europcar	88	A2
Hertz	(see 88)	
Secure Car Park	89	C5
Taxi Stand	90	E3
Underground Car Park	91	C1

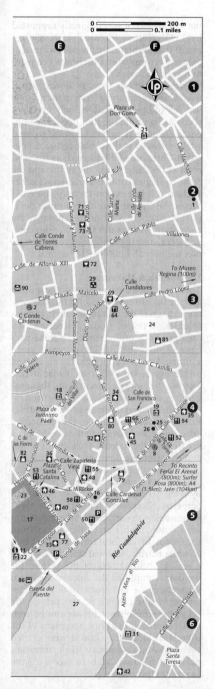

Mezquita hints, with all its lustrous decoration, at a lavish and refined age where Muslims, Jews and Christians lived side by side and enriched their city and surroundings with the heady interaction of diverse and vibrant cultures. However, it's likely that a less-glamorous reality prevailed, with medieval Córdoba no doubt a hotbed of racial and class-based tension. That said, there is no doubt that the Mezquita is captivating, despite the hordes of tourists that threaten to drown the romantic ideal.

Entrance to the Mezquita is free from 9am to 10am Monday to Saturday and 9am to 11am Sunday, when Mass is celebrated in the central cathedral, but you cannot enter the cathedral unless you are attending the Mass in its entirety. The rest of the Mezquita is unlit during this time. It is also worth taking a turn around the exterior walls at night when the lights throw the highly ornate doorways into relief.

HISTORY
The Church of St Vincent was the original building located on this site, and Arab chronicles tell how Abd ar-Rahman I bought half of the church for the use of the Muslim community's Friday prayers. However, the rapid growth of that community soon rendered the space too small and in 784 he bought the other half of the church in order to erect a new mosque. Material from Roman and Visigothic ruins were incorporated into the structure and it is often speculated that Abd ar-Rahman I designed the mosque himself with the help of Syrian architects. In 785 the mosque was opened for prayer although it was subsequently extended southwards by both Abd ar-Rahman II (821–852) and Al-Hakim II in the 960s, in order to cater for Córdoba's expanding population. Al-Hakim II also added the existing mihrab (prayer niche) and, for extra light, built a number of domes with skylights over the area in front of it. Under Al-Mansur, eastward extensions were made and the mihrab lost its central position in the south wall.

What you see today is the building's final form with one major alteration – a 16th-century cathedral right in the middle (hence the often-used description of the 'Mezquita-Cathedral'). Extensions made to the Mezquita under Abd ar-Rahman II and

Al-Mansur were partly dismantled to make way for the cathedral, which took nearly 250 years to complete (1523–1766). The cathedral thus exhibits a range of changing architectural styles and tastes from late-Renaissance through Plateresque to the extravagant Spanish baroque.

For more information on the Mezquita's architectural qualities and importance, see p68.

ORIENTATION & INFORMATION

The main entrance to the Mezquita is the **Puerta del Perdón**, a 14th-century Mudejar gateway on Calle Cardenal Herrero. There's a ticket office immediately inside on the pretty Patio de los Naranjos (Courtyard of the Orange Trees), from where a door leads inside the building itself. Beside the Puerta del Perdón is the 16th- and 17th-century tower encasing the remains of the original minaret.

A leaflet given free to visitors contains a map clearly outlining the stages of the building's construction. The first 12 east-to-west aisles inside the building comprise Abd ar-Rahman I's original 8th-century mosque, completed by his son Hisham I. It extends a little over halfway across the existing building from west to east. The mihrab is visible straight ahead from the entrance door, in the far (southern) wall. In the centre of the building is the Christian cathedral, aligned east to west and surrounded by more Islamic aisles, pillars and arches. Just past the right-hand (western) end of the cathedral, heavier, more elaborate arches mark the approach to the mihrab.

THE MOSQUE-CATHEDRAL

The Mezquita's architectural uniqueness lies in the fact that it broke with earlier precedents – namely the Dome of the Rock in Jerusalem and the Great Mosque in Damascus, with their vertical, nave-like designs – to form an infinitely spacious, democratically horizontal and sumptuously simple space. Here was a realisation of the original Islamic prayer space (usually the open yard of a desert home) transformed into 22,784 sq metre where men could pray side-by-side on the *argamasa* (a compact, reddish mixture of slaked lime and sand) floor. A flat roof, decorated with gold and multicoloured motifs, shaded them from the sun. The roof was originally supported by 1293 columns (of which only 856 remain) that dramatically imitated a forest of palms. This was truly a mezquita – 'a place to prostrate oneself'.

Originally there were 19 doors, which would have meant the interior of the mosque was full of light. Nowadays, only one door sheds its light into the dim interior, dampening the quite vibrant effect of the red-and-white voussoirs of the double arches. Subsequent Christian additions, such as the solid mass of the cathedral in the centre and the 50 or so chapels around the fringes, further enclose and impose on the airy space. At the furthest point from the entrance door, on the southern wall of the mosque, the aisles draw you towards the *qibla* (direction of Mecca) and the mosque's greatest treasure, the mihrab built by Al-Hakim II.

The Mihrab & Maksura

The bay immediately in front of the mihrab and the bays to each side form the *maksura,* the area where the caliphs and their retinues would have prayed (today it's enclosed by railings). Each of the *maksura*'s three bays has a sky-lit dome with star-patterned stone vaulting. Due to their weight the domes rest on stronger, more elaborate lobular arches. Despite their orgy of decoration, these ingenious arches are subtly interwoven to form the strongest elements of the structure. Not only functional, the decorative effect succeeds in drawing the worshipper's eye towards the mihrab, the focus of prayer and the symbolic doorway to heaven.

With nearly 1.6 tonnes of golden mosaic cubes, Cordoban artisans – instructed by a master builder sent by the Christian emperor Nicephorus Phocas from Constantinople – decorated the whole *maksura* with flower motifs and inscriptions from the Quran. Inside the mihrab a single block of white marble, sculpted into the shape of a scallop shell (symbol of the Quran) for the dome, amplified the voice of the imam throughout the vast space. In this area, reserved for the caliph's private prayer, the art of the Cordoban caliphate can be seen to have reached maturity, and many of the superlative decorative effects were carried over into Abd ar-Rahman III's extravagant palace at Medina Azahara (see Pleasure Dome & Powerhouse, p283).

PLEASURE DOME & POWERHOUSE

Legend has it that Abd ar-Rahman III built his palace-city, the **Medina Azahara** (in Arabic, Madinat al-Zahra; ☎ 957 32 91 30; Carretera Palma del Río; non-EU citizen €1.50, EU citizen free; ☿ 10am-8.30pm Tue-Sat May–mid-Sep; 10am-6.30pm Tue-Sat mid-Sep–Apr; 10am-2pm Sun year-round) for his favourite wife. She missed the snow-covered mountains of her Syrian home so he promised to make it snow for her. He then surrounded his new city with almond and cherry trees, whose fluffy white blossoms covered the ground like snow.

Legend aside, Abd ar-Rahman was probably imitating the rival Abbasid dynasty in Baghdad in building a new, opulent royal complex outside the city of Córdoba. Building started in AD 936 and chroniclers record some staggering construction statistics: 10,000 labourers setting 6000 stone blocks a day, with outer walls extending to 1518m west to east and 745m north to south.

It is almost inconceivable to think that such a city, built over 40 years, was only to last a mere 30 years before the usurper Al-Mansur transferred the seat of government to a new palace-complex of his own in 981. Then, between 1010 and 1013, the Azahara was wrecked by Berber soldiers. During succeeding centuries its ruins were plundered repeatedly for building materials. Less than one-tenth of the site has been excavated to date.

Located at the foot of the Sierra Morena, the complex spills down over three terraces with the caliph's palace on the highest terrace overlooking what would have been the court and town. The visitors' route takes you down through the city's original northern gate to the **Dar al-Wuzara** (House of the Viziers) and then to the centrepiece of the site, the **Salón de Abd ar-Rahman III**. Inside, the royal reception hall has been much restored, and the exquisitely carved stuccowork, a riot of vegetal designs, has been painstakingly repaired and returned to cover most of the wall's surface. It gives just a glimpse of the lavishness of the court, which was said to be decorated with gold and silver tiles, its halls intercepted by arches of ivory and ebony contrasting with walls of multicoloured marble. For special effect a bowl at the centre of the hall was filled with mercury so that when it was rocked the reflected light flashed and bounced off the gleaming decoration.

To reach the site with your own vehicle, follow the signs down Avenida de Medina Azahara that leads west out of Córdoba onto the A431. The Medina Azahara is signposted 8km from the city centre and there is free parking at the site, although this gets very full. Try to visit before 11am to avoid the coaches.

A taxi costs €24 for the return trip, with one hour allowed to view the site, or you can take a coach tour (for details see p286). The nearest you can get by public transport is by bus to the Cruce de Medina Azahara (Crossroads of the Medina Azahara), the turn-off from the A431, from which it's a uninspiring 3km walk, slightly uphill, to the site. City bus No 0-1 will drop you at the *cruce* – the bus departs from the northern end of Avenida de la República Argentina.

The Patio de los Naranjos & Minaret

Outside the mosque, the leafy walled courtyard and its fountain were the site of ritual ablutions before prayer, while the arcaded walls would have seen much of the ancient city's hustle and bustle. The crowning glory of the whole complex was the minaret, which at its peak towered 48m (now only 22m survive) and allowed the call to prayer to echo over the city. Now encased in its 16th-century shell, the original minaret would have looked something like the Giralda (p93) in Seville, which was practically a copy. In fact, the influence of Córdoba's minaret was reflected in all the new minarets built thereafter throughout the western Islamic world.

The Cathedral

Following the Reconquista (Christian reconquest) in 1236, the Mezquita remained largely unaltered save for minor modifications such as the Mudejar tiling added in the 1370s to the Mozarabic and Almohad **Capilla Real** (nine bays north and one east of the mihrab; now part of the cathedral). In the 16th century King Carlos I gave permission (against the wishes of Córdoba's city council) for the centre of the Mezquita to be ripped out to allow construction of the **Capilla Mayor** (the altar area in the cathedral) and *coro* (choir). However, upon seeing the results, the king realised he had made a mistake and famously regretted: 'You have built what you or others might have built anywhere, but you have destroyed something that was unique in the world'.

Subsequent additions included a rich 17th-century jasper and red-marble retable in the Capilla Mayor, and fine mahogany stalls in the choir, which were carved in the 18th century by Pedro Duque Cornejo.

If you think of the whole building as a cathedral, the forest of arches and pillars provide a superb setting for the central structures. If you see it as a mosque, the Christian additions wreck its whole conception.

Around the Mezquita

Opposite the Mezquita and next door to the regional tourist office is the **Palacio Episcopal** (Bishops' Palace; Calle de Torrijos), now a conference centre but originally the old Hospital of San Sebastian. A lovely Isabelline-style villa, with an internal patio, the palace now stages exhibitions, often of regional pottery, to which admission is free if you have a Mezquita ticket. The palace also houses the **Museo Diocesano** (Diocesan Museum; ☎ 957 49 60 85; admission €1.20; 9.30am-3pm), which has a collection of religious art. The best of this art is some outstanding medieval woodcarving, including the 13th-century *Virgen de las Huertas*.

Continuing southwest from the Mezquita, down Calle Amador de los Ríos, will bring you to the massive fortified **Alcázar de los Reyes Cristianos** (Castle of the Christian Kings; ☎ 957 42 01 51; Campo Santo de los Mártires s/n; admission Tue-Thu, Sat & Sun €2, admission Fri free; 10am-2pm & 4.30-6.30pm Tue-Sat mid-Oct–Apr, 10am-2pm & 5.30-7.30pm Tue-Sat May, Jun & Sep–mid-Oct, 8.30am-2.30pm Tue-Sat Jul & Aug; 9.30am-2.30pm Sun & holidays year-round). Built on the remains of Roman and Arab predecessors by Alfonso X in the 13th century, the castle began life as a palace, hosting both Fernando and Isabel. From 1490 to 1821 it became home for the Inquisition, later being converted into a prison that only closed in 1951. Its large terraced gardens, full of fish ponds, fountains, orange trees, flowers and topiary, were added in the 15th century and are among the most beautiful in Andalucía. They're dotted with fine archaeological remains, including mosaics, marble sarcophagi and Roman statuary. The building itself, much altered, also houses an old royal bathhouse, the Baños Califales.

Situated on the banks of the Guadalquivir, the castle overlooks the much-restored Roman bridge, the **Puente Romano**. The bridge formed part of the old medieval walls that are reputed to have been some 22km in length. These days, traffic is heavy across the bridge and the pedestrian walkways are narrow. On the other side of the river, the dour-looking **Torre de la Calahorra** (☎ 957 29 39 29; Puente Romano s/n; adult/child €4/2.50; 10am-2pm & 4.30-8.30pm May-Sep, 10am-6pm Oct-Apr) is the oldest defence tower of the city. Used as a jail for the Cordoban nobility in the 18th century and as a school for women in the 19th, it now lays extravagant claim to being the 'Living Museum of Al-Andalus' and offers a rather over-the-top multimedia tour (in Spanish) complete with headphones, models and films.

Judería

Records as old as the 2nd century AD attest to a Jewish community in Spain. Persecuted by the Visigoths, they allied with the Muslims after the Arab conquests. By the 10th century they were established as some of the most dynamic members of society, holding posts as administrators, doctors, jurists, philosophers, poets and functionaries. In fact, one of the greatest Jewish theologians, Maimónides, summarised the teachings of Judaism and completed his magnum opus, the *Mishne Torah*, which systemises all of Jewish law, before fleeing persecution to Fez. He later moved to Egypt, where he became physician to the sultan, Saladin. The importance of the community is illustrated by the proximity of the Judería (the Jewish quarter) to the Mezquita and the centres of power.

Although much diminished, what remains of the old Jewish quarter extends west and northwest from the Mezquita, almost to the beginning of Avenida del Gran Capitán. It's a maze of narrow streets and small squares, of whitewashed buildings with flowers dripping from window boxes, and wrought-iron doorways giving glimpses of plant-filled patios (see Córdoba's Hidden Heart, p287). The most famous street in the area is known as **Calleja de las Flores** (Flower Alley) and gives a picture-postcard view of the Mezquita bell tower framed between the narrow alley walls.

The medieval **Sinagoga** (Synagogue; Calle de los Judíos 20; non-EU citizen €0.30, EU citizen free; 9.30am-2pm & 3.30-5.30pm Tue-Sat, 9.30am-1.30pm Sun & holidays), built in 1315, is a beautiful little building. It has a women's gallery upstairs and is decorated with extravagant stuccowork that includes Hebrew inscriptions and intricate Mudejar star and plant patterns. The **Casa Andalusí** (Calle de los Judíos 12; admission €2.50; ☒ 10.30am-8pm May-Sep; 10.30am-7pm Oct-Apr) is a 12th-century house prettily decked out with a tinkling fountain in the patio. It has a variety of exhibits, mainly relating to Córdoba's medieval Muslim culture, but also including a Roman mosaic in the cellar.

Nearby is **Museo Taurino** (Bullfighting Museum; ☎ 957 20 10 56; Plaza de Maimónides; admission Tue-Thu, Sat & Sun €3, admission Fri free; ☒ 10am-2pm & 4.30-6.30pm Tue-Sat Oct-Apr; 10am-2pm & 5.30-7.30pm Tue-Sat May, Jun, Sep & Oct; 8.30am-2.30pm Tue-Sat Jul & Aug; 9.30am-2.30pm Sun & holidays year-round), housed in a 16th-century Renaissance mansion. It celebrates, with grim theatricality, Córdoba's legendary matadors, with rooms dedicated to El Cordobés and Manolete. Exhibits include the rather forlorn, pegged-out hide of Islero, the bull that killed the revered Manolete at Linares in 1947.

Northeast of the Mezquita

Córdoba's excellent archaeological museum, **Museo Arqueológico** (☎ 957 47 40 11; Plaza de Jerónimo Páez 7; non-EU citizen €1.50, EU citizen free; ☒ 3-8pm Tue, 9am-8pm Wed-Sat, 9am-3pm Sun & holidays), is housed in a Renaissance mansion that's now known to be the site of an original Roman villa. The museum has a wonderful collection of Iberian, Roman and Muslim artefacts and provides real insight into pre-Islamic Córdoba. A reclining stone lion takes pride of place in the Iberian section, and there is a huge collection of Roman artefacts – from large mosaics and gladiatorial tombstones to elegant ceramics and tinted glass bowls. The upstairs is devoted to medieval Córdoba, including a bronze stag, a gift to Abd ar-Rahman III from the Byzantine emperor Constantine VII, which used to grace one of the fountains at Medina Azahara.

Córdoba's most visited museum is **Museo Julio Romero de Torres** (☎ 957 49 19 09; Plaza del Potro 1; admission Tue-Thu, Sat & Sun €3, admission Fri free; ☒ 10am-2pm & 4.30-6.30pm Tue-Sat mid-Oct–Apr, 10am-2pm & 5.30-7.30pm Tue-Sat May, Jun & Sep–mid Oct, 8.30am-2.30pm Jul & Aug, 9.30am-2.30pm Sun & holidays year-round), which is devoted to local painter Julio Romero de Torres (1880–1930) who was hugely revered in Córdoba. The museum

was also the artist's studio and contains his furniture and ornaments as well as his trademark portraits full of sultry nudes and overt sexual symbolism. His voluptuous *Ofrenda al Arte del Toreo* (Offering to the Art of Bullfighting) says it all.

In the same building you will also find **Museo de Bellas Artes** (Plaza del Potro 1; non-EU citizen €1.50, EU citizen free; ☒ 3-8pm Tue, 9am-8pm Wed-Sat, 9am-3pm Sun & holidays), with a collection of mainly Cordoban artists.

The attractive old Charity hospital in which the two previous museums are housed is in a picturesque location on the famous **Plaza del Potro** (Square of the Colt). The square's heyday was in the 16th and 17th centuries when it was a hang-out for traders and adventurers. Miguel de Cervantes, who lived for a spell nearby, immortalised the square in his novel *El Ingenioso Hidalgo Don Quijote de La Mancha*, refers to it as a 'den of thieves'. In the centre stands a lovely 16th-century stone fountain, which is topped by a rearing *potro* (colt). On the western side of the square is the **Posada del Potro** (☎ 957 48 50 18; Plaza del Potro 10; admission free; ☒ 10am-2pm & 5-8pm Mon-Fri Aug-May), an inn dating back to at least 1435 and immortalised in Cervantes' *Don Quixote*. The picturesque *posada* (inn), arranged around a small animal yard, often has interesting temporary exhibits of art, artisanal artefacts and photography.

North of Plaza del Potro is the grand 17th-century **Plaza de la Corredera**, the site of Córdoba's Roman amphitheatre and later the location for horse races and bullfights, as well as Inquisition burnings. Nowadays the extensively restored square hosts rock concerts and other events (ask at the tourist office for details). A daily fruit market is held here and on Saturday there's a lively and colourful flea market selling stuff of interest mainly to locals (eg second-hand clothes, household items and bric-a-brac).

Some 500m north of the plaza is the stunning Renaissance **Palacio de Viana** (☎ 957 49 67 41; Plaza de Don Gome 2; whole house/patios only €6/3; ☒ 9am-2pm Mon-Fri, 10am-1pm Sat Jun-Sep, 10am-1pm & 4-6pm Mon-Fri, 10am-1pm Sat Oct-May), which has a staggering 12 patios and a formal garden that are a real pleasure to visit in the spring. The palace was occupied by the Marqueses de Viana until a couple of decades ago. The charge covers a one-hour guided tour of the rooms (packed with art and antiques) and access to the patios and garden. It takes about half an hour to stroll around the garden and patios.

To really immerse yourself in history, why not try a dip in the newly renovated Arab baths, **Hammam Baños Árabes** (☎ 957 48 47 46; www.hammamspain.com/cordoba in Spanish; Calle Corregidor Luis de la Cerda; bath/bath & massage €12/16; 🕙 10am-noon, 2-4pm, 6-8pm & 10pm-midnight). In its glory days Córdoba had 60 of these wonderful steamy baths where you pass from hot to tepid and cold baths and can even enjoy an aromatherapy massage. Don't forget your swimming costume, as you're not allowed to go naked. After the relaxing, and tiring, experience of getting clean it is traditional to take a glass of sweet mint tea. To cater for this the complex has an attractive tearoom, decorated with iridescent zellij tiles, where you can indulge in a range of Arabian-style sweets. Reservations for the baths and massages are required.

Plaza de las Tendillas & Around

Córdoba's busy main square features a clock with flamenco chimes, exuberant fountains and an equestrian statue – much loved by pigeons – of local lad Gonzalo Fernández de Córdoba, who rose to become the Catholic Monarchs' military right-hand man and earn the name El Gran Capitán. The streets running off from here are the main shopping zones. Calle Conde de Gondomar leads west into the broad and lengthy Avenida del Gran Capitán. The Avenida is undistinguished architecturally, but is the scene of Córdoba's evening *paseo* (stroll) and is lively enough. To the east of Plaza de las Tendillas, on Calle Claudio Marcelo, a ruined **Roman temple** has been partly restored, with 11 columns standing.

COURSES

Centro de Idiomas Larcos (☎ 957 47 11 03; www .larcos.net; Calle Manchado 9) A good private language school offering a range of Spanish courses lasting one or two weeks and longer, and varied accommodation options. A typical two-week course costs €257, and two weeks in a shared apartment costs about an extra €156.

Universidad de Córdoba (☎ 957 21 81 33; www.uco .es/webuco/ceucosa/lenguas in Spanish; Edificio E U Enfermería, Avenida de Menéndez Pidal, 5 planta, 14071 Córdoba) For information on monthly language courses (held every month except August) contact Servicio de Lenguas Modernas y Traducción Técnica at the university.

Course fees are €365 and monthly accommodation can be arranged in shared apartments (€180), university residences (€480) and lodgings with local families (€480).

TOURS

You can book an organised tour to Medina Azahara through many of the hotels, or contact the following places:

Autobús Turístico a Medina Azahara (☎ 902 20 17 74; Campo Santo de los Mártires; tour €5; 🕙 tours 11am Tue-Fri, 10am & 11am Sat & Sun) Offers a similar service to that of Córdoba Vision, travelling to the Medina. Tickets include a three-hour guided tour and an illustrated book of the site.

Córdoba Vision (☎ 957 23 17 34; Doctor Marañón 1; tour €10; 🕙 tours winter/summer 4pm/6pm Tue-Sat, 10.30am Sat & Sun) Offers a three-hour guided tour to Medina Azahara, conducted in Spanish, French and English. The ticket includes entry to the site. The bus departs from Avenida del Alcázar from in front of the Alcázar de los Reyes Cristianos. It also does a combined tour of the city and Medina for €30.

FESTIVALS & EVENTS

Spring and early summer are the chief festival times in Córdoba. The major events are:

Semana Santa (Holy Week) Every evening during Holy Week up to 12 *pasos* (the platforms on which images are carried in a religious procession) and their processions file through the city, passing along the *carrera oficial* (official course) – Calle Claudio Marcelo, Plaza de las Tendillas, Calle José Cruz Conde – between about 8pm and midnight. The climax is the *madrugada* (early hours) of Good Friday, when six *pasos* pass along the *carrera* between 4am and 6am.

Cruces de Mayo (Crosses of May; first few days of May) Squares and patios are decked with flower crosses, which become a focus for wine stalls and tapas stalls, music and merrymaking.

Concurso de Patios Cordobeses (Competition of Cordoban Patios; first half of May) Held at the same time as the patio festival (see Córdoba's Hidden Heart, p287), there's a busy cultural programme that, every three years (next in 2007), includes the Concurso Nacional de Arte Flamenco, an important flamenco competition.

Feria de Mayo (May Fair; last week of May and first days of June) Nonstop partying with concerts, a big fairground in the El Arenal area southeast of the city centre, and the main bullfighting season in the Los Califas ring on Gran Vía Parque.

Festival Internacional de Guitarra (International Guitar Festival; late June or early July) A two-week celebration of the guitar, with live performances of classical, flamenco, rock, blues and more; top names play in the Jardines del Alcázar at night.

CÓRDOBA'S HIDDEN HEART

Concealed behind heavy wooden doors or partly hidden by wrought-iron gates are many examples of a beautiful Cordoban tradition. For centuries, the patios of Córdoba have provided shade during the searing heat of summer, a haven of peace and quiet, and a place to talk and entertain.

The origin of these patios probably lies in ancient Greek megaron and the Roman atrium. The tradition, with the addition of a central water fountain, was continued by the Arabs, where the internal courtyard was an area for women to go about family life and household chores. The courtyards are decorated with potted plants – an idea conceived by desert nomads who carried pots of plants with them on their migrations – and the inevitable grapevine.

In the first half of May you'll notice 'patio' signs in the streets and alleyways, which means that you're invited to enter and view what is for the rest of the year closed to the outside world. At this time of year the patios are at their prettiest as new blooms proliferate. Many patios are entered in an annual competition, the **Concurso de Patios Cordobeses**; a map of patios open for viewing is available from the tourist office. Some of the best patios are on and around Calle San Basilio, about 400m southwest of the Mezquita. During the competition, the patios are generally open from 5pm to midnight Monday to Friday and noon to midnight Saturday and Sunday. Admission is usually free but sometimes there's a container for donations.

SLEEPING

Many lodgings in Córdoba are built around the charming patios for which the city is famous. There are plenty of places near the Mezquita, with the cheaper ones chiefly in the streets to the east. Those mentioned here are just a selection. Booking ahead during the main festivals is essential. Córdoba draws increasing numbers of visitors throughout the year, so single rooms at a decent price are in short supply. Prices are generally reduced from November to mid-March; some places also cut their rates in the hot months of July and August. Where stated, hotels do offer parking facilities but these have to be paid for at a rate of around €10 to €12 per day.

Budget

Nearly all of the following *hostales* (simple guesthouses or small places offering hotel-like accommodation) also offer rooms without bathrooms at a cheaper rate.

Hostal Lineros (☎ 957 48 25 17; www.hostallineros38 .com; Calle de Lineros 38; s/d/ste €30/49/90.15) Within spitting distance of the Plaza del Potro, the gorgeous Arab baths and the best restaurant in town, Bodegas Campos (p290), this *hostal* not only has a great location but fantastic Muslim-inspired rooms in an original Mudejar villa. There is also a *salon de té* (tearoom) in the internal courtyard.

Hostal Séneca (☎ /fax 957 47 32 34; Calle Conde y Luque 7; s/d incl breakfast €44/46) A charming and friendly villa with a marvellous pebbled patio, filled with greenery. The rambling

house has 12 rooms of different sizes and configurations.

Hostal La Fuente (☎ /fax 957 48 78 27; hostalla fuente@terra.es; Calle de San Fernando 51; d €45; P ☒) A refurbished 19th-century town house, La Fuente offers 40 decent rooms all with TV and heating. Rooms are compact, but you can stretch your legs in the hotel's courtyards. A decent breakfast is served for €3.

Hotel Maestre (☎ 957 47 24 10; www.hotelmaestre .com; Calle Romero Barros 4; s/d €30/50, apt €58; P ☒) Comfortably furnished rooms equipped with all mod cons. The helpful reception staff speak English. The same proprietors run an equally good hostal a few doors down (No 16) and have a number of attractively furnished apartments which sleep up to four people.

Hostal Osio de Córdoba (☎ /fax 957 48 51 65; Calle Osio 6; d €40; ☒) Great facilities at a very reasonable price. This hotel is a refurbished mansion with two patios and has been recommended by LP readers. The proprietor speaks English.

Hostal El Portillo (☎ /fax 957 47 20 91; Calle Cabezas 2; s/d €18/30) Another recently refurbished *hostal*, El Portillo now offers comfortable accommodation. The rooms have balconies and the friendly management tries its best to please.

Pension Augustina (☎ 957 47 08 72; Calle Zapateria Vieja 5; s/d €17/30) A simple, old-fashioned and friendly family-run *hostal* with a plant-filled patio. There are nine simple but pristine rooms.

Instalacion Juvenil Córdoba (☎ 957 29 01 66, reservations 902 51 00 00; www.inturjoven.com; Plaza de Judá Leví s/n; B&B under 26 low/high season €9.05/13.75, over 26 low/high season €13.75/18.75; 🎀 🖳) Perfectly positioned in the Judería, Córdoba's youth hostel accommodates 167 people in double, triple, quadruple and quintuple rooms, all with private bathroom. One wing is in a converted 16th-century convent.

Hostal El Triunfo (☎ 957 49 84 84; reservas@ htriunfo.com; Calle Corregidor Luis de la Cerda 79; s/d €29/55; 🅿 🎀) Facing the southern side of the Mezquita, El Triunfo has 70 rooms, some of which actually have views of the Mezquita, although these can be a bit noisy. There's also a friendly bar and restaurant.

Mid-Range

Hotel Lola (☎ 957 20 03 05; www.hotelconencantolola; Calle Romero 3; d low/high season €75/108; 🅿 🎀) A truly charming family-run hotel located in the Judería. Art Deco and antiques go hand in hand in the individually decorated rooms. What's more, you can enjoy your minibar drinks up on the roof terrace overlooking the Mezquita bell tower.

Hotel González (☎ 957 47 98 19; hotelgonzalez@ wanadoo.es; Calle Manriquez 3; d low/high season €49/66; 🎀) In a building that was once home to Córdoba's favourite artist, Julio Romero de Torres, Hotel González has 16 large rooms. The hotel's restaurant serves meals on the pretty flower-filled patio and the friendly proprietors speak fluent English.

Hotel Los Patios (☎ 957 47 83 40; www.lospatios.net; Calle Cardenal Herrero 14; d low/high season €36/84; 🎀) Unusually for a hotel opposite the Mezquita, Los Patios has managed to retain its character as well as offering good-value accommodation. It also has a reasonable restaurant that serves local dishes.

Hotel Albucasis (☎ /fax 957 47 86 25; Calle Buen Pastor 11; s/d €45/72; 🅿 🎀) Tucked in the Judería away from the tourist circus, this quiet, comfortable hotel has simply furnished, spotlessly clean rooms around a quaint courtyard.

Hotel Mezquita (☎ 957 47 55 85; hotelmezquita@ wanadoo.es; Plaza Santa Catalina 1; s/d €36/69; 🎀) Across the street from the eastern side of the Mezquita, this hotel offers 21 good rooms in a 16th-century converted mansion.

Top End

Many of Córdoba's top-end hotels find it difficult to compete in character and location with the cheaper *hostales* and small hotels. However, if you don't want to get embroiled in traffic or are just stopping for a day or two they may be a good option.

Hotel Conquistador (☎ 957 48 11 02; www.jpmoser .com/hotelconquistador.html; Calle Magistral González Francés 15; d €118/141; 🅿 🎀) An elegant 102-room hotel facing the eastern side of the Mezquita. It is the best located of top-end hotels and offers a good range of facilities and tastefully decorated rooms.

Hotel Amistad Córdoba (☎ 957 42 03 35; www.nh -hoteles.com; Plaza de Maimónides 3; s/d €106/130; 🅿 🎀 🖳) Occupying two 18th-century mansions with original Mudejar patios, the Amistad Córdoba is now part of the modern NH chain with all the requisite facilities including babysitting and Internet access.

Parador Nacional Arruzafa (☎ 957 27 59 00; cordoba@parador.es; Avenida de la Arruzafa s/n; d €113.30; 🅿 🎀 🖳) Situated 3km north of the city centre on the site of Abd ar-Rahman I's summer palace, Córdoba's Parador is a modern affair. It's situated in lush green gardens where Europe's first palm trees were planted. Some facilities are adapted for wheelchair users.

Hotel Hespería Córdoba (☎ 957 42 10 42; www .hoteles.hesperia.es; Avenida de la Confederación s/n; d €115/135; 🅿 🎀 🖳) Situated across the river with good views of the Mezquita and the Puente Romano from its rooftop bar. Although the hotel is looking a little tired, it offers a huge range of facilities. Some facilities are adapted for wheelchair users.

EATING

Found on almost every Cordoban *menú* (set menu), *salmorejo* is a thick gazpacho (chilled soup of blended tomatoes, peppers, cucumber, garlic, breadcrumbs, lemon and oil) with bits of hard-boiled egg on top. *Rabo de toro* (oxtail stew) is another favourite. Some of the top restaurants feature recipes from Al-Andalus such as garlic soup with raisins, honeyed lamb, fried aubergine and meats stuffed with dates and pine nuts. The local wine from nearby Montilla and Moriles is similar to sherry. Like sherry, it comes fino, amontillado or oloroso (see p78) and there's also the sweet Pedro Ximénez variety made from raisins.

Budget

Córdoba prides itself on its *tabernas* (taverns) – busy bars where you can usually also sit down to eat. A long walk east or north of the Mezquita will produce better options for the budget-conscious or inquisitive gourmet.

Taberna San Miguel (☎ 957 47 01 66; Plaza San Miguel 1; tapas €1.50, media raciones €3-6; ☒ closed Sun & August) Going strong since 1880, El Pisto (the barrel), as it is locally known, is one of Córdoba's most atmospheric *tabernas*. You'll find a good range of dishes here, and inexpensive Moriles wine ready in jugs on the bar.

Taberna Sociedad de Plateros (☎ 957 47 00 42; Calle de San Francisco 6; tapas/raciones €2/8; ☒ closed Sun) Run by the silversmiths' guild (Sociedad de Plateros), this well-loved restaurant in a converted convent serves a selection of tempting tapas in its light, glass-roofed patio.

Taberna Salinas (☎ 957 48 01 35; Calle Tundidores 3; tapas/raciones €2/8; ☒ closed Sun & Aug) A historic *taberna* in the lively area around Plaza de la Corredera. Dating back to 1879, the large patio restaurant fills up fast and has a lively atmosphere.

Comedor Árabe Andalusí (Calle Alfayatas 6; bocadillos €2.80) Entrances diners with its dim lighting, Arabian music and mouthwatering falafel *bocadillos* (filled long, white bread rolls). This place is a treat not to be missed.

Bar Callejón (Calle Enrique Romero de Torres; platos combinados €3-6, menú €7.20) On a pedestrian street with tables outside, looking up to Plaza del Potro, Bar Callejón does tasty omelettes (€4.30) and a range of fish dishes.

Cafetín Halal (Calle de Rey Heredia 28; mains €5-8) Another Arabian-style cafeteria, this time inside the Islamic cultural centre. Spicy dishes, many of them vegetarian, and a huge range of fruity cocktails.

Bar Santos (Calle Magistral González Francés 3; tapas/raciones €0.90/3) It might be tiny but it does a roaring trade in *bocadillos*, tapas and *raciones* (meal-sized servings of tapas). Wash down your snack with a glass of potent sangría.

Pizzaiolo (☎ 957 48 64 33; Calle San Felipe 5; pizza or pasta dishes €4-8) Made it into the Guinness World Records for having the world's longest *menú* (more than 360 dishes always available). It's bright and popular without reaching any great culinary heights.

Mid-Range

Casa Pepe de la Judería (☎ 957 20 07 44; Calle Romero 1; mains €9-15) A favourite with locals, who hang out in the small bar well into the

night. Start off with a complimentary glass of Montilla on the patio before launching into the house specials, including Cordoban-style ox tails or venison fillets.

El Churrasco (☎ 957 29 08 19; Calle Romero 16; mains €12; ☒ closed Aug) One of Córdoba's top-notch restaurants. The food is rich, the portions generous and the service attentive. Meaty dishes include *churrasco* (grilled meat in a tangy sauce) – in this case, barbecued fillet of pork with Arabian sauce (€9.60).

Almudaina (☎ 957 47 43 42; Plaza Campo Santo de los Mártires 1; mains €10-14) An elegant, atmospheric restaurant, in a 16th-century mansion – all dark wood and damask tablecloths. Almudaina serves up excellent traditional food in individual dining rooms, including on an ivy-clad patio.

Taberna Restaurante Puerta Sevilla (☎ 957 29 73 80; Calle Postrera 51; mains €8.50-15; ☒) Nestled in the shadow of the Puerta Seville, its pretty plant-hung patio framed by ancient crenellations, is this wonderfully atmospheric restaurant. The interior, divided into intimate salons, is equally attractive and the food is artistically presented. Specialities include *bacalao* (cod) tacos and duck in caramel cream.

Bandolero Restaurante (☎ 957 47 64 91; Calle de Torrijos 6; raciones €2.50-8, mains €9-14) An attractive *azulejo* (tile)-lined bar, facing the western side of the Mezquita. Serves up good *media raciones* (half-raciones) and you can sit in the bar or the restaurant patio at the back.

Los Berengueles (☎ 957 47 28 28; Calle Conde de Torres Cabrera 7; mains €7-14) A fantastic attractively decorated *azulejos*-lined fish restaurant. Choose your own fresh fish or monster prawns from the cold counter.

Amaltea (☎ 957 49 19 68; Ronda de Isasa 10; mains €6-10) Specialises in organic food and wine and there is a good range of vegetarian dishes such as a delicious green salad with avocado and walnuts or Lebanese-style tabbouleh. A haven in a vegetarian desert.

Casa Rubio (☎ 957 42 08 53; Puerta de Almodóvar 5; mains €7-15) Just inside the Almodóvar gate, this popular local bar full of Mezquita-inspired horseshoe arches serves up all the usual tapas and has a restaurant section upstairs. Serves popular local dishes such as *flamenquin* (fried veal or pork), *salmorejo* (gazpacho made from tomato) and *cordero a la miel* (lamb in honey).

Top End

Bodega Campos (☎ 957 49 75 00; Calle Lineros 32; tapas/raciones €5/11, mains €13-19; ☒ closed Sun evening) This fashionable bodega (winery) is the real McCoy with huge oak barrels and its own house Montilla. It's comprised of a cellar, wine bar and formal restaurant, all in interconnecting rooms. The restaurant, which is full of swankily dressed *cordobeses* (Córdoba locals), serves up a delicious array of meals. For a cheaper but no less enjoyable evening, try the huge plates of tapas in the bar.

El Caballo Rojo (☎ 957 47 53 75; Calle Cardenal Herrero 28; mains €10.20-17.70) Busy, big and with a reputation for Mozarabic specialities and heartwarming dishes such as white-bean stew. The upstairs terrace overlooks the Mezquita.

DRINKING & ENTERTAINMENT
Bars & Nightclubs

The magazines *Qué hacer en Córdoba?* and *Welcome & Olé!*, issued free by tourist offices, have some what's-on information, as does the daily newspaper *Córdoba*. Fliers for live bands are posted outside music bars and at the Instalacion Juvenil Córdoba (p288). Bands usually start around 10pm and there's rarely a cover charge. Most bars in the medieval city close around midnight.

Córdoba's liveliest bars are mostly scattered around the newer parts of town and come alive at about 11pm or midnight on weekends. You'll be lucky to find any action early in the week.

Bodega Guzmán (Calle de los Judíos 7) Close to the Sinagoga, this atmospheric local favourite oozes alcohol from every nook. Check out the bullfighting museum and don't leave without trying some *amargoso* Montilla from the barrel.

Casa Salinas (Calle Fernández Ruano) A cosy tapas bar serving up tapas and Montillas. Quite often the bar also stages flamenco shows.

Magister (Avenida del Gran Capitán 2) Caters to the more mature drinker, playing soporific background music and brewing beer on the spot to assure patrons the alcohol won't run out. The beer comes in five tasty varieties: blond *rubia* and *tostada*, the dark *caramelizada* and *morenita*, and the *especial*, which varies from season to season.

Jazz Café (☎ 957 47 19 28; Calle Espartería s/n; ☒ 8am-late) Black-and-white tiled floors, a dark bar with glittering optics and pictures of jazz legends such as Roberta Flack, Miles Davis and King Curtis, set the tone for this fabulous laid-back bar. It is also a haven for late-morning coffee away from the tourist hordes. Puts on regular live jazz and jam sessions.

Soul (☎ 957 49 15 80; Calle de Alfonso XIII 3; ☒ 9am-3am Mon-Fri & 10am-3am Sat & Sun) Attracts a hip and arty crowd with its retro vibe and vanguard music. It also does good coffee and toast (€1.50) for breakfast.

Surfer Rosa (☎ 957 75 22 72; Feria El Arenal 4; admission free; ☒ 11pm-late Thu-Sat) A riverbank warehouse in the Recinto Ferial El Arenal (location of the Feria de Mayo). Live bands play frequently and the recorded music is infectious.

Sala Level (Calle Antonio Maura 58; tickets €9; ☒ 8pm-late) West of the city centre in the Ciudad Jardín suburb is this busy live-band venue. Prices vary depending on the talent.

Up near the university there are a number of small bar-cafés such as the '60s-style **Velvet Café** (Calle Alfaros 29) or the popular gay haunt, **Milenium** (Calle Alfaros 33), which plays a good range of ambient House tunes.

Flamenco

Tablao Cardenal (☎ 957 48 33 20; www.tablaocardenal.com; Calle de Torrijos 10; €16.80; ☒ 10.30pm-late) Vibrates with the sound of tapping heels when its flamenco shows get going. Performances, which vary in quality, can be enjoyed on the open-air patio. Guitar players and singers also feature.

Theatre & Cinemas

Gran Teatro de Córdoba (☎ 957 48 02 37, tickets ☎ 901 24 62 46; www.teatrocordoba.com in Spanish; Avenida del Gran Capitán 3) Puts on a busy programme of events ranging from concerts and theatre to dance, and film festivals.

Filmoteca de Andalucía (☎ 957 47 20 18; www.cica.es/filmo in Spanish; Calle Medina y Corella 5; tickets €0.90; ☒ closed Sat & Sun morning & Jul & Aug) Situated at the end of a small courtyard, this art-house cinema regularly shows subtitled (sometimes in Spanish, sometimes in English) foreign films.

SHOPPING

Córdoba is known for its *cuero repujado* (embossed leather) products and silver jewellery (particularly filigree). Shops selling these crafts concentrate around the Mezquita. In the Judería, **Zoco** (Calle de los

Judíos) is a group of workshops/showrooms selling good but pricey crafts. For embossed leatherwork try **Meryan** (☎ 95 747 59 02; Calleja de las Flores), where you should be able to find a wallet or a pair of slippers for €9 to €12.

Tasteful silver shops such as **Espauliú** (Calle Cardenal González 3) sell modern silver jewellery and you can also buy wonderfully crafted pieces from the new **Museo Regina** (Plaza Luis de Venegas 1; admission €3; ✆ 10am-3pm & 5-8pm), which has dedicated exhibitions of silver jewellery.

There are also a number of excellent delicatessens in town, most notably the sumptuous **Bodegas Mezquita** (Calle Corregidor Luis de la Cerda 73), which sells a huge selection of olive oils, hams and wines. Similarly, **La Tienda del Olivo** (☎ 95 747 44 95; Calle de San Fernando 124B) sells fancy soaps made from olive oil, plus oodles of extra virgin for those tapas nights back home. For fresh food and a pleasant wander, the **Mercado** (Plaza de la Corredera) is a wonderful food hall with all manner of stalls.

Calle José Cruz Conde is the smartest central shopping street. There is also the ubiquitous **El Corte Inglés** (Avenida del Gran Capitán) to fulfil those shopping whims.

GETTING THERE & AWAY
Bus
The **bus station** (☎ 957 40 40 40; Plaza de las Tres Culturas) is behind the train station. The biggest operator, Alsina Graells, runs services to Seville (€8.60, 1¾ hours, 10 daily), Granada (€10.65, three hours, nine daily) and Málaga (€10.45, 2½ hours, five daily). It also serves Carmona (€6.75, two hours), Antequera (€7.45, 1½ hours, three daily), Cádiz (€18.35, three hours, one or two daily), and Almería (€20.10, five hours, one daily). Bacoma runs to Baeza (€8.25) and Úbeda (€8.75). Transportes Ureña serves Jaén (€6.70, 1½ hours, seven daily), while Secorbus operates buses to Madrid (€10.85, 4½ hours, six daily).

Empresa Carrera heads south, with several daily buses to Priego de Córdoba (€5.95, 1¼ hours) and Cabra (€4.30), and a couple to Zuheros (€4.30, one hour, at least two daily), Rute and Iznájar.

Car
Rental firms include **Avis** (☎ 957 47 68 62; Plaza de Colón 32), **Europcar** (☎ 957 40 34 80) and **Hertz** (☎ 957 40 20 60), with the latter two located at the train station.

Train
Córdoba's modern **train station** (☎ 957 40 02 02; www.renfe.com; Avenida de América) is 1km northwest of Plaza de las Tendillas.

Dozens of Andalucía Exprés regional trains (€7, 1½ hours) and AVEs (€24, 45 minutes) run to Seville. Options to Madrid range from several daily AVEs (€43 to €48 in *turista* (2nd class), 1¾ hours) to a middle-of-the-night *estrella* (€26 for a seat, 6¼ hours).

Several trains head to Málaga (tourist class €14 to €19.50, first class up to €23, 2½ hours) and Barcelona (€48 to €76, 10½ hours, four daily) and there is a service to Jaén (€7.65, 1½ hours, one daily). For Granada (€14, four hours) you need to change at Bobadilla.

GETTING AROUND
Bus
City buses cost around €1. Bus No 3, from the street between the train and bus stations, runs to Plaza de las Tendillas and down Calle de San Fernando, 300m east of the Mezquita. For the return trip, pick it up on Ronda de Isasa, just south of the Mezquita, or on Avenida Doctor Fleming.

Car & Motorcycle
Córdoba's one-way system is nightmarish, and parking in the old city can be difficult. Metered street parking around the Mezquita and along the riverside is demarcated by blue lines. Charges are €0.30 for 30 minutes or €1.30 for two hours, from 9am to 9pm. Overnight parking outside these hours is free. There is parking across the river, but it is not necessarily secure overnight. A tempting option (metered) is the walled space just below the Mezquita, abreast of the Puerta del Puente. This is fine by day, but not advised overnight. There is secure parking just off Avenida Doctor Fleming costing €1/6/12/45 for one hour/overnight/12 hours/24 hours. There is an underground car park on Avenida de América that has similar prices.

The routes to many hotels and *hostales* are fairly well signposted, and the signs display a 'P' if the establishment has parking. Charges for hotel parking are about €10 to €12.

Taxi
In the city centre, taxis congregate at the northeastern corner of Plaza de las Tendillas. The fare from the train or bus station to the Mezquita is around €5.

NORTH OF CÓRDOBA

The Sierra Morena rises sharply just north of Córdoba city then rolls back gently over most of the north of the province. Dark-green hills and tiny, hardworking pueblos untouched by the tourist mania of the south characterise this undulating countryside. The main CO31/N432 runs northwest into Extremadura.

LOS PEDROCHES

Los Pedroches is a sparsely populated area of scattered granite-built settlements, occasional rocky outcrops and expanses of *dehesa* (woodland pasture). The area is full of holm oak and, along with Jabugo in Huelva (see p160), is another source of quality *jamón ibérico de bellota* – ham that comes from small, fat, black pigs who gorge themselves on the October harvest of acorns. The acorns give the meat its slightly sweet, nutty flavour. Salted and cured over a period of six to 12 months, the resulting dark-pink ham is usually served wafer thin with bread and Montilla. And you can sample it in almost every Los Pedroches village.

Two absorbing places to head for, if you enjoy off-the-beaten-track destinations, are the castles at **Belalcázar** and **Santa Eufemia.** Both villages have simple, inexpensive *hostales.*

The **Castillo de los Sotomayor**, looming over remote Belalcázar, is one of the spookiest fortifications in Andalucía. Dominated by a huge top-heavy keep, with a later Renaissance palace tacked on to the side, it was built in the 15th century on the site of an Islamic fort. The castle is in private hands so you can't go inside, but it still provides a dramatic focus amid the low-lying hills. The only place to stay in Belalcázar is the simple **Hostal La Bolera** (☎ 957 14 63 00; Calle Padre Torrero 17; s/d €14/28) which also has a restaurant, although there are a number of café-bars around the Plaza de la Constitución.

Santa Eufemia, 26km east of Belalcázar across empty countryside, is Andalucía's northernmost village. The **Castillo de Miramontes**, originally Muslim, on a crag to the north above the village, is a tumbled ruin but the 360-degree views are stupendous. To reach the castle turn west off the N502 main road at Hostal La Paloma in the village, and after 1km turn right at the 'Camino Servicio RTVE' sign, from which it's a 1.5km drive uphill to the castle. The **tourist office** (☎ 957 15 82 29; Plaza Mayor 1; ⌚ 9am-2.30pm Mon-Fri) in the *ayuntamiento* (town hall) also has a leaflet (in Spanish) detailing two walks, one up to the castle and the other to the nearby *ermita* (chapel). For comfortable accommodation book into the village's **Hostal La Paloma** (☎ 957 15 82 42; Calle Calvario 6; s/d €12/24). The *hostal* does a good-value *menú* for €8.

The eastern end of Los Pedroches is occupied by the **Parque Natural Sierra de Cardeña y Montoro**, a hilly, wooded area that is one of the last Andalucian refuges of the wolf and lynx.

Buses reach most of Los Pedroches' villages from Córdoba, but to tour freely you need a vehicle.

WEST OF CÓRDOBA

ALMODÓVAR DEL RÍO

pop 7,100 / elevation 123m

The castle-crowned **Almodóvar del Río** lies 22km down the Guadalquivir valley from Córdoba and is an attractive and busy agricultural town. There is a **tourist office** (☎ 957 63 50 14; Calle Vicente Aleixandre 3; ⌚ 9am-2pm & 4-8pm Mon-Fri, 10am-2pm Sat & Sun Apr-Oct; 9am-2pm & 4-7pm Mon-Fri, 10am-2pm Sat & Sun Nov-Mar) just around the corner from the pretty central square, Plaza de la Constitución.

Almodóvar's inescapable main feature is its monumental, and sinister-looking, eight-towered **castle** (☎ 957 63 51 16; admission €3, EU citizen free Wed afternoon; ⌚ 11am-2.30pm & 4-8pm, closes at 7pm Oct-Mar) that dominates the view from miles around. The castle was built in 740 but owes most of its present appearance to post-Reconquista rebuilding. Pedro I ('the Cruel') used it as a treasure store because the castle has never been taken by force. Its sense of impregnability is still potent within the massive walls. The castle has now been over-restored by its owner, the Marqués de la Motilla, and is full of some rather silly exhibits including limp, manacled mannequins. The towers – with names such as 'the Bells', 'the School' and 'the Tribute' – have various stories attached to them and there are information placards in Spanish and English.

If you are driving, the best way to reach the castle (avoiding the crowded town centre) is to ignore signs ahead for Centro Urbano at the junction as you enter town. Instead, go right and follow the A431 ring road, signed to Posadas and Palma del Río. There is ample parking below the castle, but you can also drive up the stony approach track (there is no official parking space there but you can park). You can easily walk down into the old town centre from the castle.

Hostal San Luis (☎ 957 63 54 21; Carretera Palma del Río; s/d €23/38) is alongside the main A431 by the turn-off for Almodóvar coming from Córdoba. It has decent rooms in a separate building attached to its busy restaurant. You can get plentiful *platos combinados* ('combined plates' of seafood, omelette or meat, with trimmings) for €5 to €6. Don't be put off by the large number of trucks parked outside. For accommodation at the opposite end of the spectrum, **Hospedería de San Francisco** (☎ 957 71 01 83; www.casasypalacios.com; Avenida Pío XII 35; d low/high season €89/104; P ⚆ ⚅) in Palma del Rio, 30km southwest, offers luxurious accommodation in a converted 15th-century monastery set around a superb Renaissance patio.

In Almodóvar there are several good eating places. **Bar Tapón** (Calle Antonio Espín 18; mains €5) is just up from the tourist office and does good meat dishes such as *carne de monte* ('meat of the mountain'; local game, such as venison or wild boar). **La Taberna** (☎ 957 71 36 84; Calle Antonio Machado 24; mains €9-18 ⚆ closed Mon Sep-Jun, closed Sun Jul, closed Aug) is a good upmarket restaurant that serves tasty home-cooked fish and meat dishes.

Autocares Pérez Cubero (☎ 957 68 40 23) runs buses to/from Córdoba (€1.50, ½ hour, at least five daily).

HORNACHUELOS & PARQUE NATURAL SIERRA DE HORNACHUELOS

The pleasant village of Hornachuelos is the ideal base for spending a couple of days enjoying the quiet charms of **Parque Natural Sierra de Hornachuelos**. The park is a 672-sq-km area of rolling hills in the Sierra Morena, northwest of Almodóvar del Río. The park is densely wooded with a mix of holm oak, cork oak and ash, and is pierced by a number of river valleys that are thick with willow trees. It is renowned for its eagles and other raptors, and harbours the second-largest colony of black vultures in Andalucía.

Hornachuelos is an appealing village that stands above a small reservoir. On the reservoir bank is a charming little picnic area. The **tourist office** (☎ 957 64 07 86; Carretera San Calixto; ⚆ 8am-3pm Thu-Tue, 8am-3pm & 4-6pm Wed) is located in the sports complex on Carretera de San Calixto, the main road to the west of the centre. From Plaza de la Constitución, a lane called La Palmera, with a charming palm-tree pebble mosaic underfoot, leads up to the **Iglesia de Santa Maride las Flores** and a **mirador** (lookout) on Paseo Blas Infante.

Heading 1.5km northwest from Hornachuelos on the road to San Calixto will take you to the **Centro de Visitantes Huerta del Rey** (☎ 957 64 11 40; ⚆ 10am-2pm & 4-7pm Mon-Fri, 10am-7pm Sat). This visitors centre features interesting displays on the area and its creatures, and it also sells local produce, including honey. You can get information on any of the numerous walking trails that fan out from the centre and you can book a **guided walk** (☎ 957 33 82 33, 617-237700), hire bikes or arrange horse-riding sessions here. There is a bar-restaurant situated just by the centre car park that serves mains from €5 to €9.

Hostal El Álamo (☎ 957 64 04 76; www.hostalelalamo.com; Carretera Comarcal 141, also called Carretera de San Calixto; s/d €48/59.50; P ⚆), on the main road just west of the centre, has clean, pleasant rooms. There is also a busy bar and restaurant located in a separate unit. The restaurant does a *menú* for €6.90. Through the *hostal* it is possible to arrange a number of activities such as walking, biking and horse riding.

Casa Rural El Melojo (☎ 957 64 06 29; Plaza de la Constitución 15; d €55), located in the heart of Hornachuelos village, is a traditionally furnished house with comfortable rooms. There are substantial reductions for groups.

Just south of the road that leads into the village you'll find **Bar Casa Alejandro** (Avenida Guadalquivir 4; raciones €3.60). This bar is very popular with locals and the walls are heavy with hunting trophies; an alarmingly lifelike stuffed head of a horse protrudes from a bar-side pillar.

Autocares Pérez Cubero (☎ 957 68 40 23) runs buses to/from Córdoba (€3.20, 50 minutes, four daily Monday to Friday, one to two daily Saturday and Sunday).

SOUTH OF CÓRDOBA

The south of Córdoba province straddled the Islamic–Christian frontier from the 13th to 15th centuries and many towns and villages cluster around huge, fortified castles. The beautiful, mountainous southeast is known as **La Subbética** after the Sistema Subbético range that crosses this corner of the province. The mountains, canyons and wooded valleys of the 316-sq-km **Parque Natural Sierras Subbéticas** (www.subbetica.org in Spanish) offer some enjoyable walks. The CNIG 1:50,000 map *Parque Natural Sierras Subbéticas* is useful, but it's best to get a copy before arriving in the area (see p408). The park's **Centro de Visitantes Santa Rita** (☎ 957 33 40 34; A340) is located, not very conveniently, 10km east of Cabra.

The southern boundary of the region is demarcated by the **Embalse de Iznájar**, a long, wriggling reservoir overlooked by the village of Iznájar (see Getting Away From It All, p297). There are some good walks that can be done around the reservoir. The northern section of the park has a number of attractive settlements of which Zuheros and Priego de Córdoba are among the most appealing.

BAENA
pop 18,000

Nestled among endless serried ranks of olive trees lies the small and unassuming market town of Baena, famous through the province for its superb quality olive oil, now accredited with its own Denominación de Origen (DO; domains that consistently produce high-quality olive oils) label. The periphery of the town is populated by huge storage tanks and it is possible to visit the best oil-producing mill in the province for a guided tour.

The small **tourist office** (☎ 957 67 19 46; Calle Domingo de Henares s/n; ✆ 9am-2pm & 5-8pm Tue-Fri, 10am-2pm Sat & Sun) has limited information but tries to be as helpful as possible. It stocks a range of leaflets on the town, and a useful map.

The best reason for coming to Baena is to visit the **Museum of Olive Oil** (☎ 957 69 16 41; www.museoaceite.com; admission €1.50; Calle Cañada 7; ✆ 9am-2pm & 4-6pm Mon-Fri, 10am-2pm Sat), which is devoted to the history and production of Baena's oil. Audio-visual presentations (in Spanish) explain production methods and uses and it is possible to taste and purchase the famous oil from the museum shop.

To experience the best working olive oil mill in Córdoba, visit **Núñez de Prado** (☎ 957

AMBER NECTAR

For miles and miles across the rolling *campiña* (countryside) grow vines of the Pedro Ximénez grapes that are used to create the region's Montilla wine. Growing in soggy, rain-drenched soil under a glaring sun, the grapes thrive in conditions that would destroy other vines. In fact it is exactly these conditions that give Montilla its unusual flavours, ranging from very thin, dry almost olive tastes through to a sweet dark treacle.

Originally thought to be a type of riesling, legend has it that the Ximénez grape was imported to the region in the 16th century by a German called Peter Seimens (hence the name in Spanish, Pedro Ximénez). It yields an intensely sweet wine that is endlessly compared to sherry, much to the irritation of the vintners. The fundamental difference between the Jerez sherries and Montilla is the alcoholic potency – alcohol is actually added to Jerez wine, while Montilla grapes achieve their own high levels of alcohol (15% proof), and sweetness, from the intense summer temperatures experienced by the grapes when they are laid out to dry. Left to darken in the sun, the grapes produce a thick, golden must when crushed. What results from this was traditionally racked off into huge terracotta *tinajas*, now steel vats, for ageing. Wine that is clean and well formed goes on to become the pale, strawlike fino; darker amber wines with nutty flavours create the amontillado; and full-bodied wines become the oloroso. The wines are then aged using a *solera* system, where younger vintages are added to older ones in order to 'educate' the young wine.

You can visit **Bodegas Alvear** (☎ 957 66 40 14; Avenida María Auxiliadora 1; guided tour & tasting weekday/weekend €3.95/2.95; ✆ shop 10am-2pm Mon-Sat), in Montilla but you should call first to book. Tours take place at 12.30pm Monday to Saturday.

67 01 41; Avenida de Cervantes s/n; admission free; ☑ 9am-2pm & 4-6pm Mon-Fri, 9am-1pm Sat), where Paco Núñez de Prado himself will give you a tour of the facilities. Overall, the family owns something like 90,000 olive trees and their organic methods of farming result in a very high quality product. Unlike some other producers, there are no high-tech gimmicks here; rather, olives are still painstakingly hand-picked to prevent bruising and high acidity and are then crushed in the ancient stone mills. The mill is famous for *flor de aceite*, the oil that seeps naturally from the ground-up olives. It takes approximately 11kg of olives to yield just 1L of oil. The mill shop sells the oil at bargain prices.

Baena also has a number of quaint 16th- and 17th-century churches and a small **archaeological museum** (☎ 957 66 50 10; Casa de la Tercia, Calle Beato Domingo de Henares 5; admission €0.90; ☑ 10am-1pm & 6-8pm Tue-Fri, 10am-1pm Sat).

There are a number of good *hostales* and hotels in town. The best budget option is the newly opened **Albergue Ruta del Califato** (☎ 957 69 23 59; Calle Coro 7; per person bed/bed & half-board €15/24.20), located near the Iglesia de Santa María. It has extremely comfortable dorm rooms, a good bar-restaurant and some fantastic views. For something more upmarket, try the plush **Casa Grande** (☎ 957 67 19 05; www .lacasagrande.es/hotelbaena/hotelbaena.htm in Spanish; Avenida Cervantes 35; s/d €45/78; 🏊), a converted mansion with refurbished accommodation.

ZUHEROS & AROUND

pop 850 / elevation 625m

Rising above the low-lying *campiña* (countryside) south of the C031, Zuheros is in a dramatic location, crouching in the lee of a craggy mountain. It's approached up a steep road through a series of hairpin bends and provides a beautiful base for exploring the south of the province. Tourist information is available from **Turismo Zuheros** (☎ 957 69 47 75; Carretera Zuheros-Baena s/n; ☑ 9am-2pm & 5-8pm), a small office at the entrance to the village on the Baena road.

The Turismo has plenty of leaflets and information on walking and bike hire. It can also put you in contact with an English-speaking walking guide, Clive Jarman (☎ 957 69 47 96), who lives in Zuheros. There is a **park information point** (☎ 957 33 52 55), open occasionally in summer, a few hundred metres up the road towards the Cueva de los Murciélagos. There is a good car park at the heart of the village below the castle.

Zuheros has a delightfully relaxed atmosphere. All around the western escarpment on which it perches are *miradors* with exhilarating views of the dramatic limestone crags that tower over the village and create such a powerful backdrop for Zuheros' **castle**. The ruined Islamic castle juts out on a pinnacle and has a satisfying patina of age and decay in its rough stonework. Near the castle is the **Iglesia de los Remedios**, originally a mosque, and directly opposite the castle is the **archaeological museum** (☎ 957 69 45 45; Mirador, Zuheros; castle & museum €1.80; ☑ 10am-2pm & 5-8pm Apr-Sep; 10am-2pm & 4-7pm Oct-Mar), which houses some interesting finds from the Cueva de los Murciélagos. Guided tours take place on the hour.

Zuheros is also renowned for its local cheeses and there is a wonderful organic-cheese factory on the road entering the village. Here you can buy delicious varieties of local cheese – some cured with pepper or wood ash – complete hams, wines, olive oil and honey.

Some 4km above the village are the **Cueva de los Murciélagos** (Cave of the Bats; ☎ 957 69 45 45; admission €3.70; ☑ guided tours noon & 5.30pm Mon-Fri Apr-Sep, 12.30pm & 4.30pm Mon-Fri Oct-Mar, 11am, 12.30pm, 2pm & 5.30pm Sat & Sun year-round, extra tours Sat & Sun summer/winter 6.30pm/4pm), which were inhabited by Neanderthals more than 35,000 years ago. It is worth visiting for its Neolithic rock paintings that date back to 6000–3000 BC. Opening times in winter can be unreliable. The drive up to the caves is fantastic, as the road twists and turns through the looming mountains with spectacular views from a number of *miradors*. From one of these you actually get a weird vertiginous, aerial view of the town.

Hotel Zuhayra (☎ 957 69 46 93; Calle Mirador 10; s/d €37/47; 🏊 🍴) is a excellent base for exploring the area. The friendly proprietor Juan Ábalos (who speaks English) can also provide a great deal of information on walking routes and guided walks. Guests get free use of the village pool and it is possible to take part in cheese-making and painting workshops. The hotel's restaurant serves good mains from €4 to €9.

Another good option, recommended by LP readers, is the new **Apartamentos de Turismo Rural** (☎ 957 69 45 27; Calle Mirador 2; 4-person apt

---

DETOUR: ZUHEROS WALK

Behind Zuheros village lies the dramatic rocky gorge, the **Cañon de Bailón**, through which there is a pleasant circular walk of just over 4km (taking about three to four hours).

To pick up the trail find the **Mirador de Bailón**, just below Zuheros on the village's southwestern side, where the approach road C0241 from the A316 Doña Mencía junction bends sharply. There is a small car park here and the gorge is right in front of the *mirador* (lookout). From the car park's entrance – with your back to the gorge – take the broad stony track heading up to the left. Follow the track as it winds uphill and then curves left along the slopes above the gorge. In about 500m the path descends and the valley of the Bailón opens out between rocky walls. The path crosses the stony riverbed to its opposite bank and, in about 1km, a wired-down stone causeway that recrosses the river appears ahead. A few metres before you reach this crossing, bear up left on what is at first a very faint path. It becomes much clearer as it zigzags past a big tree and a twisted rock pinnacle up on the right.

Climb steadily, then, where the path levels off, keep left through trees to reach a superb **viewpoint**. Continue on an obvious path that passes a couple of Parque Natural notice boards and takes you to the road leading up to the Cueva de los Murciélagos. Turn left and follow the road back down to Zuheros.

€60; ☒) located just opposite the castle. The apartments represent great value for money and the proprietors are extremely helpful in arranging excursions. On the same square is the friendly **Mesón Los Palancos** (☎ 95 769 45 38; Calle Llana 43; raciones €3).

Empresa Carrera (☎ 957 40 44 14) runs buses to/from Córdoba (€4.30, one hour, at least two daily).

PRIEGO DE CÓRDOBA
pop 23,000 / elevation 650m

In the 18th century the Subbética was famous for its silk production and many of its small towns grew rich on the proceeds. Such a town is Priego de Córdoba, a sizable market town full of fancy 18th-century mansions, extravagant baroque churches and fine civic buildings. The excruciatingly narrow lanes of the Barrio de La Villa (the old Arab quarter) all converge on the handsome Balcón de Aldarve with its elevated promenade and magnificent views over the Río Salado. Two of the province's highest peaks, 1570m **La Tiñosa** and 1476m **Bermejo**, rise to the southwest.

Orientation & Information

Priego's main square is the busy Plaza de la Constitución, which merges with the smaller traffic junction of Plaza Andalucía. The helpful **tourist office** (☎ 957 70 06 25; Calle del Río 33; ☒ 10am-1.30pm & 5-7.30pm Tue-Sat, 10am-1pm Sun) is a short walk south of the central Plaza de la Constitución. The office's indefatigable chief,

José Mateo Aguilera, is an enthusiastic fount of information and the office is in a historic building that you can look around.

Sights & Activities

The town's catalogue of elegant architecture has earned it a reputation as the capital of Cordoban baroque. Golden-hued stonework and whitewashed walls characterise the buildings, and it is easy to lose yourself in the cobbled streets as you move from one sumptuous baroque church to the next.

The most notable church is the **Parroquia de la Asunción** (Calle Plaza de Abad Palomino) with its fantastic **Sagrario chapel** (sacristy) where an orgy of frothy white stuccowork surges upwards to a beautiful cupola. The sacristy (off the left-hand aisle) and the ornate *retablo* (retable) represent a high point in Andalucian baroque and are now considered national monuments. Similarly ornate are the **Iglesia de San Francisco** (Calle Buen Suceso) and **Iglesia de la Aurora** (Carrera de Álvarez), whose brotherhood takes to the streets of the town in a procession each Saturday at midnight. They play guitars and sing hymns in honour of La Aurora (Our Lady of the Dawn). All the churches normally open from 11am to 1pm.

The main area of monuments in Priego lies 200m northeast of Plaza de la Constitución and is reached by following Calle Solana on through Plaza San Pedro. At a junction with Calle Doctor Pedrajas you can turn left to visit the well-preserved 16th-century slaughterhouse, the **Carnicerías Reales** (admission

DENNIS JOHNSON

The Rock of Gibraltar (p222) as
seen from the cemetery, Gibraltar

Sacred bull (p177), Cádiz province

JOHN NOBLE

Andalucía's high-quality olive oil (p76)

OLIVER STREWE

WAYNE WALTON

Parson's Lodge (p224),
Gibraltar

Green olives of Jaén province (p345)

OLIVER STREWE

Dining alfresco, Seville (p113)

CHRISTOPHER GROENHOUT

Andalucian vineyard (p77)

MASON FLORENCE

OLIVER S

World-famous sherry of Jerez de la Frontera (p182), Cádiz province

free; 🕐 10am-1pm & 5-7pm). It has an enclosed patio and a wonderful stone staircase; exhibitions of paintings are often held here. Turning right along Calle Doctor Pedrajas takes you to Plaza de Abad Palomino, where you can visit the Parroquia de la Asunción. On the square's northern side is Priego's **castillo**, an Islamic fortress built on original Roman foundations in the 9th century and later rebuilt in the 16th century. Privately owned, and closed to the public, the castle has been the subject of much archaeological investigation, which among other things has turned up dozens of stone cannonballs.

Beyond the castle lie the winding streets of the **Barrio de La Villa**, where cascades of potted geraniums transform the whitewashed walls, especially in Calle Real and in the Plaza de San Antonio. Other pretty alleyways lead down from the heart of the *barrio* to the Paseo de Adarve, where there are fine views across the rolling countryside and mountains. On the southern edge of the *barrio* and ending in a superb **mirador** is the Paseo de Colombia, with fountains, flowerbeds and an elegant pergola.

At the opposite end of town, you will find Priego's extraordinary 19th-century fountain, **Fuente del Rey** (Fountain of the King; Calle del Río), with its large three-tiered basins continually filled with splashing water from 180 spouts. The fountain writhes with classical sculptures of Neptune and Amphitrite and when the level of the water rises to cover Neptune's modesty, the townsfolk know that it will be a good harvest. The fountain is more Versailles than provincial Andalucía and the peaceful leafy square in which it is situated is a popular place to while away an afternoon. Behind the Fuente del Rey is the late-16th-century **Fuente de la Virgen de la Salud**, less flamboyant, but further enhancing the square's delightful tranquillity. If you take the stairs to the left of the Fuente de la Virgen de la Salud you can walk to the **Ermita del Calvario** from where there are scenic views.

Also worth a visit is the **Museo Histórico Municipal** (☎ 957 54 09 47; Carrera de las Monjas 16; admission free; 🕐 10am-2pm Tue-Fri, 11am-2pm Sat & Sun), just west of Plaza de la Constitución. Here, imaginative displays exhibit artefacts dating from the Palaeolithic to medieval periods. The museum also organises archaeological tours in the area.

Sleeping

There is only a small selection of accommodation in Priego but places are seldom full.

Posada Real (☎ 957 54 19 10; Calle Real 14; d incl breakfast €39; P ✗ 🛁) A wonderful old house. Juan López Calvo and his family have lovingly restored the four rooms (each with a balcony) and one apartment, filling them with antiques and comfortable furnishings. In the summer, breakfast is served on the quaint patio.

GETTING AWAY FROM IT ALL

South of Priego de Córdoba, stranded on a dramatic promontory above a huge reservoir, is the isolated pueblo of **Iznájar**, which is dominated by its Islamic castle. Despite the poverty of the region, it is a place of outstanding natural beauty and tranquillity, where you can enjoy the beautiful scenery and indulge in a host of outdoor activities.

On the reservoir's **Valdearenas beach** is the province's most scenic camping ground, **Camping La Isla** (☎ 957 53 30 73; www.camping-laisla.com in Spanish; adult/tent/car €4/3.60/3.60; 🛁). **Club Nautico** (☎ 957 53 43 04) is close by and hires out dinghies and canoes and runs a variety of courses from its yacht club.

There are also two wonderful rural hotels offering charming accommodation to match the setting. **Cortijo La Haza** (☎ 957 33 40 51; www.cortijolahaza.com; Adelantado 119; s/d €60/70), outside the village, is a 250-year-old Andalucian farmhouse, furnished in typical fashion with wrought-iron beds and rustic furniture, with lovely views from its terraces. Check the website for comprehensive directions (and a map) giving details of how to reach it. Alternatively, the village's newly opened **Cortijo de Iznájar** (☎ 957 53 48 84; www.cortijodeiznajar.com; Valdearenas s/n; s/d €60/75; P ✗ 🛁) is in a stunning location overlooking the reservoir, and there are plans afoot for spa facilities.

Given the rural beauty and seclusion of this little corner of Andalucía it is hardly surprising to find one of Spain's most exclusive hotels here – **La Finca Bobadilla** (☎ 958 32 18 61; www .la-bobadilla.com; Loja, Granada; s/d €181/264; P ✗ 🛁) is located 20km south of Iznájar.

Villa Turística de Priego (☎ 957 70 35 03; www .villaturisticadepriego.com; Aldea de Zagrilla s/n; 2-person apt/chalet €65/105; P ⊠ �ℝ) A modern Islamic-style complex 7km north of Priego on the road to Zagrilla. The 52 self-catering chalets are arranged around a patio and gardens. Guided walks, horse riding and mountain biking can be arranged through the complex.

Río Piscina (☎ 957 70 01 86; Carretera Monturque-Alcalá La Real Km 44; d €44; P ⊠ ℝ) Located on the eastern edge of town, the Río Piscina has comfortable rooms and some good facilities, including tennis courts.

Hostal Rafi (☎ 957 54 70 27; htelrafi@arrakis.es; Calle Isabel La Católica 4; s/d €20/32; ⊠) Just east of Plaza de la Constitución, Rafi has pleasant rooms above a busy, popular restaurant (mains €6 to €9).

Eating

Priego has some good restaurants including the one at Hostal Rafi (see above).

Balcón del Adarve (☎ 957 54 70 75; Paseo de Colombia 36; mains €8-12) In a wonderful location overlooking the valley, this place is both a good tapas bar and an excellent restaurant. Specialities include *solomillo de ciervo al vino tinto con Grosella* (venison in gooseberry and red wine sauce), and *salmón en supremas a la naranja* (salmon in orange sauce).

El Aljibe (☎ 957 70 18 56; Calle de Abad Palomino; raciones €4-9, menú €6.75) Next to the Castillo, El Aljibe has a nice terrace and part of the downstairs has a glass floor through which you can view some old Islamic baths.

Bar Cafetería Río (Calle Río; raciones €6-11) A busy central option with *revueltos* (scrambled eggs), fish and meat dishes. The same people run **Pizzeria-Bagueteria Varini** (Calle Torrejón 7) just around the corner, where there's a huge range of pizzas (from €8), pasta dishes (from €4) and baguettes.

Getting There & Around

The centre of Priego can become very busy. There is parking just by the football and basketball pitches on Calle Cava north of Plaza de la Constitución. There is a small car park in Plaza Palenque along Carrera de las Monjas, the street that runs east from Plaza de la Constitución.

Priego's bus station is about 1km west of Plaza de la Constitución on Calle Nuestra Señora de los Remedios, off Calle San Marcos. Bus No 1 from the Plaza Andalucía takes you there. **Empresa Carrera** (☎ 957 40 44 14) runs buses to Córdoba (€5.95, 1¼ hours, 12 daily Monday to Friday, five daily Saturday and Sunday), Granada, Cabra and elsewhere.

Granada Province

GRANADA PROVINCE

CONTENTS

No other city embodies the romance and mystery of Islamic Spain as does Granada, the final redoubt where the Nasrid dynasty played out, in diminished but still splendid form, the last 2½ centuries of a great civilisation. No other building is so imbued with the exotic aura of sensuous indulgence as the extravagantly decorated Alhambra palace, surrounded by the exquisitely laid-out Generalife gardens. Nowhere else in Spain was blessed with such a talented myth-weaver as Washington Irving, the American who restored Granada to the world's fascinated attention with his half-fact, half-fiction *Tales of the Alhambra* back in 1823. If there's one don't-miss destination in Andalucía, this is it. But Granada is much more than the Alhambra – it's the fascinating old Islamic quarter (the Albayzín); it's the great Christian buildings such as the Capilla Real Monasterio de la Cartuja; and it's the thronged tapas bars, the busy cultural scene and the restaurants with unbelievable views. And Granada the province is much more than Granada the city: it's skiing and climbing in the snowcapped Sierra Nevada, the highest mountain range in mainland Spain; it's walking in the mystically beautiful Alpujarras valleys where the last Muslim emir, Boabdil, took refuge after losing Granada; it's exploring the northeastern Altiplano (high plain) where people still live in caves; and it's relaxing along the Costa Tropical, Granada's own slice of the Mediterranean coast.

HIGHLIGHTS

- Imbibing the legends and the beauty at the **Alhambra** (p305) and **Generalife** (p310), the exquisite palace and gardens of Spain's last Muslim dynasty

- Wandering around the **Albayzín** (p311), Granada's bohemian, warrenlike old Islamic quarter, with sunset views of the Alhambra

- Soaking up the history at Granada's **Capilla Real** (p310), burial place of the Catholic Monarchs, Isabel and Fernando

- Getting out on the town in the buzzing **bars** (p322) and **clubs** (p322) of after-dark Granada

- Exploring the beautiful, mysterious valleys of **Las Alpujarras** (p331) and climbing, walking or skiing in the snowcapped **Sierra Nevada** (p327)

- Experiencing great Granada festivals such as **Semana Santa** (p317), the **Feria de Corpus Christi** (p317) and the **Festival Internacional de Música y Danza** (p317)

- Discovering palatial elegance behind a forbidding façade at the **Castillo de La Calahorra** (p326)

POPULATION:	GRANADA AVERAGE DAILY HIGH:	ALTITUDE RANGE:
828,000	JAN/AUG 11°C/27°C	0m–3479m

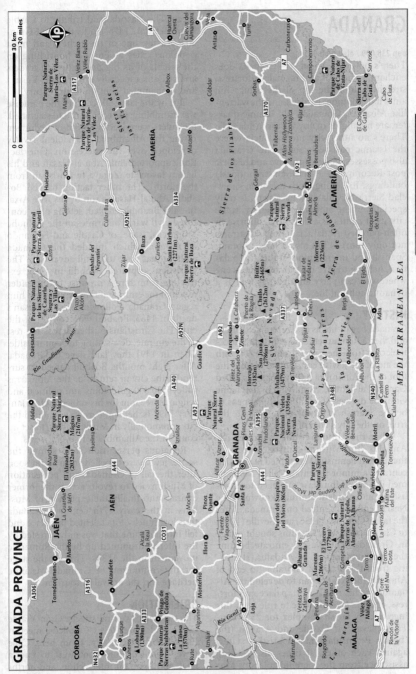

GRANADA

pop 238,000 / elevation 685m

There's no doubt about it – Granada does enchant. The Alhambra palace-fortress, stretched along the top of the Sabika hill amid its sumptuous gardens, and the warren-like Albayzín, Granada's old Islamic quarter, are highlights of any visit to Andalucía. There's no other city in Andalucía where the Islamic past feels so recent. Granada also possesses many impressive and historic post-Reconquista (Christian reconquest) buildings. Its setting, with the often snow-clad Sierra Nevada as a backdrop, is truly special, and the amount of greenery in the city itself comes as a delightful surprise in often-parched Andalucía. Granada attracts not only tourists but also a large, vibrant, Spanish and international student population, helping to give it a bar and club scene where you can party all night, as well as a dynamic cultural life.

HISTORY

Granada began life as an Iberian settlement and then a Roman settlement. Muslim forces took over from the Visigoths in AD 711, with the aid of the Jewish community around the foot of the Alhambra hill in what was called Garnata al-Jahud, from which the name Granada derives. (*Granada* also happens to be the Spanish word for pomegranate, the fruit on the city's coat of arms.)

When the Almohad state that ruled Al-Andalus (the Muslim-controlled areas of the Iberian Peninsula) crumbled in the 13th century, a minor potentate called Mohammed ibn Yusuf ibn Nasr managed to establish an independent emirate, known as the Nasrid emirate, centred on Granada. After the fall of Córdoba (1236) and Seville (1248) to Christian Castile, Muslims sought refuge in Granada. The Nasrid emirate became the final remnant of Al-Andalus, stretching from the Strait of Gibraltar to east of Almería. Ibn Nasr began to develop the Alhambra as his royal court, palace and fortress, and the Nasrids were to rule from this increasingly lavish complex for 250 years. They played off Castile and Aragón (the Iberian Peninsula's main Christian states) against each other, at times also seeking assistance from the Merenid rulers of Mo-

rocco. The Nasrids paid tribute to Castile from then until 1476. Under their rule Granada became one of the richest and most populous cities in Europe, flourishing on the talents of its big population of traders and artisans, especially under emirs Yusuf I and Mohammed V in the 14th century.

But by the late 15th century the paradise was crumbling: the economy had stagnated, the rulers were leading a life of hedonism inside the Alhambra, and violent rivalry developed over the succession. One faction supported emir Abu al-Hasan and his harem favourite, Zoraya (a Christian from the north). The other faction backed Boabdil, Abu al-Hasan's son by his wife Aixa. In 1482 Boabdil rebelled, setting off a confused civil war. The armies of the Catholic Monarchs, Isabel of Castile and Fernando of Aragón, which invaded the Granada emirate that year, took full advantage. The Christians captured Boabdil in 1483, extracting from him a promise to surrender much of the emirate if they would help him regain Granada. Following Abu al-Hasan's death in 1485, Boabdil won control of the city. The Christians pushed across the rest of the emirate, devastating the countryside. Then in 1491 they laid siege to Granada. After eight months Boabdil agreed to surrender the city in return for the Alpujarras valleys, 30,000 gold coins and political and religious freedom for his subjects. On 2 January 1492 Isabel and Fernando entered the city ceremonially in Muslim dress, to set up court in the Alhambra for several years.

Religious persecution soon soured the scene. Jews were expelled from Spain soon after the fall of Granada, and persecution of Muslims led to revolts across the former emirate and finally the expulsion of Muslims in the early 17th century. Granada thus lost much of its talented populace and fell into a decline that was only arrested by the interest drummed up by the Romantic movement in the 1830s. This set the stage for the restoration of Granada's Islamic heritage and the arrival of tourism.

ORIENTATION

The two major central streets, Gran Vía de Colón and Calle Reyes Católicos, meet at Plaza Isabel La Católica. From here, Calle Reyes Católicos runs southwest to Puerta Real, an important intersection, and north-

GRANADA'S BONO TURÍSTICO

Granada's tourist voucher, the Bono Turístico Granada (€22.50), gives admission to several of the city's major sights – the Alhambra, cathedral, Capilla Real, La Cartuja and San Jerónimo monasteries, and the Parque de las Ciencias – plus nine rides on city buses, a day pass on the City Sightseeing Granada bus, and discounts in various hotels, restaurants and additional museums. It's a worthwhile investment if you plan to stay a few days.

You can buy the Bono at the Alhambra, Capilla Real and Parque de las Ciencias ticket offices; at the **CajaGranada bank** (Plaza Isabel La Católica 6; 8.30am-2.15pm Mon-Fri) for the slightly higher charge of €24.50; by credit card over the telephone from the **Bono information line** (902 10 00 95; English spoken); or on the Internet at www.caja-granada.es (in Spanish).

When you buy your Bono you are given a half-hour time slot for entering the Alhambra's Palacio Nazaríes, as with all Alhambra tickets.

If you stay two nights or more in one of the scheme's participating hotels, paying the hotel's regular room rate, you are entitled to one free Bono per double room. Information on participating hotels (mostly three- and four-star) is available from the Bono information line and on the Internet at www.granadatur.com.

east to Plaza Nueva. The street Cuesta de Gomérez leads northeast up from Plaza Nueva towards the Alhambra on its hill-top. The Albayzín rambles over another hill rising north of Plaza Nueva, separated from the Alhambra hill by the valley of the Río Darro. Below the southern side of the Alhambra is the old Jewish district, Realejo.

Newer parts of the city stretch to the west, south and east. From Puerta Real, Acera del Darro, an important artery, heads southeast to the Río Genil. The bus station (northwest) and train station (west) are out of the centre but linked to it by plenty of buses.

INFORMATION
Bookshops
Cartográfica del Sur (Map pp304-5; 958 20 49 01; Calle Valle Inclán 2) Just off Camino de Ronda; Granada's best map shop, also good for Spanish guidebooks.
Metro (Map pp304-5; 958 26 15 65; Calle Gracia 31) Stocks an excellent range of English-language novels, guidebooks and books on Spain, plus plenty of books in French and some in German, Italian and Russian.

Emergency
Policía Nacional (National Police; Map pp312-13; 958 80 80 00; Plaza de los Campos) The most central police station.
Reporting theft (902 10 21 12) Various languages spoken.

Internet Access
Thanks to Granada's 60,000 students, Granada's Internet cafés are cheap (most charging €1 per hour) and open long hours daily.

Internet Elvira (Map pp312-13; Calle de Elvira 64; per hr €1.60, students per hr €1)
N@veg@web (Map pp312-13; Calle Reyes Católicos 55) Large Internet centre just off Plaza Isabel La Católica. Also offers fax and photocopying.
Net Realejo (Map pp312-13; Plaza de los Girones 3); Plaza de la Trinidad (Map pp304-5; Calle Buensuceso)

Internet Resources
Ayuntamiento de Granada (www.granada.org in Spanish) Town hall website with good maps and a broad range of information on what to do, where to stay and so on, with plenty of links. For tourist info, click 'La Ciudad'.
Turismo de Granada (www.turismodegranada.org) Good website of the provincial tourist office, covering the city and other places of interest in the province.

Laundry
Lavandería Duquesa (Map pp304-5; Calle Duquesa 24; 9.30am-2pm & 4.30-9pm Mon-Fri, 9.30am-2pm Sat) Service wash and dry €10.
Lavomatique (Map pp304-5; Calle Paz 19; 10am-2pm & 5-8pm Mon-Fri, 10am-2pm Sat) Wash €5; dry €3.

Medical Services
These are both central hospitals with good emergency facilities:
Hospital Clínico San Cecilio (Map pp304-5; 958 02 32 17; Avenida del Doctor Oloriz 16)
Hospital Ruiz de Alda (Map pp304-5; 958 02 00 09, 958 24 11 00; Avenida de la Constitución 100)

Money
Banks and ATMs abound on Gran Vía de Colón, Plaza Isabel La Católica and Calle Reyes Católicos.

GRANADA PROVINCE

GRANADA

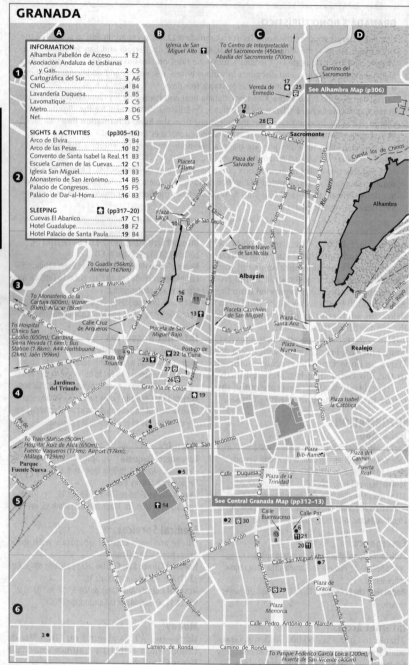

Iglesia de San
Miguel Alto

To Centro de Interpretación
del Sacromonte (450m);
Abadía del Sacromonte (700m)

Camino del
Sacromonte

Vereda de
Enmedio

See Alhambra Map (p306)

Cuesta del Chapiz

Sacromonte

Cuesta los de Chinos

Placeta
Fátima

Plaza del
Salvador

Cuesta de los Chinos

Río Darro

Alhambra

Calle Pagés

Plaza
Larga

Camino Nuevo
de San Nicolás

Albayzín

Callejón Niño
del Royo

To Guadix (56km);
Almería (167km)

Carretera de Murcia

To Monasterio de la
Cartuja (600m); Víznar
(8km); Alfacar (8km)

Placeta de San
Miguel Bajo

Placeta Cauchiles
de San Miguel

Plaza
Santa Ana

To Hospital
Clínico San
Cecilio (650m); Camping
Sierra Nevada (1.6km); Bus
Station (1.8km); A44 Northbound
(2km); Jaén (99km)

Calle Cruz
de Arqueros

Postigo de
la Cuna

Plaza
del
Triunfo

Calle de Elvira

Plaza
Nueva

Cuesta de Gomérez

Realejo

Jardines
del Triunfo

Gran Vía de Colón

Plaza Isabel
la Católica

Avenida de la Constitución

Calle San Juan de Dios

Calle Reyes Católicos

C Niño de Hierro

Calle San Jerónimo

Plaza
Bib-Rambla

Plaza del
Carmen

Puerta
Real

To Train Station (500m);
Hospital Ruíz de Alda (650m);
Fuente Vaqueros (17km); Airport (17km);
Málaga (129km)

Parque
Fuente Nueva

Calle Duquesa

Plaza de la
Trinidad

See Central Granada Map (pp312–13)

Calle
Buensuceso

Calle Paz

Calle San Miguel Alta

Plaza de
Gracia

Plaza
Menorca

Calle Pedro António de Alarcón

Camino de Ronda

Camino de Ronda

To Parque Federico García Lorca (200m);
Huerta de San Vicente (400m)

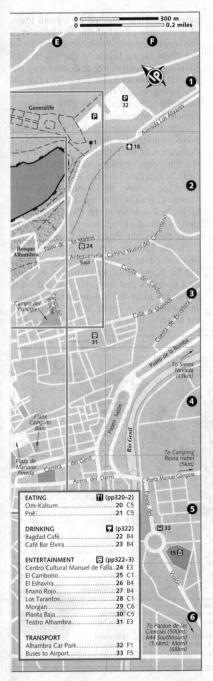

EATING 🍴 (pp320–2)
Om-Kalsum.................................20 C5
Poë...21 C5

DRINKING 🍷 (p322)
Bagdad Café...............................22 B4
Café Bar Elvira...........................23 B4

ENTERTAINMENT 🎭 (pp322–3)
Centro Cultural Manuel de Falla..24 E3
El Camborio................................25 C1
El Eshavira.................................26 B4
Enano Rojo.................................27 B4
Los Tarantos..............................28 C1
Morgan.......................................29 C6
Planta Baja.................................30 C5
Teatro Alhambra........................31 E3

TRANSPORT
Alhambra Car Park......................32 F1
Buses to Airport..........................33 F5

American Express (Map pp312–13; ☎ 958 22 45 12; Calle Reyes Católicos 31).

Post

Expendeduría No 37 (Map pp312–13; Acera del Casino 15) If stamps are all you need, avoid the post office queues by slipping around the corner to this *estanco* (tobacconist).
Main post office (Map pp312–13; Puerta Real s/n; ⏲ 8.30am-8.30pm Mon-Fri, 9.30am-2pm Sat) Often has long queues.

Tourist Information

Provincial tourist office (Map pp312–13; ☎ 958 24 71 28; www.turismodegranada.org; Plaza de Mariana Pineda 10; ⏲ 9am-9pm Mon-Fri, 10am-2pm & 4-7pm Sat, 10am-3pm Sun May-Sep; 9am-8pm Mon-Fri, 10am-1pm Sat, 10am-3pm Sun Oct-Apr) A short walk east of Puerta Real, with helpful staff, free maps and bountiful material on Granada and its province.
Regional tourist office Plaza Nueva (Map pp312–13; ☎ 958 22 10 22; Calle Santa Ana 1; ⏲ 9am-7pm Mon-Sat, 10am-2pm Sun & holidays); Alhambra (Map p306; ☎ 958 22 95 75; Alhambra ticket-office bldg, Avenida del Generalife s/n; ⏲ 8am-7.30pm Mon-Fri, 8am-2.30pm & 4-7.30pm Sat & Sun Mar-Oct; 8am-6pm Mon-Fri, 8am-2pm & 4-6pm Sat & Sun Nov-Feb, 9am-1pm holidays) Information on all Andalucía.

SIGHTS & ACTIVITIES

Most major sights are within walking distance of the city centre. There are buses if you get fed up with walking uphill.

Alhambra

Dominating the Granada skyline from its hill-top perch, the **Alhambra** (Map p306; ☎ 902 44 12 21; www.alhambra-patronato.es; admission/disabled & child under 8/EU senior/Generalife only €10/free/5/5; ⏲ 8.30am-8pm Mar-Oct; 8.30am-6pm Nov-Feb; closed 25 Dec & 1 Jan) is the stuff of fairy tales. From outside, its red fortress towers and walls appear plain if imposing, rising from woods of cypress and elm, with the Sierra Nevada forming a magnificent backdrop. Inside the Alhambra, you're in for a treat, especially in the marvellously decorated emirs' palace, the Palacio Nazaríes (Nasrid Palace), and the Generalife, the Alhambra's gardens. Water is an art form here and even around the outside of the Alhambra the sound of running water and the greenery take you to a faraway world.

This tranquillity can be completely shattered by the hordes of visitors who traipse through (an average of 6000 a day), so try to visit early in the morning or late in the afternoon or – a magical experience – make a night visit to the Palacio Nazaríes (see p307).

The Alhambra has two outstanding sets of buildings, the Palacio Nazaríes and the Alcazaba (Citadel). Also within the complex are the Palacio de Carlos V, the Iglesia de Santa María de la Alhambra, two hotels (p319), book and souvenir shops and lots of lovely gardens, including the supreme Generalife.

There's a small snack bar by the ticket office and another outside the Alcazaba but there's nowhere to sit down and eat inside the Alhambra except at the two hotels.

HISTORY
The Alhambra takes its name from the Arabic *al-qala'at al-hamra* (red castle). The first palace on the site was built by Samuel Ha-Nagid, the Jewish grand vizier of one of Granada's 11th-century Zirid sultans (whose own fortress was in the Albayzín). The Nasrid emirs of the 13th and 14th centuries turned the Alhambra into a fortress-palace complex, adjoined by a small town, of which only ruins remain. The founder of the Nasrid dynasty, Mohammed ibn Yusuf ibn Nasr, set up home on the hill-top, rebuilding, strengthening and enlarging the Alcazaba. His successors Yusuf I (r 1333–54) and Mohammed V (r 1354–59 and 1362–91) built the Alhambra's crowning glory, the Palacio Nazaríes.

After the Reconquista the Catholic Monarchs appointed a Muslim to restore the decoration of the Palacio Nazaríes. In time the Alhambra's mosque was replaced with a church, and the Convento de San Francisco (now the Parador de Granada) was built. Carlos I, grandson of the Catholic Monarchs, had a wing of the Palacio Nazaríes destroyed to make space for a huge Renaissance palace, the Palacio de Carlos V.

In the 18th century the Alhambra was abandoned to thieves and beggars. During the Napoleonic occupation it was used as a barracks and narrowly escaped being blown up. In 1870 it was declared a national monument as a result of the huge interest taken in it by Romantic writers such as

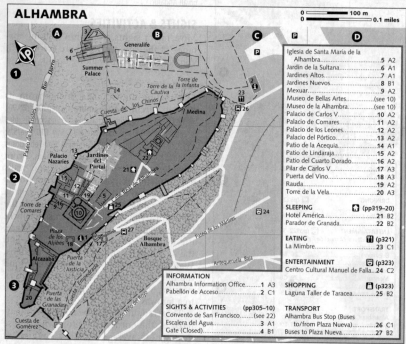

ALHAMBRA

Iglesia de Santa María de la Alhambra	**5** A2
Jardín de la Sultana	**6** A1
Jardines Altos	**7** A1
Jardines Nuevos	**8** B1
Mexuar	**9** A2
Museo de Bellas Artes	(see 10)
Museo de la Alhambra	(see 10)
Palacio de Carlos V	**10** A2
Palacio de Comares	**11** A2
Palacio de los Leones	**12** A2
Palacio del Pórtico	**13** A2
Patio de la Acequia	**14** A1
Patio de Lindaraja	**15** A2
Patio del Cuarto Dorado	**16** A2
Pilar de Carlos V	**17** A3
Puerta del Vino	**18** A3
Rauda	**19** A2
Torre de la Vela	**20** A3

SLEEPING 🛏 (pp319–20)
Hotel América	**21** B2
Parador de Granada	**22** B2

EATING 🍴 (p321)
La Mimbre	**23** C1

ENTERTAINMENT 🎭 (p323)
Centro Cultural Manuel de Falla	**24** C2

SHOPPING 🛍 (p323)
Laguna Taller de Taracea	**25** B2

TRANSPORT
Alhambra Bus Stop (Buses to/from Plaza Nueva)	**26** C1
Buses to Plaza Nueva	**27** B2

INFORMATION
Alhambra Information Office	**1** A3
Pabellón de Acceso	**2** C1

SIGHTS & ACTIVITIES (pp305–10)
Convento de San Francisco	(see 22)
Escalera del Agua	**3** A1
Gate (Closed)	**4** B1

GRANADA PROVINCE

Washington Irving, who wrote the wonderful *Tales of the Alhambra* during his stay in the Palacio Nazaríes in the 1820s. Since then the Alhambra has been salvaged and heavily restored. For more on its architectural qualities and importance, see p71.

ADMISSION

Areas of the Alhambra that can be visited at any time without a ticket include the open area around the Palacio de Carlos V and the courtyard inside it, the Plaza de los Aljibes in front of the Alcazaba, and Calle Real de la Alhambra. But the highlights of the complex – the Palacio Nazaríes and the adjacent Jardines del Partal, the Alcazaba and the Generalife – can only be entered during official opening hours and with a ticket. A maximum of between 5600 and 6600 tickets is available for each day, depending on the season and day of the week. At least 2000 of these tickets are sold at the ticket office each day, but in the busiest seasons (Easter week, July, August and September) these sell out early and you need to start queuing by 7am to be reasonably sure of getting one. Demand is high from April to October. In winter, you may well get a ticket almost immediately at any time of day or week.

It's highly advisable to book in advance (for an extra charge of €0.90). You can book up to a year ahead and there are three ways to do it:

■ In person at any branch of the BBVA bank, which has some 4000 branches around Spain and others in London, Paris, Milan and New York. This saves queuing to pick up tickets at the Alhambra ticket office. There is a convenient Granada branch of **BBVA** (8.30am-2.15pm Mon-Fri year-round & 8.30am-1pm Sat Oct-Mar) on Plaza Isabel La Católica.

■ On the Internet at www.alhambratickets .com. The website provides information in English, Spanish, French, German and Italian about tickets for the Alhambra.

■ By telephone to **Banca Telefónica BBVA** (in Spain ☎ 902 22 44 60, outside Spain ☎ 00-34-91 537 91 78; 8am-5.55pm) English speakers available.

For Internet or phone bookings you need a Visa card, MasterCard or Eurocard. You receive a reference number – you must show this number, along with your passport, national identity card or the credit card with

which you paid for the ticket, at the Alhambra ticket office when you pick up the ticket on the day of your visit. You may have to queue to pick up your ticket. You cannot buy same-day tickets by Internet or by phone or from BBVA, nor can you buy advance tickets at the Alhambra ticket office.

Every ticket is stamped with a half-hour time slot during which you must enter the Palacio Nazaríes. Once inside the Palacio Nazaríes, you can stay in there as long as you like. Each ticket is also either a *billete de mañana* (morning ticket), valid for entry up until 2pm, or a *billete de tarde* (afternoon or evening ticket), for entry after 2pm. These are the periods during which you can enter the Generalife or Alcazaba. Again, here, you can stay as long as you like. If you buy your ticket on the day of your visit at the ticket office, in busy seasons your time slot for the Palacio Nazaríes may be several hours later, and if it's an afternoon ticket you won't be able to enter the Alcazaba or Generalife until 2pm.

The Palacio Nazaríes is open for **night visits** (10-11.30pm Tue-Sat Mar-Oct, 8-9.30pm Fri & Sat Nov-Feb). For each night 400 tickets are available, at the same prices as daytime tickets, with the ticket office open from 30 minutes before the palace's opening time until 30 minutes after it. You can book ahead for night visits in exactly the same way as for day visits.

GETTING THERE & AWAY
Bus

Bus Nos 30 and 32 from Plaza Nueva both run every five to nine minutes from 7.15am to 11pm up Cuesta de Gomérez to the Alhambra, stopping near the ticket office (at the eastern end of the complex). The buses return to Plaza Nueva via a stop near the Puerta de la Justicia. No 32 continues from Plaza Nueva on a second loop through the Albayzín.

Car & Motorcycle

'Alhambra' signs on the approach roads to Granada will conduct you circuitously to the Alhambra **car parks** (per hr/day €1.35/13.50), which are just off Avenida de los Alixares, a short distance uphill from the ticket office.

Walking

There are two main ways to walk up to the Alhambra; both take 20 to 30 minutes from Plaza Nueva.

One is the path **Cuesta de los Chinos**, which leads up from Paseo de los Tristes, emerging about 50m from the ticket office. The office is in the Pabellón de Acceso (Access Pavilion), where you'll also find a tourist information office and bookshop. From the Pabellón de Acceso you can enter the Generalife, and move on from there to other parts of the complex.

The other is **Cuesta de Gomérez**, which leads up through the Puerta de las Granadas (Gate of the Pomegranates), built by Carlos I, and the Bosque Alhambra woods. Immediately after the Puerta de las Granadas, veer left up the Cuesta Empedrada path to a beautiful Renaissance fountain, the **Pilar de Carlos V**. If you already have your Alhambra ticket, take a sharp left after the fountain and enter the Alhambra without going to the ticket office, through the austere **Puerta de la Justicia** (Gate of Justice), constructed by Yusuf I in 1348 as the Alhambra's main entrance. There's an **Alhambra information office** a short distance inside this gate. For the ticket office, continue outside the Alhambra walls from the Pilar de Carlos V for about 600m.

ALCAZABA

What remains of the Alcazaba is chiefly its ramparts and several towers, the most important and tallest being the **Torre de la Vela** (Watch Tower), with a narrow staircase leading to the top terrace, which has splendid views. The cross and banners of the Reconquista were raised here in January 1492. The tower's bell rings on festive occasions only, but in the past it tolled to control the irrigation system of La Vega, Granada's plain. One of the Alhambra's many dungeons is set in the ground just inside the Alcazaba's eastern walls.

PALACIO NAZARÍES

This is the Alhambra's true gem, the most impressive Islamic building in Europe. With its perfectly proportioned rooms and courtyards, intricately moulded stucco walls, beautiful tiling, fine carved wooden ceilings and elaborate *muqarnas* (honeycomb or stalactite) vaulting, all worked in mesmerising, symbolic, geometrical patterns, the Nasrid Palace stands in marked contrast to the austere Alcazaba. Arabic inscriptions, especially the endlessly repeated '*Wa la galiba illa Allah*' ('There is no conqueror

but Allah'), proliferate in the stuccowork, which, like the wood, was originally mostly painted in bright colours.

Mexuar

This 14th-century room, through which you normally enter the palace, was used as a ministerial council chamber and as an antechamber for those awaiting audiences with the emir. The public would generally not have been allowed beyond here. The chamber has been much altered; it was converted into a chapel in the 16th century, and now contains both Muslim and Christian motifs. At its far end overlooking the Río Darro is the small, lavishly decorated Oratorio (Prayer Room).

Patio del Cuarto Dorado

From the Mexuar you pass into this courtyard, with a small fountain and the Cuarto Dorado (Golden Room) on the left. This patio was where the emirs would give audiences to their subjects. The Cuarto Dorado takes its name from its beautiful wooden ceiling, which was gilded and redecorated in the time of the Catholic Monarchs. On the other side of the patio is the entrance to the Palacio de Comares through a beautiful façade of glazed tiles, stucco and carved wood.

Palacio de Comares

Built for Emir Yusuf I, this section of the Palacio Nazaríes served as a private residence for the ruler. It's built around the **Patio de los Arrayanes** (Patio of the Myrtles), named after the hedges flanking its rectangular pool and fountains. The rooms along the sides may have been quarters for the emir's wives. Finely carved arches atop marble pillars form porticos at both ends of the patio. Through the northern portico, inside the Torre de Comares (Comares Tower), is the **Sala de la Barca** (Hall of the Boat), with a beautiful inverted boat-shaped wooden ceiling. This room leads into the square **Salón de Comares** (Comares Hall), also called the Salón de los Embajadores (Hall of the Ambassadors), where the emirs would have conducted their negotiations with Christian emissaries. The stuccowork on the walls contains repeated inscriptions in praise of Allah, and the marvellous domed marquetry ceiling contains more than 8000 cedar pieces in a pattern of stars representing Islam's seven heavens, through which the soul ascends before reaching the eighth (in the centre) where Allah resides.

The southern end of the patio is overshadowed by the walls of the Palacio de Carlos V.

Palacio de los Leones

From the Patio de los Arrayanes you move into the Palace of the Lions, another private palace-within-a-palace, built in the second half of the 14th century under Mohammed V, when the Granada emirate reached its political and artistic peak. Many other buildings in the Palacio Nazaríes were redecorated in Mohammed's reign. By some accounts the Palacio de los Leones was the royal harem.

The rooms of the palace surround the famous **Patio de los Leones** (Lion Courtyard), with its marble fountain that channelled water through the mouths of 12 carved marble lions. Carved especially for this palace, the fountain was originally brightly painted, chiefly in gold.

The Palacio de los Leones symbolises the Islamic paradise, which is divided into four parts separated by rivers (here represented by water channels meeting at the central fountain). The patio's gallery, including the beautifully ornamented pavilions protruding at its eastern and western ends, is supported by 124 slender marble columns.

Of the four halls bordering the patio, the **Sala de los Abencerrajes** on the southern side is the legendary site of the murders of the noble Abencerraj family, who favoured Boabdil in the palace power struggle and whose leader, the story goes, dared to dally with Zoraya, Abu al-Hasan's harem favourite. The room's lovely high-domed ceiling features *muqarnas* vaulting in an eight-point star formation.

At the very eastern end of the patio is the **Sala de los Reyes** (Hall of the Kings), whose inner alcoves have leather-lined ceilings painted by 14th-century Christian artists, probably Genoans. The room's name comes from the painting on the ceiling of the central alcove, thought to depict 10 Nasrid emirs. On the northern side of the patio is the **Sala de Dos Hermanas** (Hall of Two Sisters), as beautiful and richly decorated as the Sala de los Abencerrajes, and probably named after the two slabs of white marble sitting

on either side of its fountain. This may have been the room of the emir's favourite paramour. It features a fantastic *muqarnas* dome with a central star and 5000 tiny cells, reminiscent of the constellations. At its far end is the **Sala de los Ajimeces** with a beautifully decorated little lookout area, the **Mirador de Lindaraja**. Through the low-slung windows of the mirador, the room's occupants could look out over the Albayzín and countryside while reclining on ottomans and cushions.

Other Sections

From the Sala de Dos Hermanas a passageway leads through the **Estancias del Emperador** (Emperor's Chambers), built for Carlos I in the 1520s; some of them were later used by Washington Irving. From here you descend to the **Patio de la Reja** (Patio of the Grille), which leads to the pretty **Patio de Lindaraja**, originally created as a lower garden for the Palacio de los Leones. In the southwestern corner of the patio is the entrance (only sometimes open) to the **Baño de Comares**, the Palacio de Comares' bathhouse, with its three rooms lit by star-shaped skylights.

From the Patio de Lindaraja you emerge into the **Jardines del Partal**, an area of terraced gardens created in the early 20th century around various old structures, ruined and standing. The small **Palacio del Pórtico** (Palace of the Portico), from the time of Mohammed III (r 1302–09), is the oldest surviving palace in the Alhambra. You can leave the Jardines del Partal by a gate facing the Palacio de Carlos V (next to the site of the **Rauda** – the emirs' cemetery), or continue along a path to the Generalife, which runs parallel to the Alhambra's ramparts, passing several towers.

PALACIO DE CARLOS V

This huge Renaissance palace is the dominant Christian building in the Alhambra. Were it in a different setting its merits would be more readily appreciated. Begun in 1527 by Pedro Machuca, an architect from Toledo who studied under Michelangelo, it was financed from taxes on the Granada area's Morisco (converted Muslim) population. Funds dried up after the Moriscos rebelled in 1568, and the palace remained roofless until the early 20th century. The main (western) façade features three porticos divided by pairs of fluted columns, with bas-relief battle carvings at their feet. The building is square but contains a surprising two-tiered circular courtyard with 32 columns. This circle inside a square is the only Spanish example of a Renaissance ground plan symbolising the unity of earth and heaven.

Inside are two museums. The ground-floor **Museo de la Alhambra** (☎ 958 02 79 00; admission free; ☼ 9am-2.30pm Tue-Sat) has a wonderful collection of Muslim artefacts from the Alhambra, Granada province and Córdoba, with explanatory texts in English and Spanish. Highlights include the elegant Alhambra Vase, decorated with gazelles, and the door from the Sala de Dos Hermanas.

Upstairs, the **Museo de Bellas Artes** (Fine Arts Museum; ☎ 958 22 48 43) was closed for restoration in 2004 but, upon reopening, its collection is expected to remain unchanged. Check for hours at the Alhambra information office. Notable in the mainly Granada-related collection of paintings and sculptures are the carved wooden relief of the Virgin and child (c 1547) by Diego de Siloé, several 17th-century works by Alonso Cano, including the modern-looking *Ecce Homo*, and the portraits and landscapes by Granada's two early-20th-century José Marías – López Mezquita and Rodríguez Acosta.

OTHER CHRISTIAN BUILDINGS

The **Iglesia de Santa María de la Alhambra** was built between 1581 and 1617 on the site of the Islamic palace mosque. The **Convento de San Francisco**, now the Parador de Granada hotel (p319), was erected over a small Islamic palace. Isabel and Fernando were laid to rest in a sepulchre here while their tombs in the Capilla Real were being built.

GENERALIFE

The name means 'Architect's Garden'. This beautiful, soothing composition of pathways, patios, pools, fountains, trimmed hedges, tall, long-established trees and, in season, flowers of every imaginable hue, on a hillside facing the Alhambra, is the perfect place to end an Alhambra visit. The Muslim rulers' summer palace is in the corner furthest from the entrance. On the way to it you pass through the Generalife's 20th-century **Jardines Nuevos** (New Gardens). Within the palace, the **Patio de la Acequia** (Court of the Water Channel) has a long pool framed by flower beds and 19th-century fountains whose shapes sensuously

echo the arched porticos at each end. Off this patio is the **Jardín de la Sultana** (Sultana's Garden), almost as lovely and with the trunk of a 700-year-old cypress tree, where Abu al-Hasan supposedly caught his lover, Zoraya, with the head of the Abencerraj clan, leading to the murders in the Sala de los Abencerrajes of the Palacio Nazaríes. Above here are the modern **Jardines Altos** (Upper Gardens), with the **Escalera del Agua** (Water Staircase) – a set of steps with water running down beside them.

Capilla Real

Adjoining the cathedral, the **Capilla Real** (Royal Chapel; Map pp312-13; ☎ 958 22 92 39; www.capillareal granada.com; Calle Oficios; admission €3; ☼ 10.30am-1pm & 4-7pm Apr-Oct, 10.30am-1pm & 3.30-6.30pm Nov-Mar, from 11am Sun year-round, closed Good Friday) is Granada's outstanding Christian building. Spanish-history fans will enjoy this connection with the Catholic Monarchs. Commissioned by Isabel and Fernando as their own mausoleum, it was built in elaborate Isabelline Gothic style, but not finished until 1521, several years after their deaths, so they had to be temporarily interred in the Alhambra's Convento de San Francisco (p310).

The monarchs lie with three relatives in simple lead coffins in the crypt, beneath their marble monuments in the chancel. The chancel is divided from the chapel's nave by a gilded screen made in 1520 by Maestro Bartolomé of Jaén – a masterpiece of wrought-iron artisanry. The coffins, from left to right, belong to Felipe El Hermoso (Philip the Handsome; the husband of the monarchs' daughter Juana la Loca), Fernando, Isabel, Juana la Loca (Joanna the Mad) and Miguel, the eldest grandchild of Isabel and Fernando.

The marble effigies reclining above the crypt were a tribute by Carlos I to his parents and grandparents. The slightly lower of the two monuments, representing Isabel and Fernando and with a Latin inscription lauding them as 'subjugators of Islam and extinguishers of obstinate heresy', was carved by a Tuscan, Domenico Fancelli. The other monument, to Felipe and Juana, is higher, apparently because Felipe was the son of Holy Roman Emperor Maximilian. This is the work (1520) of Bartolomé Ordóñez from Burgos.

The chancel's densely decorated plateresque retable (1522), with a profusion of gold paint, is by Felipe de Vigarni. Note its kneeling figures of Isabel (lower right, with the name 'Elisabeth') and Fernando (lower left), attributed to Diego de Siloé, and the brightly painted bas-reliefs below depicting the defeat of the Muslims and subsequent conversions to Christianity. Cardinal Cisneros is there, too.

The sacristy contains an impressive small museum with Fernando's sword and Isabel's sceptre, silver crown and personal art collection, which is mainly Flemish but also includes Sandro Botticelli's *Prayer in the Garden of Olives*. Also here are two fine statues of the Catholic Monarchs at prayer by Vigarni.

Cathedral

Adjoining the Capilla Real but entered separately, from Gran Vía de Colón, is Granada's cavernous Gothic and Renaissance **cathedral** (Map pp312-13; ☎ 958 22 29 59; admission €2.50; 10.45am-1.30pm & 4-8pm Mon-Sat, 4-8pm Sun, at 7pm daily Nov-Mar). Construction of the cathedral began in 1521 and lasted until the 18th century. It was directed from 1528 to 1563 by Renaissance pioneer Diego de Siloé, and the main façade on Plaza de las Pasiegas, with four heavy square buttresses forming three great arched bays, was designed in the 17th century by Alonso Cano. De Siloé carved the statues on the lavish Puerta del Perdón on the northwestern façade, and much of the interior is also his work, including the gilded, painted and domed Capilla Mayor. The Catholic Monarchs at prayer (one above each side of the main altar) were carved by Pedro de Mena in the 17th century. Above the monarchs are busts of Adam and Eve by Cano. In the cathedral museum, be sure to see Cano's fine *San Pablo* sculpture and the golden Gothic monstrance given to Granada by Isabel La Católica.

La Madraza

Opposite the Capilla Real is part of the old Muslim university, **La Madraza** (Map pp312-13; Calle Oficios). Now with a painted baroque façade, the much-altered building retains an octagonal domed prayer room with stucco lacework and pretty tiles. The building is part of the modern university but you can take a look inside whenever it's open.

Centro José Guerrero

Just along the street from La Madraza, the **Centro José Guerrero** (Art Museum; Map pp312-13; ☎ 958 22 51 85; www.centroguerrero.org; Calle Oficios 8; admission free; 11am-2pm & 5-9pm Tue-Sat, 11am-2pm Sun) is dedicated to the most celebrated artist to come out of Granada – abstract expressionist José Guerrero (1914–91), who was born in the city but found fame in New York in the 1950s. The centre, which opened in 2000, exhibits good temporary shows as well as a permanent collection of Guerrero's dramatic and colourful canvases. It's well worth a visit.

Alcaicería, Plaza Bib-Rambla & Plaza de la Trinidad   Map pp312–13

The **Alcaicería** was the Muslim silk exchange but what can be seen here now is a 19th-century restoration that is filled with tourist shops – but it's charming in the early morning light and quiet. Its buildings, divided by narrow alleys, are just south of the Capilla Real. Southwest of the Alcaicería is the large **Plaza Bib-Rambla** with restaurants, flower stalls and a central fountain with statues of giants. This square has been the scene of jousting, bullfights and Inquisition burnings. Pedestrianised Calle Pescadería and Calle de los Mesones lead northwest to the leafy **Plaza de la Trinidad**, another lively square.

Corral del Carbón

You can't miss the lovely Islamic façade and elaborate horseshoe arch of the **Corral del Carbón** (Map pp312-13; Calle Mariana Pineda), which began life as a 14th-century inn for merchants. It has since had a chequered history, being used as an inn for coal dealers (hence its modern name, meaning 'Coal Yard') and later a theatre. It was undergoing substantial repairs in 2004 but normally is home to government offices and a government-run crafts shop, Artespaña.

Albayzín   Map pp304–5

A wander around the hilly streets and fascinating alleys of Granada's old Islamic quarter, the Albayzín, is a must. This hill, facing the Alhambra across the Darro valley, was where Granada began, as an Iberian settlement in about the 7th century BC, and where its Muslim rulers dwelt before they started to develop the Alhambra in the

GRANADA PROVINCE

CENTRAL GRANADA

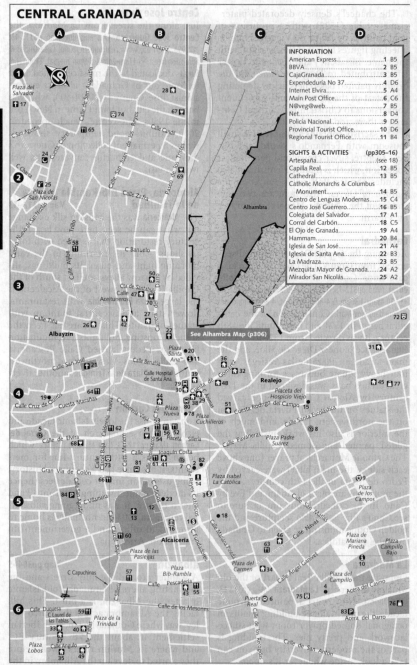

See Alhambra Map (p306)

GRANADA PROVINCE

13th century. The Albayzín's name derives from events in 1227, when Muslims from Baeza (Jaén province) moved here after their city was conquered by the Christians. It became a densely populated residential area with 27 mosques, and it survived as the Islamic quarter for several decades after the Reconquista in 1492. Islamic ramparts, houses, gates, fountains and cisterns remain, and many of the churches and villas of the Albayzín incorporate remains. The Albayzín is a favourite area for foreign students in Granada to live, and it's a marvellous area to ramble around, but to be on the safe side, stay on the major streets after dark.

Bus Nos 31 and 32 both run circular routes from Plaza Nueva around the Albayzín (Paseo de los Tristes, Cuesta del Chapiz, Plaza del Salvador, Plaza de San Nicolás, Placeta de San Miguel Bajo, Arco de Elvira) and back to Plaza Nueva about every seven to nine minutes. No 32 follows this with another loop up to the Alhambra and back. Eight times a day No 31 detours to Sacromonte mid-route. No 32 runs from 7.20am to 11pm; No 31 goes from 7.30am to 11.05pm.

ALBAYZÍN WALKING TOUR   Map p314
This tour of the Darro valley and the Albayzín, starting from Plaza Nueva, should take four or five hours, including visits to some of the sights and a stop for something to eat and drink.

Plaza Nueva extends northeast into Plaza Santa Ana, where the **Iglesia de Santa Ana (1)** incorporates a mosque's minaret in its bell tower (as do several churches in the Albayzín). Along narrow Carrera del Darro, have a look at the 11th-century Islamic bathhouse, the **Baños Árabes El Bañuelo (2**; ☎ 958 02 78 00; Carrera del Darro 31; admission free; 🕑 10am-2pm Tue-Sat), one of Granada's oldest buildings. Further along is the fascinating **Museo Arqueológico (3**; Archaeological Museum; ☎ 958 22 56 40; Carrera del Darro 43; non-EU citizen €1.50, EU citizen free; 🕑 3-8pm Tue, 9am-8pm Wed-Sat, 9am-2.30pm Sun), housed in a Renaissance mansion, the Casa de Castril. On display are finds from Granada province from Palaeolithic to Islamic times, with explanatory material in Spanish only. It's curious to find ancient Egyptian amulets (brought by the Phoenicians) so far from home.

Just past the museum, Carrera del Darro becomes Paseo de los Tristes (also called Paseo del Padre Manjón). Several cafés and restaurants here have outdoor tables and, with the Alhambra's fortifications looming above, it makes a good spot to pause. Several narrow lanes head up into the Albayzín – try Calle Candil, which leads up into Placeta de Toqueros where the **Peña de la Platería (4)** flamenco club is located (see Granada's Flamenco Scene, p323).

If you turn right at the top of Placeta de Toqueros, left at the fork soon afterwards, then left again, you emerge on Carril de San Agustín. Go left and after about 100m the street turns 90 degrees to the right. Continue 200m (initially uphill) to Plaza del Salvador, dominated by the **Colegiata del Salvador** (**5**; ☎ 958 27 86 44; admission €0.75; 🕑 10am-1pm & 4-7.30pm Mon-Sat Apr-Oct, 10.30am-12.30pm & 4.30-6.30pm Mon-Sat Nov-Mar), a 16th-century church on the site of the Albayzín's main mosque. The mosque's patio, with three sides of horseshoe arches, survives at the church's western end. From here Calle Panaderos leads west to **Plaza Larga (6)**, with lively bars.

Leave Plaza Larga through the **Arco de las Pesas (7)**, an impressive Islamic gateway in the Albayzín's 11th-century defensive wall, and

WALKING TOUR

Distance	5½km
Duration	4–5 hours

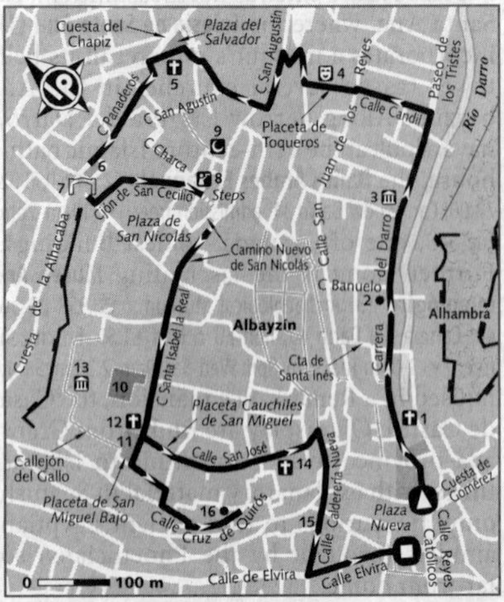

take the first street to the left, Callejón de San Cecilio. This leads to the **Mirador San Nicolás (8)**, a lookout with fantastic views of the Alhambra and Sierra Nevada. You might like to come back here later for sunset (you can't miss the trail then!), but at any time of day keep a tight hold on your belongings. Skilful, well-organised wallet-lifters and snatchers of bags and cameras operate here. One of their tactics is to distract people with 'impromptu' flamenco dance routines; another is for pillion riders on passing motorbikes to stand up and grab bags lying on the side walls of the *mirador*.

The Albayzín's first new mosque in 500 years, the **Mezquita Mayor de Granada** (**9**; ☎ 958 20 23 31; 🕑 gardens 11am-2pm, 6-9.30pm), has been built just east of Mirador San Nicolás, off Cuesta de las Cabras, to serve modern Granada's growing Muslim population. Opened in 2003, it includes an Islamic centre and gardens that have a direct view of the Alhambra and are open to the public. This open-door policy has defused opposition from some quarters to the opening of a new mosque in Granada.

Take the steps down beside the south end of Mirador San Nicolás, turn right and follow the street down to Camino Nuevo de San Nicolás. Turn right, which takes you down to the **Convento de Santa Isabel la Real** (**10**; ☎ 958 27 78 36; Calle Santa Isabel la Real 15; admission €5; 🕑 guided tours 4.30pm Fri, 10am & 11.30am Sat), founded in 1501 and with a Gothic chapel. A few more steps down the street is **Placeta de San Miguel Bajo (11)**, whose cafés and restaurants with outdoor tables are great places to relax over something to eat or drink. The plaza's **Iglesia de San Miguel (12)** is another church on the site of a former mosque. Leave Placeta de San Miguel Bajo by Callejón del Gallo, turn right at the end of this short lane and you'll come to the door of the 15th-century **Palacio de Dar-al-Horra** (**13**; Callejón de las Monjas s/n; admission free; 🕑 10am-2pm Mon-Fri), which was home to Aixa, the mother of Granada's last Muslim ruler, Boabdil. With its patio, pool, arched doorways, coffered ceilings, and friezes with decorative inscriptions, it's like a mini-Alhambra.

Return to Placeta de San Miguel Bajo and head down Placeta Cauchiles de San Miguel, which becomes Calle San José, where the lovely little **Alminar de San José (14)**; San José

GRANADA'S SACRED MOUNTAIN

Fancy some fresh air? Then make your way up to the Sacromonte district, the mysterious neighbourhood of *gitanos* (Roma people, formerly called Gypsies) that occupies the northern side of the Darro valley northeast of the Albayzín. This largely natural space has dazzling views of the Alhambra, the Sierra Nevada and the Albayzín. A city perimeter wall dating from Nasrid times snakes across the hillside above the inhabited part of Sacromonte abutting the Albayzín. Many of the dwellings here are cave homes, burrowed out of the hillside since the 18th century and mostly occupied by *gitanos*. It's interesting to stroll around the area and you can work your way up to the Iglesia de San Miguel Alto, at the top of the hill, for fine views. But make sure you're down to inhabited parts by nightfall.

Beyond the built-up area, some 700m further up the Darro valley, is the early-17th-century **Abadía del Sacromonte** (Map pp304–5; admission €2.50, ⏰ 11am-3pm & 4-6pm Tue-Sun), with a museum exhibiting *granadino* art. The abbey is connected with the name Sacromonte (sacred mountain) because the supposed remains of San Cecilio and other early Christian martyrs, considered sacred, were discovered in a nearby cave in the late 16th century. This led to the building of the monastery.

The **Centro de Interpretación de Sacromonte** (Map pp304–5; ☎ 958 21 51 20; Barranco de los Negros s/n; www.sacromontegranada.com; ⏰ 10am-2pm & 5-9pm Tue-Fri, 10am-9pm Sat & Sun summer, 10am-2pm & 4-7pm Tue-Fri & 10am-7pm Sat & Sun winter) makes a trip to Sacromonte even more worthwhile. This wide-ranging ethnographic and environmental museum and arts centre is set in large grounds planted with all manner of herbs. There are caves set up to show how *gitanos* used to live and do their traditional crafts – metalwork, pottery, weaving, basket-making etc. You'll find written accounts in English and Spanish of some of the many legends connected with the area. Also here are art exhibitions and a herbal remedy workshop. Morning is the best time to see the artists at work. The centre has an outdoor flamenco music, dance and film programme starting at 10pm on Wednesday and Friday from June to September. To get here, hop off the Sacromonte bus at the Venta El Gallo Flamenco School, 250m along the road from El Camborio cave disco (p323), and follow the signs up Barranco de los Negros to the centre. It's about a 200m uphill walk.

Bus No 31 (see p313) detours along Camino del Sacromonte eight times daily; times are posted at its stops.

Some caves on or near Sacromonte's main street, Camino del Sacromonte, are venues for expensive tourist-oriented flamenco shows or lively dance clubs (see p323).

Minaret) survives from the 11th-century mosque that stood here before the neighbouring Iglesia de San José was built in the 16th century. Calle San José meets the top of **Calle Calderería Nueva (15)**, lined by *teterías* (Arabian-style tearooms) and craft shops and full of bohemian atmosphere – stop here for an infusion or head on down to Calle de Elvira and then back to Plaza Nueva.

Alternatively, from Placeta de San Miguel Bajo, take Calle Cruz de Quirós, the street parallel to Placeta Cauchiles de San Miguel. After a couple of hundred metres this will bring you to **El Ojo de Granada (16**; ☎ 958 20 24 73; www.elojodegranada.com; admission €5; ⏰ 10.30am-8.30pm Jun-Aug, 10.30am-6.30pm Mar-May, Sep & Oct, 10.30am-5.30pm Nov-Feb), which has a camera obscura system projecting live, 360-degree views of Granada onto a screen. There's a running commentary in Spanish, English and French.

Monasterio de San Jerónimo

Five hundred metres west of the cathedral, the 16th-century **Monasterio de San Jerónimo** (Map pp304–5; ☎ 958 27 93 37; Calle Rector López Argüeta 9; admission €3; ⏰ 10am-1.30pm & 4-7.30pm Apr-Oct, 10am-1.30pm & 3-6.30pm Nov-Mar) features some beautiful stone carving and a spectacularly decorated church. Specially to be admired in the cloister are two lovely plateresque doorways carved by the monastery's chief architect, the talented Diego de Siloé. The church, in a combination of Isabelline Gothic and Renaissance styles, features an incredible profusion of brightly painted sculpture on the enormous retable and the towering vaults at the eastern end. Before it, at the foot of the steps, is the tombstone of El Gran Capitán (the Great Captain) – Gonzalo Fernández de Córdoba, the military right-hand man of the Catholic Monarchs. Statues of El Gran Capitán and his wife, the Duquesa de Sesa, at prayer stand either side of the retable.

Monasterio de la Cartuja

Another architectural gem stands 2km northwest of the centre, reached by bus No 8 from Gran Vía de Colón. **Monasterio de la Cartuja** (☎ 958 16 19 32; Paseo de la Cartuja; admission €3; ☯ 10am-1pm & 4-8pm Apr-Oct, 10am-1pm & 3.30-6pm Nov-Mar, to noon Sun mornings year-round), with an imposing, sand-coloured stone exterior, was built between the 16th and 18th centuries. It's the lavish baroque monastery church that people come to see, especially the Sagrario (Sanctuary) behind the main altar, a confection of red, black, white and grey-blue marble, columns with golden capitals, profuse sculpture and a beautiful frescoed cupola; and, to the left of the main altar, the Sacristía (Sacristy), the ultimate expression of Spanish late baroque, in effusive 'wedding-cake' stucco and brown-and-white Lanjarón marble (resembling a melange of chocolate mousse and cream). The Sacristía's cabinets, veneered and inlaid with mahogany, ebony, ivory, shell and silver by Fray José Manuel Vázquez in the 18th century, represent a high point of Granada marquetry art.

Huerta de San Vicente

The great *granadino* writer Federico García Lorca spent summers and wrote some of his best-known works at the **Huerta de San Vicente** (☎ 958 25 84 66; Calle Virgen Blanca s/n; admission €1.80, free Wed; admission only by guided tour in Spanish; ☯ 10am-12.30pm & 4-7pm Tue-Sun Oct-Mar, 10am-1pm & 5-8pm Apr-Jun, 10am-3pm Jul-Aug). The house is a 15-minute walk from the city centre and was once surrounded by orchards. Today, the **Parque Federico García Lorca** separates the house from whizzing traffic in an attempt to recreate the tranquil environment that inspired him.

The folksy house contains some original furnishings, including Lorca's writing desk and piano, some of his drawings and other memorabilia, and exhibitions connected with his life and work. A cheeky Salvador Dalí drawing of a short-haired blonde woman smoking a pipe catches the eye. To get here, head 700m down Calle de las Recogidas from Puerta Real, turn right along Calle del Arabial then take the first left into Calle Virgen Blanca.

Hammam

This Arabic-style **bathhouse** (Map pp312-13; ☎ 958 22 99 78; www.hammamspain.com/granada in Spanish; Calle Santa Ana 16; bath/bath & massage €13/20; ☯ 10am-11pm) is in an ancient house just up the street from the regional tourist office. It's the real thing with geometric mosaics, arches and latticework decorations, the scent of herbal oils in the air and soothing background music. Pools are hot and cold and a variety of massages is available. Bring a swimsuit or hire one here. You can have tea in the *tetería* from 3pm and there's a rooftop restaurant.

Parque de las Ciencias

Granada's fun, modern **Parque de las Ciencias** (☎ 958 13 19 00; Avenida del Mediterráneo s/n; adult/child under 18 museum €4/3, planetarium €1.80/1.50; ☯ 10am-7pm Tue-Sat, 10am-3pm Sun, closed 15-30 Sep), a science museum 2km south of the centre, has plenty of hands-on exhibits and a special room for children to explore basic scientific principles. The planetarium has sessions roughly every hour. Take bus No 1, 4, 5, 10 or 11 from the centre.

COURSES

With its many attractions and youthful population, Granada is a good place to study Spanish; it also has several Spanish dance schools. The provincial tourist office can provide lists for all types of schools. For more information check out www.granada spanish.org, www.spanishcourses.info and www.granadainfo.com.

Centro de Lenguas Modernas (Modern Languages Centre; Map pp312-13; ☎ 958 21 56 60; www.clm -granada.com; Placeta del Hospicio Viejo s/n) Granada University's modern languages department, in the historic Realejo district, offers a variety of Spanish language and culture programmes, from intensive beginners' courses to classes for teachers of Spanish. Its teachers are highly qualified. Intensive language courses, at all levels, start at 10 days (40 hours of classes) for €328.

Escuela Carmen de las Cuevas (Map pp304-5; ☎ 958 22 10 62; www.carmencuevas.com; Cuesta de los Chinos 15, Sacromonte) A private school that gets good reports. It teaches Spanish language and culture, and flamenco dance and guitar, all at several levels. A two-week intensive language course (30 hours' tuition) costs €273.

TOURS

Cicerone Cultura y Ocio (☎ 670-541669) Offers guided walking tours in English (2½ hours, €10) from Plaza del Carmen, in front of the *ayuntamiento*, at 10.30am daily.

City Sightseeing Granada (☎ 902 10 10 81) Granada's double-decker city tour bus. It has 15 stops outside the main sights, including the cathedral and the Alhambra. You hop on and off where you like and the ticket (€10) is valid for 24 hours. There's a smaller mini-bus that does a mini-route. You can travel on either bus with the same ticket.

Granavisión (☎ 902 33 00 02) Offers guided tours of the Alhambra and Generalife (€38), Historic Granada tours (€43) and excursions further afield.

FESTIVALS & EVENTS

Semana Santa (Holy Week) – This and Corpus Christi (below) are Granada's big two popular festivals; benches are set up in Plaza del Carmen to view the Semana Santa processions.

Día de la Cruz (Day of the Cross; 3 May) Squares, patios and balconies are adorned with floral crosses (the Cruces de Mayo; May crosses). These become the focus for typical Andalucian revelry – drinking, horse riding, polka-dot dresses and *sevillanas* (traditional Andalucian dances with high, twirling arm movements)

Feria de Corpus Christi (Corpus Christi Fair; late May 2005, mid-June 2006) Granada's big annual fair – a week of fairgrounds, drinking, bullfights and *sevillanas*.

Festival Internacional de Música y Danza (late June to early July) First-class 2½-week festival of mainly classical music and dance, with many events held in the Palacio Nazaríes, Generalife, Palacio de Carlos V and other historical sites. Tickets go on sale in May at the **festival box office** (☎ 958 22 18 44; Corral del Carbón, Calle Mariana Pineda s/n); Internet applications can be made at www.granadafestival.org.

SLEEPING

Places to stay are scattered all around the central areas, especially around Plaza Nueva. Reformed Albayzín mansions, usually with Alhambra views of some kind, provide charming mid-range and top-end options.

You should have no problem finding a room except during Semana Santa and at Christmas. From March to October book ahead to secure your choice. Parking, where offered, costs €8 to €10 per day. For apartments, check out www.granada.info.com.

Budget

At busy times rooms tend to fill up before noon, especially on Cuesta de Gomérez. Most places keep more or less the same prices year-round except for a few days over Easter.

NEAR PLAZA NUEVA　　**Map pp312–13**
Oasis Backpackers' Hostel (☎ 958 21 58 48; www .oasisgranada.com; Calle Rodrigo del Campo 13; dm €16.65;

🖳) This top-notch rest stop, just 200m from Cuesta de Gomérez, is designed for serious backpackers. Word spreads fast, so book ahead to enjoy its little luxuries: happy staff, free Internet access, rooftop terrace, personal safes, tapas tours, and a tip-top central location.

Half a dozen *hostales* (simple guesthouses or small places offering hotel-like accommodation) are strung along Cuesta de Gomérez, between Plaza Nueva and the Alhambra.

Hostal Landázuri (☎ /fax 958 22 14 06; Cuesta de Gomérez 24; s/d/tr/q €28/45/50/60; s/d with shared bathroom €20/28; P) This folksy place boasts a terrace with Alhambra views and a café. The 20 rooms have been updated and a few have a TV; triples and quads are large, bright and comfortable. It's well heated in winter. Party-goers should note that there's a 1am curfew during the week (a little later on weekends).

Hostal Britz (☎ /fax 958 22 36 52; Cuesta de Gomérez 1; s/d €32/42, with shared bathroom €19/29) The friendly, efficient Britz has 22 clean, good-sized rooms with pretty bed covers, double glazing, gleaming wooden surfaces and central heating. There's also a lift.

Hostal Venecia (☎ 958 22 39 87; Cuesta de Gomérez 2; r €32; s/d/tr/q with shared bathroom €15/28/39/52) An exceptionally welcoming place whose owners bring you a soothing herbal infusion to drink each morning. Relaxing background music plays, incense wafts, it's warm in winter and the nine rooms are all individually decorated. There are overhead fans, too.

Hostal Navarro Ramos (☎ 958 25 05 55; Cuesta de Gomérez 21; s/d €22/31, with shared bathroom €16/21) Offers 15 good, clean, plain rooms in a calm environment. The building is cool in summer; in winter, the heating is on from 6pm to midnight.

Hostal Austria (☎ 958 22 70 75; www.hostalaustria .com; Cuesta de Gomérez 4; s/d/tr/q €35/45/60/70; P ⚹) This *hostal* and **Hostal Viena** (☎ /fax 958 22 18 59; Calle Hospital de Santa Ana 2; s/d €35/45, with shared bathroom €25/37) are run by the same Austrian-Spanish family. The Austria has the better rooms, which ramble over several floors of a renovated old property with eye-catching traditional tiles. Rooms are modernised and have attractive wooden doors and shutters.

The streets between Calle de Elvira and Gran Vía de Colón, west of Plaza Nueva, have several more *hostales* worth a look if you're having difficulty finding a room.

PLAZA BIB-RAMBLA & AROUND

Map pp312–13

Some of the many *hostales* in this area fill up with university students in term time. The following should have rooms year-round.

Hostal Lisboa (☎ 958 22 14 14; www.lisboaweb.com; Plaza del Carmen 27; s/d €32/44, s with shared bathroom €19/29) A few blocks south of Plaza Nueva, this friendly place with 28 clean rooms is connected to the Hostal Britz (p317). The paintwork is in dull colours but the bathrooms sport blue-and-white tiles. All rooms have fans and winter heating, and most overlook the plaza or Calle Navas.

Hostal Sevilla (☎ 958 27 85 13; Calle Fábrica Vieja 18; r €32, s/d with shared bathroom €16/25) This friendly, clean, 14-room *hostal*, run by a young family, has some attractive tilework and lampshades. All rooms have heating.

Hostal Zurita (☎ 958 27 50 20; Plaza de la Trinidad 7; r €36, s/d with shared bathroom €18/30; P X) Friendly, super-clean Zurita has 14 quiet, pretty rooms with winter heating. Nearly all rooms have a little balcony.

Hostal Meridiano (☎/fax 958 25 05 44; hostalmeridiano@telefonica.net; Calle Angulo 9; r €37, s/d with shared bathroom €18/30, 4-/6-person apt €35/40; P X) Modernised former student residence run by a helpful couple tuned to travellers' needs. Six of the 18 attractive rooms have a bathroom; there's a bathroom for each pair of other rooms. A sitting room with free Internet access adds appeal.

Hostal Lima (☎ 958 29 50 29; Calle Laurel de las Tablas 17; s/d €30/36, r with fridge €40, 2-person ste 2 €52; P X) On a quiet side street, the Lima has bright décor, brass bedsteads, firm mattresses, winter heating and TV.

SACROMONTE

Cuevas El Abanico (Map pp304–5; ☎ /fax 958 22 61 99, 608-848497; www.el-abanico.com; Vereda de Enmedio 89, Sacromonte; s/d/tr €58/58/73, 4-person 2-bedroom cave €88; P) Something different – cave lodgings in the Sacromonte *gitano* neighbourhood. The five cave apartments are comfortable and kitted out with heating, kitchen, bathroom, hot water and outdoor terraces. There's normally a two-night minimum stay.

CAMPING

There's one camping ground in the city, which holds 600 people, and half a dozen smaller ones within a few kilometres, most of them accessible by bus.

Camping Sierra Nevada (Map pp304–5; ☎ 958 15 00 62; Avenida de Madrid 107; camping per adult/tent/car €4.80/5.45/5.45; ☢) A short walk from the bus station, 2.5km northwest of the centre, this camping ground has big, clean bathrooms and a laundry. Bus No 3 runs between here and Gran Vía de Colón in the city centre.

Camping Reina Isabel (Map pp304–5; ☎ 958 59 00 41; Carretera Granada–La Zubia Km 4; camping per adult/tent/car €4/4/4; ☢) About 5km south of the centre, Reina Isabel is clean, with good bathrooms. Take the La Zubia exit from the Ronda Sur ring road.

Mid-Range

All hotels are on Map pp312–13 unless otherwise stated.

NEAR PLAZA NUEVA

Hotel Puerta de las Granadas (☎ 958 21 62 30; www.hotelpuertadelasgranadas.com; Calle Cuesta de Gomérez 14; s/d €72/90, superior r €100-180; X 🖳) A 19th-century

---

BE WARNED! – DRIVING IN GRANADA

Vehicle access to the Plaza Nueva area, and therefore to the narrow streets leading up from Plaza Nueva to the Alhambra and Albayzín, is restricted by red lights and little black posts known as *pilonas* that block certain streets during certain times of day. Residents and other authorised drivers slot cards into a box, causing the posts to slide down into the ground to let one car (only) pass. You'll see the warning sign *'Obstáculos en calzada a 20 metros'* and will have to detour. The only exception is if you are going to stay at one of the Plaza Nueva area hotels – in which case, press the button by your hotel's name beside the *pilonas* to speak with your hotel's reception, which will be able to lower the *pilonas* for you.

It's a good idea to ask advice beforehand from your hotel about parking. Some hotels have their own parking facilities for which they might charge you anything from €7.50 per day. Alternatively, there are underground car parks such as **Parking San Agustín** (Map pp304–5; Calle San Agustín; per hr/day €1/16), just off Gran Vía de Colón, and **Parking Plaza Puerta Real** (Map pp312–13; Acera del Darro; per hr/day €1/10), as well as the Alhambra car parks (see p307).

building reformed in modern minimalist style with wooden shutters and elegant furnishings. The more expensive, luxurious rooms have a number of windows that catch divine views of the Alhambra and/or the old city roofline. Prices drop significantly mid-week. There's also a lift.

Hotel Anacapri (☎ 958 22 74 77; www.hotelanacapri .com; Calle Joaquín Costa 7; s/d €78/105; ✖) Just a minute's walk from Plaza Nueva, the Anacapri has 49 pretty rooms in varied colours, with floral bedspreads, cork floors and satellite TV. Its 18th-century patio is fitted out with cane chairs and palms. Buffet breakfast is €7.50 and the reception staff make you welcome.

Hotel Maciá Plaza (☎ 958 22 75 36; www.maciahotel es.com; Plaza Nueva 4; s/d €50/73; P ✖ 🖳) This, one of four Maciás in Granada, has 44 comfy rooms with attractive enough décor but its top location is its major draw card. Try for a double overlooking the plaza. Its single rooms are small. Rates drop to €50 a double on weekends in winter, July and August.

ALHAMBRA
Hotel América (Map p306; ☎ 958 22 74 71; www .hotelamericagranada.com; Calle Real de la Alhambra 53; s/d €70/106; 🌙 Mar-Nov; ✖) Within the Alhambra grounds, this is in an early 19th-century building. Alas, although it has a stupendous location, there are only 17 rooms, and reservations are essential. There's a leafy patio where good lunches are served.

Hotel Guadalupe (Map pp304-5; ☎ 958 22 34 23; www.hotelguadalupe.es; Avenida Los Alixares s/n; s/d €76/104; P ✖) Almost on the Alhambra's doorstep, the well-managed Guadalupe has 42 spacious, beautifully fitted-out rooms. All have views of some sort, be they of the Alhambra or the beautiful olive groves behind.

ALBAYZÍN
Casa del Capitel Nazarí (☎ 958 21 52 60; www.hotel casacapitel.com; Cuesta Aceituneros 6; s/d €73/91; ✖ 🖳) This reformed Albayzín mansion focuses on a 16th-century patio with wooden balconies and ancient pillars, and is named after the marble Nasrid-era capital on one of the pillars. Décor is quiet.

Casa del Aljarife (☎ /fax 958 22 24 25; www.granada info.com/most; Placeta de la Cruz Verde 2; r €95; ✖) A beautifully restored 17th-century house in the Albayzín, Casa del Aljarife has just four spacious, character-filled rooms, help-

ful hosts and a pretty patio where you can take breakfast in warmer weather.

Hotel Zaguán (☎ 958 21 57 30; www.hotelzaguán .com; Carrera del Darro; s €50, r €64-100; ✖ 🖳) A restored 16th-century Albayzín house, which was almost a complete ruin. Its 13 rooms are all different; some front the Río Darro. The Zaguán has a bar-restaurant, too.

REALEJO
Hotel Molinos (☎ 958 22 73 67; www.eel.es/molinos; Calle Molinos 12; s/d €50/73; P ✖) In the interesting Realejo district, the Molinos is neat, clean and tiny – it has just nine rooms and it once made the *Guinness Book of Records* as the world's narrowest hotel. Rooftop views are 360-degree.

Hostal La Ninfa (☎ 958 22 79 85; Campo del Príncipe s/n; s/d €45/65; ✖) Also in Realejo, this rustic place is covered in brightly painted ceramic stars, both outside and in. It has a pretty foyer-cum-breakfast-room and 10 clean, cosy rooms. The friendly owners speak English and German.

PLAZA BIB-RAMBLA & AROUND
Hotel Reina Cristina (☎ 958 25 32 11; www.hotelreina cristina.com; Calle Tablas 4; s/d €66/98; P ✖) The Reina Cristina, just off Plaza de la Trinidad, is a renovated 19th-century mansion that once belonged to the Rosales family, friends of Lorca. The writer spent his last days here before being arrested and subsequently murdered by the Nationalists during the civil war. Rooms are very comfortable and have satellite TV. There is also a good restaurant.

Hotel Navas (☎ 958 22 59 59; www.hotelesporcel .com; Calle Navas 22; s/d €72/96; ✖) A perfectly adequate but unexciting city-centre hotel. With 44 rooms, it's on a manageable scale, and all rooms have an external window, pastel tones, satellite TV and a safety box. Prices tumble in July and August.

Hotel Los Tilos (☎ 958 26 67 12; www.hotellostilos .com; Plaza Bib-Rambla 4; s/d €41/65; ✖) Provides comfy rooms (the 26 doubles are a good size, the four singles small). Eleven doubles overlook the plaza and there's a small but panoramic roof terrace. Buffet breakfast is €5.

Top End
ALHAMBRA
Parador de Granada (Map p306; ☎ 958 22 14 40; www .parador.es; Calle Real de la Alhambra s/n; s/d €182/228; P ✖) This is the Alhambra's San Fran-

cisco monastery, converted into a hotel. Originally built in the time of the Catholic Monarchs, whose initial burial place was here, it's the most expensive parador in Spain. You can't beat its location within the Alhambra and its historical connections. Book ahead.

ALBAYZÍN

The following hotels in the Albayzín all have English-speaking staff and offer breakfast for €10. Each one is sumptuously decorated and has its individual stamp.

Casa Morisca Hotel (Map pp312–13; ☎ 958 22 11 00; www.hotelcasamorisca.com; Cuesta de la Victoria 9; s/d interior €90/119, exterior €120/150; ▨) Occupies a late-15th-century mansion that's centred on a patio with an ornamental pool and wooden galleries. It has 14 rooms, which aren't huge but are full of atmosphere.

Hotel Carmen de Santa Inés (Map pp312–13; ☎ 958 22 63 80; www.carmensantaines.com; Placeta de Porras 7; s/d €95/105, r with sitting room €125-200; ▨) The nine rooms here, in an Islamic-era house that was extended in the 16th and 17th centuries, are furnished with antiques, and the lovely patio opens onto a garden of myrtles, fruit trees and fountains.

Hotel Palacio de Santa Inés (Map pp312–13; ☎ 958 22 23 62; www.palaciosantaines.com; Cuesta de Santa Inés 9; r €80-105, with sitting room €128-225; ▨) Has 35 rooms in an early-16th-century building, with reception installed in the Renaissance patio. Park first and walk, or take a taxi.

AROUND PLAZA ISABEL LA CATÓLICA

Hotel Palacio de Santa Paula (Map pp304–5; ☎ 902 29 22 93; www.ac-hotels.com; Gran Vía de Colón; r from €205; ℗ ▨ 🖳) This opulent and beautiful five-star hotel occupies a former 16th-century convent, some 14th-century houses with patios and wooden balconies, and a 19th-century bourgeoisie house, all with a contemporary overlay. The rooms sport every top-end luxury and the hotel has a fitness centre, sauna and Turkish bath.

EATING

After parading around the Alhambra and exploring the Albayzín warren, it's time to let loose on Granada's gastronomic scene – and with tapas bars and restaurants teeming with life, it's clear that food is a highlight of any trip here. Hearty local dishes include the typical *rabo de toro* (oxtail stew), *habas con jamón* (broad beans with ham) and *tortilla Sacromonte*, a tasty omelette (traditionally made with calf brains and bull testicles!). The well-known *granadino* custom of serving free tapas with drinks in bars is one that will have a huge impact on your waistline. The free tapas can differ enormously from bar to bar; olives in one may be a cheese roll or stylish haute-cuisine stew in another. Part of the fun is finding a tapas haunt to suit your taste. Top tapas areas include the roads off Calle de Elvira (near Plaza Nueva), south of the cathedral and Calle Navas. For terrace dining head for Plaza Nueva, Paseo de los Tristes and Plaza Bib-Rambla. Alternatively, if incense-infused *teterías* are up your street then atmospheric Calle Calderería Nueva has a muddle of choices.

A mesmerising experience is dining in the Albayzín. The reward for finding a restaurant with a terrace is a spectacular view of the Alhambra, which is theatrically floodlit at night.

Near Plaza Nueva   Map pp312–13

Café Central (☎ 958 22 97 06; Calle de Elvira; tapas €1.95, raciones €4.20-8.50) Bleary-eyed travellers can perk up with a strong morning coffee (€1.60) at this no-nonsense café opposite Plaza Nueva.

Al Andalus (☎ 958 22 67 30; Calle de Elvira; mains €3-6) Scurry off with a neatly wrapped parcel of falafel in pitta (€3) from Al Andalus and indulge in an Arabic fast-food feast.

Bodegas Castañeda (Calle Almireceros; tapas €1.60-2.20) An institution among locals and tourists alike, this place whips up classy food in a typical bodega (traditional wine bar) setting. Fill up on Spanish tortilla and *alioli* (aïoli; garlic mayonnaise).

Antigua Bodega Castañeda (Calle de Elvira; mains €6.90-13.50) If the barrels of potent 'Costa' wine from the Sierra de la Contraviesa tempt you to the point of befuddlement then sober up with a few *montaditos* (small sandwiches; €3.20 to €4.40). These slices of bread come with a variety of toppings.

Vía Colón (☎ 958 22 98 42; Gran Vía de Colón 13; mains €10-17; ⏰ 8am-1am) Decorated with cherubs and angels, this smart and popular café-bar serves up fancy crepes, coffee and snacks at the bar and meaty mains, such as the delicious *jamón ibérico de bellota* (ham made from pigs fed on *bellotas* (acorns);

€16.95). There are more seats on the terrace by the cathedral.

Jamones Castellano (cnr Calles Almireceros & Joaquín Costa) This Spanish delicatessen sells basic groceries that are ideal for picnics. Get a few slices of *jamón serrano* (mountain-cured ham) and some cheese to stuff your own *bocadillo* (filled roll).

For fresh fruit and veg head for the large, covered **Mercado Central San Agustín** (Calle San Agustín), a block west of the cathedral.

Inhale the lingering aroma of the herb and spice stalls along the Calle Cárcel Baja side of the cathedral. The bulging sacks contain everything from camomile to saffron.

Alhambra   Map pp306

Parador de Granada (☎ 958 22 14 40; Calle Real de Alhambra s/n; sandwiches from €5.05; ⌚ 11am-11pm) The effortlessly charming Parador de Granada is a swanky place to indulge in fine fare or sup a simple cup of thick hot chocolate (€2.05) as you contemplate the Alhambra's magnificence. The whole experience will leave you feeling rather special – as intended.

La Mimbre (☎ 958 22 22 76; cnr Paseo del Generalife & Cuesta de los Chinos; menú turístico €17.50) Positioned under the sheer walls of the Alhambra, La Mimbre is the obvious tourist choice but the food is palatable and it's worth taking a breather in the leafy patio dining area after all that wandering.

Albayzín

The labyrinthine Albayzín holds a wealth of eateries, all tucked away in the narrow streets – some behind gates with inconspicuous bells and missable signs.

Kasbah (Map pp312-13; Calle Calderería Nueva 4; teas €1.80-2.40) Duck into this candlelit tea den and turn heads with a cream-topped Arabic special tea (€2.40). Match it with a doubly fattening cream-and-chocolate crepe (€2.30) and think about sleeping on one of the cushion-covered benches.

Tetería As-Sirat (Map pp312-13; Calle Calderería Nueva 4; teas €2-3) For another nose-twitching incense and tea experience try this little place opposite Kasbah. Among a head-spinning variety of teas you'll find Cocktail Cleopatra (€2.75) or a fruity mango infusion (€2), which complements the honey-and-orange crepe (€3) nicely.

Restaurante Arrayanes (Map pp312-13; ☎ 958 22 84 01; Cuesta Marañas 4; mains €7-17; ⌚ from 8pm) This well-applauded Moroccan favourite cooks up a delicious lamb tagine with prunes and almonds (€10) in authentic surrounds. It doesn't serve alcohol but you won't miss it.

El Agua (☎ 958 22 33 58; Plaza Aljibe de Trillo 7; fondues per person €13.95-18.80, minimum 2 people; ⌚ 1.30-3.30pm & 8-11.30pm Wed-Mon, 8-11.30pm Tue) Wild fondue feasts are the mainstay of this first-rate restaurant. Melt along with the cheese as you dunk your chunks of juicy ham and take in the fabulous Alhambra views. After all that (and the chocolate fondue dessert) you're guaranteed to leave satisfied.

Terraza las Tomasas (Map pp312-13; ☎ 958 22 41 08; Carril de San Agustín 4; mains €16-20; ⌚ 1.30-3.30pm Mon-Tue, 1.30-3.30pm & 8.30-11pm Wed-Sat) After hunting through the Albayzín jungle, ring the little bell here and prepare to be astonished. This classy restaurant is blessed with first-rate views of the Alhambra, impeccable service and commendable food. Dishes, such as the *granadino* favourite tortilla Sacromonte (€9 for starter), are good though your mind will probably be focused elsewhere.

Plaza Bib-Rambla & Around

Café Bib-Rambla (Map pp312-13; ☎ 958 71 00 76; Plaza Bib-Rambla 3; mains from €8) Fragrant flower stalls and no traffic make pedestrianised Plaza Bib-Rambla a peaceful option for al fresco dining. So pick a pew at this café and opt for a fluffy tortilla Español (€9.50).

Cunini (Map pp312-13; ☎ 958 25 07 77; Plaza de Pescadería 14; menú €17.85) The terrace at this swanky seafood restaurant buzzes with the sound of clanking cutlery, and chatty diners tucking into a variety of aquatic delights.

Guerrero (Map pp312-13; ☎ 958 28 14 60; Plaza de la Trinidad 7; raciones €5.40-6.60) The messy tissue-strewn floor indicates punters have enjoyed their fill at this bubbly café-bar. Try one of its ample ham-and-cheese *bocadillos* (€2.10).

Poë (Map pp304-6; Calle Paz; drink & tapa €1.50) Hearty free tapas dishes, such as chicken stew with polenta, are served in small earthenware bowls at this trendy bar. Hang out with the cheery, English-speaking bar staff and enjoy the vibe.

Om-Kalsum (Map pp304-5; Calle Jardines 17; drink & tapa €1.80) Those of you on a tapas trail can decamp from Poë to Om-Kalsum in a flash and start on the Arabic-influenced tapas served here. All of the dishes are unbelievably good (and all the better considering that they're free).

Los Diamantes (Map pp312-13; ☎ 958 22 70 70; Calle Navas 26; media raciones €6) Boisterous and smoky Los Diamantes offers great food to a sophisticated crowd. Fish lovers should try the *boquerones* (anchovies; *raciones* – meal-sized servings of tapas – €8) before hopping off to the other tapas bars on Calle Navas.

DRINKING

Granada buzzes with heel-clicking flamenco dancers, bottle-clinking travellers and grooving students out on the pull. The best street for drinking is Calle de Elvira but other chilled bars line the Río Darro at the base of the Albayzín and Campo del Príncipe attracts a sophisticated bunch

Bodegas Castañeda (p320) and **Antigua Bodega Castañeda** (p320) are the most inviting bars, with swaying crowds and slopping drinks. Other entertaining bars can be found along Placeta Sillería and Calle Joaquín Costa.

La Taberna del Irlandés (Map pp312-13; Calle Almireceros) This hybrid Spanish-Irish bar melds local tipples with international flavours. Whether you choose Tetley's Bitter or wine from the Spanish coast, you're likely to leave legless.

El Círculo (Map pp312-13; Calle de Elvira) One of Calle de Elvira's treasures, El Círculo is a calm and unpretentious tapas bar with a slightly retro feel. After one of the large spirit measures you might be wishing there were more seats, though.

Bagdad Café (Map pp304-5; Coca de San Andrés; ☾ from 6pm) A dirty side street and a derelict feel won't put off those hunting for Granada's alternative scene. Strain to hear the pulsing beat through the black door and then make your way into the chilled den.

Café Bar Elvira (Map pp304-5; Calle de Elvira 85; ☾ from noon) Every man and his dog packs into this trendy joint where, happily, the spirit measures are large and the mixers are splashed almost everywhere except in the glass.

La Fontana (Map pp312-13; Carrera del Darro 19; ☾ from noon) Huddle around the pool table and listen to rock ballads at this popular joint, opposite the first bridge over the Río Darro. Leave here tipsy and you'll be stunned at the size of the Alhambra looming above.

Casa 1899 (Map pp312-13; Paseo de los Tristes; ☾ from noon) Despite its location on 'Sad People Promenade', this drinking den, with its buffed wood and bodega vibe, has a range of spirit-lifting Spanish wines and liqueurs to ensure you leave happy.

El Rincón de San Pedro (Map pp312-13; Carrera del Darro 12; ☾ from noon) Turquoise walls and slate tiles give this hip bar a cooling feel to complement the sound of the Río Darro trickling past. Gaze out of the back doors onto the greenery at the base of the Alhambra as you sip a refreshing gin and tonic (€4.50).

ENTERTAINMENT

The excellent monthly *Guía de Granada* (€0.85), available from kiosks, lists entertainment venues and places to eat, including tapas bars.

The city's large university population includes plenty of aspiring musicians who keep the gig circuit alive. Look out for posters and leaflets advertising live music and nontouristy flamenco. The bi-weekly flyer *Yuzin* lists many live-music venues, some of which are also dance clubs where DJs spin the latest tracks.

Posters listing forthcoming cultural events can be viewed on the notice board in the foyer of **La Madraza** (Map pp312-13; Calle Oficios), located opposite the Capilla Real.

Nightclubs

AROUND PLAZA NUEVA

Granada 10 (Map pp312-13; Calle Cárcel Baja; admission €6; ☾ from midnight) Stay awake with a riotous bunch late into the night at the ever-popular Granada 10. The added appeal, apart from the skimpy outfits, is that it's housed inside a plush cinema. It's wise to adopt a smarter dress code.

El Eshavira (Map pp304-5; ☎ 958 29 08 29; Postigo de la Cuna 2; www.eshavira.com; ☾ from 10pm) Just off Calle Azacayas, duck down the spooky alley, battle with the hefty door and adopt the *granadino* penchant for dark, smoky haunts that ooze cool jazz and sultry flamenco.

Enano Rojo (Map pp304-5; Calle de Elvira 91; ☾ from 10pm) Gritty and grungy Enano Rojo, with its toadstool emblem, plays jazz and funk to a hip crowd on weekends. Mid-week it's a little tamer and the later you get here the better.

ELSEWHERE

Planta Baja (Map pp304-5; Calle Horno de Abad 11; www.planta-baja.com; ☾ 12.30am-6am Tue-Sat) Deprived

GRANADA'S FLAMENCO SCENE

It's difficult to see flamenco that's not geared to tourists but some shows are more authentic than others and attract Spaniards as well as foreigners. The quality of flamenco shows depends on who is performing. If some of Granada's top professionals are dancing, you're in for a good evening. If not, you may be disappointed.

Los Tarantos (Map pp304-5; ☎ 958 22 45 25 day, 958 22 24 92 night; Camino del Sacromonte 9; admission €21) You'll find a frenzy of flamenco delights all tightly packed in a cave at Los Tarantos. It is geared towards tourists but midnight shows on Friday and Saturday draw fewer foreigners; most tour and hotel groups opt for the 10pm performance. For these shows, you can pre-book tickets through hotels and travel agencies. Wear your dancing shoes if you want to sit in the first few rows: you'll be pulled up on stage before you know it! A string of other flamenco haunts can be found at the Sacromonte caves, though some are a rip-off.

Peña de la Platería (Map pp312-13; ☎ 958 21 06 50; Placeta de Toqueros 7) Buried deep in the Albayzín warren, Peña de la Platería is a genuine aficionados' club with a large outdoor patio. Catch a 9.30pm performance on Thursday or Saturday.

Eshavira (Map pp304-5; ☎ 958 29 08 29; www.eshavira.com; Postigo de la Cuna 2) This smoky den has live flamenco some nights. Check online for the latest programme.

In summer the flamenco nights at the **Centro de Interpretación de Sacromonte** (see Granada's Sacred Mountain, p315) are well worth catching. Flamenco dancers and singers also perform in some of Granada's more highbrow venues – see below) for details.

GRANADA PROVINCE

acid jazz and lounge lovers can indulge in a well-needed music fix here. You can catch DJ Toner and DJ Vadim going back to the old school with their hip-hop and funk sessions, too.

Morgan (Map pp304-5; Calle Obispo Hurtado 15; ☺ from 1am Tue-Sat) House-hunters can find what they're looking for at Morgan, where deep house, funky house and soulful house spar on the decks.

El Príncipe (Map pp312-13; Campo del Príncipe; admission around €10) Entertaining Granada's well-dressed bunch of party girls and suave bachelors, El Principe is the place to inhale strong aftershave and show off your moves.

El Camborio (Map pp304-5; ☎ 958 22 12 15; Camino del Sacromonte 47; admission €6; ☺ from 11pm Sat & Sun) Mixing modern sounds with prehistoric surroundings, El Camborio has two dance floors with one at cave level.

Concerts & Theatre

Centro Cultural Manuel de Falla (Map p306; ☎ 958 22 00 22; Paseo de los Mártires s/n) A haven for lovers of classical music, this venue right near the Alhambra presents weekly orchestral concerts.

The **Teatro Alhambra** (Map pp304-5; ☎ 958 22 04 47; Calle de Molinos 56) and the more central **Teatro Isabel La Católica** (Map pp312-13; ☎ 958 22 15 14; Acera del Casino) both have ongoing programmes of theatre and concerts (and sometimes flamenco).

SHOPPING

A distinctive local craft is *taracea* (marquetry), used on boxes, tables, chess sets and more – the best have shell, silver or mother-of-pearl inlays. Marquetry experts can be seen at work in Laguna Taller de Taracea (Map p306), opposite the Iglesia de Santa María in the Alhambra. Other *granadino* crafts include embossed leather; guitars; wrought iron, brass and copper ware; basket-weaving; textiles and, of course, pottery. Places to look out for Granada handicrafts include the Alcaicería, the Albayzín and Cuesta de Gomérez. Also try the government-run Artespaña in the Corral del Carbón (p311).

Strum your way home with a hand-made guitar from **Manuel L Bellido** (Map pp312-13; Calle Molinos) – peer in the workshop window for a glimpse of the *guitarrero* (guitar maker) at work.

The Plaza Nueva area (Map pp312–13) is awash with jewellery vendors, selling from rugs laid out on the footpath, and ethnic clothes shops.

For general shopping, trendy clothes and ever-delightful Spanish shoes try pedestrianised Calle de los Mesones, or **El Corte Inglés** (Map pp312-13; Acera del Darro).

GETTING THERE & AWAY

Air

Iberia (Map pp312-13; ☎ 958 22 75 92; Plaza Isabel La Católica 2) flies daily to/from Madrid and Barcelona.

Bus

Granada's **bus station** (Map pp304-5; Carretera de Jaén) is located almost 3km northwest of the city centre. All services operate from here except for a few to nearby destinations such as Fuente Vaqueros (p324). **Alsina Graells** (☎ 958 18 54 80) runs buses to Córdoba (€10.65, three hours, nine daily), Seville (€16.45, three hours direct, 10 daily), Málaga (€8.30, 1½ hours direct, 16 daily) and Las Alpujarras (see p336). It also operates buses to Guadix (€4.05, one hour, up to 14 daily), Baza (€7.15, two hours, up to eight daily) and Mojácar (€14.65, four hours, two daily). Alsina handles buses heading to destinations in Jaén province and on the Granada, Málaga and Almería coasts, and to Madrid (€13.40, five to six hours, 10 to 13 daily).

Alsa (☎ 902 42 22 42; www.alsa.es) runs buses up the Mediterranean coast as far as Barcelona (€58.10 to €69.35, seven to 10 hours, five daily). It also runs buses to many international destinations.

Car & Motorcycle

Car rental is expensive. **ATA Rent A Car** (Map pp312-13; ☎ 958 22 40 04; Plaza Cuchilleros 1) has small cars for one/two/seven days for €71/83/219.

Train

The **station** (Map pp304-5; ☎ 958 20 40 00; Avenida de Andaluces) is 1.5km west of the centre, off Avenida de la Constitución. Four trains run daily to/from Seville (€17.65, three hours) and to/from Almería (€11.80, 2¼ hours) via Guadix, and six to/from Antequera (€5.85 to €6.55, 1½ hours). Three go to Ronda (€10.50, three hours) and Algeciras (€15.75, four to 4½ hours). For Málaga (€12, 2½ hours) or Córdoba (€14, four hours) take an Algeciras train and change at Bobadilla (€7, 1½ hours). Five trains go to Linares–Baeza daily (€9.45 to €18, three hours), and one or two each to Madrid (€28.50 to €45, six hours), Valencia (€40 to €62, 7½ to eight hours) and Barcelona (€49 to €125, 12 to 14½ hours).

GETTING AROUND

To/From the Airport

The **airport** (Map pp304-5; ☎ 902 40 05 00) is 17km west of the city on the A92. At least five buses daily (€3), operated by **Autocares J González** (☎ 958 49 01 64), run between the airport and a stop near the Palacio de Congresos, stopping in the centre on Gran Vía de Colón, where a schedule is posted at the outbound stop, opposite the cathedral. A taxi costs around €18 to €20.

Bus

City buses cost €0.90. Tourist offices give out a leaflet showing routes. The Bono Turístico voucher (see p303) includes nine bus rides.

Bus No 3 runs between the bus station and Gran Vía de Colón in the centre. To reach the centre from the train station, walk straight ahead to Avenida de la Constitución and pick up bus No 4, 6, 7, 9 or 11 going to the right (east). From the centre (Gran Vía de Colón) to the train station, take No 3, 4, 6, 9 or 11.

Taxi

Taxis line up on Plaza Nueva. Most fares within the city cost between €4.50 and €7.50. To call a taxi, ring **Teleradio taxi** (☎ 958 28 06 54).

AROUND GRANADA

Granada is surrounded by a fertile plain known as **La Vega**, planted with poplar groves and crops ranging from potatoes and maize to melons and tobacco. The Vega has always been vital to the city and was an inspiration to the writer Federico García Lorca, who was born and died here. The **Parque Federico García Lorca**, a memorial park between the villages of Víznar and Alfacar (about 2.5km from each), marks the site where Lorca and hundreds – possibly thousands – of others are believed to have been shot and buried by the Nationalists at the start of the civil war.

FUENTE VAQUEROS

The house where Lorca was born in 1898, in Fuente Vaqueros village, 17km west of Granada, is now the **Museo Casa Natal Federico García Lorca** (☎ 958 51 64 53; www.museogarcialorca .org; Calle Poeta Federico García Lorca 4; admission €1.80;

guided visits hourly 10am-1pm & 5-7pm Tue-Sun Apr-Jun; 10am-2pm & 6-8pm Tue-Sun Jul-Sep; 10am-1pm & 4-6pm Tue-Sun Oct-Mar). The place brings his spirit alive, with numerous charming photos, posters and costumes for plays that he wrote and directed, and paintings illustrating his poems. A short video captures him in action with the touring Teatro Barraca.

Buses to Fuente Vaqueros (€1.10, 20 minutes) by **Ureña** (☎ 958 45 41 54) leave from Avenida de Andaluces in front of Granada train station. Departures from Granada at the time of writing were at 9am and 11am, then hourly from 1pm to 8pm except 4pm, Monday to Friday, and at 9am, 11am, 1pm and 5pm on Saturday, Sunday and holidays.

EAST OF GRANADA

The A92 northeast of Granada crosses the forested, hilly Parque Natural Sierra de Huétor before entering an increasingly arid landscape. Outside Guadix the A92 veers southeast towards Almería, crossing the Marquesado de Zenete district below the north flank of the Sierra Nevada, while the A92N heads northeast across the Altiplano, Granada's 'High Plain', which breaks out into mountains here and there and affords superb long-distance views on the way to northern Almería province.

GUADIX

pop 20,000 / elevation 915m

Guadix (gwah-*deeks*), 55km from Granada, is famous for its cave dwellings – not prehistoric remnants but the homes of about 3000 present-day townsfolk. Cave living is in fact fairly widespread in eastern Granada, and Guadix has the biggest concentration of underground homes.

Information

There's a **tourist office** (☎ 958 66 26 65; Carretera de Granada s/n; 9am-3pm Mon, 9am-4pm Tue-Fri, 10am-2pm Sat) on the Granada road leaving the town centre.

Sights

At the centre of Guadix is a fine sandstone **cathedral** (admission €2; 10.30am-1pm & 2-7pm Mon-Sat, 9.30am-1pm Sun), built in the 16th to 18th centuries on the site of the town's former main mosque in a mix of Gothic, Renais-

sance and baroque styles. Nearby, **Plaza de las Palomas** is beautiful when floodlit at night.

A short distance south you'll find the 10th- and 11th-century Islamic castle, the **Alcazaba** (Calle Barradas 3; admission €1.20; 11am-2pm & 4-6.30pm Tue-Sat, 10am-2pm Sun), which gives views over the main cave quarter, the Barriada de las Cuevas, some 700m south.

The typical 21st-century cave has a white-washed wall across the entrance, a chimney and TV aerial protruding from the top, and all mod cons inside. Some have many rooms. The caves maintain a comfortable temperature of around 18°C year-round. The **Cueva Museo Municipal** (☎ 958 66 08 08; Plaza de Padre Poveda; admission €1.35; 10am-2pm & 4-6pm Mon-Sat, 10am-2pm Sun & holidays), in the Barriada de las Cuevas, recreates typical cave life.

Sleeping & Eating

Cuevas Pedro Antonio de Alarcón (☎ 958 66 49 86; www.andalucia.com/cavehotel; Barriada San Torcuato; s/d/q €36.90/55.65/88.25; P) This offers the genuine Guadix experience: sleeping in a cave. This is in fact a comfy, modern cave-apartment-hotel with a pool and restaurant. It's 3km from the town centre, along the Murcia road heading towards the A92 (look for 'Alojamiento en Cuevas' signs).

Hotel Comercio (☎ 958 66 05 00; www.hotelcomercio .com; Calle Mira de Amezcua 3; s €42.80, d €54.55-64.20;) This long-standing central hotel had a complete make-over a few years ago and offers very comfy rooms and a fine restaurant with a wide variety of medium-priced Spanish fare.

Hotel Mulhacén (☎ 958 66 07 50; www.hotelmul hacen.com; Avenida Buenos Aires 41; s/d €29.50/37.60, superior rooms €33.40/42.70; P) A straightforward place on the Murcia road 600m from the centre.

Getting There & Away

Guadix is about one hour from Granada (bus €4.05, train €5.55) and 1½ hours from Almería (bus €6.85, train €6.15 to €14); there are at least nine buses and four trains daily in each direction. At least two daily buses head to Baza (€3.25, one hour) and Mojácar (€10.50, three hours). The **bus station** (☎ 958 66 06 57; Calle Concepción Arenal) is off Avenida Medina Olmos, about 700m southeast of the centre. The train station is off the Murcia road, about 2km northeast of the town centre.

DETOUR: ORCE

The dusty Altiplano village of Orce styles itself as the 'Cradle of European Humankind'. A fossilised bone fragment possibly between one and two million years old, found in 1982 at nearby Venta Micena, may be part of the skull of an infant *Homo erectus*, an ancestor of *Homo sapiens*. If so, the bit of bone would be the oldest known human remnant in Europe. The many sceptics, however, say the 'Hombre de Orce' (Orce Man) fragment more likely came from a horse or deer and could be less than a million years old. Even so, Orce can still claim Spain's oldest evidence of human presence in the form of stone tools that are 1.3 million years old.

For most of the last four million years, much of the Hoya de Baza, the now arid basin in which the Baza-Orce area lies, was a lake. Wildlife drinking at the edge of the lake was vulnerable to attack by larger animals, and the fossilised bones of dozens of species, including mammoth, rhinoceros, sabre-tooth tiger, hippopotamus, giant hyena, wolf, bear, elephant and buffalo, relics of such encounters between one and two million years ago, have been found at Venta Micena and nearby sites.

A good selection of the finds – including enormous mammoths' teeth and a replica of the 'Hombre de Orce' fragment (the original is under lock and key in Orce *ayuntamiento* (town hall)) – are on show in Orce's interesting **Museo de Prehistoria y Paleontología** (☎ 958 74 61 01; admission €1.50; ⏰ 11am-2pm Tue-Sun year-round, 6-8pm Tue-Sun Jun-Sep, 4-6pm Tue-Sun Oct-May), in an Islamic castle just off the village's central square.

Orce makes an interesting detour if you are driving between Granada/Guadix/Baza and the Los Vélez area of northern Almería province (p396). Eighteen kilometres east of Baza on the A92N, turn north along the A330 towards Huéscar. After 23km, turn east along the SE34 for Orce (6km away).

Continuing east from Orce it's a further 30km to María, the first Los Vélez village. As you cross the empty plains between Orce and María, it's quite a thrill to know that this landscape was once roamed by the likes of mammoths, sabre-tooth tigers and elephants.

MARQUESADO DE ZENETE

This bleak, flat area between Guadix and the Sierra Nevada was a prosperous agricultural district in Islamic times. After the Reconquista it was awarded to Cardinal de Mendoza, chief adviser to the Catholic Monarchs during the war against Granada. His illegitimate son Rodrigo de Mendoza became its first *marqués* (marquis).

The main town, **Jerez del Marquesado**, is a starting point for ventures into the high Sierra Nevada. Thirteen kilometres east of Jerez, the forbidding **Castillo de La Calahorra** (admission €3; ⏰ 10am-1pm & 4-6pm Wed, other times by appointment with caretaker Antonio Trivaldo ☎ 958 67 70 98) looms above the village of **La Calahorra**. The castle was built between 1509 and 1512 by Rodrigo de Mendoza, whose tempestuous life included a spell in Italy unsuccessfully wooing Lucrezia Borgia. The building's domed corner towers and blank walls enclose an amazingly elegant Italian Renaissance courtyard which has a staircase of Carrara marble. There are at least two *hostales* and one hotel to be found in La Calahorra village, from which the A337

heads south over the **Puerto de la Ragua** pass to Las Alpujarras.

BAZA

pop 21,000 / elevation 850m

The market town of Baza, 44km northeast of Guadix, dates back to Iberian times. Its attractive Plaza Mayor is dominated by the 16th-century **Iglesia Concatedral de la Encarnación**. Baza's **tourist office** (☎ 958 86 13 25; Plaza Mayor 2; ⏰ 10am-2pm & 4-6.30pm except holidays) is in the same building as the town's good **Museo Municipal** (☎ 958 70 35 55; admission €1.20; ⏰ 10am-2pm & 4-6.30pm except holidays), whose mainly archaeological collection includes a copy of the *Dama de Baza*, a person-sized Iberian goddess statue unearthed locally in 1971 (the original is housed in Madrid's Museo Arqueológico Nacional).

Cuevas Al Jatib (☎ 958 34 22 48; www.aljatib.com; Arroyo Cúrcal s/n; 2-person cave €75-95, 4-/6-person cave €89-143; 🅿) is almost a mini-cave-resort on the edge of town, with comfortable accommodation in five caves (all with fireplace and fully equipped kitchen), plus Arab baths, tearoom, restaurant, play-cave for kids and one disabled-adapted cave! An alternative in town, about half a kilometre south of Plaza Mayor, is the friendly **Hostal Anabel** (☎ 958 86 09 98; Calle María de Luna s/n; s/d €22/38; 🔀).

The **bus station** (☎ 958 70 21 03; Calle Reyes Católicos) is 200m north of Plaza Mayor. There are about 15 buses a day to/from Guadix (€3.25, one hour) and Granada (€7.15, two hours) in one direction and Vélez Rubio (€3.65, 1½ hours) in the other.

SIERRA NEVADA

The Sierra Nevada mountain range, with mainland Spain's highest peak, Mulhacén (3479m), forms an almost year-round snowy, southeastern backdrop to Granada. The range extends about 75km from west to east, crossing from Granada into Almería province.

All the highest peaks (3000m or more) are towards the range's western (Granada) end, and it's on the northern flank of this end of the range that the Sierra Nevada ski station, Europe's most southerly and one of Spain's best, stands. In the warmer seasons the mountains and the valleys beneath them (especially Las Alpujarras, to the south) offer wonderful walking. Lonely Planet's *Walking in Spain* details eight days of good walking in the Sierra Nevada and Las Alpujarras.

The best overall maps of the area are Editorial Alpina's *Sierra Nevada, La Alpujarra* (1:40,000) and Editorial Penibética's *Sierra Nevada* (1:50,000). Both come with booklets, in English or Spanish, describing walking, biking and skiing routes.

The best period for walking in the high mountains is early July to early September: only then is the high ground reliably snow-free and the weather relatively settled. Unfortunately this doesn't coincide with the most comfortable months down in the valleys (see p331). Late June/early July and the first half of September are the best compromise periods. The Sierra Nevada is a serious mountain range: temperatures on the summits average 14°C less than in the highest Alpujarras villages. You should come well equipped, and prepared for cloud, rain or strong, icy winds at *any* time.

Nearly all the upper reaches of the Sierra Nevada are included in the 862-sq-km

Parque Nacional Sierra Nevada, the biggest of Spain's dozen national parks. This rare high-altitude environment is home to 2100 of Spain's 7000 plant species, among them unique types of crocus, narcissus, thistle, clover, poppy and gentian. Andalucía's largest ibex population (about 5000) is here, too – in summer, walkers may come across ibex anywhere above about 2800m.

Surrounding the national park, at lower altitudes, is the 848-sq-km Parque Natural Sierra Nevada, with a lesser degree of protection.

ESTACIÓN DE ESQUÍ SIERRA NEVADA

The A395 leads from Granada to the Estación de Esquí Sierra Nevada (Sierra Nevada Ski Station), with high peaks rising behind it.

The **ski station** (☎ 902 70 80 90; www.sierranevadaski.com), at Pradollano, 33km from Granada, is an ugly modern construction and very crowded on weekends and holidays in the ski season (when it has a thumping nightlife), but the skiing and the facilities are good enough to have hosted the World Alpine Skiing championships in 1996 and now a World Cup event every year. Snow conditions and weather are frequently better than in more northerly Spanish ski resorts.

Information

About 10km before the ski station is the **Centro de Visitantes El Dornajo** (☎ 958 34 06 25; ☼ 10am-2pm & 6-8pm Apr-Sep, 10am-2pm & 4-6pm Oct-Mar), with plenty of Sierra Nevada information, and maps for sale.

Activities

The ski season normally lasts from December to April or early May. *Forfaits* (lift passes; one day for €23 to €33) and accommodation cost the least in the 'promotional' periods at the beginning and end of the season, and cost the most around Christmas/New Year and other holiday periods, and on Saturday and Sunday from January to March.

The station has 67 marked downhill runs totalling 76km – four graded black (very difficult), 31 red (difficult), 24 blue (easy) and eight green (very easy). The highest start almost at the top of 3392m Veleta, the second-highest peak in the Sierra Nevada. Cable cars (€10 return for nonskiers) run up from Pradollano (2100m) to Borreguiles (2645m); other lifts go higher. There are

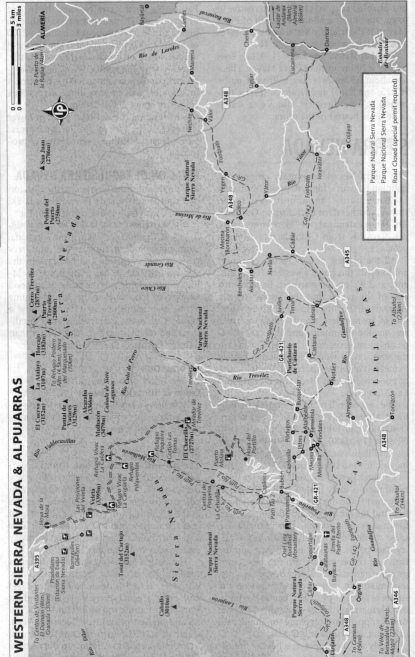

WESTERN SIERRA NEVADA & ALPUJARRAS

NOT JUST FOR SKIERS

The ski station is not just for skiers. You can ice-skate (per hour €7.50, including skate rental), ride a dog-sled (per person per half-hour €40), go snowshoeing (per two hours €34) and even toboggan on giant inner tubes (per half-hour €15). Remember that nonskiers need to wrap up just as warmly as skiers!

The Al-Andalus cable car has wheelchair access, and skiing equipment for the disabled is available near its upper station.

Outside the ski season the **Sierra Nevada Activa programme** (www.sierranevadaactiva.com) lays on a host of warmer-weather activities. Options include mountain-biking to Trevélez (one day €78) or the coast (two days €170), a four-day trek to several of the range's 3000m-plus peaks (€346), a day's horse ride to the Cañada de Siete Lagunas (€80), and canyoning on the Río Verde above Almuñécar (per day €75). In winter it offers cross-country skiing expeditions and guided ascents of the high peaks.

cross-country routes, too, and a dedicated snowboard area above Borreguiles.

Kit yourself out at the resort's numerous ski-hire shops. Skis, boots and poles cost €21 for one day; a snowboard and boots cost €24. The resort has several ski and snowboard schools: a six-hour weekend course is €57.

Sleeping & Eating

The ski station has around 20 hotels, *hostales* and apartment-hotels. None is cheap (double rooms start at around €80) and reservations are always advisable. The best deals are ski packages, bookable through the station's website or phone number, which start at around €150 per person for two days and two nights with half-board and lift passes. Book two weeks ahead, if you can.

There are only a limited number of places to stay and eat that remain open outside of the ski season.

El Lodge (☎ 958 48 06 00; www.ellodge.com; Calle Maribel 8; r €214; ✹ year-round; **P**) This luxurious 20-room hotel is constructed in Finnish pine, giving a log-cabin effect to the rooms. It has a great Basque restaurant.

Hotel Ziryab (☎ 958 48 05 12; www.cetursa.es; Plaza de Andalucía; r €118.35; ✹ late Nov–early May; **P** **☎**) A larger (147-room) top-end hotel near the foot of the resort, this is reasonably attractive, with a lot of stone and wood.

Albergue Juvenil Sierra Nevada (☎ 958 48 03 05; Calle Peñones 22; adult/under 26 incl breakfast ski season €18.35/13.75, rest of year €12.25/9.05) The youth hostel near the top of the ski station has 341 places in dorm rooms holding two to four people, including six doubles that are adapted for the disabled. It's quite a hike up

to the hostel after an evening in the resort's bars, though!

These are some of the slightly less expensive hotel/*hostal* options:

Hostal El Ciervo (☎ 958 48 04 09; www.eh.etursa.es; Edificio Penibético; r €84; ✹ Dec-Apr)

Hotel Apartamentos Trevenque (☎ 958 48 08 62; www.cetursa.es; Plaza de Andalucía 6; r €105; ✹ year-round; **P**)

For food, take your pick from 30 varied eateries in the resort and nine up on the pistes.

Getting There & Away

In the ski season **Autocares Bonal** (☎ 958 46 50 22) operates three daily buses (four on the weekends) to the ski resort from Granada's bus station (one-way/return, one hour €3.60/6.60). Outside the ski season there's just one daily (9am from Granada, 5pm from the ski station). A taxi from Granada costs about €40.

MULHACÉN & VELETA

The Sierra Nevada's two highest peaks – Mulhacén (3479m) and Veleta (3395m), even in summer usually marked out by patches of snow – rise to the southeast of the ski station. They also crown the head of the Poqueira valley in Las Alpujarras on the southern flank of the range. Mulhacén is the highest peak in mainland Spain, and its summit supports a small shrine and a roofless chapel, a few metres from the edge of a near-perpendicular 500m drop to the Hoya de Mulhacén basin. The views, on a good day, take in such incredibly distant ranges as the Rif Mountains of Morocco and the Sierra de Cazorla.

A road climbs right over the Sierra Nevada from the ski station to **Capileira**, the highest village in the Poqueira valley, but it's closed to motor vehicles (except with a special permit) between Hoya de la Mora (2550m), some 3km up from Pradollano, and Hoya del Portillo (2150m), 12km above Capileira. From about late June to the end of October (depending on the snow cover) the Parque Nacional Sierra Nevada operates a shuttle bus service, called the Servicio de Interpretación Ambiental Altas Cumbres (High Peaks Environmental Interpretation Service), giving walkers access to the upper reaches of the range. The bus service runs about 6km up the road from Hoya de la Mora (to Las Posiciones del Veleta, at 3020m), and some 21km up from Capileira (to the Mirador de Trevélez, at 2680m). Tickets (one-way/return on either route €4/6) and further information are available from the national park information posts at **Hoya de la Mora** (☎ 630 95 97 39; ✆ about 8.30am-2.30pm & 3.30-7.30pm during bus-service season) and **Capileira** (☎ 958 76 34 86, 686-414576; ✆ about 9am-2pm & 4.30-7.30pm year-round).

Many exciting walks start from the near the top ends of the bus routes: the national park information posts have leaflets summarising them. From the Posiciones del Veleta it's about 4km to the top of Veleta, an ascent of about 370m with 1½ hours' walking (plus stops); or 14km to the top of Mulhacén, with four to five hours' walking; or about 15km (five or six hours) all the way over to Mirador de Trevélez (avoiding the summits). From the Mirador de Trevélez it's around three hours to the top of Mulhacén (6km, 800m ascent), or you could reach the **Cañada de Siete Lagunas**, a lake-dotted basin below the eastern side of Mulhacén, in 1½ to two hours.

If you want to make more than a day trip of it, there are four high-mountain refuges where you can spend the night.

The **Refugio Poqueira** (☎ 958 34 33 49; per person €8.20; breakfast/dinner €3.50/10; ✆ year-round) is a modern 87-bunk refuge with a restaurant and hot showers, towards the top of the Poqueira valley at 2500m. Phone ahead, if possible. You can get here by walking 4km from the Mirador de Trevélez (about one hour), or following the Río Mulhacén for 2.3km down from the road beneath the western side of Mulhacén, then veering 750m southeast along a path to the refuge.

Sleeping in the three *refugios vivac* (simple stone or brick shelters with boards for around 12 people to sleep on) is free, and they are always open, but reservations are not possible. **Refugio Vivac La Caldera** is below the western flank of Mulhacén, a 1½-hour walk up from Refugio Poqueira; **Refugio Pillavientos** is about a 20-minute walk southwest along the road from Refugio La Caldera; **Refugio Vivac La Carigüela** is at the 3200m Collado del Veleta pass below the summit of Veleta.

Overnight camping in the mountains is permitted, but only above 1600m, at least 50m from high-mountain lakes and at least 500m from staffed refuges and vehicle tracks. You must give prior notification by email, fax or letter to the park authorities: check the latest regulations at a park information office.

You can reach the refuges and high altitudes under your own steam, without using the shuttle service. From Capileira, path No 3 with yellow marker posts (see p333) makes its way up the Poqueira valley to Cortijo Las Tomas, from which it is about 45 minutes further up to the Refugio Poqueira – about five hours' walking from Capileira in all. A good route from Trevélez is to head northwestward up to the Cañada de Siete Lagunas, from which you can ascend Mulhacén via the rocky Cuesta del Resuello ridge – around seven hours' walking from Trevélez.

MONACHIL
pop 1000 / elevation 810m
This attractive village in the foothills just 6km southeast of Granada is the biggest magnet for climbers in the area thanks to a spectacular gorge, **Los Cahorros**, just to its east. There are 300 sport and classical routes here. Los Cahorros is also good for a short walk, with a suspension bridge and waterfalls. Monachil is also the home of British-run **Ride Sierra Nevada** (☎ 958 50 16 20; www.ridesierranevada.com), a recommended mountain-bike tour firm. It offers guided biking holidays with self-catering accommodation from UK£110 (long weekend) or from UK£175 (one week). Prices include airport transfers.

Buses to Monachil (€0.75, 15 minutes) run 20 times a day (10 on Saturday, four on Sunday) from Paseo del Salón in Granada.

LAS ALPUJARRAS

The wrinkled landscape along the southern flank of the Sierra Nevada, a 70km-long jumble of valleys known as Las Alpujarras or La Alpujarra, forms one of the most picturesque crannies of all Andalucía. Arid hillsides split by deep ravines alternate with oasislike white villages set amid gardens, orchards and woodlands watered by rapid streams. It's a delightful area to explore on foot and is the starting point for some of the best routes up into the Sierra Nevada.

Despite tourism and a recent wave of northern European (chiefly British) settlers, Las Alpujarras remains a world apart, with a rare sense of timelessness and mystery. The Berber-style villages, with their winding lanes of flat-roofed, two-storey houses (the lower storey is still often used for storage and animals), and the terraced and irrigated hillsides are ubiquitous reminders of the area's flourishing Islamic past.

The main road into the Alpujarras from the west is the A348 (C333 on some signs), which leaves the N44 34km south of Granada. The GR421 turns north off the A348 just west of Órgiva to wind along the northern slopes of the Alpujarras, rejoining the A348 a few kilometres north of Cádiar. Many Alpujarras villages are within the Parque Natural Sierra Nevada but none are within the Parque Nacional Sierra Nevada.

History

In Muslim times Berber migrants to Las Alpujarras introduced silkworms (the mulberry-leaf-eating caterpillars of the silk moth). Thread spun from the silkworms' unravelled cocoons was the raw material of the thriving silk workshops of 10th- and 11th-century Almería and, later, Nasrid Granada. Together with irrigation-based agriculture, the production of silk thread supported a population of probably over 150,000 in at least 400 villages and hamlets in Las Alpujarras by the late 15th century.

On his surrender to the Catholic Monarchs in 1492, Boabdil, the last Granada emir, was awarded Las Alpujarras as a personal fiefdom. He settled at Laujar de Andarax in the eastern Alpujarras (Almería province), but left for Africa the next year. Christian promises of tolerance gave way to forced conversions and land expropriations; in 1500, Muslims rebelled across the former Granada emirate, with Las Alpujarras in the thick of things. When the revolt failed, Muslims were given the choice of exile or conversion. Most converted – to become known as Moriscos – but the change was barely skin deep. A new repressive decree by Felipe II in 1567 forbade the use of Arabic names and dress and even the Arabic language, leading to a new revolt in 1568, led by an Alpujarras Morisco named Aben Humeya. Two years of vicious guerrilla war in the Alpujarras ended only after Don Juan of Austria, Felipe's half-brother, was brought in to quash the insurrection and Aben Humeya was assassinated by his cousin Aben Aboo.

Almost the whole Alpujarras population was then deported to Castile and western Andalucía, and some 270 villages and hamlets were re-peopled with settlers from northern Spain. The other villages were abandoned. Over the following centuries, the silk industry fell by the wayside and swaths of the Alpujarras' woodlands were lost to mining and cereal growing.

Walking

The best times for walking in Las Alpujarras are April to mid-June and mid-September to early November, when the temperatures are just right and the vegetation at its most colourful.

An infinity of good walks connects valley villages or heads up into the Sierra Nevada. *Holiday Walks in the Alpujarras* by Jeremy

---

BRITISH LITERATI IN LAS ALPUJARRAS

In the 1920s Englishman Gerald Brenan settled in the Alpujarras village of Yegen with 'a good many books and a little money', to escape the weight of British traditions. His book *South From Granada* is a fascinating picture of what was then a very isolated and superstitious corner of Spain, leavened by visits from Virginia Woolf and other literati. Another Englishman, Chris Stewart, settled in Las Alpujarras in the 1990s, as a sheep farmer near Órgiva; his best-selling *Driving over Lemons* and *A Parrot in the Pepper Tree* tell entertainingly of modern life as a foreigner in Las Alpujarras.

Rabjohns is a useful English-language guide available locally. Two long-distance footpaths traverse Las Alpujarras. One is the GR-7, which crosses Europe from Greece to Tarifa (Cádiz province): you could follow it through the Granada Alpujarras from Laroles to Lanjarón in one week. The 144km GR-142 runs east from Lanjarón along the length of Las Alpujarras, then curves northwest to Fiñana on the northern flank of the Sierra Nevada in Almería province.

See p327 for information on maps.

Sleeping & Eating

It's worth booking ahead for rooms in Las Alpujarras during Semana Santa and from July to September. Many villages have apartments and houses for short-term rental; ask in information offices or check websites such as **Turgranada** (www.turgranada.com).

Most Alpujarras food is straightforward, hearty country fare, with lots of good meat and local trout. Trevélez is famous for its *jamón serrano*, but other villages produce good hams too. A *plato alpujarreño* consists of fried potatoes, fried eggs, sausage, ham and maybe a black pudding, and usually costs around €6.

'Alpujarras' or 'Costa' wine comes from the Sierra de la Contraviesa, on the south flank of Las Alpujarras, and tends to be strong and fairly raw.

ÓRGIVA

pop 5100 / elevation 725m

The main town of the western Alpujarras, Órgiva is a scruffy but bustling place. On Thursday morning, locals and the international populace (which has a big hippy–New Age element) gather to buy and sell everything from vegetables to bead necklaces at a colourful market in the upper part of town, the Barrio Alto.

The landmark 16th-century twin-towered **Iglesia de Nuestra Señora de la Expectación** (Plaza García Moreno) stands beside Órgiva's central traffic lights. The **Alsina Graells bus stop** (Avenida González Robles 67) is about 300m down the street from here. You'll find banks and ATMs on and around Plaza García Moreno.

Sleeping & Eating

Hotel & Hostal Mirasol (☎ 958 78 51 08/59; Avenida González Robles 5 & 3; s/d hostal €17.10/27.80, hotel €32.10/42.80) Near the bridge over the Río Chico

on the western side of town, the Mirasol provides plain but adequately comfortable rooms with tile floors and all-white walls. Those in the hotel section are larger and newer and have TV.

Hotel Taray (☎ 958 78 45 25; www.turgranada.com /hoteltaray; A348 Km 18.5; r from €72.45; P ⊠ �ℝ) In a rural setting about 1.5km south of the centre on the A348 running down towards the Río Guadalfeo, this best hotel in town provides pleasant pastel rooms in Alpujarras-style buildings. It has a good restaurant and a lovely big pool at the bottom of its long, grassy garden.

Camping Órgiva (☎ 958 78 43 07; www.descubrela alpujarra.com; A348 Km 18.9; camping per adult/tent/ car €4.15/3.95/3.30, cabins & bungalows from €34.45; P ℝ) This camping ground, 2km south of the centre on the A348 towards the Río Guadalfeo, has a nice pool area and a reasonably priced restaurant but the area for camping is not large.

Mesón Casa Santiago (Plaza García Moreno; mains €6-12) Good for grilled meats at indoor or outdoor tables, right in the heart of town.

Café Baraka (Calle Estación 12A; snacks & light meals €2-3) The spicy aromas tell you this pleasantly spacious café, beside the municipal car park in the upper part of town, is a little different. Come here to enjoy herbal teas, milk shakes, *shwarmas* (meat sliced off a spit and stuffed into a pitta-type bread) or a variety of sandwiches.

PAMPANEIRA, BUBIÓN & CAPILEIRA

Pampaneira pop 340 / elevation 1050m
Bubión pop 360 / elevation 1300m
Capileira pop 570 / elevation 1440m

These villages, clinging to the side of the deep Barranco de Poqueira ravine 14km to 20km northeast of Órgiva, are among the prettiest, most dramatically sited, and most touristed, in Las Alpujarras. Their whitewashed stone houses seem to clamber over each other in an effort not to slide down into the gorge, while streets decked with flowery balconies wriggle between. Capileira, the highest of the three, is the best base for walks.

Information

You'll find ATMs just outside the car park entrance in Pampaneira, and in Capileira at **La General** (Calle Doctor Castilla).
Ciber Monfí Café Morisco (see Sleeping & Eating, p333) Internet café in Bubión.

GRANADA PROVINCE

Punto de Información Parque Nacional de Sierra Nevada (☎ 958 76 31 27; Plaza de la Libertad, Pampaneira; ☽ 10am-3pm Sun & Mon, 10am-2pm & 5-7pm Tue-Sat, afternoon hours 4-6pm about mid-Oct–Easter) Plenty of information about Las Alpujarras and Sierra Nevada; maps and books for sale.

Servicio de Interpretación de Altos Cumbres (☎ 958 76 34 86, 686-414576; ☽ about 9am-2pm & 4.30-7.30pm) By the main road in Capileira: information mainly about the national park, but also on Las Alpujarras.

Sights & Activities

All three villages – like many others in Las Alpujarras – have solid 16th-century **Mudejar churches** (☽ Mass times, posted on the doors). They also have small **weaving workshops** that you can poke your head into: an interesting little one in Bubión is French-owned **Taller del Telar** (Calle Santísima Trinidad; ☽ 11am-2.30pm & 5-8.30pm), with ancient looms from Granada. Also in Bubión, don't miss the **Casa Alpujarreña** (Calle Real; admission €1.80; ☽ 11am-2pm Sun-Thu, 11am-2pm & 5-7pm Fri, Sat & holidays), beside the church. This is an excellent little folk museum in a village house that was left untouched from the 1950s until its recent adaptation – a marvellous glimpse of bygone Alpujarras life!

WALKS

Eight trails ranging from 4km to 23km (two to eight hours) are marked by colour-coded posts in the beautiful **Barranco de Poqueira**. Although their starting points can be a little hard to find, they are marked and described on the recommended Editorial Alpina map (see p327). Most routes start from Capileira.

Path No 2, a 4km circuit down into the valley and back up again, starts at the end of Calle Cerezo in Capileira. Path No 4 (8km, 3½ hours) takes you from Capileira up to the hamlet of La Cebadilla, then down the western side of the valley and back up to Capileira. To find its start, walk down Calle Cubo from Plaza Calvario at the northern end of Capileira, turn right where the street takes its second turn to the left, and follow the street out into the countryside. Fork up to the right 125m after the last village building on your right. Path No 3 continues up the valley from La Cebadilla to Cortijo Las Tomas (from which it's a steep half-hour walk up to Refugio Poqueira) then returns to Capileira following a path high on the eastern side of the valley (the full round-trip from Capileira is 19km, about eight hours).

Nevadensis (☎ 958 76 31 27; www.nevadensis.com), at the information office in Pampaneira, offers hikes and treks with knowledgeable guides, including a combined 4WD and foot ascent of Mulhacén for €35 per person.

OTHER ACTIVITIES

Nevadensis (above) is a highly experienced local firm offering a host of guided activities in the area, including mountain biking, climbing, canyoning, horse riding and snowshoeing. Horse-riders recommend rides with **Rafael Belmonte** (☎ /fax 958 76 31 35; www .ridingandalucia.com) and **Dallas Love** (☎ 958 76 30 38; dallaslove@arrakis.es); both are Bubión-based, speak English and offer trail rides lasting anywhere up to about a week. **Horizonte Vertical** (☎ /fax 958 76 34 08; www.granadainfo.com/hv; Calle Nivel 6, Bubión) will take you paragliding over some of this thrilling topography.

Sleeping & Eating

PAMPANEIRA

Hostal Ruta del Mulhacén (☎ 958 76 30 10; www.ruta delmulhacen.com; Avenida Alpujarra 6; s €25-35, d €30-45) Most of the cosy rooms at this *hostal* at the entrance to the village have balconies, and a few have their own terraces with views down the valley.

Hostal Pampaneira (☎ 958 76 30 02; Avenida Alpujarra 1; s/d €25/36) Opposite Hostal Ruta del Mulhacén, this has a friendly local owner and clean, good-sized rooms. Its **Restaurante Alfonso** (trout €5.50, menú €9) is one of the village's best-value eateries.

Restaurante Casa Diego (☎ 958 76 30 15; Plaza de la Libertad 3; mains €5-9) In decent weather the pleasant upstairs terrace makes this a good choice from the three restaurants around the plaza. Trout with ham, and local ham and eggs, are good bets towards the budget end of the menu.

BUBIÓN

Hostal Las Terrazas (☎ 958 76 30 34; www.terrazas alpujarra.com; Plaza del Sol 7; s/d €21.40/28.90, 2-/4-/6-person apt €48.15/58.85/77.05) Friendly Las Terrazas, on a street just below the main road, has neat little rooms with folksy textiles and pine furnishings, and apartments nearby.

Ciber Monfí Café Morisco (☎ 958 76 30 53; www .cibermonfi.com; Calle Alcalde Pérez Ramón 2; light dishes €3-4; ☽ closed Tue & Wed) This tea-and-coffeehouse-cum-bar in a converted village house serves up great Arabic food. With a pretty garden terrace, Internet access, log fire in winter and live music on weekend nights, it's the Poqueira valley's coolest hang-out. Try the excellent *plato Monfí* (€10), combining a vegetarian, chicken or pork brochette with rice, couscous and salads.

CAPILEIRA

Cortijo Catifalarga (☎ 958 34 33 57; www.catifalarga .com; Carretera de Sierra Nevada; s €48.15, d €64.20-92, apt from €77; mains €6-12; **P**) This charmingly renovated old farmstead is the choicest base in the Poqueira valley. The signposted 500m driveway begins 750m up the Sierra Nevada road from the top of Capileira. Chestnut beams, stone floors and Moroccan rugs set the tone, and some rooms have their own terrace. You can dine indoors or out, and hear live music some nights. The views are fabulous and so is the food – a mix of Andalucian, Arabic, Catalan, vegetarian and more.

Mesón Poqueira (☎ 958 76 30 48; Calle Doctor Castilla 11; s/d €18/24, 2-/4-/6-person apt €48/80/90) Just off the main road, friendly Mesón Poqueira, run by two almost identical brothers, has plain but decent-sized rooms, plus a bar and restaurant.

Hostal Atalaya (☎ 958 76 30 25; www.hostal atalaya.com; Calle Perchel 3; s/d incl breakfast with view €22/34, without view €17/30) The Atalaya, just 100m down the road from Mesón Poqueira, is friendly and geared to travellers, with simple but pleasant rooms and plenty of information on offer.

Finca Los Llanos (☎ 958 76 30 71; www.hotelfinca losllanos.com; Carretera de Sierra Nevada; s/d €45/72; **P** ☆) At the top of the village, Los Llanos has tasteful rooms with terracotta tile floors, folksy textiles and phone – plus a good restaurant, pool and library.

Campileira (☎ 958 76 34 19; Carretera de Sierra Nevada; dm €11.75, d €26.75, camping per person/site €3.40/ 6.40; breakfast/dinner €2.15/8.55; **P**) Some 500m up the Sierra Nevada road from the top of the village, Campileira provides clean dorms in a spacious stone building, hot showers, inexpensive meals, camping on a grassy terrace – and to top it all off, fabulous views.

Restaurante Ibero-Fusión (☎ 958 76 32 56; Calle Parra 1; salads €5-8.50, mains €7-10; ☆ 7-10.45pm) This restaurant just below the church is a change from the regular Alpujarras fare – an Andalucian, Arabic and Indian fusion, with plenty of vegetarian specialities. Think

couscous, dhal, and Saharan turkey with dates and apples.

Bar El Tilo (☎ 958 76 31 81; Plaza Calvario; raciones €4-6) Come here for good-value *raciones* such as melon and ham or *patatas a lo pobre*, a potato dish with peppers and garlic.

Shopping

All three villages have many craft shops selling, among many other things, colourful, inexpensive, homespun Alpujarras cotton rugs. In Capileira **J Brown** (☎ 958 76 30 92; Calle Doctor Castilla) sells quality handmade leather and suede clothing at good prices, including waistcoats from €50.

PITRES & LA TAHA

Pitres pop 450 / Pitres elevation 1250m

Pitres is almost as pretty as the Poqueira gorge villages, but is less touristed. The five lovely hamlets in the valley just below Pitres – **Mecina**, **Mecinilla**, **Fondales**, **Ferreirola** and **Atalbéitar** – are grouped with it in a municipality called La Taha, the old Arabic name for the administrative units into which Las Alpujarras was divided. Ancient paths between these hamlets wend their way through lush woods and orchards, to the ubiquitous tinkle of running water, and the air seems thick with accumulated centuries. A few minutes' walk below Fondales is an old Islamic bridge over the deep gorge of the Río Trevélez, with a ruined Islamic mill beside it (ask for the *puente árabe*).

Sleeping & Eating

Sierra y Mar (☎ 958 76 61 71; www.sierraymar.com; Calle Albaicín, Ferreirola; s/d incl breakfast €28/48) This really charming guesthouse is tucked away in the wonderfully tranquil little village of Ferreirola, with nine individual rooms set around multiple patios and gardens. The welcoming, multilingual Danish and Italian owners have been here since the 1980s and you couldn't ask for more helpful or knowledgeable hosts, especially when it comes to planning walks in the district.

L'Atelier (☎ 958 85 75 01; www.ivu.org/atelier; Calle Alberca 21, Mecina; s/d €28.50/42, s/d incl breakfast €30/45; ☆ restaurant 7-11pm Wed-Mon) This welcoming little French-run vegetarian guesthouse, in a centuries-old village house, serves gourmet meatless meals and has six cosy rooms and an art gallery next door. Vegetarian cookery courses happen here, too.

Balcón de Pitres (☎ 958 76 61 11; www.balconde
pitres.com; Carretera GR421 Km 51, Pitres; camping per adult/
tent/car €5.35/5.35/4.80, cabins & cottages from €45;
P ⛽) Just above the main road on the
western side of Pitres, this camping ground
is shady and fairly spacious. It has a decent, inexpensive restaurant and some nice
wooden cabins.

Refugio Los Albergues (☎ 958 34 31 76; Pitres; dm
€7-8; ⛄ closed mid-Dec–mid-Feb) Los Albergues is
a small, simple walkers' hostel in a beautiful
setting 200m (signposted) off the GR421
main road on the eastern side of Pitres. It
has an equipped kitchen, hot showers and
interesting outdoor toilets. The friendly
German owner is full of information on the
area's many good walks. There's one double
room (without/with heating €21/24).

El Jardín (☎ 689-633529; Calle Escuelas Viejas,
Pitres; mains €6.50-8; ⛄ 7-10.30pm Tue-Fri, noon-11pm
Sat & Sun approx Semana Santa–Oct) This excellent
British-run vegetarian restaurant occupies
a lovely shady garden 200m east of Pitres'
plaza. The evolving *menú* (set menu) en-
compasses staples such as lasagne and pan-
cakes and exotica such as brie Curaçao, a
hard-to-resist combination of brie, tropical
fruits and vegetables, red-pepper sauce and
coconut.

Hotel Albergue de Mecina (☎ 958 76 62 41; www
.ocioteca.com/hotelmecina; Calle La Fuente s/n, Mecina;
r €64.20; P ⛽) A tasteful 21-room hotel,
modern and comfortable but with touches
of traditional Alpujarras style.

TREVÉLEZ

pop 800 / elevation 1476m
Trevélez, set in a gash in the mountainside
almost as impressive as the Poqueira gorge,
is famous for three reasons: it's a starting
point for routes into the high Sierra Nevada;
it produces some of Spain's best *jamón serrano*, with hams trucked in from far and
wide for curing in the dry mountain air; and
it claims to be the highest village in Spain.
Other villages actually have better claims to
the 'highest' title, but the Trevélez municipality is certainly the highest on the mainland as
it includes the summit of Mulhacén.

Along the main road you're confronted
by a welter of ham and souvenir shops,
but an exploration of the upper parts reveals a lively, typically Alpujarran village.
La General bank, just above the main road,
has an ATM.

Sleeping & Eating

Hotel La Fragua (☎ 958 85 86 26; Calle San Antonio 4;
s/d €23/35) The rooms at La Fragua are pine-
furnished and comfortable, but if a walking group decides to clatter forth at 6am,
you stand little chance of sleeping through
it. The hotel is towards the top of town, a
200m walk (signposted) from Plaza Barrio
Medio. Its restaurant, **Mesón La Fragua** (mains
€6-9), a few doors away, is one of the best
in town, with items including partridge in
walnut sauce, fig ice cream, excellent pork
solomillo (sirloin) and some good vegetarian dishes.

Camping Trevélez (☎ /fax 958 85 87 35; www
.campingtrevelez.org; Carretera Trevélez-Órgiva Km 1;
camping per adult/tent/car €3.50/3/3, 2-/4-person cabins
from €16.50/36.50; P ⛽) On a terraced hillside
with lots of trees 1km out of Trevélez, the
camping ground has ecologically minded
owners and a good-value **restaurant** (vegetarian
dishes €2.50-4, meat & fish dishes €6-7.50).

Hotel Pepe Álvarez (☎ 958 85 85 03; www.andalucia
.co.uk; Plaza Francisco Abellán s/n; s/d €23/41) By the main
road at the foot of the village, some of its
rooms have a terrace overlooking the busy
plaza.

Mesón Joaquín (☎ 958 85 89 04; GR421; 3-course
menú €7) Joaquín, on the western side of the
village, is one of Trevélez's better restaurants
but mind your head on the hanging hams!

Restaurante González (☎ 958 85 85 31; Plaza
Francisco Abellán s/n; mains €5-13) This good-value
place by the main road at the foot of the
village serves trout, ham, *plato alpujarreño*
and other local fare.

EAST OF TREVÉLEZ

Seven kilometres south of Trevélez the
GR421 road crosses the low Portichuelo de
Cástaras pass and turns east into a harsher,
barer landscape, yet still with oases of greenery around the villages. The central and eastern Alpujarras have their own magic, but see
fewer tourists than the western villages.

Bérchules

pop 800 / elevation 1350m
This village 17km from Trevélez is set in a
green valley that stretches a long way back
into the hills. The area around here offers
attractive walks.

Hotel Los Bérchules (☎ 958 85 25 30; www.hotel
berchules.com; Carretera s/n; s/d €30/41; mains €6-11; P),
by the main road at the bottom of Bérchules,

has good, clean, bright rooms (all with bathtub), helpful English-speaking hosts who can help you set up all manner of activities, the best restaurant in town (try the local lamb with mint) and a cosy lounge area with a bookcase full of books on Spain.

At **La Posada** (☎ 958 85 25 41; www.laposada berchules.com; Plaza del Ayuntamiento 7; per person with private/shared bathroom €18/15) villager Miguel has adapted two sturdy old village houses to provide simple but comfortable lodgings – geared to walkers but open to all. Vegetarian breakfast and dinner are available.

Cádiar
pop 1600 / elevation 850m
Down by the Río Guadalfeo 8km south of Bérchules, Cádiar is one of the bigger Alpujarras villages. The **Alquería de Morayma** (☎ /fax 958 34 32 21; www.alqueriamorayma.com; d €57-67, 4-person apt €88-98; P ♠), 2km south of Cádiar just off the A348 towards Órgiva, is one of the most charming places to stay in Las Alpujarras – an old farmstead lovingly renovated and expanded by its *granadino* owners to provide 19 comfortable rooms and apartments, all unique. There's excellent, moderately priced food, a library of Alpujarras information, great views, fine walking available nearby, and fascinating art and artefacts everywhere. The Alquería also hosts classes in tai chi, reiki, yoga and other disciplines.

Yegen
pop 400 / elevation 1100m
Yegen, where writer Gerald Brenan made his home in the 1920s, is about 12km east of Bérchules. Parts of the valley below Yegen have a particularly moonlike quality. **Brenan's house**, just off the village square, is marked by a plaque. Several **walking routes** have been marked out locally, including a 2km 'Sendero de Gerald Brenan'.

El Rincón de Yegen (☎ 958 85 12 70; www.aldearural .com/elrincondeyegen; s/d €25/36, 4-person apt €65; mains €7-13; P ♠) is a little hotel on the eastern edge of the village. It has comfortable rooms and an excellent, medium-priced restaurant. Succumb to the pears in Contraviesa wine and hot chocolate!

Válor
pop 800 / elevation 900m
Válor, 5km northeast of Yegen, was the birthplace of Aben Humeya, leader of the 1568

rebellion, and is the setting for the biggest of several annual Moros y Cristianos (Moors & Christians) festivities in Las Alpujarras that recreate the rebellion. On 14 and 15 September, colourfully costumed 'armies' battle it out noisily from midday to evening.

Mairena
pop 300 / elevation 1050m
The unspoiled village of Mairena, 6km from Válor, enjoys superb views from its elevated position. **Las Chimeneas** (☎ 958 76 03 52; www .alpujarra-tours.es; Calle Amargura 6; d incl breakfast €60; dinner €15; ☐ ♠) is a village house renovated in charming, uncluttered style by helpful young British owners who offer guided walks, mountain biking, horse riding, painting excursions and more. They also serve good dinners using organic local produce, and can organise transport from Granada or Guadix.

East of Mairena you encounter the A337, which crosses the Sierra Nevada by the 2000m Puerto de la Ragua pass (occasionally snowbound in winter) to La Calahorra (p326).

GETTING THERE & AWAY
Buses to the Alpujarras are run by **Alsina Graells** (Granada ☎ 958 18 54 80; Órgiva ☎ 958 78 50 02; Málaga ☎ 95 234 17 38; Almería ☎ 950 23 51 68). From Granada, buses leave three times daily for Órgiva (€3.60, 1½ hours), Pampaneira (€4.40, two hours), Bubión (€4.80, 2¼ hours), Capileira (€4.80, 2½ hours) and Pitres (€4.80, 2¾ hours). Two of the buses continue to Trevélez (€5.65, 3¼ hours) and Bérchules (€6.70, 3¾ hours). Return buses start from Bérchules at 5am and 5pm and from Pitres at 3.30pm.

Alsina also runs twice-daily buses from Granada to Cádiar (€6.15, three hours), Yegen (€6.95, 3½ hours) and Válor (€7.25, 3¾ hours), a Málaga–Órgiva bus (€8.30, 3¼ hours, once daily except Sunday), and a daily Almería–Bérchules service (€7, 3¾ hours).

THE COAST

Granada's 80km coastline is rugged and cliff-lined, with spectacular views from the N340 as it winds up and down between scattered seaside towns and villages. This coast is called the Costa Tropical because of the hot-climate crops such as custard apples, avocados and mangoes that are grown where the coastal plain broadens out a bit. East of Motril, the mountains often come right down to the sea, making for some of Andalucía's better scuba diving (especially around the towns of **Calahonda** and **Castell de Ferro**, although the settlements are drab and the beaches pebbly). West of Motril the terrain is less abrupt and there are three quite attractive beach towns.

SALOBREÑA

pop 11,000

Salobreña's huddle of white houses rises on a crag between the N340 and the sea. At the top is an impressive Islamic castle and below is a long, wide dark-sand beach. It's a low-key place for most of the year but jumps in August.

Orientation & Information

Avenida García Lorca, the easterly entrance into Salobreña from the N340, leads 200m straight to the helpful **tourist office** (☎ 958 61 03 14; Plaza de Goya; ⏰ 9.30am-1.30pm & 4-7pm Tue-Sat). The Alsina Graells bus stop is diagonally across the street from the tourist office and the beach is 1km further on.

Sights & Activities

Found a 20-minute walk uphill from the tourist office, the **Castillo Árabe** (Arab Castle; admission €2.55 incl Museo Histórico; ⏰ Castillo & Museo 10.30am-1.30pm & 4-8pm) dates from the 12th century, though the site was fortified as early as the 10th century. The castle was used as a summer residence by the Granada emirs. Legend has it that Emir Mohammed IX had his three daughters, Zaida, Zoraida and Zorahaida, held captive here; Washington Irving gives a version of this story in *Tales of the Alhambra*. The inner Alcazaba, a setting for many cultural events, retains much of its Nasrid structure. You can walk along parts of the parapets. Just below the castle is the 16th-century Mudejar **Iglesia de Nuestra Señora del Rosario**, with an elegant tower and striking arched doorway. The **Museo Histórico** (Plaza del Ayuntamiento) is nearby, in the former *ayuntamiento*, below the church.

The old Muslim town spills out below the castle, ending on one side in steep cliffs. There's a **mirador** on Paseo de las Flores, below the castle.

It is possible to drive to this upper part of town (follow 'Casco Antiguo' and 'Castillo Árabe' signs) but parking can be difficult. There's also an urban bus from the lower part of town up to the Iglesia de Nuestra Señora del Rosario a few times a day (except Sunday).

Salobreña's long **beach** is divided by a rocky outcrop, El Peñón. Playa de la Charca, the eastern part, is grey sand; the western Playa de la Guardia is more pebbly.

Sleeping

Hostal San Juan (☎ 958 61 17 29; www.hotel-san-juan .com; Calle Jardines 1; d €42; ✹) An appealing tiled and plant-dotted patio-lounge greets you as you enter this spick-and-span *hostal* on a quiet street about 400m from the tourist office. The spotless rooms have pleasing wrought-iron bedsteads and bold bathroom tiling, and there's an ample roof terrace.

Hotel Avenida (☎ 958 61 15 44; www.hotelavenida tropical.com; Avenida Mediterráneo 35; d incl breakfast €85.60; P ✹ ⌨) Between the town centre and beach, this new, family-oriented hotel is the best in town, with 30 comfortable but unfussy rooms with phone, satellite TV, bathtub and safe – plus its own restaurant, elegantly decked-out bar, Jacuzzi and sun terrace.

Pensión Mari Carmen (☎ 958 61 09 06; Calle Nueva 30; s/d €20/39, d with shared bathroom €24; ✹) A 10-minute uphill walk from Plaza de Goya, the Mari Carmen has beautifully bright and clean pine-furnished rooms, some with their own terrace, and a communal terrace with great views.

Eating & Drinking

There are loads of restaurants, beach-side *chiringuitos* (small open-air eateries) and bars, and a spot of nightlife, on and near the beachfront.

Restaurant El Peñón (☎ 958 61 05 38; Paseo Marítimo s/n; mains €6-12; ⏰ closed Mon) Just by the big rock dividing Salobreña's beach, El Peñón does good medium-priced seafood and meat, and you can sit outside almost on top of the waves.

Restaurante Tropical (☎ 958 61 25 84; Paseo Marítimo; mains €7.50-15; ⏰ closed Tue) This popular semi-open-air steakhouse serves up its meat with a variety of sauces, including pineapple and curry. It's right on the corner when you hit the beachfront road coming from town.

Also recommended are the following two restaurants:

Restaurante Travesía (☎ 958 61 26 72; Calle Antequera 4; pizzas & pasta €6-9; ✆ closed Mon) Panoramic views here, a couple of minutes' walk from the foot of the castle steps.

La Bodega (☎ 958 82 87 39; Plaza de Goya; menú €8, meat & fish mains €10-20) By the tourist office, with outdoor tables and good service.

Getting There & Away

Alsina Graells (☎ 958 61 25 21) has at least six daily buses to Almuñécar (€0.95, 20 minutes), Granada (€4.90, one hour), Málaga (€6.15, 1½ hours) and Nerja (€2.95, 40 minutes), plus four to Almería (€7.40, 1½ hours) and one (except Sunday) to Órgiva (€2.75, 30 minutes).

ALMUÑÉCAR
pop 23,000

Found 15km west of Salobreña, Almuñécar may appear uninviting but there's an attractive old section around its 16th-century castle, and the town has its own life independent of tourism. Popular with Spanish tourists and a growing community of northern Europeans, it's bright and not too expensive, although the beaches are mainly pebbly.

History

The Phoenicians set up a colony called Ex or Sex here in the 8th century BC to obtain oil and wine from interior Andalucía for trade. The Roman Sexi Firmum Iulium was founded in 49 BC. It was here that Abd ar-Rahman I arrived from Damascus in AD 755, going on to found the Muslim emirate of Córdoba. Later, the town served as a coastal fortress for the Granada emirate. And it was from Almuñécar that Granada's last emir, Boabdil, with 1130 supporters, finally abandoned Spain for North Africa in 1493.

Orientation & Information

The N340 runs across the northern part of town, with the bus station just to its south. Plaza de la Constitución, the main square of the old part of town, is a few minutes' walk southwest of the bus station, with a maze of narrow streets dotted with galleries and interesting boutiques, spreading to its south and southeast.

The beachfront is divided by a rocky outcrop, the Peñón del Santo, with Playa de San Cristóbal – the best beach (grey sand and small pebbles) – stretching to its west, and Playa Puerta del Mar to the east.

There's a **tourist information kiosk** (☎ 958 63 11 25; Avenida Fenicia; ✆ 10am-2pm & 5-8pm, afternoon hours 4-7pm about Oct-Apr) along the street from the bus station near the roundabout on the N340. The **main tourist office** (☎ 958 63 11 25; www.almunecar.info; Avenida Europa s/n; ✆ 10am-2pm & 5-8pm, afternoon hours 4-7pm about Oct-Apr) is 1km southwest of the kiosk and the roundabout in the Palacete de La Najarra, just back from Playa de San Cristóbal.

Sights & Activities

Just behind the Peñón del Santo is a tropical bird aviary, **Parque Ornitológico Loro-Sexi** (☎ 958 63 02 80; adult/child €2/1.40; ✆ 11am-2pm & 5-7pm, afternoon hours 4-6pm approx Oct-Apr). The top of the hill just inland is occupied by the **Castillo de San Miguel** (☎ 958 63 12 52; adult/child €2/1.40 incl Museo Arqueológico; ✆ 10.30am-1.30pm & 5-7.30pm Tue-Sat, 10.30am-1.30pm Sun, afternoon hours 4-6.30pm approx Oct-Apr), built by the conquering Christians over Islamic and Roman fortifications. It's a circuitous climb up to the entrance (on the northern side), but the castle commands excellent views and contains an informative little museum. The **Museo Arqueológico** (☎ 958 63 12 52; Calle Málaga; ✆ 10.30am-1.30pm & 5-7.30pm Tue-Sat, 10.30am-1.30pm Sun, afternoon hours 4-6.30pm approx Oct-Apr), a few streets northeast, is in a set of 1st-century Roman underground galleries called the Cueva de Siete Palacios. It displays finds from local Phoenician, Roman and Islamic sites plus a rare 3500-year-old Egyptian amphora, probably brought by the Carthaginians. One hundred metres along Avenida de Europa from the main tourist office is the **Parque Botánico El Majuelo** (admission free; ✆ 9am-10pm), where you'll find the **Factoría de Salazones de Pescado**, which is the remains of a Carthaginian and Roman fish-salting workshop. The park plays host to Andalucía's only summer jazz festival, the international **Festival de Jazz en la Costa**, in the first half of July.

You can paraglide, windsurf, dive, sail, ride a horse or bicycle, walk, or descend canyons in and around Almuñécar and nearby La Herradura (p339). The tourist office's website and its leaflet *Sport Tourism* have information.

Sleeping

The town has around 40 hotels, *hostales* and holiday apartments.

Hotel Casablanca (☎ 958 63 55 75; www.almunecar .info/casablanca; Plaza San Cristóbal 4; s/d €44.95/64.20; P ⊠) Overlooking the Peñón del Santo and almost opposite the monument to Abd ar-Rahman I on Playa de San Cristóbal, the Hotel Casablanca has 36 spacious and attractive rooms, each with beautiful and distinctive handmade furnishings. The rooms here come with either a balcony or a picture window.

Hotel California (☎ 958 88 10 38; www.hotelcalif orniaspain.com; Carretera N340 Km 313; s/d €33/48; P) The bar, lounge, restaurant and terrace here overlook the town and sea from an elevated position just off the N340 on the northwestern edge of Almuñécar, and are decorated with colourful Andalucian-Moroccan furnishings. The friendly young English and Belgian owners, one of them an experienced and enthusiastic paraglider, have created an atmosphere and style that's a bit different. The 10 colourful rooms all have a private balcony. The hotel offers packages for paragliders combining accommodation, breakfast, car hire, guiding and retrieval for around €400 per person per week.

Hostal Plaza Damasco (☎ /fax 958 63 01 65; Calle Cerrajeros 16; s €20-30, d €36-60) This is a spotlessly clean *hostal* in the older part of the town centre, prettily adorned with flowers and tiles. All 17 rooms have bathtub. Rates depend on the season.

Hostal Altamar (☎ 958 63 03 46; Calle Alta del Mar 21; s €16-25, d €30-50) On a narrow street lined with Internet cafés in the old part of the centre, the Altamar's rooms are plain brown-and-white but comfy; there's a pleasant lounge-cafeteria where you can get breakfast. Rates depend on the season.

Eating

La Galería (☎ 958 63 41 18; Paseo Puerta del Mar 3; mains €13-18, lunch menú €15 & €25; ✕ closed Wed) Above Playa Puerta del Mar on the eastern side of town, this distinctive restaurant is run by a talented young Belgian chef, serving up tasty duck, meat and fish dishes and inventive concoctions such as wild mushroom and foie gras lasagne.

La Trastienda (Plaza Kelibia; canapés €4-5) For tapas, head to Plaza Kelibia, a pedestrian plaza in the old town filled with tables

from several bars. La Trastienda's wonderful smoked salmon, caviar and cheese canapés come with a delicious salad; it also serves *tablas* (platters) of cold meats, cheeses and smoked fish for €6 to €10.

Restaurante Calabre (☎ 958 63 00 80; Playa de San Cristóbal; mains €9-15; ✕ closed Tue) For seafood on the beach, head to the Calabre at the eastern end of Playa de San Cristóbal. There's an open-air terrace facing the waves and a nice bright glassed-in area for cooler days. Beware of items priced by the kilogram!

Drinking & Entertainment

In summer Plaza Kelibia and the beach bars along Playa Puerta del Mar buzz all night. Musical events, theatre, poetry readings and a cine club happen at the **Casa de la Cultura** (☎ 958 83 86 05; Calle Angustias Viejas).

Getting There & Away

From the **bus station** (☎ 958 63 01 40; Avenida Juan Carlos I No 1), at least six buses a day go to Almería (€8.40, two hours), Granada (€5.95, 1½ hours), La Herradura (€0.70, 15 minutes), Málaga (€5.20, 1½ hours), Nerja (€2.10, 30 minutes), and Salobreña (€0.95, 20 minutes), and one (except on Sunday) to Órgiva (€3.30, 1¾ hours).

LA HERRADURA

pop 4300

The little resort town of La Herradura, 7km west of Almuñécar along the coast, attracts paragliders from far and wide for the thermals that rise around the hills backing its pretty, horseshoe-shaped bay. It's also popular locally for water sports and seafront restaurants. La Herradura's sheltered beach is packed during July and August; a few kilometres to the west, down a 1km side road beyond the towering Cerro Gordo headland, is a popular clothing-optional beach, Playa Cantarriján. Just over on the far side of Punta de la Mona, which forms the east side of La Herradura's bay, is an attractive pleasure-boat harbour, Marina del Este.

Orientation & Information

The Alsina Graells bus stop is at the top of Calle Acera del Pilar, by the N340. This street heads south to the seafront Paseo Andrés Segovia (also called Paseo Marítimo), which runs along the bay. There's a **tourist information kiosk** (✕ 10am-2pm & 5-7pm Mon-Fri, 10am-2pm

---

DETOUR: CARRETERA DEL SUSPIRO DEL MORO

If you're OK with narrow, winding, mountain roads then, for a truly spectacular alternative to the normal N323 up from the coast to Granada, take the Carretera del Suspiro del Moro from Almuñécar, with the option of stopping off for a good walk en route. From the N340 main road through Almuñécar, turn into town at the roundabout by the tourist information kiosk. Pass McDonald's on your left and follow the street around to the right, then take the first turn-off to the right – Calle Suspiro del Moro (you may notice a small 'Otívar' sign pointing in the direction you must go). The road passes under the N340 and heads northward out of Almuñécar up the Río Verde valley. You reach the village of Otívar after 13km. Make a note of your car's kilometre reading here.

From Otívar the road winds its way endlessly upwards with ever more breathtaking panoramas and ever higher, more jagged crags appearing above. In 13km the road ascends 1000m before, relatively speaking, levelling off for the next 7km to its highest point.

Sixteen kilometres from Otívar, the signed 7.35km Sendero Río Verde walking trail starts on the western side of the road. This circular route of around 3½ hours descends nearly 400m into the deep valley of the Río Verde, with fine views and a good chance of sighting ibex as you go. At the highest point of the road, 3.5km later, another marked walk branches off to the Pico de Lopera (1485m), 2.5km west. Beyond here the landscape is generally gentler and after around 15km you start to get views of the often snowcapped Sierra Nevada to the east.

Turn left 35km from Otívar onto a road signed 'Suspiro del Moro' and in five minutes you emerge in front of the Suspiro del Moro restaurant, with Granada in view 12km to the north. You're at the Puerto del Suspiro del Moro, the 'Pass of the Moor's Sigh,' where, legend has it, the last Muslim emir of Granada, Boabdil, looked back and wept as he left the city for the final time in 1492. Follow the 'Granada' signs to continue to the city.

Sat) a few steps west of this junction along the Paseo: it's a branch of the Almuñécar tourist office, whose website, www.almunecar.info, also covers La Herradura.

Activities

For rentals, outings, classes and courses, try:

Buceo La Herradura (☎ 958 82 70 83; www.buceola herradura.com; Marina del Este) Diving.

Club Adventure (☎ 958 64 07 80; www.club-adventure .com; Calle Olmos 3) Paragliding, canyoning, mountain biking.

Club Nautique (☎ 958 82 75 14; www.clubnautique.com; Marina del Este) Diving, yachting.

Granada Sub (☎ 958 64 02 81; www.granadasub.com; Paseo Andrés Segovia 6) Diving.

Ocio Aventura (☎ 958 81 61 85; www.ocioaventura .com; cnr Calle San Miguel Bajo & Calle Dulcinea, Armilla, Granada) Paragliding, canyoning, climbing.

Windsurf La Herradura (☎ 958 64 01 43; www.wind surflaherradura.com; Paseo Andrés Segovia 34) Windsurfing, kitesurfing, canoeing, kayaking.

Some of the best dive sites can be found around Punta de la Mona and Cerro Gordo at the eastern and western ends of the bay respectively, and the Grutas de Cantarriján a little further west.

Sleeping

Hotel Sol Los Fenicios (☎ 958 82 79 00; www.tryp net.com; Paseo Andrés Segovia; s €69-128, d €94.50-174; **P** ⊠ ⊡) The best hotel in town, towards the eastern end of the beach, has a manageable 42 rooms. Nearly all have sea view and terrace or balcony, around an interior patio. Room rates depend on the season. The restaurant and café-bar have terraces overlooking the beach, too.

Also recommended:

Hostal La Caleta (☎ 958 82 70 07; Paseo Andrés Segovia s/n; d €60-72) Towards the eastern end of the beach, also with a good restaurant.

Hostal Peña Parda (☎ 958 64 00 66; Paseo Andrés Segovia 65; d €48) At the western end of the beach, with a good restaurant.

Nuevo Camping La Herradura (☎ 958 64 06 34; Paseo Andrés Segovia; camping per 2 adults, tent & car €20) Fairly basic camping ground across the street from the western part of the beach.

Eating

Most restaurants on Paseo Andrés Segovia serve good food at reasonable prices, although they mark up drinks.

Mesón El Tinao (☎ 958 82 74 88; Edificio Bahía II, Paseo Andrés Segovia; mains €12-20; ⊠ closed Mon) El

Tinao prepares excellent Alpujarras food and a few unusual dishes such as duck with raspberries.

El Chambao de Joaquín (☎ 958 64 00 44; Paseo Andrés Segovia; paella Sat & Sun €6) Paella is dished out from a giant pan at 2.30pm every Saturday and Sunday in the beachside garden here at the far eastern end of the beach. You need to book for Sunday.

Chiringuito La Sardina (☎ 958 64 01 11; Paseo Andrés Segovia; mains €9-16) Situated right on the beach, Chiringuito La Sardina is a top place for seafood.

Getting There & Away

Plenty of Alsina Graells buses head east and west along the coast and a few go to Granada. Buses go to Almería (€8.60, 3½ hours, five daily), Almuñécar (€0.70, 15 minutes, 10 daily), Granada (€6.15, two hours, five daily), Málaga (€4.55, 1¾ hours, six daily) and Nerja (€1.40, 20 minutes, 10 daily).

GRANADA PROVINCE

Jaén Province

Jaén (ha-*en*) is characterised less by the attitudes and culture of the sunny south than by those of its northern neighbour, Castilla-La Mancha. The Desfiladero de Despeñaperros pass – a gap in the Sierra Morena on Jaén's northern border – has, from time immemorial, been the most important gateway into Andalucía and the barrier between north and south. It's in this province, too, that the journey of Andalucía's 'Great River', the Guadalquivir, begins. It starts in the mountains of Parque Natural de Cazorla and rushes southwest through Córdoba and Seville until it reaches the Atlantic.

Jaén is also the olive capital of Spain – the silvery trees ripple out over the province covering nearly half of the arable land and forming the basis of a huge agricultural-estate style of farming. Olive production and the cultivation of wheat, barley and rye form the basis of the province's economy, but it's an economy that's seen better days. The Renaissance towns of Úbeda and Baeza hint at an illustrious past, where aristocratic families hobnobbed with the royal court and splashed out on expensive town planning. The lack of development, however, and the persistence of a largely agrarian economy controlled by a few wealthy landowning families has led to depressing and impoverished modern times. This is the flip-side of the tourism coin – where the Costa del Sol pulls in the punters by their millions and enjoys the rosy economic spin-off, so Jaén languishes in relative obscurity. However, the burgeoning attractions of the Parque Natural de Cazorla, perhaps the most beautiful of all of Andalucía's mountain regions, and the quaint charms of its historic towns, draw a number of discerning travellers.

JAÉN PROVINCE

HIGHLIGHTS

- Enjoying the quiet sophistication and aristocratic edge of the perfectly preserved Renaissance towns of **Úbeda** (p357) and **Baeza** (p353)

- Hiking or biking in the ruggedly beautiful mountains of **Parque Natural de Cazorla** (p365)

- Sampling city life in down-to-earth **Jaén** (p345) and lording it up in Andalucía's most impressive parador, **Castillo Santa Catalina** (p349)

- Taking a castle crawl around **Jaén** (p349), **Baños de la Encina** (p353), **Cazorla** (p363) and **Segura de la Sierra** (p369)

- Shopping till you drop and buying some of Andalucía's most authentic products – **pottery** (p362) and **esparto work** (p362), **olive-wood bowls** (p357), real aristocratic **antiques** (p362) and **olive oil** (p345)

Segura de la Sierra
Baños de la Encina
Parque Natural de Cazorla
Baeza Úbeda
Cazorla
Jaén

POPULATION: 648,000	JAÉN AVERAGE DAILY HIGH: JAN/AUG 9°C/25°C	ALTITUDE RANGE: 323m–2167m

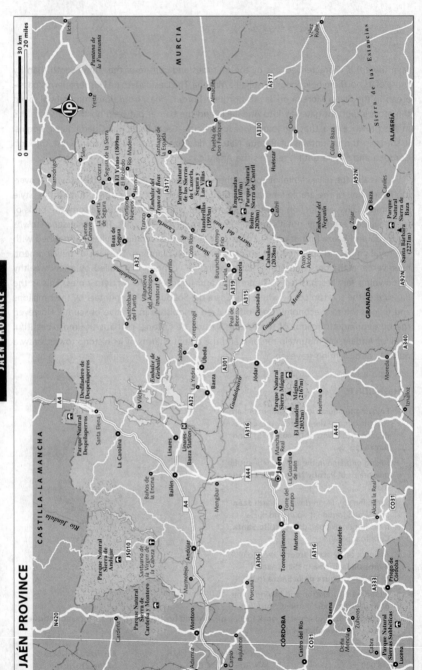

JAÉN PROVINCE

JAÉN

pop 116,000 / elevation 575m
Provincial capital and gateway to the south, Jaén is essentially a bustling market town made grand by its strategic importance in the Reconquista (Christian reconquest). Jaén was a bone of contention between the Muslims in Granada and the Castilians to the north, until the ruling emir, Mohammed ibn Yusuf ibn Nasr, struck a deal with Fernando III (El Santo; The Saint) in 1247. The deal meant ibn Nasr would pay tribute if the Christian monarch respected the borders of his shrinking kingdom. Thus Jaén became the thin end of the wedge that would eventually drive the Muslims from Granada in 1492.

Centuries of decline set in after the Reconquista, with many *jiennenses* (locals of Jaén) emigrating to Spanish colonies – hence the existence of other Jaéns in Peru and the Philippines. Subsequently, Jaén is now an impoverished populace struggling to make ends meet (a quarter of Jaén's families live on less than €100 a month). Only since the 1960s has the city seen much growth, and the opening of its first university in 1993 injected a much-needed breath of fresh air.

ORIENTATION
Old Jaén, with narrow, winding streets, huddles around the foot of Cerro de Santa Catalina, the wooded, castle-crowned hill above the western side of the city. Jaén's monumental cathedral is near the southern end of the old city. From here, Calle de Bernabé Soriano leads northeast and downhill to Plaza de la Constitución, the focal point of the newer part of the city, complete with metal palm trees that light up at night.

From Plaza de la Constitución, Calle Roldán y Marín, soon becoming Paseo de la Estación, heads northwest to the train station 1km away. This is the main artery of the newer part of town. The bus station is east off Paseo de la Estación, 250m north of Plaza de la Constitución.

INFORMATION
Bookshops
Librería Metrópolis (Calle del Cerón 17) Good for maps and Spanish-language guidebooks.

Emergency
Policía Municipal (Municipal Police; ☎ 953 21 91 05; Carrera de Jesús) Just behind the *ayuntamiento* (city hall).
Policía Nacional (National Police; ☎ 953 26 18 50; Calle del Arquitecto Berges)

ESSENTIAL OIL

In Jaén, the *aceituna* (olive) rules. You can smell the astringent odour of *aceite de oliva* (olive oil) just about everywhere you go. Over 40 million *olivos* (olive trees) stud the rolling hills of the province and occupy almost every scrap of fertile land. A third of Jaén province – more than 4500 sq km – is devoted to *olivares* (olive groves). In an average year these trees produce 900,000 tonnes of olives, most of which are turned into some 200,000 tonnes of olive oil. Thus, Jaén provides about half of Andalucía's olive oil, one-third of Spain's and 10% of that used in the entire world. You need some of the best Verde Mágina *virgen extra* (extra virgin) oil just to digest those statistics.

The olives are harvested from late November to January. Though there's some mechanisation, much is still done traditionally – by spreading nets beneath the trees, then beating the branches with sticks. The majority of Jaén's (and Andalucía's) olive groves are owned by a handful of large landowners and the dominance of this one crop in the province's economy means that unemployment in Jaén rises from 10% during the harvest to around 45% in summer. An olive picker earns about €30 a day.

Once harvested, olives are taken to oil mills to be mashed into a pulp that is then pressed and filtered. Modern machinery and stainless-steel vats have replaced mule-driven presses that once squeezed the oil through *esparto* (grass) mats. Oil that is considered good enough for immediate consumption is sold as *aceite de oliva virgen* (virgin olive oil), the finest grade and the best of the best is *virgen extra*. *Aceite de oliva refinado* (refined olive oil) is made from oil that's not quite so good, and plain *aceite de oliva* is a blend of refined and virgin oils. Expect to pay about €5 for a 750mL bottle of Verde Mágina *virgen extra* and about €11 for 2.5L. Specialist shops in Jaén (p351), Baeza (see p357) and Úbeda (p362) sell quality oil.

JAÉN

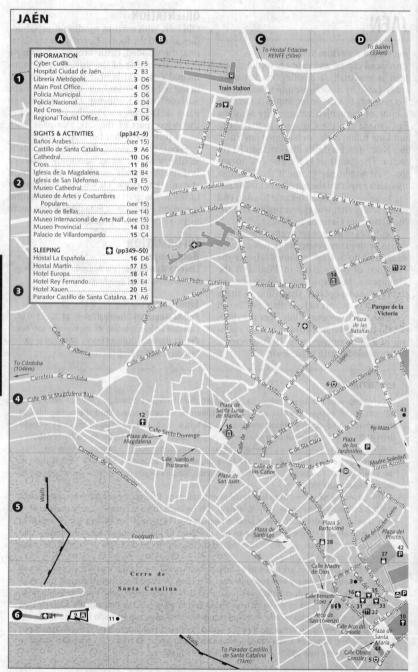

Internet Access

Cyber Cu@k (Calle de Adarves Bajos 24; per 30min €1; ⏱ 10.30am-12.30pm & 5.30pm-midnight) Found near Plaza de Toros.

Internet Resources

You'll find lots of interesting information in English, French, German and Spanish on www.promojaen.es and on the *ayuntamiento's* website at www.aytojaen.es.

Medical Services

Hospital Ciudad de Jaén (☎ 953 29 90 00; Avenida del Ejército Español) The main general hospital.
Red Cross (Cruz Roja; ☎ 953 25 15 40; Calle Carmelo Torres) Provides emergency care.

Money

There's no shortage of banks or ATMs around Plaza de la Constitución and on Calle Roldán y Marín.

Post

Main post office (Plaza de los Jardinillos; ⏱ 8.30am-8.30pm Mon-Fri, 9.30am-2pm Sat) The main post office.

Tourist Information

Regional tourist office (☎ 953 19 04 55; otjaen@andalucia.org; Calle de la Maestra 13; ⏱ 10am-7pm Mon-Fri Oct-Mar, 10am-8pm Mon-Fri Apr-Sep, 10am-1pm Sat, Sun & public holidays year-round) Helpful, multilingual staff with plenty of free information about the city and province.

SIGHTS

In the heart of the city at Plaza de Santa Maria is Jaén's major sight, the cathedral, north of which sprawls the old town, a warren of pleasantly picturesque streets. The two notable museums worth visiting are located north of the cathedral, the Palacio de Villardompardo along Calle Martínez Molina, and the Museo Provincial along the main thoroughfare, Paseo de la Estación. A day or two is needed to really take in these collections and the cathedral. And another full morning can be spent exploring the Castillo de Santa Catalina, finishing off with a memorable lunch at its restaurant.

Cathedral

For over a hundred years following the Reconquista, Christians used the old mosque for worship. It wasn't until the 16th century that the ambitious plans for Jaén's huge

cathedral (☎ 953 23 42 33; Plaza de Santa María; ☼ 8.30am-1pm & 4-7pm Mon-Sat Oct-Mar; 8.30am-1pm & 5-8pm Mon-Sat Apr-Sep; 9am-1pm & 5-7pm Sun & holidays year-round) were conceived and master architect, Andrés de Vandelvira (who was also responsible for many fabulous buildings in Úbeda and Baeza) was commissioned.

Nowadays, the magnificent twin-towered edifice dwarfs the entire city – its size and opulence fantastically visible from the hilltop eyrie of Santa Catalina (see p349). The **southwestern façade**, set back on Plaza de Santa María, was not completed until the 18th century and, with its host of statuary by Seville's Pedro Roldán, owes more to the late baroque tradition than to the Renaissance. However, the overall size and solidity of the internal and external structures retain their Renaissance roots with huge, rounded arches and clusters of Corinthian columns that lend it great visual strength.

During services the cavernous gloom throbs with intense devotion. Directly behind the main altar, the **Capilla del Santo Rostro** houses the Reliquia del Santo Rostro de Cristo, the cloth with which St Veronica is believed to have wiped Christ's face on the road to Calvary. The Reliquia was reputedly carried to Jaén from Constantinople in the 14th century. A painting of the cloth replaced the original during the Napoleonic Wars. Both the painting and the cloth were stolen during the Spanish Civil War and (ironically, considering previous Napoleonic fears) later turned up hidden in a garage outside Paris. On Friday at 11.30am and 5pm long queues of the faithful assemble to kiss the cloth. You can visit the **Museo Catedral** (Cathedral Museum; admission €3; ☼ 10am-1pm & 4-7pm Tue-Sat) in the mausoleum beneath the chapter house for an excess of religious art and artefacts.

North of the Cathedral

Steep, narrow alleyways disappear in a warren northwest from the cathedral up Calle de la Maestra, Calle Madre de Dios and Calle Martínez Molina into the heart of the old Arab quarter. Calle Madre de Dios, running into Calle Aguilar takes you through the **Arco de San Lorenzo** all the way up to the handsome Renaissance **Palacio de Villardompardo** (Villardompardo Palace; ☎ 953 23 62 92; Plaza de Santa Luisa de Marillac; non-EU citizen €1.50, EU citizen free;

☼ 9am-8pm Tue-Fri, 9.30am-2.30pm Sat & Sun, closed holidays), housing two museums and what are claimed to be the largest Arab baths open to visitors in Spain. There are pamphlets, in French and English, giving some information on the baths and the museums.

The complex is Jaén's most rewarding attraction and houses one of the most intriguing collections of artefacts and archaeological remains to be found under one roof in Andalucía. The signposted tour of the palace leads you first over a glass walkway revealing Roman ruins, into the bowels of the building and into the **Baños Árabes** (Arab Baths). The 11th-century baths are in a remarkably good state of preservation, with horseshoe arches and star-shaped skylights. After the Reconquista, suspicious of what they considered to be a decadent and vice-inducing habit (that nurtured the practise of the Muslim faith), the Christians converted the baths into a tannery. The baths then disappeared altogether in the 16th century, when the Conde (Count) de Villardompardo built a palace over the site, and were only rediscovered in 1913.

Emerging from the baths, the route takes you through the palace's numerous salons divided into different exhibits of the **Museo de Artes y Costumbres Populares** (Museum of Popular Art & Customs). The collection is wonderfully comprehensive and you can easily while away an entire morning running the whole gamut of hideously harsh rural life including shoe-making, pre-industrial construction, cloth weaving, lace-making, ironmongery and every aspect of the Andalucian home. It also sheds light on the very recent hardships endured by the majority of people in the province.

The most recent addition to the *palacio* is the **Museo Internacional de Arte Naïf** (International Museum of Naïf Art). The work and collection of the museum's founder, Manuel Moral, a native of Jaén province, forms the basis of the display, which complements the folk exhibits of the Museo de Artes y Costumbres Populares. Village life and the countryside are constant themes in the brilliantly coloured and witty paintings.

A short walk west of the Palacio de Villardompardo is Jaén's oldest church, the **Iglesia de la Magdalena** (Calle Santo Domingo; admission free; ☼ 9am-12.30pm & 5-8pm). Originally a mosque, it now has a Gothic façade and interior. Its tower is the mosque's minaret, reworked in the 16th century. The outstanding internal feature is the retable. Behind the church is a lovely Islamic courtyard with Roman tombstones and a pool used for ritual ablutions by Muslims before prayer.

Jaén's other most notable museum is the **Museo Provincial** (☎ 953 25 06 00; Paseo de la Estación 27; non-EU citizen €1.50, EU citizen free; ◷ 3-8pm Tue, 9am-8pm Wed-Sat, 9am-3pm Sun), which has Spain's finest collection of 5th-century BC Iberian sculptures. Found in Porcuna, the sculptures show a clear Greek influence in their fluidity of form and graceful stylised design. Every year new finds are added and it is hoped that this will eventually become the principal museum of Iberian art in the country. The rest of the exhibits include a collection of Roman and Islamic artefacts including ceramics, mosaics and sculpture. Admission to the museum also gets you into the upstairs **Museo de Bellas Artes**, which exhibits a supremely mediocre range of 19th- and 20th-century Spanish art.

Some 200m northeast of the cathedral is the huge bulwark of the 13th-century **Iglesia de San Ildefonso** (Plaza de San Ildefonso; admission free; ◷ 8.30am-noon & 7-8pm), the 'home church' of Jaén's patron saint, the Virgen de la Capilla, and the second-largest church in the city. An inscription on the bottom (northeastern) end of its exterior marks the spot where the Virgin is believed to have appeared on 10 June 1430. Her much-venerated image stands in a special chapel. Free guided tours can be arranged through the **Guide Organisation** (☎ 953 25 44 42).

Castillo de Santa Catalina

Spectacularly sited, Jaén's **castillo** (☎ 953 12 07 33; admission €3; ◷ 10am-2pm & 5-9pm Tue-Sun Apr-Sep, 10am-2pm & 3.30-7pm Tue-Sun Oct-Mar), a former Islamic fortress, is perched atop the cliff-girt Cerro de Santa Catalina, the high hill that towers above the city. Inside the castle a signposted route takes you around the keep, the chapel and the dungeon, while audio-visual gimmicks explain each point of interest – the best (and most amusing) being the manacled prisoner whose hologrammed face comes to life and details his miserable fate at the hands of the evil Napoleonic invaders. There is also a short, incredibly superficial film on Jaén's history but the kids may enjoy the

three-D glasses and it only lasts 15 minutes. Unfortunately, all this enjoyment is only to be had in Spanish. Past the castle at the end of the ridge stands a large **cross** from where there are magnificent views over the city and the olive groves beyond.

If you don't have a vehicle for the circuitous 4km drive up from the city centre, you can take a taxi (€6). You can walk (about 40 minutes from the city centre) by heading uphill from the cathedral to join Calle de Buenavista. Go up right and at a junction with Carretera de Circunvalación, cross over; a short distance along to the right, take the path that heads off steeply uphill to the left.

FESTIVALS

Semana Santa (Holy Week) Celebrated in a big way, with processions through the old city by members of 13 *cofradías* (brotherhoods). The week climaxes in the early hours of Good Friday.

Feria y Fiestas de San Lucas (10-18 October) This is Jaén's biggest party, complete with concerts, funfairs, bullfights and general merrymaking leading up to the saint's day (for San Lucas) on 18 October.

SLEEPING

Jaén's hotels are incredibly mediocre. Budget options are very basic and from May to October mosquitoes can be a nuisance, so arm yourself with plenty of insect repellent. Prices in several places rise a bit during Semana Santa and the Feria y Fiestas de San Lucas. Some hotels do offer parking but this has to be paid for at around €7 to €10 per day.

Parador Castillo de Santa Catalina (☎ 953 23 00 00; www.parador.es in Spanish; d €113.30; P ✗ ✤) If you want character, this is the only place worth checking into. Part of the Santa Catalina castle complex, the hotel has an incomparable setting, theatrical vaulted halls and huge fireplaces. Rooms are incredibly comfortable with four-poster beds, Islamic tiled details and all mod cons. There is also an excellent restaurant (p350), well worth a trip even if you are not a guest.

Hotel Rey Fernando (☎ 953 25 18 40; Plaza de Coca de la Piñera 5; s/d €48/61; P ✗) The modern, comfortable, nicely furnished Rey Fernando is a blessing for the weary traveller in Jaén. It also has a lovely tiled tapas bar and a huge restaurant.

Hotel Europa (☎ 953 22 27 00; www.husa.es; Plaza de Belén 1; s/d €34/56.50; P ✗) Struggling to rise above the budget range, Hotel Europa has adequate rooms, each with TV and – wait for it – a safe! Located just off Avenida de Granada it is one of the most convenient options for drivers.

Hotel Xauen (☎ 953 24 07 89; www.hotelxauenjaen .com; Plaza del Deán Mazas 3; s/d €40/55; P ⊠ ⬜) More central than Hotel Europa and popular with the business crowd, the Xauen has good facilities and spacious, well-appointed rooms – if you can get over the shocking '70s leather chairs in the foyer.

Hostal Estacion RENFE (☎ 953 27 46 14; Plaza de Jaén por la Paz s/n; s/d €28.50/36; P ⊠) Although the exterior of this new *hostal* (a simple guesthouse or small place offering hotel-like accommodation) opposite the train station is not the most attractive, inside it offers efficient and comfortable accommodation for short stays and overnighters. The *hostal* also has its own good restaurant.

Hostal Martín (☎ 953 24 36 78; Calle Cuatro Torres 5; s/d €20/30) In a narrow street just east of Plaza de la Constitución, this very basic budget *hostal* has adequate rooms without bath. However, it does have a good central location near some of the best nightspots.

Hostal La Española (☎ 953 23 02 54; Calle Bernardo López 9; s/d €26/32) A budget option near the cathedral, in the heart of the old town. The interior is grimly Gothic with its creaking spiral staircase, drab furnishings and lukewarm welcome. It's close to some good tapas bars – although you may need to fortify yourself with a few *vinos tintos* (red wines) to take the edge off this place.

EATING

There is not a lot of money sloshing around Jaén for eating out and, therefore, there is not a great restaurant scene. Most *jiennenses* eat out at the good selection of authentic and atmospheric tapas bars. The best of these are on Calles del Cerón, Arco del Consuelo and Bernardo López, all near the cathedral. The other restaurant strip is the short Calle Nueva, off Calle Roldán y Marín.

Casa Vicente (☎ 953 23 28 16; Calle Francisco Martín Mora; menú €30) Found in a restored mansion with a patio, Casa Vicente is one of the best restaurants in town. It has a great bar where you can take a tipple with tapas or sit down in the patio or interior dining-room (the best option in winter) to enjoy specialities

such as the *cordero mozárabe* (lamb with honey and spices).

Parador Castillo de Santa Catalina (☎ 953 23 00 00; www.parador.es in Spanish; menú €23) A superb experience akin to travelling back in time. Dine in the authentically recreated medieval dining room amid suits of armour and vast wall tapestries. The atmosphere is solemn and formal, the service dutifully obsequious and the menu suitably traditional.

Casa Antonio (☎ 953 27 02 62; Calle de Fermín Palma 3; menú €30) Another highly regarded restaurant now rivalling Casa Vicente as the best in town. Serves up *jiennense*-style classics with a more-modern twist.

Taberna La Manchega (☎ 953 23 21 92; Calle Bernardo López 12; platos combinados €4; ⏰ 10am-5pm & 8pm-1am Wed-Mon) A terrific bar with an atmospheric dining room in the cellar. It's over a century old, and the ambience is boisterous and unpretentious and the food cheap and tasty.

Mesón Río Chico (☎ 953 24 08 02; Calle Nueva 2; menú €8) A top choice, and very popular. The downstairs *taberna* (tavern) serves delicious tapas and *raciones* (meal-sized servings of tapas) of meat, *revueltos* (scrambled eggs) and fish. There is a more-expensive restaurant upstairs.

La Gamba de Oro (☎ 953 24 17 46; Calle Nueva 5; raciones €3-6) Just along the street from Río Chico, the rather unattractive-looking La Gamba is a terrific seafood place, despite being miles from the sea. There are baskets underfoot for discarded shells, and a selection of fried fish costs from €4 to €8.

Mesón Nuyra (☎ 953 27 31 31; Pasaje Nuyra s/n; mains €10-14) Located in a passageway off Calle Nueva, this small, rustic restaurant (lots of terracotta tiles and wedgy wooden chairs) is a more formal place. However, it offers well-cooked, well-priced meals.

Yucatán Café Bar (Calle de Bernabé Soriano; platos combinados €5) The Yucatán is a popular, modern café serving up breakfast for €2.50. It also serves sandwiches and hamburgers for around €2.

DRINKING & ENTERTAINMENT

Jaén stages numerous excellent (read: untouristy) cultural events featuring local and national performers. The tourist office has monthly programmes of concerts, dance, film and theatre performances.

Several of the establishments on Calle Nueva are also excellent if you are on a tapas tour. The main nightlife zone is further away, towards the train station and university – the students add some zip to the bar life.

Taberna La Manchega (☎ 953 23 21 92; Calle Bernardo López 12; ☼ 10am-5pm & 8pm-1am Wed-Mon) La Manchega has entrances on both Calle Arco del Consuelo and Calle Bernardo López and has been in action since the 1880s.

Bar del Pósito (Plaza del Pósito 10) An entertaining place on the pleasant little square off Calle de Bernabé Soriano. It's a regular hang-out for Jaén's cultural movers and you may even be buttonholed by the odd poet reciting quite serious stuff.

El Azulejo (Calle de Hurtado 8) Another place with good atmosphere.

Iroquai (☎ 953 24 36 74; Calle de Adarves Bajos 53) Usually has live rock, blues, flamenco or fusion on Thursday (look out for its posters) and plays good music other nights.

Paddy O'Hara (Calle de Bernabé Soriano 30) Has all the trappings of a trans-national Irish bar and the Irish beers to go with it, but any Irish music is likely to be piped pop-folk. However, it does good tapas to make up for it.

Chubby Cheek (☎ 953 27 38 19; Calle de San Francisco Javier 7) Caters to a slightly older set and has live jazz most weekends.

For general socialising, several atmospheric old bars are clustered just northwest of the cathedral on Calle del Cerón and narrow Calles Arco del Consuelo and Bernardo López. Among them are **La Barra** (Calle del Cerón 7) and **El Gorrión** (Calle de Arco del Consuelo 7).

SHOPPING

The main shopping areas focus on Calle Roldán y Marín, Paseo de la Estación and Calle de San Clemente (off Plaza de la Constitución). Jaén's trademark olive oil can be bought at **Almacenes del Pósito** (Plaza del Pósito) or the **Museo del Olivo** (Calle Martínez Molina 6). A big *mercadillo* (flea market) is held on Thursday morning at the **Recinto Ferial** (Exhibition Site; Avenida de Granada), northeast of Plaza de la Constitución. You can buy almost any type of fresh food at the large, modern **Mercado Central San Francisco** (Calle de los Álamos).

GETTING THERE & AWAY
Bus

From the **bus station** (☎ 953 25 01 06; Plaza de Coca de la Piñera), Alsina Graells runs buses to Granada (€6.25, 1½ hours, 14 daily), Baeza (€3.15, 45 minutes, 11 daily Monday to Saturday), Úbeda (€3.75, 1¼ hours, 12 daily Monday to Saturday), and Cazorla (€6.50, two hours, two daily). The Ureña line travels up to Córdoba (€6.70, 1½ hours, seven daily) and Seville (€15.25, three hours, three to five daily). Other buses head for Málaga (€13.90, one daily), Almería (€25.85, at least one daily), Madrid (€19.20, five daily Monday to Saturday) and many smaller places in Jaén province.

Car & Motorcycle

Jaén is 92km north of Granada by the fast A44. This road continues to Bailén where it meets the Córdoba–Madrid A4. To get to or from Córdoba, take the A306 via Porcuna.

Viajes Sacromonte (☎ 953 22 22 12; Paseo de la Estación 12), in the Pasaje Maza arcade, is a car-rental agent as well as a general travel agent. **Avis** (☎ 953 28 09 37; Avenida de Madrid) and **Atesa** (☎ 953 28 16 40; Calle Ortega Nieto 9) have local offices.

Train

Jaén's **train station** (☎ 953 27 02 02; www.renfe .com; Paseo de la Estación) is at the end of a branch line and there are only five departures most days. A train leaves at 8am for Córdoba (€7.65, 1½ hours, one daily), Seville (€14.70, three hours, one daily) and Cádiz (€22, 4¾ hours, one daily). There are also trains to Madrid (€19.90, four hours, four daily).

GETTING AROUND

There's a **bus stop** (Paseo de la Estación) south of the train station: bus No 1 will take you to Plaza de la Constitución, the central point for all city buses, for €1.

Driving in Jaén can be stressful due to the one-way road system and the weight of traffic. If you end up in the centre, there is underground parking at Plaza de la Constitución and at **Parking San Francisco** (off Calle de Bernabé Soriano) near the cathedral. Costs are €0.90 per hour or €12 for 24 hours.

Taxis gather on Plaza de la Constitución, Plaza de San Francisco, near the cathedral, and at the bus and train stations. Call **Radio Taxis** (☎ 953 22 22 22).

JAÉN PROVINCE

NORTH OF JAÉN

The road (A4) north out of Andalucía to Madrid passes through indifferent countryside to the north of Jaén until the hills of the Sierra Morena appear on the horizon. Ahead lies the Desfiladero de Despeñaperros, the 'Pass of the Overthrow of the Dogs'. The Christian victors of the battle at nearby Las Navas de Tolosa (1212), are said to have tossed from the cliffs many of their Muslim enemies.

The full drama of the pass is not appreciated until the last minute, when the road from the south descends suddenly and swoops between rocky towers and wooded slopes to slice through tunnels and defiles.

PARQUE NATURAL DESPEÑAPERROS

Road and rail have robbed the Desfiladero de Despeñaperros of much of its historic romance, but the splendid hill country to either side is one of Spain's most beautiful and remote areas. If you're travelling this way there are a few places, not far off the highway, that are worth a visit.

Clothed with dense woods of pine, holm oak and cork trees from which protrude dramatic cliffs and pinnacles of fluted rock, the area around the pass is now a natural park, home to deer and wild boar, and maybe the occasional wolf and lynx. There are no local buses, so you need your own transport to get the most out of the area. The main visitor centre is the **Centro de Visitantes Puerta de Andalucía** (☎ 953 66 43 07; Carretera Santa Elena a Miranda del Rey; ⊙ 10am-2pm & 4-8pm Apr-Sep; 10am-2pm & 3-7pm Oct-Mar) on the outskirts of **Santa Elena**, the small town just south of the pass. The centre has information and maps on walking routes in the area.

Santa Elena is an ideal base for exploring the park and has shops, bars and cafés. **Hotel El Mesón de Despeñaperros** (☎ 953 66 41 00; fax 953 66 41 02; meson@serverland.com; Avenida de Andalucía 91; s/d €25/38.60), at the north end of town, has comfy rooms and a busy restaurant. Alternatively, in La Carolina, 12km south of Santa Elena, there is the more fancy **La Perdiz** (☎ 953 66 03 00; www.nh-hoteles.es in Spanish; Autovía de Andalucía, salida Km.268; s/d €74/79; P ✂ 🖳 🐾), part of the NH chain, which offers every possible amenity and is set amid lovely gardens.

For campers, **Camping Despeñaperros** (☎ 953 66 41 92; campingdesp@navegalia.com; camping per 2 people, tent & car €12) has a great location among pine trees and the helpful owner can advise on walking in the area. You can also contact a park guide direct (☎ 610-282531).

Several buses from Jaén run on weekdays to La Carolina, from where **La Sepulvedana** (☎ 953 66 03 35) runs about four or five buses

---

DETOUR: PARQUE NATURAL SIERRA DE ANDÚJAR

Thirty-one kilometres north of Andújar on the J-5010 is the 13th-century **Santuario de la Virgen de la Cabeza**. It is tucked away in the secluded Parque Natural Sierra de Andújar, and is the scene of one of Spain's biggest religious events, the Romería de la Virgen de la Cabeza. The original shrine was destroyed in the Civil War when it was seized by 200 pro-Franco troops. The shrine was only 'liberated' in May 1937 after eight months of determined Republican bombardment.

On the last Sunday in April nearly half a million people converge to witness a small statue of the Virgin Mary – known as La Morenita (The Little Brown One) – being carried around the Cerro del Cabezo for about four hours from around 11am. It's a festive, emotive occasion: children and items of clothing are passed over the crowd to priests who touch them to the Virgin's mantle.

There are two small *hostales* (simple guesthouses or small places offering hotel-like accommodation), the **Hotel la Mirada** (☎ 953 54 91 11; d €50) and **Pensión Virgen de la Cabeza** (☎ 953 12 21 65; d €35), near the sanctuary that provide a good base for exploring the 740-sq-km park. The park is said to have the largest expanse of natural vegetation in the Sierra Morena. Full of evergreen and gall oaks, the park is home to plenty of bull-breeding ranches, a few wolves, lynx and boars, plus deer, mouflon and various birds of prey. Information is available from the **Centro de Visitantes** (☎ 953 54 90 30), at Km 12 on the road from Andújar to the Santuario de la Virgen de la Cabeza, and from Andújar's **tourist office** (☎ 953 50 49 59; Plaza de Santa María; ⊙ 8am-2pm Tue-Sat Jul-Sep, 10am-2pm & 5-8pm Oct-Jun).

Buses run daily from Jaén to Andújar (€3.80, four daily) and there are buses from Andújar to the sanctuary on Saturday and Sunday.

to Santa Elena, weekdays only. It's best to check the current schedules.

BAÑOS DE LA ENCINA

One of Andalucía's finest castles, the **Castillo de Burgalimar** (☎ 953 61 32 00; admission free; ☉ 9am-8pm), dominates the quiet ridge-top town of Baños de la Encina. The town is a few kilometres north of unexciting Bailén. Built in AD 967 on the orders of the Cordoban caliph Al-Hakim II, the castle has 14 towers and a large keep entered through a double horseshoe arch. The interior of the castle has an unprotected parapet (not for the faint-hearted!) encircling the walls, with dramatic views across the countryside. The castle fell to the Christians in 1212 just after the battle of Las Navas de Tolosa. For info – and the key to the castle – ask at the **tourist office** (☎ 953 61 41 85; Callejón del Castillo 1; ☉ 8.30am-2pm Mon-Fri).

Several mansions and churches – including the **Ermita del Cristo del Llano**, with its spectacular rococo decoration reminiscent of Granada's Alhambra (p305) – make a ramble through Baños' old streets worthwhile. The **Restaurante Mirasierra** (Calle Bailen 6; mains €6-8) serves good fish and meat dishes.

EAST OF JAÉN

BAEZA

pop 15,000 / elevation 790m

Situated atop an escarpment overlooking wide tracts of fertile land, the Romans called this town 'Beatia', meaning 'happy or fortunate'. Baeza (ba-*eh*-thah) is the smaller twin of Úbeda (only 9km away) and together the towns represented the bridgehead of the Christian advance on Muslim Granada.

Baeza was one of the first Andalucian towns to fall to the Christians (1227), but little is left of its Muslim heritage after years of Castilian influence. The richness of its architecture, however, belies any suggestion that there is little of architectural interest in Andalucía outside the Islamic period. Instead, a handful of rich, fractious families left a staggering catalogue of perfectly preserved Renaissance churches and civic buildings.

Orientation & Information

The heart of town is Plaza de España, with the long, wide Paseo de la Constitución stretching to its southwest.

The bus station is about 700m east of Plaza de España on a street officially called Avenida Alcalde Puche Pardo.

The **tourist office** (☎ 953 74 04 44; otbaeza@andalucia.org; Plaza del Pópulo; ☉ 9am-6pm Mon-Fri, 10am-1pm & 4-6pm Sat Oct-Mar, 9am-7pm Mon-Fri, 10am-1pm & 5-7pm Sat Apr-Sep, 10am-1pm Sun year-round), which has loads of information, is in a beautiful 16th-century appeal court on Plaza del Pópulo, just southwest of Paseo de la Constitución. The Internet is available at **Speed Informatica** (Portales Tundidores 2; per hr €1.80; ☉ 10.30am-2pm & 5.30-8pm) on the north side of Paseo de la Constitución, and the main post office is on Calle Julio Burell.

You'll find banks and ATMs on Paseo de la Constitución and to the east of Plaza de España on Calle San Pablo.

Sights

All of Baeza's sights cluster around the central Plaza de España and by extension Plaza de la Constitución. You can take them all in during a leisurely day's stroll. The opening hours of some of the buildings are unpredictable so check at the tourist office first.

PASEO DE LA CONSTITUCIÓN & AROUND

Honey-coloured churches and huge mansion palaces characterise the whole of Baeza's historic centre, leaving the lonely **Torre de los Aliatares** (Tower of the Aliatares), on Plaza de España, as one of the few remnants of Muslim Bayyasa (as the town was called by the Muslims). The tower somehow survived Isabel la Católica's 1476 order to demolish the town's fortifications, meant to end the feuds between the Benavide and Carvajal noble families. The small Plaza de España is the centre of the town and merges with the sprawling, cafe-lined **Paseo de la Constitución**, once Baeza's marketplace and bullring.

On Plaza del Pópulo is the old entrance to the city, the **Puerta de Jaén** (Jaén Gate), which is connected to the huge **Arco de Villalar** (Villalar Arch). The arch was erected by Carlos I in 1526 to commemorate the crushing of a serious insurrection in Castilla that had threatened to overthrow his throne. The arch dominates **Plaza del Pópulo**, also called Plaza de los Leones after the **Fuente de los Leones** (Fountain of the Lions) at its centre. The fountain, made up of carvings from the Iberian and Roman village of Cástulo, is topped by a statue reputed to represent

BAEZA

0 ———————— 200 m
0 ———————— 0.1 miles

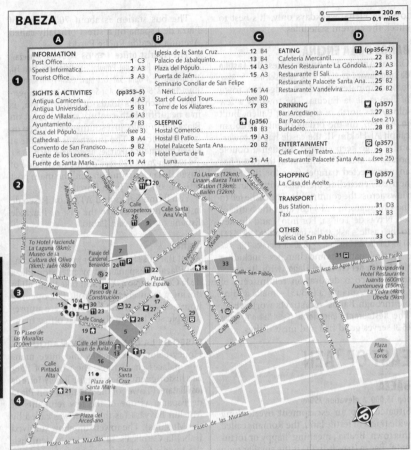

INFORMATION		
Post Office	1	C3
Speed Informatica	2	A3
Tourist Office	3	A3

SIGHTS & ACTIVITIES	(pp353–5)	
Antigua Carnicería	4	A3
Antigua Universidad	5	A3
Arco de Villalar	6	A3
Ayuntamiento	7	B3
Casa del Pópulo	(see 3)	
Cathedral	8	A4
Convento de San Francisco	9	B2
Fuente de los Leones	10	A3
Fuente de Santa María	11	A4
Iglesia de la Santa Cruz	12	B4
Palacio de Jabalquinto	13	B4
Plaza del Pópulo	14	A3
Puerta de Jaén	15	A3
Seminario Conciliar de San Felipe Neri	16	A4
Start of Guided Tours	(see 30)	
Torre de los Aliatares	17	B3

SLEEPING	(p356)	
Hostal Comercio	18	A3
Hostal El Patio	19	A3
Hotel Palacete Santa Ana	20	B2
Hotel Puerta de la Luna	21	A4

EATING	(pp356–7)	
Cafetería Mercantil	22	B3
Mesón Restaurante La Góndola	23	A3
Restaurante El Sali	24	B3
Restaurante Palacete Santa Ana	25	B2
Restaurante Vandelvira	26	B2

DRINKING	(p357)	
Bar Arcediano	27	B3
Bar Pacos	(see 21)	
Burladero	28	B3

ENTERTAINMENT	(p357)	
Café Central Teatro	29	B3
Restaurante Palacete Santa Ana	(see 25)	

SHOPPING	(p357)	
La Casa del Aceite	30	A3

TRANSPORT		
Bus Station	31	D3
Taxi	32	B3

OTHER		
Iglesia de San Pablo	33	C3

Imilce, an Iberian princess and the wife of the notorious Carthaginian general, Hannibal. On the southern side of the square is the lovely 16th-century plateresque (primarily a decorative genre, with effects resembling those of silverware) **Casa del Pópulo**, formerly a courthouse, it's now Baeza's tourist office. On the eastern side of the square stands the **Antigua Carnicería** (Old Slaughterhouse), a beautiful building with a Renaissance gallery that must rank as the one of the most elegant tanning sheds in the world!

Through the Puerta de Jaén and along to the **Paseo de las Murallas**, a path loops around the old city walls to a point near the cathedral. From here, Baeza's fantastic escarpment position can be easily appreciated.

PLAZA DE SANTA MARÍA

This square is typical of all the town's squares, surrounded on all sides by mansions and churches and designed to be a focus of religious and civic life. This is evident by the location of the **Seminario Conciliar de San Felipe Neri** on the square's northern side. This seminary now houses the Universidad International de Andalucía.

Following the Reconquista, the mosque was naturally rebuilt as Baeza's new **cathedral** (Plaza de Santa María; admission free, donations welcome; 10.30am-1pm & 4-6pm Oct-Mar, 10.30am-1pm & 5-7pm Apr-Sep), initiating the transformation of the town into a Castilian gem. The cathedral itself is an aesthetic hotchpotch of features, although the overall style is pure

16th-century Renaissance, clearly visible in the **main façade** on Plaza Santa María. The cathedral's oldest feature is the 13th-century Gothic-Mudejar **Puerta de la Luna** (Moon Doorway) at the western end, which is topped by a 14th-century rose window.

A lavish baroque retable backs the main altar and a 13th-century Romanesque-Gothic Crucifixion sculpture – rare in Andalucía – stands high on the retable of the adjacent Capilla del Sagrario. At the cathedral's western end, the grille on the **Antiguo Coro** (Old Choir) is one of the masterpieces of Jaén's 16th-century wrought-iron supremo, Maestro Bartolomé. There's a slot to the right of the grille, by an unremarkable painting – if you pop a coin into the slot the painting will slide noisily aside to reveal a large, silver 18th-century **Custodia del Corpus** used in Baeza's Corpus Christi processions.

Outside the cathedral on the pretty square is the handsome **Fuente de Santa María**, a fountain built in the shape of a miniature triumphal arch in 1569 by *baezano* (Baeza local) Ginés Martínez.

PLAZA SANTA CRUZ

Down Cuesta San Felipe Neri is Baeza's most extraordinary palace, **Palacio de Jabalquinto** (Plaza Santa Cruz; admission free; ☻ 10am-2pm & 4-6pm Thu-Tue, patio only). Probably built in the early 16th century for one of the Benavides clan, it has a spectacularly flamboyant façade typical of Isabelline Gothic style. The patio has been undergoing restoration for some time, but you can capture the sense of grandeur in its Renaissance-style marble columns, two-tiered arches and elegant fountain. A fantastically carved baroque stairway ascends from one side.

Opposite the palace is the tiny **Iglesia de la Santa Cruz** (Plaza Santa Cruz; admission free; ☻ 11am-1.30pm & 4-6pm Mon-Sat, noon-2pm Sun), one of the first churches to be built in Andalucía after the Reconquista. It was one of the last in Spain, and one of the very few in Andalucía, to be built in the Romanesque style, and its round-arched portals and semicircular apse set it apart. Inside are enchanting traces of the mosque that the church replaced. Opening times are not very reliable.

Next door to the Jabalquinto is Baeza's **Antigua Universidad** (Old University; ☎ 953 74 01 54; Calle del Beato Juan de Ávila; admission free; ☻ 10am-1pm & 4-6pm Thu-Tue), founded in 1538 and a fount

of progressive ideas that generally ran counter to the conservative tendencies of Baeza's dominant families. It closed in 1824 and since 1875 the building has housed an *instituto de bachillerato* (high school). The main patio, with its elegant Renaissance arches, is open to the public as is the classroom of poet Antonio Machado (see p44), who taught French at the high school from 1912 to 1919.

NORTH OF PASEO DE LA CONSTITUCIÓN

A block north of the Paseo is the **Ayuntamiento** (Town Hall; ☎ 953 74 01 54; Pasaje del Cardenal Benavides 9), with a marvellous plateresque façade. The four finely carved balcony portals on the upper storey are separated by the coats of arms of Felipe II (in the middle), the magistrate Juan de Borja, who had the place built, and that of the town. The building was originally a courthouse and prison (entered by the right- and left-hand doors respectively).

A short walk from the *ayuntamiento* is the ruined and controversially restored **Convento de San Francisco** (Calle de San Francisco). One of Andrés de Vandelvira's masterpieces, it was conceived as the funerary chapel of the Benavides family. Devastated by an earthquake and sacked by French troops in the early 19th century, it is now partly restored. At the eastern end, a striking arrangement of curved girders traces the outline of its dome over a space adorned with Renaissance carvings. The cloister, occupied by the Restaurante Vandelvira (p356), is worth a look, too.

Activities

Horse riding can be organised through Hotel Hacienda La Laguna (p356).

Tours

Pópulo Servicios Turísticos (☎ 953 74 43 70; Plaza de los Leones 1; adult/children under 12 €6/free; ☻ 10am & 5pm Mon-Sat, 11am Sun) Guided tours take about two hours and start from opposite the tourist office. The tour is fairly run of the mill (and your Spanish needs to be pretty good to enjoy it), but in a place with so much history and detail to every building it really fills in the background. However, this will not be everyone's cup of tea as some people may just want to wander around and enjoy the atmosphere of the place.

Festivals & Events

Semana Santa (Holy Week) A typically big, picturesque celebration complete with devotional processions.

Feria (mid-August) A happy carnival procession of *gigantones* (papier-mâché giants), together with fireworks and a huge funfair.

Romería del Cristo de la Yedra (7 October) An image of the Virgen del Rosell is carried from the Iglesia de San Pablo through Baeza's streets, accompanied by a singing and dancing crowd. In the afternoon, a colourful procession follows the image to La Yedra village, 4km to the north, to continue celebrations there.

Sleeping

Some prices will rise by a few euros from about June to September.

Hotel Puerta de la Luna (☎ 953 74 70 19; www .hotelpuertadelaluna.com in Spanish; Calle Canónigo Melgares Raya s/n; d Mon-Thu/Fri-Sun €95/110; P ✕ ⊠ ⊠) A fantastically luxurious mansion hotel with real character and a wonderful range of facilities. The cobbled Mudejar patio (where you can have breakfast) with its manicured hedges leads into beautifully furnished salons with welcoming fireplaces. Bedrooms are kitted out with antiques and lush damask sheets. There is also a lovely restaurant, funky bar, Turkish bath, spa, gym and library.

Hotel Palacete Santa Ana (☎ /fax 953 74 16 57; info@palacetesantaana.com; Calle Santa Ana Vieja 9; s/d €42/66; ✕) A stylish hotel within a restored 16th-century mansion. The rooms are beautifully furnished and the lounges, dining salons and hallways are veritable galleries of fine art. The nearby restaurant of the same name (below) is also under the same management.

Hotel Hacienda La Laguna (☎ 953 76 51 42; www .ehlaguna.com/hotel in Spanish; Puente del Obispo s/n; d low/ high season €58/64; P ✕ ⊡ ⊠) An enormous hacienda 10 minutes' drive from Baeza. The complex houses its own museum of olive oil – the Museo de la Cultura del Olivo (p357) – and has 18 stylishly furnished rooms and an excellent restaurant, La Campana, which is worth visiting even if you are not staying at the hotel. The ranch also has a stable that provides horse riding.

Hospedería Fuentenueva (☎ 953 74 31 00; www .fuentenueva.com; Paseo Arco del Agua s/n; s/d €43/72; ✕ ⊠) This former women's prison is now a beautifully restored small hotel, all subdued oranges and salmon-pink. The 12 rooms are large, comfortable and bright, with modern marble bathrooms. Rates include breakfast.

Hostal Comercio (☎ 953 74 01 00; Calle San Pablo 21; d €30-35) Atmospherically gloomy and creaky, this friendly family-run *hostal* gives a gra-cious welcome. It has decent, old-fashioned rooms, some with their own little entrance hall. The poet Antonio Machado stayed in room 215 in 1912.

Hotel Juanito (☎ 953 74 00 40; juanito@juanitobaeza .com; Paseo Arco del Agua s/n; s/d €34/54; ✕) Next to a petrol station and opposite Baeza's football ground, this is hardly an optimum location. However, the rooms are comfortable and there is heating and a TV. Its restaurant (below) is one of the most celebrated in the province.

Hostal El Patio (☎ 953 74 02 00; fax 953 74 82 60; Calle Conde Romanones 13; d with bathroom €28) Baeza's cheapest *hostal* occupies a dilapidated 17th-century mansion that has a covered patio. The place has a romantic air of decline about it, but some rooms are drab and poorly lit. There are cheaper rooms without a bathroom.

Eating

Baeza has a whole host of good-quality restaurants and the tourist office can give you small booklet (in Spanish only) detailing a tapas trail.

Restaurante Vandelvira (☎ 953 74 81 72; Calle de San Francisco 14; mains €7-16; ⊗ closed Sun night & Mon) Installed in part of the restored Convento de San Francisco (p355), this is a classy restaurant with bags of character. If you want to spoil yourself you might try the partridge pâté salad or the *solomillo al carbón* (char-grilled steak).

Restaurante Juanito (☎ 953 74 00 40; Paseo Arco del Agua s/n; mains €30; ⊗ closed Sun night & Mon night) The proprietors, Juan Antonio Salcedo and his wife, Luisa, have been dishing up traditional Jaén fare for four decades in this acclaimed eatery. People travel far and wide to sample its specialities, but popularity has a price and the service is sometimes lacking.

Cafetería Mercantil (Portales Tundidores 18, Paseo de la Constitución; raciones €6-9) The vast terrace of this busy café spills out into the Paseo and is a fantastic place to while away the morning or early evening. This is your chance to sample *criadillas* (testicles) or *sesos* (brains), and watch the machinations of the local clientele.

Restaurante Palacete Santa Ana (☎ 953 74 16 57; Calle Escopeteros 12; menú/à la carte €15/24) A large restaurant and bar complex that occupies several floors and is run by the same management as the hotel (above). Serves up

JAÉN PROVINCE

regional specialities that are usually complemented by the local olive oil. Reservations are required.

Mesón Restaurante La Góndola (☎ 953 74 29 84; Portales Carbonería 13, Paseo de la Constitución; mains €8-14) A terrific local atmospheric restaurant helped along by the glowing, wood-burning grill behind the bar, cheerful service and good food. Try *patatas baezanas*, a vegetarian delight that mixes a huge helping of sautéed potatoes with mushrooms.

Restaurante El Sali (☎ 953 74 13 65; Pasaje del Cardenal Benavides 15, menú/à la carte €12/30; ♡ closed Wed) Fantastic outdoor tables opposite the imposing *ayuntamiento*. Serves up lots of fresh fish and the local *pipirrana* (*jamón* – ham – and vegetables).

Drinking & Entertainment

Nightlife in Baeza is generally limited to a few lively bars.

Burladero (Calle de la Barbacana s/n) Pleasant bar for a decent drink.

Bar Arcediano (☎ 953 74 81 84; Calle de la Barbacana s/n; raciones €7-10) Another place for a decent drop on the same side of the street as Burladero.

Bar Pacos (☎ 953 74 70 19; Calle Canónigo Melgares Raya 7; raciones €6-9) A more elegant option in the Hotel Puente de la Luna.

Café Central Teatro (☎ 953 74 43 55; Calle Obispo Narvaez 19) Often has live bands.

Restaurante Palacete Santa Ana (☎ 953 74 16 57; Calle Escopeteros 12) Stages some excellent flamenco nights.

Shopping

For quality olive oil visit **La Casa del Aceite** (Paseo de la Constitución 9), which sells a huge selection along with other products such as soap, ceramics and olive-wood bowls. Another good place, and worth the trip to have a look around the museum, is the **Museo de la Cultura del Olivo** (☎ 953 76 51 42; Complejo Hacienda la Laguna, Puente del Obispo; adult/child €2.50/1.50; ♡ 10.30am-1.30pm & 4.30-7pm Tue-Sun) located outside Baeza in the Hotel Hacienda La Laguna (p356).

Getting There & Around

From the **bus station** (☎ 953 74 04 68; Paseo Arco del Agua), Alsina Graells runs daily buses to Jaén (€3.15, 45 minutes, 11 daily), Úbeda (€0.75, 30 minutes, 15 daily) and Granada (€9.10, five daily). There are also buses to Cazorla (€3.40, 2¼ hours, two daily), Córdoba (€8.25), Seville (€16.40) and Madrid (€18.80).

The nearest train station is **Linares-Baeza** (☎ 953 65 02 02), located 13km northwest of town, where a few trains a day leave for Granada, Córdoba, Seville, Málaga, Cádiz, Almería, Madrid and Barcelona. Buses connect with most trains from Monday to Saturday. A taxi to the train station costs €12.

Parking in Baeza is fairly restricted, but there are parking spots around the Paseo de la Constitución and in Pasaje del Cardenal Benavides. Taxis wait for fares in Paseo de la Constitución.

ÚBEDA

pop 33,000 / elevation 760m

Sophisticated and stately, Úbeda (*oo*-be-dah), like its rival Baeza, became a Castilian bulwark on the inexorable Christian march south. As Fernando III reclaimed and reconquered Muslim Andalucía, aristocratic families such as the Molinas, de la Cuevas and Cobos benefited from their part in the campaign. They were rewarded with huge estates, ownership of which would mould the character of the province and even endure today. Shoring up their influence in the Castilian court, they siphoned off huge sums of money for conspicuously expensive civic projects and, in the 16th century, with the appointment of Don Francisco Cobos to privy secretary (in effect, prime minister), Úbeda became a centre of culture and power.

Orientation

Most of Úbeda's splendid buildings – the main reason for visiting the town – are among the maze of narrow, winding streets and expansive squares that constitute the old town, in the southeast. The cheaper accommodation and the bus station are about 1km away, in the drab new town to the west and north. The better accommodation is concentrated in the *casco antiguo* (old quarter). Plaza de Andalucía marks the boundary between the two parts of town.

Information

You'll find the biggest concentration of banks and ATMs on Plaza de Andalucía and nearby Calle Rastro.

Centro de Salud (Health Centre; ☎ 953 02 86 00; Calle Explanada s/n) In the new part of town, with an emergency section.

ÚBEDA

0 — 200 m
0 — 0.1 miles

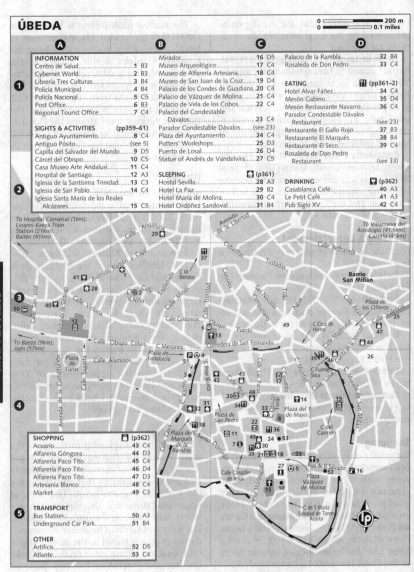

INFORMATION
Centro de Salud...............................1 B3
Cybernet World..............................2 B3
Librería Tres Culturas.....................3 B4
Policía Municipal............................4 B4
Policía Nacional..............................5 C5
Post Office.....................................6 B3
Regional Tourist Office..................7 C4

SIGHTS & ACTIVITIES (pp359–61)
Antiguo Ayuntamiento..................8 C4
Antiguo Pósito..........................(see 5)
Capilla del Salvador del Mundo.....9 D5
Cárcel del Obispo........................10 C4
Casa Museo Arte Andalusí............11 C4
Hospital de Santiago....................12 A3
Iglesia de la Santísima Trinidad....13 C3
Iglesia de San Pablo....................14 C4
Iglesia Santa María de los Reales
    Alcázares................................15 C5
Mirador.......................................16 D5
Museo Arqueológico....................17 C4
Museo de Alfarería Artesana........18 C4
Museo de San Juan de la Cruz......19 D4
Palacio de los Condes de Guadiana..20 C4
Palacio de Vázquez de Molina.......21 C4
Palacio de Vela de los Cobos........22 C4
Palacio del Condestable
    Dávalos..................................23 C4
Parador Condestable Dávalos......(see 23)
Plaza del Ayuntamiento................24 C4
Potters' Workshops......................25 D3
Puerto de Losal...........................26 D4
Statue of Andrés de Vandelvira.....27 C5

SLEEPING (p361)
Hostal Sevilla..............................28 A3
Hotel La Paz................................29 B2
Hotel María de Molina..................30 C4
Hotel Ordóñez Sandoval..............31 B4

Palacio de la Rambla....................32 B4
Rosaleda de Don Pedro................33 C4

EATING (pp361–2)
Hotel Alvar Fáñez........................34 C4
Mesón Gabino.............................35 D4
Mesón Restaurante Navarro.........36 C4
Parador Condestable Dávalos
    Restaurant.............................(see 23)
Restaurante El Gallo Rojo.............37 B3
Restaurante El Marqués................38 B4
Restaurante El Seco......................39 C4
Rosaleda de Don Pedro
    Restaurant.............................(see 33)

DRINKING (p362)
Casablanca Café..........................40 A3
Le Petit Café................................41 A3
Pub Siglo XV...............................42 A3

SHOPPING (p362)
Acuario.......................................43 C4
Alfarería Góngora.........................44 D3
Alfarería Paco Tito.......................45 C4
Alfarería Paco Tito.......................46 D4
Alfarería Paco Tito.......................47 D3
Artesanía Blanco..........................48 C4
Market..49 C3

TRANSPORT
Bus Station.................................50 A3
Underground Car Park..................51 B4

OTHER
Artificis.......................................52 D5
Atlante..53 C4

Cybernet World (Calle Niño 22; per 30min €1; ⏰ 11am-2pm & 4.30-10pm) Lots of computers, and full of teenagers.
Hospital Comarcal (☎ 953 02 82 00; Carretera de Linares Km 1) The main hospital, found on the northwestern edge of town.
Librería Tres Culturas (☎ 953 75 26 25; Calle Rastro 7) Sells a selection of maps, including maps of Cazorla, and some guidebooks.

Policía Municipal (☎ 953 75 00 23; Plaza de Andalucía) Found in the busy centre.
Policía Nacional (☎ 953 75 03 55; Plaza Vázquez de Molina) Occupies the Antiguo Pósito.
Post office (Calle Trinidad 4; ⏰ 8.30am-2.30pm Mon-Fri, 9.30am-1pm Sat)
Regional tourist office (☎ 953 75 08 97; otubeda@ andalucia.org; Calle Baja del Marqués 4; ⏰ 9am-2.45pm &

4-7pm Mon-Fri, 10am-2pm Sat) Located in the 18th-century Palacio Marqués de Contadero, in the old town.

Sights

Nearly all of Úbeda's main sights are located within the *casco antigua*, which can be thoroughly explored in a day or two. It is quite helpful to concentrate on the different plazas (Plaza Vazquez de Molina, Plaza del Ayuntamiento and Plaza del 1 de Mayo) with another morning or afternoon set aside to root around the Barrio San Millán (the pottery quarter) and do a spot of shopping.

PLAZA VÁZQUEZ DE MOLINA

Following the success of the Reconquista, Úbeda's aristocratic lions lost no time jockeying for power in the Castilian court. In the 16th century, Francisco de los Cobos y Molina secured the post of privy secretary to King Carlos I and was later succeeded by his nephew Juan Vázquez de Molina. Exposed to the cultural influences of the Italian Renaissance that were then seeping into Spain, and benefiting from the wealth and privilege of high office, the Molina family turned their attention to self-aggrandizing civic projects in their home town. They commissioned what are now considered to be some of the purest examples of Renaissance architecture in Spain, prompting the Catalan art critic and philosopher Eugenio D'Ors (1881–1954) to later compare the town with the Italian cities of Ferrara and Brescia.

The purity of Renaissance lines is best expressed in the **Capilla del Salvador del Mundo** (☎ 953 75 81 50; entrance on southern side; adult/child €2.25/1, last hour free; ⏰ 10am-2pm & 4.30-7pm), the first of many works executed in Úbeda by celebrated architect Andrés de Vandelvira (see Master Builder, p360). A pre-eminent example of the plateresque style, the chapel's **main façade** is modelled on Diego de Siloé's Puerta del Perdón at Granada's cathedral (p311). The classic portal is topped by a carving of the transfiguration of Christ, flanked by statues of St Peter and St Paul. The underside of the arch is an orgy of classical sculpture, executed by French sculptor Esteban Jamete, depicting the Greek gods – a Renaissance touch that would have been inconceivable a few decades earlier. Viewed at night, the whole façade leaps out in dynamic 3D.

Inside, the sacristy glitters with symbolic carvings, again by Jamete. Having worked on Fontainebleau, Jamete gave the sacristy some French flair with huge swags and medallions all topped off by the huge frescoed dome modelled on the Capilla Mayor in Granada (see p311). The church's main retable, by Alonso de Berruguete, was damaged in the civil war and only one statue, the *Transfiguración del Monte Tabor* (Transfiguration on Mount Tabor), is original. However, the rest has been painstakingly and skilfully restored.

This is not your typical parochial church, but instead the private funereal chapel of the Cobos family (their crypt lies beneath the nave) – a small indication of Francisco's wealth that, at one time, exceeded that of King Carlos I himself. Today the church is still privately owned by the Seville-based Duques de Medinaceli, descendants of the Cobos, and one of Andalucía's major landowning families.

In fact, the whole beautifully proportioned plaza (180m long), with its excess of architecture, was the family precinct. Next door to the Capilla stands the **Palacio del Condestable Dávalos**, originally the house of the church's chaplain and a palace by any other name. Partly remodelled in the 17th century, the mansion is now Úbeda's luxurious parador (p361). To the west the huge **Palacio de Vázquez de Molina** (☎ 953 75 04 40; ⏰ 10am-2pm & 5-9pm), now Úbeda's *ayuntamiento*, was built by Vandelvira for Juan (Francisco's nephew and successor to the post of privy secretary), whose coat of arms surmounts the doorway. The uncluttered façade, deeply Italian-influenced, has superbly harmonious proportions. The **Museo de Alfarería Artesana** (admission €1.80; ⏰ 10.30am-2pm & 5-7pm Tue-Sat, 10.30am-2pm Sun) is devoted to Úbeda pottery, a craft whose green glaze dates back to Islamic times.

Facing the Palacio de Vázquez de Molina is the site of Úbeda's old mosque, now dominated by the **Iglesia Santa María de los Reales Alcázares** although the picturesque cloisters mark the original site of the Muslim ablutions fountain. The church has been closed for restoration for several years so check with the tourist office for details of its reopening. Next door to Santa María stands the **Cárcel del Obispo** (Bishop's Prison), where nuns who stepped out of line used to be incarcerated. It is now a courthouse. Under the trees in front is a **statue of Andrés de Vandelvira**,

JAÉN PROVINCE

MASTER BUILDER

Born in 1509 in Alcaraz (in Castilla-La Mancha), 150km northeast of Úbeda, Andrés de Vandelvira almost single-handedly brought the Renaissance to Jaén province. Influenced by the pioneering Renaissance architect Diego de Siloé, Vandelvira designed numerous marvellous buildings in Úbeda, Baeza and Jaén, which add up to an outstanding and contained catalogue of Renaissance architecture. His work spanned all three main phases of Spanish Renaissance architecture: the ornamental early Renaissance phase known as plateresque (primarily a decorative genre, with effects resembling those of silverware), as seen in the **Capilla del Salvador del Mundo** (p359), with its predilection for sculpted coats of arms; a much purer line and classic proportions emerged in the later **Palacio de Vázquez de Molina** (p359); and in his last building, the **Hospital de Santiago** (p360; completed in 1575, the year he died), Vandelvira displays almost as much sobriety as Juan de Herrera's El Escorial (near Madrid), the paradigm of the austere Spanish late Renaissance.

---

the man who made Úbeda worth visiting. By the statue, fronting the main square, the 16th-century **Antiguo Pósito**, originally a communal store for surplus grain, is now the local headquarters of the Policía Nacional.

East of the square, 150m along Baja de El Salvador, a **mirador** (lookout) gives fine views across the olive fields, overshadowed by the snow-capped Cazorla mountains in the distance.

NORTH OF PLAZA DE VÁZQUEZ DE MOLINA

North of Úbeda's main plaza a warren of winding streets gives way to a series of elegant squares, each lined with ever-more mansions and churches. The first of these is the broad **Plaza del Ayuntamiento**, overlooked from its northwestern corner by the **Palacio de Vela de los Cobo**. This palace can be visited (admission free) by prior arrangement with the tourist office.

Another of the town's best mansions is the 17th-century **Palacio de los Condes de Guadiana**, three blocks up Calle Real (once Úbeda's main commercial street), with some elegant carving around the windows and balconies. For an insight into a typical mansion home visit the recently opened **Casa Museo Arte Andalusí** (☎ 619-076132; Calle Narvaez 11; admission €1.50; ☼ 10.30am-2.30pm & 4-8.30pm), which is full of period antiques. It also stages flamenco shows every Saturday night from 10pm onwards.

Northeast of the Plaza del Ayuntamiento is the even bigger Plaza del 1 de Mayo, originally the town's market square and bullring. It was also the iniquitous site of Inquisition burnings, which local worthies used to watch from the gallery of the **Antiguo Ayuntamiento** (Old Town Hall) in the southwestern corner. Along the northern side of the square is the **Iglesia de San Pablo** (admission free; ☼ 7-9pm), with a fine late-Gothic portal (1511).

Just north of the Iglesia de San Pablo, a 14th-century Mudejar mansion houses the **Museo Arqueológico** (☎ 953 75 37 02; Calle Cervantes 4; admission free; ☼ 3-8pm Tue, 9am-8pm Wed-Sat, 9am-3pm Sun), with exhibits from Neolithic to Islamic times. A second smaller museum, the **Museo de San Juan de la Cruz** (☎ 953 75 06 15; Calle del Carmen; admission €1.20; ☼ 11am-1pm & 5-7pm Tue-Sun) is dedicated to the 16th-century mystic, poet and religious reformer St John of the Cross who founded the breakaway monastic order of Carmelitos Descalzos (Barefoot Carmelites). He did this, against opposition, in an effort to return to the austerity and contemplative life from which he felt mainstream Carmelites had lapsed.

The museum is housed in the Oratorio de San Juan de la Cruz, where St John died of gangrene in 1591. In a reconstructed monk's cell, a lifelike figure of St John sits at his writing table – perhaps musing on 'the dark night of the soul'. Nearby is a cabinet containing his letters, plus a couple of his fingers! Visits, guided by Spanish-speaking monks, last about half an hour.

North of the museum the impressive **Puerta de Losal** takes you down into the **Barrio San Millán**, Úbeda's famous potters' quarter, with **potters' workshops** located on Calle Valencia. Alternatively, if you turn left at the gate and walk down Calle Fuente Seca and then Calle Cruz de Hierro to link up with Corredera de San Fernando, past the unusual baroque **Iglesia de la Santísima Trinidad**, you will eventually reach Vandelvira's last architectural project, the **Hospital de Santiago** (☎ 953 75 08 42;

Calle Obispo Cobos; admission free; ☺ 8am-3pm & 4-10pm Mon-Fri, 11am-3pm & 6-10pm Sat & Sun). Completed in 1575 it is a very grand and sober affair, and has often been dubbed the Escorial of Andalucía. It now acts as Úbeda's cultural centre, housing a library, municipal dance school and an exhibition hall.

Tours

Artificis (☎ 953 75 81 50; adult/child €6/free; ☺ tours 11am & 5pm, afternoon tours at 6pm Jun-Sep) With Artificis, tours of Úbeda's monuments take about two hours (commentary in Spanish). If you ring ahead it is possible to book tours spoken in English, French and Italian. It also runs tours in nearby Baeza.

Atlante (☎ 953 79 34 22; adult/child €6/free; ☺ tours 11am & 5pm, afternoon tours at 6pm Jun-Sep) Atlante runs similar tours to Artificis. A combined tour of Úbeda and Baeza is €10 and there is also a theatrical night-time tour (winter/summer 7pm/10pm).

Festivals & Events

Semana Santa (Holy Week) Solemn brotherhoods, devotional processions and lots of atmospheric drama.

Festival Internacional de Música y Danza Ciudad de Úbeda (May) Varied music and dance performances throughout the month of May.

Fiesta de San Miguel (27 September to 4 October) Celebrates the capture of the town in 1233 by Fernando III, with firework shows, parades, concerts, a flamenco festival, a bullfighting season and more.

Sleeping

Úbeda's budget accommodation is rather dreary although perfectly adequate; hotels then make a quantum leap to establishments that are comfortable and full of character, with many housed in old palaces.

Palacio de la Rambla (☎ 953 75 01 96; Plaza del Marqués de la Rambla 1; d/ste incl breakfast €99.50/112) Úbeda's best palace conversion, the Palacio de la Rambla offers eight fantastic rooms crammed with antiques in the home of the Marquesa de la Rambla. The ivy-clad patio is wonderfully romantic and entry is restricted to guests only. Breakfast can be served in your room. The hotel is closed in July and August.

Parador Condestable Dávalos (☎ 953 75 03 45; www.parador.es in Spanish; Plaza Vázquez de Molina; s/d €106/119; P ☒) A fabulous parador in Úbeda's prime location, looking out over the wonderful Plaza Vázquez de Molina. The hotel itself is a historic monument, previously the Palacio del Deán Ortega. It has,

of course, been comfortably modernised and is appropriately luxurious. The restaurant is the best in town.

Hotel María de Molina (☎ 953 79 53 56; www.hotel -maria-de-molina.com in Spanish; Plaza del Ayuntamiento; s/d €52/83.50; ☒) An attractive hotel housed in a 16th-century palacio on the picturesque Plaza Ayuntamiento. Well-appointed rooms are arranged around a typical patio and the hotel has an excellent restaurant (p362).

Rosaleda de Don Pedro (☎ 953 79 51 47; www .husa.es; Calle Obispo Toral 2; d €57; P ☒ ☒) Part of the Husa hotel chain, the Don Pedro offers good three-star facilities in a central old town location. It also has a good restaurant (p362) and the only pool in the historic centre. Some facilities are adapted for wheelchair users.

Hotel Ordóñez Sandoval (☎ 953 79 51 87; Calle Antonio Medina 1; s/d €53/66; P) The family home of Amalia Perez Ordóñez, this 19th century *palacio* now has three vast bedrooms open to guests. Amalia is a gracious and helpful hostess, checking on guests at breakfast and trying valiantly with her huge English dictionary to communicate with even the worst Spanish linguists.

Hostal Sevilla (☎ 953 75 06 12; Avenida Ramón y Cajal 9; s/d €20/33) Situated in the modern town, Úbeda's *hostales* (all located near each other) are rather grim in appearance. However, the best of the bunch, the Sevilla, is a pleasant family-run *hostal*, offering good-value rooms with heating.

Hotel La Paz (☎ 953 75 08 48; www.hotel-lapaz.com in Spanish; Calle Andalucía 1; s/d €35/54; ☒) Located in an anonymous part of the modern town, La Paz appears a huge '60s monstrosity. Inside, however, its rooms are comfortable and fairly well-appointed with neat if unimaginative pine furnishings.

Eating

Parador Condestable Dávalos (☎ 953 75 03 45; Plaza Vázquez de Molina; mains €12-17, menú €25) A deservedly popular restaurant serving up delicious elegant dishes. Despite the price this is the place in which to eat in Úbeda and even off-season the dining room buzzes happily in the evening. Try the local specialities: *carruécano* (green peppers stuffed with partridge) or *cabrito guisado con piñones* (stewed kid with pine nuts).

Mesón Restaurante Navarro (☎ 953 79 06 38; Plaza del Ayuntamiento 2; raciones €4-9, mains €8-14) Popular, smoky and noisy, the Navarro is a cherished local favourite. Taking your tapas at the bar is the order of the day but in summer it is nice to sit out on the plaza and enjoy the excellent and varied *raciones* and *bocadillos* (filled long white bread rolls) from €1.50 to €4.50. Note that the sign just says 'Mesón Restaurante'.

Restaurante El Seco (☎ 953 79 14 52; Calle Corazón de Jesús 8; menú €12) Located on a pretty square filled with orange trees, El Seco is a mid-priced, old town option although the food here is of a higher standard than most including the steaming *carne de monte* (usually venison) with a rich tomato sauce or lightly grilled trout with mixed vegetables.

Restaurante El Gallo Rojo (☎ 953 75 20 38; Calle Manuel Barraca 3; mains €9-12) Just off the northern end of Avenida Ramón y Cajal, this is one of the best places in the new part of town. The *menú* (set menu) is good value and this cheerful restaurant has outdoor tables.

Mesón Gabino (☎ 953 75 75 53; Calle Fuente Seca; mains €6-10) A wonderfully atmospheric cellar restaurant where the dining room is intercepted by stone pillars. It is a good spot to eat if you have been wandering in the potters' quarter and it serves up solid fare, including salads and egg dishes.

Restaurante El Marqués (☎ 953 75 72 55; Plaza del Marqués de la Rambla; platos combinados €8-12; ☻ 2-4pm Tue-Fri, 2-4pm & 8.30-11pm Sat & Sun) Run by the Hotel María de Molina (p361), this vast restaurant with its massive stone arches and stained-glass skylights, serves up local specialities such as oven baked lamb with fresh vegetables and salmon with wild asparagus. In summer the best place to eat is outside at the tables in the attractive cobbled plaza.

Both the **Rosaleda de Don Pedro** (☎ 953 79 51 47; www.husa.es; Calle Obispo Toral; menú €20) and the **Hotel Alvar Fáñez** (☎ 953 79 60 43; Calle Juan Pasquau 5; menú €20) have good restaurants. Both restaurants serve menus full of mountain fare – freshwater fish, heaps of vegetables and hearty meat dishes.

Drinking & Entertainment

Quiet and introverted Úbeda does not have much of a nightlife and off-season most of the town's youth seem to hang out at pizza parlours and Internet cafés. Most of the action takes place in the modern town.

Le Petit Café (Avenida Ramón y Cajal 26) An elegant and popular café that gets full to bursting in the late afternoon. Speciality teas, coffees and fruit cocktails come accompanied by a huge range of *tortas* (tarts), biscuits, pastries and ice creams.

Casablanca Café (☎ 953 79 27 88; Redonda de Santiago) If Úbeda had a Hotel California this would be its bar. Jukeboxes, Americana, retro lights, a huge billiard table and an old gas pump create a twilight atmosphere. On quieter Sunday and Monday nights the bar is full of men contemplating the dregs in their glasses, serenaded by endless sad songs.

Pub Siglo XV (Calle Prior Blanca 5) The only bar in the old town, this atmospheric joint sometimes stages live flamenco or bands. However, in low season it is randomly closed.

Shopping

The typical emerald-green glaze on Úbeda's attractive pottery, and the tradition of embroidering coloured patterns into *ubedíes* (esparto mats), both date back to Islamic times. The potters' quarter still retains three original kilns from this period (there are only six left in the whole of Spain).

Several workshops sell pottery in the San Millán barrio (district), northeast of the old town, and the potters are often willing to explain some of the ancient techniques they use. These include adding olive stones to the fire to intensify the heat, which results in a more-brilliant glaze. **Alfarería Paco Tito** (Calle Valencia 22, Calle Fuente Seca 17 or Plaza del Ayuntamiento 12) is the largest concern, but several others on the same street, and nearby **Alfarería Góngora** (Cuesta de la Merced 32), are worth a look. Smaller pottery pieces that you could comfortably carry home start at about €6.

For esparto mats and baskets, costing from about €5, visit **Artesanía Blanco** (Calle Real 47) in the old town. The nearby **Acuario** (Calle Real 61) has some good antiques, and bits and pieces of fine tiling. You'll find olive oil for sale in shops and supermarkets all over town.

The main shopping streets are Calle Mesones and Calle Obispo Cobos, between Plaza de Andalucía and the Hospital de Santiago.

Getting There & Around

BUS

The **bus station** (☎ 953 75 21 57; Calle San José 6) is located in the new part of town. Alsina Graells runs to Baeza (€0.75, 30 minutes, 15 daily), Jaén (€3.75, 1¼ hours, 12 daily Monday to Saturday), Cazorla (€2.95, 45 minutes, up to

10 daily) and to Granada (€9.70, seven daily). Bacoma goes to Córdoba (€8.75, four daily) and Seville (€16.95, four daily). Other buses head to Málaga (€17.40) and Madrid (€18.35), and small places around Jaén province.

CAR & MOTORCYCLE
There is now a convenient underground car park in Plaza de Andalucía (one hour €1, 12 hours €8). You can park for free in the narrow streets of the old town and in the streets that radiate from Plaza de Andalucía although it is not always easy to find a spot.

TRAIN
The nearest station is **Linares-Baeza** (☎ 953 65 02 02), 21km northwest of town, which you can reach by Linares-bound buses. For information on trains, see p357.

CAZORLA
pop 8200 / elevation 836m
Busy, bustling Cazorla is a fairly large, modern rural town with an appealing unpretentious air about it. A halfway house between the passive landscape of the plains and the great rugged swathe of mountain and valley that unfolds enticingly to the north and east, the town is the official gateway to the Parque Natural de Cazorla. The park begins dramatically amid the cliffs of **Peña de los Halcones** (Falcon Crag) that tower above the town.

Cazorla becomes crowded during Spanish holiday times and on weekends from spring to autumn.

Orientation
The A319 from the west winds up into Cazorla and is known as Calle Hilario Marco. This road ends at Plaza de la Constitución, the often frantically busy main square of the newer part of town. The second important square is Plaza de la Corredera, 150m south of Plaza de la Constitución. It is reached along Calle Doctor Muñoz, Cazorla's narrow, but shop-lined, main street. Plaza de Santa María, 300m further southeast and reached along even more narrow, winding streets, is the heart of the oldest part of town, and stands directly below the castle and crags.

Information
You'll find several banks with ATMs on and between Plaza de la Constitución and Plaza de la Corredera.

Centro de Salud Dr José Cano Salcedo (Health Centre; ☎ 953 72 10 61; Calle Ximénez de Rada 1)
Information kiosk (Calle Hilario Marco; ☼ 10am-2pm & 5-9pm summer, 10am-2pm & 4-8pm winter) As you come into town along the A310 from the west, the kiosk is located on the right-hand side, just past the sharp right-hand bend.
Municipal tourist office (☎ 953 71 01 02; Paseo del Santo Cristo 17; ☼ 10am-1pm & 5.30-8pm) Found 200m north of Plaza de la Constitución. It has information on the park and town.
Policía Local (Local Police; ☎ 953 72 01 81) In the *ayuntamiento*, just off Plaza de la Corredera.
Post office (Calle Mariano Extremera 2; ☼ 8.30am-2.30pm Mon-Fri, 9.30am-1pm Sat) Behind the town hall, just off Plaza de la Corredera.
Quercus (☎ 953 72 01 15; www.excursionesquercus.com in Spanish; Plaza de la Constitución 15; ☼ 10am-2pm Mon-Fri, 10am-2pm & 5-8pm Sat & Sun) This privately run company provides some tourist information and sells maps, Spanish-language guidebooks and souvenirs. It also offers excursions into the park (see p369).

Sights
Cazorla's history, like that of most of Jaén province, is one of rich landowning classes. The central square, **Plaza de la Corredera**, is the civic centre of the town, where the elegant **ayuntamiento** dominates the square with its landmark clock tower. The plaza, much like the rest of the town, is full of life. Canyon-like streets radiate south to the **Balcón de Zabaleta**. This little *mirador* (lookout) is like a sudden window in a blank wall – it has stunning views over the town and up to the **Castillo de la Yedra** (Castle of the Ivy).

The dramatic castle is of Roman origin, though it was largely built by the Muslims, then restored in the 15th century after the Reconquista. Much money has been spent on a modern restoration, and the castle now houses the **Museo del Alto Guadalquivir** (Museum of the Upper Guadalquivir; non-EU citizen €1.50, EU citizen free; ☼ 3-8pm Tue, 9am-8pm Wed-Sat, 9am-3pm Sun & holidays), a mishmash of art and local artefacts. Included are a reconstructed traditional kitchen, models of old oil mills and a chapel featuring a life-sized Romanesque-Byzantine Crucifixion sculpture. The shortest way up to the castle is from the attractive **Plaza de Santa María**, starting along the street to the right of the ruined **Iglesia de Santa María**. The devastated church was built by Vandelvira and wrecked by Napoleonic troops in reprisal for Cazorla's tenacious resistance. It is now used for occasional open-air concerts.

In Plaza de Santa María you can while away a pleasant hour or two in the early evening amid the café tables and ancient plane trees, overlooking the 400-year-old fountain, the **Fuente de las Cadenas**.

Festivals

La Caracolá (14 May) The image of Cazorla's patron saint, San Isicio (a Christian apostle supposedly stoned to death at Cazorla in Roman times), is carried from the Ermita de San Isicio to the Iglesia de San José.

Fiesta de Cristo del Consuelo (17-21 September) Fireworks and fairgrounds mark Cazorla's annual fiesta. On the first day a 17th-century painting of the Cristo del Consuelo (Christ of Consolation), which was rescued from Napoleonic destruction, is carried in a procession.

Sleeping

CAZORLA

Molino la Farraga (☎ 953 72 12 49; www.molinolafar raga.com; Calle Camino de la Hoz s/n; d €64; 🏊) Just up the valley from the Plaza de Santa María is the tranquil old mill of La Farraga, nestling amid forested slopes that are crisscrossed by rivers. Inside, understated comfort is the order of the day with lots of dark mahogany colours – a welcome relief from the Hansel and Gretel pine-kitsch of most *casas rurales* (village houses or farms with rooms to let).

Villa Turística de Cazorla (☎ 953 71 01 00; Ladera de San Isicio; 2-/4-person villa €70/120; P 🍴 🏊) A lovely Andalucian-style tourist village offering 32 comfortable villas with living rooms and terrace. Around the hotel there are pleasant walks into the park, a good-sized swimming pool and a children's play area.

Albergue Juvenil Cazorla (☎ 953 72 03 29; www .inturjoven.com; Plaza Mauricio Martínez 6; high season under 26/over 26 €13.75/18.35; 🏊) Cazorla's spick-and-span youth hostel is housed in a 16th-century convent, 200m uphill from Plaza de la Corredera. It has places for 120 people in rooms holding between two and six, most with shared bathrooms.

Hotel Ciudad de Cazorla (☎ 953 72 17 00; Plaza de la Corredera 9; s/d incl breakfast €59/70.75; P 🍴 🏊) Jarring somewhat with its surroundings on the Plaza de Corredera, Cazorla's newest hotel has not found favour with the locals. However, it has 35 modern rooms with all the requisite facilities.

Hotel Guadalquivir (☎ 953 72 02 68; www.hguadal quivir.com in Spanish; Calle Nueva 6; s low/high season

€27/30.50, d low/high season €37/42; 🍴) Cheap 'n' cheerful, the Guadalquivir has comfortable, if cheesy, rooms with pine furniture, TV and heating. The singles can be a bit cramped but the hotel is good value for money, in a good location.

Camping Cortijo San Isicio (☎ 953 72 12 80; per person/tent/car €3.50/3/2.50; 🕓 Mar-Oct) A charming camping ground amid pine trees, off the Quesada road 4km southwest of central Cazorla. It has room for just 54 people. The access road is narrow and twisting.

LA IRUELA

More accommodation can be found in or around the nearby village of La Iruela, which is 1km out of Cazorla in the direction of the park.

Hotel de Montaña Riogazas (☎ 953 12 40 35; www.riogazas.com in Spanish; Carretera de La Iruela al Chorro Km 4.5; s/d €45.50/61.75; P 🍴 🏊) An attractive lodge-style option in a pleasant rural setting. Through its affiliation with Quercus, the hotel can arrange any excursions you may want to undertake.

Hotel Sierra de Cazorla (☎ 953 72 12 25; www.hotel sierradecazorla.com in Spanish; Travesía del Camino de La Iruela 2; s/d €45.50/61.75, apt 2-4 people €67.30, 4-6 people €81.60, 6-8 people €94; P 🍴 🏊) A sprawling modern hotel redeemed by its scenic surroundings. Again, all things pine dominate the furnishings but the pool is fantastic, sited in the shadow of a huge craggy mountain. The hotel also administers the Don Pedro apartments, which consist of one-, two- and three-bedroom apartments accommodating up to eight people. The apartments are excellent value for groups. They're light and airy, which is great in summer but a bit chilly when it rains although some of the apartments have fireplaces. Furnishings are adequate and comfortable, if not the height of fashion.

Eating

In late summer or autumn, after rain, locals disappear into the woods to gather large, delicious, edible mushrooms that they call *níscalos*. If these appear in your restaurant, get your share.

Restaurante La Sarga (☎ 953 72 15 07; Plaza del Mercado s/n; mains €8-12, menú €18; 🕓 closed Sep) Cazorla's best restaurant, serving up well-prepared local specialities. Many of these involve game, such as the *caldereta de gamo*

(venison stew) or the *lomos de venado con miel* (venison with honey).

La Cueva de Juan Pedro (Plaza de Santa María; raciones €9) An ancient, wood-beamed place hung with countless clumps of garlic and drying peppers, serves up traditional Cazorla fare such as *conejo* (rabbit), *trucha* (trout), *rin-rán* (a mix of salted cod, potato and dried red peppers), *jabalí* (wild boar), *venado* (venison) and even mouflon. All are available as *raciones*, prepared in a variety of ways.

Mesón Don Chema (☎ 953 72 00 68; Calle Escaleras del Mercado 2; mains €7-9) Down a lane off Calle Doctor Muñoz, this cheerful place serves up good-value local fare, such as the sizzling *huevos cazorleña*, a mixed stew of sliced boiled eggs and chorizo with vegetables.

Several of the bars on Cazorla's three main squares serve good tapas and *raciones*, including **Bar Las Vegas** (Plaza de la Corredera 17; raciones €6), where you can try *gloria bendita* (blessed glory), a tasty prawn-and-capsicum *revuelto* (scrambled eggs). The Las Vegas has the town's best breakfast *tostadas* (toasted bread often served with toppings), too.

La Montería (Plaza de la Corredera 18) has tapas of *choto con ajo* (veal with garlic) while the *plato olímpico* (Olympic plate) is a good way to sample a selection of its tapas. Other tapas stops include bright **Café-Bar Rojas** (Plaza de la Constitución 2) and down-to-earth **Taberna Quinito** (Plaza de Santa María 6).

A daily **market** is held in Plaza del Mercado just down from Plaza de la Constitución.

Getting There & Around

Alsina Graells runs buses to/from Úbeda (€2.95, 45 minutes, up to 10 daily), Jaén (€6.50, two hours, two daily) and Granada (€11.85, 3½ hours, two daily). The main stop in Cazorla is Plaza de la Constitución; the tourist office has timetable information. A few buses run from Cazorla to Coto Ríos (€3.05, two daily Monday to Saturday) in the park. It makes stops at Arroyo Frío and Torre del Vinagre.

There is a convenient car park in Plaza del Mercado, below Plaza de la Constitución.

PARQUE NATURAL DE CAZORLA

Cazorla's chief attraction, and one of the biggest draws in the whole province, is the lushly wooded, 2143-sq-km Parque Natural de las Sierras de Cazorla, Segura y Las Villas (to give it its full title). It is the largest natural park in Spain and its corrugated, craggy mountain ranges – although not extraordinarily high – are memorably beautiful, as is the huge snaking 20km reservoir in its midst. The park is also the origin of the Río Guadalquivir, Andalucía's longest river. It rises between the Sierra de Cazorla and Sierra del Pozo in the south of the park and flows northwards into the reservoir, from which it emerges westbound, heading for the Atlantic Ocean.

The park's numerous attractions include enjoyable walking, picturesque villages, and better prospects of seeing wildlife than almost anywhere else in Andalucía. Red and fallow deer, wild boar, mouflon and ibex are all here in good numbers (partly because they are protected in order to be hunted). You may even see deer or boar on some of the roads. Some 140 bird species nest in the park, including several types of eagle, vulture and falcon, and efforts are being made to reintroduce the majestic lammergeier (bearded vulture).

The best times to visit the park are in the spring and autumn when the vegetation is at its most colourful. In winter the park is often covered in snow. When walking, go properly equipped, with enough water and appropriate clothes. Temperatures up in the hills are several degrees lower than down in the valleys, and the wind can be cutting at any time.

Exploring the park is a lot easier if you have a vehicle, but some bus services exist (see p371) and there are plenty of places to stay inside the park. If you don't have a vehicle to get to the more-remote places you do have the option of taking guided excursions to those areas.

The park is hugely popular with Spanish tourists and attracts an estimated 600,000 visitors a year – some 50,000 of them during Semana Santa. The other peak periods are July and August, and weekends from April to October.

Information

The main park information centre is at Torre del Vinagre (p367). There are seasonal tourist offices at Cortijos Nuevos, Hornos, Santiago de la Espada, Segura de la Sierra, Orcera and Siles. Tourism offices in Cazorla also provide information on the park.

Lonely Planet's *Walking in Spain* details three of the best Cazorla walks. Other good hiking guides are *Walking in Andalucía* by Guy Hunter-Watts, which details walks of between 5km and 15km, or for Spanish speakers, *Senderos de Pequeño Recorrido – Parque Natural de Cazorla* by Justo Robles Álvarez.

The best maps are Editorial Alpina's 1:40,000 *Sierra de Cazorla*, covering the southern third of the park (€5.40) and *Sierra de Segura*, covering the northern two-thirds (€7.40). Selected walking and mountain-bike routes are specially marked and described in accompanying booklets. Quercus also produces an excellent driving map (1:100,000) of the park, *Parque*

Natural de las Sierras de Cazorla, Segura y Las Villas (€2.70), showing all the points of interest.

The Sierra de Cazorla map is available in English. You may be able to get these and other maps and guides at the Torre del Vinagre information centre (p367) and at some shops in Cazorla town, but do not rely on it. See p408 for information on buying maps before you arrive.

The South of the Park

The park begins just a few hundred metres up the hill east of Cazorla town. The footpaths and dirt roads working their way between the pine forests, meadowlands, crags and valleys of the Sierra de Cazorla offer

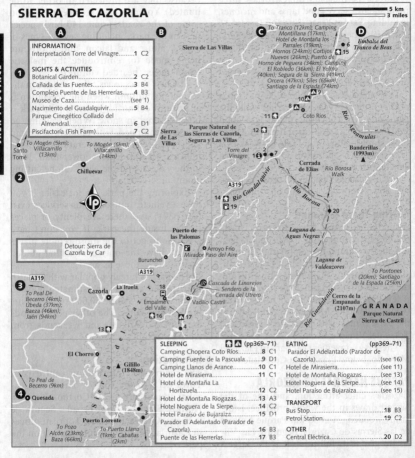

SIERRA DE CAZORLA

0 —— 5 km
0 —— 3 miles

INFORMATION
Interpretación Torre del Vinagre........1 C2

SIGHTS & ACTIVITIES
Botanical Garden....................................2 C2
Cañada de las Fuentes........................3 B4
Complejo Puente de las Herrerías......4 B3
Museo de Caza................................(see 1)
Nacimiento del Guadalquivir.............5 B4
Parque Cinegético Collado del
Almendral..6 D1
Piscifactoría (Fish Farm).....................7 C2

Detour: Sierra de Cazorla by Car

To Tranco (12km); Camping Montillana (17km); Hotel de Montaña los Parrales (19km); Hornos (24km); Cortijos Nuevos (26km); Puerto de Horno de Peguera (34km); Camping El Robledo (36km); El Yelmo (40km); Segura de la Sierra (41km); Orcera (47km); Siles (65km); Santiago de la Espada (74km)

Embalse del Tranco de Beas

Sierra de Las Villas

Coto Ríos

Río Aguamulas

Parque Natural de las Sierras de Cazorla, Segura y Las Villas

Banderillas (1993m)

Torre del Vinagre

Cerrada de Elías
Río Borosa Walk
Río Borosa

A319
Río Guadalquivir

Laguna de Aguas Negras

Puerto de las Palomas

Arroyo Frío
Mirador Paso del Aire

Burunchel

Laguna de Valdeazores

To Pontones (20km); Santiago de la Espada (25km)

A319
Cascada de Linarejos
Sendero de la Cerrada del Utrero

La Iruela
Cazorla
Empalme del Valle
Vadillo Castril

Cerro de la Empanada (2107m)

GRANADA
Parque Natural Sierra de Castril

To Peal De Becerro (4km); Úbeda (37km); Baeza (46km); Jaén (94km)

El Chorro

Gilillo (1848m)

Río Guadalentín

Quesada

Puerto Lorente

To Pozo Alcón (23km); Baza (66km)

To Puerto Llano (1km); Cabañas (2km)

To Peal de Becerro (9km)

Santo Tomé

To Mogón (5km); Villacarrillo (13km)

To Mogón (6km); Villacarrillo (14km)

Chilluevar

Sierra de Las Villas

JAÉN PROVINCE

DETOUR: SIERRA DE CAZORLA BY CAR

This 60km itinerary is a good introduction to the parts of the park nearest Cazorla town. Much of it is on unpaved roads, but it's all quite passable for ordinary cars, if a little bumpy in places. Allow two hours for the trip – longer if you stop lots and have a picnic.

Head up first to La Iruela and turn right along Carretera Virgen de la Cabeza soon after entering La Iruela. You reach the **Merenderos de Cazorla** *mirador* (lookout), with fine views over Cazorla, after about 700m. After another 4km you pass the Hotel de Montaña Riogazas; 7km further is **El Chorro**, a gorge that's good for watching Egyptian and griffon vultures.

Just beyond El Chorro, keep on the current track, ignoring another dirt road forking down to the right. The track you are on winds around over the **Puerto Lorente** (Lorente Pass) and, after 12km, down to a junction. Take the right fork here and after a couple of hundred metres a 'Nacimiento del Guadalquivir' sign points down some steps towards the river on your left. A plaque on the far bank marks the official source of the Guadalquivir. In dry periods you can apparently identify the stream emerging from underground. The road heads a short distance past the Nacimiento to the **Cañada de las Fuentes** picnic area.

From Cañada de las Fuentes, return to the junction just before the Nacimiento and head northward, with the infant Guadalquivir on your right – a beautiful trip down the wooded valley with the river bubbling to one side and rugged crags rising all around. It's 11km to the **Puente de las Herrerías**, a bridge over the Guadalquivir supposedly built in one night for Queen Isabel la Católica to cross during her campaigns against Granada. Here the road becomes paved, and 3km further on, past the large Complejo Puente de las Herrerías camping ground, you reach a T-junction. Go left and after 400m, opposite the turning to Vadillo Castril village, is the start of the **Sendero de la Cerrada del Utrero**, a beautiful 2km marked loop walk passing imposing cliffs, the **Cascada de Linarejos** (Linarejos Waterfall) and a small dam on the Guadalquivir – a great chance to get out and stretch your legs.

One kilometre further on from the turning to Vadillo Castril is the left-hand turn to the Parador El Adelantado hotel (which is 5km up a paved side road) and after another 2.5km you're at Empalme del Valle junction, from which it's 17km back to Cazorla.

plenty of scope for day walks or drives, with fine panoramas. The park's abrupt geography rising to 2107m at the summit of the **Cerro de la Empanada**, and descending to 460m, makes for rapid and dramatic changes in landscape.

The main A319, east from Cazorla, doesn't enter the park until Burunchel, 7km from Cazorla. From Burunchel it winds 5km up to the 1200m Puerto de las Palomas, with the breezy **Mirador Paso del Aire** a little further on. Five twisting kilometres downhill from here is Empalme del Valle, a junction where the A319 turns north towards the park's first major centre, **Arroyo Frío**. From here the road follows the north-flowing Guadalquivir.

An interesting detour from Empalme del Valle will take you to the source of the mighty river near **Cañada de las Fuentes** (see Detour: Sierra de Cazorla by Car, above). From here you can continue a further 8km to Cabañas, which at 2028m is one of the highest peaks in the park. It is a two-hour round-trip walk

from the road at Puerto Llano, and the route loops round the southern end of the hill and approaches the summit, which offers superb views from the southeast.

Further good walks in the south of the park are to be had in the **Sierra del Pozo**, which rises above the eastern side of the upper Guadalquivir valley, and in the **Barranco del Guadalentín**, a deep river valley further east. The latter is particularly rich in wildlife, but you need either your own vehicle, or a guide with one, to reach these areas.

Continuing along the A319 from Arroyo Frío, the road continues down the Guadalquivir valley to Torre del Vinagre where you will find the park's **Centro de Interpretación Torre del Vinagre** (Information Centre; ☎ 953 71 30 40; Carretera del Tranco Km 51; ☷ 11am-2pm & 5-8pm Apr-Sep, 11am-2pm & 4-7pm Oct-Mar). Built as a hunting lodge for Spain's high and mighty (including General Francisco Franco) in the 1950s, it now offers a rather dry display on the park's ecology. Note that the centre has useful toilets (the only

WALK THE WALK

The most popular walk in the Parque Natural de Cazorla follows the Río Borosa upstream. It goes through scenery that progresses from the pretty to the majestic, via a gorge and two tunnels (a torch is useful) to two beautiful mountain lakes – an ascent of 500m in the course of 12km from Torre del Vinagre. Although it can get very busy on weekends and at holiday times, this 24km, seven-hour walk (return, not counting stops) is popular for good reason.

A road signed 'Central Eléctrica', east off the A319 opposite the Centro de Interpretacion Torre del Vinagre, crosses the Guadalquivir after about 500m. Within 1km of the river, the road reaches a **piscifactoría** (fish farm), with parking areas close by. The marked start of the walk is on your right, shortly past the fish farm.

The first section is an unpaved road crisscrossing the tumbling, trout-rich river over bridges. After about 4km, where the road starts climbing to the left, take a path forking right. This takes you through a beautiful 1.5km section where the valley narrows to a gorge (the **Cerrada de Elías**) and the path changes to a wooden walkway. You re-emerge on the dirt road and continue for 3km to the **Central Eléctrica**, a small hydroelectric station.

The path passes between the power station and the river, and crosses a footbridge, where a 'Nacimiento de Aguas Negras, Laguna de Valdeazores' sign directs you ahead. About 1.5km from the station, the path turns left and zigzags up into a **tunnel** cut into the cliff. This tunnel allows water to flow to the power station. A narrow path, separated from the watercourse by a fence, runs through the tunnel, which takes about five minutes to walk through. Then there's a short section in the open air before you enter a **second tunnel**, which takes about one minute to get through. You emerge just below the dam of **Laguna de Aguas Negras**, a picturesque little reservoir surrounded by hills and trees. Cross the dam to the other side of the lake then walk about 1km south to reach a similar-sized natural lake, the **Laguna de Valdeazores**.

You can do this walk as a day trip from Cazorla if you take the bus to Torre del Vinagre (see p371). Be sure to carry plenty of water with you.

easily accessible public toilets in the park). In an adjoining building is the **Museo de Caza** (Hunting Museum; admission free; ☺ 11am-2pm & 5-8pm Apr-Sep, 11am-2pm & 4-7pm Oct-Mar), with a welter of stuffed wildlife, plus ibex and deer heads staring dolefully from the walls. A more-cheerful place to spend some time is the **botanical garden** exhibiting the park's extraordinarily rich flora, including some species that are unique to the area.

Beyond Torre del Vinagre is Coto Ríos and the beginning of the **Embalse del Tranco de Beas** reservoir. This is as far as many people venture from Cazorla. The main concentration of accommodation and visitor facilities in the park is dotted along the road up to this point and the most popular day hike, up the Río Borosa (see Walk the Walk, above), is accessible from it. The bus from Cazorla only goes this far and to explore the park further you will need your own transport.

The North of the Park

From Coto Ríos the road follows the edge of the huge, wide reservoir with tantalising glimpses through the trees. On a sunny day it is quite beautiful, and just 7km north of Coto Ríos, on a spur of land between the A319 and the reservoir, you will find the **Parque Cinegético Collado del Almendral**, a large enclosed game park where ibex, mouflon and deer are kept. A 1km footpath leads from the parking area to three *miradors* where you might see animals – your chances are best at dawn and dusk. Fifteen kilometres further north, the A319 crosses the dam that holds back the reservoir near the small village of Tranco. Beyond this the valley widens out and the hills become less rugged.

Twelve kilometres north of the dam at Tranco, the A319 runs into a T-junction from which the A317 winds 4km up to Hornos, a village atop a high rock outcrop with panoramic views. About 10km northeast of Hornos on the A317 is the **Puerto de Horno de Peguera** junction. One kilometre up the road to the north (towards Siles), a dirt road turns left at some ruined houses to the top of **El Yelmo** (1809m), one of the most distinctive mountains in the northern part of the park. It's 5km to the top – an ascent of 360m. At a fork after 1.75km, go right (the left fork goes down to El Robledo and Cortijos Nuevos). Both the climb and the summit of El Yelmo afford superb long-distance views. You should see griffon vultures wheeling around the skies and, on the weekend and holidays, paragliders and hang-gliders. The road is OK for cars, if narrow, but is also a good walk (about six to seven hours round-trip).

SEGURA DE LA SIERRA

Easily the most spectacular village in the park, Segura de la Sierra sits perched on a 1000m-high hill crowned by an Islamic **castle**. It's 20km north of Hornos: turn east off the A317 4km after Cortijos Nuevos. Although it's a short distance, the incredibly sinuous road that winds endlessly upwards begins to make you feel like you'll never reach the town. Characterised largely by its Islamic heritage, the village actually dates way back to Phoenician times and ultimately became part of the Christian frontline of defence when it was taken from the Muslims in 1214.

As you approach the upper, older part of the village, there's a **tourist office** (☎ 953 12 60 53; 10.30am-2pm & 6.30-8.30pm), beside the Puerta Nueva, an arch that was one of four gates of Islamic Saqura. The two main attractions, the **castle** and the **Baño Moro** (Muslim Bath), are normally left open all day every day, but you should check at the tourist office first (especially for the castle).

You can walk or drive up to the castle, which is at the top of the village. If you're walking, take the narrow Calle de las Ordenanzas del Común to the right after the **Iglesia de Nuestra Señora del Collado**, parish church. After a few minutes you'll emerge beside Segura's tiny bullring (which has seen famous fighters such as Enrique Ponce during the October festival), with the castle track heading up to the right. All the way up wonderful views of the surrounding countryside unfurl and if you climb the three-storey castle keep you get a bird's-eye view across to El Yelmo, about 5km to the south-southwest. You can drive most of the way up to the castle by heading past the parish church and around the perimeter of the village.

Segura's other attraction, the **Baño Moro**, is located just off the central Plaza Mayor. Built around 1150, probably for the local ruler Ibn ben Hamusk, it has three elegant rooms (for cold, temperate and hot baths), with horseshoe arches and barrel vaults

studded with skylights. Nearby is the **Puerta Catena**, the best preserved of Segura's four Islamic gates; from here you can pick up the way-marked GR-147 footpath to the splendidly isolated village of **Río Madera** (a 15km downhill hike).

Tours

A number of outfits offer guided trips to some of the park's less accessible areas, plus other activities such as horse riding and biking. Nearly all the hotels and camping grounds in the park can arrange these excursions for you. The main operators are:

Quercus (☎ 953 72 01 15; www.excursionesquercus.com in Spanish; Plaza de la Constitución 15, Cazorla) Offers 4WD trips with English- and French-speaking guides from its Cazorla base and from Torre del Vinagre to *zonas restringidas* (areas where vehicles are not normally allowed, with chained-off tracks). The trips cost €19 per person for a half day or €33 for a full day. Quecus also offers guided hikes and *'caza fotográfica'* (photographic hunting) outings. Quercus can also be contacted through the Torre del Vinagre information centre.

TurisNat (☎ 953 72 13 51; www.turisnat.org in Spanish; Paseo del Santo Cristo 17, Cazorla) Provides similar 4WD excursions to those offered by Quercus. Trips cost €21 per person for a half day to €45 per person for a whole day.

Tierraventura (☎ 953 72 20 11; www.tierraventura cazorla.com in Spanish; Calle Ximénez de Rada 17, Cazorla) Multiadventure activities including quad biking, canoeing, hiking and rock climbing.

Excursiones Bujarkay (☎ 953 71 30 11; www.swin .net/usuarios/jcg; Calle Borosa 81, Coto Ríos) Offers walking, 4WD, biking and horse-riding trips with *guías nativos* (local guides). Prices are detailed on the company's website and it also has a roadside kiosk in Arroyo Frío.

Sleeping & Eating

The park has plenty of accommodation but few places in the budget range, except for camping grounds, of which there are at least 10 (you can get details of these from the Cazorla tourist office). During peak visitor periods it's worth booking ahead. Camping is not allowed outside the organised camping grounds. These don't always stick to their published opening dates and from October to April you should ring ahead or check with one of the tourist offices. Most of the restaurants in the park – except small, casual roadside cafés – are part of the hotels or *hostales*. For excellent coverage of nearly all the hotels and camping grounds in the park visit www .turismoencazorla.com (in Spanish).

Hotel Noguera de la Sierpe (☎ 953 71 30 21; Carretera del Tranco Km 44.5; s/d €63/97; P ✕ 🛒) This hotel is a haven for hunting junkies and is run by an equally fanatical proprietor who has decorated the place with plenty of stuffed animals and suitably macho photos of his exploits. The hotel is housed in a converted *cortijo* (country property) and overlooks a picturesque lake. There are also five self-contained chalets for rent (four-person chalet costs €130). You can arrange riding sessions at the hotel's stables (first half-hour free, then per hour €12) and there is a good rustic restaurant.

Hotel Paraíso de Bujaraiza (☎ 953 12 41 14; www.paraisodebujaraiza.com in Spanish; Carretera del Tranco Km 59; s/d €50/60; P ✕ 🛒) A lovely small hotel located right on the reservoir. It has its own beach, where you can hire canoes. The rooms are attractive and comfortable and it is a scenic spot to stop for lunch, as the restaurant looks out over the huge expanse of water.

Parador El Adelantado (Parador de Cazorla; ☎ 953 72 70 75; www.parador.es in Spanish; at end of JF7094, near Vadillo Castril; s/d €80.90/97.10; P ✕ 🛒) One of the less-attractive *parador* (one of the Paradores de Turismo, a chain of luxurious hotels, often in historic buildings) offerings although its lovely pine forest setting, grassy garden and fine pool go a long way to compensate. Only nine of the 33 rooms have views, so be sure to ask for one of these.

Hotel de Montaña La Hortizuela (☎ 953 71 31 50; Carretera del Tranco Km 53; s/d €33/55; P ✕ 🛒) A cosy, 27-room hotel in a tranquil setting 1km off the main road, down a signed track. The hotel has comfortable rooms and a worthwhile restaurant serving a *menú* at €9. The turn-off is 2km north of Torre del Vinagre.

Los Enebros (☎ 953 72 71 10; Carretera del Tranco Km 37, Arroyo Frío; s/d €48/78, 4-/12-person apt €93/153; P ✕ 🛒) Located at the northern end of Arroyo Frío, this tourist complex has a hotel, apartments, chalets and a small camping ground. The accommodation is a bit rough and ready, definitely appealing to the outdoor spirit, but there is a huge range of activities available from horse-riding and hiking to canoeing. There are also two pools and a playground. Some facilities are adapted for wheelchair users.

El Parral (☎ 953 72 72 65; Carretera del Tranco Km 37, Arroyo Frío; 4-person apt €40.30; P ✕ 🛒) Another pleasant complex of attractive stone-faced,

self-catering apartments. All apartments have spacious rooms, well-equipped kitchens and bathrooms, and scenic terraces.

Hotel de Mirasierra (☎ 953 71 30 44; www.hotel mirasierra.com in Spanish; Carretera del Tranco Km 51; s/d €30/45; P ✕ 🛒) A slightly cheaper option, in a refurbished modern hotel. The rooms are adequate but nothing special, although the hotel restaurant has a very well-deserved reputation and is a good spot to stop for lunch.

Bar El Cruce (☎ 953 49 50 03; Puerta Nueva 27, Hornos; s/d €12/24) At the entrance to the village of Hornos, this cheerful bar (with a lovely garden terrace) serves up good food and offers decent rooms. The bar also has information on apartments to rent.

Hotel de Montaña Los Parrales (☎ 953 12 61 70; www.turismoencazorla.com/parrales.html in Spanish; Carretera del Tranco Km 78; s/d €25/35; P ✕) North of Tranco along the road towards Hornos, Los Parrales is an extremely pleasant hotel with a fabulous position overlooking the reservoir. The interior is tastefully decorated in cheerful blues and yellows, with a sweet rustic dining room with chequered tablecloths. Run by Excursions Bujarkay, you can arrange any number of activities through the hotel.

There is very limited accommodation in Segura de la Sierra and it is advisable to book ahead on weekends and in the summer holidays.

Albergue Jorge Manrique (☎ 953 48 04 14; Calle Francisco de Quevado 1, Segura de la Sierra; d with/without bathroom €22/19; ✕) This is the only hotel in Sierra de la Segura, but it is a nice place to stay and caters for a range of budgets, with new studio flats. It can also pack lunches for hikers.

Los Huertos de Segura (☎ 953 48 04 02; anton peer@arrakis.es; Calle Castillo 11, Segura de la Sierra; 2-/4-person apt €54/60; P ✕) Excellent self-catering studio rooms and apartments with terrific views. The friendly owners are a good source of information about organised tours and walking in the area.

The best restaurants in Segura are the **El Mirador Messia de Leiva** (Calle Postigo 2; menú €8) located in the upper town near Los Huertos, and **La Mesa Segureña** (☎ 953 48 21 01; www .lamesadesegura.com in Spanish; Calle Postigo 13, Segura de la Sierra; mains €7-12; ✕ closed Sun night & Mon) run by artist Ana María. La Mesa Segureña also rents out very attractive, good-value apartments in the jigsaw-like town for a minimum of two nights (studio apartment €54, two-bedroom apartment €84).

CAMPING

Complejo Puente de las Herrerías (☎ /fax 953 72 70 90; near Vadillo Castril; per person/tent/car €4/3.60/3.60, 2-/12-person cabins €43.60/143.40; P ✕ ♨) This is the largest camping ground in the park, with room for about 1000 people. It also has a small hotel with 11 double rooms, and self-catering cabins. There's also a restaurant, and you can arrange horse riding, canoeing, canyoning and climbing. It's possible to walk here from the Empalme del Valle bus stop by following the signed Sendero de El Empalme del Valle path (1.5km), then the signed Sendero de la Fuente del Oso path (1.4km).

Just off the A319 are three medium-sized camping grounds beside the Guadalquivir: the first is **Camping Chopera Coto Ríos** (☎ 953 71 30 05; 2 people, tent & car €12.80), with a rather cramped but shady camping ground by the side road into Coto Ríos; then **Camping Llanos de Arance** (☎ 953 71 31 39; 2 people, tent & car €15.30), just across the Guadalquivir; and **Camping Fuente de la Pascuala** (☎ 953 71 30 28; 2 people, tent & car around €13.90), beside the A319. In Tranco the nearest camping ground, **Camping Montillana** (☎ 953 12 61 94; per person/tent/car €3.20/3.40/4.55), is located 4km north of the town. To camp near Segura de la Sierra, look for **Camping El Robledo** (☎ 953 12 61 56; Segura de la Sierra; per person/tent/car €3.35/4.20/3.35), about 4km east of Cortijos Nuevos on a road leading up to El Yelmo.

Getting There & Around

BUS

Two buses are run daily (except Sunday) by **Carcesa** (☎ 953 72 11 42) from Cazorla's Plaza de la Constitución to Empalme del Valle (€1.20, 30 minutes), Arroyo Frío (€1.60, 45 minutes), Torre del Vinagre (€3.05, one hour) and Coto Ríos (€3.05, one hour and 10 minutes). Pick up the latest timetable from the tourist office or from Quercus (p369).

No buses link the northern part of the park with the centre or south, and there are no buses to Segura de la Sierra. However, coming from Jaén, Baeza or Úbeda, you could get an Alsina Graells bus to La Puerta de Segura (leaving Jaén daily at 9.30am and returning from La Puerta at 3pm). From La Puerta the best bet is a **taxi** (☎ 953 48 08 30, 619-060409) onwards to Segura de la Sierra (€12).

CAR & MOTORCYCLE

Approaches to the park include the A319 from Cazorla, roads into the north from Villanueva del Arzobispo and Puente de Génave on the A32, and the A317 to Santiago de la Espada from Puebla de Don Fadrique in northern Granada province. There are at least seven petrol stations in the park.

JAÉN PROVINCE

Almería Province

Much of the mystery and attraction of Andalucía comes from its complex past, with an enduring legacy of nearly 900 years of Islamic rule and integration. All over the region this past is being restored in a frenzy of romantic reconstruction but Almería stands apart, almost devoid of monumental sights with the exception of the huge Alcazaba. And yet this most eastern corner of the province is the closest to North Africa in character and geography.

Almería city, the coastal capital, is almost an extension of Morocco, with signposting in Spanish and Arabic and ferry-loads of immigrant labourers filling the streets down by the seafront and along Calle Real. The name 'Almería' comes from the Arabic *al-mariyya* (the watchtower), in reference to the enormous Alcazaba. However, it has also been suggested, rather romantically, that the etymology may come from *al-miraya* (the mirror) – reflecting North Africa back to itself.

Receiving over 3000 hours of annual sunshine, Almería is the hottest and driest place in Europe, with large expanses of mountainous semidesert. Inland, the wooded Alpujarras give way to a succession of mountain ranges, their slopes pierced by the ravines of often dry river beds. Eastwards these arid mountains meet the coast on the Cabo de Gata peninsula, where magnificent beaches are strung between dramatically rugged cliffs and headlands that are interspersed with attractive coastal towns.

HIGHLIGHTS

- Hiking around the dramatic **Cabo de Gata** (p387) peninsula, enjoying Almería's wild, rugged beaches
- Hanging out in Almería's coolest hotels in hedonistic **Agua Amarga** (p389)
- Soaking up Islamic history in Almería's **Alcazaba** (p375)
- Donning a pit helmet and heading underground at **Cuevas de Sorbas** (p383) for one of the best caving excursions in Andalucía
- Having fun in **Mojácar's** (p390) pretty pueblo and its booming beach resort
- Enjoying the contrasting landscapes of the wooded Almerian **Alpujarras** (p383) and the arid mountains of the **Tabernas** (p382) area

ALMERÍA PROVINCE

| ■ POPULATION: 546,000 | ■ ALMERÍA AVERAGE DAILY HIGH: JAN/AUG 13°C/25°C | ■ ALTITUDE RANGE: 0m–2609m |

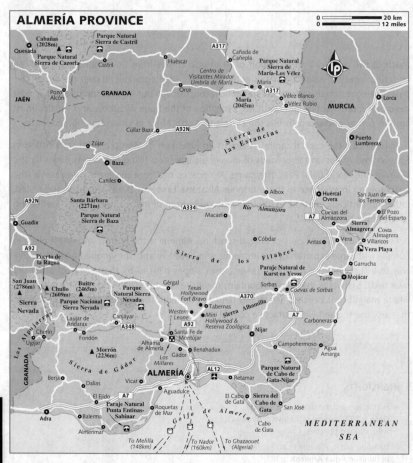

ALMERÍA PROVINCE

0 — 20 km
0 — 12 miles

ALMERÍA

pop 177,000

The cliff-ringed Alcazaba (citadel) dominates Almería and its sea approaches. It is the most dramatic reminder of the city's long-lost glory, when merchants from Egypt, Syria, France and Italy thronged its streets. Initially a port for the Cordoban caliphate it soon became the most important outlet of Al-Andalus, being both the headquarters of the Omayyad fleet and its admiral. Almería once raked in revenues that far surpassed any other Andalucian seaport.

Today the ruined castle is all that remains of the city's former glory. Following the Reconquista (Christian reconquest), the city began a long, slow decline, exacerbated by the shifting of naval interests to the Atlantic ports and the Americas. By 1658, after a devastating earthquake, a census revealed the city had only 500 inhabitants. However, these days the hardworking *almerienses* (Almería locals) are turning things around with a flush of agri-dollars from the booming *plasticultura* (see The Plastic Sea, p384) industry and a concerted drive to market the region as an alternative to the Costa del Sol.

ORIENTATION

Old and new Almería lie to either side of the Rambla de Belén, a *paseo* (walk) that runs down the centre of Avenida de Federico

García Lorca. A broad, airy boulevard, Rambla de Belén is punctuated by water channels, fountains, palm trees and dramatic sculptures, and descends gently towards the sea above the course of a once-dry river bed. East of Rambla de Belén lies Almería's architecturally bland commercial district. West of the Rambla lies the city centre, the cathedral, the Alcazaba and the oldest and most interesting streets and plazas. The old city's main artery, Paseo de Almería, leads diagonally north from Rambla de Belén to a busy intersection called Puerta de Purchena. The bus and train stations sit side-by-side on the Carretera de Ronda, a few hundred metres east of the seaward end of Rambla de Belén.

INFORMATION
Bookshops
El Libro Picasso (☎ 950 23 56 00; Calle Reyes Católicos 17 & 18) An excellent bookshop with separate departments facing each other across the street. It stocks a vast range of books and maps of all kinds.

Emergency
Policía Local (Local Police; ☎ 950 21 00 19; Calle Santos Zárate 11) Just off Rambla de Belén.
Policía Nacional (National Police; ☎ 950 22 37 04; Avenida Mediterráneo 201) At the northern end of Avenida Frederico García Lorca.
Red Cross (Cruz Roja; ☎ 950 22 22 22) Call this number to request an ambulance.

Internet Access
Café La India (☎ 950 26 88 21; Paseo Marítimo 87; ☺ 8am-2am; per hr €1.80) Inconveniently located about 1.5km southeast of the Rambla, but one of the only real cybercafés in town.
Voz y Datos (Bus Terminal, Carretera de Ronda; per hr €2 ☺ 9am-2pm & 4.30-8.30pm Mon-Fri, 9.30am-2pm Sat) Two handy computers in the main bus terminal.

Medical Services
Hospital Torrecárdenas (☎ 950 01 61 00; Pasaje Torrecárdenas) This is the main public hospital, located 4km northeast of the city centre.

Money
There are numerous banks on Paseo de Almería. There is also a Banco de Andalucía with an ATM in the bus terminal.

Post
Post office (Plaza de Juan Cassinello 1; ☺ 9am-8pm Mon-Fri & 9am-1.30pm Sat) Just off Paseo de Almería.

Tourist Information
Municipal tourist office (☎ 950 28 07 48; Rambla de Belén, Avenida de Federico García Lorca s/n; ☺ 10am-1pm & 5.30-7.30pm Mon-Fri, 10am-noon Sat) Found below ground level, but not very well signed. It has a very useful range of information, and helpful staff.
Regional tourist office (☎ 950 27 43 55; Parque de Nicolás Salmerón s/n; ☺ 9am-7pm Mon-Fri, 10am-2pm Sat & Sun) Provides yet more free leaflets and brochures.

SIGHTS
Almería's enormous Alcazaba is the city's main sight and can be explored thoroughly in a good half day. The old town tumbles down it's eastern slope and is the location of most of the city's cafés and bars. Other notable sights are the cathedral to the south, and the archaeological collections in the Biblioteca Pública and Archivo Histórico Provincial to the east.

Almería's beach is located a good kilometre out of town but can be crowded in the summer. A better alternative is a day or two in the Parque Natural Cabo de Gata-Níjar (p385), an easy day trip from Almería.

Alcazaba
The **Alcazaba** (☎ 950 27 16 17; Calle Almanzor s/n; non-EU citizen €1.50, EU citizen free; ☺ 10am-2pm & 5-8pm May-Sep; 9.30am-1.30pm & 3.30-7pm Oct-Apr, closed 25 Dec & 1 Jan) is Almería's premier attraction: a monstrous fortress that rises austerely from impregnable cliffs to dominate the city. Built in the 10th century by Abd ar-Rahman III, the greatest caliph of Al-Andalus, the simple 'watchtower' transformed the seaport into a major metropolis and a flourishing locus for trade. Not quite an Alhambra (p305) – earthquake and the ravages of time have spared little of the original splendour of the interior – it is nonetheless an imposing place.

The huge interior is divided into three separate compounds and originally contained the civic centre in the lowest area, the **Primer Recinto**. Houses, baths, water storage chambers and all the necessities for city life have now been replaced by some rather windswept rose gardens. From the battlements you can see the **Muralla de la Hoya** (also known as Muralla de Jairán) – a fortified wall built in the 11th century by Jairán, Almería's first *taifa* (small kingdom) ruler – which descends the valley on the northern side of the Alcazaba and climbs

ALMERÍA

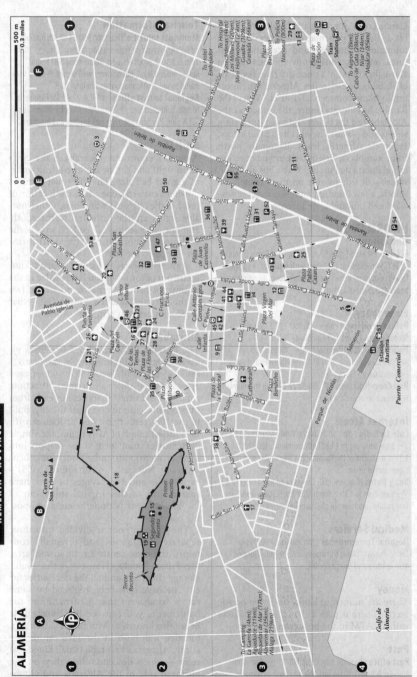

500 m
0.3 miles

To Camping
La Garrofa (4km);
Aguadulce (11km);
Roquetas de Mar (17km);
Almerimar (35km);
Málaga (219km)

Cerro de
San Cristóbal

Avenida de
Pablo Iglesias

Puerta de
Purchena

Plaza del
Carmen

Plaza de
la Flores

Plaza
Constitución

Plaza de
la Catedral

Calle de la Reina

Plaza San
Sebastián

Plaza
San Sebastián

Rambla del Obispo Orbera

Plaza de
Juan
Cassinello

Paseo de Almería

Plaza
Pablo
Cazard

Plaza
Virgen
del Mar

Plaza
Bendicho

Parque de Nicolás

Puerto Comercial

Golfo de
Almería

Estación
Marítima

Avenida de la Estación

To Hotel
Embajador

To Hospital
Torrecárdenas (4km);
Los Millares (20km);
Mini Hollywood (25km);
Níjar (29km);
Granada (166km)

Plaza
Barcelona

To Policía
Nacional (300m)

Plaza de
la Estación

Train
Station

To Airport (8km);
Cabo de Gata (30km);
Níjar (34km);
Mojácar (85km)

Rambla de Belén

Rambla de Belén

Avenida de Federico García Lorca

Avenida de Federico García Lorca

Golfo de
Almería

To Beach (500m); Eolo (700m); Café
La India (1km); Albergue Juvenil
Almería (1.2km)

Avenida del Cabo de Gata

Paseo Marítimo

the slopes of Cerro de San Cristóbal opposite, a parched and barren hill crowned with a ruined church and a giant **statue of Christ**.

Deeper within the fortified walls is the **Segundo Recinto**. On the northern side of the enclosure you will find the ruins of the Muslim rulers' palace, **Palacio de Almotacín**. It's named after Almotacín (r 1051–91), under whom medieval Almería reached its peak. Inside, the **Ventana de la Odalisca** (Concubine's Window) is romantically named for a slave girl who, legend says, leapt to her death after her Christian lover had been thrown from the same window.

Also within the compound are the preserved **Aljibes Califales** (Caliphal Water Cisterns) and a chapel, the **Ermita de San Juan**, converted from a mosque by the Reyes Católicos (Catholic Monarchs).

At the highest point of the Alcazaba, within the **Tercer Recinto**, is a fortress that was added by the Catholic Monarchs. It has been well restored and from its walls there are breathtaking views across the city and the sea.

Museums

Still closed to the public (since 1993) the saga of the Museo Arqueológico and its notable collection of Los Millares archaeological finds continues. Check with the tourist office for up-to-date news. It is most likely that the entire collection will be relocated to a new site, but in the meantime you will have to divide yourself between the **Biblioteca Pública** (Calle Hermanos Machado; admission free; ☉ 9am-2pm Mon-Fri, 9.30am-1.30pm Sat) and the **Archivo Histórico Provincial** (Calle Infanta 12; admission free; ☉ 9am-2.30pm Mon-Fri). The former houses some prehistoric finds, while Iberian and Roman artefacts are located at the latter.

To see the city's permanent art collection, visit the **Centro de Arte – Museo de Almería** (950 26 64 80; Plaza Barcelona; admission free; ☉ 11am-2pm & 6-9pm Mon-Fri, 6-9pm Sat, 11am-2pm Sun), which also stages temporary exhibitions.

ACTIVITIES

Almería's long, grey-sand beach southeast of the city, fronting the Paseo Marítimo, is not particularly exciting. However, the well-organised **Eolo** (☎ 950 26 17 35, 670-391480; www.eolo-wind.com; Avenida del Cabo de Gata 185) has English-speaking staff who can help you get out of town and explore some of the

ALMERÍA PROVINCE

dramatic cliffs and beaches of the Parque Natural Cabo de Gata-Níjar. It organises a huge array of guided kayaking, windsurf-ing or catamaran trips ranging from €39 to €90, or you can simply rent equipment (one hour/one day for €9/€30) and Eolo will even deliver it to the park for you.

WALKING TOUR

With the exception of the Alcazaba, Almería is not a monumental city, but there are plenty of interesting distractions in its meandering streets. The main arterial road leading from the south to the Alcazaba, called Calle de la Reina, once divided the old Muslim medina and the quarter of La Musalla, which was originally a large orchard. Turn right into Calle Bailén and walk about 150m to reach Almería's fortresslike **cathedral** (**1**; Plaza de la Cat-edral; admission €2; ☉ 10am-5pm Mon-Fri, 10am-1pm Sat) with its embattled walls and six formidable towers, all designed to withstand constant piratical raids. Fronted by ranks of towering palms its one notable decorative feature is the exuberant **Sol de Portocarrero**, a splendid 16th-century relief of the sun carved on the eastern (Calle del Cubo) end of the building.

The cathedral's vast, spacious interior – dominated by three huge naves – is trimmed

with jasper and local marble. The chapel behind the main altar contains the tomb of the cathedral's founder, Bishop Diego Vil-lalán. The bishop's broken-nosed image is a work of 16th-century architect and sculptor Juan de Orea, as are the choir, with its wal-nut stalls, and the Sacristía Mayor. A door in the south wall opens onto a small Re-naissance courtyard crammed with shrubs and flowers.

Head back to Calle de la Reina and take a turn west along Calle Almedina, which will take you deep into a narrow labyrinth of original Muslim-era streets to the **Iglesia San Juan** (**2**; Calle San Juan; ☉ hours of service). This is the city's old mosque, complete with its 11th-century mihrab. From here it is just a five-minute walk to the entrance of the **Alcazaba** (**3**; p375) on Calle Almanzor.

Calle Almanzor heads east to the site of the old Arab *souq* (market), now **Plaza Constitución** (**4**; also known as Plaza Vieja), a charming 17th-century arcaded square hung with vivid bougainvillea. Almería's endearingly theatrical-looking **ayuntami-ento** (**5**; city hall) is on its northwest side. The centre of the plaza is filled with tall palm trees that encircle the bone-white **Monumento a los Colorgos** (**6**; Monument to the Redcoats), which commemorates the execution in 1824 of 24 liberals who took part in a rebellion against the despotic rule of Fernando VII.

From the plaza, walk about 300m north-east up Calle de las Tiendas. Here, you'll pass

WALKING TOUR	
Distance	2.6km
Duration	3–4 hours

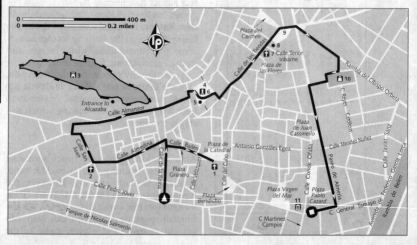

La Pantilla —
Calle San Pedro &
Calle San Pablo
Nerja.

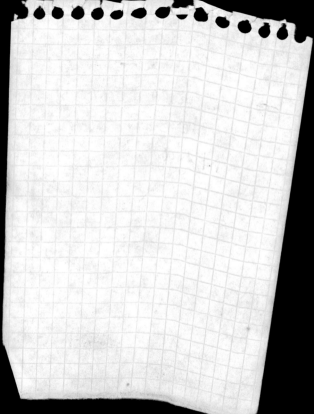

another of Juan de Orea's ecclesiastical triumphs, the **Iglesia de Santiago** (7; Church of St James; Calle de las Tiendas; ☽ hours of service), before arriving at the extremely well preserved **Aljibes Árabes** (8; Arab Cisterns; ☎ 950 27 30 39; Calle Tenor Iribarne 20; admission free; ☽ 10am-2pm Mon-Fri), built by Jairán in the 11th century to supply the city's water. A stone's throw from here, further along Calle de las Tiendas, is the old city gate of **Puerta de Purchena** (9). Al-Zagal, the city's last Muslim ruler, surrendered here to the Christians in 1490, and it's now a busy road junction at the heart of the modern city.

To take a break for lunch, walk about 200m from the gate down Rambla de Obispo Orbera, turning right at Calle de los Reyes Católicos to get to the covered **mercado central** (10; market; ☽ 8am-2pm). The market is a great spectacle and has some good eateries nearby, including Comidas Sol de Almería (p380) and El Quinto Toro (p380). After lunch head down the Paseo de Almería, and after 500m turn right into Calle General Tamayo, walking one block to reach the contemporary **Centro Andaluz de la Fotografía** (11; ☎ 950 00 27 00; Calle Conde Ofalia 30; admission free; ☽ 11am-2pm & 6-9pm Mon-Fri, 7-10pm Sat). This is Andalucía's first photography museum and is housed in a lovely 18th-century convent. The exhibitions are interesting rather than ground-breaking, and with so little else to see in the city it is worth going to.

FESTIVALS & EVENTS
Feria de Almería (late August) runs for ten days and nights with music, bullfights, fairground rides, exhibitions and full-on partying.

SLEEPING
Budget
Hostal Sevilla (☎ 950 23 00 09; Calle de Granada 23; s/d incl breakfast €32.10/48.15; ❄) The best of the budget *hostales* (simple guesthouses or small places offering hotel-like accommodation) the Sevilla is a cheerful and efficient place that offers clean rooms with the added bonus of TV.

Hostal Bristol (☎ 950 23 15 95; Plaza San Sebastián 8; s/d €30/40) A more ramshackle place than the Sevilla with an *azulejo* (tile) entrance and comfortable, old-fashioned charm. Rooms are adequate.

Hotel La Perla (☎ 950 23 88 77; fax 950 27 58 16; Plaza del Carmen 7; s/d €45/60; ❄) Recently refurbished La Perla now provides good-value

accommodation. The renovations may be a bit slapdash in places but the rooms are comfortable enough.

Hostal Nixar (☎ /fax 950 237 255; Calle Antonio Vico 24; s/d €27/44.50) This well-kept place is located in the shadow of the Muralla de la Hoya. However, it has rather gloomy décor that is matched occasionally by the welcome. You have to ring for entrance, even in the middle of the day.

Albergue Juvenil Almería (☎ 950 26 97 88; fax 950 27 17 44; Calle Isla de Fuerteventura s/n; under 26/over 26 €13.75/18.75) Clean and well-kept, the Albergue can accommodate 170 people, nearly all in double rooms. It's 1.5km east of the city centre, beside the stadium and three blocks north of Avenida del Cabo de Gata. Take bus No 1 'Universidad' from the eastern end of Rambla del Obispo Orbera and ask the driver for the *albergue*, or for the stadium.

Camping La Garrofa (☎ 950 23 57 70; www.la garrofa.com; camping per person/tent/car €3.80/3.80/3.80, bungalow low/high €40/75; ☽ year-round) An attractive camping ground on the coast, 4km west of town on the Aguadulce road. In addition to the camping ground there are some two-bedroom self-catering bungalows (sleeping up to five people) and you can arrange a host of activities at the site.

Mid-Range & Top End
In this range you can count on satellite TV, air-con in summer and heating in winter.

Hotel AM Torreluz (☎ 950 23 49 99; www.amtorreluz .com; Plaza de las Flores 5; s/d €68.80/91.45; P ❄ ☒) A grand four-star place with lots of brass and marble and a huge sweeping staircase. It's definitely a favourite with business clientele and has all the trimmings. Note that it's under different management to its namesake neighbours (the two-star and three-star hotels of Hotel Torreluz). Prices are reduced by up to 40% on weekends.

Hotel AM Congress (☎ 950 23 49 99; www.amtorre luz.com; Plaza de las Flores 5; s/d €55.50/59.60; P ❄) An off-shoot of the AM Torreluz, the Congress is a brand new three-star hotel located in a bustling part of the old town. It provides a good level of service with a rather corporate flavour.

Gran Hotel Almería (☎ 950 23 80 11; www.gran hotelalmeria.com; Avenida Reina Regente 8; s/d €108/135; P ❄ ☒) Very conveniently located right on the sea front, it is impossible to miss the ostentatious Gran Hotel. Despite its four stars and a website that declares you will receive 'awesome' service during your time there, the AM Torreluz hotel is better value. Still you can't beat this location and the sea views from the comfortable, modern rooms.

Hotel Torreluz (☎ 950 23 43 99; www.torreluz.com; Plaza de las Flores 2 & 3; s/d in 2-star €38.80/57.30, in 3-star €55.50/74; **P**) Comprises separate but adjacent hotels of two and three stars under the same management, located in the very pleasant Plaza de las Flores. Despite a rather chilly corporate atmosphere the prices are very reasonable and rooms have every convenience. Reception is located in the three-star hotel.

NH Ciudad de Almería (☎ 950 18 25 00; nhciudad-de almeria@nh-hotels.com; Calle Jardín de Medina s/n; d €80-131; **P**) Going for the modern minimalist look, the NH is a well-appointed chain hotel, even if it doesn't quite pull off the style-statement of the year. As it's opposite the bus and train stations it also makes for a good stopover.

Hotel Costasol (☎/fax 950 23 40 11; www.hotelcosta sol.com; Paseo de Almería 58; s/d €51.50/70.90;) A fairly ordinary mid-range hotel with comfortable rooms (we're not sure about the brown carpets) and friendly service. It is also in a very central location. Parking is available in a nearby municipal car park (€7 per day).

EATING

Restaurante Valentín (☎ 950 26 44 75; Calle Tenor Iribarne 19; mains €10-15; closed Mon & Sep) A secluded little restaurant with stylish service. Dark wood and exposed brickwork create an intimate atmosphere and the food is good, too, although the *langosta* (lobster) will set you back €52.

Casa Sevilla (☎ 950 27 29 12; Calle Rueda López; menú €24; closed Sun & 1st-15th Aug) A *tour de force* of Andalucian cuisine and wine (the same people own La Vinoteca next door). Specialities include *bacalao a la almeriense* (cod in a spicy tomato sauce) and Argentinian beef, and there are over 8000 bottles of wine from which to choose. The restaurant is inside the Galería Almericentro shopping centre.

Comidas Sol de Almería (Calle Circunvalación, Mercado Central; menú €8.30; closed Sun) A fun little restaurant opposite the busy covered market. At lunch, hungry shoppers stream in here to tuck into the extensive and hearty daily menú. There is also a large patio out the back, dotted with flowering oleanders.

La Encina Restaurante (☎ 950 27 34 29; Calle Marín 3; menú €26; closed Sun) Conveniently close to the Alcazaba, La Encina is a neat little restaurant serving up solid Spanish cuisine with an inventive edge. A very reliable option.

Casa Puga (Calle Jovellanos 7; tapas €1) This bar has few rivals as Almería's best tapas bar. Shelves of ancient wine bottles and traditional *azulejo* wall covering set the tone for a roaring lunch.

El Quinto Toro (☎ 950 26 15 21; Calle de los Reyes Católicos; tapas €1.80) Close to the market, this dark, atmospheric tapas bar has a faithful following devoted to its tasty tapas.

Mesa España (☎ 950 27 49 28; Calle Mendez Nuñez 19; tapas €1.80, fondue €18.15) A busy tapas bar-cum-restaurant with bar seating up-front and red banquettes at the back. A great stop in the evening, especially for the fun fondues.

La Charka (☎ 950 25 60 45; Calle Trajano 8) A very popular tapas bar in Almería's busiest evening spot. A big bar, wooden chairs and tables and real 'saucers' of tapas (rather than plates) provide just the right amount of nibbles to keep the clientele guzzling. A great spot to graze before moving on to some late-night bars.

DRINKING

Capri Cafetería y Confitería (☎ 950 23 76 85; Calle Méndez Nuñez 14) If you need to put up your feet late in the afternoon, prop up the chrome bar at the Capri where you can tuck into a range of delicious pastries or enjoy a cool granita.

Almedina Tetería (Calle Almedina; 11am-11pm Wed-Sun) Alternatively, enjoy a mint tea at the Almedina where you can also get a good couscous or a henna tattoo.

Molly Malone (Paseo de Almería 56; 8am-11pm) Despite its classical façade, this is a great bar. Spit-and-sawdust décor – lots of dark wood and old London theatre posters – fades in the fog of cigarette smoke. It is also a great spot for breakfast (€2.50).

Desatino (Calle Trajano 14; 8pm-late) A trendy bar with mirrored windows, playing Cuban rumbas. It doesn't fill up until late.

La Charka (☎ 950 25 60 45; Calle Trajano 8) This tiny, but popular tapas bar is opposite Destino.

Other popular bars on Calle Antonio González Egea include **El Cafetín**, the **Irish Tavern** and **Taberna El Postigo**.

ENTERTAINMENT

A dozen or so music bars are clustered in the streets between the post office and the cathedral. Some of them open from late afternoon.

Peña El Taranto (☎ 950 23 50 57; Calle Tenor Iribarne 20) In the renovated Aljibes Árabes (Arab Water Cisterns) this is Almería's top flamenco club. Live performances (€20), open to the public, often happen on weekends. Ring for details or check at the tourist office.

Georgia Café Bar (☎ 950 25 25 70; Calle Padre Luque 17; ☼ 8pm-late) The Georgia Café Bar has a terrific ambience. It has been open for more than 20 years and it stages the occasional live jazz, although even the piped music is great.

GETTING THERE & AWAY
Air

Almería's **airport** (☎ 950 21 37 00; www.aena.es) receives charter flights from several European countries. Scheduled services go to/from Düsseldorf with **LTU** (☎ 950 21 37 80; www.ltu.de), to London Gatwick with **GB Airways** (☎ 950 21 38 98; www.gbairways.com) and to Barcelona, Madrid and Melilla with **Iberia** (☎ 950 21 37 90; www.iberia.com). You can pick up inexpensive outbound international fares from agencies such as **Viajes Cemo** (airport ☎ 950 21 38 47; Roquetas de Mar ☎ 950 33 35 02) or **Tarleton Direct** (airport ☎ 950 21 37 70; Mojácar ☎ 950 47 22 48; Roquetas de Mar ☎ 950 33 37 34).

Boat

From Almería's Estación Marítima (passenger port), **Trasmediterránea** (☎ 950 23 61 55, 902 45 46 45; www.trasmediterranea.es) sails to/from Melilla three times daily Tuesday to Friday and twice daily Saturday to Monday, from June to September, with daily sailings from October to May. The trip takes up to eight hours. The cheapest passenger accommodation, a *butaca* (seat), costs one-way €29; the fare for a car starts at €122.50 for a small vehicle. The Moroccan lines **Ferrimaroc** (☎ 950 27 48 00; www.ferrimaroc.com), **Comarit** (☎ 950 23 61 55; www.comarit.com in Spanish) and **Limadet** (☎ 950 27 07 71) sail to/from Nador, the Moroccan town neighbouring Melilla, with similar frequency to Trasmediterránea. Prices vary between €26.80 to €31 for a one-way adult fare and €126.48 to €137 for a car.

You can buy tickets for all sailings at the Estación Marítima.

Bus

Daily departures from the **bus station** (☎ 950 26 20 98) include buses to Guadix (€6.85, 1¼ hours, nine daily), Granada (€9.40 to €16.80, 2¼ hours, 10 daily), Málaga (€13.55, 3¼ hours, 10 daily), Seville (€26.70, five hours, two daily) and Murcia (€4.65, 2½ hours, 10 or more daily). There are daily buses to Madrid (€21, seven hours, five daily), Jaén (€25.85, five hours, one or two daily), Córdoba (€20.10, five hours, one daily) and Valencia (€30.20 to €37.35, 8½ hours, five daily). For buses to places within Almería province, see Getting There & Away information in individual destination sections.

The bus station is extremely efficient and clean. There are clean toilets, an ATM, Internet access (p375) and automatic left-luggage lockers (per day €4.50). Renfe has a travel centre in the terminal, where you can book onward tickets, and there is a helpful **information desk** (☼ 6.45am-10.45pm) that will direct you to the right ticket booth for your destination.

Train

You can buy tickets at the town centre **Renfe** (☎ 950 23 18 22; www.renfe.es; Calle Alcalde Muñoz 7; ☼ 9.30am-1.30pm Mon-Fri & 9.30am-1pm Sat) office, as well as at the **train station** (☎ 902 24 02 02). Direct trains run to/from Granada (€11.80, 2¼ hours, four daily), Seville (€28.25, 5½ hours, four daily) and Madrid (€31 to €36.50, 6¾ to 10 hours, twice daily). All trains go through Guadix (€6.15 to €14, 1¼ to 1¾ hours).

GETTING AROUND
To/From the Airport

The airport is 8km east of the city, off the AL12; the No 20 'Alquián' bus (€0.80) runs between the city (the western end of Calle del Doctor Gregorio Marañón) and the airport every 30 to 45 minutes from 7am to 10.30pm, but less frequently on Saturday and Sunday. It runs from the airport to the city every 30 to 45 minutes from 7am to 10.08pm Monday to Friday, and from 7am to 11.03pm on Saturday and Sunday.

Car & Motorcycle

There are several car rental agencies in the city. Avis, Europcar and Hertz have desks at the airport. A good-value local company, **Auriga** (☎ 902 20 64 00; www.aurigacar.com), has an office in the bus terminal.

Almería has the same difficult streetside parking like most Andalucian cities. Parking for 30 minutes will cost you €0.20 and an hour is €1.05. There are, however, large underground car parks situated beneath the Rambla de Belén and on the eastern side of the Rambla at its seaward end. Fees at these car parks are €1 for one hour and €10 for 24 hours.

Taxis

There are taxi stands (☎ 950 22 61 61; night taxis ☎ 950 42 5757) on Puerta de Purchena and Paseo de Almería and at the bus and train stations.

NORTH OF ALMERÍA

LOS MILLARES

You need to be an archaeology enthusiast to consider a visit to **Los Millares** (☎ 608-903404; admission free; 🕙 9.30am-4pm Tue-Sat Apr-Sep, 10am-2pm Wed-Sat Oct-Mar), 20km northwest of Almería between the villages of Gádor and Santa Fé de Mondújar. Your own transport is necessary as there is no viable public transport and the site is a 1.5km trek from the main road.

The site covers 190,000 sq metres and stands on a 1km-long spur between the Río Andarax and Rambla de Huéchar. It was a town that was possibly occupied from around 2700 BC to 1800 BC, during a period when the Río Andarax was navigable from the sea. The town's metalworking people may have numbered up to 2000 during optimum periods of occupation. They hunted, bred domestic animals and grew crops; their skills included pottery and jewellery-making, and certain finds indicate trading links with other parts of the Mediterranean.

The site is enclosed within four lines of defensive walls (reflecting successive enlargements of the settlement). Inside lie the ruins of the stone houses typical of the period. Outside the living area are the ruins (and some reconstructions) of typical passage graves (domed chambers entered by a low passageway) of the Neolithic and pre-Bronze Age period.

Do not be discouraged by a notice on the roadside wall of the gatehouse stating that you should contact the Delegación de Cultura de Almería for permission to enter the site. It is essential, however, that before you leave for the site you check that someone will be on duty at the Los Millares **gatehouse** (☎ 608 95 70 65) to let you in. To get here, take the A92 north from Almería to Benahadux, then head northwest on the A348. Signs indicate the Los Millares turning, shortly before Alhama de Almería.

THE WILD WEST

North of Benahadux, Almería's increasingly savage semidesert landscape resembles the deeply riven 'badlands' of the American West. In the 1960s and '70s, makers of Western movies spotted the resemblance and shot dozens of films here, including *A Fistful of Dollars*, *The Magnificent Seven* and *The Good, the Bad and the Ugly*. Locals played Indians, outlaws and cavalry, while Clint Eastwood, Raquel Welch and Charles Bronson took centre stage. Movie makers come here less often now, but the surviving shells of three Wild West sets remain as tourist attractions, of a sort.

Mini Hollywood (☎ 950 36 52 36; adult/child €17/9, ticket includes Reserva Zoológica; 🕙 10am-9pm Apr-Oct, 10am-7pm Tue-Sun Nov-Mar), the best known and most expensive of these sets, is 25km from Almería on the Tabernas road and has all the features you'd expect of a Wild West movie town. Youngsters love every minute of it, but adults may have to grit their teeth through the mock bank hold-up, shoot out and hanging, which is staged at noon and 5pm (and 8pm from mid-June to mid-September). Rather bizarrely, adjoining the Wild West town is the **Reserva Zoológica** with lions, elephants and numerous other species of African and Iberian fauna.

Three kilometres further towards Tabernas, then a few minutes along a track to the north, **Texas Hollywood Fort Bravo** (☎ 950 16 54 58; www.texashollywood.com; adult/child €10.50/6.50; 🕙 10am-10pm) boasts a Western town, a stockaded fort, a Mexican village and Indian tepees. There's also **Western Leone** (☎ 950 16 54 05; admission €9; 🕙 9.30am-sunset Apr-Sep, 9.30am-sunset Sat & Sun year-round) on the A92 about 1km north of the A370 turning. Both of these sights played a part in some of the same films as Mini Hollywood and have a more authentic if slightly worn-out air (which extends itself to their approach tracks, so it's best to drive slowly).

NÍJAR & SORBAS

Famous for providing the inspiration for Federico García Lorca's poetic drama, *Blood Wedding* (from a real-life tale of jilted love and revenge), the small town of Níjar is also well known for producing some of Andalucía's most attractive and original glazed pottery and colourful striped rag rugs known as *jarapas*.

From the top end of Calle García Lorca, the narrow Calle Carretera leads into the heart of old Níjar and to **Plaza la Glorieta** and the church of **Santa María de la Anunciación**. Beyond Plaza la Glorieta, up Calle Colón, is the delightful **Plaza del Mercado** with a huge central plane tree and a superb blue-tiled fountain with large fish-head taps.

Accommodation is limited, but **Hostal Asensio** (☎ 950 36 10 56; Calle Parque 2; s/d €18/36) has bright, pleasant rooms. Cheap eats can be had in the popular **Café Bar La Curva** (Calle Parque; platos combinados €6), which is diagonally opposite Hostal Asensio. For a more picturesque spot head for **Café Bar Glorieta** (Plaza la Glorieta; plato combinados €4.80) or across the plaza to **Bar Restaurante El Pipa** (Plaza la Glorieta; bocadillos €2.40).

Shops and workshops selling pottery and rugs line the main street, Calle García Lorca, and are dotted along the adjoining **Barrio Alfarero** (Potters' Quarter) along Calle Las Eras, off Calle García Lorca. Most notably, **La Tienda de los Milagros** (Calle Lavadero 2) is the workshop of British ceramicist Matthew Weir and his wife, who produces quality *jarapa* rugs. A good regional delicatessen is **La Pita** (☎ 950 36 03 43; Calle Parque s/n), and for some hefty, designer garden furniture in wrought iron and monster terracotta pots look in at the warehouse of **Knupfer.Leiber** (☎ 950 38 01 10; Calle García Lorca 11).

Níjar is served by two buses a day (one only on Saturday), but the times that are scheduled make a return day trip from Almería impossible. Driving, Níjar is 4km north of the A7, 31km northeast of Almería. There are parking bays all the way up Calle García Lorca, but check for parking restriction signs.

Another pottery town, Sorbas, lies about 34km by road from Níjar and can be reached from here by a pleasant drive through the compact mountains of the Sierra de Alhamilla. More excitingly, Sorbas stands along the edge of a dramatic limestone gorge in the Paraje Natural de Karst en Yesos, where water erosion over millions of years has resulted in the stunning **Cuevas de Sorbas** (☎ 950 36 47 04; www.cuevasdesorbas.com; adult/child €10.50/6.50; 🕓 guided tours 10am-8pm Apr-Oct). The excellent guided tours, complete with pit helmets and lights, can be organised through the town's **tourist office** (☎ 950 36 44 76; Calle Terraplén 9; 🕓 10.30am-2.30pm Wed-Sun) or through the **Centro de Visitantes Los Yesares** (☎ 950 36 44 81; Calle Terraplén s/n; 🕓 11am-2pm & 5-8pm). Both of these are located on the road into town. Tours are only run on request and at least a day's notice is required.

The only accommodation option is the motel-style **Hostal Sorbas** (☎ 950 36 41 60; s/d €25/40; **P**) on the main road right at the entrance to the village. For food, the best options are **Cafetería Caymar** (Plaza de la Constitución; tapas €1.80) or the good-quality **Restaurante el Rincón** (☎ 950 36 41 52; Plaza de la Constitución; mains €8-14) next door. Both are on the charming central plaza.

There are buses from Almería to Sorbas and back (€3.40, 1¾ hours, four Monday to Friday).

LAS ALPUJARRAS

West of the small spa town of Alhama de Almería, the A348 winds up the Andarax valley into the Almería section of the Alpujarras (for more information on the Alpujarras, see p331).

The landscape is at first relentlessly barren, with arid, serrated ridges stretching to infinity. However, it gradually becomes more vegetated as you approach Fondón, where the small **Camping Puente Colgante** (☎ 950 51 42 90; camping per person/tent/car €2/2/2; 🕓 year-round) is located.

For information on walking routes and refuges in the Sierra Nevada mountains, which rise from the north side of Las Alpujarras, visit the **Centro de Visitantes Laujar de Andarax** (☎ 950 51 35 48; 🕓 10.30am-2.30pm Thu & Fri, 10.30am-2.30pm & 6-8pm Sat & Sun), on the A348, just west of Laujar de Andarax.

Laujar de Andarax
pop 1800 / elevation 920m
This pleasant 'capital' of the Almería Alpujarras is where Boabdil, the last emir of Granada, settled briefly after losing Granada. It was also the headquarters of Aben Humeya, the first leader of the 1568–70

Morisco uprising, until he was assassinated by his cousin Aben Aboo. Today the town produces Almería's best wine.

SIGHTS & ACTIVITIES

To sample some of the local *vino* (wine), pop into the shop at **Cooperativo Valle de Laujar** (8.30am-noon & 3.30-7.30pm Mon-Sat) where you can sample the cooperative's own wines and *digestifs* and buy good local produce. You'll find it 2km west of town on the A348.

Laujar de Andarax itself is not remarkable but there is a handsome **Casa Consistorial** (town hall) on the central Plaza Mayor de la Alpujarra, with three tiers of arches crowned by a distinctive belfry. Otherwise, the large 17th-century brick **Iglesia de la Encarnación** is the only other building of note, with its minaret-like tower and a lavish golden retable.

A signposted road leads 1km north to **El Nacimiento**, a series of waterfalls in a deep valley, with a couple of restaurants nearby. On weekends the falls are full of weekending Spaniards who rock up to use the purpose-built barbecues under the trees. It is possible to purchase meat and wood at the falls although most people usually bring their own.

The falls are the starting point for some walking trails that the Centro de Visitantes can tell you about.

SLEEPING & EATING

Hostal Fernández (☎ 950 51 31 28; Calle General Mola 2; s/d €16/31) Just off the main square, Plaza Mayor de la Alpujarra, this is a friendly place overlooking the square and the valley. It also has an excellent restaurant (mains €9) that serves local wines.

Hotel Almirez (☎ 950 51 35 14; almihost@larural.es; s/d €32/42) About 1km west of town on the A348, the Almirez is a nicely situated modern hotel with comfortable rooms. It has a bar and a large restaurant that offers a reasonable *menú* (set menu) for €8.40.

A popular bar is the **Fonda Nuevo Andarax** (☎ 950 51 31 28; Calle General Mola 4; d €33; raciones €3.50), which also has rooms above the restaurant.

GETTING THERE & AWAY

A bus to Laujar (€4.70, 1¼ hours, one daily) leaves Almería bus station at 9am Sunday to Friday, starting back from Laujar at 3.45pm. To get from Laujar to the Granada Alpujarras, take a bus to Berja, then another to Ugíjar or beyond.

THE PLASTIC SEA

Farmers have transformed Almería's barren coastland into one of Europe's most intensive horticultural zones. It's an area canopied with a sea of rippling polythene greenhouses, which rely on underground aquifers for irrigation. This industry has brought untold wealth to parts of Almería province since the 1970s, giving the town of El Ejido, west of Almería, Spain's highest ratio of bank branches to population.

Despite this green gold mine, there is the inevitable flip side – ugly acres of plastic, diminishing aquifers, and enormous quantities of nonbiodegradable rubbish (20,000 tons annually). In addition, El Ejido, the capital of *plasticultura,* is a continual scene of tension between Spaniards and the Moroccan labourers on whom the industry now relies. This situation is vividly expressed in the opening chapter of the recently published travelogue *Andalus: Unlocking the Secrets of Moorish Spain,* by Jason Webster.

The environmental price on Almería's precious water resources became evident when the Partido Popular (PP) national government (1996–2004) planned to divert water from the Río Ebro in northern Spain to keep the show on the road. This was strongly opposed by Ebro area inhabitants and by ecologists concerned about the large Ebro delta. The plan has since been shelved under the newly inaugurated Partido Socialista Obrero Español (PSOE) government. Instead, the world's second-largest desalination plant is being built at Carboneras on Almería's east coast, to ensure that Europe's driest desert continues to put food on the table.

To see for yourself you can take the bizarre 'Plastic-fantastic' tour offered by **Hola-Almeria** (☎ 627 46 03 01; sergitocv@yahoo.es; tours in English & Spanish €15), which takes you to a good old veg auction in El Ejido before commencing a tour of greenhouses in the locality and ending with tapas on the beach at Balerma.

COSTA DE ALMERÍA

WEST OF ALMERÍA

There are two neat and orderly but run-of-the-mill beach resorts to be found to the west: **Aguadulce**, 11km from Almería, and **Roquetas de Mar**, 17km from Almería, further around the coast. Both do a sizable northern-European package-holiday trade and have facilities for various water sports, including windsurfing at Roquetas. **Almerimar**, further west, is popular with Spanish vacationers and has the best windsurfing conditions on Andalucía's Mediterranean coast.

The wetlands of the **Paraje Natural Punta Entinas-Sabinar**, between Roquetas and Almerimar, are a good place to see greater flamingos and other water birds – around 150 species have been recorded there. A vast area west of Almería and a lesser one to its east are covered in plastic-sheeted greenhouses (see The Plastic Sea, p384).

PARQUE NATURAL CABO DE GATA-NÍJAR

East of Almería city the stark, volcanic hills of the Sierra del Cabo de Gata tumble down to a sparkling turquoise sea around the Cabo de Gata peninsula. Some of Spain's most beautiful and least crowded beaches are strung between the awesome cliffs and capes of the dramatic Parque Natural Cabo de Gata-Níjar. With just 100mm of rain in an average year, Cabo de Gata is the driest place in Europe. Yet the area supports over 1000 varieties of animal and plant wildlife that thrive in the arid, salty environment. The area's scattered settlements of whitewashed, flat-roofed houses add to its haunting character.

You can walk along the coast for 61km all the way from Retamar (east of Almería city) around the southern tip of Cabo de Gata and then northeast to Agua Amarga, but in summer there's very little shade (the route is described in Lonely Planet's *Walking in Spain*). It's worth doing for the feeling of being in a real wilderness – the area is still very wild and you are likely to be walking in splendid isolation amid some extraordinary scenery.

It's recommended to call ahead for accommodation anywhere on Cabo de Gata during Easter and July and August. Camping is only allowed in official camping grounds.

The Editorial Alpina 1:50,000 map *Cabo de Gata-Níjar Parque Natural* is the best for the area. See p390 for information on getting to the various villages on the peninsula.

Information

About 2.5km before Ruescas on the road from Almería is **Centro de Interpretación Las Amoladeras** (☎ 950 16 04 35; Carretera Cabo de Gata-Almería, Km 7; ✆ 10am-2pm & 5.30-9pm mid-Jul–mid-Sep; 10am-3pm Tue-Sun mid-Sep–mid-Jul), the main information centre for the Parque Natural Cabo de Gata-Níjar, which covers Cabo de Gata's 60km coast plus a thick strip of hinterland. The centre has displays on the area's fauna, flora and human activities, as well as tourist information and maps.

El Cabo de Gata

Officially called San Miguel de Cabo de Gata, this is the main village on the western side of the promontory. In summer the coarse, sandy beach attracts day-trippers from Almería, giving it a holiday atmosphere. But out of season, the place is windswept, shuttered and deserted.

South of the town is the **Salinas de Cabo de Gata**, an area of soupy salt-extraction lagoons. In spring, many greater flamingos and other water birds call in at the salt pans while migrating from Africa to breeding grounds further north. With more arrivals in August there can be as many as 1000 flamingos on the pans. Autumn brings the largest numbers of birds as they pause on their return south. A good place to watch the birds is in the hide that's found in a wood-fenced area just off the road 3km south of the village.

Another flamingo-viewing spot, where you'll probably get closer to the birds, is the small lagoon where the stream **Rambla de Morales** reaches the beach, 2km northwest of El Cabo de Gata village.

A good way to explore the wide, flat area is on a bike (two hours/one day €4/13), which can be hired in El Cabo de Gata at the **Oficina de Información** (☎ 950 38 00 04; Avenida Miramar 88; ✆ 10am-2.30pm & 5.30-9pm).

SLEEPING & EATING

Camping Cabo de Gata (☎ /fax 950 16 04 43; camping per person/site €4/7.35, bungalow €6; ✆ year-round; **P** ✆) Probably the best place to stay in El Cabo de Gata, this extremely well-run camping ground is close to the beach. It

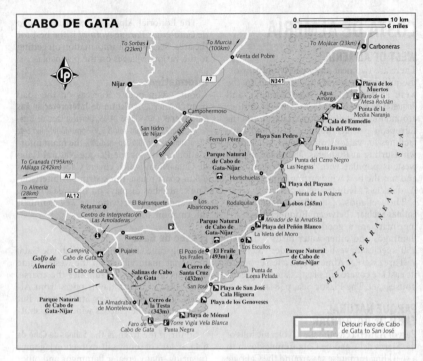

CABO DE GATA

has all the necessary amenities, including a restaurant and 250 sites. You will find it 2km down a signposted side road southwest of Ruescas.

Blanca Brisa (☎ /fax 950 37 00 01; www.blancabrisa .com; Las Joricas 49; s/d €38.50/64.50; P) A big peach-coloured, modern hotel with comfortable (if cold-looking) rooms, at the entrance to the village. It has a large, decent restaurant (one of the few restaurants in town) with *platos combinados* for about €5.

Hostal Las Dunas (☎ 950 37 00 72; Calle Barrio Nuevo 58; s/d €38.50/55; P) A family affair with well-kept, modern rooms and crazy balustraded balconies in carved marble.

El Naranjero (☎ 950 37 01 11; Calle Iglesia 1; mains €9.50-25; ♥ closed Sun) Located at the entrance to the village, this is one of the closest things you'll find to a proper restaurant in El Cabo de Gata. It specialises in fish and seafood and pulls in the punters at lunch time.

La Goleta (☎ 950 37 02 15; mains €5-20; ♥ closed Mon Oct-Jun & Nov) Right on the beachfront at the southern end of town, with a marquee and tables on the beach. Good seafood, and great views on summer days.

Faro de Cabo de Gata & Around

Salt collected from the *salinas* (salt lagoons) is piled up in great heaps at La Almadraba de Monteleva. This desolate-looking village has an equally desolate-looking church, the **Iglesia de las Salinas**, whose extremely tall tower dominates the area for miles around.

South of La Almadraba the coast becomes abruptly more rugged and the perilously narrow road winds airily around the sharp cliffs. It soon reaches the lonely lighthouse of the **Faro de Cabo de Gata** on the southern tip of the peninsula. From here a *mirador* (lookout) has a view over the jagged reefs of the **Arrecife de las Sirenas** (Reef of the Mermaids).

There is an **information cabin** (♥ 10am-2pm & 4.30-8.30pm May-Sep, 10am-3pm Oct-Apr) that has some information on the park, but it is randomly closed in the off-season. You can pick up information here about the boat trips around the peninsula that are run by **El Cabo a Fondo** (reservations ☎ 637 44 91 70). The trips are a wonderful way to view the dramatic coastline.

San José

Along with Mojácar Playa (p390), San José is Almería's answer to the Costa del Sol, although somewhat more tastefully executed with low-rise developments and a neat little marina. Situated on the edge of the Parque Natural Cabo de Gata-Níjar, there are a host of healthy outdoor activities available, which is one of the reasons Spaniards flock here for the holidays and long weekends. The resort centres around a small, sandy bay with a harbour at its eastern end, representing the village's origins as a fishing cove.

Drivers from El Cabo de Gata will have to head inland and turn off in an easterly direction towards Ruescas. After about 61km you will hit the San José–Níjar road. Turn right and after a further 7km you will reach San José.

ORIENTATION & INFORMATION

The road that enters the town eventually becomes San José's main street, Avenida de San José with the beach, Playa de San José, a couple of blocks down to the left. On Avenida de San José, in the main block of shops and cafés, just before the central Plaza Génova, you'll find a **natural park information office and visitor centre** (☎ 950 38 02 99; ☺ 10am-2pm & 5-9.30pm Mon-Sat, 10am-2pm Sun). It sells maps and a range of books, souvenirs and craft work.

Also on Avenida de San José, in the village centre, are a Caja Rural bank, an ATM and a Spar supermarket. For a good selection of second-hand books and for local information try **David the Bookman** (Avenida de San José; ☺ 10.30am-2pm & 5-10pm Sat-Thu), located above the little Moroccan gift shop Aladino.

ACTIVITIES

The information office can tell you about bicycle rental, boat trips, 4WD tours and diving. For horse riding, book a 45-minute lesson (€21.05) at the **Cortijo el Sotillo** (below), or take a cross-country ride to Playa de los Genoveses (€44.65, 2½ hours) or further into the Parque Natural (€62.50, 3½ hours). Almería's **Eolo** (☎ 950 26 17 35, 670-391480; www .eolo-wind.com; Avenida del Cabo de Gata 185, Almería) also organises activity trips to the Parque Natural.

SLEEPING

Hostal Doña Pakyta (☎ 950 61 11 75; fax 950 61 10 62; Calle del Correo; d with sea view low/high season €115/151; P ☒) Huge picture windows with magnificent views of the sea greet you as you enter the cool, white lobby of Doña Pakyta. Rooms are large and spacious and continue the blue and white theme. A room with a terrace is a must (those without are only €10 cheaper) to enjoy the wonderful views.

Hostal Sol Bahía (☎ 950 38 03 07; fax 950 38 03 06; Avenida de San José; d low/high season €35/60; ☒) and its sister establishment **Hostal Bahía Plaza** (Avenida de San José) across the street, are in the centre of San José and have 34 attractive, clean rooms with TV, in bright, modern buildings.

Hotel Cortijo el Sotillo (☎ 950 61 11 00; Carretera Entrada a San José s/n; s low/high season €66/100, d low/high season €90/124; P ☒ ☒) A fun ranch-style complex full of shouting children with a host of great facilities and on-site riding (see above). The house is an authentic 19th-century *cortijo* (country property) and has an excellent restaurant serving regional cuisine.

DETOUR: FARO DE CABO DE GATA TO SAN JOSÉ

There is no road between Faro de Cabo de Gata and San José but there is a wonderful walking/cycling track that hugs the coastline for 8.5km. Take the left-hand turning at Café Bar El Faro, which leads up to the dramatically sited **Torre Vigía Vela Blanca**, an 18th-century watchtower atop 200m cliffs. The cliffs have wonderful windswept views.

Just before the tower you will see a track leading off down the coast to **Playa de Mónsul**, which is about 3km away. Huge, black volcanic outcrops provide a backdrop to the secluded sandy beach whose volcanic nature contributes to some excellent submarine scenery (great for snorkelling). Out of the cove and a further 2.5km across the black, stony landscape will bring you to **Playa de los Genoveses**, a broad, 1km strip of fine yellow sand, with shallow waters, and rocky headlands at each end, which is preceded by a startlingly green field of agaves. The track continues for a further 4km before descending to the large San José cove and its modern tourist development.

See Lonely Planet's *Walking in Spain* for more detail on walking the Cabo de Gata coast.

Albergue Juvenil de San José (☎ 950 38 03 53; fax 950 38 02 13; Calle Montemar s/n; bunks €8; ❤ Apr-Sep) A friendly, non-Inturjoven youth hostel run by the local municipality. It also opens over the Christmas and New Year period and long weekends. To find it, head towards Camping Tau but turn right after crossing a dry river bed, then take the first left up the hill.

Camping Tau (☎ /fax 950 38 01 66; e@parque natural.com; camping per adult/child/tent/caravan €4/ 3.50/4.75/5.50; ❤ Apr-Sep) This shady camping ground, set 250m back from the beach, has room for 185 people and is very popular with families. Follow the 'Tau' sign pointing left along Camino de Cala Higuera as you approach central San José from the north.

When high-season numbers make accommodation scarce you may want to try the spick-and-span **Hostal Costa Rica** (☎ 950 38 01 03; fax 950 38 00 59; Avenida de San José; d low/high season €51.35/64.20; ⊠)), which is on the main drag near Hostal Sol Bahía.

Plenty of apartments are available for rent (ask at the tourist office or look for signs); two people can pay as little as €18 a day for a few days' stay off-season, though it costs more like €60 during July and August.

EATING

La Gallineta (☎ 950 38 05 01; Pozo de los Frailes; mains €8-18; ❤ 8pm-late Tue-Sun, closed mid-Jan–end-Feb) A small, elegant restaurant 4km north of San José. Serves equally elegant food with an international twist, making it popular with weekending city folk. Try the prawns in mango purée (€7.50) or the fillet of beef in a thick Pedro Ximénez gravy (€18).

Hotel Cortijo el Sotillo (☎ 950 61 11 00; Carretera Entrada a San José s/n; mains €8-14) The huge, echoing dining room of the *cortijo* is nearly always full of noisy, satisfied diners (eating lunch up to 5pm in the afternoon). The kitchen serves up hearty regional cuisine, which makes it a good place if you fancy a change from seafood. Reservations are recommended.

Mesón El Tempranillo (☎ 950 38 00 59; Puerto de San José 6-7; mains €9-15) One of a number of good fish restaurants found beneath a string of colourful awnings near the harbour. Eat out on the shaded veranda that overlooks the beach.

Restaurante El Emigrante (☎ 950 38 03 07; Avenida de San José; fish & meat mains €6-12) Under

the same ownership as the Bahía *hostales* (p387), Emigrante is a somewhat ordinary but dependable option in the centre of town. Breakfast of orange juice, toast and coffee costs €3.

Another good fish eatery is **La Cueva** (☎ 950 38 01 54; Puerto Deportivo 3, 4 & 5; mains €8-14), next door to Méson El Tempranillo.

GETTING AROUND

There is a reasonable amount of parking on Avenida de San José, north side of the main beach, and at the harbour. Taxis can be contacted on ☎ 950 38 97 37 or ☎ 608 05 62 55.

San José to Las Negras

The rugged coast northeast of San José has only two small settlements, the odd fort and a few beaches before the village of Las Negras (17km from San José, as the crow flies). The road spends most of its time diverting inland.

The hamlet of **Los Escullos** has a short, mainly sandy beach and a restored old fort, the Castillo de San Felipe. You can walk here from San José along a track from Cala Higuera. **La Isleta del Moro**, 1km further northeast, is a tiny fishing village on the western arm of a wide bay, with the Playa del Peñón Blanco stretching to its east.

From here, the road climbs to a good viewpoint, the **Mirador de la Amatista**, before heading inland past the former gold-mining village of Rodalquilar. About 1km past Rodalquilar is the turning for **Playa del Playazo**, 2km away along a level track. This attractive, sandy beach stretches between two headlands, one topped by the Batería de San Ramón fortification (now a private home). From here you can walk along the coast to Camping La Caleta and Las Negras.

The tiny but engaging village of **Las Negras** stands above a pebbly beach that runs north towards Punta del Cerro Negro, an imposing headland of volcanic rock.

SLEEPING & EATING

Hotel Los Escullos (☎ 950 38 97 33; d incl breakfast low/ high season €51/85; ⊠) A small hotel near the beach with reasonable rooms (all with TV). It also has a restaurant serving limited fare between €8 and €15.

Camping Los Escullos (☎ 950 38 98 11; camping per 2 people, tent, car & electrical hook-up €18.70; ❤ year-round;

P **☎**) A large, moderately shaded place 900m back from the Los Escullos beach. It has a pool, restaurant, grocery store and ATM, and bikes for hire.

Casa Café de la Loma (La Isleta del Moro; s/d €30/42 Sep-Jul, s/d €36/48 Aug) Found on a small hill above the village, this is a friendly, relaxed place with terrific views. In summer a restaurant opens and offers vegetarian dishes as well as a general *menú*.

The largest settlement along this stretch of coast is the hamlet of Las Negras, which has good hostal accommodation, camping facilities and one or two eateries.

Hostal Isleta del Moro (**☎** 950 38 97 13; fax 950 38 97 64; s/d €21/43) In a superb location overlooking La Isleta de Moro's harbour. The *hostal* also has a good restaurant that serves fresh seafood.

Hostal Arrecife (**☎** 950 38 81 40; Calle Bahía 6, Las Negras; s/d €26/38) A very well-maintained small *hostal* on the main street in Las Negras. The rooms are cool and quiet and some of them have sea views from their balconies.

Camping La Caleta (**☎** 950 52 52 37; camping per adult/child/tent/car €4.60/3.45/4.50/4.75; ☼ year-round; **P** **☎**) Lies in a valley 1km south of Las Negras, in a separate cove. It can be fiercely hot in summer, but there is a good pool.

Other accommodation in Las Negras consists of holiday apartments and houses to let, but you may find a few signs offering rooms by the night. For food, try **Restaurante La Palma** (**☎** 950 38 80 42; mains €5-10), a relaxed shack overlooking the beach, playing good music and serving excellent fish at medium prices.

Another option is **Pizza y Pasta** (**☎** 950 38 80 97; Calle San Pedro; mains €5-6; ☼ Mar-Nov), a friendly Italian restaurant with checked tablecloths and a small patio. After filling up, pop across the road to the perpetually busy **Cerro Negro** (Calle San Pedro), whose outside tables are invariably occupied by hippies or bright young things chilling out with a cold beer.

Agua Amarga

The most northerly settlement on the eastern side of Cabo de Gata, Agua Amarga, is a scruffy, laid-back, flip-flop-scuffed village with a certain *je ne sais quoi*, which has made it popular with uber-cool young professionals. Sandy streets, surfer shops and boho-chic make this just about the most fashionable fishing village on the coast.

DETOUR: LAS NEGRAS TO AGUA AMARGA

There's no road along this cliff-lined and secluded stretch of the Cabo de Gata coast, but walkers can take an up-and-down path of 11km (four to five hours). **Playa San Pedro**, one hour's walk from Las Negras, is the site of a ruined hamlet whose buildings (including a castle) once housed an international colony of two or three dozen hippies and the occasional wandering naturist. It's 1½ hours' walk on from San Pedro to **Cala del Plomo**, a beach with another tiny settlement. You could stop at the little **Cala de Enmedio** beach, half an hour after Cala del Plomo, before heading on for about one hour to reach Agua Amarga.

There are boats for hire on the long sandy beach and 3km east (up the Carboneras road) is a turning to a cliff-top lighthouse, the **Faro de la Mesa Roldán** (1.25km away), from where there are spectacular views. From the car park by the turning you can walk down to the naturist **Playa de los Muertos**.

Drivers from Las Negras to Agua Amarga must head inland through Hortichuelas. From the bus shelter on the eastern side of the road in Fernán Pérez, you head northeast for 10km on a new tarmac road until you meet the N341. Turn right here for Agua Amarga.

SLEEPING & EATING

miKasa (**☎** 950 13 80 73; www.hotelmikasa.com; Carretera Carboneras s/n; d low season €80-138, d high season €157-174; **P** **☎** **☎**) Chic and understated is the only way to describe the slick interior of miKasa. Coir matting, colonial recliners, discreet balconies and intimate rooms attract a savvy crowd of professionals who rush down here from Madrid for long weekends. Cold and heated swimming pools, Jacuzzi baths and a small health spa make this Almería's most romantic hideaway.

Hotel Family (**☎** 950 13 80 14; fax 950 13 80 70; Calle La Lomilla; d without/with sea views €70/100) At the other end of town from miKasa (above), and at the opposite end of the spectrum, is Hotel Family, run by Michéle and René. It's set amid trees and is unpretentious and relaxed. The hotel is renowned for its excellent four-course *menú* (€16).

Hostal Restaurante La Palmera (☎ 950 13 82 08; Calle Aguada s/n; d low/high season €70/80; ✹) Breezy, beachfront location in the middle of the action. La Palmera has 10 pleasant rooms, with prices depending on the views. The restaurant (mains €6.60 to €15) has a nice beach terrace and is the town's most popular place for lunch.

Hotel El Tio Kiko (☎ 950 13 80 80; www.eltiokiko.com; Calle Embarque; d low/high season €135/150; P ✹ ☎) El Tio Kiko is a top-of-the-range large hotel where all rooms enjoy lovely views over the bay. The style is something akin to Mexican-adobe with lots of wood and white.

La Villa (☎ 950 13 80 90; Carretera Carboneras s/n; mains €18-20; ☽ 8.30am-late, closed Wed) Right next door to miKasa (p389) and run by the same family, La Villa offers the same stylish environment and a quality international *menú* influenced by the family's extensive travels. Meals can be taken outside around the atmospheric pool.

Café Bar La Plaza (☎ 950 13 82 14; Calle Ferrocarril Minero; platos combinados €5.50) Located in the village square, this is a cheerful, down-to-earth favourite with the locals. Try the fish soup for authentic local taste.

Getting There & Away

Buses run from Almería to El Cabo de Gata (€2.10, 30 minutes, 10 daily), San José (€2.40, 1¼ hours, four daily Monday to Saturday), Las Negras (€3.40, 1¼ hours, one daily Monday to Saturday) and Agua Amarga (€3.70, 1¼ hours, one daily Monday to Friday). Bus schedules can be obtained from Almería city tourist offices or from Almería bus station.

To reach Faro de Gata you will need your own car. Alternatively you can hire bicycles in El Cabo de Gata at the **Oficina de Información** (☎ 950 38 00 04; Avenida Miramar 88; ☽ 10am-2.30pm & 5.30-9pm) for an easy ride. If you are touring the park by car, the only petrol station is halfway along the Ruescas–San José road. San José has a couple of car-rental agencies.

MOJÁCAR
pop 5900

There are two Mojácars: old Mojácar Pueblo, a jumble of white, cube-shaped houses on top of a steep-sided hill 2km inland, and Mojácar Playa, a modern coastal resort 7km long but only a few blocks wide. Mo-

jácar Pueblo is dominated by tourism, but retains its picturesque charms and can still captivate with its mazelike streets, and balconies swathed in bougainvilleas. Mojácar Playa is a relentless strip of hotels, apartments, shops, bars and restaurants, but the predominantly low-rise buildings give it a cheerful, airy appeal. There is a good, long beach and a lively summer scene, but life slows down here from October to Easter.

From the 13th to 15th century, Mojácar Pueblo stood on the Granada emirate's eastern frontier and suffered several Christian attacks, including a notorious massacre in 1435, before finally succumbing to the Catholic Monarchs in 1488. Tucked away in an isolated corner of one of Spain's most backward regions, it was decaying and almost abandoned by the mid-20th century before its mayor lured artists and others with give-away property offers.

Orientation

Mojácar is divided into two distinct areas: the *playa*, the developed beachfront running for several kilometres, and the pueblo, the old village located on a hilltop 2km inland. To reach the pueblo from the *playa* turn inland at the roundabout by the huge shopping centre, Parque Comercial. Regular buses run from the pueblo to the *playa* and vice versa.

Information

In Mojácar Pueblo, both Banesto and Unicaja (across the square) have ATMs, as does Banco de Andalucía which is located in the Parque Comercial.

Centro Medíco (Medical Centre; ☎ 950 47 51 05; Parque Comercial, Mojácar Playa; ☽ 10am-1pm & 5.30-8pm) Deals with all manner of medical complaints. English and French are spoken.

Information booth (☎ 950 47 87 26; Paseo del Mediterráneo, Mojácar Playa; ☽ 10am-2pm & 5-7.30pm Mon-Fri, 10.30am-1.30pm Sat Apr-Sep) Opposite the Parque Comercial.

Policía Local (☎ 950 47 20 00; Calle Glorieta, Mojácar Pueblo) In the same building as the tourist office.

Post office (Calle Glorieta, Mojácar Pueblo; ☽ 12.30-2.30pm Mon-Fri & 10am-noon Sat) In the same building as the tourist office.

Tinta y Papel (☎ 950 47 27 92; Centro Comercial, Plaza Nueva, Mojácar Pueblo) Located on the first floor of the shopping centre, this handy stationary shop sells maps of the region and some tourist books.

Tito's (☎ 950 61 50 30; Playa de las Ventánicas, Mojácar Playa; per hr €3; ☺ 10am-8.30pm, closed when raining) Internet access is available at this lively outdoor bar overlooking one of the beaches along Mojácar Playa.

Tourist office (☎ 950 47 51 62; fax 950 61 51 63; info@mojacar.es; Calle Glorieta, Mojácar Pueblo; ☺ 10am-2pm & 5-7.30pm Mon-Fri, 10.30am-1.30pm Sat) The office is just north of Plaza Nueva and is very helpful.

Sights & Activities

Seeing the pueblo is mainly just a matter of wandering around the quaint streets with their flower-decked balconies, and browsing through the boutiques. There are great views from the public terraces of **Mirador del Castillo**, at the top of the village. The fortress-style **Iglesia de Santa María** (Calle Iglesia) is just south of Plaza Nueva and dates from 1560. On Calle La Fuente is the remodelled, though still expressive **Fuente Mora** (Moorish Fountain), a fine example of the Spanish-Islamic tradition of enhancing function with artistry. An inscription records the last Muslim governor's noble plea for Mojácar Muslims to be allowed to remain in their home. The plea was made to the Catholic Monarchs who usurped the governor in 1488.

Apart from Mojácar Playa's long, sandy main beach, a number of more secluded beaches are strung out to the south of the town. Some of those beyond the **Torre de**

Macenas, an 18th-century fortification, are naturist beaches. For good windsurfing equipment (per hour €12), canoeing, sailing and water-skiing (per session €20) check out **Samoa Club** (☎ 666-442263, 950 47 84 90; Playa de las Ventánicas, Mojácar Playa), on one of the beaches on Mojácar Playa. For some exciting quad biking (one hour €35) in the Cabrera mountains contact **Mojácar Quad Treks** (☎ 600 25 83 85, 637 92 55 05; Paseo del Mediterráneo).

Festivals & Events

Moros y Cristianos (weekend nearest 10 June) re-enacts the Christian conquest of Mojácar, along with dances, processions and other festivities.

Sleeping

MOJÁCAR PUEBLO

Hostal Mamabel's (☎ /fax 950 47 24 48; www.mamabels.com; Calle Embajadores 5; d/ste €65/87) An exquisite, small hotel hugging the very edges of the pueblo. The rooms are seemingly piled on top of each other, and all are individually styled with antiques. Some have fantastically precipitous views from their windows and terraces.

La Fonda del Castillo (☎ 950 47 30 22; www.elcastillomojacar.com; Mirador del Castillo; d €48-54; ☒) This laid-back *hostal* manages to stay just the right side of characterful. Peeling paint and a bit

---

THE MOORS' LAST SIGH

Driven from the heady heights of Granada in 1492, the remaining Andalucian Muslims retreated east to Almería's and Granada's Alpujarra valleys, Mojácar, Murcia and Valencia. However, over the next century they were inexorably pressurised to convert to Christianity or emigrate to North Africa.

As the Inquisition got going, the Muslim community was banned from reading or writing Arabic and in 1490s mass conversions were forced upon them. Many did convert (becoming known as Moriscos), but this conversion was superficial and revolts ensued over the years. In 1609 the Inquisition finally sought the official expulsion of the Moriscos and over the next few years some 300,000 (some say three million) Muslim Spaniards were expelled from Al-Andalus.

The refugees were only permitted to take belongings that they could carry, and they arrived at the ports, 'tired, in pain, lost, exhausted, sad, confused, ashamed, angry, crestfallen, irritated, bored, thirsty and hungry' as Father Áznar Cardona observed. Children under seven were not allowed to travel directly to Islamic lands, forcing many families to give them up to Christian orphanages. The arrival of the refugees in the ancestral homeland was far from comfortable – dressed as Europeans, with many of them having forgotten their Arabic mother-tongue, they were quickly labelled the 'Christians of Castile'.

Interestingly, when photographer Kurt Hielscher arrived in Mojácar in the early 20th century he found the local women dressed in black, wearing veils over their faces. At the entrance of the village there was sign stating 'Mojácar, Kingdom of Granada' as though the last 400 years had never happened.

ALMERÍA PROVINCE

of damp do nothing to eclipse the bohemian atmosphere. Bedrooms and bathrooms are neat and all have fantastic views. There is a bar, Café Bar Mirador del Castillo (p394), in front of the house, with some rooms above it. More rooms are around a courtyard (with a pool in the middle) at the back.

Hostal Arco Plaza (☎ 950 47 27 77; fax 950 47 27 17; Calle Aire Bajo 1; s/d €42/54; ✦) Found just off Plaza Nueva this centrally located *hostal* has 16 rooms painted in pretty pastel shades. Bedrooms also have TVs and the management is incredibly friendly and efficient.

Pensión El Torreón (☎ 950 47 52 59; Calle Jazmín 4; d with shared bathroom €50) Another attractive *hostal* in a buzzing part of town, allegedly the birth house of Walt Disney. Locals maintain that Disney was the love-child of a village girl and a wealthy landowner. There are great views from the bougainvillea-draped balconies of the *hostal's* five rooms.

MOJÁCAR PLAYA

Almost everything here is on Paseo del Mediterráneo, the main road running along the beach.

Hotel Río Abajo (☎ 950 47 89 28; www.mojacar .info/rio-abajo/ in Spanish; Calle Río Abajo; d low/high season €45.10/57.10; P ✦) Nestling amid trees in a residential cul-de-sac on the edge of the Lagunas del Río Aguas, this has to be the most tranquil hotel on the *playa*. Nineteen blue and white pueblo-style chalets are dotted among lush gardens, with direct access to the broad, sandy beach. It's a fantastic place for kids and there are even swings in the gardens.

Hotel Felipe San Bernabé (☎ 950 47 82 02; fax 950 47 27 35; Playa Las Ventanicas; d low/high season €45/66; P ✦) Completely different from the Río Abajo, this is a swish (and good value) hotel with well-appointed rooms. Set back from one of the better beaches, the hotel's main feature is its excellent restaurant (p393).

Parador de Mojácar (☎ 950 47 82 50; www.parador .es; Paseo Mediterráneo; s/d €78.60/98.40; P ✦ ✦) A few hundred metres south of the Parque Comercial, Mojácar's *parador* (one of the Paradores de Turismo, a chain of luxurious hotels, often in historic buildings) is a modern building with lavish gardens and is well located for the golf course.

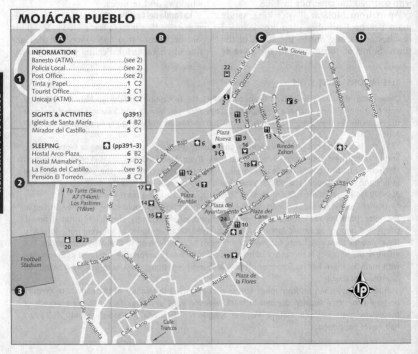

MOJÁCAR PUEBLO

INFORMATION
Banesto (ATM)..........................(see 2)
Policía Local.............................(see 2)
Post Office................................(see 2)
Tinta y Papel.............................**1** C2
Tourist Office............................**2** C1
Unicaja (ATM)...........................**3** C2

SIGHTS & ACTIVITIES   (p391)
Iglesia de Santa María................**4** B2
Mirador del Castillo....................**5** C1

SLEEPING   (pp391–3)
Hostal Arco Plaza.......................**6** B2
Hostal Mamabel's.......................**7** D2
La Fonda del Castillo................(see 5)
Pensión El Torreón.....................**8** C2

Hotel El Puntazo (☎ 950 47 82 65; Paseo del Mediterráneo 257; 3-star d low/high season €59.80-115.70, 1-star d low/high season €45-56.90; **P** ⊠ ⚑) The sprawling Puntazo comprises separate but adjacent hotels of one and three stars, under the same management. It has comfortable (if soulless) modern rooms and arranges plenty of activities, making it popular with families.

Eating

El Horno (☎ 950 47 24 48; Calle Embajadores 5, Mojácar Pueblo; menú €12.90, mains €10.50-16) The stylish restaurant of Hostal Mamabel's (p391) offers the best home-cooked food in Mojácar, including a tasty couscous. The location also offers some of Mojácar's most exciting views. Definitely not to be missed.

La Taberna (☎ 647 72 43 67; Plaza del Cano 1, Mojácar Pueblo; tapas & platos combinados from €4) A thriving little restaurant inside a warren of cavelike rooms. This setup encourages intimate dining spaces full of hubbub. The tapas are extremely well prepared and there are plenty of tasty vegetarian options. There's also an enormous house kebab that arrives on its own scaffolding!

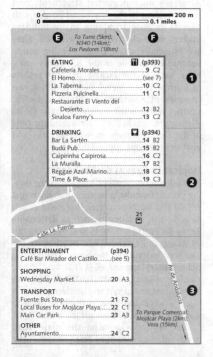

```
                                          200 m
0                                         0.1 miles

         E    To Turre (5km);        F
              N340 (14km);
              Los Pastores (18km)

    ┌─────────────────────────────────────┐
    │ EATING                    🍴 (p393)  │
    │ Cafetería Morales...............9 C2 │    ❶
    │ El Horno.....................(see 7) │
    │ La Taberna....................10 C2  │
    │ Pizzeria Pulcinella...........11 C1  │
    │ Restaurante El Viento del            │
    │   Desierto....................12 B2  │
    │ Sinaloa Fanny's...............13 C2  │
    │                                      │
    │ DRINKING                  🍸 (p394)  │
    │ Bar La Sartén.................14 B2  │
    │ Budú Pub......................15 B2  │
    │ Caipirinha Caipirosa..........16 C2  │    ❷
    │ La Muralla....................17 B2  │
    │ Reggae Azul Marino............18 C2  │
    │ Time & Place..................19 C3  │
    └─────────────────────────────────────┘

                                 21
                                 🚏

   Calle La Fuente

    ┌─────────────────────────────────────┐
    │ ENTERTAINMENT               (p394)   │
    │ Café Bar Mirador del Castillo..(see 5)│
    │                                      │
    │ SHOPPING                             │
    │ Wednesday Market..............20 A3  │    ❸
    │                                      │
    │ TRANSPORT                            │
    │ Fuente Bus Stop...............21 F2  │
    │ Local Buses for Mojácar Playa..22 C1 │
    │ Main Car Park.................23 A3  │
    │                                      │
    │ OTHER                                │
    │ Ayuntamiento..................24 C2  │
    └─────────────────────────────────────┘

              To Parque Comercial;
              Mojácar Playa (2km);
              Vera (15km)
```

Hotel Restaurante Felipe San Bernabé (☎ 950 47 82 02; Playa Las Ventanicas, Mojácar Playa; mains €11-16) A plush conservatory-style restaurant decked out in cool whites and greens. Pristine white tablecloths and big wine glasses set the mood for some excellent Spanish cooking. There's a good selection of fish dishes and you can also get good-value tapas in the bar area.

Los Pastores (☎ 950 46 80 02; Cortijo Cabrera, Turre; mains €9-16; ☸ closed Mon) It's an epic journey to reach this modest eatery, but it is worth it, especially on the weekends (when it is advisable to book two days in advance). The cosy publike interior belies the excellent cooking – home-made pastas, grilled sea breams, giant king prawns – and a commendable wine list. From Mojácar head towards the A7 *autovía* (toll-free dual carriageway). Turn left (through a large stone gateway) after about 10km, at the sign for Cortijo Grande. Drive a further 8km past the golf course and up to Cabrera at the top of the hill. There are occasional signs for the restaurant en route.

Restaurante El Viento del Desierto (Plaza Frontón, Mojácar Pueblo; mains €5-6) This good-value Moroccan restaurant can be found just by the church. It is well regarded by the locals and makes a nice change from tapas, although it also does standard Spanish dishes such as pork fillet with mushrooms or rabbit in mustard.

Sinaloa Fanny's (☎ 950 47 22 73; Rincón Zahori, Mojácar Pueblo; meat & fish mains €7.80; ☸ closed Wed Oct-May) A laid-back Mexican joint run by the affable Steve, who has lived in Mojácar for 20 years. Reputed to have the largest selection of tequilas in Spain, the restaurant also has slow Internet access, a pool table and vertiginous terraces.

Maskó (☎ 950 47 22 47; Parque Comercial, Mojácar Playa; ☸ 8am-late) A real Italian-run café with good viscous coffee and a huge selection of pastries, cakes, ice creams, sandwiches and snacks. Open almost all the time, this place is the main rendezvous in town and is perpetually busy.

For cheap eats you should check out the cheerful **Pizzeria Pulcinella** (Cuesta del Castillo, Mojácar Pueblo; pizzas €6, pasta from €6.50), which has good views over the *playa*. For breakfast (from €2.50 to €3) – when everything else is firmly closed – try **Cafetería Morales** (Plaza Nueva, Mojácar Pueblo).

Drinking & Entertainment

Classical music, live comedy acts and jazz concerts are staged at the lively **Café Bar Mirador del Castillo** (☎ 950 47 30 22; Mirador del Castillo, Mojácar Pueblo; ☿ 11am-11pm or later). There's a throng of busy summer bars in Mojácar Pueblo but some of the better ones include the Mexican-style **Caipirinha Caipirosa** (Calle Horno), **Reggae Azul Marino** (Calle Enmedio), the more pretentious **Budú Pub** (Calle Estación Nueva) and, next door, **La Muralla** (Calle Estación Nueva) with the most romantic views from its *mirador* terrace. For good conversation and late-night drinking, the stylish **Time & Place** (Plaza de la Flores) keeps going to the early hours, while **Bar la Sartén** (Calle Estación Nueva) keeps going even longer, with a terrific stir of conversation and character. All the bars are open evenings only from 8pm until late.

Alternatively, just hang out in the beachfront bar of the moment, **La Mar Salada** (Paseo del Mediterráneo 62, Mojácar Playa; ☿ 10am-late Mon-Fri, 11am-late Sat) or the lively, long-established **Tito's** (☎ 950 61 50 30, Playa de las Ventánicas; ☿ Apr-Oct), on one of the beaches on Mojácar Playa, which features live music, including jazz.

Getting There & Away

BUS

Long-distance buses stop at the Parque Comercial and at the Fuente bus stop at the foot of Mojácar Pueblo. The tourist office has bus timetables.

Alsa Enatcar (☎ 902 42 22 42; www.alsa.es) runs daily buses to/from Murcia (€8.70, 2½ hours, four daily), Almería (€5.50, 1¾ hours, two daily), Granada (€14.65, four hours, two daily) and Madrid (€29.15, eight hours, two daily). There's a bus to Málaga daily except Sunday and holidays. For Almería, Granada and Murcia you buy tickets on the bus; for Málaga and Madrid you must book at a travel agency such as **Viajes Cemo** (☎ 950 47 28 35; Paseo del Mediterráneo, Mojácar Playa), 2km south of the Parque Comercial (Pueblo Indalo bus stop). Buses to Alicante, Valencia and Barcelona go from Vera, 16km north, which is served by several daily buses from Mojácar (€1.20, 50 minutes, nine daily).

CAR & MOTORCYCLE

Mojácar is 14km east of the A7. A winding, scenic coastal road approaches Mojácar from Agua Amarga and Carboneras to the south.

Getting Around

A local bus service (€0.75) runs a circuit from the southern to the northern end of Mojácar Playa, then back to the Parque Comercial, up to the pueblo (stopping near the tourist office), then back down to the *playa*. It runs every half-hour from 9am to 11.30pm, April to September, and every hour from 9.30am to 7.30pm, October to March, reaching the pueblo in 15 minutes.

Parking in Mojácar Playa is along the seaward side of the main road. In Mojácar Pueblo you should follow the one-way system along Avenida de Paris to reach the main car park, at Plaza Rey Alabez. Mojácar's Wednesday market takes over the car park. It is not advisable to leave your car in this car park overnight on Tuesday night, when parking is transferred to the nearby football stadium for the duration of the market. Taxis (☎ 950 47 81 84) hang about in Plaza Nueva. There are several car rental offices strung out along Mojácar Playa.

VERA & AROUND

pop 6400 / elevation 102m

Almería's once neglected stretch of coast from Mojácar to the provincial border with Murcia is now attracting many holidaymakers, both clothed and unclothed. They are especially attracted to the big sandy beaches either side of the Río Almanzora. Here, one of the largest naturist resorts in Europe is still developing within a vast complex of apartments, villas and hotels. Further north is the darkly dramatic Costa Almagrera, backed by the brooding hills of the Sierra Almagrera, where locals (and visitors) thin out appreciably.

Mojácar to Cuevas de Almanzora

Five kilometres north of Mojácar is the fishing port of **Garrucha**, a bustling holiday resort with a fun harbour where there is a clutch of good fish restaurants such as **Restaurante Rincón del Puerto** (☎ 950 13 30 42; Puerto Deportivo s/n; raciones €6-10). There are beaches at the southern entrance to the town. The cosmopolitan **Hotel Tikar** (☎ 950 61 71 31; www.hoteltikar .com; Carretera Garrucha-Vera s/n; d €89/115; P ✷), with its excellent restaurant and modern rooms in burnt orange and blue, is the best place to stay, even if it is set back off the beach.

Just beyond Garrucha the main road heads inland for 8km to **Vera**. There is little to interest the visitor in Vera itself other than the handsome **Iglesia de la Encarnación**. In front of the church is a charming, pedestrianised square, a haven amid Vera's otherwise traffic-logged streets. The town has a complicated one-way traffic system and, if you plan to stop off during the busy morning period, it's best to park on the outskirts and walk in.

For some child-friendly fun, head inland to the **Parque Acuático Vera** (☎ 950 46 73 37; www.aquavera.com in Spanish; Carretera Vera-Villaricos; adult/child €13/8; ☼ 11am-6pm 18 May-end Jun & 1 Sep-17 Sep, 10.30am-7.30pm Jul & Aug). Children also enjoy poking around in the troglodyte dwellings at **Cuevas de Almanzora**, a busy agricultural town lying 6km north of Vera. The caves, which are known properly as the **Cuevas del Calguerín** (☎ 950 45 66 51, 639 10 19 48; admission €5; ☼ guided visits 11am, 2pm, 4pm & 9pm, in Spanish only), pock-mark several layers of cliff-face on the northern outskirts of the town (follow signs for 'Cuevas Históricas'). The price for the cave tour is fairly stiff for what you get, but it is fascinating nevertheless. There are 8600 caves (some permanently inhabited), and the tour provides an insight into cave life.

The town's other big attraction is the handsome **Castillo Marqués de Los Vélez** at the heart of the town, which houses a **Museo Arqueologíco** and the **Museo Antonio Manuel Campoy** (☎ 950 45 80 63; admission free; ☼ 10am-1.30pm & 5-8pm Tue-Sat, 10am-1.30pm Sun). The latter exhibits a large and fascinating selection of art works, from the outstanding private collection of Antonio Manuel Campoy, a native of Cuevas who was one of Spain's greatest 20th-century art critics.

There is not much accommodation in Cuevas itself, but the large **Cuatro Vientos** (☎ 950 45 62 28; Avenida Atrales 21; s/d €20/40; P ✷), opposite the bus station, has reasonable rooms.

Vera Playa & The Sierra Almagrera

Back on the coast, Vera Playa comprises the good beaches to either side of the mouth of the Río Almanzora and is exuberantly naturist. There is big money to be made in putting a roof over the unclothed, it seems. Huge frothy-looking developments are springing up, and complexes such as **Vera Playa Club** (☎ 950 46 74 75; Carretera de Garrucha a Villaricos; d from €180) and a clutch of equally expensive apartments shut off the beaches from the main road, although there are access points for all.

The big **Camping Almanzora** (☎ /fax 950 46 74 25; Carretera de Garrucha a Villaricos; camping per adult/child/tent/car €4/3.40/4/3.87) has a *zona naturista* for naturists and a *zona textiles* for the clothed, although the beach is healthily all-embracing.

Just to the north is the pleasant village of Villaricos, which heralds a sudden return to traditional buildings after the vast architectural confections of Vera Playa. It has a pebbly beach and a smart little harbour at its northern end. Close by, **Diving Vivariva** (☎ 950 46 75 72; Puerto de la Esperanza 7) runs diving trips and courses in the crystal clear waters of the Almagrera coast. Hire of a boat and equipment costs around €45 while a 'Discover Scuba' course is around €85.

The **Hostal Restaurante Playa Azul** (☎ 950 46 70 75; Calle Barea 62; s/d €24/48) is a well-kept small hotel with balconied rooms, which is renowned for its excellent restaurant. The next best hotel is the **Hostal Restaurante Don Tadeo** (☎ /fax 950 46 71 05; Calle Baria 37; s/d €24/36), which was undergoing renovations at the time of writing.

You'll need your own transport to explore further north from here. The road winds on for 8km between the coast and the gaunt, wrenched-looking slopes of the Sierra Almagrera. Amid these dark, shaley hills silver, lead, bauxite and iron ore were mined from the 1830s to the 1950s. There is a rare sense of isolation along the coast until the road reaches the village of El Pozo del Esparto. Beyond El Pozo, San Juan de los Terreros is the last resort before the border with Murcia.

Getting There & Away

There are plenty of buses between Almería and Vera (€6, 2¾ hours, 10 daily) and between Mojácar, Garrucha (€0.80, 30 minutes, nine daily) and Vera (€1.20, 50 minutes, nine daily). Several buses also travel between Mojácar, Vera and Cuevas de Almanzora (€2.05, 15 minutes) but there are no regular bus connections to Villaricos and north along the Almagrera coast. In July and August there are infrequent connections to Villaricos from Vera. Schedules change each year so it's best to contact **Vera bus station** (☎ /fax 950 39 04 10).

LOS VÉLEZ

VÉLEZ BLANCO & AROUND

pop 2300 / elevation 1070m

Sixty kilometres inland from Vera is the intriguing district of Los Vélez. Its main settlements are three small towns – Vélez Rubio, Vélez Blanco and María, which nestle in the shadow of the remote Sierra de María range. Much of the range is protected, in the Parque Natural Sierra de María-Los Vélez. Vélez Blanco, with its dramatic castle overlooking a scramble of red-tiled houses, is easily the most attractive and interesting of the towns.

Information

At Vélez Blanco's **Centro de Visitantes Almacén del Trigo** (☎ 950 41 53 54; Avenida del Marqués de los Vélez; ☽ 10am-2pm Tue, Thu & Sun, 10am-2pm & 4-6pm Fri & Sat), information on walking routes, refuges and other attractions is available. The centre is on the northern edge of town. If arriving by car from the south, reaching it is easier by following the main road that bypasses Vélez Blanco, then entering the town by its northern access road. Another natural park visitor centre, the **Centro de Visitantes Mirador Umbría de María** (☎ 950 52 70 05) is 2km west of María off the A317 and has similar opening times to the Vélez Blanco office.

In Vélez Blanco there is a post office on Calle Clavel and an ATM at the start of Calle Vicente Sánchez, at the eastern end of Calle La Corredera (the main street). The ATM is behind a solid metal grille, so don't get your hand stuck.

Sights

Vélez Blanco is crowned by the very imposing **Castillo de los Fajardo** (☎ 607 41 50 55; adult/child €1/0.50; ☽ 11am-2pm & 5-7pm Mon, Tue, Thu & Fri, 11am-4pm Sat, Sun & holidays). The castle seems to spring naturally from its rocky pinnacle and confronts, across the tiled roofs of the village, the great sphinxlike mountain butte of La Muela. The castle is built over an earlier Islamic fort and dates from the 16th century. The interior is now rather bare, as the impoverished owners sold off the decorations (including the fabulous carved white marble Patio de Honor) in 1904 to American millionaire George Blumenthal. If you're really determined, you

can see the lovely patio next time you're in New York, where it has been reconstructed in The Metropolitan Museum of Art.

A stroll around Vélez Blanco is rewarding, not least for its delightful maze of streets and its many attractive houses. From the far end of the tree-lined main street, Calle La Corredera, you can head up Calle Vicente Sánchez to reach the castle. On the way, Calle Palacio, the first left, is a good example of Vélez Blanco's stylish domestic architecture, all overhanging tiles and handsome wrought-iron balconies.

Just south of Vélez Blanco on the road from Vélez Rubio, signs point to the **Cueva de los Letreros** (A317; admission free). The district has several groups of 7000-year-old rock paintings, but it's at this ancient rock shelter that you'll find the most outstanding of these paintings. They include the now ubiquitous Indalo figure (used all over the province as a sign of good luck). For a close-up look, contact the **Centro de Visitantes Almacén del Trigo** (☎ 950 41 53 54; Avenida del Marqués de los Vélez; ☽ 10am-2pm Tue, Thu & Sun, 10am-2pm & 4-6pm Fri & Sat) and arrange a time for them to open the iron fence around the shelter for you. From the A317 you can drive 500m along the signposted dirt track, then it's a 10-minute walk up to the shelter.

The upland town of **María** is a plain little place but has a fine position against the awesome backdrop of the Sierra de María. It's a good base from which to explore the mountains. The town is surrounded by almond groves that are a glorious froth of pink and white blossom in spring.

About 6km west of María, the A317 heads north onto a high plateau towards the lonely village of **Cañada de Cañepla**, from where it continues, by a superbly scenic road, into the Parque Natural de Cazorla (p365).

Sleeping & Eating

Hostal La Sociedad (☎ 950 41 50 27; Calle Corredera 5, Vélez Blanco; d €30) Right in the centre of Vélez Blanco, this *hostal* has comfortable rooms run by the same management as the popular **Bar Sociedad** (Calle Corredera; tapas €1.50, menú €9) just across the road.

Hotel Velad Al-Abyadh (☎ 950 41 51 09; www.hotel velad.com; Calle Balsa Parra 28, Vélez Blanco; s/d with view €58/64; ☑ ☒) At the entrance to Vélez Blanco from Vélez Rubio, al-Abyadh is a mock hunting lodge full of rustic artefacts and exposed brickwork. Rooms are comfortable and many of them have spectacular views. The hotel also has a good restaurant.

Casa de los Arcos (☎ 950 61 48 05; Calle San Francisco 2, Vélez Blanco; d/ste €45/64.30) Located close to the information office in Vélez Blanco, this converted mansion has comfortably renovated rooms that overlook a scenic gorge. The hotel also runs tours to the Cueva de los Letreros (these tours are also open to open to nonguests).

Mesón el Molino (☎ 950 41 50 70; Calle Curtidores 1, Vélez Blanco; fish & meat mains €12-15; ⏰ closed Thu evening) Tucked away up a narrow lane near the centre of Vélez Blanco is this superb restaurant, with big displays of raw beef and hung hams. The patio has a gurgling stream channelled through it. Choice ranges from partridge and duck, to steak and hake.

Restaurante Los Vélez (Calle Balsa Parra 15, Vélez Blanco; mains €8-10), along the street from Hotel Velad Al-Abyadh, does satisfying meals.

In Vélez Rubio and María the following two hotels are the best accommodation options, although it would be preferable to stay in Vélez Blanco, if you can.

Hotel Jardín (☎ 950 41 01 06; N342, Vélez Rubio; s/d €18/30) A huge 1960s building on the old main road at the eastern end of Vélez Rubio. Although rather ugly, it is still the best hotel in town and has a friendly bar that serves food.

Hotel Sierramaría (☎ 950 41 71 26; www.hotelsierra maria.com; Paraje la Moratilla, María; s/d €36/58) The Sierramaría is a large, modern motel-style place in María, with superb mountain views. It is reached along a left turning, just before Hostal Torrente.

Getting There & Away

Alsina Graells (☎ 968 29 16 12) runs buses each way through Vélez Rubio to Granada (€9.40, 3½ hours, three daily), Guadix (€6.85, 2½ hours, three daily) and Murcia (€6.60, 2¼ hours, four daily).

Enatcar (☎ 902 42 22 42) has a bus that runs from Almería to Vélez Rubio (€10, 2¼ hours, one daily), Vélez Blanco (€10.25, 2½ hours, one daily) and María (€10.70, 2½ hours, one daily).

Autobuses Giménez García (☎ 968 44 19 61) has a bus from María to Vélez Blanco, Vélez Rubio and Lorca.

The bus stop in Vélez Rubio is on Avenida de Andalucía at the junction by Hostal Zurich.

ALMERÍA PROVINCE

Directory

CONTENTS

ACCOMMODATION

The Sleeping sections for larger towns and cities in this book are split into Budget, Mid-Range and Top End sections. The budget bracket covers places where a typical room for two people costs under €60; mid-range is for places where rooms for two cost between €60 and €110; and the top end is for places where rooms for two cost more than €110.

The budget range includes the more economical hotels as well as most *hostales, hospedajes* and *pensiones* (all types of guesthouses), hostels and camping grounds. There are plenty of attractive and comfortable places to stay in this range. Most rooms, in all types of establishment, now have a private bathroom (with at least a toilet, a washbasin and either a shower or

PRACTICALITIES

■ Spain uses the metric system for weights and measures.

■ Like other continental Europeans, the Spanish indicate decimals with commas and thousands with points.

■ Most prerecorded video tapes on sale in Spain use the PAL image registration system common to most of Western Europe and Australia. PAL is incompatible with the NTSC system used in North America and Japan.

■ Electric current in Spain is 220V, 50Hz, as in the rest of continental Europe. Plugs have two round pins.

■ Among the major daily national newspapers, the liberal-left *El País* is hard to beat for solid reporting. Every sizable Andalucian city has at least one daily paper of its own.

■ Dozens of commercial radio stations fill the FM band, but you might prefer the several stations of RNE (Radio Nacional de España): RNE3 plays admirably varied pop, RNE2 is classical. *El País* publishes province-by-province wavelength guides in its *Cartelera* (What's-on) section.

■ Switch on the TV in your hotel room and you'll probably get six or eight free-to-air channels including the state-run TVE1 and TVE2, the national independent channels Antena 3 and Tele 5, and a couple of local channels. Infinite permutations of international satellite channels crop up on some TVs.

a bathtub) and all accommodation listed in this book provides private bathrooms unless stated otherwise.

Mid-range covers lodgings whose rooms are generally a bit bigger and more attractively designed and furnished, with a few more touches of comfort. They are also likely to have more spacious and better-equipped public areas and facilities – swimming pools, gardens, lounge areas, bars, cafés, restaurants and the like. Top-end establishments will have all these facilities and standards in higher degree. The mid-range and top-end categories include many places whose charming design or architecture (from ancient palaces to hip contemporary minimalism), or their spectacular location, add greatly to their attractions – these characterful lodgings are the ones you are most likely to remember after your trip.

Most places to stay have separate prices for *temporada alta* (high season), *temporada media* (shoulder season) and *temporada baja* (low season).

High season depends on where in Andalucía you are, and every hotel seems to have its own unique twist to seasonal prices, but in most places high season is some part of the summer. On the coast, July and August is the typical high season; inland, it's more likely to be May, June and September, when temperatures are more pleasant. In many places the Christmas–New Year period, Semana Santa (Holy Week) and local festivals that attract lots of visitors are also high season – or even *temporada extra* (extra-high season).

Low season is typically November to February; and shoulder season whatever is neither high nor low.

Accommodation prices given in this book are high-season prices unless stated otherwise – so you can expect some pleasant surprises at other times. Differences between low- and high-season prices vary from place to place: you might pay 40% less in winter in one place, or 10% less in another.

Most places to stay display a chart of room prices according to season in the reception area or somewhere reasonably prominent. But many establishments, especially the cheaper ones, vary their prices according to demand and they are free to charge less than the posted prices, which they quite often do, or more, which happens less often.

In the low season there's generally no need to book ahead, but when things get busier it's advisable to do so, and at peak periods it can be essential if you want to avoid a wearisome search for a room. Often, all that's needed is a phone call with an indication of what time you'll arrive. Occasionally you'll be asked for a credit card number: this is a safeguard for the hotel in case you fail to show without having cancelled.

Camping

Andalucía has over 130 officially registered *campings* (camping grounds). Some are well located in woodland or near beaches or rivers, others are stuck away near main roads on the edges of towns and cities. None are near city centres.

The camping grounds are officially rated 1st class (1ªC), 2nd class (2ªC) or 3rd class (3ªC). Facilities range from reasonable to very good, though any camping ground can be crowded and noisy at busy times. Even a 3rd-class ground is likely to have hot showers, electrical hook-ups and a cafeteria. The best camping grounds have heated pools, supermarkets, restaurants, laundry service and children's playgrounds. Some cater for under 100 people, others can take over 5000.

Camping grounds usually charge per person, per tent and per vehicle – typically €3 to €4 for each. Children usually pay a bit less. Some grounds close from around October to Easter.

With certain exceptions – such as many beaches and environmentally protected areas – it is permissible to camp outside camping grounds (though not within 1km of official ones). Signs may indicate where wild camping is not allowed. You'll need permission to camp on private land.

Casas Rurales

An ever-growing number of *casas rurales* provides increasing options for staying in the Andalucian countryside. These *casas rurales* are usually comfortably renovated village houses or farmhouses, with just a handful of rooms. Some have meals available; some just provide rooms; some offer self-catering accommodation. Prices typically range between €15 and €25 per person per night.

Tourist offices and their websites can usually provide leaflets on local country accommodation and direct you to any local agencies where you can book. **Rural Andalus** (☎ 952 27 62 29; www.ruralandalus.es; Calle Montes de Oca 18, 29007 Málaga) represents around 450 rural properties including some hotels. It's particularly strong on rural areas of Málaga province, but houses are offered in most parts of Andalucía. **Red Andaluza de Alojamientos Rurales** (Andalucian Country Lodgings Network; www.raar.es) offers about 300 rural accommodation possibilities. **Rustic Blue** (☎ 958 76 33 81; www.rustic blue.com; Barrio la Ermita, 18412 Bubión, Granada) offers a range of rural cottages, farmhouses and village houses, mainly in inland areas of Granada and Málaga provinces (Las Alpujarras, La Axarquía, the Ronda area and so on).

Hospedajes, Hostales & Pensiones

These types of place are mainly inexpensive guesthouses, typically a town or city house with between six and 12 rooms. *Hostales* are not to be confused with hostels. They are generally a grade better than *hospedajes* and *pensiones*, and the best *hostales* are as good as budget, or even some mid-range, hotels. They rarely provide meals of any kind, however.

Most rooms have private bathroom, though there are still some places where some of the rooms share bathrooms.

Hostels

Most of Andalucía's 20-odd youth hostels (*albergues juveniles*, not to be confused with *hostales*) are affiliated to **Inturjoven** (Instalaciones y Turismo Joven; ☎ reservations 902 51 00 00; www .inturjoven.com), the official Andalucian youth hostel organisation. Inturjoven hostels are mostly good, modern places with a large number of twin rooms as well as small dormitories with bunks. Though they are sometimes full of large, noisy school groups, they provide a decent standard of accommodation at an inexpensive price. Most rooms have private bathrooms. Hostels don't have cooking facilities but they do have *comedores* (dining rooms), usually serving meals at low prices. You can book places in any Inturjoven hostel through the Inturjoven website, on Inturjoven's reservations line or through the hostel itself.

Prices for a bed in any Inturjoven hostel, including breakfast, in the low/mid/high season are €9.05/11.65/13.75 for under-26s and €12.25/16.20/18.35 for people aged 26 or over. The periods of the different seasons vary from hostel to hostel: there's full detail on the website.

To stay in an Inturjoven hostel you need a youth hostel card. If you don't already have one from a youth hostel or hostel organisation in your own country, you can get a Hostelling International (HI) card, valid till 31 December of the year you buy

it, at any Inturjoven hostel or any of the 140 or so other hostels in the Red Española de Albergues Juveniles (REAJ), the Spanish affiliate of HI. For the HI card, you pay in instalments of €3.50 for each of the first six nights you spend in a hostel, up to €21.

International backpackers hostels have not yet taken off in a big way in Andalucía. So far there are just a couple in places such as Granada and Cádiz.

Hotels

Hoteles range from simple places where a double room could cost €30, up to superluxury places where you would pay €300. Officially they're classified from one to five stars, depending on their facilities. Even in the cheapest hotels, there'll probably be a restaurant.

Some of Andalucía's most charming lodgings are small- or medium-sized hotels occupying old town houses or mansions, or country properties with pleasant gardens and pools. These tend to be atmospheric places to stay and their manageable scale makes for more personal attention.

Some places to stay have a range of rooms at different prices – standard rooms, suites, rooms with and without terrace, interior and exterior rooms, and so on. Many places have rooms for three, four or more people where the per-person cost is much lower than in a single or double – good news for families. Checkout time is nearly always noon.

Note that *una habitación doble* (a double room) might have one *cama matrimonial* (double bed) or two *camas individuales* (single beds). If one or the other option is important to you, specify it.

Rental Accommodation

In many places in Andalucía there are well-equipped, self-catering apartments, houses and villas to rent. A simple one-bedroom apartment for two or three people might cost as little as €25 a night, though more often you're looking at twice that or more, and prices can jump further in high season. These options are worth considering if you plan to stay several days or more, in which case there will usually be discounts from the daily rate.

Tourist offices and their websites can supply lists of places for rent, and in Britain the travel sections of the broadsheet press

OLD-FASHIONED LUXURY

Spain's paradors, officially Paradores de Turismo, are a chain of 89 high-class hotels dotted all around the country (16 of them in Andalucía). Many – such as those at Carmona, Jaén, Úbeda and Granada – are in historic buildings such as castles, mansions or monasteries, and are highly atmospheric places to stay. Singles/doubles in the low season start at around €63/80 at the least expensive paradors and in the high season you're looking at about €95/120 – even more at Parador de Granada (p319), which is the most expensive parador in Spain. Special offers can make paradors more affordable and there are often deals for the over-60s and 20- to 30-year-olds. Check out the offers at www.parador.es, or by contacting the Paradores de Turismo's central reservation service, the **Central de Reservas** (☎ 91 516 66 66; fax 91 516 66 57; Calle Requena 3, 28013 Madrid) or one of its 20 overseas booking offices (listed on the website).

carry private ads for such places. British-based house and villa agencies (don't expect low prices) include the following:

Individual Travellers Spain (☎ 08700 780194; www .indiv-travellers.com)

Magic of Spain (☎ 0800 9803378; www.magictravel group.co.uk)

Simply Spain (☎ 020-8541 2222; www.simply-travel .com)

Spain at Heart (☎ 01373-814222; www.spainatheart .co.uk)

Travellers' Way (☎ 01527-559000; www.travellers way.co.uk)

Also see Casas Rurales (p399) for options of staying in the Andalucian countryside.

BUSINESS HOURS

Banks generally open from 8.30am to 2pm Monday to Friday and 9am to 1pm Saturday, and post offices from 8.30am to 8.30pm Monday to Friday and 9am to 1.30pm Saturday. There are of course some local and seasonal variations.

Most shops and nongovernment offices (such as travel agencies, airline offices and tour companies) open from 9am or 10am to 1.30pm or 2pm and 5pm to 8pm or 9pm, Monday to Saturday, though some skip the Saturday evening session. Large supermarkets, department stores and *centros comerciales* (large, purpose-built shopping centres) normally stay open all day, from 9am to 9pm, Monday to Saturday.

Restaurants typically open from between 12.30pm and 1.30pm to between 3.30pm and 4pm, and in the evening from between 7.30pm and 8.30pm to between 11pm and midnight. Many have one weekly closing day (often Monday).

CHILDREN

Travelling with children in Andalucía is easy. You can get just about everything you need, and Andalucians as a rule are very friendly to children. Any child whose hair is less than jet black will get called *rubia* (blonde) if she's a girl, *rubio* if he's a boy. Children accompanied by adults are welcome at all kinds of accommodation, and in virtually every café, bar and restaurant. Andalucian children stay up late and at fiestas it's commonplace to see even tiny ones toddling the streets at 2am or 3am. Visiting kids like this idea too, but can't always cope with it quite so readily.

If you need a *cuna* (cot) in a hotel, one should be available. Highchairs in restaurants are not so common. Safety seats are available for hire cars: you're certainly given the option when booking a hire car on the Internet. Safety seats in taxis are rarer. Andalucians generally have a slack attitude to using safety seats and wearing seat belts, though this is slowly changing with stepped-up traffic law enforcement, especially on the major coastal roads.

A few of the top-end hotels will be able to help arrange childcare. Nappy changing facilities are rare and breast-feeding in public is unusual, though discreet breast-feeding is no problem.

As well as the obvious attraction of the beaches, playgrounds are plentiful. Special attractions such as water parks and aquariums are spread over the region but abound in Málaga province and especially along the Costa del Sol: see the Andalucía for Kids itinerary (p16). Another feature of Andalucía that excites many young 'uns is the visibility of wildlife such as dolphins, apes, deer, vultures and wild boar: check the Wildlife Watch itinerary (p16) for recommended viewing locations.

Along the Mediterranean coast older children might like to try windsurfing: there are facilities at several Costa del Sol resorts, La Herradura (p340) and Roquetas de Mar (p385). The generally gentler winds on the Med make it more suitable for beginners than the Atlantic coast, but more adventurous young adults can try windsurfing or kitesurfing at blowy Tarifa and other spots on the Cádiz coast (see p204) or have a go at surfing on the Cádiz coast at El Palmar (see p199). Andalucía is bursting with other activity possibilities: see the Andalucía Outdoors chapter (p61) for more ideas.

Children benefit from cut-price or free entry at many sights and museums. Those under four years of age travel free on Spanish trains and those aged four to 11 normally pay 60% of the adult fare. Lonely Planet's *Travel with Children* has lots of practical advice, and first-hand stories from many Lonely Planet authors and others.

CLIMATE CHARTS

There's a difference between the coastal and interior climates. Inland, the weather can be pretty inclement from November to February and frying hot in July and August. On the coasts, temperatures are more temperate in winter and not quite so hot in summer. And with the prevailing winds coming from the Atlantic Ocean, western Andalucía is damper than the east.

Andalucian weather is less predictable than you might imagine. Only June, July and August are certain to be more or less rain-free. Winter (November to February) can be predominantly dry and warm (raising the danger of drought) or subject to weeks of rain, with the possibility of flooding.

For tips on the best times to travel in Andalucía, see p9.

COURSES

Taking a course in Andalucía is a great way not only to learn something but also to meet people and get an inside angle on local life. Many of the universities and schools offering language courses (see p403) also offer other courses in Spanish history, literature and culture.

Dance

Andalucía is dance-mad and a good place for professional dancers to hone their skills

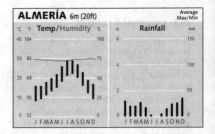

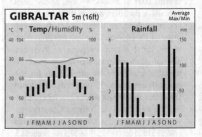

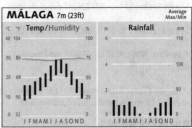

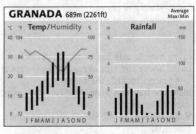

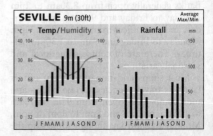

or for beginners to sample flamenco or other types of dance. See the Courses sections for Seville (p106) and Granada (p316) for information on courses in Spanish dance and/or guitar. The magazine *El Giraldillo* (available from tourist offices) carries ads for dance classes and courses.

Language

The teaching of Spanish to foreigners is a booming business in Andalucía and new language schools are springing up all the time. The **Instituto Cervantes** (www.cervantes.es in Spanish) has a great deal of information on Spanish-language courses in Andalucía. With branches in over 30 cities around the world, it exists to promote the Spanish language and the cultures of Spanish-speaking countries. It's mainly involved in teaching Spanish and in library and information services.

Spanish Directory (www.europa-pages.com/spain) is a good Internet source on language courses.

Seville (p106), Granada (p316) and Málaga (p237) are the most popular places in Andalucía to study Spanish, but there are schools in many other attractive and interesting towns such as Cádiz (p171) and Córdoba (p286), and even in some mountain villages such as Cómpeta (p271) in Málaga province. Courses sections throughout this book will point to recommended colleges, and tourist offices can usually supply plenty of info on language schools in their areas.

University courses often last a term, though they range from two weeks to a year. Private language schools are generally more flexible about when you can start and how long you study. Most places cater for a wide range of levels, from beginners up. Many courses have a cultural component as well.

University courses offer some of the best value, with a typical four-week course of 20 one-hour classes a week for around €500 to €600. Many places offer accommodation with families, in student lodgings or in flats – generally from around €300 a month with no meals to €700 to €1000 for full board. Shared apartments are often the cheapest option at around €180 a month.

Things to think about when choosing a course include how intensive it is (this varies at different schools), class sizes, who the other students are likely to be and whether you want organised extracurricular activities. Recommendations from previous stu-

dents count for a lot in selecting your school. It's also worth asking whether a course will lead to any formal certificate. The Diplomas Oficiales de Español como Lengua Extranjera (DELEs) are qualifications awarded by Spain's Ministry of Education and Science (for a complete beginner, approximately 40 hours of classes are required to achieve the most basic DELE qualification).

It's easy to arrange private classes in many places: check notice boards in universities and language schools, or small ads in the local press. Expect to pay around €15 per hour for individual private lessons.

Outdoor Activities

You can do it all in Andalucía. Courses in outdoor activities include snowboarding, skiing, windsurfing, kitesurfing, rock climbing, diving and more. See the Andalucía Outdoors chapter (p61) for details.

CUSTOMS

Duty-free allowances for entering Spain from outside the EU include 2L of wine, 1L of spirits and 200 cigarettes or 50 cigars. Duty-free allowances for travel between EU countries were abolished in 1999. Limits on imports and exports of duty-paid goods between other EU countries and Spain include 110L of beer, 90L of wine, 10L of spirits, 800 cigarettes and 200 cigars.

DANGERS & ANNOYANCES

Andalucía is generally a pretty safe place. The main thing you have to be wary of is petty theft (which of course may not seem so petty if your passport, money and camera go missing).

To safeguard your money, keep only a limited amount as cash and the bulk in more easily replaceable forms such as plastic cards or travellers cheques. If your accommodation has a safe, use it. For carrying money on the street the safest thing is an unobtrusive money belt or wallet that you can keep under your clothes. Watch out for people who touch you or seem to be getting unwarrantedly close, in any situation. When using ATMs be wary of anyone who offers to help you, even if your card is stuck in the machine.

Most risk of theft occurs in tourist resorts and big cities, and when you first arrive in a city and may be unaware of danger signs.

The main things to guard against are pickpockets, bag snatchers and theft from cars. Anything visible in a car in Spain is at risk. If anything valuable does get stolen or lost and you want to make an insurance claim, you'll need to report it to the police and get a copy of the report.

Terrorism

The Basque terrorist organisation ETA occasionally explodes bombs or commits murders in Andalucía, as in other parts of Spain. The country has of course also been victim to terrorism. Before travelling to Spain, you can consult your country's foreign affairs department for any current warnings.

DISABLED TRAVELLERS

Some Spanish tourist offices in other countries (see p412) provide a basic information sheet with useful addresses for disabled travellers, and can give details of accessible accommodation in specific places.

Wheelchair accessibility in Andalucía is improving as new buildings meet regulations requiring them to have wheelchair access. The Spanish-language guidebook for disabled people, *Guía Valinet* (sold at www .valinet.org) lists 321 recommended Spanish hotels with wheelchair access, many of them in Andalucía. Many mid-range and top-end hotels are now adapting rooms and accesses for wheelchair users. Nearly all Andalucian youth hostels have rooms adapted for the disabled. However, poor accessibility is still the norm in other budget accommodation.

Some beaches are equipped for the disabled. Fuengirola (in Málaga province), for instance, has equipped two beaches with specially adapted showers and sunbed areas, reserved toilets and parking, and aluminium wheelchairs that can be taken into the sea without going rusty. The website www .mma.es/en/costas/guia_playas has information in Spanish on disabled access for hundreds of beaches.

These two UK-based organisations have more travel information for the mobility impaired and the disabled:

Holiday Care (☎ 0845 1249974; www.holidaycare.org.uk; 7th fl, Sunley House, 4 Bedford Park, Croydon, Surrey CRO ZQP) Produces an information pack on Spain for people with special needs. Tips range from accommodation with disabled access to equipment-hire services, to advice on tour operators and getting to your destination in Spain.

Radar (☎ 020-7250 3222; www.radar.org.uk) Run by, and for, disabled people. Its excellent website has links to travel and holiday-specific sites.

DISCOUNT CARDS

Student, teacher and youth cards can get you worthwhile discounts on airfares and other travel and reduced prices at some museums, sights and entertainment venues.

The International Student Identity Card (ISIC), for full-time students, and the International Teacher Identity Card (ITIC), for full-time teachers and academics, are issued by colleges and student travel organisations such as STA Travel.

Anyone under 26 can get a Euro<26 card (Carnet Joven in Spain), which is available in Europe to people of any nationality, or an International Youth Travel Card (IYTC or GO25 card), available worldwide. These give similar discounts to the ISIC and are issued by many of the same organisations. Benefits for Euro<26 card holders in Andalucía include 20% or 25% off many train fares, 20% off some ferry fares, 10% to 20% off some bus fares with the Alsa, Socibus, Secorbus and Daibus companies, 10% to 15% off rooms at many places to stay, 10% off some car rentals, and discounts at some museums.

For information, see www.istc.org and www.euro26.org. One place you can obtain these cards in Andalucía is **Asatej Viajes** (Map pp98-100; ☎ 902 44 44 88; www.asatej.com in Spanish; Calle O'Donnell 3, Seville).

EMBASSIES & CONSULATES
Spanish Embassies & Consulates

Following is a list of Spanish embassies and consulates in selected countries:

Australia Canberra (☎ 02-6273 355; www.embaspain.com; 15 Arkana St, Yarralumla, ACT 2600); consulate in Melbourne (☎ 03-9347 1966); consulate in Sydney (☎ 02-9261 2433)

Canada Ottawa (☎ 613-747 2252; www.embaspain.ca; 74 Stanley Ave, Ontario K1M 1P4); consulate in Montreal (☎ 514-935 5235); consulate in Toronto (☎ 416-977 1661)

France Paris (☎ 01 44 43 18 00; www.amb-espagne.fr; 22 Ave Marceau, 75381, Cedex 08); consulate in Paris (☎ 01 44 29 40 00; www.cgesparis.org; 165 Blvd Malesh-erbes, 75840); consulate in Lyon (☎ 04 78 89 64 15); consulate in Marseille (☎ 04 91 00 32 70); consulate in Toulouse (☎ 05 34 31 96 60)

Germany Berlin (☎ 030-254 00 70; www.spanischebots chaft.de; Lichtensteinallee 1, 10787); consulate in Düsseldorf (☎ 0211-43 90 80); consulate in Frankfurt am Main (☎ 069-959 16 60); consulate in Munich (☎ 089-98 47 90)

Ireland Dublin (☎ 01-269 1640; www.mae.es/embajadas
/dublin; 17A Merlyn Park, Balls Bridge, 4)
Italy Rome (☎ 06-684 04 01; www.amba-spagna.com;
Palacio Borghese, Lardo Fontanella di Borghese 19, 00186);
consulate in Rome (☎ 06-687 14 01; Via Campo Marzio 34,
00186); consulate in Genoa (☎ 010-56 26 69);
consulate in Milan (☎ 02-632 88 31); consulate in Naples
(☎ 081-41 11 57)
Japan Tokyo (☎ 3-3583 8531; embespjp@mail.mae.es;
1-3-29, Roppongi, Minato-ku, 106-0032)
Morocco Rabat (☎ 07-633900; ambespma@mail.mae.es;
Rue Aïn Khalouiya, Rte Des Zaërs Km 5.3, Suissi);
consulate in Casablanca (☎ 02-220752); consulate in Tangier
(☎ 09-937000)
The Netherlands The Hague (☎ 070-302 49 99;
ambespnl@correo.mae.es; Lange Voorhout 50, 2514 EG);
consulate in Amsterdam (☎ 020-620 38 11)
New Zealand See Australia.
Portugal Lisbon (☎ 213-472 381; embesppt@correo
.mae.es; Rua do Salitre 1, 1269); consulate in Lisbon
(☎ 213-472 792; Rua do Salitre 3, 1269); consulate in
Porto (☎ 225-363 915); consulate in Vila Real de Santo
António (☎ 281-544 888)
UK London (☎ 020-7235 5555; embespuk@mail.mae.es;
39 Chesham Plc, SW1X 8SB); consulate in London
(☎ 020-7589 8989; www.conspalon.org; 20 Draycott Plc,
SW3 2RZ); consulate in Edinburgh (☎ 0131-220 18 43);
consulate in Manchester (☎ 0161-236 1262)
USA Washington DC (☎ 202-452 0100; www.spainemb.org;
2375 Pennsylvania Ave NW, 20037); consulate in Washington
(☎ 202-728 2330; 2375 Pennsylvania Ave NW, 20037);
consulate in Boston (☎ 617-536 2506); consulate in Chicago
(☎ 312-782 4588); consulate in Houston (☎ 713-783 6200);
consulate in Los Angeles (☎ 213-938 0158); consulate in
Miami (☎ 305-446 5511); consulate in New Orleans
(☎ 504-525 4951); consulate in New York (☎ 212-355
4080); consulate in San Francisco (☎ 415-922 2995)

Embassies & Consulates in Spain

All foreign embassies are in Madrid, but
many countries also have consulates in Andalucian cities, especially Seville. Embassies
and consulates include the following:
Australia Madrid (☎ 91 441 60 25; www.spain.embassy
.gov.au; Plaza del Descubridor Diego de Ordás 3); consulate
in Seville (Map pp98-100; ☎ 954 22 09 71; Calle Federico
Rubio 14)
Canada Madrid (☎ 91 423 32 50; www.canada-es.org;
Calle de Núñez de Balboa 35); consulate in Málaga (Map
pp232-3; ☎ 952 22 33 46; 1st fl, Plaza de la Malagueta 2)
France Madrid (☎ 91 423 89 00; www.ambafrance-es.org;
Calle Salustiano Olózaga 9); consulate in Seville (Map pp98-
100; ☎ 954 29 32 00; www.consulfrance-seville.org;
Plaza de Santa Cruz 1)
Germany Madrid (☎ 91 557 90 00; www.embajada-al

emania.es; Calle de Fortuny 8); consulate in Málaga
(Map pp232-3; ☎ 952 36 35 91; Edificio Eurocom, Calle
Mauricio Moro Pareto 2)
Ireland Madrid (☎ 91 436 40 93; Paseo de la Castellana 46);
consulate in Fuengirola (☎ 952 47 51 08; Galerías Santa
Mónica, Avenida de los Boliches); consulate in Seville
(Map pp98-100; ☎ 954 21 63 61; Plaza de Santa Cruz 4)
Italy Madrid (☎ 91 423 33 00; Calle Lagasca 98);
consulate in Seville (Map pp98-100; ☎ 954 22 85 76;
Calle Fabiola 10)
Japan Madrid (☎ 91 590 76 00; www.embjapon.es;
Calle de Serrano 109)
Morocco Madrid (☎ 91 563 10 90; www.maec.gov.ma
/madrid; Calle de Serrano 179); consulate in Algeciras
(Map p213; ☎ 956 66 18 03; Calle Teniente Maroto 2);
consulate in Seville (Map pp88-90; ☎ 954 08 10 44; Pabel-
lón de la Naturaleza, Camino de los Descubrimientos s/n,
Isla de la Cartuja)
The Netherlands Madrid (☎ 91 353 75 00; www.embaja
dapaisesbajos.es; Avenida del Comandante Franco 32, Madrid);
consulate in Seville (Map pp98-100; ☎ 954 22 87 50;
Calle Placentines 1)
New Zealand Madrid (☎ 91 523 02 26; Plaza de la
Lealtad 2)
Portugal Madrid (☎ 91 782 49 60; www.embajada
portugal-madrid.org; Calle Pinar 1); consulate in Madrid
(☎ 91 577 35 85; Calle Lagasca 88); consulate in Seville
(Map pp88-90; ☎ 954 23 11 50; Avenida del Cid 1)
UK Madrid (☎ 91 700 82 00; www.ukinspain.com;
Calle de Fernando el Santo 16); consulate in Málaga
(Map p232-3; ☎ 952 35 23 00; Edificio Eurocom,
Calle Mauricio Moro Pareto 2)
USA Madrid (☎ 91 587 22 00; www.embusa.es; Calle de
Serrano 75); consular agency in Fuengirola (☎ 952 47 48
91; Apartment 1C, Avenida Juan Gómez 8); consular agency
in Seville (Map pp88-90; ☎ 954 23 18 85; Paseo de las
Delicias 7)

FESTIVALS & EVENTS

Andalucians indulge their love of colour, noise, crowds, pageantry, dressing up and partying at innumerable exuberant local fiestas. Every little village and every city barrio (district or quarter) holds several festivals every year, each with its own unique twist. Many fiestas are religion-based but still highly festive.

Most places hold their *feria* (main annual fair) in summer, with concerts, parades, fireworks, bullfights, fairgrounds, dancing and an all-night party atmosphere.

You'll find information on the most important local events in city and town sections throughout this book and tourist offices can supply detailed information. The following are the outstanding region-wide celebrations:

January
Día de los Reyes Magos (Three Kings' Day; 6 January) Children receive gifts in commemoration of the gifts brought by the Three Kings to the baby Jesus; in many towns, Reyes Magos *cabalgatas* (cavalcades) tour the streets the evening before, tossing sweets to the crowds.

February/March
Carnaval (Carnival) Fancy-dress parades and general merry-making happen in many places (wildest in Cádiz), usually ending on the Tuesday 47 days before Easter Sunday.

March/April
Semana Santa (Holy Week) The biggest event of Spain's religious calendar: the week leading up to Easter Sunday sees parades of lavishly bedecked holy images, long lines of *nazarenos* (penitents), and big crowds lining the streets, in almost every city, town and village. In major cities there are daily processions from Palm Sunday to Easter Sunday. Seville's celebrations are the most lavish and intense; Málaga, Granada, Córdoba, Arcos de la Frontera, Jaén, Baeza and Úbeda also stage spectacular processions.

May
Cruces de Mayo (May Crosses; 3 May & around) Crosses are placed in squares and patios in many towns, notably in and around Granada and Córdoba. Decorated with flowers, the crosses become the focus for temporary bars, food stalls, music and dancing.

June
Hogueras de San Juan (Bonfires of San Juan; 23 June) Bonfires and fireworks, especially on beaches, are the heart of this midsummer celebration; many thousands of people camp overnight along Andalucía's beaches.

July
Día de la Virgen del Carmen (16 July) On this feast day of the patron of fisherfolk, the Virgin's image is carried into the sea, or paraded upon it amid a flotilla of small boats, at many coastal towns.

FOOD

The Eating sections for some larger towns and cities in this book are split into Budget, Mid-Range and Top End sections. The budget bracket covers places where a typical main dish is under €8; mid-range is where a typical main dish is between €8 and €14; and the top end is places where typical mains cost more than €14.

For an introduction to Andalucian food, see p74.

GAY & LESBIAN TRAVELLERS

Andalucía's liveliest gay scenes are in Málaga, Torremolinos, Seville and Granada, but there are gay-and-lesbian-friendly bars or clubs in all major cities. Some Spanish receptionists have difficulty understanding that two people of the same sex might want to share a double bed. One lesbian traveller suggested that to avoid confusion and wasted time, it can be a good idea for one of the pair to do the checking in before the other appears.

Websites such as www.gayinspain.com, www.guiagay.com (in Spanish) and www.cogailes.org have long listings of bars, clubs, discos, beaches, bookstores and associations. Gayinspain and Cogailes have message boards too. Cogailes is the site of the **Coordinadora Gai-Lesbiana** (☎ 932 98 00 29), a Barcelona-based gay and lesbian organisation that operates a free national information telephone line in English, Spanish and Catalan on ☎ 900 60 16 01, from 6pm to 10pm daily.

The **Asociación Andaluza de Lesbianas y Gais** (Map pp304-5; Calle Lavadero de las Tablas 15, Granada) runs the **Teléfono Andaluz de Información Homosexual** (☎ 958 20 06 02). The **Federación Colega** (www.colega web.net) works for Andalucian gay and lesbian solidarity, rights and acceptance, and has branches in all eight provincial capitals.

Andalucian law allows gay as well as heterosexual couples to register as de facto couples for tax, social security and health benefits. Of the 400 couples who registered in Seville between 2000 and 2004, 65 of them were gay or lesbian. Some couples turn the registration formalities into a ceremony or celebration – something akin to gay weddings.

HOLIDAYS

Everywhere in Spain has 14 official holidays a year – some are holidays nationwide, some only in one village. The list of holidays may change from year to year. If a holiday date falls on a weekend, sometimes the holiday is moved to the Monday. If a holiday falls two days away from a weekend, many Spaniards take the intervening day off too – a practice known as making a *puente* (bridge).

The two main periods when Spaniards go on holiday are Semana Santa (Holy Week, leading up to Easter Sunday) and the six weeks from mid-July to the end of August. At these times accommodation in resorts can be scarce and transport heavily booked.

There are usually nine official national holidays:

Año Nuevo (New Year's Day) 1 January
Viernes Santo (Good Friday) 25 March 2005, 14 April 2006
Fiesta del Trabajo (Labour Day) 1 May
La Asunción (Feast of the Assumption) 15 August
Fiesta Nacional de España (National Day) 12 October
Todos los Santos (All Saints' Day) 1 November; traditional day for paying respect to the dead.
Día de la Constitución (Constitution Day) 6 December
La Inmaculada Concepción (Feast of the Immaculate Conception) 8 December
Navidad (Christmas) 25 December

In addition, regional governments normally set three holidays, and local councils a further two. The three regional holidays in Andalucía are usually these:

Epifanía (Epiphany) or **Día de los Reyes Magos** (Three Kings' Day) 6 January – see p406
Día de Andalucía (Andalucía Day) 28 February
Jueves Santo (Holy Thursday) 24 March 2005, 13 April 2006

The following are often selected as local holidays by town halls:

Corpus Christi 26 May 2005, 15 June 2006
Día de San Juan Bautista (Feast of St John the Baptist, King Juan Carlos I's saint's day) 24 June
Día de Santiago Apóstol (Feast of St James the Apostle, Spain's patron saint) 25 July

INSURANCE

A travel-insurance policy to cover theft, loss and medical problems is a good idea. Travel agents will be able to make recom-

mendations. Check the small print: some policies specifically exclude 'dangerous activities', which can include scuba diving, motorcycling, even trekking. You may prefer a policy that pays doctors or hospitals directly, rather than you having to pay on the spot and claim later. If you have to claim later, make sure you keep all documentation. Check whether the policy covers ambulances or an emergency flight home.

Buy travel insurance as early as possible. If you buy it in the week before you leave home, you may find, for example, that you are not covered for delays to your trip caused by strikes.

Paying for your airline ticket with a credit card often provides limited travel accident insurance, and you may be able to reclaim payment if the operator doesn't deliver.

See p427 for more information on health insurance and p424 for motor insurance.

INTERNET ACCESS

Most travellers make constant use of Internet cafés and free web-based email such as **Yahoo** (www.yahoo.com) or **Hotmail** (www.hotmail.com), or the email component of Lonely Planet's **ekno global communication service** (www.ekno.lonelyplanet.com). There are plenty of Internet cafés in large and small towns throughout Andalucía, with a typical charge of around €2 per hour.

For those travelling with a notebook or hand-held computer, a small but growing number of hotels in Andalucía now provide Internet connections in rooms. You should be aware that your modem may not work once you leave your home country. The safest option is to buy a reputable 'global' modem before you leave home, or buy a local PC-card modem if you're spending an extended time in any one country. For more information on travelling with a portable computer, see www.teleadapt.com.

For some recommended websites giving information on Andalucía, see p12.

LEGAL MATTERS

Article 17 of the Spanish constitution determines that anyone who is arrested must be informed immediately, in a manner understandable to them, of their rights and the grounds for the arrest. Arrested people are entitled to the assistance of a lawyer during police inquiries or judicial investigations. If an arrested person does not appoint their own lawyer, they must be allotted a duty lawyer. For many foreign nationalities including British citizens, the police are also obliged to inform an arrested person's consulate immediately. Arrested people are likely to be held in a police cell until a formal statement answering the charges against them is taken, although by article 17 they may not be compelled to make a statement. Within 72 hours of arrest, the person must be brought before a judge or released. A lawyer to safeguard the arrested person's rights, and if necessary an interpreter, must be present when the statement is taken and when the arrested person goes before the judge.

Further useful information on Spanish legal procedures and lawyers is published on the website of the UK embassy in Madrid (www.ukinspain.com): select 'Consular Information' then 'Information Leaflets'.

Drugs

Spain's once liberal drug laws were severely tightened in 1992. The only legal drug is cannabis, and then only for personal use – which means very small amounts. Public consumption of any drug is illegal. It would be very unwise to smoke cannabis in hotel rooms or guesthouses.

Travellers entering Spain from Morocco, especially with a vehicle, should be prepared for intensive drug searches.

Police

Spain has three main types of police. The **Policía Nacional** (National Police; ☎ 091) cover cities and bigger towns, some of them forming special squads dealing with drugs, terrorism and the like. A further contingent is to be found shuffling paper in bunkerlike police stations called *comisarías*. The **Policía Local** (Local Police; ☎ 092), also known as Policía Municipal, are controlled by city and town

---

LEGAL AGE

- Voting: 18
- Driving: 18
- Drinking: 16
- Sex: 13 (for both heterosexual and homosexual, but sex between under-15s and over-18s is illegal)

---

halls and deal mainly with minor matters such as parking, traffic and bylaws. They wear blue-and-white uniforms. The responsibilities of the green-uniformed **Guardia Civil** (Civil Guard; ☎ 062) include roads, the countryside, villages and international borders.

If you need to go to the police, any of them will do, but you may find the Policía Local are the most approachable.

MAPS

Michelin's 1:400,000 *Andalucía* is excellent for overall planning and touring, with an edition published each year. It's widely available in and outside Andalucía – look at petrol stations and bookshops.

Maps provided by tourist offices are often adequate for finding your way around cities and towns. So are those in phone directories, which come with indexes of major streets. For something more comprehensive, most cities are covered by one of the Spanish series such as Telstar, Escudo de Oro, Alpina or Everest, all with street indexes – available in bookshops. Check their publication dates, though.

On the Internet, **Multimap** (www.multimap.com) and **Andalucía There's Only One** (www.andalucia.com) have searchable street maps of Andalucian cities and towns.

If you are going to do any walking in Andalucía you should arm yourself with the best possible maps. Spain's Centro Nacional de Información Geográfica (CNIG), the publishing arm of the Instituto Geográfico Nacional (IGN), published a useful *Mapa Guía* series of national and natural parks, mostly at 1:50,000 or 1:100,000 and produced in the 1990s. The CNIG also covers about three-quarters of Andalucía in its 1:25,000 *Mapa Topográfico Nacional* maps, most of which are up to date. Both the CNIG and the Servicio Geográfico del Ejército (SGE; Army Geographic Service) publish 1:50,000 series: the SGE's, called *Serie L*, tends to be more up-to-date (most of its Andalucía maps have been revised since the mid-1990s). CNIG maps may be labelled CNIG, IGN or both.

The Junta de Andalucía, Andalucía's regional government, also publishes a range of Andalucía maps, including a *Mapa Guía* series of natural and national parks. These have been published recently and are widely available, although perhaps better for vehicle touring, with a scale of 1:75,000. Their covers are predominantly green, as opposed to the CNIG *mapas guía* which are mainly red or pink. Other Junta maps include 1:10,000 and 1:20,000 maps covering the whole of Andalucía – good maps but sales outlets for them are few.

The best maps for walkers in the Sierra Nevada, Las Alpujarras, Parque Natural de Cazorla and the Cabo de Gata area are the 1:40,000 and 1:50,000 maps published by Editorial Alpina.

Local availability of maps is patchy, so it's a good idea to try to obtain them in advance. **Stanfords** (☎ 020-7836 1321; www.stanfords .co.uk; 12-14 Long Acre, London WC2E 9LP, UK) has a good range of Spain maps and you can order them online. In Spain, seek out any specialist map or travel bookshops: several are recommended in this book's destination chapters. **LTC** (Map pp98-100; ☎ 954 42 59 64; ltc -mapas@sp-editores.es; Avenida Menéndez Pelayo 42-44, 41003 Seville) is the best map shop in Andalucía, selling most Junta maps as well as SGE and CNIG maps.

The **CNIG** (www.cnig.es) has sales offices in Andalucía's eight provincial capitals, including the following:

Granada (Map pp304-5; ☎ 958 90 93 20; Avenida Divina Pastora 7 & 9)

Málaga (Map pp232-3; ☎ 952 21 20 18; Calle Ramos Carrión 48)

Seville (Map pp88-90; ☎ 955 56 93 20) Avenida San Francisco Javier 9, Edificio Sevilla 2, 8°, módulo 7)

MONEY

Spain's currency is the euro (€), which is made up of 100 cents. It comes in coins of one, two, five, 10, 20 and 50 cents and one and two euros, and notes of five, 10, 20, 50, 100, 200 and 500 euros. See the inside back cover for exchange rates.

You can get by very well in Andalucía with a credit or debit card enabling you to make purchases direct and to withdraw cash euros from *cajeros automáticos* (ATMs), which are extremely common. But it's wise to take more than one card (if you have them) and a few travellers cheques too. The combination gives you a fallback if you lose a card.

See p10 for an introduction to costs in Andalucía.

Cash & Travellers Cheques

Cash and travellers cheques can be exchanged at virtually any bank or exchange office. Banks are plentiful and tend to offer the best rates. Exchange offices – usually indicated by the word *cambio* (exchange) – exist mainly in tourist resorts. Generally they offer longer opening hours and quicker service than banks, but worse exchange rates.

Travellers cheques usually bring a slightly better exchange rate than cash, though that may be offset by the charges for buying them in the first place. Thomas Cook, Visa and American Express (Amex) are widely accepted brands with efficient replacement policies. Amex offices cash their own travellers cheques commission-free, but you might still stand to gain by going to a bank or exchange office because their exchange rates may be more favourable.

In many places, the more money you change, the better the exchange rate you'll get. It's always worth checking commissions first, and confirming that exchange rates are as posted (posted rates may not have been recently updated). Commissions may depend on how many cheques, or how much in total, you're cashing. A typical commission is 2% to 3%, with a minimum of €4 or €5. Places that advertise 'no commission' usually offer poor exchange rates. If you get most of your cheques in fairly large denominations (the equivalent of €100 or more), this reduces any per-cheque commission charges.

In Spain you usually can't use travellers cheques like money to make purchases.

Credit & Debit Cards

Not every establishment accepts payment by card. You will normally be able to make payments by card in mid-range and top-end accommodation and restaurants, and larger shops; but you cannot depend on it elsewhere. You may be asked for ID such as your passport when you pay by card.

After you take into account the commissions, handling fees, exchange rate differentials and other methods banks have of taking your money from you, visitors from outside the euro zone will get most value for their pound, dollar or whatever by making purchases by *tarjeta de crédito* (credit card) or debit card, with ATM withdrawals as second-best value. Obtaining euros by exchanging travellers cheques or non-euro cash gives less value for your money.

Make sure you keep a note of the numbers to call for reporting a lost or stolen card.

Taxes & Refunds

Spanish value-added tax (VAT) is called IVA (*ee*-ba; *impuesto sobre el valor añadido*). On accommodation and restaurant prices, it's 7% and is usually (but not always) included in the prices that you'll be quoted. On retail goods and car hire, IVA is 16%. As a rule, prices given in this book include IVA. Some accommodation places will forget about IVA if you pay cash and don't require a receipt. To ask 'Is IVA included?', say '*¿Está incluido el IVA?*'.

Visitors resident outside the EU are entitled to a refund of the 16% IVA on purchases costing more than €90.15 from any shop if they are taking them out of the EU within three months. Ask the shop to give you an invoice showing the price and IVA paid for each item and the name and address of the vendor and purchaser. Then present both the invoice and goods to the customs booth for IVA refunds at the airport or port from which you leave the EU. The officer will stamp the invoice and you hand it in at a bank in the airport or port for the reimbursement. Some retailers offer a slightly simplified version of this procedure via refund services such as **Global Refund** (www.globalrefund.com) or **Premier Tax Free** (www.premiertaxfree.com).

Tipping

Spanish law requires menu prices to include the service charge, and tipping is a matter of personal choice – most people leave some small change if they're satisfied, and 5% is usually plenty. Porters will generally be happy with €1.50. Taxi drivers don't have to be tipped but a little rounding up won't go amiss.

NAMES WITHOUT NUMBERS

Locating a hotel, café or tourist office is not always as easy as you might expect in Andalucía. Not every building has a street number. One way this is shown in addresses is by the abbreviation s/n, which stands for *sin número* (without number). Another method is to locate a place by reference to the kilometre markers on the highway it stands on – for example 'Carretera N340 Km 55,' which means that the place is at the Km 55 marker on highway N340.

POST

At 2004 rates, a postcard or letter weighing up to 20g costs €0.52 from Spain to other European countries, and €0.77 to the rest of the world. *Certificado* (registered) mail costs an extra €2.19. *Urgente* service, which means your mail may arrive two or three days quicker than normal, costs around €2 extra for international mail.

Stamps are sold at most *estancos* (tobacconist shops with 'Tabacos' in yellow letters on a maroon background), as well as at *oficinas de correos* (post offices). It's quite safe to post mail in the yellow street *buzones* (postboxes) as well as at post offices. Mail to or from other Western European countries normally arrives within a week; to or from North America within 10 days; to or from Australia and New Zealand within two weeks.

Poste restante mail can be addressed to you at Poste Restante (or better, Lista de Correos, the Spanish name for it), anywhere in Spain that has a post office, with the name of the province following that of the town. This will be delivered to the place's main post office unless another one is specified in the address. Take your passport when you go to pick up mail. Every Spanish address has a five-digit postcode, use of which may help your mail arrive a bit quicker.

SOLO TRAVELLERS

Unfortunately for solo travellers, a single room normally costs well over half the price of a double room. Budget travellers can cut accommodation costs by staying in youth hostels, which have the additional advantage of providing ready-made company and helpful travel tips. But true backpackers hostels, real gathering places for international travellers, as opposed to youth hostels which may be dominated by groups of teenagers, are thin on the ground: Granada and Cádiz have the two best ones that we know of – Oasis Backpackers' Hostel (p317) and Quo Qadis (p172).

Despite Andalucians' reputation for being gregarious, it is possible for solo travellers to feel left out of some of the fun. You can't expect the locals to want to get to know every foreigner who passes through and Andalucian accommodation is not, in general, terribly conducive to getting to know other guests. Bars can be a good place to meet people but women need to be wary as many bars are the domain of macho males or those on the lookout for a tourist woman. This obviously is less the case in sophisticated places such as central parts of Málaga, Granada and Seville. Of course, if you're gregarious, self-assured and can speak a bit of Spanish, you'll get by just fine.

Solo travellers need to be watchful of their luggage when on the road and should stay in places with safe boxes for their valuables so as not to be burdened with them when out and about. One big drag of travelling alone is when you want to take a quick dip in the sea and there's no-one to keep an eye on your valuables!

TELEPHONE & FAX

Spain has no telephone area codes. Every phone number has nine digits and for any call within Spain you just dial all those nine digits. If calling Spain from another country, dial your international access code, followed by Spain's country code ☎ 34, followed by all nine digits of the local number. The international access code for calls from Spain is ☎ 00.

The first digit of all Spanish fixed-phone numbers is ☎ 9. Numbers beginning with ☎ 6 are mobile phones.

Andalucía is fairly well provided with blue street payphones, which (as long as they are not out of order) are easy to use for both international and domestic calls. They accept coins and/or *tarjetas telefónicas* (phonecards) issued by the national phone company Telefónica. Phonecards come in €6 and €12 denominations and are sold at post offices and *estancos*. Coin payphones inside bars and cafés – usually green – are normally a little more expensive than street payphones. Phones in hotel rooms can be a good deal more expensive: managements set their own rates, so ask about costs before using one.

Costs

A three-minute payphone call costs around €0.10 within your local area, €0.30 to other places within the same province, €0.45 to other Spanish provinces and around €1 to Spanish mobile phones (which are numbers starting with ☎ 6). All these calls are 10% to 20% cheaper (about 30% cheaper to mobile numbers) from 8pm to 8am Monday to Friday, and all day Saturday and Sunday. A three-minute payphone call to other EU countries or the USA costs about €1, and to Australia €4.50.

Calls to Spanish numbers starting with ☎ 900 are free. Numbers starting with ☎ 901 to ☎ 906 are per-per-minute numbers and charges vary; a common one is ☎ 902, for which you pay about €0.35 for three minutes from a payphone.

Calls from private lines cost about 25% less than calls from payphones.

A variety of discount cards are available which can significantly cut call costs, especially for international calls. Most of these are not slot-in cards but cards that work through special access numbers. If you're thinking of buying one, look closely into call costs (including any taxes payable, such as IVA) and try to establish exactly where you can use the card.

Fax

Most main post offices have fax service: sending one page costs about €1.50 within Spain, €6.20 elsewhere in Europe and €12 to North America or Australasia. However, you'll often find cheaper rates at shops or offices with 'Fax Público' signs.

Mobile Phones

Spaniards adore *teléfonos móviles* (mobile phones). Shops on every high street and in every shopping centre sell phones at bargain prices and if you are going to be in the country for more than a few days, it's worth considering buying a Spanish mobile. Amena, Movistar and Vodafone are all widespread and reputable brands. You need to understand the detail of advertised deals, however: if, for example, a phone with a call credit of €50 is on sale for €40, you will usually find that in order to qualify for the €50 free credit you will have to buy further credit at normal rates.

If you're considering taking a mobile from your home country to Spain, you should find out from your mobile network provider whether your phone is enabled for international roaming, and what the costs of voice calls and text are likely to be. It can also be useful to know the charges that people calling you will have to pay. Don't forget to take a continental adaptor for your charger plug.

The website www.gsmcoverage.co.uk provides coverage maps, lists of roaming partners and links to phone companies' websites.

Reverse-charge & Information Calls

Dial ☎ 1009 to speak to a domestic operator, including for *una llamada por cobro revertido* – a domestic reverse-charge (collect) call.

To make an international reverse-charge call via an operator in the country you're calling, dial the following numbers:

Australia (☎ 900 99 00 61)
Canada (☎ 900 99 00 15)
France (☎ 900 99 00 33)
New Zealand (☎ 900 99 00 64)
UK (☎ 900 99 00 44)
USA AT&T (☎ 900 99 00 11); MCI (☎ 900 99 00 14); Sprint (☎ 900 99 00 13)

Codes for other countries are often posted up in payphones. Alternatively, you can usually get an English-speaking international operator on ☎ 1005 or ☎ 1008.

For Spanish directory inquiries you need to dial ☎ 11822; these calls cost €0.22 plus €0.01 per second.

For international directory inquiries dial ☎ 11825; the cost is €1 plus €0.75 per minute.

TIME

All mainland Spain is on GMT/UTC plus one hour during winter, and GMT/UTC plus two hours during the country's daylight-saving period, which runs from the last Sunday in March to the last Sunday in October. Most other Western European countries have the same time as Spain year-round, the major exceptions being Britain, Ireland and Portugal. Add one hour to these three countries' times to get Spanish time.

Spanish time is normally USA eastern time plus six hours, and USA pacific time plus nine hours. But the USA tends to start daylight saving time a week or two later than Spain, so you must add one hour to the time differences in the intervening period.

In the Australian winter subtract eight hours from Sydney time to get Spanish time; in the Australian summer subtract 10 hours. The difference is nine hours for a few weeks in March.

Morocco is on GMT/UTC year-round, so is two hours behind Spain during Spanish daylight saving time, and one hour behind at other times of year.

For further information see World Time Zones, p430.

TOILETS

Public toilets are not common, but it's OK to wander into many bars and cafés to use their toilet even if you're not a customer. It's worth carrying some toilet paper with you as many toilets lack it.

TOURIST INFORMATION
Tourist Offices in Spain

All cities and many smaller towns and even villages in Andalucía have at least one *oficina de turismo* (tourist office). Staff are generally knowledgeable and increasingly well versed in foreign languages. Offices are usually well stocked with printed material. Opening hours vary widely.

Tourist offices in Andalucía may be operated by the local town hall, by local district organisations, by the government of whichever province you're in, or by the regional government, the Junta de Andalucía. There may also be more than one tourist office in larger cities, each offering information on the territory it represents. The Junta de Andalucía's environmental department, the Consejería de Medio Ambiente, also has visitors centres located in many of the environmentally protected areas (*parques naturales* and so on).

You'll find details of useful tourist offices in destination sections throughout this book.

Spain's national tourism authority is **Turespaña** (☎ 91 343 36 46, tourist information ☎ 901 30 06 00; www.spain.info; Calle José Lázaro Galdiano 6, 28036 Madrid). The Andalucian regional tourism authority is the Junta de Andalucía's **Consejería de Turismo, Comercio y Deporte** (Map pp88-90; ☎ 955 06 51 00; www.juntadeandalucia.es/turismocomercio ydeporte; tourist information www.andalucia.org; Torretriana, Isla de la Cartuja, 41092 Seville).

Tourist Offices Abroad

You can get information on Andalucía from Spanish national tourist offices in 23 countries, including the following:

Canada (☎ 416-961 3131; www.tourspain.toronto.on.ca; Suite 3402, 2 Bloor St W, Toronto M4W 3E2)

France (☎ 01 45 03 82 57; www.espagne.infotourisme
.com; 43 rue Decamps, 75784 Paris, Cedex 16)
Germany (☎ 030-882 6036; berlin@tourspain.es;
Kurfürstendamm 63 5.0G, 10707 Berlin) Also branches in
Düsseldorf, Frankfurt am Main & Munich.
Italy (☎ 06-6920 0453; www.turismospagnolo.it;
Piazza di Spagna 55, 00187 Rome)
Japan (☎ 3-3432 6141; www.spaintour.com; Daini
Toranomon Denki Bldg, 4F, 3-1-10 Toranomon, Minato-Ku,
Tokyo 105)
The Netherlands (☎ 070-346 59 00; www.spaansver
keersbureau.nl; Laan Van Meerdervoor 8A, 2517 AJ The
Hague)
Portugal (☎ 21-354 1992; lisboa@tourspain.es;
Avenida Sidónio Pais 28-3º Dto, 1050-215 Lisbon)
UK (☎ 0906-364 0630; www.tourspain.co.uk;
22-23 Manchester Sq, London W1M 5AP)
USA (☎ 212-265 8822; www.okspain.org; 35th fl, 666
Fifth Ave, New York, NY 10103) Also branches in Chicago,
Los Angeles and Miami.

You'll find details of the other offices on the
Turespaña website (www.spain.info).

VISAS

Citizens of EU countries, Switzerland, Nor-
way, Iceland and Liechtenstein need only
carry their passport or national identity document in order to enter Spain. Citizens of
many other countries, including Australia,
Canada, Japan, New Zealand, Singapore and
the USA, do not need a visa for visits of up to
90 days but must carry their passport.

Nationalities required to obtain a visa to
visit Spain at the time of writing include South
Africa, Russia, Morocco, India and Pakistan.
Consult a Spanish consulate well in advance
of travel if you think you need a visa. The
standard tourist visa issued when necessary
is the Schengen visa, which is valid not only
for Spain but for all the 14 other countries
that are party to the Schengen agreement,
which abolished controls at borders between
these countries in 2000. The other Schengen
countries are Austria, Belgium, Denmark,
Finland, France, Germany, Greece, Iceland,
Italy, Luxembourg, the Netherlands, Nor-
way, Portugal and Sweden. You must apply
for the visa in person at a consulate in your
country of residence. In the UK, single-
entry visas for a 30-day stay cost UK£17.25;
multiple-entry visas for 90-day stays cost
UK£24.15. A multiple-entry visa will save
you time if you plan to leave Spain – say for
Gibraltar or Morocco – and then re-enter.

WOMEN TRAVELLERS

Women in Spain are just about on an
equal footing with men these days. By and
large women work, contribute to the family purse, have their own money to spend
and share in the decision-making in the
home. Sexual equality has been slower
coming to Spain than in many other parts
of the Western world and the new-found
confidence of women is striking. Women
occupy positions of power and authority
in all sectors. Young women in general can
hold their own and are unafraid to stand up
for themselves, although of course there are
situations where this results in unpleasant
consequences. Spain has its share of abused
girls and women.

Men under about 35, who have grown
up in the post-Franco era, are less sexually
stereotyped than their older counterparts
whose thinking and behaviour towards
women is still directed by machismo.

Women travellers should be ready to ignore any stares, catcalls and unnecessary
comments, though in fact harassment is not
frequent. Learn the word for help *(socorro)*
in case you need to draw other people's
attention. You do still need to exercise common sense about where you go solo. Think
twice about going alone to isolated stretches
of beach or country paths, or down empty
city streets at night. A lone woman, for example, would be better to forget wandering
around the uninhabited parts of Granada's
Sacromonte area. It's highly inadvisable for
a woman to hitchhike alone – and not a
great idea even for two women together.

Topless bathing and skimpy clothes are
de rigueur in many coastal resorts, but
people tend to dress more modestly elsewhere. As in France and Italy, many Spanish women like to get really dressed and
made up. You can feel very obvious on a
Sunday when they take to the plazas and
promenades for the afternoon *paseo* (walk)
and you're in your casual gear.

Each province's national police headquarters has a special Servicio de Atención
a la Mujer (SAM), literally Service of Attention to Women. The national **Comisión
de Investigación de Malos Tratos a Mujeres** (Commission of Investigation into Abuse of Women; emergency
☎ 900 10 00 09; ◷ 9am-9pm Mon-Fri, 9am-3pm Sat)
maintains an emergency line for victims of
physical abuse anywhere in Spain.

Transport

GETTING THERE & AWAY

AIR

Airports & Airlines

Málaga's airport is the main international airport in Andalucía. Almería, Seville, Jerez de la Frontera and Gibraltar also receive some international flights. Andalucía's other airport, Granada, receives internal Spanish flights only.

Airlines flying into Andalucía, with local telephone numbers in Andalucía or Spain, include the following:

Aer Lingus (www.flyaerlingus.com; airline code EI; ☎ 902 50 27 37; hub Dublin)

Air Canada (www.aircanada.com; airline code AC; ☎ 91 563 93 01; hub Toronto)

THINGS CHANGE...

The information in this chapter is particularly vulnerable to change. Check directly with the airline or a travel agent to make sure you understand how a fare (and ticket you may buy) works and be aware of the security requirements for international travel. Shop carefully. The details given in this chapter should be regarded as pointers and are not a substitute for your own careful, up-to-date research.

Air Europa (www.air-europa.com; airline code UX; ☎ 902 40 15 01; hub Madrid)

Air France (www.airfrance.com; airline code AF; ☎ 901 11 22 66; hub Paris)

Air Nostrum See Iberia.

Air Plus Comet (www.aircomet.com; airline code MPD; ☎ 91 203 63 00; hub Madrid)

Air Scotland (www.air-scotland.com; airline code GRE; ☎ 952 04 88 38; hub Edinburgh)

Air-Berlin (www.airberlin.com; airline code AB; ☎ 901 11 64 02; hub Palma de Mallorca)

Alitalia (www.alitalia.it; airline code AZ; ☎ 902 10 03 23; hubs Milan, Rome)

American Airlines (www.aa.com; airline code AA; ☎ 902 11 55 70; hub Dallas)

Basiq Air (www.basiqair.com; airline code HV; ☎ 902 11 44 78; hubs Amsterdam, Rotterdam)

Bmibaby (www.bmibaby.com; airline code WW; ☎ 902 10 07 37; hubs Cardiff, East Midlands, Manchester, Teesside)

British Airways (www.ba.com; airline code BA; ☎ 902 11 13 33, in Gibraltar ☎ 79300; hub London Heathrow)

Brussels Airlines (www.flysn.com; airline code SN; ☎ 902 90 14 92; hub Brussels)

CityJet (www.cityjet.com; airline code WX; ☎ 952 04 88 38; hub Dublin)

Continental Airlines (www.continental.com; airline code CO; ☎ 901 10 15 22; hub Houston)

Delta Air Lines (www.delta.com; airline code DL; ☎ 91 749 66 30; hub Atlanta)

EasyJet (www.easyjet.com; airline code EZY; ☎ 902 29 99 92; hubs Bristol, Liverpool, London Luton, London Stansted, Newcastle)

Finnair (www.finnair.com; airline code AY; ☎ 952 04 83 28; hub Helsinki)

Flybe (www.flybe.com; airline code BE; ☎ 952 04 88 38; hub Southampton)

GB Airways (www.gbairways.com; airline code BA; ☎ 902 11 13 33, in Gibraltar ☎ 79300; hub London)

Germanwings (www.germanwings.com; airline code 4U; ☎ 91 514 08 25; hub Cologne)

Hapag-Lloyd (www.hlf.de; airline code X3; ☎ 902 48 05 00; hubs Munich, Stuttgart)

Hapag-Lloyd Express (www.hlx.com; airline code X3; ☎ 902 02 00 69; hub Cologne)

Iberia (www.iberia.com; airline code IB; ☎ 902 40 05 00; hub Madrid)

Jet2 (www.jet2.com; airline code LS; ☎ 902 02 02 64; hub Leeds-Bradford)

DEPARTURE TAX

Taxes are always included in the cost of your ticket: they depend where you are flying to and from but generally range between about €8 and €20 per flight.

LTU (www.ltu.de; airline code LT; ☎ 901 33 03 20; hubs Düsseldorf, Munich)

Lufthansa (www.lufthansa.com; airline code LH; ☎ 902 22 01 01; hub Frankfurt)

Monarch Airlines (www.flymonarch.com; airline code ZB; ☎ 952 04 83 47, in Gibraltar ☎ 47477; hubs London Gatwick, London Luton, Manchester)

My TravelLite (www.mytravellite.com; ☎ 902 02 01 91; hub Birmingham)

Portugália Airlines (www.flypga.com; airline code NI; ☎ 952 04 88 38; hub Lisbon)

Regional Air Lines (airline code FN; ☎ 952 04 82 02; hub Casablanca)

Royal Air Maroc (www.royalairmaroc.com; airline code AT; ☎ 91 548 78 00; hub Casablanca)

Ryanair (www.ryanair.com; airline code FR; ☎ 807 22 00 22; hubs Dublin, London Stansted)

SAS (www.sas.se; airline code SK; ☎ 952 04 81 73; hubs Copenhagen, Stockholm)

Spanair (www.spanair.com; airline code JK; ☎ 902 13 14 15; hubs Barcelona, Madrid)

Swiss (www.swiss.com; airline code LX; ☎ 901 11 67 12; hub Zürich)

Thomsonfly (www.thomsonfly.com; airline code TOM; ☎ 091 41 44 81; hub Coventry)

Transavia (www.transavia.com; airline code HV; ☎ 902 11 44 78; hub Amsterdam)

Virgin Express (www.virgin-express.com; airline code TV; ☎ 902 88 84 59; hub Brussels)

Tickets

Some of the best-value tickets to Andalucía are available on the Internet (through agencies or direct from airlines), but it can also be worth making a few phone calls or visiting a couple of travel agents to see what deals are available.

For flights heading out of Andalucía, including last-minute and standby seats, it's well worth trying the following local travel agencies, all of which have offices at Málaga airport:

Flightline (☎ 902 20 22 40; www.flightline.es)

Servitour (☎ 902 40 00 69; www.servitour.es)

Travelshop (☎ 95 246 42 27; www.thetravelshop.com)

Viajes Mundial Schemann (☎ 902 10 06 05) For flights to Germany.

Advertisements in local foreign-language papers such as *Sur in English* are worth a look too.

Australia & New Zealand

As there are no direct flights from Australia or New Zealand to Spain, you have to fly to Europe via Asia, the Middle East or (less often) America, changing flights at least once.

Cheap fares are advertised in the Saturday editions of the *Age* in Melbourne and the *Sydney Morning Herald*, and in the *New Zealand Herald* travel section. Sydney–Málaga return tickets on mainstream airlines through reputable agents start at around A$2000 for February departures, and A$2500 for August. The cheapest Auckland–Madrid fares may be via the USA. Expect to pay around NZ$2500 for a return flight during the low season. Round-the-world tickets can sometimes be cheaper.

The following are well-known agents for cheap fares, with branches throughout both countries:

Flight Centre Australia (☎ 133 133; www.flightcentre.com .au); New Zealand (☎ 0800 243 544; www.flightcentre.co.nz)

STA Travel Australia (☎ 1300 733 035; www.statravel.com .au); New Zealand (☎ 0508 782 872; www.statravel.co.nz)

For online fares try www.travel.co.nz and www.travel.com.au.

Continental Europe

Except for very short hops, air fares often beat overland alternatives on cost.

FRANCE

Charter or discounted return flights year-round from Paris to Málaga or Seville start at around €200 to €250. Airlines flying direct are Air France and Iberia. Air Europa offers competitive fares, with a connection at Madrid.

Recommended ticket agencies:

Anyway (☎ 0892 893 892; www.anyway.fr)

Nouvelles Frontières (☎ 0825 000 747; www.nouvelles -frontieres.fr)

OTU Voyages (www.otu.fr) Student and youth travel specialist.

Voyageurs du Monde (☎ 01 40 15 11 15; www.vdm .com)

GERMANY

The budget German airlines Germanwings (Cologne–Málaga) and Hapag-Lloyd Express

(Cologne–Seville) provide the possibility of bargain flights. Some good fares from various German cities are available too on Air Berlin and LTU (both to Málaga, Almería and Seville), Hapag-Lloyd (Málaga and Almería) and Lufthansa (Málaga). You can usually find a return flight year-round in the region of €250.

Recommended ticket agencies:

Expedia (www.expedia.de)

Just Travel (☎ 089 747 3330; www.justtravel.de)

STA Travel (☎ 01805 456 422; www.statravel.de) For travellers aged under 26.

THE NETHERLANDS & BELGIUM

The no-frills airlines are Basiq Air (Amsterdam and Rotterdam to Málaga) and Virgin Express (Brussels–Málaga). Also check the fares on Brussels Airlines (Brussels–Seville) and Transavia (Amsterdam, Rotterdam or Maastricht to Málaga, Seville or Almería). A recommended ticket agency is **Airfair** (☎ 020-620 5121; www.airfair.nl).

PORTUGAL

Portugália Airlines flies daily nonstop between Lisbon and Málaga. One-way fares compare very poorly with the buses, but return tickets are worth considering.

Morocco

Morocco's Regional Air Lines flies direct between Málaga and Tangier (daily), and Málaga and Casablanca (several days weekly). Iberia flies daily nonstop from Melilla, the Spanish enclave on the Moroccan coast, to Málaga, Almería and Granada.

Spain

Flying within Spain is most worth considering if you're in a hurry and you're making a longish one-way trip or a return trip.

Spain's biggest airline, Iberia, flies daily (in some cases several times a day) nonstop from Madrid and Barcelona to all five Andalucian airports, and from Bilbao and Valencia to Seville and Málaga. With a connection in Madrid or Barcelona, you can fly to any Andalucian airport from any airport in Spain. Normal Iberia one-way/return fares from Madrid to Seville, for instance, are around €100/150. Barcelona to Málaga fares are around €120/230.

Air Europa flies nonstop on the following routes: Madrid–Málaga, Barcelona–Seville,

Palma de Mallorca–Granada, Palma de Mallorca–Seville and Bilbao–Málaga. Spanair flies Barcelona–Málaga, Madrid–Jerez de la Frontera, Madrid–Málaga, Madrid–Seville and Palma de Mallorca–Málaga. Both these airlines offer connections at Madrid to and from many other Spanish cities. Their standard fares are similar to Iberia's, but they're worth checking for special deals.

The UK & Ireland

The weekend national newspapers have ads and information on cheap fares. In London also try the *Evening Standard, Time Out* and the free magazine *TNT*.

An ever-changing array of no-frills airlines flies to Málaga from around Britain. In most regions of the country you have several possible departure airports – for example, in northern England you can depart from Manchester, Liverpool, Leeds-Bradford, Newcastle and Teesside. Return fares range between about UK£40 and UK£300 on most routes year-round and depend on how far ahead you book. From London airports, no-frills flights to Málaga are on EasyJet; from western England or Cardiff, you can choose between EasyJet, Bmibaby or Flybe; from the English midlands, Bmibaby, EasyJet, My TravelLite and Thomsonfly; from northern England, Bmibaby, EasyJet and Jet2; from Scotland, EasyJet and Air Scotland; from Northern Ireland, EasyJet.

Monarch Airlines is not a no-frills airline but often has competitive fares on flights to Málaga from Gatwick, Luton or Manchester, which can be booked online. British Airways and Iberia, too, are worth checking for London fares, as is Air Europa (if you're willing to make a connection in Madrid). Ryanair, Aer Lingus and CityJet fly Dublin–Málaga direct.

The only no-frills airlines that fly to other Andalucian airports are MyTravelLite (Birmingham to Almería) and Ryanair (London Stansted to Jerez de la Frontera). Monarch flies to Gibraltar from London Luton and British Airways and Iberia have direct flights from London Gatwick to Seville and Almería. British Airways flies Gatwick–Gibraltar.

Also worth looking into are charter flights. These can be among the cheapest of all flights, though you must often fly back within a fairly short period (one or two weeks is typical), and arrival and departure times can be inconvenient.

Recommended travel agencies include the following:

Avro (☎ 0870 458 2841; www.avro.com) Charter and scheduled flights.

First Choice (☎ 0870 850 3999; www.firstchoice.co.uk) Mainly charter flights.

Flight Centre (☎ 0870 890 8099; flightcentre.co.uk)

Flightbookers (☎ 0870 010 7000; www.ebookers.com)

Quest Travel (☎ 0870 442 3542; www.questtravel.com)

Sky Deals (☎ 0800 975 5477; www.skydeals.co.uk)

Spanish Travel Services (☎ 020-7874 0990; www.apatraveluk.com)

STA Travel (☎ 0870 160 0599; www.statravel.co.uk) For travellers under the age of 26.

Travel Bag (☎ 0870 890 1456; www.travelbag.co.uk)

It's also worth trying some of the following online ticket agencies:

www.airline-network.co.uk
www.dialaflight.com
www.expedia.co.uk
www.lastminute.com
www.opodo.co.uk

The USA & Canada

The only direct flights between North America and Andalucía at the time of writing are the twice-weekly flights between New York and Málaga by the Spanish airline Air Plus Comet. Plenty of flights with transfers in Madrid or another European city are available on airlines such as Delta, Continental, American Airlines, Air Canada, Iberia, British Airways, Air France, Lufthansa, Air Europa and Spanair. Fares via Barcelona, London, Paris or Frankfurt are not necessarily more expensive than via Madrid. Booking well ahead, you should be able to get a New York–Málaga round-trip ticket for about US$700 in low season or US$1000 to US$1200 in high season. Round trips from Montreal or Toronto to Málaga range from about C$1000 to C$1700. For flights from the Pacific coast, add a couple of hundred dollars. Booking just a week or two before travel can add hundreds of dollars to all prices.

Discount travel agents in the USA are known as consolidators. San Francisco is the ticket consolidator capital of America, although some good deals can be found in Los Angeles, New York and other big cities. The *New York Times, Los Angeles Times, Chicago Tribune* and *San Francisco Chronicle*

all produce weekly travel sections in which you'll find a number of travel agency ads.

The following agencies are recommended for online bookings from the USA:

www.cheaptickets.com
www.expedia.com
www.itn.net
www.lowestfare.com
www.orbitz.com
www.sta.com (For travellers under the age of 26.)
www.travelocity.com

Travel Cuts (☎ 800 667 2887; www.travelcuts.com) is Canada's national student travel agency. For online bookings from Canada try www.expedia.ca and www.travelocity.ca.

LAND

Bus

Bus travel to Andalucía from other countries except Portugal often works out no cheaper than flying. From within Spain, bus is sometimes quicker or cheaper than the train, but it's sometimes slower or more expensive – it depends on the route.

Main bus companies serving Andalucía include the following:

Alsa (☎ 902 42 22 42; www.alsa.es)

Alsina Graells (☎ 902 33 04 00; www.alsinagraells.es in Spanish)

Anibal (☎ 902 36 00 73; www.anibal.net in Spanish)

Continental Auto (☎ 902 33 04 00; www.continental-auto.es in Spanish)

Daibus (☎ 902 27 79 99; www.daibus.es in Spanish)

Dainco (☎ 95 490 78 00; www.dainco.es)

Damas (☎ 959 25 89 00; www.damas-sa.es in Spanish)

Eurolines (www.eurolines.com) France (☎ 08 36 69 52 52); Germany (☎ 069 7903219); Spain (☎ 902 40 50 40); the UK (☎ 0870 514 3219) A grouping of over 30 bus companies from different countries.

Eva Transportes (in Portugal ☎ 289-899 700; www.eva-bus.com)

La Sepulvedana (☎ 91 530 48 00; www.lasepulvedana.es in Spanish)

Secorbus/Socibus (☎ 902 22 92 92; www.socibus.es in Spanish)

CONTINENTAL EUROPE

Eurolines runs to several Andalucian cities from France, Germany, Switzerland, Italy, the Czech Republic and Belgium. The Spanish company Alsa is the Eurolines operator on many of these routes. A Paris–Granada trip, for example, costs €115/210 one-way/return (24 hours each way).

From Portugal, the main services are by Eurolines/Alsa with daily services from Lisbon's Terminal Rodoviário Arco do Cego to Seville (€35, 7½ hours) via Evora and Badajoz, and to Málaga (€51, nine hours) via Faro, Huelva, Seville, Cádiz, Algeciras and the Costa del Sol. Anibal runs three times weekly from Lisbon to Málaga (€47, 12 hours) via Evora, Badajoz, Seville, Cádiz, Algeciras and the Costa del Sol. There's also a thrice-weekly Damas/Eva Transportes service from Lisbon to Seville (€28, 4½ hours) via Beja, Serpa and Aracena, plus two daily Damas/Eva buses from Lagos to Seville (€17, 5½ hours) via Albufeira, Faro and Huelva.

MOROCCO

Eurolines and Alsa run several weekly buses between Moroccan cities such as Casablanca, Marrakesh and Fès, and Seville, the Costa del Sol, Málaga, Granada and Jaén, via Algeciras–Tangier ferries. The Málaga–Marrakesh trip, for example, takes 19 to 20 hours for around €85/140 one-way/return.

SPAIN

From Madrid, buses running to Cádiz, Córdoba, Huelva, Jerez and Seville are operated by Socibus/Secorbus; to Málaga, the Costa del Sol and Algeciras by Daibus; to Granada by Continental Auto; and to Jaén by La Sepulvedana. Most leave from Madrid's **Estación Sur de Autobuses** (☎ 91 468 42 00; Calle Méndez Álvaro; metro Méndez Álvaro). The trip from Madrid to any of Seville, Granada or Málaga,

for example, takes around six hours for between €13 and €18. The Barcelona–Granada trip takes between seven and 10 hours for between €60 and €70.

Routes down the Mediterranean coast from Barcelona, Valencia and Alicante to Almería, Granada, Jaén, Córdoba and Seville, are mainly operated by Alsa and its associated companies such as Bacoma and Enatcar. The other main route into Andalucía, operated by Alsa and Dainco, is from northwestern Spain (Galicia, Asturias and Cantabria) via Castilla y León and Extremadura to Seville and Cádiz.

All these services go at least daily, often several times daily.

THE UK

Eurolines runs two or three times weekly from London's Victoria coach station to all the main Andalucian cities. The trip takes 33½ hours to Granada (€129/232 one-way/return), 36 hours to Seville (€136/245) and 35 hours to Málaga (€136/245).

Car & Motorcycle

For information on the paperwork needed for taking a vehicle to Andalucía and general information on driving in Andalucía and the rest of Spain, see p423. Normally there are no customs or immigration checks when entering Spain overland from France or Portugal.

Spain's main roads are good and you could drive to Andalucía in a day, if you

ROAD DISTANCE CHART (KM)

	Almería	Barcelona	Bilbao	Cádiz	Córdoba	Gibraltar	Granada	Huelva	Jaén	Madrid	Málaga	Seville
Almería	---											
Barcelona	809	---										
Bilbao	958	620	---									
Cádiz	484	1284	1058	---								
Córdoba	332	908	796	263	---							
Gibraltar	346	1124	1110	127	314	---						
Granada	166	868	829	297	166	256	---					
Huelva	516	1140	939	219	232	291	350	---				
Jaén	228	804	730	367	104	336	99	336	---			
Madrid	563	621	395	663	400	714	434	632	335	---		
Málaga	219	997	939	265	187	127	129	313	209	544	---	
Seville	422	1046	933	125	138	197	256	94	242	538	219	---

wish, from any corner of the country. Note that the highway numbers of many important roads in Spain changed in 2004. Published maps may not always be up-to-date with these changes. In this book we use only the new numbers.

The main highway from Madrid to Andalucía is the A4/AP4 to Córdoba, Seville and Cádiz. For Jaén, Granada, Almería or Málaga, turn off at Bailén.

From the ferry ports at Santander or Bilbao or the French border at Irún, the most direct route is to head for Burgos, from which it's a pretty straight 240km to Madrid. The main Irún–Bilbao and Bilbao–Burgos highways are each subject to tolls of about €12.

The AP7/A7 leads down the Mediterranean side of Spain from La Jonquera on the French border as far as Almería. Tolls total around €45 between La Jonquera and Alicante and toll-free alternative roads tend to be busy and slow, but between Alicante and Almería there are no tolls. Branch off the A7 along the A92N for Granada and Málaga (no tolls). It's possible to drive from

Barcelona to Málaga in eight hours (though at a sane pace it's closer to 11 hours).

The A66/AP66/N630 heads all the way down to Seville from Gijón on Spain's north coast, through Castilla y León and Extremadura.

THE UK

If you just want to drive *in* Andalucía, it normally works out easier and more economical to fly and rent a car there. But if you plan to stay for several weeks and want a car most of the time, driving from home might work out cheaper. The options for getting your vehicle from Britain to continental Europe are threefold: you can use Eurotunnel – the Channel Tunnel car train from Folkestone to Calais; or put your vehicle on a cross-channel ferry to France; or use the direct vehicle ferries from England to Bilbao or Santander in northern Spain (from which it's possible to reach Andalucía in one long day).

Using Eurotunnel or a ferry to France, then driving pretty hard to Andalucía, should cost between UK£600 and UK£800 for a return trip for two people, including

APPROACHES TO ANDALUCÍA

TRANSPORT

petrol, food and one night's accommodation each way en route. To this, add about UK£75 each way for road tolls if you use the quickest routes. **Eurotunnel** (www.eurotunnel .com; France ☎ 03 21 00 61 00; Spain ☎ 91 630 73 15; the UK ☎ 0870 535 3535) runs around the clock, with up to four crossings (35 minutes) an hour. You pay for the vehicle only. Return fares booked a minimum 14 days ahead are around UK£300 for a car and UK£150 for a motorcycle. Please see p421 for details of the ferry options, and the previous section for a summary of routes through Spain.

In the UK, further information on driving in Europe is available from the **RAC** (☎ 020-8917 2500; www.rac.co.uk) or the **AA** (☎ 0870 600 0371; www.theaa.com).

Train

Rail companies serving routes to Andalucía include the following:

Caminhos de Ferro Portugueses (Portuguese Railways; in Portugal ☎ 808 208 208; www.cp.pt)

Eurostar (reservations in the UK ☎ 0870 518 6186, information in the UK ☎ 0870 160 0052; www.eurostar.com)

Renfe (Red Nacional de los Ferrocarriles Españoles, Spanish National Railways; in Spain ☎ 902 24 02 02; www.renfe.es)

SNCF (French National Railways; in France ☎ 36 35; www.sncf.com)

CONTINENTAL EUROPE

All of the routes from France to Andalucía involve at least one change of train (usually in Madrid). The only direct train between France and Madrid is the overnight sleeper train No 409 from Paris Austerlitz to Madrid Chamartín. Standard one-way/return couchette fares are around €110/190. Trains from Madrid (usually Atocha station) get you to the main Andalucian cities in a few hours for between €28 and €65.

No railway crosses from Portugal into Andalucía, but trains run along the Algarve to Vila Real de Santo António, where there's a ferry across the Río Guadiana to Ayamonte in Andalucía.

You can travel from Lisbon to Seville, or vice versa, in about 16 hours by changing trains (and waiting four or five hours at night) at Cáceres in Spain's Extremadura. Departure from Lisbon's Santa Apolónia station is around 10pm daily. The *turista* (2nd-class) seat fare from Lisbon to Seville is €49.65 one-way.

Direct trains run at least three times a week from cities in Switzerland and northern Italy to Barcelona, where you can transfer to an Andalucía-bound train.

SPAIN

Spain's national railway company Renfe provides quick, reliable trains to Andalucía from Madrid and points along the Mediterranean coast. From most other parts of Spain you can reach Andalucía by train in a day. The fastest services are the AVE (Alta Velocidad Española) trains covering the 471km from Madrid to Seville, via Córdoba, in around 2½ hours, reaching speeds of 280km/h.

Most long-distance trains have 1st- and 2nd-class carriages, usually called *preferente* and *turista*, respectively. Basic long-distance daytime trains are called *diurnos*. More comfortable, marginally more expensive trains with fewer stops are called InterCity. Even more comfortable and expensive trains are called Talgo, and a Talgo 200 is a Talgo that uses the high-speed AVE line for part of its journey to destinations such as Málaga, Cádiz, Huelva and Algeciras. The fastest and most expensive way to go is to take the AVE itself on the Madrid–Córdoba–Seville line. Overnight trains are usually classed as *estrella* (with seats, couchettes and sleeping compartments) or *trenhotel* (a sleek, expensive, sleeping-car-only train).

On most trains you don't need to book in advance, but on busy services it's advisable to do so. The fare you pay between two places depends on the type of train, the class you travel in, and sometimes the time of day. Examples of one-way *turista*-class seat fares include the following:

Route	Fare (€)	Duration (hr)
Barcelona-Granada	49	12-14
Cáceres-Seville	14.65	5¾
Madrid-Córdoba	26-43	1¾-6¼
Madrid-Málaga	32.50-54	4¼-7¼
Madrid-Seville	51-65	2¼-3¼

Return train fares are generally 20% less than two one-way fares. Children aged under four years travel free; those from four to 11 (to 12 on some trains) get 40% off the cost of seats and couchettes. The Euro<26 card (see p404) gives 20% or more off long-distance and regional train fares.

THE UK

The simplest and quickest route from London to Andalucía (about 24 hours) involves the Eurostar Channel Tunnel service from Waterloo to Paris, changing there from the Gare du Nord to the Gare d'Austerlitz, taking an overnight sleeper-only train to Madrid's Chamartín station, changing to Atocha station and taking an AVE or Talgo 200 to Andalucía. The best services to central and western Andalucía use the expensive AVE line for at least part of their route. It costs around UK£250 return to Seville if you book 30 days ahead (a little less to Málaga or Granada). To cut costs, and add time, you can take more economical trains from Paris to Madrid and from Madrid to Andalucía.

For information and bookings on rail travel from Britain, contact **Rail Europe** (☎ 0870 584 8848; www.raileurope.co.uk) or Eurostar.

SEA
Morocco

You can sail to Andalucía from the Moroccan ports of Tangier and Nador, as well as Ceuta or Melilla (Spanish enclaves on the Moroccan coast). The routes are: Melilla–Almería, Nador–Almería, Melilla–Málaga, Tangier–Gibraltar, Tangier–Algeciras, Ceuta–Algeciras and Tangier–Tarifa. All routes usually take vehicles as well as passengers. The most frequent sailings are to and from Algeciras. Usually there are at least 16 sailings a day plying the route between Algeciras and Tangier (1¼ to 2½ hours) and 16 between Algeciras and Ceuta (35 minutes). Extra services are put on during the peak summer period (mid-June to mid-September) when hundreds of thousands of Moroccan workers return home from Europe for holidays. The Tangier–Tarifa route may be restricted to people with EU passports or EU residence papers during this period.

Anyone travelling to Morocco for the first time should consider sailing to Ceuta or Melilla rather than Tangier. The hustlers around the port at Tangier can be hard to handle and it's much more painless to sail to Ceuta or Melilla. The border crossing into Morocco itself is more straightforward from Melilla than from Ceuta, but sailings to Melilla can take eight hours and are much less frequent (just one a day from Almería and one a day from Málaga for most of the year). Passenger seat fares to Melilla are little more than to

Algeciras or Ceuta, but if you want a cabin or are taking a car, it gets more costly.

The most prominent ferry company, with sailings from Tangier and Ceuta to Algeciras, Melilla to Málaga and Melilla to Almería, is the Spanish government-run **Trasmediterránea** (www.trasmediterranea.es; Spain ☎ 902 45 46 45; Tangier ☎ 039-931142; the UK ☎ 0870 499 1305). The other main operators to Algeciras are **EuroFerrys** (☎ 956 65 11 78; www.euroferrys.com) and, from Ceuta only, **Buquebus** (☎ 902 41 42 42). There's little price difference between the rival lines. One-way passenger fares from Algeciras are around €26 to Tangier and €21 to Ceuta. Two people with a small car pay around €130 to Tangier and €150 to Ceuta.

If you're taking a car, book well ahead for August or Easter travel. Anyone crossing from Morocco to Spain with a vehicle should be prepared for rigorous searches on arrival at Ceuta and Melilla and on the mainland.

For further details see the Getting There & Away sections for Algeciras (p214), Almería (p381), Gibraltar (p226), Málaga (p243) and Tarifa (p210).

The UK
PORTSMOUTH–BILBAO

P&O Ferries (www.poferries.com; Spain ☎ 902 02 04 610; the UK ☎ 0870 520 2020) operates a ferry from Portsmouth to Bilbao. As a rule, there are two sailings a week except for a few weeks in January (when there's no service) and the month of February (when it's once weekly). Voyage time varies between 28 and 35 hours.

Standard return fares for two people with a car range from around UK£450 to UK£800 depending on the season, including the cheapest cabin accommodation. The ferries dock at Santurtzi, about 14km northwest of central Bilbao.

PLYMOUTH–SANTANDER

Brittany Ferries (www.brittanyferries.com; Spain ☎ 942 36 06 11; the UK ☎ 0870 556 1600) operates a twice-weekly car ferry from Plymouth to Santander (24 hours sailing time), between mid-March and early November. For two people with a car, return fares range from about UK£500 to UK£900.

VIA FRANCE

The quickest and busiest ferry route, with around 60 crossings daily at peak times, is Dover–Calais, operated by **P&O Ferries**

TRANSPORT

TRANSPORT

(www.poferries.com; France ☎ 08 25 12 01 56; the UK ☎ 0870 520 2020), **SeaFrance** (www.seafrance.com; France ☎ 08 25 82 6000; the UK ☎ 0870 571 1711) and the ultrafast **Hoverspeed** (www.hoverspeed.co.uk; France ☎ 008 0012 111211; the UK ☎ 0870 240 8070), which takes 40 to 45 minutes. Fares are volatile and you should research the latest offers. In August a Dover–Calais return ticket for a car and two people can cost UK£130 to UK£250 with SeaFrance or up to UK£350 with Hoverspeed. Winter fares are lower.

Other routes include Newhaven–Dieppe (Hoverspeed), Portsmouth–Caen (Brittany Ferries) and Portsmouth–Cherbourg/Le Havre (P&O Ferries).

Ferrysavers (☎ 0870 990 8492; www.ferrysavers.com) offers an online booking service and comparisons of cross-Channel sailing options.

GETTING AROUND

AIR

There are no internal flights operating between Andalucian cities.

BICYCLE

Andalucía is good biking territory, with wonderful scenery and varied terrain. Plenty of lightly trafficked country roads, mostly in decent condition, enable riders to avoid the busy main highways. Road biking here is as safe as anywhere else in Europe provided you make allowances for some Spanish drivers' love of speed. Off the paved roads, endless thousands of kilometres of tracks, including old railway lines adapted by bikers and hikers, await mountain bikers. Day rides and touring by bike are particularly enjoyable in spring and autumn, avoiding weather extremes. See p66 for an introduction to cycling and mountain biking in Andalucía.

If you get tired of pedalling, it's often possible to take your bike on a bus (usually you'll just be asked to remove the front wheel). To take a bike on a train, you must comply with numerous conditions. On long-distance trains you have to be travelling overnight in a sleeper or couchette, and you have to remove the pedals and pack the bike in a specially designed container. Regional trains are less strict but not all of them have space for bicycles. Ask before buying tickets. Bikes are generally permitted on *cercanías* (suburban trains).

Bicycles, often *bicis todo terreno* (mountain bikes), are increasingly available for hire in main cities, coastal resorts and inland towns and villages which attract tourism. Prices range from €10 to €20 a day. Buying a decent mountain bike will cost you anywhere upwards of €200 from a bike shop in any medium-sized town. Cheaper bikes are sold in hypermarkets and department stores, among other places.

Bike lanes on main roads are rare, but cyclists are permitted to ride in groups up to two abreast. Helmets are obligatory outside built-up areas.

BUS

Buses, mostly modern, comfortable and inexpensive, run just about everywhere in Andalucía except the smallest villages. Buses make their way along some unlikely mountain roads to provide a connection between remote villages and their nearest town. The bigger cities are connected to

MAIN BUS COMPANIES

Company	Website (in Spanish)	Telephone	Main destinations
Alsina Graells	www.alsinagraells.es	☎ 902 33 04 00	Almería, Córdoba, Granada, Jaén, Málaga, Seville
Casal	-	☎ 954 99 92 90	Aracena, Carmona, Seville
Comes	-	☎ 902 19 92 08	Algeciras, Cádiz, Granada, Jerez, Málaga, Ronda, Seville
Damas	www.damas-sa.es	☎ 959 25 89 00	Huelva, Seville
Linesur	www.linesur.com	☎ 954 98 82 20	Algeciras, Écija, Jerez, Seville
Los Amarillos	www.losamarillos.es	☎ 902 21 03 17	Cádiz, Jerez, Málaga, Ronda, Seville
Portillo	-	☎ 956 65 10 55	Algeciras, Costa del Sol, Málaga, Ronda
Transportes Ureña	-	☎ 957 40 45 58	Córdoba, Jaén, Seville

SELECTED MAIN BUS ROUTES

Route	One-way fare (€)	Duration (hr)	Distance (km)	Frequency (daily)
Granada-Almería	9.40	2¼	166	10
Málaga-Cádiz	18.05	6	265	4
Málaga-Córdoba	10.45	2½	187	5
Málaga-Granada	8.65	2	129	18
Málaga-Seville	13.05	2½	219	12
Seville-Cádiz	9.30	1½	125	11
Seville-Córdoba	8.60	1½	138	10
Seville-Granada	16	3	256	10
Seville-Huelva	6.10	1¼	94	18

TRANSPORT

each other by frequent daily services; on less frequented routes services may be reduced (or occasionally nonexistent) on Saturday and Sunday.

Larger towns and cities usually have one main *estación de autobuses* (bus station) where all out-of-town buses stop. In smaller places, buses tend to operate from a particular street or square, which may be unmarked. Ask around; locals generally know where to go. See the boxed text for a list of the main bus companies operating routes within Andalucía.

During Semana Santa (Holy Week), July and August it's advisable to buy long-distance bus tickets a day in advance. On a few routes, a return ticket is cheaper than two singles. Travellers aged under 26 should inquire about discounts on intercity routes.

The boxed text shows one-way fares and journey times on selected main routes. For much more detail see this book's city and town sections.

CAR & MOTORCYCLE

Andalucía's good road network and inexpensive rental cars make driving an attractive and practical way of getting around.

Bring Your Own Vehicle

Bringing a vehicle of your own to Andalucía makes the most sense if you plan to stay more than a couple of weeks. For information on routes from the UK and through Spain to Andalucía, see p418. Petrol (around €0.90 per litre in Spain) is widely available. In the event of breakdowns, every small town and many villages have a garage with mechanics.

When driving a private vehicle in Europe proof of ownership (a Vehicle Registration Document for cars registered in the UK), driving licence, roadworthiness certificate (MOT), and either an insurance certificate or a Green Card (see Insurance, p424) should always be carried. Also ask your insurer for a European Accident Statement form, which can simplify matters in the event of an accident.

If the car is from the UK or Ireland, remember to adjust the headlights for driving in mainland Europe (motor accessory shops sell stick-on strips which deflect the beams in the required direction).

In the UK, further information on driving in Europe is available from the **RAC** (☎ 020-8917 2500; www.rac.co.uk) or the **AA** (☎ 0870 600 0371; www.theaa.com).

Driving Licence

All EU countries' licences (pink or pink-and-green) are accepted in Spain. (But note that the old-style UK green licence is not accepted.) Licences from other countries are supposed to be accompanied by an International Driving Permit although, in practice, for renting cars or dealing with traffic police your national licence will suffice. The International Driving Permit, valid for 12 months, is available from automobile clubs in your country.

Hire

If you plan to hire a car in Andalucía, it's a good idea to organise it before you leave.

As a rule, local firms at Málaga airport or on the Costa del Sol offer the cheapest deals. You can normally get a two-door aircon economy-class car from local agencies for around €110 to €120 a week in August or around €100 a week in January. A larger four-door vehicle should be around €130 to €140 in August or €120 in January. Many of these local firms offer Internet booking and you simply go to their desk in or just outside the airport on arrival. In general, rentals away from the holiday *costas* (coasts) are more expensive.

Well established local firms with branches at Málaga airport (and, in most cases, other coastal towns too) include the following:

Centauro (☎ 902 10 41 03; www.centauro.net)
Crown Car Hire (☎ 952 17 64 86; www.crowncarhire .com)
Helle Hollis (☎ 952 24 55 44, in the UK ☎ 0871 222 7245; www.hellehollis.com)
Holiday Car Hire (☎ 952 24 26 85; www.holidaycarhire .com)
Niza Cars (☎ 952 23 61 79; www.nizacars.es)

Spain's national tourism authority, **Turespaña** (www.spain.info), has town-by-town listings of car rental companies on its website.

An alternative to dealing direct with a local rental company is to go through online brokers such as **Holiday Autos** (www.holiday autos.co.uk), **Transhire** (www.transhire.com), **Carjet** (www .carjet.com) or **Sunny Cars** (www.sunnycars.de, www .sunnycars.nl). These firms act as intermediaries between you and the local agencies, offering a wide variety of vehicle options and pick-up locations and the comfort of dealing with a company that offers a degree of across-the-board certainty about insurance and other factors. You'll usually wind up paying a bit more than if you rent direct from a local company.

The third and usually most expensive option is to rent from one of the major international rental companies, giving assuredly high standards of service:

Avis (in Spain ☎ 902 13 55 31; www.avis.com)
Europcar (in Spain ☎ 902 10 50 30; www.europcar.es in Spanish)
Hertz (in Spain ☎ 902 40 24 05; www.hertz.es)
National/Atesa (in Spain ☎ 902 10 01 01; www.atesa.es)

To rent a car you need to be aged at least 21 (23 with some companies) and to have held a driving licence for a minimum of one year (sometimes two years). Under-25s have to pay extra charges with many firms.

It's much easier, and often obligatory, to pay for your rental with a credit card.

As always, check the detail of exactly what you are paying for. Some companies will throw in extras such as child seats and the listing of additional drivers for free; others will charge for them. See the following section for some tips on rental-car insurance.

Insurance

Third-party motor insurance is a minimum requirement throughout Europe. If you live in the EU, your existing motor insurance will probably provide automatic third-party cover throughout the EU: this is certainly the case with all UK car insurance policies. But check with your insurer about whether you will also be covered for medical or hospital expenses or accidental damage to your vehicle. You might have to pay an extra premium if you want the same protection abroad as you have at home. A European breakdown assistance policy such as the AA Five Star Service or RAC European Motoring Insurance, entitling you to roadside assistance or towing, emergency repairs and 24-hour telephone assistance in English, is also a good investment.

The Green Card is an internationally recognised document showing that you have the minimum insurance cover required by law in the country visited. It is provided free by insurers. If you're carrying an insurance certificate that gives the minimum legal cover, a Green Card is not essential, but it has the advantage of being easily recognised by foreign police and authorities.

If you are renting a vehicle in Andalucía, the routine insurance provided by the rental company may not cover much beyond basic third-party requirements. For insurance against theft of your rented vehicle or damage to it through collision or vandalism, or injury or death to driver or passengers, you may need to ask the rental company for extra coverage. Check the conditions carefully before committing yourself to a rental agreement.

Road Conditions

Spanish roads have one of the highest death rates in Europe and a love of high speed among many drivers has to be one factor in the casualty rate. Drivers from other countries need to be prepared for other road users to be travelling faster than they might be used to, especially on *autovías* (toll-free dual carriageways) and even in heavy traffic.

TRANSPORT

PARKING

Street parking space can be hard to find during working hours (about 9am to 2pm Monday to Saturday and 5pm to 8pm Monday to Friday). You'll often have to use underground or multistorey car parks, which are common enough in cities, and well enough signposted, but not cheap (typically around €1 per hour or €10 to €15 for 24 hours). Underground and multistorey car parks are generally more secure places to park than the street, though. City hotels with their own parking usually charge for the right to use it, at similar rates to underground car parks.

Blue lines on the street usually mean you must pay at a nearby meter to park during working hours (usually around €0.50 an hour). Yellow lines mean no parking. Take care not to park in prohibited zones, even if other drivers have (you risk your car being towed and paying around €60 to have it released).

Road Rules

As elsewhere in continental Europe, drive on the right and overtake on the left. The minimum driving age is 18 years. Rear seat belts, if fitted, must be worn. Children under three must sit in child safety seats. The blood-alcohol limit is 0.05% (0.03% for drivers with a licence less than two years old) and breath-testing is carried out on occasion. The police can, and do, carry out spot checks on drivers so it pays to have all your papers in order. Nonresident foreigners may be fined on the spot for traffic offences. You can appeal in writing (in any language) to the Jefatura Provincial de Tráfico (Provincial Traffic Headquarters) and if your appeal is upheld, you'll get your money back – but don't hold your breath for a favourable result. Contact details for each province's traffic headquarters are given on the website of the **Dirección General de Tráfico** (www.dgt.es). Click on 'Direcciones y Teléfonos' then on 'Donde Realizar Trámites,' then select the province you are in.

The speed limit is 50km/h in built-up areas, 90km/h or 100km/h outside built-up areas, and 120km/h on autopistas (toll highways) and autovías.

In Spain it's compulsory to carry two warning triangles (to be placed 100m in front of and 100m behind your vehicle if you have to stop on the carriageway), and a reflective jacket, which must be donned if you get out of your vehicle on the carriageway or hard shoulder outside built-up areas.

It's illegal to use hand-held mobile phones while driving.

LOCAL TRANSPORT

Cities and larger towns have efficient bus systems, but you often won't need to use them because accommodation, attractions and main transport terminals are usually within fairly comfortable walking distance of each other. All Andalucía's airports except Jerez are linked to city centres by bus – in Málaga's case also by train. Gibraltar airport is within walking distance of downtown Gibraltar and of the bus station in La Línea de la Concepción, Spain.

Taxis are plentiful in larger places and even many villages have a taxi or two. Fares are reasonable – a typical 3km trip should cost about €3 (airport runs cost a bit extra). Intercity runs are around €0.60 per kilometre. You don't have to tip taxi drivers but a little rounding up doesn't go amiss.

TRAIN

Renfe (☎ 902 24 02 02; www.renfe.es), Spain's national railway company, has an extensive and efficient rail system in Andalucía linking all the main cities and many smaller places. Trains are at least as convenient, quick and inexpensive as buses on many routes.

See p420 for information on long-distance trains linking Andalucía with other parts of Spain. These can be used for journeys within Andalucía as well, on routes such as Córdoba–Málaga, Córdoba–Seville–Cádiz and Córdoba–Ronda–Algeciras. Generally more frequent services between Andalucian destinations are provided by the cheaper, one-class *regional* and *cercanía* trains. *Regionales* run between Andalucian cities, stopping at towns en route. They're classed, in descending order of speed and price, as Tren Regional Diésel (TRD), Andalucía Expres (AE) and basic Regional (R) trains. *Cercanías* are commuter trains that link Seville, Málaga and Cádiz with their suburbs and nearby towns.

Good or reasonable train services, with at least three direct trains running each way daily (often more), service the following routes: Algeciras–Ronda–Bobadilla–Antequera–Granada, Córdoba–Málaga,

SELECTED MAIN TRAIN ROUTES

Route	One-way fare (€)	Duration (hr)	Distance (km)	Frequency (daily)
Granada-Almería	11.80	2¼	166	4
Málaga-Cádiz	21.25	5-6	265	5 (change at Bobadilla & Dos Hermanas)
Málaga-Córdoba	14-19	2½	187	9
Málaga-Granada	12	2½	129	3 (change at Bobadilla)
Málaga-Seville	13.15	2½	219	5
Seville-Cádiz	8.40-22.50	1½	125	9
Seville-Córdoba	7-25	¾-1½	138	21
Seville-Granada	17.65	3¼	256	4
Seville-Huelva	6.40-15.50	1½	94	4

Málaga–Torremolinos–Fuengirola, Seville–Jerez de la Frontera–El Puerto de Santa María–Cádiz, Seville–Córdoba, Seville–Huelva, Seville–Bobadilla–Málaga and Seville–Antequera–Granada–Guadix–Almería.

Services on other routes tend to be infrequent and they often involve changing trains at the small junction station of Bobadilla in central Andalucía, where lines from Seville, Córdoba, Granada, Málaga and Al-

geciras all meet. But with a little perseverance you can reach a surprising number of places by train, including Jaén, the Sierra Norte of Sevilla province and the Sierra de Aracena.

The boxed text shows one-way fares and journey times on selected routes (fares on some routes vary according to the type of train). For more detail see this book's city and town sections.

Health Dr Caroline Evans

CONTENTS

BEFORE YOU GO

Prevention is the key to staying healthy while abroad. Some predeparture planning will save you trouble later on. See your dentist before a long trip, carry a spare pair of contact lenses and glasses, and take your optical prescription with you. Bring medications in their original, clearly labelled, containers. A signed and dated letter from your physician describing your medical conditions and medications, including generic names, is also a good idea. If carrying syringes or needles, be sure to have a physician's letter documenting their medical necessity.

INSURANCE

If you're an EU citizen, an E111 form, available from health centres or, in the UK, post offices, covers you for most medical care. The E111 will not cover you for non-emergencies or emergency repatriation home. So even with an E111, you will still have to pay for medicine bought from pharmacies, even if prescribed, and perhaps for a few tests and procedures. An E111 does not cover private medical consultations and treatment in Andalucía; this includes nearly all dentists, and some of the better clinics and surgeries. Non-EU citizens should find out if there is a reciprocal arrangement for free medical care between their country and Spain.

If you do need health insurance, strongly consider a policy that covers you for the worst possible scenario, such as an accident requiring an emergency flight home. Find out in advance if your insurance plan will make payments directly to providers or reimburse you later for overseas health expenditures. The former option is generally preferable, as it doesn't require you to pay out of pocket in a foreign country.

RECOMMENDED VACCINATIONS

No vaccinations are necessary for Spain. However, the WHO recommends that all travellers should be covered for diphtheria, tetanus, measles, mumps, rubella and polio, regardless of destination. Since most vaccines don't produce immunity until at least two weeks after they're given, visit a physician at least six weeks before departure.

INTERNET RESOURCES

The WHO's publication *International Travel and Health* is revised annually and is available online at www.who.int/ith. Other useful websites:

www.ageconcern.org.uk Advice on travel for the elderly.
www.fitfortravel.scot.nhs.uk General travel advice for the layperson.
www.mariestopes.org.uk Information on women's health and contraception.
www.mdtravelhealth.com Travel health recommendations for every country; updated daily.

IN TRANSIT

DEEP VEIN THROMBOSIS (DVT)

Blood clots may form in the legs during plane flights, chiefly because of prolonged immobility. The chief symptom of Deep Vein Thrombosis (DVT) is swelling or pain of the foot, ankle or calf, usually but not always on just one side. When a blood clot travels to the lungs, it may cause chest pain and breathing difficulties. Travellers with any of these symptoms should immediately seek medical attention.

HEALTH

To prevent the development of DVT on long flights you should walk about the cabin, contract the leg muscles while sitting, drink plenty of fluids and avoid alcohol and tobacco.

IN ANDALUCÍA

AVAILABILITY OF HEALTH CARE

If you need an ambulance call ☎ 061. For emergency treatment go straight to the *urgencias* (casualty) section of the nearest hospital.

Good health care is readily available and *farmacias* (pharmacies) offer valuable advice and sell over-the-counter medication. In Spain, a system of *farmacias de guardia* (duty pharmacies) operates so that each district has one open all the time. When a pharmacy is closed, it posts the name of the nearest open one on the door.

TRAVELLER'S DIARRHOEA

If you develop diarrhoea, be sure to drink plenty of fluids, preferably an oral rehydration solution such as Dioralyte. If diarrhoea is bloody, persists for more than 72 hours or is accompanied by a fever, shaking, chills or severe abdominal pain, you should seek medical attention.

ENVIRONMENTAL HAZARDS
Altitude Sickness

Lack of oxygen at high altitudes (over 2500m) affects most people to some extent. Symptoms of Acute Mountain Sickness (AMS) usually develop during the first 24 hours at altitude but may be delayed up to three weeks. Mild symptoms include headache, lethargy, dizziness, difficulty sleeping and loss of appetite. AMS may become more severe without warning and can be fatal. Severe symptoms include breathlessness, a dry, irritable cough (which may progress to the production of pink, frothy sputum), severe headache, lack of coordination and balance, confusion, irrational behaviour, vomiting, drowsiness and unconsciousness. There is no hard-and-fast rule as to what is too high: AMS has been fatal at 3000m, although 3500m to 4500m is the usual range.

Treat mild symptoms by resting at the same altitude until recovery, usually a day or two. Paracetamol or aspirin can be taken for headaches. If symptoms persist or become worse, however, *immediate descent is necessary;* even 500m can help. Drug treatments should never be used to avoid descent or to enable further ascent.

Diamox (acetazolamide) reduces the headache of AMS and helps the body acclimatise to the lack of oxygen. It is only available on prescription and those who are allergic to sulfonamide antibiotics may also be allergic to Diamox.

In the UK, fact sheets are available from the **British Mountaineering Council** (www.thebmc.co.uk; 177-179 Burton Rd, Manchester, M20 2BB).

Bites & Stings

Bees and wasps only cause real problems to those with a severe allergy (anaphylaxis). If you have a severe allergy to bee or wasp stings carry an 'epipen' or similar adrenaline injection.

In forested areas you should watch out for the hairy reddish-brown caterpillars of the pine processionary moth. They live in silvery nests up in the pine trees and, come spring, leave the nest to march in long lines (hence the name). Touching the caterpillars' hairs sets off a severely irritating allergic skin reaction.

Some Andalucian centipedes have a very nasty, but non-fatal sting. The ones to watch out for are those composed of clearly defined segments, which may be patterned with, for instance, black and yellow stripes.

Jellyfish, with their stinging tentacles, generally either occur in large numbers or hardly at all, so it's fairly easy to know when not to go in the sea.

The only venomous snake that is even relatively common in Spain is Lataste's viper. It has a triangular-shaped head, is up to 75cm long, and grey with a zigzag pattern. It is found in dry, rocky areas, usually away from humans. Its bite can be fatal and needs to be treated with a serum which state clinics in major towns keep in stock.

Mosquitoes are found in most parts of Europe. They may not carry malaria but can cause irritation and infected bites. Sand flies are found around the Mediterranean beaches. They usually cause only a nasty itchy bite, but can also carry a rare skin disorder called cutaneous leishmaniasis. Use a DEET-based insect repellent to prevent both mosquito and sand fly bites.

Scorpions are found in Spain and their sting can be distressingly painful but is not considered fatal.

Check for ticks if you have been walking where sheep and goats graze as they can cause skin infections and other more serious diseases.

Heat Exhaustion & Heat Stroke

Heat exhaustion occurs following excessive fluid loss with inadequate replacement of fluids and salt. Symptoms include headache, dizziness and tiredness. Dehydration is already happening by the time you feel thirsty – aim to drink sufficient water to produce pale, diluted urine. Replace lost fluids by drinking water and/or fruit juice, and cool the body with cold water and fans. Treat salt loss with salty fluids such as soup or add a little more table salt to foods than usual.

Heat stroke is a much more serious condition, resulting in irrational and hyperactive behaviour and eventually loss of consciousness and death. Rapid cooling by spraying the body with water and fanning is ideal treatment, and emergency fluid and electrolyte replacement by intravenous drip is recommended.

Water

Tap water is generally safe to drink in Spain, but the city of Málaga is one place where many people prefer to play it safe drinking bottled water. Do not drink water from rivers or lakes as it may contain bacteria or viruses that can cause diarrhoea or vomiting.

TRAVELLING WITH CHILDREN

Make sure children are up to date with routine vaccinations, and discuss travel vaccines well before departure as some vaccines aren't suitable for children under one year old.

WOMEN'S HEALTH

Travelling during pregnancy is usually possible but always seek a medical check-up before planning your trip. The most risky times for travel are during the first 12 weeks of pregnancy and after 30 weeks.

SEXUAL HEALTH

Condoms are widely available but emergency contraception may not be, so take the necessary precautions. When buying condoms, look for a European CE mark, which means they have been rigorously tested. Remember to also keep them in a cool, dry place so that they don't crack and perish.

HEALTH

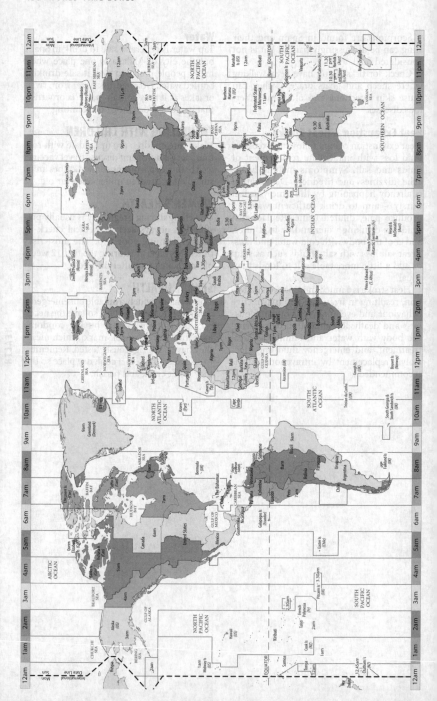

Language

CONTENTS

Spanish, or Castilian (castellano), as it is often and more precisely called, is spoken throughout Andalucía. English isn't as widely spoken as many travellers expect, though you're more likely to find people who speak some English in the main cities and tourist areas. Generally, however, you'll be better received if you try to communicate in Spanish.

For a more comprehensive guide to the Spanish language than we're able to offer here, pick up a copy of Lonely Planet's Spanish Phrasebook.

ANDALUCIAN PRONUNCIATION

Spanish spelling is phonetically consistent, meaning that there's a clear and consistent relationship between what you see in writing and how it's pronounced. In addition, most Spanish sounds have English equivalents, so English speakers shouldn't have much trouble being understood.

Andalucians don't pronounce Spanish quite the same way as speakers from other parts of Spain, or as it is taught to foreigners. Local accents vary too, but whether you choose to use mainland pronunciation or learn the following rules, you're sure to get your message across.

Vowels

a	as in 'father'
e	as in 'met'
i	as in 'marine'
o	as in 'or' (without the 'r' sound)
u	as in 'rule'; the 'u' is not pronounced after **q** and in the letter combinations **gue** and **gui**, unless it's marked with a diaeresis (eg *argüir*), in which case it's pronounced as English 'w'
y	at the end of a word or when it stands alone, it's pronounced as the Spanish **i** (eg *ley*); between vowels within a word its sound is somewhere between the 'y' in 'yonder' and the 'g' in 'beige', depending on the region

Consonants

As a rule, Spanish consonants resemble their English counterparts, with the exceptions listed below.

While the consonants **ch**, **ll** and **ñ** are generally considered distinct letters, **ch** and **ll** are now often listed alphabetically under **c** and **l** respectively. The letter **ñ** is still treated as a separate letter and comes after **n** in dictionaries.

b	soft, as the 'v' in 'van'; also (less commonly) as in 'book' when word-initial or when preceded by a nasal such as **m** or **n**
c	as 'k' before **a**, **o** and **u**; as 's' when followed by **e** or **i** (not 'th' as in standard Castilian)
ch	as in 'choose'
d	as in 'dog' when initial or preceded by **l** or **n**; elsewhere as the 'th' in 'then', and sometimes not pronounced at all – thus *partido* (divided) becomes 'partio'
g	as in 'go' when initial or before **a**, **o** and **u**; elsewhere much softer. Before **e** or **i** it's a harsh, breathy sound, similar to the 'ch' in Scottish *loch* (written as 'kh' in our guides to pronunciation).
h	always silent
j	as the 'ch' in the Scottish *loch* (written as 'kh' in our guides to pronunciation)
ll	similar to the 'y' in 'yellow' but often closer to a 'j' in Andalucía

LANGUAGE

ñ   as the 'ni' in 'onion'

q   always followed by a silent **u** and
either **e** (as in *que*) or **i** (as in *aquí*);
the combined sound of 'qu' is like
the 'k' in 'kick'

r   a rolled 'r' sound; longer and stronger
when initial or doubled

s   often not pronounced at all, especially
when not initial; thus *pescados* (fish)
can be pronounced 'pecao' in
Andalucía

v   the same sound as Spanish **b** (see
earlier)

x   as the 'x' in 'taxi' when between two
vowels; as the 's' in 'say' before a
consonant

z   pronounced as 's' (not 'th' as in
standard Castilian); **z** is often silent
when at the end of a word

Word Stress

Stress is indicated by italics in the pronunciation guides included with all the words
and phrases in this language guide. In general, words ending in vowels or the letters
n or **s** have stress on the next-to-last syllable,
while those with other endings have stress
on the last syllable. Thus *vaca* (cow) and
caballos (horses) both carry stress on the
next-to-last syllable, while *ciudad* (city) and
infeliz (unhappy) are both stressed on the
last syllable.

Written accents indicate a stressed syllable,
and will almost always appear in words that
don't follow the rules above, eg *sótano* (basement), *porción* (portion).

GENDER & PLURALS

In Spanish, nouns are either masculine or
feminine, and there are rules to help deter-
mine gender (there are of course some exceptions). Feminine nouns generally end
with **-a** or with the groups **-ción**, **-sión** or **-dad**.
Other endings typically signify a masculine
noun. Endings for adjectives also change to
agree with the gender of the noun they
modify (masculine/feminine **-o**/**-a**). Where
both masculine and feminine forms are included in this language guide, they are
separated by a slash, with the masculine
form first, eg *perdido/a*.

If a noun or adjective ends in a vowel, the
plural is formed by adding **s** to the end. If
it ends in a consonant, the plural is formed
by adding **es** to the end.

ACCOMMODATION

I'm looking for ...	Estoy buscando ...	e·stoy boos·kan·do ...
Where is ...?	¿Dónde hay ...?	don·de ai ...
a hotel	un hotel	oon o·tel
a boarding house	una pensión/ residencial/ un hospedaje	oo·na pen·syon/ re·see·den·syal/ oon os·pe·da·khe
a youth hostel	un albergue juvenil	oon al·ber·ge khoo·ve·neel

I'd like a ... room.	Quisiera una habitación ...	kee·sye·ra oo·na a·bee·ta·syon ...
double	doble	do·ble
single	individual	een·dee·vee·dwal
twin	con dos camas	kon dos ka·mas

MAKING A RESERVATION

(for phone or written requests)

To ...	A ...
From ...	De ...
Date	Fecha
I'd like to book ...	Quisiera reservar ... (see the list under 'Accommodation' for bed and room options)
in the name of ...	en nombre de ...
for the nights of ...	para las noches del ...
credit card ...	tarjeta de crédito ...
number	número
expiry date	fecha de vencimiento
Please confirm ...	Puede confirmar ...
availability	la disponibilidad
price	el precio

How much is it per ...?	¿Cuánto cuesta por ...?	kwan·to kwes·ta por ...
night	noche	no·che
person	persona	per·so·na
week	semana	se·ma·na

Does it include breakfast?

¿Incluye el desayuno?	een·kloo·ye el de·sa·yoo·no

May I see the room?

¿Puedo ver la habitación?	pwe·do ver la a·bee·ta·syon

I don't like it.

No me gusta.	no me goos·ta

It's fine. I'll take it.

OK. La alquilo.	o·kay la al·kee·lo

I'm leaving now.
 Me voy ahora. me *voy* a·o·ra

full board	*pensión completa*	pen·*syon* kom·*ple*·ta
private/shared bathroom	*baño privado/ compartido*	*ba*·nyo pree·*va*·do/ kom·par·*tee*·do
too expensive	*demasiado caro*	de·ma·*sya*·do *ka*·ro
cheaper	*más económico*	mas e·ko·*no*·mee·ko
discount	*descuento*	des·*kwen*·to

CONVERSATION & ESSENTIALS

When talking to people familiar to you or younger than you, it's usual to use the informal form of 'you', *tú*, rather than the polite form *Usted*. The polite form is used in all cases in this guide; where options are given, the form is indicated by the abbreviations 'pol' and 'inf'.

Hello.	*Hola.*	o·la
Good morning.	*Buenos días.*	bwe·nos *dee*·as
Good afternoon.	*Buenas tardes.*	bwe·nas *tar*·des
Good evening/ night.	*Buenas noches.*	bwe·nas *no*·ches
Goodbye.	*Adiós.*	a·*dyos*
Bye/See you soon.	*Hasta luego.*	as·ta *lwe*·go
Yes.	*Sí.*	see
No.	*No.*	no
Please.	*Por favor.*	por fa·*vor*
Thank you.	*Gracias.*	*gra*·syas
Many thanks.	*Muchas gracias.*	moo·chas *gra*·syas
You're welcome.	*De nada.*	de *na*·da
Pardon me.	*Perdón/ Discúlpeme.*	per·*don* dees·*kool*·pe·me

(before requesting information, for example)

Sorry.	*Lo siento.*	lo see·*en*·to

(when apologising)

Excuse me.	*Permiso.*	per·*mee*·so

(when asking permission to pass, for example)

How are things?
 ¿Qué tal? ke tal
What's your name?
 ¿Cómo se llama Usted? ko·mo se *ya*·ma oo·ste (pol)
 ¿Cómo te llamas? ko·mo te *ya*·mas (inf)
My name is ...
 Me llamo ... me *ya*·mo ...
It's a pleasure to meet you.
 Mucho gusto. moo·cho *goos*·to
Where are you from?
 ¿De dónde es/eres? de *don*·de es/e·res (pol/inf)
I'm from ...
 Soy de ... soy de ...

Where are you staying?
 ¿Dónde está alojado? *don*·de es·ta a·lo·*kha*·do (pol)
 ¿Dónde estás alojado? *don*·de es·tas a·lo·*kha*·do (inf)
May I take a photo?
 ¿Puedo hacer una foto? *pwe*·do a·*sair* oo·na *fo*·to

DIRECTIONS
How do I get to ...?
 ¿Cómo puedo llegar a ...? ko·mo *pwe*·do lye·*gar* a ...
Is it far?
 ¿Está lejos? es·ta *le*·khos
Go straight ahead.
 Siga/Vaya derecho. see·ga/va·ya de·*re*·cho
Turn left.
 Doble a la izquierda. do·ble a la ees·*kyer*·da
Turn right.
 Doble a la derecha. do·ble a la de·*re*·cha
I'm lost.
 Estoy perdido/a. es·toy per·*dee*·do/a
Can you show me (on the map)?
 ¿Me lo podría indicar (en el mapa)? me lo po·*dree*·a een·dee·*kar* (en el *ma*·pa)

here	*aquí*	a·*kee*
there	*allí*	a·*yee*
avenue	*avenida*	a·ve·*nee*·da
street	*calle/paseo*	ka·lye/pa·se·o
traffic lights	*semáforos*	se·*ma*·fo·ros
north	*norte*	*nor*·te
south	*sur*	soor
east	*este*	*es*·te
west	*oeste*	o·*es*·te

HEALTH
I'm sick.
 Estoy enfermo/a. es·toy en·*fer*·mo/a
I need a doctor.
 Necesito un médico (que habla inglés). ne·se·*see*·to oon *me*·dee·ko (ke *a*·bla een·gles)

LANGUAGE

EMERGENCIES

Help!	¡Socorro!	so·ko·ro
Fire!	¡Incendio!	een·sen·dyo
Go away!	¡Vete!/¡Fuera!	ve·te/fwe·ra
Call ...!	¡Llame a ...!	ya·me a
an ambulance	una ambulancia	oo·na am·boo·lan·sya
a doctor	un médico	oon me·dee·ko
the police	la policía	la po·lee·see·a

It's an emergency.
Es una emergencia.   es oo·na e·mer·khen·sya
Could you help me, please?
¿Me puede ayudar,   me pwe·de a·yoo·dar
por favor?   por fa·vor
I'm lost.
Estoy perdido/a.   es·toy per·dee·do/a
Where are the toilets?
¿Dónde están los baños?   don·de es·tan los ba·nyos

Where's the hospital?
¿Dónde está el hospital?   don·de es·ta el os·pee·tal
I'm pregnant.
Estoy embarazada.   es·toy em·ba·ra·sa·da
I've been vaccinated.
Estoy vacunado/a.   es·toy va·koo·na·do/a

I'm allergic to ...	Soy alérgico/a a ...	soy a·ler·khee·ko/a a ...
antibiotics	los antibióticos	los an·tee·byo·tee·kos
penicillin	la penicilina	la pe·nee·see·lee·na
nuts	las frutas secas	las froo·tas se·kas
peanuts	los cacahuetes	los ka·ka·we·tes

I'm ...	Soy ...	soy ...
asthmatic	asmático/a	as·ma·tee·ko/a
diabetic	diabético/a	dya·be·tee·ko/a
epileptic	epiléptico/a	e·pee·lep·tee·ko/a

I have ...	Tengo ...	ten·go ...
a cough	tos	tos
diarrhea	diarrea	dya·re·a
a headache	un dolor de cabeza	oon do·lor de ka·be·sa
nausea	náusea	now·se·a

LANGUAGE DIFFICULTIES

Do you speak (English)?
¿Habla/Hablas (inglés)?   a·bla/a·blas (een·gles) (pol/inf)
Does anyone here speak English?
¿Hay alguien que   ai al·gyen ke
hable inglés?   a·ble een·gles

I (don't) understand.
Yo (no) entiendo.   yo (no) en·tyen·do
How do you say ...?
¿Cómo se dice ...?   ko·mo se dee·se ...
What does ... mean?
¿Qué quiere decir ...?   ke kye·re de·seer ...

Could you please ...?	¿Puede ..., por favor?	pwe·de ... por fa·vor
repeat that	repetirlo	re·pe·teer·lo
speak more slowly	hablar más despacio	a·blar mas des·pa·syo
write it down	escribirlo	es·kree·beer·lo

NUMBERS

1	uno	oo·no
2	dos	dos
3	tres	tres
4	cuatro	kwa·tro
5	cinco	seen·ko
6	seis	says
7	siete	sye·te
8	ocho	o·cho
9	nueve	nwe·ve
10	diez	dyes
11	once	on·se
12	doce	do·se
13	trece	tre·se
14	catorce	ka·tor·se
15	quince	keen·se
16	dieciséis	dye·see·says
17	diecisiete	dye·see·sye·te
18	dieciocho	dye·see·o·cho
19	diecinueve	dye·see·nwe·ve
20	veinte	vayn·te
21	veintiuno	vayn·tee·oo·no
30	treinta	trayn·ta
31	treinta y uno	trayn·ta ee oo·no
40	cuarenta	kwa·ren·ta
50	cincuenta	seen·kwen·ta
60	sesenta	se·sen·ta
70	setenta	se·ten·ta
80	ochenta	o·chen·ta
90	noventa	no·ven·ta
100	cien	syen
101	ciento uno	syen·to oo·no
200	doscientos	do·syen·tos
1000	mil	meel
5000	cinco mil	seen·ko meel

SHOPPING & SERVICES

I'd like to buy ...
Quisiera comprar ...   kee·sye·ra kom·prar ...
I'm just looking.
Sólo estoy mirando.   so·lo es·toy mee·ran·do

May I look at it?
¿Puedo mirar(lo/la)?   pwe·do mee·rar·(lo/la)
How much is it?
¿Cuánto cuesta?   kwan·to kwes·ta
That's too expensive for me.
Es demasiado caro   es de·ma·sya·do ka·ro
para mí.   pa·ra mee
Could you lower the price?
¿Podría bajar un poco   po·dree·a ba·khar oon po·ko
el precio?   el pre·syo
I don't like it.
No me gusta.   no me goos·ta
I'll take it.
Lo llevo.   lo ye·vo

Do you   ¿Aceptan ...?   a·sep·tan ...
accept ...?
 credit cards   tarjetas de   tar·khe·tas de
        crédito   kre·dee·to
 travellers   cheques de   che·kes de
 cheques   viajero   vya·khe·ro

less   menos   me·nos
more   más   mas
large   grande   gran·de
small   pequeño/a   pe·ke·nyo/a

I'm looking for   Estoy buscando ...   es·toy boos·kan·do
the ...
 ATM   el cajero   el ka·khe·ro
        automático   ow·to·ma·tee·ko
 bank   el banco   el ban·ko
 bookstore   la librería   la lee·bre·ree·a
 chemist/   la farmacia   la far·ma·sya
 pharmacy
 embassy   la embajada   la em·ba·kha·da
 laundry   la lavandería   la la·van·de·ree·a
 market   el mercado   el mer·ka·do
 post office   los correos   los ko·re·os
 supermarket   el supermercado   el soo·per-
                mer·ka·do
 tourist office   la oficina de   la o·fee·see·na de
        turismo   too·rees·mo

What time does it open/close?
¿A qué hora abre/cierra? a ke o·ra a·bre/sye·ra
I want to change some money/travellers cheques.
Quiero cambiar dinero/   kye·ro kam·byar dee·ne·ro/
cheques de viajero.   che·kes de vya·khe·ro
What is the exchange rate?
¿Cuál es el tipo de   kwal es el tee·po de
cambio?   kam·byo
I want to call ...
Quiero llamar a ...   kye·ro lya·mar a ...

airmail   correo aéreo   ko·re·o a·e·re·o
letter   carta   kar·ta
registered mail   correo   ko·re·o
        certificado   ser·tee·fee·ka·do
stamps   sellos   se·lyos

TIME & DATES
What time is it?   ¿Qué hora es?   ke o·ra es
It's one o'clock.   Es la una.   es la oo·na
It's seven o'clock. Son las siete.   son las sye·te
midnight   medianoche   me·dya·no·che
noon   mediodía   me·dyo·dee·a
half past two   dos y media   dos ee me·dya

now   ahora   a·o·ra
today   hoy   oy
tonight   esta noche   es·ta no·che
tomorrow   mañana   ma·nya·na
yesterday   ayer   a·yer

Monday   lunes   loo·nes
Tuesday   martes   mar·tes
Wednesday   miércoles   myer·ko·les
Thursday   jueves   khwe·ves
Friday   viernes   vyer·nes
Saturday   sábado   sa·ba·do
Sunday   domingo   do·meen·go

January   enero   e·ne·ro
February   febrero   fe·bre·ro
March   marzo   mar·so
April   abril   a·breel
May   mayo   ma·yo
June   junio   khoo·nyo
July   julio   khoo·lyo
August   agosto   a·gos·to
September   septiembre   sep·tyem·bre
October   octubre   ok·too·bre
November   noviembre   no·vyem·bre
December   diciembre   dee·syem·bre

TRANSPORT
Public Transport
What time does   ¿A qué hora   a ke o·ra
... leave/arrive? sale/llega ...?   sa·le/ye·ga ...?
 the bus   el autobus   el ow·to·boos
 the plane   el avión   el a·vyon
 the ship   el barco   el bar·ko
 the train   el tren   el tren

 the airport   el aeropuerto   el a·e·ro·pwer·to
 the train station la estación de   la es·ta·syon de
        tren   tren
 the bus station la estación de   la es·ta·syon de
        autobuses   ow·to·boo·ses

the bus stop	la parada de autobuses	la pa·ra·da de ow·to·boo·ses
the luggage check room	la consigna	la kon·seeg·na
taxi	taxi	tak·see
the ticket office	la taquilla	la ta·kee·lya

The ... is delayed.

| *El ... está retrasado.* | el ... es·ta re·tra·sa·do |

I'd like a ticket to ...

| *Quiero un billete a ...* | kye·ro oon bee·lye·te a ... |

Is this taxi free?

| *¿Está libre este taxi?* | e·sta·lee·bre es·te tak·see |

What's the fare to ...?

| *¿Cuánto cuesta hasta ...?* | kwan·to kwes·ta a·sta ... |

Please put the meter on.

| *Por favor, pong el taxímetro.* | por fa·vor pon·ga el tak·see·me·tro |

a ... ticket	un billete de ...	oon bee·lye·te de ...
one-way	ida	ee·da
return	ida y vuelta	ee·da ee vwel·ta
1st class	primera clase	pree·me·ra kla·se
2nd class	segunda clase	se·goon·da kla·se
student	estudiante	es·too·dyan·te

Private Transport

I'd like to hire a/an ...	Quisiera alquilar ...	kee·sye·ra al·kee·lar ...
4WD	un todoterreno	oon to·do·te·re·no
car	un coche	oon un ko·che
motorbike	una moto	oo·na mo·to
bicycle	una bicicleta	oo·na bee·see·kle·ta

Is this the road to ...?

| *¿Se va a ... por esta carretera?* | se va a ... por es·ta ka·re·te·ra |

Where's a petrol station?

| *¿Dónde hay una gasolinera?* | don·de ai oo·na ga·so·lee·ne·ra |

Please fill it up.

| *Lleno, por favor.* | ye·no por fa·vor |

I'd like (20) liters.

| *Quiero (veinte) litros.* | kye·ro (vayn·te) lee·tros |

diesel	diesel	dee·sel
leaded (regular)	gasolina normal	ga·so·lee·nor·mal
petrol	gasolina	ga·so·lee·na
unleaded	gasolina sin plomo	ga·so·lee·na seen plo·mo

(How long) Can I park here?

| *¿(Por cuánto tiempo) Puedo aparcar aquí?* | (por kwan·to tyem·po) pwe·do a·par·kar a·kee |

ROAD SIGNS

Acceso	Entrance
Aparcamiento	Parking
Ceda el Paso	Give Way
Despacio	Slow
Desvío	Detour
Dirección Única	One-way
Frene	Slow Down
No Adelantar	No Overtaking
Peaje	Toll
Peligro	Danger
Prohibido Aparcar/ No Estacionar	No Parking
Prohibido el Paso	No Entry
Vía de Accesso	Exit Freeway

Where do I pay?

| *¿Dónde se paga?* | don·de se pa·ga |

I need a mechanic.

| *Necesito un mecánico.* | ne·se·see·to oon me·ka·nee·ko |

The car has broken down (in ...).

| *El coche se ha averiado (en ...).* | el ko·che se a a·ve·rya·do (en ...) |

The motorbike won't start.

| *No arranca la moto.* | no a·ran·ka la mo·to |

I have a flat tyre.

| *Tengo un pinchazo.* | ten·go oon peen·cha·so |

I've run out of petrol.

| *Me he quedado sin gasolina.* | me e ke·da·do seen ga·so·lee·na |

I've had an accident.

| *He tenido un accidente.* | e te·nee·do oon ak·see·den·te |

TRAVEL WITH CHILDREN

I need ...	Necesito ...	ne·se·see·to ...
Do you have ...?	¿Hay ...?	ai ...
a car baby seat	un asiento de seguridad para bebés	oon a·syen·to de se·goo·ree·da pa·ra be·bes
a child-minding service	un servicio de cuidado de niños	oon ser·vee·syo de kwee·da·do de nee·nyos
a children's menu	un menú infantil	oon me·noo een·fan·teel
a creche	una guardería	oo·na gwar·de·ree·a
(disposable) diapers/nappies	pañales (de usar y tirar)	pa·nya·les (de oo·sar ee tee·rar)
an (English-speaking) babysitter	un canguro (de habla inglesa)	oon kan·goo·ro (de a·bla een·gle·sa)

formula (milk)	leche en polvo	*le·*che en *pol·*vo
a highchair	una trona	oo·na *tro·*na
a potty	un orinal	oon o·*ree·*nal
	de niños	de *nee·*nyos
a stroller	un cochecito	oon ko·che·*see·*to

Do you mind if I breast-feed here?

| ¿Le molesta que dé | le mo·*les·*ta ke de |
| de pecho aquí? | de *pe·*cho a·*kee* |

Are children allowed?

| ¿Se admiten niños? | se ad·*mee·*ten *nee·*nyos |

Also available from Lonely Planet:
Spanish Phrasebook

Glossary

For terms for food, drinks and other culinary vocabulary, see p80. For additional terms and information about the Spanish language, see the Language chapter on p431.

alameda – avenue or *paseo* lined (or originally lined) with *álamo* (poplar) trees

albergue juvenil – youth hostel; not to be confused with *hostal*

alcázar – Islamic-era fortress

artesonado – ceiling with interlaced beams leaving regular spaces for decorative insertions

autopista – toll highway

autovía – toll-free dual carriageway

AVE – Alta Velocidad Española; the high-speed train between Madrid and Seville

ayuntamiento – city or town hall

azulejo – tile

bahía – bay

bailaor/a – flamenco dancer

bandolero – bandit

barrio – district or quarter (of a town or city)

biblioteca – library

bici todo terreno (BTT) – mountain bike

bodega – cellar, winery or traditional wine bar likely to serve wine from the barrel

buceo – scuba diving

bulería – upbeat type of flamenco song

buzón – yellow postbox

cabalgata –cavalcade

cajero automático – automated teller machine (ATM)

calle – street

callejón – lane

cama individual – single bed

cama matrimonial – double bed

cambio – currency exchange

campiña – countryside (usually flat or rolling cultivated countryside)

camping – camping ground

campo – countryside, field

cantaor/a – flamenco singer

cante jondo – 'deep song', the essence of flamenco

capilla – chapel

capilla mayor – chapel containing the high altar of a church

carnaval – carnival; a pre-Lent period of fancy-dress parades and merrymaking

carretera – road, highway

carril de cicloturismo – road adapted for cycle touring

carta – menu

casa de huéspedes – guesthouse

casa rural – a village house or farmhouse with rooms to let

casco – literally 'helmet'; used to refer to the old part of a city *(casco antiguo)*

castellano – Castilian; the language also called Spanish

castillo – castle

caza – hunting

centro comercial – large, purpose-built shopping centre

cercanía – local train serving suburbs and nearby towns

cerro – hill

cervecería – beer bar

chiringuito – small, often makeshift bar or eatery, usually in the open air

choza – traditional thatch hut

Churrigueresque – ornate style of baroque architecture named after the brothers Alberto and José Churriguera

cofradía – see *hermandad*

colegiata – collegiate church, a combined church and college

comedor – dining room

comisaría – station of the Policía Nacional

consigna – left-luggage office or lockers

converso – Jew who converted to Christianity in medieval Spain

copla – flamenco song

cordillera – mountain chain

coro – choir (part of a church, usually in the middle)

corrida de toros – bullfight

cortes – parliament

cortijo – country property

costa – coast

coto – area where hunting rights are reserved for a specific group of people

cruce – cross

cuenta – bill (check)

cuesta – sloping land, road or street

custodia – monstrance (receptacle for the consecrated Host)

dehesa – woodland pastures with evergreen oaks

Denominación de Origen – domains that consistently produce high-quality wines

diurno – basic long-distance daytime train

duende – the spirit or magic possessed by great flamenco performers

duque – duke

duquesa – duchess

embalse – reservoir

ermita – hermitage or chapel

escalada – climbing
estación de autobuses – bus station
estación de esquí – ski station or resort
estación de ferrocarril – train station
estación marítima – passenger port
estanco – tobacconist
estrella – overnight train with seats, couchettes and
sleeping compartments

farmacia – pharmacy
faro – lighthouse
feria – fair; can refer to trade fairs as well as to city, town
or village fairs
ferrocarril – railway
fiesta – festival, public holiday or party
finca – country property, farm
flamenco – means flamingo and Flemish as well as
flamenco music and dance
fonda – basic eatery and inn combined
frontera – frontier
fuente – fountain, spring

gitano – the Spanish word for Roma people, formerly
called Gypsies
Guardia Civil – Civil Guard; police responsible for roads,
the countryside, villages and international borders. They
wear green uniforms.
guía nativo – local guide

hammam – bathhouse
hermandad – brotherhood (which may include women),
in particular one that takes part in religious processions;
also *cofradía*
hospedaje – guesthouse
hostal – simple guesthouse or small place offering
budget hotel-like accommodation; not an *albergue juvenil*
(youth hostel)
hotel – hotel

infanta – daughter of a monarch but not first in line to
the throne
infante – son of a monarch but not first in line to the
throne
IVA – *impuesto sobre el valor añadido*; the Spanish
equivalent of VAT (value-added tax)

jardín – garden
judería – Jewish barrio in medieval Spain
Junta de Andalucía – executive government of
Andalucía

latifundia – huge estate
lavandería – laundry
levante – easterly wind
librería – bookshop

lidia – the modern art of bullfighting on foot
lista de correos – poste restante
lucio – pond or pool in the Doñana *marismas*

madrugada – the 'early hours', from around 3am to dawn;
a pretty lively time in some Spanish cities!
marismas – wetlands, marshes
marisquería – seafood eatery
marqués – marquis
medina – Arabic word for town or inner city
mercadillo – flea market
mercado – market
mezquita – mosque
mihrab – prayer niche in a mosque indicating the direction
of Mecca
mirador – lookout point
morisco – Muslim converted to Christianity in medieval Spain
moro – 'Moor' or Muslim (usually in a medieval context)
movida – the late-night bar and club scene that emerged
in Spanish cities and towns after Franco's death; a *zona
de movida* or *zona de marcha* is an area of a town where
young people gather to drink and have a good time
mozárabe – Mozarab; Christian living under Islamic rule
in medieval Spain
Mudejar – Muslim living under Christian rule in medieval
Spain; also refers to their decorative style of architecture
muelle – wharf, pier
muladí – Muwallad; Christian who converted to Islam, in
medieval Spain

nazareno – penitent taking part in Semana Santa
processions
nieve – snow
nuevo – new

oficina de correos – post office
oficina de turismo – tourist office
olivo – olive tree

palacio – palace
palo – literally 'stick'; also refers to the categories of
flamenco song
panadería – bakery
papelería – stationery shop
parador – one of the Paradores de Turismo, a chain of
luxurious hotels, often in historic buildings
paraje natural – natural area
parque nacional – national park
parque natural – natural park
paseo – avenue or parklike strip; walk or stroll
paso – literally 'step'; also the platform an image is carried
on in a religious procession
peña – a club; usually for supporters of a football club or
flamenco enthusiasts *(peña flamenca)*, but sometimes a
dining club

pensión – guesthouse
pescadería – fish shop
picadero – stable
pícaro – dice trickster and card sharp, rogue, low-life scoundrel
pinsapar – forest of *pinsapo* (Spanish fir)
pinsapo – Spanish fir
piscina – swimming pool
plateresque – early phase of Renaissance architecture noted for its decorative façades
playa – beach
plaza de toros – bullring
Policía Local – Local Police; also known as Policía Municipal. Controlled by city and town halls, they deal mainly with minor matters such as parking, traffic and bylaws. They wear blue-and-white uniforms.
Policía Municipal – Municipal Police; see *Policía Local*
Policía Nacional – National Police; responsible for cities and bigger towns, some of them forming special squads dealing with drugs, terrorism and the like.
poniente – westerly wind
pozo – well
preferente – 1st-class carriage on a long-distance train
provincia – province; Spain is divided into 50 of them
pueblo – village, town
puente – bridge
puerta – gate, door
puerto – port, mountain pass
puerto deportivo – marina
punta – point

quinto real – the royal fifth: the 20% of the bullion from the New World to which the Spanish Crown was entitled

rambla – stream
Reconquista – the Christian reconquest of the Iberian Peninsula from the Muslims (8th to 15th centuries)
refugio – shelter or refuge, especially a mountain refuge with basic accommodation for hikers
regional – train running between Andalucian cities
reja – grille; especially a wrought-iron one over a window or dividing a chapel from the rest of a church
Renfe – Red Nacional de los Ferrocarriles Españoles; Spain's national rail network
reserva – reserve
reserva nacional de caza – national hunting reserve
reserva natural – nature reserve
retablo – retable (altarpiece)
ría – estuary
río – river

romería – festive pilgrimage or procession
ronda – ring road

s/n – *sin numero* (without number); sometimes seen in addresses
sacristía – sacristy, the part of a church in which vestments, sacred objects and other valuables are kept
salina – salt lagoon
Semana Santa – Holy Week, the week leading up to Easter Sunday
sendero – path or track
sevillana – a popular Andalucian dance
sierra – mountain range
Siglo de Oro – Spain's cultural 'Golden Century', beginning in the 16th century and ending in the 17th century

taberna – tavern
tablao – flamenco show
taifa – one of the small kingdoms into which the Muslim-ruled parts of Spain were divided during parts of the 11th and 12th centuries
taquilla – ticket window
taracea – marquetry
tarjeta de crédito – credit card
tarjeta telefónica – phonecard
teléfono móvil – mobile telephone
temporada alta – high season
temporada baja – low season
temporada extra – extra-high season
temporada media – shoulder season
terraza – terrace; often means an area with outdoor tables at a bar, café or restaurant
tetería – Arabian-style tearoom with low seats around low tables
tienda – shop, tent
tocaor/a – flamenco guitarist
torre – tower
trenhotel – sleek, expensive, sleeping-car-only train
turismo – means both tourism and saloon car; *el turismo* can also mean the tourist office
turista – 2nd-class carriage on a long-distance train

v.o. – *versión original*; foreign-language film
v.o.s. – *versión original subtitulada*; foreign-language film subtitled in Spanish
valle – valley

zoco – large market in Muslim cities
zona de protección – protected area
zona restringida – restricted area

Behind the Scenes

THIS BOOK

The first two editions of *Andalucía* were written by John Noble and Susan Forsyth, who were joined by Des Hannigan and Heather Dickson on the third edition. This fourth edition was written by John Noble, Susan Forsyth, Paula Hardy and Heather Dickson. The Health chapter was written by Dr Caroline Evans.

THANKS from the Authors

John Noble Thank you to the hoteliers of the Sierra Norte de Sevilla for their hospitality and the people of Cádiz for their warmth; Gabbi Wilson and her team for their painstaking, careful and helpful editing (while at the same time coping with all the demands of converting a book to the 'new look') and Marion Byass and the cartographers for producing excellent maps (ditto on the new look); and last but not least, thanks to Susan, Izzy and Jack for putting up with life with a Lonely Planet writer!

Susan Forsyth Thanks to all of the tourist office staff on my beat for this new edition of *Andalucía*. Special thanks go to Karen Abrahams of Casas Karen and Zoe of Hotel Madreselva, both in Los Caños de Meca, and Alan and Pepa of Casa No 6 in El Puerto de Santa María. To my children Isabella (14) and Jack (12) *muchísimas gracias* for putting up with all those Sundays at home while Mum was writing. To John Noble, co-author and coordinator, thanks for your herculean efforts. At least I kept the meals coming!

Paula Hardy Thank you to everyone involved in gleaning the myriad information that goes into a Lonely Planet guide, from all the helpful tips and criticisms of our readers to the production folk at the other end of the process.

In particular thanks to Heather Dickson for commissioning me and always being available to answer queries and stave off writer's hysteria. Thanks also to John Noble for his guiding hand in his capacity as coordinating author. To those on the ground, in particular the tourist offices in Jaén, Málaga and Almería, heartfelt thanks for sharing your time and patiently answering an endless series of questions. For Costa gossip thank you Raphael Serrano. Thanks also to Virginia Irurita, Theresa Montero, Juan Antonio Llorente, Sarah Jaboor and to the best tourist office representative, Elka Azopardi. Last, but never least, thanks to my dad and my sister who keep the home fires burning for the family gypsy.

CREDITS

Andalucía 4 was commissioned and developed in Lonely Planet's London office by Heather Dickson. Production was coordinated in Melbourne by Gabbi Wilson (editorial), Marion Byass (cartography) and Indra Kilfoyle (layout). Overseeing production were Rachel Imeson (Project Manager) and Mark Griffiths (Regional Cartographer). Cartography for this guide was developed by Adrian Persoglia. Thanks also go to Stefanie Di Trocchio.

Editorial assistance was provided by Nancy Ianni, Thalia Kalkipsakis, Kate McLeod, Maryanne Netto,

---

THE LONELY PLANET STORY

The story begins with a classic travel adventure: Tony and Maureen Wheeler's 1972 journey across Europe and Asia to Australia. There was no useful information about the overland trail then, so Tony and Maureen published the first Lonely Planet guidebook to meet a growing need.

From a kitchen table, Lonely Planet has grown to become the largest independent travel publisher in the world, with offices in Melbourne (Australia), Oakland (USA), London (UK) and Paris (France).

Today Lonely Planet guidebooks cover the globe. There is an ever-growing list of books and information in a variety of media. Some things haven't changed. The main aim is still to make it possible for adventurous travellers to get out there – to explore and better understand the world.

At Lonely Planet we believe travellers can make a positive contribution to the countries they visit – if they respect their host communities and spend their money wisely.

Joanne Newell and Elizabeth Swan. Cartographic assistance was provided by Hunor Csutoros, Jim Ellis, Joelene Kowalski and Jacqui Saunders, with map checking by Daniel Fennessy. Layout assistance was provided by Margie Jung.

The language chapter was prepared by Quentin Frayne and the climate charts were produced by Csanad Csutoros. The cover was designed by Annika Roojun and book was indexed by Gabbi Wilson.

And last but not least, *muchas gracias* to our brilliant team of authors.

THANKS from Lonely Planet

Many thanks to the travellers who used the last edition and wrote to us with helpful hints, useful advice and interesting anecdotes:

A Toya Albert, Karin Almbladh, Kate Anderson, Robert Aronson, Arne Augedal **B** Arntraud Bacher, Ernie Badcock, Justine Baird, Joan Ball, Dr Elaine Barry, Aparna Baskaran, Amir Bergman, Andrew Berns, Suman Bolar, Samantha J Bond, Glenn Boyes, Graeme Brock, Daniel A Brown, Andrew Browne **C** Mauro Carlieri, Jason Christie, Andre Clarenberg, Ian Coldicott, Fred Crabtree, P Cuypers **D** Anna Dackenberg, Anthony Daprian, Steve Deegan, Joan Deive, Chris Deloddere, A Delwel, Elizabeth Downing, Dermot Duncan **E** Robert Eastham, Jennifer M Edie, Daniel Eisenberg, Henrike Evers **F** Luke Fisher, Marilyn Ford **G** Peter Gebert, Eugene Gholz, Roz Gordon, Teresa Goss, Lindsay Grant, P Grimes **H** Jack Harvey, Ian Hedge, John Holman, Andy Hopkinson, Gaye Huddant, D Hurlin **J** Heather Johnston **K** Amanda Kliefoth, Deirdre Kuit **L** Jo Lane, Silja Longhurst, Artioli Lorenzo **M** Lukas Martin, Aviva Mayers, Andrew McCloy, Sandra Moorhead, E P Mycroft **N** A E Normington **O** Tracy O'Donnell, Ray Ossen **P** Lee Patmore, Clive Paul, Marianne Persson, Reiner Peters **Q** Shazia Qureshi **R** Ine Raangs, Paul Ratcliffe, Sikha Ray, Jason Riley, Melanie Riopelle, K Ronich, Helen Ross, Joe Ross, Oonagh Ross **S** Fatima Sales, Julian Sanders, Harvey Sapir, Matthew Scanlon, Sara Schneider, Steffi Schott, Morag Scott, Rachel Senior, Sonia Sereno, Helen Shone, Jaqueline Smith, Vikki Stein, Lynn Stephenson, Angus Stewart, Rafael Iglesias Stoutz, John Strachan, Gillian Sutton **T** Jon Taplin, Paul Taylor, Jocelyne Tobe **V** Giusi Valentini, Barend van de Kraats, Bibeche van der Weide, Sofie Verbrugge, Raf Vermeyen **W** Martin Walser, Louise Watson, Sue Weatherill, Gwyn Welles, Andre Wiederhold, Tom Wolff **Z** R A Zambardino, Mara Zepeda, Ernesto Zimmermann

Carol: 086 825 0262.

Index

INDEX

INDEX

INDEX

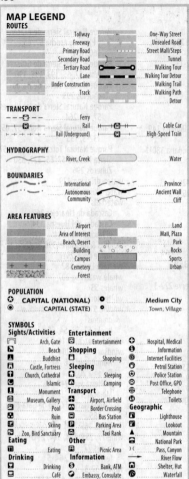

MAP LEGEND

ROUTES

Tollway	One-Way Street
Freeway	Unsealed Road
Primary Road	Street Mall/Steps
Secondary Road	Tunnel
Tertiary Road	Walking Tour
Lane	Walking Tour Detour
Under Construction	Walking Trail
Track	Walking Path
	Detour

TRANSPORT

Ferry	
Rail	Cable Car
Rail (Underground)	High-Speed Train

HYDROGRAPHY

River, Creek	Water

BOUNDARIES

International	Province
Autonomous	Ancient Wall
Community	Cliff

AREA FEATURES

Airport	Land
Area of Interest	Mall, Plaza
Beach, Desert	Park
Building	Rocks
Campus	Sports
Cemetery	Urban
Forest	

POPULATION

○ CAPITAL (NATIONAL)	● Medium City
◉ CAPITAL (STATE)	● Town, Village

SYMBOLS

Sights/Activities
- Arch, Gate
- Beach
- Buddhist
- Castle, Fortress
- Church, Cathedral
- Islamic
- Monument
- Museum, Gallery
- Pool
- Ruin
- Skiing
- Zoo, Bird Sanctuary

Eating
- Eating

Drinking
- Drinking
- Café

Entertainment
- Entertainment

Shopping
- Shopping

Sleeping
- Sleeping
- Camping

Transport
- Airport, Airfield
- Border Crossing
- Bus Station
- Parking Area
- Taxi Rank

Other
- Picnic Area

Information
- Bank, ATM
- Embassy, Consulate
- Hospital, Medical
- Information
- Internet Facilities
- Petrol Station
- Police Station
- Post Office, GPO
- Telephone
- Toilets

Geographic
- Lighthouse
- Lookout
- Mountain
- National Park
- Pass, Canyon
- River Flow
- Shelter, Hut
- Waterfall

LONELY PLANET OFFICES

Australia
Head Office
Locked Bag 1, Footscray, Victoria 3011
☎ 03 8379 8000, fax 03 8379 8111
talk2us@lonelyplanet.com.au

USA
150 Linden St, Oakland, CA 94607
☎ 510 893 8555, toll free 800 275 8555
fax 510 893 8572, info@lonelyplanet.com

UK
72–82 Rosebery Ave,
Clerkenwell, London EC1R 4RW
☎ 020 7841 9000, fax 020 7841 9001
go@lonelyplanet.co.uk

Published by Lonely Planet Publications Pty Ltd
ABN 36 005 607 983

4th Edition – Jan 2005

First published – Jan 1999

© Lonely Planet 2004

© photographs as indicated 2004

Cover photographs by Alamy Images: flamenco dancers, Seville, Pere Conner (front); Plaza de España, Seville, Paul Bernhardt (back). Many of the images in this guide are available for licensing from Lonely Planet Images: www.lonelyplanetimages.com.

Printed through Colorcraft Ltd, Hong Kong.
Printed in China.